India
A TRAVEL GUIDE

Dear Sandy,

with best wishes
Sudhir & family.

India
A TRAVEL GUIDE

ARUNA DESHPANDE

Crest Publishing House

(A JAICO ENTERPRISE)
G-2, 16 Ansari Road, Darya Ganj
New Delhi-110 002

INDIA—A TRAVEL GUIDE
ISBN 81-242-0171-4

First Edition : 2000

Published by:
CREST PUBLISHING HOUSE
(A Jaico Enterprise)
G-2, 16 Ansari Road, Darya Ganj,
New Delhi-110 002

Printed by:
Saurabh Print - O - Pack
A - 16, Sec. 4, Noida

Dedicated

to my beloved husband, Mr. Jagdish Deshpande,
without whose cooperation this book
could not have been written.

Contents

PREFACE

This book stands in a class of its own since it has followed no beaten track. It is unique and of its own type. It won't be an exaggeration to say that it is for the first time that such a book has been written on Indian tourism. It is a complete and at the same time compact book or better say a concise encyclopaedia which gives a bird's eye-view of India in general—its people, their history, their culture, manners and beliefs, their life patterns, their religions, their modes of entertainment i.e. dance and music both the classic as well as the current, and what not—in fact every thing a stray traveller, native or foreigner, may desire to know. It practically describes every facet of India and is not merely a booklet of information about hotels and motels and places of interest. An effort has been made to introduce its reader with a brief history of the place he intends to tour, to the socio-cultural pattern of the people thereof to help make him feel at home amongst them.

Naturally the compilation of such an immense information about every nook and corner of India was an arduous task. Several persons and institutions were instrumental in the compilation of this book uppermost among whom stands Mr. S.C. Sethi, Director, Crest Publishing House, New Delhi. His unmitigated support and guidance, professional approach and effort to bring out the book in, if not complete, near-immaculate form deserve sheer praise. I am particularly thankful to him for his exemplary patience and philosophic calm over my not being able to keep the time schedule as I had been shuttling between Delhi and Mumbai on professional errands too frequently. I feel indebted and express my gratitude.

I must also thank Mr. Sameer Banerjee and Mr. Girish Purvar of A.H. Wheeler & Co., Allahabad, to whom goes the credit of introducing me to Mr. Sethi who ultimately translated the dream of this book into reality.

However, the moving spirit all along had been my husband, Mr. Jagdish Deshpande, and also his friend, Mr. Vijay Kanhere, who were persistently pestering me to write this book. Their stubbornness and constant reminders which ultimately pulled me out of the cosy comfort of my laziness were sometimes rather irritating. But these irritants more than often were lovely and affectionate particularly their threat to go on hunger-strike if I did not sit down and start writing.

My thanks to Mrs. Sushma Powdwal, Deputy Librarian, S.N.T.D. Women's University, Juhu, for suggesting me varied books on the topic and also making them available to me. And I must acknowledge that I owe my knowledge to my workplace—Trade Wings, Institute of Management, Mumbai—which was my second home for 18 years. My special thanks to Ms. Preeti Nazare and Mr. Rajan Dani of Trade Wings who gave me a chance to teach tourism.

Last but not the least, I express my gratitude to Dr. S.P. Mittal who enabled me to travel world wide and have a visa of global tourism, and Mr. Vinno Ubhayakar, Managing Director, Trade Wings Ltd. for his unfailing inspiration and professional guidance and making me understand the vital standing of Indian Tourism on the world map.

ARUNA DESHPANDE

FOREWORD

Having travelled the length and breadth of India many times over in the past fifty years I could perhaps claim the ability to write a travel and tourism guide myself, but being otherwise occupied I can only marvel at the tremendous effort made by Aruna Deshpande to collect a vast amount of information about India that eminently answers every question any foreign tourist would ask, and every Indian tourist should ask. Our record in domestic tourism is not particularly commendable. For the affluent Indian, tourism is holidaying abroad. This is because we often take the wonder, beauty, history and culture of our country for granted, and go in search of landscapes abroad before we have cared to admire at the mountains and monasteries of Ladakh, the palms and rivers of Kerala, the breathtakingly beautiful Konkan coast or the forests and gentle culture of the North-East. It is time everyone explored every facet of India and went beyond the usual trip to the Taj Mahal.

Tourism is a multi-billion dollar global industry today, generating enormous wealth and large scale employment. By any account, India should have had a substantial share of it. The sad truth is that India's place is on the fringes in the vast sphere of international tourism. There are many reasons for India not becoming an inevitable destination for the international tourist, one of the more important being lack of infrastructure.

The development of infrastructure for tourism means the providing of comfort and hospitality to tourists of every hue, be they religious pilgrims, students, families or luxury lovers. This comes not only by building five-star or small budget hotels and running the trains or flying the aircrafts on time. Facilities for reservations, gathering information and above all safety and security go a long way in conveying that we

really care for tourists. The better the facilities less the danger of having unsuspecting tourists duped by touts, or female travellers molested.

Those who visit Indian homes never forget the warmth and graciousness of Indian hospitality. We should ponder over why this civilized behaviour disappears when it comes to the service sector. The tourist is generous if he is served well, and to that extent, every tourist guide must behave as a cultural ambassador of India through whom the tourist gathers impressions and information of our country. Comfortable transport should not just be for the rich. Clean and hygienic food should be cooked well and priced reasonably. Lodgings should be clean and aesthetic, no matter the category. Every satisfied and happy tourist becomes the biggest advertisement for Indian tourism.

To carry forward the heritage of our past we must educate ourselves about it and share it with the rest of the world in a contemporary context. This is what tourism is about, and it includes monuments, entertainment, food and other aspects of our culture all bound together by efficient and well maintained facilities.

Aruna Deshpande has made her work a part of this process. With her long experience in the travel trade and her interaction with tourists from all over the world she has developed a keen sense of the kind of information everyone would seek to obtain. In this new era of greater communication and information a dedicated effort such as the compilation of this book can open vast vistas for those who want to explore beyond the confines of their small worlds. It can indeed be a *vade mecum* for domestic and international tourists.

New Delhi.   **George Fernandes**
29th July, 2000

FOREWORD

The last century witnessed dramatic growth in the tourism sector to make it the centre stage of economic activity and a significant feature of national economics. At the dawn of the 21st century, Tourism is already the fastest growing and largest employment generating sector. The Information Technology Revolution has given unprecedented impetus to this sector and opened the floodgates of opportunities. India's position in the IT sector has tremendously increased the international awareness about this country and more and more people want to know and experience this ancient land.

Mrs. Aruna Deshpande's efforts through this book fulfil this new yearning for knowledge of this country. The choice of subjects and information is very apt and precise and satisfies most of the tourism queries on India. The book renders a great service to the tourists as well as students of tourism.

I am confident that this book will help in creating widespread awareness about our civilization, culture and tourist treasure. It is to me an invaluable contribution to a motherland from a caring citizen of the country.

Ashish Kumar Singh
Managing Director
Maharashtra Tourism Development Corporation Ltd.

FOREWORD

Mrs. Aruna Deshpande, began her career with us in February, 1978, as an Assistant in our Rail Ticketing Department. From the very beginning, she took keen interest in her work and soon rose to head the Department. But, since her heart and interest was in Tourism, she was transferred to our Inbound Tours Division. This opportunity encouraged her to channel all her energies and efforts in developing new ideas and introducing new destinations in the country. She continued to show tremendous progress in working independently. In between, in 1982, she took leave to complete the "German language" course at the University of Munich, and, on her return after completing her studies, she re-joined our Tours Division. Her knowledge of German language helped us to substantially increase our business from Germany. Though, she left us in 1996, Aruna continued to be associated with Tourism and particularly in giving lectures on Tourism to aspiring students. Her thorough knowedlge of Tourism destinations in our country and of the infrastructural facilities available in these areas helped her immensely to compile this highly useful book on Tourism. She has taken great care to incorporate all relevant details and facts covering almost all the States in our Country. This book, therefore, will not only be excellent reference material to Tour Operators, but, also be a great help to students who wish to complete special courses in Tourism.

Vinoo Ubhayakar
Managing Director
Trade-Wings Ltd.

INDIA AND ITS GEOGRAPHY

India is one of the oldest civilisations with a Kaleidoscopic variety and rich cultural heritage. The name India is derived from its great river "Indus". India lies to the north of the equator between 8°4' and 37°6' north latitude—68°7' and 97°25' east longitude.

India occupies a strategic position in Asia, looking across the seas to Arabia and Africa on the west; Burma, Malaysia and the Indonesian Archipelago on the east. Geographically, the Himalayan ranges keep India apart from the rest of Asia.

DIMENSIONS

Distance from North to South	3214 Km
Distance from East to West	2933 Km
Length of coastline	7516.6 Km
Length of land frontier	15,200 Km
Total geographic land area	32,87,263 Sq.Km
Percentage of earth's surface covered by India	2.4%

LOCATION

India, a land of variety and beauty occupies a strategic position in Asia, the Himalayan ranges and Nepal separate India from Tibet and China. The boundary line between India and China is called the McMahon line. In the east are Bangladesh and Mynamar, in the west Pakistan and in the south lies the Indian ocean and Sri Lanka, Gulf of Mannar and Palk straits separates India from Sri Lanka. Kanyakumari constitutes the southern tip of the Indian peninsula where it gets narrower and loses itself into the Indian Ocean.

Geographically, the mainland comprises seven regions—
- Northern mountains including the Himalayas and the north-eastern mountain ranges,
- The Indo-gangetic plain,
- The desert,
- Central highlands and peninsular plateau,

1

- East coast,
- West coast and
- Bordering seas and islands

ISLANDS

Andaman & Nicobar : Andamans is the northern cluster of 204 islands and Nicobar southern of 19 small islands. They constitute the Union Territory of Andman and Nicobar islands with Port Blair as its capital.

Lakshadweep : Lakshadweep is a group of 27 coral islands scattered in the Arabian Sea 300 km to the west of Kerala coast. Only 10 of these are inhabited. Together they form the Union Territory of Lakshadweep with Kavaratti island as its capital.

CLIMATE

India has three main seasons :

1.   Rainy season or Monsoon : *June to October*

There are two types of monsoon—the south-west monsoon which is from June to September.

The north-east monsoon which is from October to December and is confined to the east coast particularly on Tamil Nadu.

Assam, Arunachal Pradesh, Meghalaya, Sikkim and the northern parts of West Bengal, westren ghats and the Himalayan slopes are the regions which receive heavy rainfall above 200 cm annually.

Kutch and western Rajasthan and southern Haryana, south-east Punjab and Laddakh are the regions which receive scanty rainfall less than 50 cm annually.

Jaisalmer is the driest area which receives only 10 cm rainfall.

Cherapunji in Meghalaya is the wettest place in the world which receives the maximum amount of rainfall—as high as 1080 cm annually.

2.   Summer : *April to June*

During the summer, the mountains and hill resorts are cool and pleasant. Barmar in west Rajasthan remains the hottest with temperature shooting up to 50^0 c during day time.

3.   Winter : *October to March*

The Himalayan regions are the coldest, particularly Drass and Kargil in Laddakh where temperature falls below 4^0c.

CLIMATE

Average Temperature in °C and rainfall in mm

Month :		J	F	M	A	M	J	J	A	S	O	N	D
Agra	max	22	26	32	38	42	41	35	33	33	33	30	22
169 m	min	7	10	16	20	27	29	27	26	24	19	12	8
	rain	15	10	11	5	10	60	210	265	152	25	2	4
Ahmedabad	max	28	31	36	40	41	37	33	32	33	35	33	30
53 m	min	11	14	18	23	26	27	26	24	23	21	16	12
	rain	4		1	2	5	100	315	213	164	13	5	1
Ajanta/	max	28	31	36	38	40	35	30	29	30	32	30	29
Ellora	min	12	14	20	24	25	24	22	21	21	20	16	14
275 m	rain	3	3	4	7	16	140	190	145	180	163	32	9
Amritsar	max	18	22	28	34	39	40	36	34	34	32	27	20
234 m	min	5	7	12	16	22	25	26	25	23	17	9	5
	rain	38	10	26	10	11	32	168	168	106	55	10	15
Bangalore	max	25	30	32	33	33	29	27	27	28	28	26	25
920 m	min	14	16	18	21	21	20	18	19	19	19	16	15
	rain	3	10	6	45	117	80	117	147	144	185	54	16

Month:		J	F	M	A	M	J	J	A	S	O	N	D
Bhopal	max	26	29	34	38	41	37	32	29	30	31	29	26
	min	10	12	16	21	26	25	23	23	22	24	12	11
	rain	17	5	10	3	11	137	430	308	230	37	15	6
Bhubane-	max	27	32	35	38	39	35	32	31	31	31	29	28
swar	min	14	18	22	25	27	26	25	25	25	23	18	15
45m	rain	12	25	16	12	61	225	302	336	305	265	51	3
Bombay	max	28	28	30	32	33	32	30	30	30	32	32	31
11m	min	19	19	22	24	27	26	25	24	24	25	23	21
	rain	2	1		2	16	522	710	440	295	88	21	2
Calcutta	max	27	30	34	36	36	34	32	32	32	32	29	27
6m	min	12	17	22	25	27	27	26	26	26	24	18	13
	rain	14	24	26	44	121	258	301	305	291	160	35	3
Kochi	max	31	31	31	31	32	29	28	28	28	29	30	30
(Cochin)	min	22	23	26	26	23	24	24	24	24	24	24	23
Sea-level	rain	10	34	50	140	364	756	572	385	235	333	185	36
Darjeeling	max	8	11	15	18	19	19	20	20	20	18	15	11
2134m	min	1	3	8	11	14	14	14	15	15	12	7	3
	rain	22	27	52	107	185	522	714	572	416	116	14	5

Month :		J	F	M	A	M	J	J	A	S	O	N	D
Jodhpur 224m	max	25	28	33	38	42	41	36	34	35	36	31	26
	min	10	11	16	22	27	29	27	25	24	20	14	10
	rain	6	5	2	2	6	32	122	145	46	7	3	2
Kathmandu 1331m	max	18	20	24	27	29	29	27	28	27	26	22	19
	min	1	3	7	11	14	19	20	20	18	13	6	1
	rain	16	26	31	62	69	285	318	360	365	63	13	3
Leh 3521m	max	-3	1	6	12	16	20	25	24	21	15	8	2
	min	-14	-12	-6	-2	1	7	10	10	5	-1	-7	-11
	rain	10	8	8	5	5	5	13	15	8	3	3	5
Lucknow 111m	max	23	25	33	38	41	39	35	33	33	33	30	24
	min	8	11	16	21	26	27	27	26	25	20	13	9
	rain	24	17	9	6	12	95	298	302	182	40	1	5
Madras 16m	max	29	31	33	35	38	38	36	35	34	32	29	29
	min	19	20	23	26	28	27	26	26	25	24	22	21
	rain	24	7	15	25	52	52	85	124	117	266	309	140
Mandu 634m	max	24	28	34	38	40	36	32	28	29	31	28	26
	min	8	10	15	20	26	24	23	22	21	18	12	9
	rain	8	1	4	4	12	146	315	268	221	48	22	3

Month :		J	F	M	A	M	J	J	A	S	O	N	D
Mount Abu 1195m	max	18	21	25	29	32	29	24	23	24	27	24	21
	min	6	11	16	20	22	21	18	18	18	17	14	11
	rain	6	7	60	67	11	90	632	665	249	13	8	3
Mysore 770m	max	27	31	34	34	33	29	27	28	29	28	27	26
	min	16	17	20	21	21	20	20	20	19	20	18	16
	rain	3	6	12	65	156	61	72	80	150	180	67	15
Udhaga-mandalam Ooty 2286m	max	18	20	22	22	22	18	20	17	18	19	18	18
	min	4	5	8	10	11	11	11	11	10	10	8	6
	rain	26	12	30	108	173	139	177	128	110	214	127	59
Panaji 57m	max	31	31	32	33	33	31	29	29	29	31	33	32
	min	18	29	23	25	27	24	22	24	24	23	22	20
	rain	2	-	4	17	18	500	900	345	277	122	20	37
Port Blair 79m	max	29	30	31	31	31	29	29	29	29	29	29	29
	min	23	22	23	24	24	34	24	25	24	24	24	23
	rain	29	26	3	71	363	590	435	437	516	329	205	157
Pune 559m	max	31	33	36	38	37	32	28	28	30	32	31	30
	min	11	12	17	21	22	23	22	22	21	19	15	12
	rain	2	-	2	16	35	103	185	105	126	92	37	5

Month :		J	F	M	A	M	J	J	A	S	O	N	D
Puri	max	26	28	30	31	32	32	30	31	31	31	29	27
Sea-level	min	16	20	24	27	28	27	26	26	26	25	21	17
	rain	9	20	14	12	63	186	295	256	258	242	75	8
Shillong	max	15	16	22	24	24	24	24	24	24	22	19	16
1496m	min	4	5	11	14	16	16	17	18	17	13	8	5
	rain	15	29	60	136	325	545	395	335	315	220	35	6
Shimla	max	8	10	14	19	23	24	21	20	20	18	15	10
221m	min	-1	3	7	11	15	16	15	15	14	11	7	2
	rain	65	48	57	38	54	148	415	385	195	45	7	24
Srinagar	max	5	7	14	19	24	29	31	30	28	22	15	10
1768m	min	-2	-1	3	7	11	14	18	18	12	5	-0	-2
	rain	74	71	91	94	61	35	58	60	38	30	10	33
Trichy	max	29	33	36	38	38	36	36	35	34	32	30	28
88m	min	21	21	23	27	27	27	26	25	25	24	23	21
	rain	18	8	8	70	80	34	42	107	108	175	160	71
Thiruvana-	max	30	31	33	32	32	29	29	29	30	30	29	30
nthapuram	min	20	22	24	25	25	24	23	23	23	23	22	21
Trivandrum	rain	20	20	44	122	249	331	215	165	123	271	207	73
Sea-level													

Month:		J	F	M	A	M	J	J	A	S	O	N	D
Udaipur 582m	max	23	28	32	36	39	36	32	29	31	32	29	26
	min	7	9	15	20	25	25	24	23	22	19	11	8
	rain	9	4	4	3	5	87	195	205	120	16	5	3
Varanasi 76m	max	23	27	33	39	42	39	36	32	33	33	29	23
	min	8	12	17	22	27	27	26	26	25	21	12	9
	rain	19	18	9	5	14	116	301	305	185	55	9	7
Visakha-patnam 3m	max	27	28	31	34	35	34	32	32	32	31	29	28
	min	17	18	23	26	28	27	26	26	26	25	21	18
	rain	7	15	9	13	54	88	22	132	165	259	91	18

India became independent in 1947 and a republic in 1950 with a parliamentary form of democratic government, elected on the basis of universal adult franchise. India, world's largest democracy, is a union of 25 States and seven union territories.

THE POLITY : India, a sovereign socialist secular democratic republic, is governed in terms of a constitution, adopted by a constituent Assembly on November 26, 1949 and put into force in January 26, 1950. The Constitution of India provides for a single and uniform

citizenship for whole country. The constitution offers all citizens individually and collectively some basic freedoms. These are 1) right to equality, 2) right to freedom of speech and expression, 3) right against exploitation, 4) right to freedom of conscience and free profession, practice and propagation of religion, 5) right of any section of citizens to conserve their culture, language or script and right of minorities to establish and administer educational institutions of their choice and 6) right to constitutional remedies for enforcement of fundamental rights.

Fundamental duties enjoin upon a citizen among other things to abide by the constitution, to cherish and follow noble ideals which inspired our national struggle for freedom, to defend the country and render national services when called upon to do so and to promote harmony and spirit of common brotherhood amongst all people transcending religious, linguistic and regional or sectional diversities.

NATIONAL FLAG : The national flag is a horizontal tricolour deep saffron at the top, white in the middle and dark green at the bottom in equal proportion. In the centre of white band is a wheel, in navy blue—it s design is that of the wheel which appears on the abacus of the Sarnath lion stupa of Emperor Ashoka. It has 24 spokes. The design of the national flag was adopted by the Constituent Assembly of India on July 22, 1947. Its use of display is regulated by the Indian flag code.

NATIONAL ANTHEM : The song Jana-Gana-Mana, composed in Bengali by Nobel laureate Rabindranath Tagore was adopted in its Hindi version by the Constituent Assembly as the national anthem of India on January 24, 1950. It was first sung on December 27, 1911 at the Calcutta session of the Indian National Congress. The complete song consists of five stanzas. The first stanza contains the full version of the National Anthem.

NATIONAL SONG : The song Vande Mataram, composed by Bankim Chandra Chatterji, was a source of inspiration to the people in their struggle for freedom. It has an equal status with Jana-Gana-Mana. The first political occasion when it was sung was the 1896 session of the Indian National Congress

NATIONAL BIRD : The Indian peacock, the national bird, is a colourful, swan-sized bird, with a fan-shaped crest of feathers, a white patch under the eye and a long, slender neck. It is fully protected under the Indian wildlife (Protection) Act, 1972.

NATIONAL ANIMAL : The magnificent tiger is a striped animal. It has a thick yellow coat fur with dark stripes. The combination of grace, strength, agility and enormous power has earned the tiger its pride of place as the national animal of India.

NATIONAL FLOWER : Lotus

NATIONAL CALENDAR : The National calendar based on the Saka era with Chaitra as its first month and a normal year of 365 days was adopted from March 22, 1957 along the Georgian Calendar for official purposes.

FORESTS

With a wide range of climatic conditions from the torrid to the arctic India has a rich and varied vegetation which only a few countries of comparable size possess.

Nearly 22.8% of total land area is covered by forest. This constitutes 2% of the world's forest area. India can be divided into eight distinct floristic regions, namely, the western Himalayas (extend from Kashmir to Arunachal Pradesh through Nepal, Sikkim, Bhutan, Meghalaya and Nagaland and the Deccan Peninsula); the eastern Himalayas (extend from Sikkim eastwards and embracing Darjeeling, Kurseong and the adjacent tract); Assam (Brahmputra and the Surma valleys with evergreen forests); the Indus plain (plains of Punjab, western Rajasthan and northern Gujarat); the Ganga plain (only a small area supports forests of widely differing types; the Deccan (the entire land of the Indian Peninsula); Malabar (covering the excessively humid belt of the mountain country parallel to the west coast of the peninsula; and the Andmans (rich in evergreen, mangrove, beach and diluvial forests)

TYPES OF FORESTS

Evergreen Forests (Tropical) : These are found in the area where rainfall ranges between 200-300 cm, e.g. Western Ghats and sub-Himalayan regions. These are coniferous forests with trees having neddle-shaped leaves and provide Teak, Rosewood, Ebony and Bamboo.

Decidious Forests (Monsoon) : These are found in the area where rainfall ranges between 150 - 200 cm, e.g. parts of Deccan Plateau stretching over Maharashtra, Madhya Pradesh and Karnataka. They provide fine timber such as Teak, Sal and Sandalwood.

Dry Forests : These are found in the deserts of Rajasthan and south of Punjab where rainfall ranges between 75-100 cms.

Hill Forests : These are found in southern India and the Himalayan regions and provide timber like Oak, Deodar, Pines and Chi.

Tidal Forests (Mangrove) : These are found in coastal plains which are generally submerged, particularly on river deltas on the east coast, (the Ganga, the Mahanadi and the Godavari). The forests on the Gangetic delta in Bengal are called Sunderbans after the Sundari trees found in these forests.

MOUNTAINS

THE HIMALAYAS : Highest in the world, the Himalayas cover a distance of about 2500 km and an area of about 500,000 sq.km. It has the world's highest peak Mount Everest.

PATKAI : The Patkai and allied mountain ranges run along the Indo-Bangladesh-Burma border and are collectively called Purvachal or eastern mountains.

ARAVELLI : A range in north-western India is one of the oldest mountains in the world. The present Aravalli ranges are only a remnant of the gigantic one that had existed in pre-historic times with several of its summits rising above the snow line and nourishing glaciers of stupendous magnitude feeding many great rivers.

VINDHYAN : The Vindhyan range traverses nearly the whole width of peninsular India. It covers a distance of about 1050 km with an average elevation of 300 meters.

SATPURA : The Satpura range covers a distance of 900 km with peaks rising about 1000 meters. It is triangular in shape with its apex at Ratnapuri and two sides running parallel to the Narmada and Tapti rivers.

SAHYADRI OR WESTERN GHATS : These ranges with an average height of 1200 meters is about 1600 km long and runs along the Deccan plateau from the mouth of the river Tapti to Kanyakumari, the southernmost point of India. It overlooks the Arabian Sea and catches the full force of the monsoon winds, thus precipitating heavy rains on the west coast.

EASTERN GHATS : Bordering the east coast of India, these are cut by the powerful rivers into discontinuous blocks of mountains. In its northern parts between the Godavari and the Mahanadi rivers it rises about 1000 meters.

DESERTS

The deserts can be divided into two parts—the great desert and little desert. The great desert forms a part of Thar desert which extends over Pakistan in the west from the edge of Runn of Kutch beyond the Luni river northward. The whole of the Rajasthan-Sind frontier runs through this.

The little desert extends from the Luni between Jaisalmer and Jodhpur upto the northern wastes. Between the great and the little deserts lies a zone absolutely sterile, consisting of rock land and cut by limestone ridges. The arid zone in the country occupies nearly 12% of land which accounts for 3.2 lakh sq. km. Besides, there are 70,000 sq. km. of cold deserts in Ladakh.

RIVERS

Rivers in India may be classified as 1) Himalayan, 2) Peninsular, 3) Coastal and 4) those of the inland drainage basin.

The Himalayan rivers are perennial as they are generally snow-fed and have reasonable flow throughout the year. During the monsoon the Himalayas receive very heavy rain and the river carry the maximum quantity of water causing floods.

The peninsular rivers are generally rain-fed and, therefore, fluctuate in volume. A large number of the streams is non-perennial. The coastal streams, especially on the west coast, are short in length and have limited catchment area. The streams of the inland drainage basin of western Rajasthan are few and far between. They drain towards the individual basins or salt lakes like the Sambhar or are lost in the sands having no outlet to the sea. The Luni is the only river of this category that drains into the Runn of Kutch.

The Ganga sub-basin which is part of the larger Ganga-Brahmputra-Meghana basin is the largest in India receiving waters from an area which comprises one-quarter of the total area of the country (7500 sq. km). The Ganga flows through Uttar Pradesh, Bihar, West Bengal and then enters Bangladesh. The Ganga is joined by a number of the Himalayan rivers including the Yamuna, the Ghagra, the Gomati, the Gandak and the Kosi. Among the important rivers flowing north from central India into the Yamuna are Chamba, Betwa and Sone.

The Brahmaputra and the Barak flowing from east to west in north-eastern regions have immense water resources. The Ganga and the Brahmputra carry 61% of the total water of the country's rivers.

The Godavari in the southern Peninsula has the second largest river basin covering 10% of the area of India. Next is the Krishna basin while the Mahanadi has the third largest basin. The basin of the Narmada in the uplands of the Deccan flowing to the Arabian Sea and the Kaveri in the south falling into the Bay of Bengal are about the same size.

The two other river systems, small but agriculturally important, are the Tapti in the north and the Pennar in the south. These west coast rivers are of great importance as they contain as much as 11% of the country's water resources irrigating about 10% of the land area.

There are 14 major river basins, each with drainage area of above 20,000 sq. km., 44 medium basins.

The total water in all river systems of India has been estimated roughly at 16,45,000 million cubic metres.

TABLE OF STATES, UNION TERRITORIES, CAPITALS AND LANGUAGES

State	Capital	Main Language
Andhra Pradesh	Hyderabad	Telugu
Arunachal Pradesh	Itanagar	Assamese
Assam	Dispur	Assamese
Bihar	Patna	Hindi
Delhi	Delhi	Hindi
Goa	Panaji	Konkani, Marathi
Gujarat	Gandhinagar	Gujarati
Haryana	Chandigarh	Hindi
Himachal Pradesh	Shimla	Hindi, Pahari
Jammu & Kashmir	Srinagar in summer Jammu in winter	Dogri, Kashmiri
Karnataka	Bangalore	Kannada
Kerala	Thiruvananthapuram	Malyalam
Madhya Pradesh	Bhopal	Hindi
Maharashtra	Mumbai	Marathi
Manipur	Imphal	Assamese
Meghalaya	Shillong	Assamese
Mizoram	Aizawal	Assamese
Nagaland	Kohima	Assamese
Orissa	Bhubaneshwar	Oriya
Punjab	Chandigarh	Punjabi
Rajasthan	Jaipur	Rajasthani
Sikkim	Gangtok	Nepali
Tamil Nadu	Chennai	Tamil
Tripura	Agartala	Assamese
Uttar Pradesh	Lucknow	Hindi
West Bengal	Calcutta	Bengali

UNION TERRITORIES

State	Capital	Main Language
Andman & Nicobar Islands	Port Blair	Bengali, Tamil
Chandigarh	Chandigarh	Punjabi
Dadra & Nagar Haveli	Silvassa	Gujarati
Daman and Diu	Daman	Gujarati
Lakshadweep	Kavaratti	Malayalam
Pondicherry	Pondicherry	Tamil

HOW TO REACH INDIA

In India there is an ancient Sanskrit dictum : *"Atithi Devo Bhava"*
—Treat a guest as if he were God himself.

For thousand of years this land of magic and mystique has lured
distant travellers and we have been treating everybody as God.

For information and assitance regarding travel and accommodation
contact the Government of India Tourist Office or visit the Government
of India website at **http//www.tourindia.com** *or* **e-mail:
Tourism@x400.nicgw.nie.in.**

India can be reached by air, sea or road. However, in recent years,
over 97% of all tourists have been arriving by air. India has direct air
link with all five continents except South America. Over 50 international
carriers fly to and through India. The four major international airports
are Mumbai, Delhi, Chennai and Calcutta. Other small international
airports are Varanasi & Patna (from Nepal), Hyderabad and
Thiruvananthapuram. The charter flights bringing foreign tourists to the
country are now allowed to operate to Goa, Agra, Varanasi, Jaipur and
Bangalore. The minimum payment to the Indian tour operator by the
foreign charter operator is US$ 400 per person effective from April 1,
1998. However, from the SAARC countries and Mynamar the amount
to be paid is 50% of the aforesaid. International airports offer a range
of services like restaurants, business centres, rest rooms and phone
booths.

The time difference in India is GMT plus 5 hours in winter &
4 hours in summer time. Throughout India there is only one Indian
Standard Time with no change in summer or winter.

AIRPORTS

The international airports in the metro cities offer a range of
services ensuring that the traveller on business trip can continue working
while waiting to board an international connecting flight, or when
transferring from one international flights to another. These include
restaurants, business centres, rest rooms and handy telephone booths.
Business centres are equipped with state-of-the-art equipment including
word processors and telefax.

All airports have 'left luggage' facilities, porters and metered taxis. At Delhi and Mumbai 'prepaid' taxis are available. There are duty-free shops at all international airports.

Baggage Loss or Damage Claims : If your baggage is mishandled or lost in transit
— Obtain a certificate to this effect from the Airline, and
— Have the certificate countersigned by customs, indicating specifically the unutilised portion of the free allowance.

INDIA BY SHIP : There are no longer any passenger liners operating to India. However, some parts like Mumbai, Chennai, Goa and Cochin are stops for luxury liners round the world cruises. The most well-known is Q.E.II, Semester at Sea from Pittsburgh, Song of Flower, Ocean Pearl, Royal Viking Sun and Golden Oddessey.

INDIA BY ROAD : India has a wide network of roads and travel by road is an exciting experience. Tourists who wish to travel in India in their own cars or coaches or trailers often bring their vehicles overland or overseas.

Vehicles covered by Triptyques or Carnets issued by any internationally recognised automobile association or club affiliated to the Alliance Internationale de Tourisme, Geneva, are allowed free of import duty for a period of six months only. Import of vehicles under Customs Carnets are permitted only in the case of bonafide tourists and foreigners visiting India mainly on a holiday.

For obtaining release from Customs, besides production of a customs carnet, the tourist must be personally present and produce to the Customs the foreign registration certificate of the vehicle to be imported. Vehicles imported under a Customs carnet must be re exported within six months.

ICMV's : International Certificate for Motor Vehicles, valid for one year, can be obtained by tourists from the Licensing Authority or from an Automobile Association / Club of their country of residence. Tourists are advised to obtain such certificates to facilitate the movement of their vehicles through the various States of India.

IDP : International Driving Permit, valid for one year, can be obtained from the Licensing Authority or from an authorised Automobile Association / Club of their country of residence. The IDP acts as a driving licence during its validity.

The Third Party Insurance is compulsory in India and must be taken before putting the vehicle on the road in case of its arriving by sea and immediately after arrival by the land route.

In the case of tourists importing their own cars/coaches/vehicles, it is advisable for them or their agent to contact in advance one of the following automobile association regarding the rules and regulations :

(a) Western India Automobile Association and Federation of the Indian Automobile Associations, Lalji Narainji Memorial Building, 76 Veer Nariman Road, Mumbai 400 020, Phone – 204 1085.

(b) Automobile Association of Upper India, Lilaram Buliding, 14F Connaught place, New Delhi 100 001, phone 331 2323.

(c) Automobile Association of Eastern India, 13 Promothesh Baru Sarai, Calcutta 700 019, phone 755131

(d) Automobile Association of Southern India, 187, Anna Salai, Chennai, Phone 8268661

(e) UP Automobile Association, 32A Mahatma Gandhi Marg, Allahabad, Phone 600332.

Car Rent : Cars self driven or with chauffeurs are available easily in India. All Airports have 'car rent' counters. Cars can be rented from the transport counters of hotels or by calling a rental company. All State governments operate inter-city or inter-State bus services. Local buses are operated within city limits. Also Rikshaws, metered taxis, tourist taxis are easily available at all major tourist destinations.

CUSTOMS REGULATION

For purposes of customs, a 'Tourist' is defined as a person not normally resident of India, who enters India for a period up to six months in the course of any twelve months period for legitimate non-immigration purposes, such as touring, recreation, sports, health, family reasons and pilgrimage.

There are two channels for Customs clearance :

Green Channel : Green Channel is for passengers not having any dutiable articles or unaccompanied baggage.

Red Channel : Red Channel is for passengers having dutiable articles or high value articles to be entered on Tourist Baggage Re-Export form. These articles have to be re-exported at the time of departure. Failure to re-export as per list on TBRE form will involve payment of duty leviable thereon.

Customs Assistance/Grievances : If you have any complaints, comments or suggestions regarding customs contact :

— The Assitant Collector of Customs in the custom wing, open 24 hours, at the international airport.

For detailed information and registering complaint, write to :

— The Commissioner of Customs,
   New Customs House, New Customs House Road, Near IGT
   Terminal II, New Delhi-110037.

Special Assistance

Emergency Health Services. Ambulance : PH 102

Airport Emergency Services

— 24 hours emergency medical aid is available at all international
   airports for passengers needing medical care on arrival.

VISA REQUIREMENTS

Indian Visas are available from Indian Consular Offices around the
world on payment. They should posses a valid National Passport except
in the case of nationals of Bhutan and Nepal who may carry only suitable
means of identification.

Tourist Visa : A multi-entry visa, valid for 180 days, is granted
for the purpose of tourism. The visa is valid for entry into India within
six months from the date of issue.

Collective Visa : The facility also exists for the issue of collective
visas to group tours consisting of not less than four members and
sponsored by a travel agency recognised by the Government of India.
Such groups may split into smaller groups for visiting different places
in India after obtaining a collective 'licence to travel' from the
Immigration authorities in India. However, they must reassemble and
depart as the original groups.

Transit Visa : Transit visas are granted by Indian Missions abroad
for a maximum period of 15 days.

Exemption from Registration : Foreigners coming on tourists
visas for 180 days or a shorter period are not required to register
themselves with any authority in India. They can move about freely
in the country, except to restricted / protected areas and prohibited
places. Nationals of Bangladesh are exempted from registration up to
six months. They have to register themselves thereafter. Individuals
without nationality or of undetermined nationality should have valid
passports, identity of documents or sworn affidavits along the visa for
which they should apply at least two months in advance.

Family passports issued by other governments are recognised
without discrimination.

Landing permit Facility : No landing permit facility is available
to any foreign tourist landing without a visa. A limited facility exists
only for group tours consisting of four or more members and sponsored
by a travel agency recognised by the Government of India.

Childern below the age of 12 of foreigners of Indian origin may be granted a landing permit by the immigration authorities up to a period of 90 days to see their relatives, in case they happen to come without a visa.

Tourist Groups : A tourist group arriving by air, ship, chartered or scheduled flight may be granted a collective landing permit for a period up to 30 days by the immigration authorities on landing, provided the group is sponsored by a recognised travel agency, a pre-drawn itinerary is presented along with details of passport etc. of the members and the travel agency gives an undertaking to conduct the group.

VISA EXTENSION : Tourist Visas are available for a maximum period of 180 days. No extension beyond six months is provided as a rule.No charges are levied for Visa extension within the maximum period of 180 days.

If the visa for stay in India is for more than 180 days, a registration certificate and residential permit should be obtained from the nearest Foreigner's Regional Registration Office within 14 days of arrival. All persons, including Indian nationals are required to fill in a disembarkation card at the time of arrival.Foreigners registered at the FRRO are required to report any change of addresses.

Please write the types of visas and exit formalities before currency regulation.

EXIT FORMALITIES : Every foreigner who is about to depart finally from India shall surrender his certificate of registration either to the Registration Officer of the place where he is registered or of the place from where he intends to depart or to the immigration officer at the port/check post of exit from India.

The following are the addresses of the Foreigner's Regional Registration Offices :

New Delhi :
1ˢᵗ floor, Hans Bhavan, Tilak Bridge, New Delhi 110 001.
PH 331 9489; FAX 375 5183

Mumbai :
Annexe II. 3ʳᵈ floor, Crawford market, Mumbai 400 001
PH 2121169; FAX 2620721

Calcutta :
Office of Deputy Commissioner of Police, Security Control, 237 Acharya Jagdish Chandra Bose Road, Calcutta – 700 020
PH 2470549; FAX 2470549

Chennai :
Shastri Bhawan Annex. NO 26, Haddows Road, Nungakkam, Chennai 600 006, PH 8277036; FAX 8277036.

OTHER TYPES OF VISAS : If a foreigner wishes to come to

India for a purpose other than tourism, he should obtain an appropriate visa out of the followings :

Business Visa : A foreigner can obtain multiple entry business visa for five years.

Student Visa : A student visa can be obtained on production of proof of admission and means of substance while in India. This visa is valid for one year but is extended for the duration of the course.

Conference Visa : Delegates coming to attend international conferences in India can be granted Conference Visa to cover the conference.

Trekking/Mountaineering Expeditions : Foreigners wishing to undertake trekking, botanical expeditions, canoe rafting etc. in a team may be granted visas for the required duration on presentation of full details.

Sports : Sports teams or individual sportsmen wishing to participate in international sports events being held in India may be granted sports visas for the required duration on presentation of full details.

Journalists /Media : Foreign journalists, media men, documentary and feature film makers may obtain necessary visas after due formalities from the Indian Embassy.

Employment Visa : Foreigners desirous of coming to India for employment should apply for Employment Visas, initially granted for one year but can be extended up to the period of the contract.

CURRENCY REGULATIONS

Tourists are not allowed to bring Indian currency into the country or take it out of the country. Unlimited amounts of foreign currency or traveller's cheques are allowed into the country, but any amount more than US$ 1000, should be declared on arrival and a certificate obtained from the Customs.

All money should be changed at official banks or through official money changers. The tourist receives a currency exchange form for each transaction. These forms are important as they may be required for re-exchange while leaving India.

Most major international credit cards – Visa, American Express, Diner's are accepted in international hotels, shops and restaurants.

INCOME TAX CLEARANCE : If a person not domiciled in India intends to stay in India for more than 120 days, an Income Tax clearance certificate is required in order to leave the country. This document will prove that the person's stay in India was financed by his own money and not by working or selling his goods.

The foreign section of the Income Tax department issues these certificates on being shown the person's passport, visa extension form and the currency exchange receipts which have been used by him.

HEALTH REGULATION

Foreign tourist should be in possession of the Yellow Fever Vaccination Certificate confirming to international health regulations, if they are not originating or transmitting through Yellow Fever endemic countries.

AIDS TEST : Foreigners visiting India for more than one year have to undergo an AIDS test in any one of the nearest survelliance centres. In case a foreigner is found to be infected with the AIDS virus, he is deported. Foreigners having HIV-free certificates issued within one month before their arrival from any one of the WHO collaborating laboratories are exempted from the AIDS test.

FOREIGN TRAVEL TAX

Passengers embarking on journeys to any place outside India will have to pay Rs 500 as foreign Travel Tax and Rs 150 on journeys to Afghanistan, Bangladesh, Butan, Burma, Nepal, Pakistan, Sri Lanka and Maldevis.

No tax is payable on journeys by ship from Rameswaram to Talaimanar and in case of transit passengers provided they do not leave the customs barrier. Transit passengers travelling by air who have to leave on account of mechanical trouble are also exempt from FTT provided they continue their journey by the same aircraft and flight number by which they arrived. Transit sea passengers leaving the ship for sightseeing/shopping during the ship's call at any of the Indian ports will not be required to pay FTT.

INLAND AIR TRAVEL TAX

An Inland Air Travel Tax is levied at 15% of the basic fare, on all passengers embarking on an inland air journey. Passengers paying their air fare in foreign currency will be exempt from payment of this tax. In addition, infants, cancer patients, the blind and the invalids are exempt after fulfilling certain conditions in the relevant notifications.

GUIDES

Trained English and foreign language speaking guides are available at fixed charge at all important tourist offices.

IMMIGRATION

PASSPORT : Citizens of all countries require a valid Passport or valid travel documents and valid visa granted by Indian Mission abroad for entering India except Nepalese or Bhutanese citizens who proceeding from their respective countries need no passport or visa but should possess suitable identification documents.

ARRIVAL FORMALITIES : If the visa for stay in India is more than 90 days Registration Certificate and Residential Permit should be obtained from the nearest Foreigner's Registration Offices within 7 days of the arrival. Personal appearance is absolutely necessary at the time of registration, extension or exit as required by the law of the land. Four photos are also required for registration. The foreigners registered at Foreigner's Registration Office are required to report change of their addresses. They have also to inform the Registration Offices regarding their absence for more than 15 days.

DEPARTURE FROM INDIA : All persons except nationals of Nepal and Bhutan leaving by road or rail have to fill an Embarkation card at the time of departure. All Tourists have to get their Registration Certificates endorsed by the appropriate registration authorities and surrender these and other residential permits at the place of Registration Office before departure.

RESTRICTED AND PROTECTED AREAS : Military installations and Defence Organisations and Research Organisations are considered protected areas where permits are generally not given to foreigners.

PHOTOGRAPHY RESTRICTIONS : Photography is prohibited in places of military importance, railway stations, bridges, airports and other military installations.

EXPORTS OF ANTIQUITIES : Antiquities include sculpture, painting or other works of art and craftsmanship, illustrative of science, art, crafts, religion of bygone ages and historical interest which have been in existence for not less than one hundred years.

Also manuscripts, or other documents of scientific, historical, literary or aesthetic value in existence for not less than seventy five years an art treasures, not necessarily antiquities, but having regard to the artistic and aesthetic value cannot be exported out of India .

RESTRICTIONS PERTAINING TO EXPORT OF ARTICLES MADE FROM ANIMALS : The Government of India is concerned about the conservation of its endangered and rare fauna. As such export of all wild animals indigenous to the country and articles made from such listed animals like skin, repetiles, furs, ivory, rhino horns, trophies etc., have been totally banned.

SOME COMMON CUSTOMS AND TRADITIONS

NAMASKAR

Namaskar or Namaste is the form of greeting used to welcome the guest. While doing namaskar, both the palms are placed together and raised near the heart but below the face to greet the person. It is believed that the hands symbolise one mind, or the self meeting the self. While the right hand represents higher nature, the left hand denotes worldly or lower nature.

TILAK OR TIKKA

Tilak or Tikka is a ritual mark on the forehead. It can be put in many forms as a sign of blessing, greeting or auspiciousness. The Tilak is usually made out of red vermilion paste (kumkum) which is a mixture of turmeric, alum, iodine, camphor etc. It can also be of sandalwood paste (chandan) blended with musk. The Tilak is applied on the spot between the brows which is considered the seat of wisdom and mental concentration and is very important for worship. This is the spot on which yogis meditate to become one with the Brahma—The supreme soul of the universe, self-existent, absolute and eternal from which all things emanate and to which all return. It also indicate the point at which the spiritual and mystical 'Third Eye' opens. All thoughts and actions are said to be governed by this spot. Putting of the coloured mark symbolizes the quest for the 'opening' of the third eye.

All rites and ceremonies of the Hindus begin with a Tilak topped with a few grains of rice placed on this spot with the index finger or the thumb. The same custom is followed while welcoming or bidding farewell to guests or relations.

ARATI

Arati is performed as an act of veneration and love. It is often performed as a mark of worship and to seek blessings from God, to welcome the guests, on birthdays, family members on auspicious occasions or to welcome newly wedded couple.

For performing Arati, five small lamps called niranjans are filled with ghee or oil and arranged in a small tray made of metal. A wick is made out of cotton wool and placed in the lamps. A conchshell filled with water, auspicious leaves or flowers, incense or lighted camphor are also placed in the tray. The lamps are lit and the tray is rotated in a circular motion in front of the deity or the person to be welcomed.

The purpose of performing Arati is to ward off evil effects and the malefic influence of the 'evil eye'. This is the highest form of veneration Hindus show to anyone.

GARLANDING

Flower garlands are generally offered as a mark of respect and honour. They are offered to welcome the visitors or in honour to the Gods and Goddesses. The garlands are generally made with white jasmine and orange marigold flowers. They are weaved in thread tied in the end with the help of the knot.

LIST OF RESTRICTED AND PROTECTED AREAS
AND AUTHORITIES THAT CAN GRANT PERMITS

Restricted/Protected Areas	Authority that can grant permit	Remarks
ASSAM : Kaziranga National Park, Manas National Park, Guwahati and Kamakhya Temple, Sibsagar, Jatibga Bird Sanctuary.	MHA and all FRROs, all Indian Missions abroad, Home Comr. Assam Govt., New Delhi and Trade advisor Govt.of Assam, Calcutta.	Entry upto Guwahati by Air only. Journey to Sibsagar by national highway and to Jatinda by train.
MEGHALAYA : Shillong, Barapani, Cherrapunji, Mawsynram, Jakeran, Ranikor, Thadlaskein, Nartiang, Tura and Siju.	MHA and all FRROs, all Indian Missions abroad, Home Comr., Meghalaya.	Journey upto Guwahati by Air only.
MANIPUR : Loklak Lake, Imphal, Moirang INA Memorial, Keibul Deer Sanctuary and Waithe Lake.	All Indian Missions abroad. All FRROs and MHA, State Govt. of Manipur.	Calcutta to Imphal by Air only.
ANDMAN & NICOBAR ISLANDS : Municipal area, Port Blair, Havelock Island, Long, Neil Island, Mayabunder, South Cinque, Red Skin, Mount Harriet and Madhuban.	MHA and All FRROs, All Indian Missions abroad, Immigration officer, Port Blair.	
LAKSHADWEEP : Bangaram	Administrator, Lakshadweep : MHA Cochin Office.	
SIKKIM : Gangtok, Rumtek, Phodang, Pemayangtse. Zongri in West Sikkim. Tsangu Lake in East Sikkim. Mangan, Tong, Singhik. Chungthang. Lachung and Yumthang. Gangtok, Rumtek, Rhongdong.	MHA, All FRROs, All Indian Missions abroad and immigration officers at airports at Mumbai, Calcutta, Chennai and New Delhi. Chief Secretary, Home Secretary/Secretary (Tourism) Govt.of Sikkim, Gangtok, I.G. Govt. of Sikkim, Siliguri,	Individual tourists not permitted, 15 days allowed. Groups allowed for 15 days trekking and are to be accompanied by a liaison officer.

Restricted/Protected Areas	Authority that can grant permit	Remarks
	Dy. Director (Tourism) Sikkim Govt.New Delhi, Asst Resident Comr., Govt of Sikkim, Calcutta Tourism officer, Rangpo, Dy. Comr., Darjeeling, Dy. Secy., Under Secy., Home Dept., Govt. of West Bengal, Calcutta.	
MIZORAM : Vairangte, Thingdawl and Aizawl	Home Commr.Govt of Mizoram, Aizwal, All FRRO's at Delhi, Mumbai and Calcutta, Chief Immigration officer, Chennai and all Indian mission abroad.	Tourist groups may travel on the identified tour circuits only. Individual tourists ᵛnot permitted, 10days allowed.
HIMACHAL PRADESH : Poo Khab-Sumdho- Dhankar-Tabo Gompa- Kaza. Morang-Dabling	MHA/Govt.of H.P/DM/ SDM Concerned/ITBP. Spl. Commissioner (Tourism) Resident Commissioner. Govt of H.P., New Delhi DG of Police, H.P.Shimla	For Trekking only.
ARUNACHAL PRADESH : Itanagar, Ziro, Along, Pasighat, Miao and Namdapha	Home Comr., Govt of A.P. Itanagar, All FRROs at Delhi, Bomaby, Calcutta, Chief Immigration officer, Chennai, all Indian Missions abroad.	Tourist groups may travel on identified tour circuits only.
UTTAR PRADESH : Nanda Devi sanctuary, Niti Ghati and Kalindi Khat in Chamoli, ˙Uttar Kashi districts. Adjoining area of Milam Glacier.	MHA/Govt of U.P. / DM/ SDM concerned.	

HINDUSTANI FOR THE TOURIST

The Basic Vocabulary

WHO ?—Cavn ?   : WHAT ?—Kay-aah ?
WHEN ?—Kab ?   : HOW ?—Kai-Sah ?
WHY ?—Queon ?   : WHERE ?—Kidhar ?
THERE—Udahar   : HERE—Idhar
NO—Na-heehn   : YES—Hahn
INSIDE—Andar   : OUTSIDE—Bah-her
LESS—Kam   : MORE—Zey-add-ah
QUICKLY and SOON—Jaldi
OFTEN—Ak-sar
MORNING — Subha; AFTERNOON — Dopahar; EVENING —
Sham
NIGHT — Rat; TODAY — Aj; DAY — Din; WEEK — Hafta;
MONTH — Mahina; YEAR — Sal
SUNDAY — Ravivar; MONDAY — Somvar; TUESDAY —
Mangalvar; WEDNESDAY — Budhvar; THURSDAY — Guruvar;
FRIDAY — Shukravar; SATURDAY — Shanivar.

1 — Ek; 2 — Do; 3 — Tin; 4 — Char; 5 — Panch; 6 — Chhai;
7 — Sat; 8 — Aath; 9 — Nau; 10 — Das; 11 — Gyara; 12 — Barah;
13 — Terah; 14 — Chaudah; 15 — Pandhrah; 16 — Sola; 17 — Satrah;
18 — Atharah; 19 — Unnis; 20 — Bees; 100 — Sau; 200 — Do Sau;
1000 — Hazar.

HOW MUCH ?—Kitna? Kit-Nah?
THANK YOU — Shukriya, Shook-ree-yah or Dhanyavad
PLEASE — Mayher-banee karkay or Kirpya
HOW ARE YOU ? — Aap kai-say hein?
ALL RIGHT — Atch-chah or Theek
THAT MUCH — Oot-nah
AS MUCH — Jit-nah
WHOSE ? — Kiss-kah ?
HOW LONG ? — Kit-nah-lumbah ?
EXCUSE ME — Maaf-kar-nah
PLEASE REPEAT — Maher-baanee kar-key phir bowl-ee-eh
HOW DO YOU DO ? — Aap kai-sae-hein?
GOOD BYE — Atch-chah, Chalte hein
WHOM ? — Kiss-ko ?
HOW MANY ? — Kit-ney ?

HOW BIG ? — Kit-nah-barrah ?
GOOD MORNING/DAY/AFTERNOON/NIGHT — Naam-astay

PRONOUNS WITH USEFUL VERBS

I am — Mayn Hoon; We are — Hum hein; You are — Toom Ho; They are — Way hein.
He, She, — Voh; It is — Yeh hei.

ALL ABOUT YOURSELF

My name is — May-rah naam ————— hai
I have come from —— — Maiyn—— se aya hoon
My passport number is —— — May-rah passport number—hai

SHOPPING

How much is this ? — Iska kya dam hai ?
That is very expensive — Bahut mehanga hai

AT THE HOTEL

What is the room charge ? — Ek din ka kiraya kya hai ?
Is there hot water ? — Kya kamre mei garam pani hai ?
Is there a large room ? — Bara kamra hai ?
Please clean the room — Yeh kamra saaf karwa dijiye
Please give me a bill — Bill dijiye
Do you have a reservation for me ? — Kya aap nay may-ray lee-eh jug-ah rocki hei?

BASIC FOOD ITEMS

Meat—Mas; Prawns—Jhinga; Fish—Macchli; Chicken—Murgah; Vegetable—Sabzi; Potato—Aaloo; Aubergine—Baigan; Cabbage—Band Gobhi; Cauliflower—Phool gobi; Ladies Finger—Bhindi; Carrots— Gajar; Peas—Matar; Onion—Piaz; Spinach—Sag; Ginger—Adrak; Hot spices—Garam masala; Turmeric—Haldi; Clove—laung; Chilli—Mirch; Bay leaf—Tej patta; Cumin—Jeera; Mustard—rai; Apple—Seb; Banana—Kela; Coconut—Nariyal; Lemon—Nimbu; Mango—Aam; Orange—Santra; Pineapple—anannas.

GOVT OF INDIA TOURIST OFFICES

AGRA
191, The Mall, Agra – 282 001
Uttar Pradesh.
Tel (0562) 363377, 363959

AURANGABAD
Krishna Vilas,
Station Road
Aurangabad – 431 005,
Maharashtra.
Tel(02432) 331217

BANGALORE
KFC Building,
48, Church Street,
Bangalore – 560 001,
Karnataka
Tel/Fax: (08) 5585417

BHUBANESWAR
B/21, BJB Nagar
Bhubaneswar – 751 014
Orissa.
Tel: (0674) 432203

CALCUTTA
"Embassy" 4, Shakespeare
Saroni, Calcutta – 700 071,
West Bengal.
Tel (033) 2421402, 2421475,
2425813
Fax: (033) 2823521

CHENNAI
154, Anna Salai,
Chennai – 600002,
Tamil Nadu
Tel (044) 8524295, 8524785,
8522193
Fax: (044) 8522193

GUWAHATI
B.K. Kakati Road,
Ulubari, Guwahati – 781 007
Assam.
Telefax (0361) 547407

HYDERABAD
3-6-369/A,
30, Sandozi Building

2nd Floor, 26, Himayatnagar
Hyderabad – 500 029
Andhra Pradesh
Tel: (040) 7630037.

IMPHAL
Old Lambulane, Jail Road,
Imphal – 795 001, Manipur
Tel/Fax: (0386) 221131

JAIPUR
State Hotel, Khasa Kothi,
Jaipur – 302 001,
Rajasthan
Tel/Fax: (0141) 372200

KHAJURAHO
Near Western Group
of Temples,
Khajuraho – 471606,
Madhya Pradesh
Tel: (076861) 42347/48

KOCHI
Willingdon Island,
Kochi – 682 009
Kerala.
Tel (0484) 668352

MUMBAI
123M, Karve Road,
Opp Churchgate
Mumbai – 400 020
Maharashtra.
Tel (022) 2032932, 2033144,
2033145, 2036854.
Fax: (022) 2014496

NAHARALAGUM
Sector"C",
Naharalagum-791110
Arunachal Pradesh.
Tel (03781) 44328

NEW DELHI
88, Janpath,
New Delhi – 110 001
Tel: (011) 3320432, 3320005,
3320109, 3320008,
3320266

Fax: (011) 3320109.
Domestic Airport Counter
Tel: (011) 5665296
International Airport Counter
Tel: (011) 5691171
PANAJI (GOA)
Comunidae Building,
Church Square,
Panaji – 403 001
Goa.
Tel: (0832) 223412
PATNA
Sudama Place,
Kankarbagh Road
Patna – 800 020
Bihar
Tel/Fax: (0612) 345776
PORT BLAIR
VIP Road, 189, II Floor

Junglighat,
PO Port Blair – 744103
Andaman & Nicobar Islands.
Tel: (03192)33006
SHILLONG
Tirot Singh Syiem Road
Police Bazar,
Shillong – 793 001
Meghalaya
Tel/Fax: (0364)225632
TIRUVANANTHAPURAM
Airport Counter,
Tiruvananthapuram, Kerala
Tel: (0471) 451498
VARANASI
15-B, The Mall
Varanasi – 221002
Uttar Pradesh
Tel: (0542) 343744.

INDIAN TOURIST OFFICES ABROAD

AUSTRALIA
Level 2, Piccadilly
201, Pitt Street, Sydney,
New South Wales 2000
PHONE : (02) 9264 4855
E Mail :
intour@ozemail.com.au
CANADA
60, Bloor Street (West),
Suite 1003, Toronto,
Ontario M4 N3 N6
PHONE : (416) 962 3787/88
FAX : (416) 962 6279
FRANCE
13, Boulevard Haussmann
F – 75009 Paris
PHONE :0033 1 45 233045
FAX : 0033 1 45 233345
GERMANY
Baseler St. 48
D – 60329
Frankfurt A Main 1
PHONE : 0049 69 242 9490

FAX : 0049 69 242 9497
Website : http: //
www:indiatourism.com
ITALY
Via-Albricci-9, Milan 21022
PHONE : 0039 2 8053506
FAX : 0039 2 72021681
JAPAN
Pearl Building, 9-18 Ginza,
7 Chome, Chuo-Ku,
Tokyo 104
PHONE : 0081 33 571 5179
FAX : 0081 33 571 5235
NETHERLANDS
Rokin 9-15,
1012 KK Amsterdam
PHONE : 0031 20 6208991
FAX : 0031 20 6383059
Website:http://
www.qqq.com./india/
SINGAPORE
20, Kramat Lane
#01 01A United House

Singapore 228 773
PHONE : 0065 235 3800
FAX : 0065 235 8677

SPAIN

C/O Embassy of India
Avenida PIO XII 30-32
Madrid –28016
PHONE : 0034 1 3457339
FAX : 0034 1 3457340

SWEDEN

Sveavagen 9-11, 8th Floor
S II 157,Stockholm 11157
PHONE : 0046 8 215081/
                          101187
FAX : 0046 8 210186
E mail :
director@indiatouristoffice.se

UAE

Post Box 12856,
NASA Building
A1 Maktoum Road,
Deira, Dubai
PHONE : 0044171 437 3677
FAX : 0044171 494 1048
E mail :
goirto@emirates.net.ae

UK

7 Cork Street,
London WIX 2AB
PHONE : 0044 171 437 3677
FAX : 0044171 491 1048

USA

3550 Wilshire Boulevard
Room 204, Los Angeles
California 90010
PHONE : 001 213 330 8855
FAX : 001 213 380 6111

NEW YORK

1270, Avenue of America
Suite 1808 (18th Floor)
New York, NY 10020
PHONE : 001 212 586 4901/
                          2/3
FAX : 001 212 582 3274
E-mail :
goitony@tourindia.com
Website:http:/ /
www.tourindia.com

ISRAEL

E –5, 4-Kaulman
Street, Tel Aviv 68012
PHONE : 00972 3 5101407
FAX : 00972 3 5100894

RUSSIAN FEDERATION

20, Petrovskie Building 1
Suite 32 - Moscow
PHONE : 007 095 200358/
                          2003579
FAX : 007 095 200 3071

SOUTH AFRICA

PO Box No 412 452,
Craig Hall 2024
Johannesburg
PHONE 0027 11 3250880
FAX : 0027 11 3250881

INDIA : A CULTURAL VOYAGE

Jawaharlal Nehru, the first Prime Minister of India has said: "India, it is said, is religion, philosophical, speculative, metaphysical, unconcerned with this world,and lost in dreams of the beyond hereafter. So we are told,and perhaps those, who tell us so would like India to remain plugged in thoughts and entangled in speculation,so that they might possess this world and the fullness thereof, unhindered by these thinkers, and take their joy of it. Yes India has been all this,but also much more than this.She has known the innocence and insouciance of childhood, the passion and abandon of youth, and the ripe wisdom of maturity that comes from long experience of pain and pleasure, and over and over again she has renewed her childhood and youth and age. The tremendous inertia of the age and size have weighed her down, degrading customs and evil practices have eaten into her, many a parasite has clung to her and sucked her blood, but behind all this lie the strength of ages and the subconscious wisdom of an ancient race. For we are very old, and trackless centuries whisper in our ears, yet we have known how to regain our youth again, through the memory and dreams of those past ages endure with us. It is not some secret doctrine and esoteric knowledge that has kept India vital and going through long ages, but a tender humanity, a varied and tolerant culture, and a deep understanding of life and its mysterious ways".

The Indian culture shall live as long as the sun rises in the sky always making new paths more human.The great periods in the Indian culture are marked by a widespread access of spiritual vitality derived from a greater process of assimilation. Indian culture is the dawn of human culture.

India's recorded civilization is one of the oldest and longest in the course of world history, with a kaleidoscopic variety and rich cultural heritage. Indian mythology is part and parcel of the religious way of day to day life.

In India, the history of cultural heritage has its starting point from Vedic period until the seals of Mohenjadaro are clearly and indubitably deciphered. The discovery of Indus Valley Civilization extended the knowledge of Indian history beyond the Vedic age in both material as well as spiritual realms.

The history of India dates back with a record of unbroken civilization of 5000 years and has been broadly divided into three distinct periods :

— Ancient.
— Medieval.
— Modern.

ANCIENT INDIA

INDUS VALLEY CIVILISATION (3000 B.C.- 1500 B.C.)

This civilization flourished on the banks of the river Indus. Ruins of this civilization are still found at Lothal near Ahmedabad; Kalibangan in Rajasthan, Banwali in district Hissar; Ropar near Chandigarh; Mohenjodaro in Larkana district of Sind now in Pakistan; and Harrappa in Montgomery district of Punjab, now in Pakistan. This ancient culture, was highly developed, urban and sophisticated with trade relations with Sumeria and Babylon.

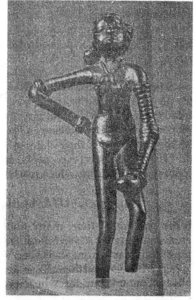

Early vedic culture dates back to 2500 B.C. to 2000 B.C. The Aryans were semi-nomadic pastoral people who originally inhabited the area around Caspian sea in Central Asia and entered the country around 2000 B.C. They first settled down in Punjab and later spread all over the Gangetic plains. They built towns and cities along the Gangetic plains, spreading their culture and Sanskrit language far and wide. The Aryans are said to be originators of the Hindu civilization. The Hindu holy book Rig Veda is claimed to be the oldest scripture of the world. The Upanishads, the Brahmanas, the Aryankas, Manu Smriti and Puranas are also believed to be scripted during this period. Their concepts of social classes or castes were fundamental to the development of later Indian societies. Being lovers of nature, Aryans worshipped the sun, water, fire etc.

There were six religious books of the Aryans which reveals their beliefs, customs and culture.

(1) **The Vedas** : There are four Vedas, viz., (I) Rig Veda : It is the oldest among the Vedas and contains 1028 hymns in the form of prayers to God (II) Samveda deals with music (III) Yajurveda deals with sacrifices, rituals and formulae (IV) Atharveda deals with medicine

(2) **The Upanishads** : These are the main source of Indian philosophy and theology. There are about 300 known Upanishads.

(3) **The Brahmanas** : These throw light on socio-political life of the Aryans and form the basic of their religion.

(4) **The Aranyakas** : These are the concluding portion of the Brahmanas and are essentially treatises on mysticism and philosophy.

(5) **Manu Smriti** : Manu was the great law giver in the Aryan period and his book Manu Smriti deals with the laws of inheritance, duties of kings and his subjects.

(6) **The Puranas** : These give religious and historical details of the Aryan civilisation and contain discourses on legends, rituals, traditions and moral codes. They are 18 in number.

Later Vedic Period (2000 BC - 700 BC)

More developed than the early Vedic period, the tiny tribal settlements were replaced by strong kingdoms. There was a growth of big cities like Ayodhya, Indraprastha and Mathura.This was called the Brahmanical age, and came very near the modern form of Hindusim. The society was divided into four castes, initially based on occupation but later became hereditary.

(I) Brahmins (priestly class) (II) Kshatriyas (military class) (III) Vaishyas (business or trading class) (IV) Shudras (labour class).

The Epic Age : It was the epic age that the Aryan tribes established themselves in the whole of northern India. The Mahabharata and Ramayana are the two great epics of this period.

The Rise of Brahmanism : During the later Vedic period the observance of religion was made very complicated by the addition of several rituals. Consequently only Brahmins could perform religious rituals and ceremonies.

The revolt against Brahmanism : As Brahmins monopolised religion, the other castes revolted against the Brahmanical exploitation.

The world of today owes much to the ancient Hindus as the concept of Zero, the decimal system, algebra, the abstract concept of numbers and the present system of numerals trace their origin to them, and were conveyed to the western world through the Arabs and the Greeks.

In the 6th century B.C. Eastern India saw the birth of two great religions of the world—Buddhism and Jainism. This was a result of the revolt against the supremacy of Brahmanical priests, several schools of philosophy opposing Brahmanism developed. The movement was spearheaded by the Kshatriyas of the royal families of Magadha who later helped in the propagation of Buddhism and Jainism. The great Emperor Ashoka embraced Buddhism and spread the faith in India and Sri Lanka. Buddhist religion and art later spread over the whole of South East Asia and to China, Japan and Korea.

Magadh Empire (600 BC - 400 BC)

During the following century the great kingdom of Magadha, south of the lower Ganga river was established. From a small kingdom it became a major power in North India, embracing the districts of Patna and Gaya in Bihar. Its capital was Patliputra.

Important rulers of Magadha dynasty
— Haryanka Dynasty
— Bimbisara Dynasty (542 BC – 493 BC)
— Ajata Shatru Dynasty (493 BC– 461 BC)
— Shishunga Dynasty
— Nanda Dynasty

Haryanka dynasty was originally founded in 566 BC by the grandfather of Bimbisara, but the actual foundation of the Magadha empire was laid by Bimbisara and Ajata Shatru who annexed the neighbouring territories and established it as the centre of the political activity in North India.

Bimbisara converted the Magadha kingdom into an empire.

A son of Bimbisara killed his father and became the ruler of Magadha. He annexed Vaishali and Kosala and increased the boundaries of his empire.

Shishunga ruled for about half a century. Kingdoms of Vatsa, Avanti and Kosala were annexed to Magadha.

Nanda dynasty was founded by Mahapadma.

Alexander invaded India in 326 BC and fought with Porus – the king of Punjab on the bank of the river Jhelum. Link between India and West was initiated by Alexander's invasion.

THE MAURYAN EMPIRE (321 BC – 289 BC)

Chandragupta Maurya was the founder of the Mauryan Empire who overthrew the Nandas. He expelled Greeks from Punjab and Sind and brought under his rule the whole of North India from Patliputra to Hindkush mountains in the north-west and to Narmada in the south. Chnadragupta became the first Indian king who can be called as national ruler. He set up an centrally based system of administration helped by a council of ministers. Megasthenes, a Greek Ambassador to Chandragupta's court wrote Megasthenes' account of India called 'INDICA' in Greek detailing the Mauryan dynasty and the capital city of Patliputra.

ASHOKA THE GREAT (273 BC – 232 BC)

Ashoka was the grandson of Chandragupta and son of Bindusara. His empire covered territory from Hindukush to Bengal and extended over Afghanistan, Baluchistan, Kashmir and to the Valley of Nepal. Royal palaces, stupas, 'monastries and cave dwellings were built throughout the kingdom. Gurukulas and Buddhist monastries developed with royal patronage. Kautilya's Artahshastra, Bhadranahu's Kalpa Sutra, Buddhist texts like Katha Vatthu and Jain texts such as the Bhagwati Sutra, Acharanga Sutra and Dava Kalik are some of the important literature of this era. University of Taxila was developed during this period.

In 265 BC Ashoka invaded Kalinga. It was the widespread massacre and bloodshed and destruction during the war which horrified Ashoka and he embaraced Buddhism.

The empire broke 50 years after the death of Ashoka because of weak successors, oppression by officials in outlying areas leading to revolt and policy of Ahimsa.

GUPTA DYNASTY (320 AD – 520 AD)

Important rulers

Chandrgupat I (320 AD - 335 AD) was the founder of the dynasty in Magadha.

Samudragupta (335 AD -375 AD) who never suffered defeat in the battlefield defended India from foreign invaders.

Chandragupta II (375 AD -415 AD) removed foreign rule completely from India.

The golden age of India was reached under the Guptas. In this period literature, the art, music, sculpture and architecture reached unprecedented heights, much of which is evident even today.

Kalidasa, Aryabhatta, Varah Mihira and Brahmgupta, the great mathematician and astronomers lived during this period.Kumatila Bhatta and Shankaracharya the great preachers of Hinduism, Dhanwantri the great physician also lived during this period.

Harshavardhan (606 AD – 647 AD) was the last Hindu king of Northern India. He moved his capital from Thaneswar to Kannauj. He established a strong empire conquering Bengal,Malwa,eastern Rajasthan and the whole of Gangetic plain up to Assam. Hieun Tsang, a Chienese traveller who came to India during his reign and stayed with him for long studying Hindu and Buddhist scriptures, wrote a detailed account of India as he witnessed it.

After Harshavardhan, the Rajputs emerged as a powerful force in western and central India. Prithaviraj Chauhan was an important ruler. Jai Chand Rathor was the last Rajput king who was defeated and killed by Muhammad Ghori and the kingdom of Delhi fell to Ghori.

In 712 AD the north west was occupied by Arab Muslim invaders and in 1001, a Turkish sultan, Mahmud (971-1030) took Islam eastwards into Punjab and beyond. After the 12ᵗʰ C., the Ghurids (from Afghanistan) captured India and   established kingdom. They established a powerful sultanate at Delhi until a Mongol invasion from north west in 1398 greatly reduced its power.

MEDIEVAL INDIA

From 12ᵗʰ C., the conquerors stayed on to rule pockets of territories in North India, until the Mughals came. This period started with the raids by Mahmud of Ghazni and the establishment of the Sultanate of Delhi. This period is divided into five parts :

— The Slave Dynasty (1206 A.D.- 1290 A.D.) ˙
— The Khilji Dynasty (1290 A.D. - 1320 A.D.)
— The Tughlaq Dynasty (1320 A.D. - 1414 A.D.)
— The Sayyed Dynasty (1414 A.D. - 1450 A.D.)
— The Lodhi Dynasty (1451 A.D. - 1526 A.D.)

The Slave Dynasty : Founded by Qutub-ud-Din Aibak, important rulers were Shamas-uddin Iltutmish (1210 AD - 1236 AD); Razia Sultan (1236 AD -1239 AD), first and the only Muslim woman who ruled over India; Nasir-uddin- Mahmud (1246 AD - 126 AD)

The Khilji Dynasty : It was founded by Sultan Jalaluddin Khilji who annexed the Rajput Kingdoms. Alauddin Khilji killed his uncle Sultan Jalaluddin and succeeded in 1296.Last king was Khusro of Khilji dynasty to rule the kingdom

The **Tughlaq Dynasty** : It was founded by Ghiasuddin Tughlaq (1320-1325) who was succeeded by Mohammed-bin- Tughlaq (1320-1414). He introduced coins of brass and copper. Tughlaq Dynasty was ended by the invasion of India by Timur (a Turk) in 1398.

The **Sayyed Dynasty** : Timur ruled Delhi for about 37 years. The last Sayyed king abdicated in favour of Balban Lodhi.

The **Lodhi Dynasty** : Afghan Sardar Balban Lodhi established his kingdowm after the invasion of Timur. Sikander Lodhi (1489-1517) and Ibrahim Lodhi (1517-1526) were the important rulers of the Lodhi Dynasty.

The 14th C also saw the foundation of the Sikh religion.

The Mughal Dynasty (1526-1707-1857)

(1) Babar : (1526-1530) He defeated Ibrahim Lodhi in the first Battle of Panipat in 1526 and became Emperor of Delhi. He was the founder of the Mughal Empire. (2) Humayun (1530 - 1556) son of Babar ascended the throne in 1530 (3) Sher Shah Suri (1540 - 1545) defeated and expelled Humayun. He introduced a brilliant administration, issued the coin called 'Rupia' and built the great Grand Trunk Road linking Peshawar to Calcutta. (4) Akbar (1556 - 1605) Eldest son of Humayun, was the first Muslim ruler who seperated religion from politics and the attitude towards the Hindus (5) Jehangir (1605 - 1627), son of Akbar, ascended the throne after Akbar's death in 1605 and was known for strict administration of justice. (6) Shahjahan (1628 - 1658) son of Jahangir, ascended the throne after the death of his father, built TAJ MAHAL, a symbol of love for his wife Mumtaz. (7) Aurangzeb (1659 - 1707) son of Shahjahan, is known for keeping his father under home arrest until death and ruling strictly according to Muslim religious laws and demolishing several Hindu temples.

In 1739 Nadir Shah, a Persian king, invaded India and broke-up Mughal empire He took Kohinoor diamond with him. The Marathas became powerful after the departure of Nadir Shah. Shivaji played a pivotal role in curtailing the muslim domination.

This period resulted in the absorption of new cultural strains of Arab, Afghan, Turkish and Persian origin which can be seen in the art, architecture and literature of the North.

Hindu Revival (1649-1748 AD)

The Marathas became powerful under the leadership of Peshwas. Balaji Vishwanath Bajirao I conquered Deccan kingdoms and aspired to bring Delhi and Punjab under the control of Marathas.

MODERN INDIA

The Portuguese sailor, Vasco-da-Gama, discovered the sea route to India and landed at Calicut in 1498 AD. By 16th C the Portuguese had established trading posts in India and retained a monopoly of trade with India until 17th C when the Dutch, the English and the French companies also set up their trading centres.

Thousands of years ago the Phoenician traders took back with them spices from the west coast. Trade with the west from the west and the east coast of India has gone on since time immemorial.

Captain Alfonso de Albuquerque conquered Goa in 1510.

Dutch followed them in 1595, the English in 1600 and finally the French arrived in 1664. Soon the companys' functions expended to political fields.

The East India company was founded in 1660 through a charter signed by Queen Elizabeth I—primarily to face the Dutch opposition, but finally the British were successful in destabilising the French and the Portuguese and ruled over India for 150 years. Robert Clive was instrumental in laying the foundation of the British Empire in India. He defeated French in the Carnatic war and foiled the French dreams of having an Empire in India.

By 1799, the East India Company had become the dominant power in India. By the Charter Act 1833, the company ceased to be a trading company and became an administrative power. By 1849 virtually the whole of Indian sub-continent was under British control.

INDIAN FREEDOM STRUGGLE

The year 1857 witnessed the major out-beak of armed defiance by Indian rulers—big and small—against the British domination.

It was the first war of independence called the Sepoy Mutiny or the revolt.On May 10, 1857, soldiers at Meerut refused to touch the new Enfield rifle cartridges which were said to have a greased cover made of animal fat. The soldiers along with other civilians went on a rampage, broke jails, murdered the English people and marched to Delhi. Delhi's local soldiers also meanwhile revolted and proclaimed the 80-years old Bahadur Shah Zafar as Emperor of India, but soon he was imprisoned by the Britishers. On March 29, 1857, Mangal Pandey killed two British officers on parade at Barrackpore. The present Indian soldiers refused to obey the orders to arrest Mangal Pandey and countrywide revolt broke out from Lucknow, Ambala, Burhanpur and Meerut.

Queen Victoria issued a proclamation on November 1, 1858 declaring India under the British crown.

Indian National Union was formed in1884 by A.O.Hume, an Englishman in association with various Indian national leaders. He called for a conference at Pune in December 1885. The conference received unanimous support of all Indian leaders who decided to rename the Indian National Union as the Indian National Congress.The India's independence struggle was launched under the presidentship of W.C.Banerjee in Bombay.

By early 20th C its more radical members had began to question Britian's right to rule India.

On October 16, 1905 the partition of Bengal came into effect to destroy the political influence of the educated middle class, reducing the province of Bengal in size by creating a new province of East Bengal. In 1906, an All India Muslim League was set up under the leadership of Aga Khan, Nawab Salimullah of Deccan and Nawab Mohsin-ul-Mulk. They supported partition of Bengal which led to communal differences between the Hindu and the Muslims.

The arrival of M.K. Gandhi gave the freedom struggle new focus and new direction. Gandhiji tried to bring all threads of Indian society together—castes, religions, communities and classes. Under his leadership a swadeshi movement was started on August 7, 1905 to boycott the British goods. Bonfires of foreign goods were conducted in all major cities all over India.

Governor-General Lord Minto introduced Minto Morley reforms which widened rift between the Hindus and the Muslims.

Gandhiji dominated the Indian political scene from 1918 to 1947 and his philosophy of non-violence became most important weapon to uproot the British rule from India. Indian hopes for independence were crushed by the Rowlatt Acts of 1919 which authorised imprisonment without trial. Gandhi gave a call in 1919 for Satyagraha against Rowaltt Act.

On13th April 1919, over 400 people were massacred and thousands wounded at Jallianwalla Bagh at Amritsar during a public meeting. It became the turning point in Indo-British relations.

Khilafat Movement : During the First World War the safety and welfare of Turkey were threatened by the British, weakening the position of the Sultan of Turkey and Caliph. The Caliph was looked upon by the Muslims as their religious head. The two brothers Mohammed Ali and Shaukat Ali launched an anti-British movement in 1920 calling it the Khilafat Movement. Maulana Abdul Kalam Azad also joined the movement which was supported by Gandhiji paving the Congress way for Hindu-Muslim unity.

Swaraj Party : Gandhiji's decision to call off the agitation caused frustration in the masses. Leaders like Motilal Nehru, C.R.Dass and N.C. Kelkar organised the Swaraj party. They emphasised the need for entering into legislative councils by contesting elections.

Simon Commission : The British Government appointed the Simon Commission in November 1927 to review and report as to what type of a representative government could be introduced in India.As all the members of this commission were English, the Indian leaders decided to boycott it.

It was in 1920 that a non-cooperation movement was launched under the leadership of Gandhiji.

The Dandi March or the Salt Satyagraha March from Sabarmati Ashram to a small village Dandi sparked off the spirit of patriotism all over country. The Government used repressive measures against satyagrahis and almost 1,00,000 people went to jail.

Based on the report of the Simon Commission, Britain passed the Government of India Act in 1935 introducing a new federal constitution, but this satisfied none. Congress won the election of 1936 and in 1939 when the Viceroy declared India to be at war with the Nazi Germany without having consulted local leaders, Congress ministers resigned in protest.

Mohammed Ali Jinnah of Muslim League raised a demand for a separate country to Muslims in 1940.

The Congress leadership launched Quit India Movement from 1942 to 1945. Gandhiji asked the British to quit India and gave a call for "DO OR DIE" to the countrymen.

A British Cabinet mission visited India and envisaged the establishment of a constituent assembly to frame constitution and provide an interim government. The constituent Assembly met in December 1946 and Dr. Rajendra Prasad was elected as president.

On June 3, 1947 Lord Mountbatten announced partition and gave birth to Pakistan. A long and troubled series of negotiations, punctuated by rioting and bloodshed finally brought full independence to India in 1947.

India was partitioned on 15th August 1947 in accordance with the Indian Independence Act of 1947.Lord Mountbatten was appointed as Governor-General of free India and M.A. Jinnah as the first Governer-General of Pakistan.

The price of Hindu-Muslim enmity was the partitioning of the country. India retained the States with Hindu majority and the Muslim dominated areas in the east and northwest became a separate country called Pakistan.

C. Rajgopalachari became the first and the only one Indian Governor-General of India in 1948.

Pandit Jawaharlal Nehru became the first Prime Minister of independent India.

He addressed the midnight session of the constituent Assembly in New Delhi. As the clock struck midnight, India awoke to life and freedom. On the evening of August 14 Union Jacks came down from flag poles all over the country. The bars, restaurants and clubs, once reserved for the British only where Indians and dogs were not allowed were thronged by the natives. The India tri-colour was hoisted over the Red Fort.

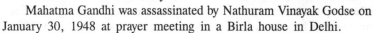

But India was also burning, there was bloodshed all over the country.

Mahatma Gandhi was assassinated by Nathuram Vinayak Godse on January 30, 1948 at prayer meeting in a Birla house in Delhi.

Dr. Ambedkar and his colleagues took three years to draft the constitution which made India a republic and came into force on January 26, 1950.

In 1955, 554 states whose treatise with the paramount power of Great Britian had lapsed and who held two-fifth of the country's land and population signed the Instrument of Accession and became a part of Independent India. The integration of India's princely States into the union was achieved by Sardar Vallabhbhai Patel.

India has faced three aggressions since independence—two from Pakistan (1965 and 1971) and one from China (1962).

Lok Sabha elections have been held for 14 times so far.

Two of India's Prime ministers were assassinated—Mrs. Indira Gandhi in New Delhi in 1984 and Mr. Rajiv Gandhi in Chikmagalur in 1987.

On December 3, 1984 in Bhopal 2500 people died and 2000 were seriously affected when they inhaled the poisonous gas which spread over the city in atmosphere due to the accident at Union Carbide, an insecticide plant.

India opted for five years plans for economic and social development. Planning in India derives its objectives and social promises from Directive Principles of State policy enshrined in the Constitution. Planning Commission was set up in 1950 to prepare the blueprint of development, taking an overall view of the needs and resources of the country.

The country registered impressive growth in many sectors but poverty continues to remain a grave concern. Therefore, a self-employment programme 'SWARANJAYANTI GRAM SWAROJGAR YOJANA' for the rural poor was launched on April 1, 1999. This programme aims at establishing a large number of micro enterprises covering all aspects of self-employment.

The Industrial policy Resolution of 1948 marked the beginning of the evolution of Indian industrial policy. The resolution defined broad contours of the policy and delineated the role of the State in industrial development both as an entrepreneur and as an authority.

Space Research. The space research programme has come a long way from a modest beginning with the Nicke Appache rocket launched with sodium vapour payload on November 21, 1963.

The education policy of the government in the post-independence era has been to provide free and compulsory education to all children at least up to elementary stages. Adult education and women's education programmes have been launched to bring about total literacy by 2005. The progress of women has always been the focal point in development planning since independence.

Telecom has emerged as the very essence of progress in India by being the backbone of industrialisation and urbanisation. Telecom has an impact on every facet of our life. It has virtually changed the ways we think and work. Telecom revolution along with the phenomenal progress made in the penetration of communication facilities in various sectors has made inroads into new sectors. Telecom is indeed a symbol of India's march into the new Millennium.

Unity in diversity is not just a slogan in India. It is a way of life. We live in different regions, follow different faiths, speak different langauges and yet through our fairs, festivals and rites and rituals that we celebrate together, we convey our message : WE ARE ALL ONE AND UNITED.

THE RACES IN INDIA

The greatest drama of coalescing by various races has been enacted on the Indian soil since times immemorial. The present population is the amalgamation of races which arrived in India over a period of time. This racial division is made on the basis of physical and biological differences among the people such as the structure and build of the body, colour of the skin, form of head and face and the formation of nose and the colour and form of eyes and hairs.

NEGRITOS OR NEGROIDS : These are supposed to be the oldest people to have come to India from Africa and are represented by the tribal groups such as Irulas, Kodars, Paniyans and Kurumbas. They are trible groups and still survive in the Andaman Islands living in the hills and jungles where they have retained their language.

PRO-AUSTRALOIDS OR AUSTRICS : These people who arrived probably after the Negritos are believed to be the builders of the Indus valley civilization as their skeletons have been discovered from the burial grounds both at Mohenjodaro and Harappa. They cultivated rice, vegetable and made sugar from sugarcane. Austrics tribes spread over whole of India and then passed on to Burma, Malaya and the islands of South East Asia. Their language has survived in the Kol or Munda speech —Mundri current language in Eastern and Central India.

MONGOLOIDS : This race is mainly concentrated in the mountainous region of Himalaya particularly in Ladakh, Sikkim, Arunachal Pradesh and other parts of Northern India. Generally they are people of yellow complexion, oblique eyes, high cheekbones, spare hair and medium height.

DRAVIDIANS : This race comprises three types: Paleo mediterranean, the true mediterranean and oriental mediterranean. They came from south-west Asia and were architect of the Indus valley civilisation along with the Proto Australoids. They introduced metal culture in India roughly between 2500 BC and 1500 BC.

43

THE WESTERN BRACHCEPHALS : These people consist of the Alpinoids, the Dinarics, the Armenoids and the nordics. They came to India along three main routes passing through Baluchistan, Sind, Kathiawar, Gujrat, Maharashtra, Karnataka and Tamil Nadu; The Ganga valley and the delta; and Chitral, Gilgit, parts of Kashmir and Nepal. They still exist in the form of Coorgis and the Parsis.

NORDIC ARYANS : These are the people who left Central Asia some 5000 years ago and settled in Mesopotamia for some centuries. Nordic Aryans were a branch of Indo-Iranians who came to India between 2000 BC and 1500 BC. Their first main concentration was in the north-western part of the country and then they spread to the Ganga valley and beyond. They are now mostly represented among the upper castes of northern India.

TRIBAL POPULATION IN INDIA

ASSAM : Abors, Khasis, Mikirsa and Nagas.

ARUNACHAL PRADESH : Apatamis

MADHYA PRADESH : Baiga, Bhils, Gonds, Kol and Murias.

RAJASTHAN AND GUJARAT : Bhils

GARHWAL AND KUMAON REGIONS OF U.P. : Bhotias and Khas.

ANDHRA PRADESH AND ORISSA : Chenchus.

HIMACHAL PRADESH : Gaddis.

MEGHALAYA : Garos

NILGIRI AND TAMIL NADU : Kotas and Todas.

MANIPUR : Kuki.

SIKKIM : Lepchas

TRIPURA : Lushais.

BIHAR AND ORISSA : Kurukh or Oarons. Santhal in Bihar only.

ANDAMAN AND NICOBAR ISLANDS : Onges, Sentinelese and Shompens.

KERALA : Uralis.

MAHARASHTRA : Warlis.

LANGUAGES OF INDIA

Sanskrit, the classical language of India, is believed to be the language of the God. All major languages of the world are believed to have their origin in the Sanskrit language.

Manu wrote the tenets of Indian life—regulations in behaviour for individuals to develop their powers and potentialities and build a healthy society—in Sanskrit.

Vyasa wrote Mahabharata—he evoked the Goddess of language. Valmiki Ramayana; Kalidas Shakantulam and Kumar Sambhar and before these all the vedas and the Puranas were all written in Sanskrit.

The elements which form the present languages come from Negroid, Austric Sino-Tibet an, Dravidian and Indo-Aryan languages which interacted on one another through the centuries.

PRESENT LANGUAGES

India has 18 officially recognised languages since 1992.

HINDI is the official language of the country as it is widely spoken in various dialects. Numerically the biggest of the Indo-Aryan family it covers a number of Dialects like Brajbhasha, Bundeli, Awadhi, early Marwari of Rajasthan and Maithili and Bhojpuri. It is the official language in seven states.

ENGLISH is the second official language and is spoken throughout the country.

ASSAMESE is an Indo-Aryan language and is the official language of Assam. Assamese has developed as a literary language since 13th century.

BENGALI the official language of West Bengal, is one of the leading Indo-Aryan languages. It emerged as a separate language around 1000 AD.

GUJRATI the official language of Gujarat, is also an Indo-Aryan language which emerged around 1200 AD. It is now one of the most developed Indian languages.

KANNADA is the official language of of Karnataka and belongs to the Dravidian family. Kannada emerged as an independent language in ninth century. It has rich literature.

KASHMIRI is a language of the Indo-Aryan group and is sopken all over Kashmir. It is written in the Pers-Arabic script.

MALYALAM is a branch of the Dravidian family and is the official language of Kerala. It is the youngest language of the Dravidian family, which emerged in 10th century. It has rich literature.

MARATHI is the official language of Maharashtra and belong to Indo-Aryan family. Its literacy career began in 13th century.

ORIYA is a branch of Indo-Aryan family and is the official language of Orissa. It came into existence in 10th century, but its literacy career began only in the 14th century.

PUNJABI is a branch of Indo-Aryan family and is in existence since 15th century. It is written in the Gurumukhi script.

SANSKRIT : The classical language of India and the oldest in the world. The Rig Veda, the oldest book in the world is written in Sanskrit.

SINDHI : Branch of the Indo-Aryan family, Sindhi has preserved some of the archaic features of the old Indo-Aryan language. Sindi uses the Pers-Arabic script in Pakistan. Speakers in India use mainly Devnagri script.

TAMIL : The oldest of the Dravidian language is the State language of Tamil Nadu. Tamil literature goes back to the centuries before the Christian Era. It represents certain new literacy types which are not found in Sanskrit or any other language.

TELUGU : Numerically the biggest of the Dravidian language, it is the State language of Andhra Pradesh. Next to Hindi, it is the biggest linguistic unit in India. Telugu is found recorded from the seventh century AD.

URDU is the State language of Jammu and Kashmir. The name Urdu is derived from Azaban-e-Urdu–Muala which means the language of the camp or court. Urdu and Hindi have proceeded from Khariboli, speech of Delhi and the surrounding areas since the 13th century. Sir Sayyed Ahmed Khan (1817 - 1898) started a revival of Urdu as the language of the Muslims in India and modern Urdu was born.

MANIPURI is the common language among the people of the valley and the hills of Manipur and have large number of dialects among the tribes.

NEPALI is though the language of Nepal but is related to the languages of North India. It is spoken in parts of U.P, Bihar, West Bengal and Assam.

KONKANI is the official language of Goa but is spoken by thousands of Konkanis in Maharashtra and Karnataka.

RELIGIONS OF INDIA

All the major religions of the world are being practised in India. India gave birth to countless minor cults and regional sects. Indian philosophy has influenced intellectuals of other cultures outside India throughout the ages.

In 1947, the Britishers divided the Indian sub-continent into India and Pakistan on the basis of religion but today India has more Muslim population than Pakistan and is considered having the third largest Muslim population in the world.

HINDUISM

Hinduism often called as the religion of divine origin is one of the oldest living religions of the world. Beginning of the Hindu religion starts with the Vedic period. Hinduism is based on the eternal truth of life. No other religious tradition is so eclectic, so diversified in its theoretical premises, as well as its practical expressions as Hinduism. It is the only major religion which has not been traced to a specific founder and the only one which does not have a "holy book" as the one and the only scriptural authority.

Shrutis' are the very soul of Hindusim. They mean that which had been heard or revealed. These Shrutis are known as Vedas which have all spiritual knowledge of the eternal truth. There are four Vedas.

RIG VEDA : It is the oldest among the Vedas and contains 1028 hymns in the form of prayers to Gods. It is not possible to fix an accurate date of the composition, imagined to be much earlier than 2000 BC.

SAMVEDA : It deals with music

YAJURVEDA : It deals with sacrifices, rituals and formulae

ATHARVEDA : It deals with medicine

THE UPANISHADS : Upanishads form the part of the **Vedas** and are the real foundations of Hinduism. All orthodox schools of Hinduism look upon Upnishads as base. There are about 300 known Upanishads.

THE BRAHMANAS : These throw light on socio-political life of the Aryans and form the basic of their religion.

THE ARANYAKAS : These are the concluding portion of the

47

Brahmanas and are essentially treatises on mysticism and philosophy.

MANUSMRITI : Manu was the great law giver in the Aryan period and his book Manusmriti deals with the laws of inheritance, duties of King and his subjects and principles of living in a society.

THE PURANAS : They give religious and mythological details of the Aryan civilisation and contain discourses on legends, rituals,traditions and moral codes.

THE EPICS

The great epics of Hindus are the Ramayana, the Mahabharata, the Yogavasishta and Harivansha. They are friendly compositions and teach the greatest of truth in easier terms.

Ramayana written by Sage Valmiki is considered as Adi Kavya of Sanskrit literature. Ramayana is the epic-poem based on the story of Lord Rama (one of the incarnations of God Vishnu). The main theme describes elaborately the character of Rama and is believed to be written in 1500 B.C.

The Ramayana represents the highest glory of the Indian culture. It is a story of a great human being who suffered for his moral conducts but sets an ideal for the humanity.

Mahabharata is an encyclopedia of Indian culture written by Sage Ved Vyasa before 400 AD.

It is about war between two rival families Kauravas and Pandavas, both descendants of King Bharata. It is based on real events and is the oldest history of ancient India.

RELIGIOUS CONCEPTS OF HINDUISM

DHARMA : Dharma is not religion exactly as the term denotes. The nearest equivalent English word to explain DHARMA is RIGHTEOUSNESS. Truth being eternal is Dharma and all that which makes human life better, proper and peaceful. Hinduism is a faith that has very few DOs and DON'Ts, yet it permits the greatest freedom of worship. It maintains that each person must be guided by his or her own individual spiritual search and experience and does not accept dictatorship in religious guidance. Hinduism believes that 'Brahma' is the absolute universal cosmic soul beyond time and space being neither male nor female.

TRINITY : Hinduism believes that there are three main functions of the cosmic soul manifested in three divinities :

CREATION	PRESERVATION	DESTRUCTION
Brahma	Vishnu	Shiva

These three divinities are jointly known as TRINITY.

ISHWARA OR BRAHM : **"Creator"** of the Universe.

The mystic syllable OM is the symbol of Brahma. OM is also the first mystical cosmic sound creating, when uttered, waves of celestial peace around. Brahma is shown with four heads facing all four directions symbolizing that he has breathed the entire universe. He sits on a Lotus which is a symbol of purity as the Lotus usually grows in muddy water but remains untouched by the mire from which it emerges.

VISHNU : The **"preserver"** is depicted either standing or lying in the lap of "Sheshnag" a gigantic snake with a thousand heads

signifying "Ananta" i.e. infinity. (symbolic of cosmic energy). He is bluish in colour which again symbolises infinity. He holds a Chakra in one hand denoting that he maintains Dharma—righteousness and order in the universe; Shankha or counch in the second for removal of ignorance; Gada or mace is the third for removing the evil in the world and Lotus in the fourth symbolising beauty and purity. The vehicle of Vishnu is Garuda, the giant eagle king of all spieces of birds. (All Hindu Gods and Goddesses have some animal or bird as vehicle which entitles them to same veneration as the divinities in worship. Vishnu has taken ten avataras or incarnations in various shapes to eradicate evil and re-establish DHARMA in the world. The avataras are—KURMA (tortoise), VARAHA (boar), NARASIMHA (man-lion), VAMANA (dwarf), PARSURAMA (the angry man who eliminated all fighting tribes in the world 21 times when they started misusing their might to oppress the weak), RAMA (the perfect man), KRISHNA (the divine statesman and the guiding spirit of the Mahabharata), the BUDDHA (the compassionate) and KALKI (the avatar yet to appear).

THE TEN INCARNATIONS OF VISHNU

NAME	FORM	MYTHOLOGICAL DETAIL
Matsya	Fish	Vishnu took the form of a fish to rescue Manu (the first man). during the rain and the floods that submerged the entire world described in all religions.
Kurma	Tortoise	Vishnu became a tortoise to rescue all the treasures lost in the Flood including the divine nectar (Amrita) which made God immortal. The gods put Mount Kailasa on the Tortoise back and when he reached the bottom of the ocean, they put the divine snake round the mountains and churned the ocean with the mountain by pulling the snake. They suceeded in bringing out the nectar, the other treasures, and the Goddess Lakshmi, Vishnu's consort.
Varaha	Boar	Vishnu appeared again in the form of a boar, sacred pig to raise the earth from the ocean's floor where it had been thrown by a demon, Hiranyakush.
Narasimha	Half-man Half-lion	Having persuaded Lord Brahma to grant him a wish that he may not be killed either in day or in night, by man or beast, in sky or on earth, inside the house or outside or by any arm the demon king Hiranyakashpu started oppressing the people in the world. Even Gods failed to control him. It was then that Vishnu burst out of a pillar in the Demon's palace at dusk, when it was neither day nor night in the form of half-man and half-lion and killed Hiranyakashapu

with His nails putting him in his lap while sitting midway on the door-step.

Vamana	A dwarf	Bali, a demon king, had attained supernatural powers through asceticism. Vishnu appeared before him in the form of a dwarf and asked him for three steps long piece of land. Bali took a vow to give this much land to him. But thereafter the dwarf assumed gigantic figure and measured the whole earth in one step, the heavens in the second and asked where to put the third step. Bali bowed down in veneration and asked the dwarf incarnation to put his third step on his head and oblige him.
Parsurama	Rama with the axe	Vishnu (Parsurama) was incarnated as the son of saint Jamadagni. Parsurama killed king Sahastrabhu for robbing his father of all his cattle. The king's sons killed Jamadagni. Parsurama took revenge by killing all male Kshatriyas, the fighting class, twenty one times in succession.
Rama	The King of Ayodhya	Vishnu took birth as Rama, son of King Dashrath of Ayodhya to rescue the world from the demon king Ravana of Lanka. His wife Sita is a model of faithful wife while Hanuman, the monkey-faced god was his helper.
Krishna	Chariot driver for Arjuna	Krishna, the guiding spirit of the Mahabharata and depicted as driving the chariot of Arjuna in the war againat evil is an integral part of Hindu ethos and is worshipped by one and all—literate or illiterate, rich or poor, pions or even impious. He had given to the world the message of the BHAGVAD GITA, highlighting

The Buddha

Kali

Riding on
a horse

the theory of KARMA (Action) and the great lesson that "those who worhsip other Gods with faith and devotion will also come to ME but by other paths and therefore all should live in peace and love."

Vishnu again took birth as Gautam Siddhartha, son of king Suddhodava of Kapilvasthu in 6th century BC to preach selflessness, virtue and wisdom as the only path to NIRVANA i.e. conquest of self and subsequent sorrow and mortality. Buddhism remained dominant in India untill the 6th C AD and stressed on compassion for animals and end to sacrifice.

Vishnu's incarnation as KALI to destroy the present evil in the world is yet to take place.

SHIVA : Third of the TRINITY, Shiva is beneficial and maleficient. He represents the power which destroys and regenerates the cosmos after

its destruction, and constantly destroys and regenerates during cosmic activity. He is also known as MAHADEV or MAHAYOGI, the patron of all saints and yogis. Known also as NATARAJA, the greatest dancer and the origin of all dances and music, his dance depicts the dance of cosmic energy. He is shown either sitting in meditation or standing with one foot on a man's body. He has four arms. In one hand he holds a drum, symbol of creativity, in the second a flame—symbol of

destruction, the third in pose of benediction to all, and the fourth pointing to the body under His foot. The circle of fire behind him symbolises the continuity and eternal motion of universe. The flame in hand also stands for knowledge which destroys ignorance; the foot on body shows that Shiva is the MASTER of all for HE has conquered the passions of man. Around his neck is a snake and a serpant—snake standing for passions which destroy and the serpant for wisdom and knowledge. His hair are braided and studded with jewels—hair symbolises strength and jewels virtues and spiritual knowledge. Goddess Ganga on Shiva's head denotes purity and the crescent through the waxing and waning of the moon the movement of time. His third eye depicts that He is seeing all and opens it only when He destroys the evil. The ashes with which He is shown covered gives the message that all worldly life ends in ash. The Tiger skin that he wraps around his waist represents pride which like the Tiger, springs out of us and has to be suppressed. The Shiva Lingam represents that He is the endless pillar of cosmic power. Nandi—the bull, vehicle of Shiva, facing the idols of Shiva at all temples, symbolizes the ATMAN (Soul) of a man yearning for Parmatman (God).

SARASWATI : The consort of Brahma is the embodiment of learning and wisdom. In her hand she holds the Veena symbolic of Rta, the order in the cosmic universe and of Nada—Brahman. She sits on lotus or peacock. Peacock symbolises the ego which is to be suppressed.

LAKSHMI : The consort of Vishnu, Lakshmi is the goddess of prosperity. She sits on lotus and holds lotus flowers in her hands emphasising the importance of pure living.

PARVATI : The consort of Shiva, symbolises cosmic energy in the form of Shakti, the world's mother who is power and energy by which the great God creates, preserves and destroys the world and recreates a new.

GANESH : Son of Shiva and Parvati he is considered as the remover of obstacles. His elephant head denotes superior intelligence and the snake around his waist the cosmic energy.

DURGA : Formed when all Gods pooled their energies and elements at one place. DURGA represents the consolidated strength of all Gods and good. She was formed when the demons became all powerful and uncontrollable. She fought and killed them all. If enraged Her complexion turns black and She is called KALI.

SAMSARA : It is a concept of rebirth, the theory of reincarnation of soul which is a fundamental belief of Hinduism. The cycle of birth and rebirth is called Samsara. Every soul is believed to go through the endless cycle of birth, death and rebirth till it reaches perfection in earthly life when it attains MOKSHA or LIBERATION. The soul then becomes one with the "Brahm", the universal spirit and the soul is not born again.

KARMA : Hinduism is based on the law of KARMA and KARAMPHAL or ACTION returned by an equivalent reaction i.e. the law of cause and effect.

DHARMA : The main aim of Hindu is to get free from the cycle of birth, death and rebirth. The first step is to perform one's DHARMA or DUTY with righteousness and discipline together with moral and spiritual excellence. Each person's dharma is different from another's depending on his occupation, moral and spiritual development, age and marital status.

THE THREE PATHS

Hindusim offers three paths for attaining the MOKSHA, permanent dissolution of one's soul in the cosmic spirit i.e. GOD—Bhakti Yoga or devotional worship of any form of God's manifestations through prayers and rituals; Karma Yoga, or path of 'Nishkama Karma' i.e. fulfilcation of one's duties towards everyone upon this earth caring not for the rewards or results; and lastly the Gyana Yoga or the path of knowledge achieved through intuitive intellect in its sublime and evolved form.

VARNASHRAMAS (DIVISION OF LIFE)

The conception of four Ashrams in the life of an individual is as old as the Vedic age. A person's life is divided into four stages and in each stage he performs specified functions.

BRAHMACHARYA ASHRAM : (Five to Twenty Five years). This period is devoted enrich studies and achievement of knowledge. The teacher becomes the spiritual parent and inculcate in him the virtues of obedience and reverence. The life of the student is austere and well-regulated from sunrise to sunset. During this period absolute celibacy is practised.

GRAHASTHA ASHRAM : (25 to 75 years) The next stage is Grihastha Ashram i.e. married life to perform duties towards society through procreation, earning wealth and performing all socio-religious duties within the limits of moral law. the wife is an equal partner in every phase of life thereby.

VANPRASTHA ASHRAM : After discharging all duties and obligations as a householder, the individual enters the Vanaprastha stage wherein he dedicates himself to a life of spiritual contemplation.

SANYAS ASHRAM : The last stage of life. Herein one renounces all possessions, affections and attachments and becomes a racluse giving up all types of intercourses with society.

Certain rivers and towns are particularly sacred to Hindus.

7 Holy Rivers : the Ganga, Yamuna, Indus and mythical Saraswati in the north and the Narmada, Godavari and Kaveri in the peninsula.

7 Holy Places/Towns : Haridwar, Mathura, Ayodhya and Varanasi in the north and Ujjain, Dwarka and Kanchipuram to the south.

Holy Abodes : Badrinath, Puri and Rameshwaram Dwarka are both holy abode and holy places/towns.

HINDUISM IN MODERN INDIA

The advent of the British and their rule exposed India to new influences from the West—western liberalism and humanism, christianity, scientific thought and technology. Hinduism once again showed its power to assimilate elements from other traditions and cultures retaining its own basic values and character.

While social reforms like the stoppage of 'SATI PRATHA' (burning of the wife with the husband's body at his pyre) was brought about by Raja Ram Moahn Roy. In the 19th century Ramakrishna Parmahansa and his disciple Swami Vivekananada infused new vigor into Hinduism. Ramakrishna example that the ideas of unity, tolerance and universal love had to be lived and not just understood. Vivekananda was the first to carry the message of Hinduism to Europe and America. The Ramakrishna mission and the Vedanta Society, founded by Vivekananda, continue to present Hinduism in a rational and non-dogmatic manner.

In the 20th century Mahatama Gandhi and Rabindranath Tagore became exponents and expressed the deepest truths of the ancient traditions in the context of the modern age.

BUDDHISM

Every fourth person in the world is said to be a Buddhist. Spread over almost entire Aisa, China, the far eastern countries—Sri Lanka it was in India that the light of Buddhism was first kindled.

Gautama Buddha was born in 566 BC in the village of Lumbini near Kapilvastu in Nepal. His father Suddhodhana was the king of Kapilvastu. His mother Mahadevi died seven days after his birth. He had married

Yashodhara and had a son Rahul. He renounced worldly life at the age of 29 in search of eternal peace after seeing a diseased man, an old man, a corpse and an ascetic. He meditated under a Peepal tree for six years and attained NIRVANA or ENLIGHTENMENT at the age of 35. He realised that the great peace is within ones own heart and one must seek it there.

He gave his first sermon at Sarnath. He taught that everything in world is impermanent and transient, without substance and life is full of sufferings. Sorrow can be removed only if desire and craving are renounced. He taught four Noble truths that is 1) at the core of life is misery, pain and suffering; 2) Thus suffering is caused by selfish desire and craving for finite existence and transient mundane happiness; 3) cessation of desires to attain Nirvana; 4) and the "noble eightyfold paths" of right understanding, right thought, right speech, right action, right livelihood, right effort, right mindfulness and right teachings for that.

The Buddha set up an order of monks, the Sangha to preach his teachings.

Buddhists believe that the Buddha, the Dhamma (Buddhist doctrine) and the Sangha are three jewels of Buddhism.

The five precepts laid for man or women to practice are to abstain from injury to all living beings; to abstain from stealing; to abstain from unchaste living; to abstain from falsehood; and to abstain from liquor and drugs

After the Buddha's mahanirvana at the age of 80, 18 schools of Buddhism sprang up.

Buddhist sacred literature comprises the Hinayana Pali canon, the Tripitaka and the Mahayana canon written mostly in Sanskrit which has been translated into Chisnese, Japanese, Tibetan and other major languages.

Buddhism has inspired some of the finest masterpiece of architecture, sculptures and paintings. The stupa of Sanchi and Amravati, the frescos of Ajanta, the remains of the university of Nalanda, the monastries of Bodh Gaya and Rajgir.

JAINISM

About the same time as the Buddha was preaching his dharma, and in the same region, another religious tradition was being established. Vardhmana, better known by his title Mahavira ("Great Hero") was an elder contemporary of the Buddha.

Jainism is a religion started by Vardhamana Mahavira in the 6th century BC. He was the son of a cheftain. He renounced his worldly life at the age of 30 and became a monk. After 12 years of penance, he attained the state of highest knowledge and became a Jina, the victorious one.

The next 30 years he spent in spreading his doctrine of AHIMSA or NON-VOILENCE to any living being as causing injury was considered by him as the greatest sins.

The vedic period ceased to be sublime and satisfy the philosophical and ethical needs of the community. It had become ritualistic. The origin of Jainism is not clear. Traditionally it is associated with 24 saints known as Tirtankaras. Rishabhadeva was the first Tirthankara. He was mentioned in the Rigveda, Upanishads and Bhagvata Purana. This indicates that Jainism was as old as the Vedic religion. Parsavanatha, the 23rd Tirtahnkara is regarded as the real founder of the Jainism. He was the son of king of Vaishali in Bihar and enjoined on his followers four vows—namely AHIMSA, SATYA, ASTEYA (non-stealing) and APARIGRAHA (non-acquisition). The parents of Vardhamana Mahavira were the followers of Parsvanatha. The next 24th and the last Tirthankara was Vardhmana Mahavira himself. He was born in 599 BC. He married a Princes called Yashoda and had a daughter by her. After the death of his parents Vardhamana renounced the world at the age of 30 and wandered all over eastern India in search of truth. In the thirteenth year of his wanderings, he attained VALANJANA, the highest spiritual knowledge. Subsequently he became a Jina (conqueror) and Mahavira (the great hero).

He did not believe in God and rejected the needs and the authority of the Brahmanas. According to him, man is the architect of his own destiny and need not crave for the mercy of God or any other person.

Jainism also believes in JIVA, the individual soul, which goes through cycles of birth and death and attains MOKSHA after breaking the bondage of Karma.

The Jains are divided into two groups - the Digambaras and the Shvetambaras. In Digambaras monks remain in the nude and in Shetambaras they are clad in white.

Avoidance of violence in thought and deed is enjoined on all.Orthodox Jains eat before sunset to avoid harming insects. In the ascetic traditions of Jainism, their festivals and rituals are austere.

Jainism has influenced Hinduism by way of non-violence and vegetarianism. Some of the important virtues enjoined on all Jains are forgiveness, charity, simple living, contented living, observance of truth, fasting, detachment self-control, humanity and continence.

Jainism accepted many celestial beings of the Hindu pantheon and deities like Saraswati, the goddess of learning, are carved on the walls of their temples. Jains have made valuable contribution in the development of Indian culture, philosophy, literature, paintings and architecture. Their poetry is often excessively didactic i.e. morally constructive. Their sculpture is of a very high quality and some of the images of Tirthankaras are technically perfect. The greatest glory of Jain religious art lies in the temple architecture, particularly at Girnar, Palitan and Mount Abu.These temples reveal a breadth of aesthetic sensitivity and feelings for ornamentation reminiscent of the finest specimen of a classical Hindu and Buddhist architecture.

SIKHISM

Sikhism was founded by Guru Nanak in the 15th century. Nanak (1469–1539), the founder, belonged to Punjab. Nanak was attracted from his childhood towards Hindu as well as Muslim saints and poets. He had visited the sacred places of the Hindus and Muslims including Mekka.

Sikhism is a reformed offshoot of Hinduism. Sikhism, based on the concept of Unity of God, was one of the most powerful sects of its time which rejected the rigid Hindu rituals and formalities and adopted an independent ethical system. He began to preach his message of Unity of God. He attracted many followers and soon came to be known as Guru Nanak. His disciples came together and a new religious tradition was born. The term Sikh is derived from the Sanskrit word Shishya (disciple).

He taught the fatherhood of God and brotherhood of man. He preached that all religions taught the same truth. Guru Nanak's divine revelation showed a new path, a new vision which anyone of any religion could follow—the path of truth, devotion and service to mankind.

Sikhism is monotheistic faith and Parbrahma, the supreme being —is designated as EK ONKAR. The Sikh faith is opposed to miracles of any kind. It places great emphasis on hard work, family life like upholding moral values and social obligations. Sikhs believe in rebirth but reject caste divisions. The military tradition introduced by Guru Gobind Singh has resulted in their joining the armed forces in large numbers.

Every Sikh wears five articles beginning with the letter 'K' – Kara (Bangle of iron); Kesh (long hair); Kangha (comb); Kachcha (short drawers); Kripan (short sword).

Sikhism tried to build a bridge between the teachings of Hinduism and Islam. Sikhism has no classical language and used the local Punjabi dialect to convey its teaching to the masses.

ZOROASTRIANISM

Zoroastrianism was the religion of Persia (Iran) till 7th century. When the Arabs converted the whole region to Islam. Some people came to India to preserve their religion and settled on its west coast in Gujarat.

The Zoroastrian people in India are known as Parsis as they came from Pars in Iran.

The founder of this religion was Zoroaster. The Avesta and prayers of Zoroaster and his disciples and the language is similar to Sanskrit language of the Hindu sacred books.

Ahura Mazda is believed to be the supreme Lord and wise creator. The Sun is his emblem and fire is his symbol on earth. Great veneration is extended for this reason to fire kept burning in their temples but it is not worshipped.

According to this religion, life is a great blessing of the God and man has to do duty to Him, to others and to himself. Hard work service and charity are enjoined on all, as is the importance of living a good and happy life, full of virtue. They have always adhered strictly to their ancient faith. In their agiaries (fire temple) the sacred flame is always kept burning. The Parsis still retain their Iranian physical features. They are a rather exclusive community and do not allow non Parsis inside the temple. The office of the dastur (priest) is hereditary. The dasturs are dressed entirely in white and they are held in great esteem. Although the Parsis are conservative in their religion, they have identified themselves with their fellow countrymen in other areas. They have contributed to the development of education and scientific and industrial progress of India.

Udawada on Mumbai-Delhi route is the sacred city for Parsis .

ISLAM

Islam was founded by Prophet Muhammad in 570-632 AD. Muhammad was born at Mecca in 570 AD. His mother died when he was four. As a boy, he earned a paltry living doing odd jobs with traders in caravans. He married Khadijah, a wealthy widow at the age of 25, who had employed him. Muhammad was distressed with the prepetual fighting between various tribes and often sought solitude in the desert and the mountains. He had his first mystical experience at the age of 40. The archangel Gabrile appeared before him in a vision, hailed him as the Rasu—messenger of God and called upon him to proclaim the glory of Allah. Gabrile repeated his message in several dreams and showed Muhammad a written text which later became the Holy Quraan. The year 622 AD, which marks the lowest point in the personal fortunes of Muhammad and also the beginnings of his remarkable success, has been adopted as the starling point of the Muhammedan calender. The Islamic calendar is dated from this migration (Hegira). In Medina, Muhammad founded a new religion—Islam. Eight years later the Prophet returned to Mecca and defeated his opponents in battle. He died in 632 AD.

The Arabs had trade relations with the south on India long before the advent of Islam during the early years of Hegira. Their mosque was built in Changanore. Islam was brought to India by Arab traders and invaders in the 8th century. Islam thereafter spread through persuasion and force.

Quran is the sacred book of the Muslims. Basic doctrines of Islam are simple—Unity of Allah (God) and Mohammed being Allah's prophet; Allah will recompense everyone according to his action on the day of Judgement; recitation of Kalma; Namaz five times a day; Roza during Ramzan; Haaj to Mekka; Zakat (charity).

There are no castes in Islam but there are about 72 sects but most important are Shias and Sunnis.

Islam gave to India arts of enamelling, calligraphy and the illuminated manuscripts. A fresh architecture—the Indo-Sarenic; Mughal schools of paintings in beautiful Persian-Hindu style, new ragas and some new musical instruments. New classical form of dance—Kathak and Unani system of medicine developed besides new types of dresses, food, manners and literature.

CHRISTIANITY

Christianity came to India earlier than to Europe, the Syrian Christians of Kerala tracing the origin of the early Malabar Church to St.Thomas, an apostle of Christ who came to India and died near Madras. The Syrian rites of the church that they have followed have given their name. Other legends describe Saint Bartholomwe as the first Christian missionary in India. Latin historians in the middle ages have made frequent references to Christian settlements in India.

Historically, however, Christian missionary activity can be said to have begun with the arrival of Saint Francis Xavier in 1542. His tomb in Goa is still visited by thousands of Catholics every year.Saint Francis Xavier was succeeded by Portuguese missionaries.During this period there were forcible conversions and destruction of Hindu temples.Some of them visited Akbar's court, and even entertained the hope of converting the emperor.

In the 18th century, Protestant missionaries, especially from Denmark, Holland and Germany, started their work in India. The British conquest naturally gave the Angkican Church an advantage over others.

During British rule, foreign missionaries spread all over the country, especially to tribal areas.

Indian social reformers, like Keshab Chandra Sen of the Brahma Samaj, realised that Christianity had enriched India's religious life in many ways. Ramakrishna lived as a Christian for several months. A Christian poet, Michael Madhusudan-Dutt, is regarded as one of the pioneers of modern Bengali poetry. Later, Tagore paid homage to Jesus Christ in several poems. Mahatma Gandhi was deeply influenced by Christianity. His writings and speeches are full of excerpts from the New Testament.

The Christian Church and community has contributed greatly in the social welfare and educational fields and in spreading of teaching in English language.

INDIAN MUSIC

Music is one of the oldest and finest forms of human expression. The Vedas are set to a distinctive melody that has been passed down through the centuries in an unbroken oral tradition.

According to a Hindu legend, music is a divine gift to man. Sarasvati, consort of Brahma, is the goddess of music and all five arts. She holds a Vina (seven-stringed instrument) in one hand and plays it with another. The Svarga (heaven) has Gandharvas, The singers, Kinnars the instrumentalists and Apsaras, the dancers.

Panini (500 BC) made one of the earliest references to music. The Mahabharata mentions the seven Sabras, the Jatakas mention the four great sounds. The earliest musical theory is included in the chapter of the Natya Shastra of Bharata. The Vaishnava and Saiva Bhakti saints of Tamil of the 18th and 19th century spread love of music through devotional hymns.

In medieval times Saangdeva (1210-1247 AD) of Devagiri in his Sangita Ratnakar showed his knowledge of south and north Indian forms of music.

The Muslim kings in the 14th and 15th centuries introduced Iranian models which differentiated it from Carnatic music. Tansen (1550 - 1610 AD) became a legend in the realm of music.

BASIC PRINCIPLES OF MUSIC

NADA : The chief property of music is Nada — Na means Prana of life — breath and Da means Agni or fire. The conception of Nada is inseparably connected with the intangible elements of breathing system and physical expellation of sound or nada Brahma.

SHRUTI : Shruti means sound that is capable of being distinctly heard by the ear. The gamut of seven blocks notes called the Saptaka (equivalent of the octave in western music) they are sa-re-ga-ma-pa-dha-ni. These Saptakas are further divided into 22 shrutis on which Indian music is based.

RAGA : Raga is the basis melody in Indian music. The term Raga is defined in various ways. Raga means passion and each note is associated with a mood, emotion or passion. Some translate it as a tune while others as air and as melody. Different combinations of octave gives rise to Ragas. There are still others 108 pure ragas. Any combination of two or more Ragas are called Misra (mixed) ragas which are numerous. Ragas have to be rendered at the right time of the day and in some cases in the right season as they are supposed to be associated with a particular time and season. All music has to be played in a variety of Talas (time measures) which are produced by hand and fingers on various types of drums. One requires practice under a guru for perfection.

There are two major systems of classical music today—the Hindustani and the Carnatic. However, the common thing among both is that they are based on the same shrutis. As performed today, the Hindustani and Carnatic genres of music are so different in practical approach that a listener whose ears are turned to one will not automatically appreciate the aesthetics of the other. Though sharing the history, science, theory and structure, the seeming paradox of these two systems turning out so differently can be explained by looking into four factors: regional, linguistic, technical and socio — political. In practical terms Carnatic music is imbued with a pre-dominance of devotional character Hindustani music has a virtuous quality that stems from its refinement as a chamber in the Mughal court art.

There are various types of melodies. The Kiratana and Kriti are two most important in Carnatic system. Some other Hindustani systems are Thumri (love songs), Tappa, Gazal (love lyrics) and Dadra.

Indian musical instruments present a large variety originating thousands years ago some coming from Arabia and Iran. The main varieties of instruments in use are :

— **String Instruments :** Played by the finger nail such as Dilruba, Sarod, Sitar, Sarangi, Rabab, Esraj and the Tambur which provide no melody but a resonant droning accompaniment.

— **Wind Instruments :** These came into existence in ancient times. The Buffalo horn is the oldest. Brass horn; Conch shells, flute (murali) and Nadaswaram.

— **Percussion instruments** : The drum takes the first rank and is one of the oldest and most important musical instruments. There are about 290 varieties of drums, some important ones being the Mridanga; Tabla (set of two drums); Pakhawaj and Tambourines of various kinds.

Indian music is like a river ever fluid and subtly changing. Indian music is attracting increasing patronage in the West as well as in the Far East. It is receiving the recognition that was long overdue.

PRESERVERS OF THE INDIA'S MUSICAL CULTURE

Thyagaraja, Muthuswami, Deekshithar and Shyam Shastri, popularly known as the trinity of Carnatic music, laid the foundation for the development of Carnatic music with their innumerable compositions in hundreds of ragas. These compositions paved way for the present concept of a stage programme.

The well known exponents of Violin are Dr. N. Rajam, V.G.Jog (Hindustani), Prof. T.N.Krishnan, Lalgudi G.Jayaraman, M.S. Gopalakrishnan, V.V. Subramanyam and Dr. I.Subramanyam (Carnatic).

Bhismillah Khan is the legendary exponent of Shehnai. Shemmangudi R. Srinivasa Iyer, M.S.Subbulakshmi, D.K.Pattammai, Palghat K.V.Narayanaswami (Carnatic), Gangubai Hangal, Bhimsen Joshi, Kishori Amonkar, Jasraj are the most shining vocalists of Indian music.

Three instrumentalists handling stringed instruments Ali Akbar Khan (Sarod) Ravi Shankar (Sitar) and Vilayat Khan (Sitar) have achieved global eminence. Veena Doraiswamy Iyengar and Amjad Ali Khan (Sarod) have also made remarkable contribution. Zakir Hussain, the most well-known tabla player, is innovative in his renditions and is totally committed to his instrument—Tabla.

M.S. Subbulakshmi excels in devotional singing. She has been honoured with Sangeet Kalanidhi, Bharat Ratna, Sangeet Academy awards and has won international acclaim for her classical vocal renditions. Pandit Jawaharlal Nehru had called her the 'Queen of Songs'. Nation thrives on her notes on Bhakti. M.S. Subbulakshmi is known across the nation as the mellifluous voice that wakes up the deity with her suprabhatam.

Girija Devi is part of the great thumri tradition of Benaras and has been instrumental in bringing respectability to the thumri form. At present she is settled in Benaras teaching students at home and in the music faculty of the Benaras Hindu University.

Lata Mangeshkar, K.J.Yesudass and S.P. Balasubramanyam have made significant contributions in popularizing semi-classical music thereby attracting new sections towards serious music.

INDIAN DANCES

DANCE is an outward expression of deep inner feelings.

The tradition of the performing arts in India has its roots in the Vedas in which ritual manifested itself through music and dance. Dance is perhaps one of the earliest fine arts evolved by mankind and considered as part of the religion as the first dance performed is believed to be the cosmic dance of Shiva at the creation of the universe. The belief is that dancing came into being at the beginning of all things. The Indian mind having traversed all regions of knowledge surrender to the bliss of Dance of Shiva who plays, longs and creates. Blinded by the beauty, he rushes frolics, dances and whirls. Lord Shiva is Natraja, Lord of Dances, the cosmos is his theatre—he himself is actor and audience. The figure of Natraja is adorned as the prime source of Indian dance.

The Natyashastra, an ancient treatise on dramaturgy, explains that when the written texts became the monopoly of the educated few the gods appealed to Lord Bramha, the creator, and urged him to promulgate a fifth Veda, in the form of audiovisual art that would be accessible to all irrespective of caste or formal education. Thus the natya Veda was conceived drawing contents and teachings from the four Vedas and presenting the quintessence of all five arts including music, painting and dance.

In India religion, philosophy and mythology cannot be divorced from their art forms. Dance and music are tied inextricably to ceremony of any kind—wedding, birth, coronation, religious procession—all are occasions for singing and dancing.

The three main divisions in the classical form of dancing are :

— Nritta or Pure dance which is performed with attractive movements of the body.
— Nritya - Conveys the meaning of the song by means of Abhinaya or Face movements, Hast mudra or hand gestures.
— Natya means drama where hand and facial gestures are added in the enactment of drama—combination of both—acting and dancing.

BHARAT NATYAM

Indian dancing has an unbroken tradition. Bharat Natyam is the oldest form of dance practised in Tamil Nadu, Tanjore and Chennai. Dance is done to the accompaniment of musical instruments. Originated in ancient times near Tanjore as temple dance of devadasis. It has been the most common national and classical dance art of India whose principles and techniques were systematised and codified about 1800 years ago in Bharat Muni's Natya Shastra. This ancient treaties has been followed by practitioners of Bharat Natyam to date. Modes of presentations have changed from time to time and from region to region but still it is fresh and fascinating and it commands admiration. Usually performed solo, there are many postures as specified in the Bharat Natya sastra.

Bharat Natyam consists of two major hand positions, 12 hand movements; 13 symbolic gestures of head; nine of the neck; nine of the eyeballs; seven of the eyebrows; six of chins; fingers; wrists and arms etc.

Dancer enacts the various roles of characters appearing in episode, themes and stories in the mythology. The dancer has to express through movements the moods of passion, heroic sentiment, fear, anger, hatred, tenderness, laughter, amazement and peace.

Bharat Natyam has been the mother of the other classical dance systems in India.

It has also been the main source of inspiration for the allied arts of sculpture, paintings and icon making.

KALAKSHETRA in Chennai is an important centre of training which was started by the late Rukmini Devi, a pioneer and one of the most renowned figures in the world of performing arts in India.

KATHAK

The Kathak school in north India gave the fullest expression to the classical dance. Kathak has its roots in Katha or Story. Kathak is a dance style full of skill and drama. In its emotional expression, Kathak possesses a fund of subjects and lyrics gleaned from sacred legends and mythology. Story-tellers, attached to temples in North India, used to narrate stories from epics. Later they started adding mime and gestures to recitation. The next stage in its evolution came in the 15th and 16th centuries with the popularisation of the Radha-Krishna legend. During Mughal rule Kathak became a court dance and received encouragement.

Kathak became popular during Mughal times and was added to the repertoire of "nautch" girls and degraded to coarse suggestiveness and indecent gestures and movements.

It was taken out from the temples to the courts. Jaipur, Lucknow and Benaras became the centres. While Jaipur gave predominance to pure dance with emphasis on rhythm, the Lucknow one drifted into erotics.

The Kathak programme is made up of three main items :
— Amada - a dance salutation
— Tarahas - a series of intricate and complex steps
— Gathas - interpretation through guestures of stories.

Tabla, Pakhawaj and Sarangis are generally used for rhythm.

Kathak is executed to instrument of music. A string of small bells (ghunghroos) are tied around both ankles of the dancer which mark the beat and timing of the foot thereby creating sweet sounds interwoven with rhythms within rhythms.

KATHAKALI

Kathakali is indigenous to Kerala. It is unique in many respects, it is based on miming in which performers remain silent. For themes, Kathakali draws upon the inexhaustible treasure house of Indian mythology. Kathakali is originated probably in the 13th or 14th century as a type of village or folk dance enacting stories and episodes from epics. In Kathakali the art of make-up is a hereditary vocation. The actor does not speak up but express himself through highly complicated and scientifically ordained mudras and steps, closely following the text being sung from the background of the stage. Mythological heroes like Pandavas, King Nala and divine personage like Krishna and Indra wear this make-up. In Kathakali, the elaborate costume, the strange mask make up, the gorgeous crowns are reminiscent of its folk traditions. The costume consists of multi-pleated billown white skirts, the long sleeved tunics and real ornamented plates and yards of cloth garlands ending up in rosettes. Dialogue is combined with dance to bring myth and legend to life in the temple courtyards of Kerala.

The vocabulary for the performer is only hast mudras (Stylised hand guestures) facial gestures and nritta. Together with the exotic quality of the spectacle and the intricate abhinaya system and the rhetorical text rendered in classical style to the accompaniment of drums— Kathakali performance transports a spectator to an unwordly atmosphere peopled by gods, demons and other super humans.

Originally, based on Natya Shastra, this dance form derived replenishment from Hastalakshana Deepika and Ahinaya Darpana. Kathakali presents in both Tandava and Lasya style of dancing. The three fundamentals of Indian dancing laid down in Natya Shastra form the basis of this dance form. Kathakali is considered to be a highly synthetic art form, combining in itself the rudiments of its earlier forms.

Poet Vallathvi can be said to be the fountainhead of all inspiration in regard to today's Kathakali. He authored many scripts. 'Kerala Kalamandalam' at Cheruthuruthy on the bank of Bharata-puzha is the premier institution in this regard.

ODISSI

Odissi dance had originated in the 2nd century BC during the reign of the Jain King Karavela who himself was an expert dancer and musician. It consists of one long theme starting from the invocation to the deities, the earth and the guru, and ending with a highly technical finale of pure dance.

In the early 17th century, a class of boys known as Gotipuas came into being. They dressed as dancing girls and danced in the temples with grace in its uniqueness with the most important elements—the Bhangimas and Karanas. The Bhangimas are the basic poses and the Karanas the basic dance unit.

Odissi dance is done in stages so as to bring to the fullest its beautiful stances of posture and the art of interpretation. The dance poses had been the themes of carvings on the temple walls. Temples have brought to the posterity thousands of postures in sculpture. We know from inscriptions and related literature that at the Shiva temple at Bhubaneshwar handmaidens of God were encouraged and assisted to preserve this form of classical dance. At about the same time the Vishnu temple at Jagannatha Puri also introduced the tradition of temple dancing. In those days Maharis were held in great esteem and enjoyed a good social status.

Popular devotion to Sri Krishna is embodied in Jayadeva's unique Sanskrit love poem, Geet Govinda and its verses were interpreted by every representative of Orissa's culture when he became a singer, dancer or devotee.

This dance form is very soft and lyrical. Many of the dances at present are based on theme of love of Radha and Krishna.

The Odissi dance has been preserved not only by the great gurus, their descendants but the temples have brought to posterity thousands of examples in sculpture.

KUCHIPUDI

Kuchipudi is a dance drama of Andhra Pradesh. Kuchelapuram is the birth-place of this style since the times of the Satvahana kings in the 2nd century BC.

The excavations of sculptures from Kunchpudi in Krisha district indicates that there are two main schools of dance—Devadasi and Kelika. The Vaishnava movement helped in the evolution of Kuchipudi and shaped it up as Bhagwata dance mela. Its forms are woven around realistic as well as conventional values.

In all aspects it is akin to Bharata Natyam. Tirtha Naryana and Siddendra Yogi evolved this style. It was a male prerogative. In recent years women have taken to it but it is mostly a solo dance. Vembhati Chinasatyam is the most popular guru today.

MANIPURI

Manipuri is a form of group dance wherein girls wear coloured ankle-deep satin skirts that are heavily emboridered and ornamented with sequins and tiny ventilating mirrors. This costume is mirror to the natural beauty of eastern frontier of Assam where Manipuri dance evolved in the most charming art form.

According to a legend, once when Lord Shiva and His consort Parvati visited this beautiful region, they found Radha and Krishna dancing the Ras. Parvati got so much enamoured that she expressed her desire to dance with Shiva who agreed. And then accompanied by heavenly music, the eternal couple danced to the glory of the universe. From 15th to the 18th century, Vaishnavism came to be adopted in Manipur and this ushered a new era in the development of this style. The dance form is mostly ritualistic. It has preserved the dance drama technique which draws heavily on the rich lore of legend and mythology. The numbers presented are Lai Haroba and Ras Leela. The former deals with the creation of the God and later on Krishna Leela. Drums play an important role and the Poonang Cholom item is a must in any performance. Manipuri is tender and reticent on the one hand and an extremely vigorous form of dance on the other hand. A continuity of movement and a restraint of power are underlying features of the Manipuri style.

KODIYATTAM

This is always a long drawn out affair and may take anywhere from a few days to a number of weeks. It is both entertainment and edification. The Vidhushaka (Jester) rules the root. He moralises but his satire and innuendo have very often no relevance to the theme of the play.

KRISHNANTTAM

It is a dance drama associated with the Krishna legend. The Zamorin king of Calicut named Mahadevan in the middle of the 17th century AD had composed eight dramatic lyrical plays dealing with Krishna's life which even today are presented for successive nights. The style is almost akin to Kathakali.

OTTAN THULLAL

It is performed solo and because of its ready mass appeal, it is also known as poor man's Kathakali. Kunjan Nambiar evolved it and highlighted the social conditions of his time, the distinctions of class and the weaknesses and whims of the rich and the great. The dialogue is in simple Malyalam and therefore ensures mass appeal.

YAKSHAGANA

It originated from one of the very early dramas known as Bahu Nataka composed by Pakkuribi Somnath in about 1250 AD. It portayed several varieties of Shiva Lila and later took the form of Yakshagana and became common to rural India. It is an admixture of dance and drama. Its heart lies in A Gana meaning music. The language is local and the themes are based on Hindu mythology and legends. There is always Suthra (conductor) and a Vidhushaka (jester) in it.

CHAU

A dance dedicated to Shiva and Shakti it is exclusively performed by men. It originated in Seraikela, a former princely state in Orissa. It is a three-day ceremonial worship in a Shiva temple followed by a grand procession and the dancers interpret mythology, the sacred history, legend and nature.

MOHINI ATAM

A solo classical dance of Kerala based on Kathakali it presents lasya and tandava style. Starting at a medium tempo, the performer increases the speed gradually to reach a thrilling climax of grace and strength combining the design of foot work posture, varied arm movements and mudras.

FOLK DANCES

Folk dances are generally spontaneous and are the creation of people's imagination and desire for artistic and emotional expression. Folk dances, unsupported by written words, are established by sociological impacts, customs and traditions.

SOUTH INDIA

Kolattam : This dance is performed to celebrate the birthday of Lord Rama by young girls with lacquered stick held in hands.Originating from Tamil Nadu, this dance form is popular throughout India.

Vasant Atam : This is performed to welcome the spring. Little boys and girls bring Mango buds and sing, dance in chorus to the accompaniment of symbols hand-claps and dholuk, extolling the mother godesses—the Earth.

Kummi Dance : A dance of Tamil Nadu, it is performed during the Hindu new year of the south which falls in January just after the Pongal festival. Groups of young girls dance with varying steps and clapping hands using their little making steps in a circle.

Oatam Tudal : It is a type of pantomic akin to Kathakali dance. It is performed by a single artist accompanied by a singer, a drumer and a cymbal player and narrates select excerpts from Malyalam literature in an enchanting manner.

Kaikottikali : A folk dance of Kerala—the songs of which are generally based on mytological stories. The women and girls dance in circles with slow and measured speed.

Tappattikkali : Performed in Kerala by young girls and women during the festival of Lord Shiva. One of the elder women in the group commences the song and leads the dancer while the others, repeating what she sings, follow her movements in a circle.

NORTH INDIA

Kajri : It is an occasion when the peasants in north India propitiate the Vedic God Indra and pray for the nourishment of the earth and fire and a successful harvest. It is performed in rainy season.The dance movements follow the songs that are accompanied by the rhythmic beat of dholak and the cymbals.

Nautanki : Popular folk dance of Uttar Pradesh. It narrates mythological stories and also comments on the present day social problems.

Ras Lila : A dance form which originated in Mathura and Vridavan. It depicts the childhood, boyhood and youth of Lord Krishna. It is accompanied by the background music consisting of drums, cymbals and flute.

Karan : Karan is a dance which originate in Shahbad to worship the trees marking the end of harvesting. The dance festival begins with fasting during the day. Women dressed in bright colours and men in their best apparel stand in rows and commence singing and dancing to the beat of the drum.

In the Himalayn ranges dances are performed in celebration of the autumn festival of Dussehra. In Kumaon people dance and sing glorifying their history. Chappeli is another type of dance performed at weddings and spring time.

Kullu the valley of gods : People dance in procession during weekly fairs and festivals—the biggest being in spring and autumn at Dussehra time.

Rauf : It belongs to Jammu and is performed by women during harvesting season. **Hikat** is another dance of Jammu in which girls and boys express sheer joy and exuberance.

Bhangara : It is the most popular and best known dance of Punjab performed on all festive occasions. It is symbolic of exuberance and gaiety associated with the nature of people living in this part of India. Bhangara is performed especially on Baisakhi festival to celebrate the harvest in March.

Gangore dance : It is peculiar to Rajasthan and is performed in veneration to Parvati (Gauri) the eternal consort of Lord Shiva during Gangaur festival.

Khayal is a folk dance drama of rural Rajasthan based on the legendary love of Dhola and Maru which originated in the 10th century AD.

WESTERN INDIA

Dhandya Ras : It is the most popular dance of Gujarat. Singing in chorus the dancers form an intricate series of movements holding hands and moving round in a circle. It is also played sometimes with the sticks with timing akin to that of a pair of drums.

Garba : It is believed to be a gift to Saurashtra from Assamese princess Usha, the grand daughter in-law of Lord Krishna. Village dancers, carrying decorated pitchers and pots of clay, dance around houses ushering in the festival of Dussehra invoking fertility and prosperity. Dance stepping is simple and is done by groups bending to right–left and forward accompanied by songs.

Tamasha : It is an operative folk dance of Maharashtra. The players sing and narrate stories with mime. Men make forceful movements while women sing in high tones as they dance.

TRIBAL DANCES

Tribal population is found all over the country. Born in natural surroundings they are vivid, temperamental and filled with zest for living. Costumed in colourful apparel tribal dances carry songs which mirror the sociological, psychological and historical moorings.

PRESERVERS OF INDIAN CLASSICAL DANCE CULTURE

Rukmi Devi and Bala Saraswati are known as the queens of Bharata Natyam. Binda Din Maharaj, Kolkadin, Aachan Maharaj, Gopi Kishan are the maestros of Khatak.

Pritima Bedi was the famous odissi dancer and founder of the prestigious 'Nrityagram' school of dancing.

Birju Maharaj, the famous Kathak dancer, belongs to the Kalka Bindodin gharana of Kathak. He is a teacher at Kathak Kendra in Delhi. Birju Maharaj conceived a number of dance-dramas like Malti-Madhav, Kumarsambav and Shan-e-Awadh.

Sonal Mansingh has made her name in Odissi dancing. Coming from a respected Gujarati family she started her career as a Bharatanatyam dancer. At present she is involved with the making of tele films.

Mrinali Sarabhai is a famous Kathakali dancer. 'Marushya', the life of a Man, was her first innovative performance. She gave a new interpretation to Tagore's Bhanusingher, Padavali and Tasher Desh in Bharatnatyam and Kathakali. At present she runs the Darpana Dance Academy at Ahmedabad with her daughter Mallika.

INDIAN PAINTINGS

Hindu legends and myths mention the making of Poraiture Chitralekha is mentioned as the first woman painter who was an accomplished portraitist. Such paintings were to be found in palaces of Kosala and Magadha. Walls were decorated with coloured murals representing human beings, animals, religious paintings were being made on cloth or wood.

Paintings in early times was one of the nine basic crafts and cannon which was laid down in handbooks such as Vatsayana's Kamsutra.

The earliest Indian paintings are pre-historic and primitive - hunting scenes were drawn on walls - witness of which are still in existence in some caves and can be seen at Kaimur ranges at Madhya Pradesh.

Stone age paintings are found in Vindhian hills, some near village Sinhanpur - Madhya Pradesh, Mirzapur in Uttar Pradesh, Bihar and Tamil Nadu. They depict in a realistic way like animals running or leaping, birds flying warriors in pursuit and resemble paintings found at Cogul in Spain and in Africa.

Paintings on the pottery began from Indus valley.

The earliest paintings of Ajanta date back to the 1st century BC and the latest to the 8th century. The spirit of the compassionate Buddha is their Jataka tales elaborated the vicissitudes of these incarnations and the Ajanta artists painted them in sinuous line and sensitive colour. City, countryside and forests, men and women of every type, Fauna and floras all are mentioned in these murals Brush and chisel accompanied the message of peace and Ajanta became a fountainhead of Asian paintings and murals. Other school and style flourished in Kashmir and South India from 6th to 19th centuries. Mural tradition in Chalukyan - Badami (6th century AD); Pallava Panamalai (7th century AD); Pandyan Sittannavasal (9th century AD); Chola Tanjaore (12th century AD); Lepakshi of Vijayanagara (16th century AD) and the murals of Kerala reaching to middle of the 19th century. A later painting had come down from mural surface to miniature style spread to western India and is seen in numerous illuminated manuscripts.

With the decay of Buddhism (in the 7th c.) art of painting declined.

Other schools and styles also flourished in Kashmir and South India from 6th to the 9th centuries. The Bengal Pala school flourished for 500 years till 125 which produced small paintings and miniature executed on palm-leaf manuscripts, the most important painters being Bhipals and Dlimana.

With the decay of Buddhism (in the 7th c.) art of painting declined some examples of these Pala school paintings (12th c.), some Jain book illustrations (15th c.), some Brahmanical frescoes at Ellora (12th c. or earlier) have survived.

The Gujarati school flourished from the beginning of the 12th c. to the 17th c. was greatly supported by the Jains and was mostly confined to illustrations in Jain palm leaf manuscripts and miniatures.

With the establishment of Mughal rule in India (1550 - 1880 AD), new style of paintings came into existence. Foreign artists made their way to India during Akbar's time and the famous ones are Farrukh, Beg, Bad-al-Samand and Mir Sayed Ali. The famous Indian painters of the time are Bassawan, Daswanth and Kesudasa. Forty famous artists lived in Akbar's time who were also Indian and Persian artists - one man doing drawings and the another the colouring, a third one for the details. Artists received further momentum when Akbar commissioned the translation and illustration of Indian texts like Ramayana and Mahabharata.

The Mughal kalam suffered due to Aurangazeb's rigid observance of the Islamic command, but the Mulsim rulers of Bijapur, Golconda and Hyderabad were great patrons of art and paintings - a Deccani school was established in the south which had traits of Mughal paintings. Local schools at Tanjavur and Mysore also grew up and later reached its zenith in the first half of the 19th c. under the patronage of the ruler Raya Krishnadevraya Wodeyar and the painters of Tanjavur school did portraiture on ivory.

Declines of patronage in the Mughal court at Delhi artists moved to a more congenial environment and were welcomed by the rulers of Rajasthan.

Rajasthani school (1550 - 1900 AD) of paintings, murals, miniatures came into existance. Frescoe paintings was done on the walls of palaces at Jaipur, Udaipur, Bikaner and Jodhpur.

Another branch of Rajasthani school was at orcha and Datia Bundelkhand. Most of these paintings have the themes of the Krishna stories, Raslila and Hindu religious subjects.

There are also the Pahari schools which celebrated local kalams

—they were Kangra, Nurpur, Chamba, Bhasoli, Jammu and Garwali.

Strong presence of British era and western academicians become popular. The modern period of paintings begins with the inspiration of Rabindranath Tagore and E.B. Havell who started Calcutta-Bengal school of paintings. Some of the famous painters are Nandlal Bose, and S.N. Ganguli.

Ravi Varma of Travancore became well known because of his style subjects painted in eastern style. Later schools of art were established in many important cities in the country.

INDIAN SCULPTURES

The Indus valley civilisation "3000 BC and possibly 5000 BC" cites specimen of beads, animals carved on limestone trees and some human figures, a small stone dancing, an exquisitely bronze girl and the bust of a priest with a shawl with a tre-foil pattern. Terracotta is the medium for objects used in rituals like the mother goddess figurines as well as for recreation like toys.

The figurine of the dancing girl that has come down to us testifies to good knowledge of bronze casting and indicates the fascination for the faminine figure pointing to the close relation between sculpture and dance in the Indian tradition.

Ashoka period (274-236 BC). The remains of some sculptures of this period still exist in Sarnath. From about 200 to 100 BC sculptures of deities of forests, trees, Yakshas and Yakshinis began to be made in sandstone. Great achievement in sculpture was attained in the carvings of Buddhist stupas and Chaytyas on the columns, gateway and railings which represent Jataka stories and scenes from the Buddha's life in Sanchi.

During the Kushan period, Gandhra school of sculpture came into being with its realistic scenes of daily life—most famous are the delicately carved stupas of Buddha. Mathura as the capital of Kushan's kingdom from 300-150 BC, produced large primitive stone images.

The age of imperial Gupta (300-510 AD) achieved stabilisation of the icons of Buddha and prefect masterpieces such at Sarnath. The wonderful torso of a Bodhisttva (now at Victoria Albert museum) and the collossal copper Buddha of Sultanganj were made around 450 AD. The Dasavatara temple at Deogarh—on the Nagara style of the Gupta period is a magnificent specimen of Gupta art and the temple still has the wonderful carvings on the doors.

The eastern Chalukyas created some fine sculptures of dance in the temple of Vijayawada region. This age also created magnificent sculptures on Hindu themes like the incarnations of Vishnu in the late

5th century temple of Deogarh and the powerful representation of the boar incarnation salvaging the earth, hewn from the rock of Udayagiri.

The Vakatakas of the Deccan were the contemporaries of the Guptas and under their patronage fine sculptures came up in abundance, mostly Buddhist at Ajanta and Hindu at Ellora. The achievement of the great range from the lightness flying figures and the elegant rhythmic balance of dancing groups such as one at Aurangabad to the majesty and wealth of symbolic meaning of the figure of Mahesha at Elephanta. The western Chalukyan continued these trends creating gloating figures and dancing Shiva at Badami, Aihole and Pattaadakal. The eastern Chalukyas created some fine sculptures of dance in the temples at Vijayawada region.

Beginning with 8th century Hindu fervour for cutting pillared halls and images had reached its climax and created Ajanta and Ellora caves (where there are 12 Buddhist caves also). The huge images of the Kailasa temple are carved in high relief. It had taken a century to complete. During this time, the Jain saints carved colossal free standing statues of their Tirthankaras and saints at Gwalior Fort.

At Sravanbelagola lies the free standing 19-meter high stone image of Gomateswara carved in 983 AD.

There are some other sculptures in Orissa temples at Puri (750 AD); Bhubaneshwar (8th - 10th century AD) and Konarak (13th century AD). They are in the forms of wheel of the Sun God's chariot and are of the finest examples.

Under Pala and Sena kings of Bengal (730 - 1125 AD), Buddhist images were made in black polished stones.

The Chandela rulers (800-1204 AD) erected Khajuraho group of temples with remarkable carvings of male and female figures in erotic poses.

Exquisite marble temples of the Jains at Dilwara and Girnar with richly carved ornamented motifs on ceilings, walls and pillars were also created during this period.

The South Indian Chola temples at Thanjavur incorporate excellent sculptured carvings. The bronze sculpture of the Chola ruler is famous particularly for the figure of Shiva in the Tandava dance pose and some statues of goddesses and lampbearers.

Moving further south, the great achievement of the Pallava dynasty (eight century) was the gigantic tableau at Mahabalipuram where the mouments of rockcut belongs to the earliest phase of Dravidian temple architecture which flourished from 600 to 750 AD. Mythological episodes, epic battles demons, gods, animals, all vividly depicted on the wall sculptures are breathtakingly real and beautiful.

During 1100 and 1345 AD came the richly carved and meticulously fine workmanship of sculpture of the Hoysala type of temples most famous being at Belur and Halebid.

In 15th the Vijayanagara kingdom (1350 - 1565 AD) created remarkable creations at Hampi.

Kerala made unique achievements in sculpture in wood.

From medieval period onwards this art declined from royal patronage due to Muslim rulers.

Exposed to global influences the Indian sculpture today is though experiencing changes and using various styles and also using new materials like steel and fibreglass but no new distinctive school or style has been evolved.

INDIAN ART, HANDICRAFTS AND SHOPPING

India's vast cultural diversity has resulted in a treasure trove of handicrafts. The cultural exuberance and composite tradition that makes this blend has found full expression in heart-warming creations of master craftspersons. These creators are extraordinary and have inherited and honed ancestral skills to perfection. India is also a country where time honoured traditions coexist in prefect harmony with the best of modernity.

An inextricable part of the great Indian shopping scene are the local fairs held periodically all over the country, street side bazars with their pavement stalls, and in dimly lit shops that invariably surround many of the country's ancient monuments. In Mumbai's Chor Bazar (Thieves Market), it is literally possible to buy everything from a pin to an elephant and an antique, if one is lucky. The bazar around Char Minar in Hyderabad is crowded with shops, where heavily veiled women bargain for real pearls and glass bangles. Each state in the country has something to offer, for crafts are essentially the inter-relationship between materials available and local traditions.

METAL CRAFT

The line dividing craft and fine arts is practically indistinguishable in the metal craft of India. Gold silver, brass, copper and bell metal are shaped into intricately designed images, idols, jewellery and utility items, having a finish and style unique in appeal.

GOLD & SILVERWARE : The princely States of India demanded not only enamelled jewellery but also enamelled utensils such as wine, cups, finger bowls, pill boxes etc., in both gold and silver repousse, sometimes studded with jewels.

The craftspersons of India excel in this art. With the evolution of new tools, technique and skills, they are now better equipped to cater to modern tastes.

Fully geared to meet modern market demands, today the gold and silver plated articles produced are usually plain or, even when ornamented are devoid of extensive encrustation. Portions of silver articles are sometimes covered with gold water. The designs thus formed are known as GANGA JAMUNA pattern from the Ganga and the Jamuna rivers which meet at Allahabad and flow together.

LUCKNOW : The former seat of the Nawabs of Avadh produces an extensive range of gold and silver-plated articles in a multitude patterns. The design resembles those found in Kashmir. Owing to strong Islamic influence, still prevailing, most of the articles are highly ornamented with repousse work depicting hunting and jungle scenes and floral motifs.

BRASS AND COPPERWARE : India is the largest brass and copper making region in the world with thousands of establishments spread all over. For articles made out of one or more pieces of metal, the copper or brass sheet is first marked out by a pair of compass and the piece or pieces cut off by a scissors called KATRI.The required shape is made by alternate heating and hammering and is finally turned on the lathe. The final polish to the article is gives on the lathe itself.

MORADABAD : The city famous for utensils, both utility and ornamental, made of white metal and electroplated brass and copper. The engraving is either "SADA'(plain)" or "SIA KALAM". Modern streamlined articles of Swedish design in polished brass or burnished copper are also made here, satisfying the demand for modern accessories and sophisticated interior decoration.

VARANASI : In Uttar Pradesh it is the first city in India for the multitude of its cast and sculptured mythological images and emblems in brass and copper as well as household utensils.

In recent years Mirzapur has also emerged as one of the important brass industries of Uttar Pradesh. Goods produced have an all over India market, with a portion being exported to other countries.

Some of the most beautiful and interesting metalwork of India for daily as well as for ceremonial purposes are crafted in Kashmir, Bihar, West Bengal, Assam, Orissa, Tamil Nadu and Kerala.

METAL ORNAMENTATION

Metal ornaments have been a rave in all ages and times. The attractive contrasts in colours and textures of metals has led to the evolution of the metal ornamentation through techniques like inlay, overlay, appliqué, fixing of colours etc.

BIDRI : Bidri, a form of surface ornamentation, takes its name from the city of Bidar situated north-west of Hyderabad. The work is in black colour which never fades and is relived with silver and gold inlay. In Lucknow the art of manufacturing Bidri is believed to have been introduced during the time of the Nawabs of Avadh. The Emperor at Delhi bestowed on them the dignity of the fish (Mahi Murattib). Lucknow Bidri, therefore, abounds in fish motifs, flora and fauna and vine leaf patterns.

ENAMELLING : Enamelling is the art of colouring and ornamenting the surface of the metal by using over it various mineral substances. The beauty of the article depends on the skill and resources of the worker and the excellence of the material employed. The range of colours obtained on gold is much greater than that on silver, copper and brass. Three forms of enamelling are known to exist. These include the "CLOISONNE OF JAPAN AND CHINA", the "CHAMLEVE PATTERN" extensively practised in Lucknow and Varanasi and Jaipur specialises in enamelled trays and trinket boxes.

POTTERY & STONE CRAFT

POTTERY : Eye-catching articles of functional and decorative value are fashioned by the skilful potters of India. The craftsperson of KHURJA in Uttar Pradesh have evolved a style of their own by raising the pattern with the use of thick slips into a light relief.Glazes in warm shades of autumnal colours like orange, brown, and light red have also been developed by them. Floral designs in sky blue are worked against blue background. A type of pitches like a pilgrim's bottle, decorated in relief by a thick slip is especially of Khujra.

RAMPUR SURAHIS : Water pots are noted for their uniform green—blue glaze with plain surface, the base being prepared from red clay. Excellent water containers are made in MEERUT and HAPUR which stand out with their striking designs of flowing lines and floral patterns, often capped by wire shaped spouts.

A very special kind of earthenware peculiar to NIZAMABAD in Azamgarh district is distinguished by its dark lustrous body. This sheen is obtained by it into a solution of clay and vegetable matter, dried, then rubbed with a vegetable oil, and fired. Scintillating silver ornamentation is done by incising the pattern on the surface after baking and rubbing in mercury and tin.

ALWAR, JAIPUR and BIKANER in Rajasthan are famed for these products. KANGRA in Himachal is rich in clay wares all throughout the valley while KHANAPUR in Belgaum district of Karnataka is noted for its large sized containers and jars. KUTCH and SAURASHTRA in Gujarat are known for their beautiful earthenware.

TERRACOTTA

Literally meaning baked earth, Indian baked ware of the southern region like large size containers, jars, stools, dresses, tiles etc. have a traditional stamp on them.

POTTERY (CERAMICS) : Beautiful pottery and other ware made of ceramics, is also one of India's famous buys of Rajasthan. It is produced in intriguing white-glazed colour with hand-painted blue-flower designs.

STONE CRAFT AND MARBLE INLAY WORK

It's amazing how odd blocks of stone are cut shaped, inlaid and polished into beautiful objects of everyday use by the skilful craftspersons of India.

HAMIRPUR district in Uttar Pradesh has nurtured a sizeable stone carving industry with its rich deposits of beautiful soft stone. The stone is many coloured with the predominance of a lovely red shade. Marble is also used especially for making statues. In VARANASI the work is done by a community called "RAIDAS".The range of items include tableware, plates, glasses, bowls, food containers, candle stands etc.

AGRA is famous for its superb inlay work in marble, drawing inspiration from the TAJ MAHAL. The designs are either foliage or floral intertwined with geometrical patterns. Model in marble of Taj, vases, boxes, lamps, plates, bowls and pitchers in delicately moulded shapes and fine carvings are some of the popular items produced here. Intricate friezes and trellis or Jali work done in an eye catching range of patterns is also an speciality of this place.

VRINDAVAN near Mathura has marble as well as alabaster products. Some objects are embossed with semi-precious stones or synthetic gems.

A dark brown stone with yellow spots and lines called "SANGE -RATHEK" is found in JHANSI and its neighbourhood from which lampshades, incense stick stands, small medicine grinders are made.

MIDNAPUR in West Bengal is an important traditional region for stoneware and the main centre is SIMULPUR.

BIHAR'S very ancient tradition in stone carving is proved by the magnificent sculpture of the Mauryan period.

TAMIL NADU has a great tradition in stone carving of icons of classical excellence.

RAJASTHAN may be called the land of marble with its stone in various colours and textures.

WOOD CRAFT

WOOD CARVING : Painstaking carved and inlaid, the wooden articles of Uttar Pradesh are quite a rave with all lovers of wood carvings.

SAHARANPUR is known for its carvings in hard sheesham wood and particularly for its famous "VINE LEAF" pattern. The range of designs include floral, geometric and figurative decoration, in addition to the traditional "ANGURI" and "TAKAI" carvings "JALI" (fretted ornamentation), brass, copper and ivory inlay work. Bone and plastic are now being used as low cost substitutes for Ivory since extracting of Ivory is banned in India.

The States of Jammu & Kashmir, Uttar Pradesh, Gujarat, Karnataka and Kerala have developed distinctive styles of wood carvings.

Rajasthan is noted for its Sandel wood and Rosewood besides heavy ornamental furniture

WOOD LACQUERING : Lacquering on wood not only lends colour and sparkel to the products, but also smoothens out the contours thereby imparting a lustrous fineness

India is well-known for ornamental lacquering involving intricate patterns like "ZIG ZAG" and "DANA" work, "ATISHI" "ABRI" or "CLOUD" and "NAKSHI".

In VARANASI a number of lacquered toys and miniature kitchen utensils for children to play with are made.

SCULPTURES : The artistic woodcarvings of southern India draws inspiration from the old Indian tradition of worship. Apart from marvellous prototypes of various gods and goddesses, the wall plaques, statues and toys made of Rosewood, Sandelwood and Teakwood are mesmerising to behold.

PRECIOUS AND SEMI-PRECIOUS STONES

India's fame in precious and semi-precious stones was well established before the arrival of the British. The land that spells royalty is the home of nameless precious and semi-precious stones like "MOTHER OF PERALS", "RUBIS", "SAPPHIRES", "LAPIS", "LAZULI", "AQUAMATINES", "AMETHYSTS" and others. The process of transforming a rough stone into a shapely object of beauty and lustre calls for a great degree of skill in which Indian craftsmen are adept to the core.

COSTUME JEWELLARY : For the hi-fashion women of today there is nothing quite like the offbeat style of self adornment — pick the style that suits most. For, with the passing of centuries, the old appears offbeat today, having an irresistible lure for women the world over.

India is one of the most important countries for the manufacture and export of costume jewellary. It has the largest productions base for glass beads.

VARANASI is famous for its glass beads made from glass rods.

PURDILPUR is famous for black glass beads.

MATHURA is noted for lovely glass beads, striking glass and wooden beads in necklaces together with "RUDRAKSHA" (sacred seeds associated to Lord Shiva) and "TULSI" (basil) in a variety of interesting combinations.

FEROZABAD has a rich selection of fragile and delicate lightweight beads.

German Silver jewellery created to modern tastes is made in AGRA,

MEERUT produces exquisite metal jewellery.

Silver ornaments are especially popular in Rajasthan.

KARNAL in Haryana produces hollow silver beads

ROHTAK has well made peasant jewellery.

Graceful head ornaments are made at Maharashtra.

TRIBAL JEWELLARY : India, has a large tribal population. Their jewellery is a major attraction within the country as well as abroad. The adornment fashioned form flowers, leaves, stones of creepers and fruits are unbelievably charming, sheels, seeds and berries - rudraksha being the most celebrated.

Shell bracelets of West Bengal, specially filigreed gold bracelets will, for certain, capture your heart.

PAINTINGS

Rock paintings in caves are the earliest specimen we have of folk art, as conventionally understood

FLOOR PAINTINGS : When we come to a later period, we find a definite established tradition of paintings on various objects, particularly floors, walls and on intimate objects of everyday use, and in most instances the act being associated with some ritual. The origin of painting is traced to a moving legend recorded in Chitralakshana— the earliest Indian treatise on painting. When the son of king's high priest died, Lord Brahma (the creator) asked the king to paint a likeness of the boy so that He could breathe life into him again. This is how the first painting was made.

The Chola rulers in the south, made use of "KOLAM" floor designs. These decorations done only by women are amongst the most expressive folk-arts. They are known by different names in different parts of the country, "ALPANA" in Bengal and Assam; "ARIPANA" in Bihar, "MANDANA" in Rajasthan, "RANGOLI" in Maharashtra & Gujarat; "CHOWKPURANA" in Uttar Pradesh and "KOLAM" in Tamil Nadu. The Rajasthani "MANDANA" is equally rich. Floor paintings in Andhra are known as "MUGGULU" and Himachal Pradesh has its own distinctive floor paintings with GEOMATRICAL PATTERNS.

WALL PAINTINGS : The paintings on wall have deeper themes; also narrative in a series of panels. Apart from their decorative purpose, they also constitute a form of visual education like picture books from which one learns of one's heritage.

Wall paintings in Punjab, outer Delhi and Rajasthan are usually made at festivals and special occasions like marriages.

Folk Paintings in Rajasthan attained a high standard and artists won great fame in this art. The themes are from epics and heroic Rajput tales. In the kumaon, the usual wall pictures are known as "BAR-BOOND" (dash and dot). The pattern is done by first putting down a number of dots to make the outline of design, then joining them together by lines in different colours. This calls for intense concentration and immense patience, for an error in a single dot or dash can upset the entire composition. Each pattern is known by the number of dots used. One is known as "MASTI BARAMAT" design, a composition of ten dots and the colours used are yellow, voilet and green. There are all over designs of roses and jasmines covering the entire wall.

PHAD PAINTINGS : Phad paintings are predominantly yellow, red and green coloured long scrolls carried by the "BHOPAS", itinerant balladers of Rajasthan, who narrated in song the legend of PABUJI—a local hero—on auspicious occasions to the accompaniment of the folk instrument "RAVANHATTA" made by the Joshis of Shahpur, near Bhilwara. Phads are now also available in smaller panels portraying tales from epics.

MUGHAL MINIATURE PAINTINGS : Of all the art forms in the Mughal period, miniature paintings are painstakingly painted creations that depict the events and lifestyles of the Mughals in their magnificent palaces. Other painting include portraits or studies of wildlife and plants. This art is still alive and popular in Rajasthan and Uttar Pradesh.

MADHUBANI : The wall paintings of Madhubani are joyous expressions of the women of Madhubani in Bihar. The lively composition and the vibrant colours used to paint them are generally drawn from Indian mythology.

TEXTILES

The textiles of India demonstrate skilful weaving techniques, inimitable colour combinations and fascinating designs that make them a class apart in domestic and overseas markets.

BROCADE TEXTILES : Extreme softness, vivid colours and translucent texture characterises the silk weaving of India.

VARANASI : An important weaving centre is famous not only for its "BROCADE" or "KINKAB" (superb weaving in gold and silver), but also for the wide variety of techniques and styles. The brocades are distinguished by apt poetic names like "CHAND TARA" (Moon and stars), "DHUPCHHAON" (Sunshine and shade), "MAZCHAR" (ripples of silver), "MORGALA" (peacock's neck), "BULBUL CHASAM" (nightingale's eyes).

Varanasi is also famous for the "TANCHOI" Saree which resembles a fine miniature. Its origin can be traced to three Indian Parsi brothers by the name of CHOI. In Tanchoi sarees the designs are always floral with interspersing of birds.

MUBARAKPUR is one of the important silk weaving centres in the area.

"JAMDANI" or "FIGURED MUSLIN" traditionally woven in Dacca is now the speciality of TANDA in Faizabad. The cotton fabric is brocated with cotton and sometimes with Zari threads.

Each region has its typical technical silks and variations and the silk of Mysore, Kanchipuram, Murshidabad and Kashmir are as well known as the cotton sarees of Bengal or the cotton and silk Maheshwaris of Madhya Pradesh.

The famous IKAT technique is used in the PATOLAS of Gujrat and Orissa.

EMBROIDERY

In the field of ornamentation, embroidery alone can match jewellery in splendour. It is an expression of emotions, rendered with patient labour which induces grace and elegance into articles of everyday use.

Noor Jehan, wife of the Mughal Emperor is said to have introduced the art of CHICKEN to Uttar Pradesh.

The chicken work of Lucknow patterned on lace is delicate and subtle. The stitch by its sheer excellence provides ornamentation to the material. The charm lies in the minuteness of the floral motifs, stitches used are satin stitch, button hole stitch, dar stitch, knot stitch, netting and appliqué work which brings a charming shadowy effect on lace.

Embroidery done in metal wires by "KALLABUT" or "ZARI" as it is popularly called, is in a class by itself. The heavier and more elaborate work is called "ZARDOZI". The ground material used is heavy silk, velvet or satin. Salma sitara, badla, katoru, seed pearls are used for decoration. Kamdani, a lighter needle work done on lighter material, produces a lovely glittering effect, especially in designs known as HAZARA BOOTI, thousands dots, done with zari thread. Kamdani is used for weaving apparel such as scarves, veils, caps etc.

HAND BLOCK PRINTING

The fabric is further decorated by printing designs on it. Hand block printing in India was the chief occupation of the Chhipas—a community of printers. They used metal or wooden blocks to print designs on the fabric by hand. This technique is in vogue even today.

Besides Rajasthan, Uttar Pradesh is also a veritable treasure-house of traditional designs which range from the classical "BOOTIES", known as "DOTS OF KANAUJ" to the universal Mango, to the tree of life.

The great colour belt in India extends from the interior of Sind through the desert of Kutch, Kathiawar, Rajasthan and Gujarat. Rajasthan and Gujarat are particularly noted for its ABANDHANI design.

ETHNIC DRESSES : Smile, but do not laugh if you see a young French woman wearing a Kashmiri Shikara dress or Rajasthani Ghagra and Choli. India being a land of various communities, you can be sure of falling to temptations of buying at least half a dozen ethnic dresses from various parts of the country. These are freely available in respective local markets.

FURNITURE

CANE AND MOONJ: For those, who prefer ethnic with the raw look, India offers a superb selection of baskets made of MOONJ GRASS. These are available in attractive blends of traditional designs and modern functional utility.

Durable and decorative cane furniture and other articles made here are a major draw as items for export. World imports of basketwork and related products are quite substantial.

DECORATIVE WORK : Patra furniture is plated with white metal which is intricately carved and engraved. This exquisite metal work which once adorned the furniture in the palaces of royalties, is popular even today and is the pride of Rajasthan.

Lac furniture from Gujarat is exquisite in variety and embellished with workmanship called "SANKHEDA".

From Kashmir and many parts of Rajasthan, come exquisitely cavred furniture.

CARPETS

Pleasing to the eye and soothing to mind, the floor coverings of India are heart-winners.

The main centers are Bhadohi, Agra, Amritsar, Jaipur, Gwalior and Kashmir. Being mostly export oriented, the weavers can produce almost any design. However they have a few distinctive designs of their own like the Taj Mahal. The carpets are so exquisitely made that they are often used as wall hangings. Improvements in the techniques of washing, have given them a mere lustrous shine.

The Mughal emperor provided patronage to this art and raised it to lofty heights with Agra being one of the oldest carpet centres. Today, it is a compact industry and does both traditional as well as modern designs.

The "CALLING OUT" or "PHER BOLAN" system still prevails in Agra. The master weaver alone follows the design and keeps calling out to the weavers about colours to be used for each knot.

High quality carpets are produced mostly in three varieties— Persian(ispahan and Kashan), Turkoman and Aubusson (French).

Indo-Ispahan is done with the long leaf and flower and the Indo-Kashan with the small leaf and flower.

In the Indo-Turkoman the Mohra Bokhara is made with the typical octagonal patterns. An interesting point in its colouring is the use of the same colour in different shades.

The carpets of India are universally admired not only for their original patterns, fine wool and rich colours, but also for being produced in sizeable quantities of acceptable commercial quality.

The carpet industry in Shahjehanpur is barely a century old and here, both cotton and woollen carpets are made. The woollen ones being in three sizes, the ordinary with 16 knots, medium with 25 knots and the best with 36 knots. The designs are based on old Persian styles. In one of the more exciting ones, the overall ground colour is a clear soft scarlet and field covered with flattened irregularly lineated diamond shapes of warm golden yellow, apparently separated, yet imperceptibly linked.

DURRIES

The brilliantly coloured durries are also an expression of the imagination of the craftspersons of India. Exciting colours, forms. shapes and vibrant images characterise this delightful art form.

JUTE FLOOR COVERING and RUNNERS : Being an important centre of world's jute production, the craftsmen of West Bengal have made use of this product extensively in an exquisite manner to create several types of floor carving with several hues, sizes and designs, which represent Indian skill par excellence. Moreover, it is for certain, that it will not pinch your pocket.

The Department of Tourism plays an important role in keeping alive many festivals throughout the country. At each of these, shopping plays a key role.

INDIAN TEMPLES

Temple is a place of worship. Hindu temple was centre of all community life and towns grew up around temples. The great temples took many years to build and gave employment to thousands of skilled and unskilled workers. Hundreds of others were employed in the service of the deity and perform the daily rituals of the temple, which can be witnessed even today.

Originally the main plan of Hindu Temples (always facing east) was very simple there was just a small 'garbagriha' (sanctum sanctorum) housing the deity to whom the temple was dedicated above which rose the 'sikhara' (spine-like tapering tower), then a (antarala) vestibule, the worshippers standing in the open space in front of the shrines. Sometimes there was a small chamber behind the shrine. Gradually additions were made—a platform for worshippers which developed into a pillared hall (mandapa) to which in time a pillared porch (ardha-maddapa) was added as were other sections for various purposes connected with temple and its ceremonies.

The Silpasastras (ancient books on architecture) mention three styles of temples—the Nagara (of North India), the Dravida (of South India—the Dravida country) and the Vesara (Chalukyan or Karnataka) which combine the features of both styles and spread to all parts of the country even as far as Gujarat and Orissa.

One of the earliest existing temples is at Sanchi in Madhya Pradesh of the early Gupta period, almost Grecian in design, with a flat roof. Other temples of the same style can be seen in Deogarh stone temple and Bhitargaon brick temple dating back to 6th century AD.

The development of temple architecture in stone can best be seen in the early Chalukyan temples at Badami in Karnataka. At Badami are the temples of the earlier cave or rock-cut variety and at Pattadakal are the 7th century shrines both of the northern Nagara and the southern Dravidian style and Aihole is the cradle of 70 temples dating back to 7th century AD.

From 650 to 850 AD, the cut temples were created from the living rock temples at Ellora, the chief and most stupendous is Kailasa temple.

Under the Chandela rulers of Jajakabhuti, a number of Brahmanical and jain temples were built, mostly in the Nagara style at Khajuraho. The sculptures in the temple are elaborate and animated with their impressive forms and beautiful workmanship.

In the Hoysala or later Chalukyan period (1000 to 1300 AD), the Hoysala kings—who were great lovers and patrons of temple architecture and sculpture, commissioned star-shaped temples, the finest being the Chanakesvara at Belur (AD 1111) and the Hoysalesvara temple.

The great style of temple architecture in South India was the Dravidian style which flourished in Tamil Nadu and was indigenous and developed by five great dynasties of rulers:

1. The Pallavas (600 - 900 AD) started the great achievement in temple buildings. Temples built than can still be seen at Tiruchirapalli, Nellore, Guntur, Chengalpattu, Mamallapuram and Kancipuram groups (640 - 690 AD)

2. The Cholas (900 - 1150 AD) made magnificent Brigadheeswara temple at Thanjavur. Gangaikondacholapuram and Koran Gunta (930 - 940) at Srinvasanallur with their physical proportions and sense of dignity and power. The gopurams of some are splendid specimen of sculpture.

3. The Pandyas (1150 - 1350) Gopurams began to acquire special consideration during this period and set pattern for all later Dravidian gopurams. The outstanding examples are Jamuksvara —Chidambaram (eastern gateway 1300 AD) and the Kumbakonam (1350 AD) temples. They also introduced flower motifs in the capital pillar.

4. The Vijayanagar Kings (1336 - 50 AD) set up some of the beautiful temples at Hampi in Vijaynagar the capital city, the ruins of which lay scattered there today. They had the finest example of a temple in the great Vithala temple with its long courtyard, ornamental and musical pillars which when struck emit notes. Subsidiary buildings, the lovely ratha is carved out of a single monolith, the stone wheels of which once revolved the Kalamandapa and Hazare Rama (commenced 1513 AD). The other temples at Vellore, Kumbakonam, Srirangam, Kamedipuram and Verinjipuram and other two at Tadapatri, the chital Venkata Ramanaswami and the Ramaligesvara.

5. The Madurai (1600 - 1700 AD) under the Nayaka, made a great contribution to temple architecture. The main temple developed into subsidiary structures with colossal gopurams.

A large number of temples being were in this style. The most famous and typical are the Meenakshi Sundaresvarar temple at Madurai and the Ranganatha temple at Srirangam with its 1000 pillars. The architectural beauty of Ramesvaram temple with its 1200 meter long richly carved corridors and the Nataraja temple (17th century) at Chidambaram.

In Kerala, the temples have a unique style of sloping roof in the shape of contour. Some well-known temples are at Tirkothithanam, Brypur, Tirumandikkara and the modern temple at Maatancheri.

Towards the south of the State. Dravidian style temples exist at Vizhinjam, the Guhanthaswami temple (AD 1000) at Kanyakumari, the Suchindram with its beautiful stone mandapam in which the details of the conventional old wooden structures of Kerala are exquisitely translated into carvings on stone.

The other temples are Padmanabhaswami at Trivandrum (14th century). There is very little difference in the development of Hindu and Jain temples, the growth of the latter being parallel to each other's. The jain temple, in keeping with the need for privacy and seclusion during rituals, had enclosed rooms in place of the open pillared mandaps of the Hindu temple.

The Andhra kings were Buddhist and their two capitals Srikakulam and Amravati became centres of religious architecture. The Pallavas built one of the earliest free standing Buddhist temples in India, not later than the middle of the first century AD at Srikap (Now in Pakistan), the ruins of which are still to be seen there.

At Osian, amongst the ruins are several Jain temples, the one of Mahavira being a typical shrine of that period.

In the 10th century the Jain Ganga dynasty ruled in the Mysore region, and a group of temples were built by them at Sravanbelgola. The monolithic 17 m. tall statues of Gomateswara is outstanding and its massive size attracts attention form miles around.

In Mudbidri (near Mangalore) are Jain temples of the 12th century based on wooden architectural styles.

The Dilwara temples at Mount Abu of the 11th to 13th centuries have intricate lace-like carvings on pillars, arches and ceilings. The marble pendant hanging from the dome in the Tejpala temple is unique. Several Jain temples can be seen at Achalgarh and Kumbharia nearby.

One of the most impressive architectural achievements amongst Jain temples are the 15th century Ranakpur temples. The massive Chaumukh temple dedicated to Adinath has 29 halls and 1444 carved pillars, not two of which are alike.

Palitana, in Gujarat, with its 863 temples atop Shatrunjaya Hill was a great centre of Jain architecture going back to the 11th century but suffered wide-spread destruction during the Muslim invasions. Many of the temples seen today were rebuilt from the 16th century onwards.

The Chandranatha temple of the 15th century is of the Chalukyan style with gables roof similar to those of Kerala temples.

Strong patronage and observance of religion in the day-to-day life produced temples all over India even in the smallest towns and villages.

MUSEUMS AND ART GALLERIES

Museums and art galleries are the treasure houses of Indian cultural heritage and display collections of artefacts, scientifically classified transporting visitors on a quick fulfilling journey to ancient times of imperial dynasties to view for themselves the wonder that was India.

The British in the 19th century set up a number of institutions to explore and document the wealth of material available in the country. Among these were the Archaeological Survey of India and Geological Survey of India. Simultaneously, they began to view Indian art and culture as integral to the country's heritage and deemed it necessary to house collections in suitable institutions. Thus in 1875 the first museum, the Indian Museum was established in Calcutta.

Museums also serve as the important audio-visual means of education. The development of museums in all their ramifications is considered important as they promote national integration and international understanding.

Museums all over the country exhibit objects that range from finds at archaeological sites, miniature paintings, royal memorabilia to India's finest traditional crafts.

The NATIONAL MUSEUM in New Delhi exhibits a range from terracotta figure of the 5th and 6th century BC to exquisitely damascened i.e. ornamented swords of the Mughal period.

Also in New Delhi, the **CRAFTS MUSEUM** displays the folk art of India. Periodical exhibitions include textiles, wooden sculptures of coastal India and other thematic subjects.

JAIPUR'S CITY PALACE, itself an object of wonder, houses a collection of royal memorabilia, as do the museums in other parts of Rajasthan, Bikaner Jodhpur, Jaisalmer, Alwar and Bundi. Each of these princely States whose rulers were great patrons of art and miniature paintings in distinctive styles of their own forms the nucleus of many a museum's treasure.

In Gujarat, the city of Ahmedabad has a sprinkling of museums, all private caollections of an individual or a family. The SHEREYAS MUSEUM OF FOLK ART, The CALICO TEXTILE MUSEUM OF

TEXTILES, the KITE MUSEUM, each display another facet of the rich heritage of craft traditions of Gujarat. Vadodara's museum is housed in an old palace and includes extremely rare bronze figurines.

In the north, Jammu's two museums display a valuable collection of miniature paintings known as "PAHARI" or hill school. Srinagar's **S P S MUSEUM** is the only place in India where one can see stone sculptures of deities executed in the distinctive style that was a hallmark of Kashmir from 7th to 11th century AD.

BHOPAL'S MUSEUM revolves around the considerable tribal skill of Madhya pradesh, the focus of which is dhokra figures, made in the lost wax technique out of bell metal.

PUNE'S RAJA (DINKAR) KELKAR MUSEUM is the lifelong collection of one man whose theme was the celebration of everyday life in art. Inkpots, cooking vessels and betal nut crackers all display the wealth of everyday art.

Hyderabad's most famous is the **SALAR JUNG MUSEUM** again a personal collection which features priceless treasures as also whimsical objects.

Trivandrum has a museum whose building is probably the most photographed edifice in the city. Objects displayed inside are exquisitely carved bronze temple figures.

Cochin has a number of museums that were built by the Dutch as palaces and by local rulers. A small museum on the outskirts of the city is the **MUSEUM OF NATURAL HISTORY**. Sound and light show brings to life all the figures exhibited ranging from classical dancers to Portuguese traders.

Calcutta too has a museum that was the personal collection of one family at **MALLICK'S PALACE**. It is impossible to give a brief account of a subject that requires a full volume itself.

HOTELS IN INDIA

The hotel sector forms one of the most important segments of the tourism industry. To give impetus to this sector, the government provides tax benefits and other incentives. The industrial policy has now placed hotels and tourism related activities as a priority industry. Foreign investment and collaborations are now facilitated under the new economic policy. Up to 51% foreign equity is granted automatically. Non-resident Indians are allowed cent per cent investment.

The diversity of accommodation ranges from deluxe hotels comparable to the world's most luxurious, to budget hostelries affordable by the most modest tourists.

The State and Union Territories have set up Directorate of Tourism and many have set up Tourism Development Corporations also. They run medium and low-priced accommodation such as Tourist Bungalows, Tourist Motels, Tourist Homes, Tourist Reception Centres, Tourist Hotels and Youth Hostels in the State concerned.

FIVE STAR AND DELUXE HOTELS : Major metropolitan cities have a number of deluxe hotels, some of which are part of international chain. All important tourist destinations do have at least one deluxe hotel classified as five star deluxe where the facilities include central air-conditioning, sumptuous decor that usually takes as its theme local art traditions, health clubs and a choice of dining that includes Indian, continental and Chinese cuisine. Facilities for business traveller encompass secretarial service, telex, fax and mini conference rooms. Accommodation in all deluxe hotels can be booked internationally by telex or through a travel agent.

HERITAGE HOTELS : A new classification standard of heritage hotels has been introduced to cover functioning hotels in palaces, havelis, castles, forts and residences built prior to 1950. As the traditional structures reflect the ambience and lifestyles of the bygone era and are immensely popular with the tourists. The scheme aims at ensuring that such properties, landmarks of our heritage are not lost due to decay and non-use. The scheme aims at bringing such properties into the approved sector. Forty-six properties have been classified in the heritage hotel category providing a capacity of 1,292 rooms so far. Guidelines have also been formulated for the conversion of heritage properties into heritage hotels and their approval is at project planning stage.

BUDGET HOTELS : Each metropolitan city has wide range of budget hotels. Classified according to the facilities they offer, these hotels range from four star down to one star. An excellent choice in the budget range is the State government run hotels which normally are conveniently located and have uniform standards of comfort.

BEACH RESORT HOTELS : These span every taste and budget. Luxury hotels have prime location, the decor enhancing the natural setting, and cuisine based on local seafood specialities. Lower down the line, the simple beach hotels and cottages cater to the budget traveller.

HILL RESORTS : The keynote of hill resort hotels is cosy comfort. Pine panelled and centrally heated deluxe resorts are usually open throughout the year in contrast to budget hotels which are ideal for the summer. Many budget hotels in hill resorts cater to trekkers. At such places extensive arrangements can be made for treks, including the hiring of equipment. Resorts hotels are generally seasonal. Attractive off-season rates are often offered. This is coupled with quiet surroundings which provide excellent value for money.

Wildlife sanctuaries have yet another type of resort. Located close to if not actually within the game park, wildlife resorts cater specifically to wild life enthusiasts and offer kind of related service. It is here that forest rangers, guides and motor vehicles can be hired for wildlife viewing. Most resorts, whether luxury or the budget variety, have an ambience that highlights the surroundings.

TOURIST BUNGALOWS / TRAVELLER'S LODGES : They offer comfortable lodging and meals. The tourist often has a choice between a dormitory and a self sufficient room with attached bathroom. A restaurant or a dining hall, often with an attached bar is a possible feature.

REST HOUSES / DAK BUNGALOWS : Introduced in the days of the British Raj, they are primarily meant for government officials on tour, though tourists may also stay in them under certain conditions. They are generally near national highways and are convenient for tourists travelling by road.

RAILWAY RETIRING ROOMS : Because of their ideal location, these rooms are extremely convenient for tourists planning on early train departure. Possession of a railway ticket or an Indrail Pass is generally required to avail this facility.

HOUSEBOATS : These fully furnished and staffed floating houseboats are moored on the Srinagar's Dal and Nagin lakes and on the backwaters of the Kerala.

PAYING GUEST ACCOMMODATION : In order to augment the accommodation facilities at major tourist centres, paying guest accommodation scheme has been introduced. So far, 1,472 units have been registered. This scheme is open to house owners having letable rooms of requisite standard. Paying guest accommodation committees have been constituted in different regions. A directory of paying guest accommodation units has also been brought out by the department.

BUSINESS CONFERENCES AND CONVENTIONS

India as a business-cum-conference centre is rapidly gaining worldwide attention. The Indian economy is fast opening up to an era of liberalisation and provides numerous opportunities for foreign business to visit India.

Several towns and cities in India have excellent hotels offering state-of-the-art conference facilities. Major hotels have business centres which provide secretarial services, telex and telefax, translation / interpretation facilities and conference rooms. In Addition, specially designed floors of major hotels are reserved for business visitors. Parties or banquets can be specially catered for the busy business traveller. These can also be theme-based for memorable launch function.

SELECT CONFERENCE DESTINATIONS

VENUE	CAPACITY	VENUE	CAPACITY
DELHI		**MUMBAI**	
Ashok Hotel	2500	Centaur Juhu Beach	700
The Hillton	500	Hotel President	600
Le Meridien	550	The Leela Kempinski	250
Hyatt Regency	600	The Oberoi Towers	800
Radisson	400	The Taj Mahal	500
Samrat	200	Ramada	1000
Taj place Intercontinental	1400	Centaur Airport	380
The Oberoi	350	Holiday Inn	250

Taj Mahal	300	The Aguada Hermitage	30
Maurya Shereton	800	Majorda Beach Resort	630
Hotel Vasant Continental	300	Goa Renaissance Resort	600
Centaur	200	The Leela Beach	350
Claridges	350	The Sarovar Park Plaza	130
Hotel Imperial	550	The Taj Holiday Village	50
Hotel Kanishka	400	The Oberoi	175
Hotel Surya	650	Ramada Inn Palm Grove	290
Qutub Hotel	265	**CALCUTTA**	
BANGALORE		Taj Bengal	300
Hotel Ashok	550	The Oberoi Grand	800
Taj Residency	650	The Airport Ashok	330
Windsor Manor Shereton	375	**VARANASI**	
West End Hotel	650	Clarks	70
Gateway Hotel on	300	Hotel Raj Ganes	90
Residency Rd.		Varansi Ashok	250
Guestline Hotels		**BHUBANESHWAR**	
and Resorts	200	Hotel Kalinga Ashok	225
Taj West End	600	The Oberoi	210
CHENNAI		**KHAJURAHO**	
Connemara Hotel	400	Hotel Chandela	180
Taj Coromondal	450	**HYDERABAD**	
Chola Shereton	450	Taj Residency on	
Park Shereton	400	Banjara Hill	275
Fisherman's Cove	135	The Krishna Oberoi	700
The Trident	585	Hotel Bhaskar palace	700
Holiday Inn Crown Plaza	1500	Grand Kakatiya Hotel	
AGRA		and Towers	600
Mughal Shereton	170	**JAIPUR**	
Hotel Agra Ashok	200	Hotel Clarks Amer	300
Hotel Clarks Shriaz	860	Hotel Jaipur Ashok	90
GOA		Hotel Jai Mahal Palace	425
Cidade-de-Goa	160	The Rambagh Palace	440
Fort Aguada Beach Resort	175		

CUISINES AND DINING CHOICES

For Indians food is a gift of gods and is treated with respect. Based on pragmatic medical precepts evolved over centuries of experimentation and observation, Indian food is aimed at nourishing the body and is pleasing to the mind and eyes. Ingredients of each meals are based on six rasas or flavours—sweet, salty, bitter, astringent, sour and pungent— each ingredient believed to have particular physical benefit on application of the right proportionate use.

Indian Cuisine is considered to be one of the three great distinctive cuisine's of the world, the other two being the Chinese and the French.

Indian cuisine aims to satisfy needs of the tongue and body, from sweet to sour bitter or hot, from heating to cooling foods, from food for the body to food for the brain. Within these parameters, each region has nurtured its own culinary tastes using different combination of spices. No country in the world has developed such elaborate and tasty range of vegetarian cuisine as India.

Characteristic of all Indian cooking is the inspired use of spices. Immense care is taken to ensure that spices enhance rather than dominate the basic flavour and they do not diminish nutritive value.

Indian curry contains pieces of mutton, chicken or fish in a sauce based on the famous onions, tomatoes, yogurt or coconut milk enriched by three or 12 condiments. Some of the more celebrated culinary traditions of India originated in the royal courts of the Mughals, in Oudh and Hyderabad. All the three cuisines can be sampled at speciality restaurants as well as regional food festivals that deluxe hotels hold periodically.

While mutton, chicken and fish are served throughout the country, the frequency with which they make their appearances differs. In Kashmir, mutton is the chief attraction in the 24-course banquet, WAZWAN, each dish being cooked in a different way seperate from the other. Of all coastal States in the country Goa, Kerala and Bengal have culinary traditions with a preponderance of fish with Goa and Kerala making profuse use of coconuts. Goan seafood delights include Crab, lobsters, tiger prawns and shellfish, all accompanied by rice and washed down with excellent wine and wermouth of local manufacture. Kerala, as all other southern States, is noted for its variety of crisp

PANCAKES — DOSA and STAEMED RICE CAKES — IDLI made from pounded rice.

DAHI (CURD) is part of almost every Indian menu. Served to mitigate the chilly "hotness" of some dishes, it is often mixed with vegetable or fruit and is lightly spiced to create the **'RAITAS'** of the north and the **'PACHADIS'** of the south.

In many parts of the country, **THALI** meals are the norm. These largest platters contain up to a dozen dishes in individual servings, consisting of meat chicken, vegetables — with gravy or dry, pulses and accompaniments and widely served.

Some of India's best, ovened culinary traditions are the **TANDOORI** cooking best known and loved. TANDOOR is the Indian oven, a homely clay lined cylinder filled with sizzling coals. Restaurants that serve Tandoori food often have a section where cooking is done by the simple expedient of wielding a metal stick. As the heat of the oven reaches 600^0 c. cooking time is counted in minutes and seconds. Tandoori meats use no oil and are normally accompanied by yougart dips.

Some of India's best loved dishes are favourite of every family as for **SARSON KA SAAG,** prepared from green mustard leaves simmered all night long on a coal fire. It is available only in the winter.

There are also the interesting dishes of the Parsis. **'DHANSAK'**, meat cooked with five different dals and an unusual blend of spices and **'PATRANI MACHI'** lightly spiced fish steamed in banana leaves, are just two examples.

Chutneys and pickles—sweet, sour or hot, or all three, whip the appetite and add relish to a meal. Every conceivable ingredient can be used: mint, coriander, mango, ginger and lime.

'PAPADS', roasted or fried savory crisps, are also popular meal adjuncts. Made of previously rolled and dried lentil or rice dough they provide the crunchiness considered essential to repast.

PAU BHAJI is a passion in Mumbai where roadside stalls have a cauldron of simmering vegetables which are served with a bun. **BHELPURI** in Mumbai and **CHAAT** in Delhi are roadside snacks of crunchy morsels tempered with piquant seasonings.

To describe **INDIAN SWEETS** as merely being made of milk, reduced milk or cottage cheese and sugar syrup is an oversimplification of a highly specialised branch of cooking. Sweet traditions in Bengal, Bikaner and Delhi are famed throughout the country.

Finally, there is the satisfying ritual of the after-meal PAN (BETEL), a must for any true connoisseur of Indian food. Lauded for its digestive and medicinal properties, it is a fragrant combination of betal leaf, aerca nut, catechu, cardamom, clove and a choice of a whole host of other exotic ingredients of varying flavours, effects and strengths.

Non-alcoholic beverages include the countrywide favourite in **NIMBU PANI** a squeeze lime over sugar or salt served in water or soda. Yougart and water are vigorously churned to make **BUTTER MILK**, a delicious accompaniment to Indian meals. Bottled fizzy drinks include various brands of indigenous lime, orange and cola.

Other **FRUIT-BASED DRINKS**—apple, guava, mango, tomato— are available in tetrapack and tins.

SODA and **MINERAL WATER** are also widely available.

India's alcoholic beverages include gin and rum which are comparable to the finest internationally as well as whisky. India's dozens of brands of BEER encompass very good pilsners and largers available in bottles. Liquor is available at most restaurants especially those in hotels. It is either imported or made in India.

In addition there are local variations like ASHA and KASTOORI, the saffron liquor of Rajasthan and FENI, the strong brew of Goa usually available in the concerned States.

Although the local food of the region is available at many restaurants, the cuisine of Punjab has become standard Indian fare in most of the middle and high priced restaurants throughout the country. Similarly Udipi restaurants serve vegetarian South Indian cuisine all over India at low prices.

Every major hotel offers, a choice between **INDIAN, CONTI-NENTAL, CHIENESE, ITALAIN** and **FRENCH** delights in the speciality restaurants.

Western style confectionery—chocolates, cakes, cookies and marzipan are available in the pastry shop confectioneries in all metro cities.

TEA : The cup that cheers is a must for millions all over the world every morning and Assam is a leader in production of tea.

Indian Tea! Flavour of Darjeeling and Assam tea has reached across oceans in all continentals. A cup of tea that cheers and cares. Tea is an ideal beverage that files into the healthy way of life—tempers the spirits, calms the mind, prevents drowsing, enlightens and refreshes the body and clears perceptive faculties. Tea is taken in various forms as a health giving drink with and without milk and sugar.

Easily available everywhere in India—on footpaths, from small restaurants to restaurants in five star hotels, bus depots, at taxi stands, railway stations, airports and at the place you name it.

ANY TIME IS TEA TIME IN INDIA.

INDIAN WILDLIFE

Indian tradition perhaps the most ancient in the history of man, dating back to the Vedic age and documented as early as 3rd century BC in the edicts of Emperor Ashoka, have stressed importance for all forms of life.

India, a unique subcontinent has vast variations in geography, climate and vegetation. As a consequence there is exciting diversity in habitat and wildlife. The mighty Himalayas, the highest mountains in the world, offer a wide spectrum of landscapes and wildlife. Tropical forest in its eastern extremity contrasts with the pine and coniferous wooden of the western Himalayas. Natural cover varies with altitudes and these evergreen forests are bounded with high alpine meadows nearer the snowline and temperate forests of short trees in the lower elevations. In the foothills are deciduous trees, with shrubs, bamboos, fern and grass.

The northern plains, the course of the holy rivers Ganga and Yamuna: the great Thar desert in the west; the Sunderbans; the marshy swamplands in the delta of the Ganga and Brahmputra in the east; the ancient volcanic rock of the Deccan plateau lying in the rain shadows of the hills and the western Ghats with their dense, luxuriant forests—all provide fascinating variations in habititats. These sustain over 350 species of mammals, 2,100 kings of birds - local and migratory, nearly 350 species of reptile and countless insects.

The need for conservation of the environment and the forests has excercised the minds of Indian rulers from the earlier times. In the 3rd century BC, the Emperor Ashoka issued edicts to protect forests and natural wealth.

Later during the reign of Emperor Chandragupta Maurya 'forests free from fear'—were identified and protected. In more recent times, it was the administrators and princely rulers who demarcated and reserved forests as private preserves. Today many of these form the nucleus of India's wildlife sanctuaries and parks.

106

The demands of a rapidly increasing population continue to put pressure on surviving forests in India. Vast herds of black buck, that roamed the northern and western plains 50 years ago, are now found only in sanctuaries and around the villages of the Bishnoi tribe, who protect them.

The Project Tiger initiated in 1973, is today a massive attempt at the conservation of the tiger and its total environment. It covers 23 National parks and sanctuaries and its success in India has gone up significantly since it was launched.

India, currently has around 80 national parks and 441 sanctuaries dotted around the country. While some are inaccessible many have excellent facilities for visitors. Depending on the area and terrain, wildlife watching provides its own excitement. It may be done from elephant back, from watch towers or even a boat - and the thrill of spotting herds of wild elephant, deer, a rihno or even a tiger, in its natural environment, is very difficult to match.

Sl. No.	Name of National Park/ Sanctuary, State and Dist.	Area and best time for visiting the Reserve	Nearest Airport (A) and Railway Station (R) and their distances from the reserve	Species Found
1.	Dachigam National Park J&K Srinagar	141 Sq. km. April-Nov.	(A) Srinagar 22 km (R) Jammu 200 km.	Leopard, Black bear, brown bear, serow, musk, deer, hangul.
2.	Corbett National Park Uttar Pradesh Nainital/ Garhwal	520.82 Sq. km. November to May	Pantnagar (R) Ramnagar (Nainital) 51 km.	Elephant, tiger, panther, sloth bear, nilgai, sambar, chital, wild boar, porcupine, pea-fowl, red jungle folw, partridge, crocodiles, goral and chousingha.

Sl. No.	Name of National Park/ Sanctuary, State and Dist.	Area and best time for visiting the Reserve	Nearest Airport (A) and Railway Station (R) and their distances from the reserve	Species Found
3.	Dudhwa National Park Uttar Pradesh Lakhimpur Kheri	498.29 Sq. km. November to May	(R) Lucknow to Dudhwa 4 km.	Tiger, Panther, sloth bear, sambar, swamp deer, chital, hog deer, barking deer, nilgai, peafowl, jungle-fowl, partridge, etc.
4.	Desert Sanctuary Rajasthan, Jaisalmer, Barmer.	3162 Sq. km. All the year.	(R) Jodhpur Jaisalmer 32 km.	Great Indian Bustard, black-buck, chinkara.
5.	Sariska National Park Rajasthan-Alwar	765.80 km. All the year. except July, August, Sept.	(R) Jaipur 108 km Alwar 21 km.	Tiger, panther, hyena, jungle cat civet, sambar, nilgai, chowsingha, partridge, green pigeon, red spurfowl.
6.	Keoladeo Ghana National Park Rajasthan-Bharatpur	28.73 sq. km. 1 October to end of February.	(R) Agra 50 Bharatpur 2 km. 176 km. from Delhi, 176 km from Jaipur, 52 km from Agra, 35 km from Mathura.	Siberian Crane, comorant, stork, spoon bill, quail coot, heron, teal, tern, sambar, chital, blackbuck, wild boar, civet etc.

Sl. No.	Name of National Park/ Sanctuary, State and Dist.	Area and best time for visiting the Reserve	Nearest Airport (A) and Railway Station (R) and their distances from the reserve	Species Found
7.	Ranthambore National Park Rajasthan, Sawai Madhopur	392 Sq. km. All the year except July, August and Sept.	(A) Jaipur 145 km (R) (Sawai) Madhopur 11 km.	Tiger, Panther, hyena, jungle cat civet, sambar, chital, nilgai, bear, wild boar, partridge, green pigeon, red spurfowl etc.
8.	Manas Tiger-Reserve Assam Barpeta	2840 Sq. km. November to April	(R) Guwahat Barpeta 40 km.	Elephant, tiger, panther, gaur, wild buffalo, rhino, golden langur, civet, cat otter, swamp deer, hog deer, sambar, pigmy hog, wild boar, great pied horn-bill, florican.
9.	Kaziranga National Park Assam-Jorhat	430 Sq. km. Nov. to April.	(A) Guwahati 217 km (R) Jorhat	Great Indian one-honed, rhino, wild buffalo, elephant, aur, leopard cat, wild boar, civet, otter, swamp deer, sambar, tiger, python, pelican, part-ridge, florican.

Sl. No.	Name of National Park/ Sanctuary, State and Dist.	Area and best time for visiting the Reserve	Nearest Airport (A) and Railway Station (R) and their distances from the reserve	Species Found
10.	Namdapha National Park Margherita, Arunachal Pradesh.	180.7 Sq. km. October to March.	(A) Dibrugarh 163 km (R) Ledo 56 km.	Tiger, Leopard, clouded leopard, snow leopard, Gaur, goral, takin, hoolock gibbon, slow loris, musk deer, binturong, red panda, Assamese macaque, horn bill, jungle fowl, pheasants.
11.	Keibul Lam Jao National Park, Manipur Central	40 Sq. km. December to May	(A) Imphal 32 km (R) Dimapur 229 km.	Brow-antiered deer, wild boar and water birds.
12.	Wild ass sanctuary in and around the little Rann of Kutch Gujarat Surendranagar	4841 Sq. km. January to mid-June	(A) Ahmedabad 156 km. (R) Dhrangadhra 25 km. Bajana 10 km	Wild ass, nilgai, wolf, chinkara.
13.	Bandhavgarh National Park Madhya Pradesh Shahdol	105.40 Sq. km. November to June.	(A) Jabalpur 170 km (A) Khajuraho 210 km. (R) Umaria 30 km.	Tiger, panther, gaur, chital, sambar, nilgai, chinkara, bar-king deer, bear, wild boar, and a variety of upland birds.

Sl. No.	Name of National Park/ Sanctuary, State and Dist.	Area and best time for visiting the Reserve	Nearest Airport (A) and Railway Station (R) and their distances from the reserve	Species Found
14.	Palamau Tiger reserve Bihar Daltonganj	1026 Sq. km. All the year.	(A) Ranchi 180 km. (R) Chipadohar 80 km.	Elephant, panther, wild boar, barking deer, gaur, chital sambar, peafowl, etc.
15.	Kanha National Park Madhya Pradesh Mandla and Balaghat.	1945 Sq. km. March to June.	(A) Nagpur 270 km. (R) Jabalpur 170 km, Nagpur 260 km, Chiri-dongri 110 km.	Tiger, Panther, gaur, barasingha chital, Sambar, blackbuck, chousingha, barking deer, mouse deer, nilgai, wild dog, boar.
16.	Gir National Park and Sanctuary Gujarat, Junagadh	1412.13 Sq. km. December to mid-June.	(A) Keshod 86 km. (A) Rajkot 186 km. Sasan Gir (W. Rly) Village is near the rail-way station.	Asiatic lion, panther, striped hyena, sambar, nilgai, chital, chousingha, chinkara, wild boar, crocodile.
17.	Simlipal National Park Orissa Mayurbhanj	2200 Sq. km. Winter	(A) Bhubaneswar 350 km (R) Baripada 50 km.	Tiger, elephant, gaur, chital, leo-pard, mouse deer, flying squirrel and muggar.

Sl. No.	Name of National Park/ Sanctuary, State and Dist.	Area and best time for visiting the Reserve	Nearest Airport (A) and Railway Station (R) and their distances from the reserve	Species Found
18.	Bhitrarknkika Wildlife Sanctuary Orissa Baleshwar	170 Sq. km. mid-October to mid-April.	(A) Bhubaneswar 190 km. (R) Bhadrak 77 km.	Salt water crocodile, monitor lizards, snakes, leopard, fishing cat, hyena, wild pig, water birds, ridley sea turtle.
19.	Chilika Sanctuary Orissa-Puri	400 Sq. km. December to February.	(A) Bhubaneswar 100 km. (R) Balgaon right on the banks of Chilika.	Flamingo, duck, bar-headed sandpiper, plover, ruddy shelduck, gull, tern, white-bellied sea eagle, dolphins, fishing cat, black buck, chital.
20.	Sunderbans National Park West Bengal, 24-Parganas.	1330.10 Sq. km. September to May.	(A) Dum-Dum 112 km. (R) Port Canning 48 km.	Tiger, different species of deer, wild boar, estuarine, crocodile, gangetic dolphin.
21.	Jaldapara Wildlife Sanctuary West Bengal-Jalpaiguri	100 Sq. km. October to May.	(A) Bagdogra 13 km from Siligury (R) Hashimara 20 km Birpara 20 km.	One horned rhino, tigers, wild elephants, deer, swamp deer, hog deer, wild pig, wild pig, birds, peafowl, etc.

Sl. No.	Name of National Park/ Sanctuary, State and Dist.	Area and best time for visiting the Reserve	Nearest Airport (A) and Railway Station (R) and their distances from the reserve	Species Found
22.	Nagarjunasagar Srisailam Sanctuary Andhra Pradesh Guntur, Prakasam, Kurnool, Mahbubnagar and Nalgonda.	3568 Sq. km. October to June.	(A) Hyderabad (R) Hyderabad 100 km.	Tiger, Panther, sloth bear, wild boar, chital, sambar, nilgai, blackbuck, jackal, fox, wolf and mugger crocodile.
23.	Ranganthitoo Bird Sanctuary Karnataka, Mysore.	27 Sq. km. July to August.	(A) Bangalore 110 km. Srirangapatnam (R) 10 km	Open billed stork, white ibis, little egret, cattle egret, darter, coromorant, pond heron, river tern, spoon bill, crocodile etc.
24.	Vedanthangal Water Birds Sanctuary Tamil Nadu.	0.3 Sq. km. November to February.	Meenambakkam (A) 70 km. (R) Chingleput 28 km.	Different water birds
25.	Nagarhole National Park, Karnataka, Coorg.	643.39 Sq. km. October to March.	(A) Bangalore 220 km. (R) Mysore 90 km.	Elephant, tiger, panther, chital, Sambar, sloth bear, jungle fowl, partridge etc.

Sl. No.	Name of National Park/ Sanctuary, State and Dist.	Area and best time for visiting the Reserve	Nearest Airport (A) and Railway Station (R) and their distances from the reserve	Species Found
26.	Banipur National Park Karnataka, Mysore.	874.20 Sq. km. March to August	(A) Bangalore 190 km (R) Mysore 65 km.	Elephant, tiger, gaur, sambar, chital, barking deer, wild dog, wild boar, jackal sloth bear, panther, chousingha, Malabar squirrel.
27.	Mudumalai Sanctuary Tamil Nadu, the Nilgiris	321 Sq. km. February to June.	(A) Coimbatore 160 km. (R) Ooty 64 km.	Elephant, gaur chital, sambar, tiger, panther, sloth bear, wild dog etc.
28.	Annamalai Wildlife Sanctuary Tamil Nadu, Coimbatore.	958.6 Sq. km. February to June.	(A) Coimbatore 80 km. (R) Pollachi 35 km.	Elephant, gaur, chital, sambar, tiger, panther, sloth bear, wild dog, etc.
29.	Periyar National Park Kerala, Idukki.	777 Sq. km. October to April.	(A) Cochin 200 km, (R) Madurai 140 km.	Elephant, tiger panther, sloth bear, wild dog, gaur, nilgai, wild boar, sambar and barking deer.

TOURISM VARIETIES IN INDIA

WHITE RIVER RAFTING

Himalayan ranges, stretches 2,700 km in an unbroken range along the Indian sub-continent's northern frontier. The snowfed mountain rivers trace their origin in the Himalayas, descend from their icy high cliffs fed by innumerable streams they race along torturous, boulder — strewn beds cutting deep gorges, and breaking into silvery white rapids, twisting and turning, makes India a paradise country for cater sportsmen.

From Ladakh in the north to Sikkim in the east, these river waters are synonymous with adventure and are finest white rafting of the world.

The holy Ganga and Yamuna rivers, the Indus and its tributaries —the Chenab, Beas and Satluj, the Zanskar, the Sharada and the Teesta —all provide exciting sites for river rafting and running.

The Government of India tourist offices, IRRA (Indian River Runners Association) and IAPRO (Indian Association of Professional Rafting Outfitters) are three bodies, which oversee the white rafting operations in India. All rafting expeditions, are in concurrence with the safety standards, rescue procedures and general river and camps ethics as per international standards.

The provisions for white river rafting in India are comparable with the standards of safety followed internationally. Equipment provided is of highest standards — helmets, lifejackets/rafts with buoyancy equivalent to US/ Canadian lifeguard standards. Also carried are first aid kits, pumps and repair kits. In case of accidents, medical backup supporting teams are ready to assist. Children below 14 years of age are normally not allowed to take part in the sport. Non-swimmers are restricted in certain sections of the river.

RIVER RAFTING ROUTES

RIVER	GRADE	BASE CAMP	NEAREST AIRPORT	MAJOR ROAD JUNCTION	BEST SEASON
Ganga	III—IV	Beasi/Shiv puri	Dehradun 111 km	Rishikesh 70 km	Oct -April
Indus	II — IV	Karu	Leh 30 km	Leh 30 km	July- Sept
Zanskar	IV	Padam	Srinagar-Leh	kargil 165 km	Aug-Sept
Chenab	IV — V	Kishtwar	Jammu 229 km	Kishtwar	Nov-March
Satluj	IV — V	Rampur Bushair	Shimla 132 km	Rampur Bushair	Oct -April
Beas	III — V	Kullu	Bhuntar 10 km	Kullu	April-June
Yamuna	II — V	Kalsi	Dehradun 50 km	Dehradun	Oct -May
Sharda	II — V	Tanakpur	Pantnagar 156 km	Tanakpur	Oct -April
Teesta	IV	Dikchu	Bagdodra 160 km	Gangtok 35 km	Oct -April

TREKKING IN THE HIMALAYAS

The foothills of the Himalayas offers spectacular opportunities for trekkers.

Himalayan flora is unique. It encompasses forests of all types — tropical swampy forests, decidious forests, coniferous forests, rhododendron forests, alpine meadows and even hot and cold deserts.

HANDY HINTS

ACCESSIBILITY : The foothills of the northern Himalayas, from Delhi are not more than five to six hours by road or by rail. From Delhi one can reach Rishikesh, Jammu, Pathankot, Chandigarh and Kalka which are roadheads to Garhwal hills, Kashmir valley, Kishtwar, Ladakh, Chamba and Manali. Shimla is the stepping stone for Kinnur Sipti, Nahan and Renuka. For trekking routes in the Garhwal region Dehradun and Rishikesh are the ideal gateways. Leh is the starting point for treks in Ladakh. Guwahati is gateway to Arunachal Pradesh.

BEST SEASON : For north-east regions—late September to April/ May; Garhwal, Kumaon and Himachal Pradesh—all year around.

TREKKING EQUIPMENT : Necessary help is available at Indian Association of Tour Operators, 404 Padma Tower II, 22 Rajendra Place, New Delhi 110008. PH 5750034, 5716562 or Indian Mountaineering Foundation, Benito Juarez Road, New Delhi 110021. PH 461211, FAX 6883412.

ACCOMMODATION : In the absence of fixed accommodation, a bed can be availed on the spot depending upon the place where the trekkers want to camp.

CARE FOR ECOLOGY : The care is to be taken to preserve the fragile ecological balance. Carry waste disposal bags to prevent littering and use liquified petroleum gas or kerosene or local wood for cooking purposes. Respect for local customs and traditions along the route is essential.

ESSENTIAL NEEDS : Basic personal items to be carried include a waterproof rucksack, sleeping bag, foamed mattress, walking boots, rain proof jacket, torch, spare batteries, waterflask, matchbox, and medicines. For higher altitudes the additional requirements are tents, feather jacket, heavy woollens, kitchen equipment and tined foodstuff, on well-frequented trek routes at lower heights food and bottled mineral water is generally available.

PRE-TREK PRECAUTIONS : Most important, get a map, compass and information from someone who has done the route. Pre-trek arrangements, in case of treks to remote areas, should include insurance, rescue and evacuation measures, apart from informing the local authorities of planned route.

PHYSICAL FITNESS : Select a route depending on fitness level and time available. Health should be of reasonable level. Trekking routes are graded according to anticipated level of exertion and degree of difficulty. These factors determine the choice of itinerary and requirement of special equipment and trained personnel.

TREKKING OPTIONS AT A GLANCE

TREKKING AREA	ENTRY POINT	TREK ITINERARY
Ladakh Zanskar via Lahaul	This region can be approached through Manali, Rohtang Pass, Leh and Upshi, also from kargil	To Leh (11,00 ft.) via Padam (3,505 m) or the Chacharla in Zanskar, also from Umasila in Kishtwar, Udaipur in

TREKKING AREA	ENTRY POINT	TREK ITINERARY
	which is on the Srinagar Zojila, Kargil Leh highway	Lahaul over Sersank and Poat la and from Lahaul to Zanskar over Shingola Pass. The Kashmir valley also has very scenic routes. Days option 3 — 6 weeks.
Himachal Manikaran to Sipti	By road from Manali/ Kullu onwards to the road-head at the Manikaran hot springs	From Manikaran to Pulga rest house along Parvati river. Continue via Khiranga and Mantalai glacier to reach Pin Parvati Pass (5320 m) on Kullu Sipti divide. Descend to roadhead at Dhankar in Sipti. Days Option — 10/11 days.
Garhwal Uttarkashi	This region can be reached by road from Dehradun, Chamba, Tehri and then onward to Uttarkashi to reach the road head at Kalyani trout hetachery.	From Kalyani to Agora and Dodi Tal. Next day cross Darwa Top (4115 m) and descend to Hanuman Chatti, two days to reach Yamunotri and Saptrishi Kund. Return via Barkot and Mussoorie. Days Option — 9/10 days.
North-East Himalayan view	Sikkim and Darjeeling can be reached by air upto bagdodra and onwards by rail to Darjeeling. Arunachal can be reached by air upto Tezpur and then onwards by road.	A 26 km drive from Darjeeling (2134 m) to Maneshanganj. Moderate trek to Batasi, Tonglu, Sandkphu (3636 m) and return route famous for view of Kanchenchanga, Everest and rhododendrons.

MOUNTAINEERING IN THE HIMALAYAS

Himalayas, stretching across the northern borders of India, from west to east with its hundreds of peaks offers unlimited opportunities for mountaineering in the Himalayas.

Mountaineering as a sport is said to have begun in the Himalayas in 1883 when W.W. Graham, an European came to Himalayas for the purpose of climbing.

The Indian Mountaineering Foundation was born in 1957 as a non-profit organisation, to organise support and provide a base for mountaineering expeditions like skiing, rock climbing, trekking at high altitude and to promote, encourage, support and execute schemes of all kinds of adventure.

Today, as many as 100 mountaineering expeditions venture into the Himalayas every year. Improved road communications, reliable weather forecasting and well-organised search and research facilities make Himalayas most challenging as well as among the safest mountains in the world.

WINTER SPORTS

Himalayas provide fertile ground for winter sports. Joshimath, traditionally a pilgrim centre, is now being developed as a skiing resort for Garhhwal.

A ropeway is underconstruction to take vision from the town at 6,000 ft. to the slopes at Auli and Gorsain near Kuari Pass at 12,000 ft. The panorama of Himalayan snow peaks from Kuari is perhaps the most splendid in the world.

Gulmarg in Kashmir is India's most popular and best developed skiing resort with the most modern equipment. Ice skating is also available at Gulmarg.

Narkhanda near Shimla provides skiing slopes from January to April.

Kurfi and slopes of Rohtang Pass are also sites for skiing.

Shimla offers facilities for ice-skating, ice-hockey, fissure skating and speed skating.

HELI SKIING

India is the first Asian country to offer Heli Skiing facilities.

Heli skiers are dropped at the top of a mountain or ridge by a helicopter saving them the arduous task of climbing up. It requires experience and careful prior study of physical features, cornices, crecasses, wind direction and potential avalanche hazard areas.

The beautiful Himalayan ranges of Kashmir is a good place for Heli Skiing.

HANG GLIDING

Hang Gliding has recently been introduced in India. It is adventure sport propelled by wings of aluminium canvassed colourful nylon, Hang-gliders, suspended from their precarious position on the undercarriage of the glider, begin their journey, executing exquisite swooping movements with skill of those born to fly.

Centres earmarked for hang gliding are :
● Srinagar valley in Jammu & Kashmir
● Billing, Kangra, Dharamshala, Shimla and Kausali in Himachal Pradesh
● Pune, Kamshet on Mumbai — Pune highway
● Talegaon, Satar, Singarh, Murud, Jangira in Maharashtra
● The Nilgiri hills in Tamil Nadu
● Mhow, Indore in Madhya Pradesh
● Chamundi hills and areas around Bangalore
● Mysore in Kanataka
● Shillong in Meghalaya

Hang gliding clubs in India are centred at Pune, New Delhi, Mumbai, Chandigarh, Shimla, Deolai, Bangalore and Kalahati. Most of the clubs have their own hang-gliders which are indigenously manufactured by Raj Hans Aero sports Ltd. at Mysore.

ROCK CLIMBING

Plenty of rocks and hills, stiff climbs and sheer mountain sides which are spread over Indian sub-continent offers limitless opportunities for rock-climbing all year around.

Major centres for rock-climbing are :
● Foothills of Himalayas in Kashmir and Himachal Pradesh
● Foothills in the Garhwal Himalayas
● Foothills in the Aravellis near Delhi
● Western ghats around Pune
● Chamundi hills and rock formation along the Bangalore - Mysore highway
● Mount Abu and Sariska in Rajasthan

Rock climbing is becoming popular as adventure sport in India. It is necessary to have a professional climber if the terrain is unfamiliar or climber is a beginner.

MOTOR RALLIES

From hilly and mountainous terrain to beaches, deserts and forest treks, India offers an exciting terrain for running motor rallies. Motor rallies are held all over India annually whose dates can be obtained from the nearest Automobile Association of India.

Important Car Rallies are :

● Himalayan Car Rally, sponsored by the Himalayan Rally Association — Mumbai.

● Karnataka 1000 Rally, organised by Karnataka Motor Sport Club

● The Rally D'Endurance, organised by Indian Automative Sports Club

BALLOONING

Ballooning is considered as a most fancy sport in India.

A balloon is 1,000 sq. yards of ripstop nylon, an average Balloon is 50 feet wide 70 feet high and 57,000 cubic feet in volume, large versions are also available. The Balloon is attached to the basket by steel ropes, the basket itself is made of resilient wicker and strengthened by a crossweave of metal ropes. Cylinders of propane or butane fire burns located at the mouth of the Balloon. When cold air is blown into its mouth by a fan and the burners lit, a jet flame furnish the hot air that gets the balloon airborne. By regulating hot and cold air, the pilot can steer the balloon along any chartered course. Commercial balloon rides are yet to be made available in India. Balloonists require permission from the Balloon Club of India before floating out.

The Balloon Club of India at Delhi's Safdarjung Airport is the tail off point and headquarters for this aero-sport.

The Indian International Balloon festival is held every November and attracts participants from all over the world.

CAMEL SAFARIES

Camel Safaries trace their origin to the age of overland trade between India and China when caravans would journey along the established trade routes laden with the herbs and jewels. The latest activity in the Thar desert is the camel safari. Route navigation in the desert is an acquired art and the caravans are required to be trained in riding of camels, reading of the stars and the shifting of the sands of the terrain.

The best safaris are held in the heart of the Thar, around Jodhpur, Jaisalmer and Bikaner, Besides desert heartland, other options for the Camel safari is the Shekawati region visiting towns like Ramgarh, Nawalgarh, Dundlod, Mandawa and Churu.

Safari organisers attempt to recreate the atmosphere of old caravan's journeys. Musicians accompany the caravan and halts are called outside some village where local people are invited to enjoy campfire hospitality.

YOGA — THE WAY TO JOY, HAPPINESS AND BLISS

The Sanskrit word yoga literally means 'to add' or 'union'. So Yoga is the vehicle through which the Yogi (one who practices Yoga) is united with the divine spiritual dimension.

If mankind is to save itself from its own aggressive tendencies, the path open is through the science of Yoga. Bodily exercises (asanas) breath control (pranayam) and mind control (dhyana) are all helpful to conquer physical and mental ills. The role of the mind in the creation of health and ill-health has been well emphasised by Ayurveda physicians.

Yoga is believed to be of pre-Aryan origin. There are even archaeological evidences to show that Yogic disciplines flourished around the Indus Valley Civilisation which existed some 5000 years ago. One of the six systems of orthodox Indian philosophy said to have been founded by rishi Yajnavalka, later systemised by Patanjali in his Yogasutra. It stored to teach disciplined meditation, certain rules of bodily and mental self discipline by which the soul (Jivatman) could attain supereme knowledge for mystic union with God (Paramatman).

Its chief forms are :

Hatha Yoga — is through subjugation of body and channelizing the flow of energy (Prana) in the right direction towards self-knowledge.

Raja Yoga — is the restraint of fluctuations in the consciousness (chitta)

Karma Yoga — is bringing salvation through work

Bhakti Yoga — through faith and devotion

Gayana Yoga — through knowledge

Mantra Yoga — through the use of mantras

The Laya Yoga — salvation through soundless sound by activizing the Spiritual centres (Chakras) in the body.

Yoga removes physical and mental tensions as these tensions are result of difference and dualities. The purpose of yoga is to enable us to rise above all senses of duality in whatever field we are.

International Yoga week is celebrated at Rishikesh every year. Contact the government of India tourist office for details.

GOLF

India was the first country outside Great Britain to take up the game of golf. The Royal Calcutta Golf Club, established in 1829, is the oldest golf club in India.

In India you can play golf almost anywhere. This outdoor sport is widely played by a cross-section of people and courses are often set against dramatic backgrounds, in the hills, in the high Himalayas, in metropolitan cities and in small towns, by the sides of lakes and forests or surrounded by tea estates, out in the desert and in old British cantonments.

A LIST OF MAJOR GOLF COURSES

PLACE	STATE	NO. OF HOLES
Bangalore Golf Club	Karnataka	18
Ootacamund Gymkhana Club	Tamil Nadu	18
Kodaikalan Golf Club	Tamil Nadu	18
Madras Gymkhana Club	Tamil Nadu	18
Hyderabad Golf Club	Andhra Pradesh	18
Bombay Presidency Golf Club	Maharashtra	18
Poona Golf Club	Maharashtra	18
Delhi Golf Club	Delhi	18
Chandigrh Gold Club	Chandigarh	18
Royal Calcutta Golf Club	West Bengal	18
Shillong Golf Club	Meghalaya	18
Srinagar Golf Club	Srinagar	18
Gulmarg Golf Club	Gulmarg	18
Naldhera Golf Club	Naldhera	9
Cosmopolitan Club	Chennai	18

Golfing in India has come a long way and a large number of Indian players now compete on the International circuit.

INDIAN ROADWAYS

There were highways, trade routes and ancillary roads in India from the earliest times; an ancient caravan route linked prehistoric settlements here and there along the north-west to Baluchistan and on route via Iran to Mesopotamia, a flourishing trade being carried on among the regions it touched. When exiled, Lord Rama incarnation of God and Prince of Ayodhya, took the known route to the Narmada (via Chiturkut—now Chitrakoot) and across the Chhatisgarh district and then Godavari to South India to Sri Lanka. Buddhist texts mention trunk and other roads in the period 700-185 BC—one main route going from Savatthi (Srivasti) to Patitthana (Paithan) with 6 halting places at important towns: another also from Savatthi went to Rajagraha (now Rajgir) and other branched off from it, one going to Bharakaccha (now Bharuch) on the western sea shore. A route that ran south-east-west went from Patliputra (now Patna) to the mouth of Sindhu and on to Iran.

In Ashoka's time roads led to all Buddhist sites and missionaries were sent as far as Kashmir and the deep south. The Qutb Shahi rulers of Golconda (1494-1687) built roads and bridges and provided halting places and caravan sarais for travellers. Sher Shah Suri (1537 - 45) repaired the Mauryan rajapatha and built 1,700 sarais along it. Many roads under the Mughals were good and well maintained. Under the British only trunk routes and major roads in cities and towns were kept in good repair, new roads being made for military, political and administrative reasons.

CURRENT ROAD STRUCTURE IN INDIA

Despite the enormity of the country, travel by road is a common choice and also the only way of communication.

All major cities of India are linked by National Highways from Kashmir to Kanyakumari and from Gujarat to Assam. National highways are connected by sub-routes from all the cities and towns.

They connect major ports, foreign highways, capitals of States and major towns including highways, required for strategic movement for the defence of India.

The National Highway Authority constituted on 15 June 1989 is responsible for the construction and maintenance of the National highways. Country has 56 important national highways with total length of 34, 000 km and longest national highway is NH -7 (2369 km)

The State roadways corporations run regular bus services as well as tourist buses and deluxe coaches. Private transport operators play important role in the transport system in India by providing all available types of vehicles varying from regular to luxury cars / coaches of International standard, even imported vechiles on hire. Taxis and small auto rikshasws are easily available in all metropolitan cities and all over India. Now, Hire-and Drive, Rent-a-car services have also been made possible in major cities.

Approximate roads network length	:	720, 37 km.
Highest road in India	:	Khardungla (leh - Manali)
Longest road in India	:	Grand Trunk Road - runs from Calcutta to Amritsar, passing through Varanasi, Allahabad, Kanpur, Agra, Delhi, Ambala. Originally this road connected Lahore and Calcutta .

ROAD LENGTH IN INDIA AS ON 13 MARCH 1995

	Surfaced	Unsurfaced	Total
Andhra Pradesh	98,348	9,83,894	1,71,785
Arunachal Pradesh	5,598	6,262	11,860
Assam	11,444	56,646	68,090
Bihar	33,811	54,043	87,854
Goa	4,691	2,612	7,303
Gujarat	95,356	13,155	10,811
Haryana	25,048	2,112	27,160
Himachal Pradesh	13,727	16,199	29,926
Jammu & Kashmir	7,760	4,830	12,590
Karnataka	94,539	45,229	1,39,768
Kerala	40,752	98,568	1,39,320
Madhya Pradesh	1,27,308	83,717	2,11,025
Maharashtra	1,64,324	60,649	2,24,973
Manipur	3,274	7,256	10,530
Meghalaya	3,500	4,221	7,721
Mizoram	2,875	3,702	6,577
Nagaland	3,882	8,998	12,880
Orissa	41,633	1,68,255	2,09,888

	Surfaced	Unsurfaced	Total
Punjab	45,118	11,921	57,039
Rajasthan	69,576	60,509	1,30,085
Sikkim	1,522	302	1,824
Tamil Nadu	1,38,472	66,003	2,04,475
Tripura	4,537	10,169	14,706
Uttar Pradesh	1,17,570	96,576	2,14,146
West Bengal	36,457	25,203	61,660
UNION TERRITORIES			
Andman & Nicobar Islands	841	30	871
Chandigarh	1,632	—	1,632
Dadra & Nagar Haveli	411	98	509
Delhi	20,409	2,356	22,765
Pondicherry	1,854	836	2,690

NATIONAL HIGHWAYS

N.H.numbers, passing route and total length in km (Sub-routes not included)

1 : Delhi-Ambala-Jalandhar-Amritsar-Indo Pak border (456 km).
2 : Delhi-Mathura-Agra-Kanpur-Allahabad-Varanasi-Mohania-Barhi-Palsit-Baidyabati-Bara-Calcutta (1,490 km).
3 : Agra-Gwalior-Shivpuri-Indore-Dhule-Nasik-Thane-Mumbai (1,161 km).
4 : Junction with N.H. 3 near Thane-Pune –Belgaum-Hubli-Bangalore-Ranipet-Chennai (1,235 km).
5 : Junction with N.H. 6 near Baharagora-Cuttak-Bhubanesh-war-Vishakhapatnam-Vijayawada-Chennai (1,533 km).
6 : Surat-Dhule-Nagpur-Raipur-Sambalpur-Baharagora-Calcutta (1,932 km).
7 : Varanasi-Mangawan-Rewa-Jabalpur-Lukhana-Don-Nagpur-Hyderabad-Kurnool-Bangalore-Krishangiri-Salem-Dindigul-Madurai-Kanyakumari (2,369 km).
8 : Delhi-Jaipur-Ajmer-Ahmedabad-Vadodara-Mumbai (1,428 km).
9 : Pune-Sholapur-Hyderabad-Vijaywada (791 km).
10 : Delhi-Fazilka-Indo-Pak border (403 km).
11 : Agra-Jaipur-Bikaner (582 km).
12 : Jabalpur-Bhopal-Khilchipur-Aklera-Jhalwar-Kota-Bundi-Devil-Tonk-Jaipur (890 km).

13 : Sholapur-Chatradurga (491 km).

14 : Bewar-Sirohi-Radhanpur (450 km).

15 : Pathankot-Amritsar-Bhatinda-Ganganagar-Bikaner-Jaisalmer-Barmar-Samakhiali (near Kandla) (1,526 km).

16 : Nizamabad-Mancherei-Jagadalpur (460 km).

17 : Panvel-Mahad-Panji-Karwar-Mangalore-Cannanore-Calicut-Ferokh-Kuttipuram-Pudu Ponnani-Chowghat-Cranganur junction with N.H. 47 near Edapally (1,269 km).

18 : Junction with N.H. 7 near Kurnool-Nandyal-Cuddapah-junction with N.H. 4 near Chittoor (369 km).

19 : Ghazipur-Balia-Patna (240 km).

20 : Pathankot-Mandi (220 km).

21 : Junction withN.H.22 near Chandigarh-Ropar-Bilaspur-Mandi-Kullu-Manali (323 km).

22 : Ambala-Kalka-Shimla-Narkanda-Rampur-Chini-Indo-Tibet border near Shipki La (459 km).

23 : Chas-Ranchi-Rourkela-Talcher junction with N.H. 42 (459 km).

24 : Delhi-Bareilly-Lucknow (418 km).

25 : Lucknow-Kanpur-Jhansi-Shivpuri (319 km).

26 : Jhansi-Lakhandon (396 km).

27 : Allahabad-Mangawan (93 km).

28 : Junction with N.H. 31 near Barauni-Mazaffarpur-Pipra-Gorakhpur-Lucknow (570 km).

29 : Gorakhpur-Ghazipur-Varanasi (730 km).

30 : Junction with N.H. 2 near Mohania-Patna-Bachtivarpur (230 km).

31 : Junction with N.H. 2 near Bahri-Bakhtiarpur-Mokameh-Purnea-Dalkota-Siliguri-Sivok-Cooch Beahr-North Salmara-Nalbari-Charali Amingaon junction with N.H.37 (1,125 km)

32 : Junction with N.H.no 2 near Gobindpur-Dhanbad-Jamshedpur (179 km).

33 : Junction with N.H. 2 near Barhi-Ranchi junction with N.H. 6 near Baharagora (352 km).

34 : Junction with N.H. 31 near Dalkoa-Berhampur-Barast-Calcutta (443 km).

35 : Barasat-Bangaon-Indo Bangladesh border (61 km).

36 : Nowgong-Dabaka-Dimapur (Manipur Road) (170 km).

37 : Junction with N.H. 31 B near Golapara-Guwahati-Jorhat-Kamargaon-Makum-Saikhoaghat (680 km).

38 : Makum-Ledo-Lekhapani (54 km).

39 : Numaligarh-Imphal-Palei-Indo Burma border (436 km).
40 : Jorahat-Shillong-Indo Bangladesh border near Dawki (161 km).
41 : Junction with N.H. 6 near Kolaghat-Haldia Port (511 km).
42 : Junction with N.H. 6 near Sambalpur-Angul junction with N.H. 5 near Cuttak (261 km).
43 : Raipur-Vizianagaram junction with N.H. 5 (551 km).
44 : Shillong-Passi Badarpur-Agartala-Sabroom (630 km).
45 : Chennai-Tirichirapalli-Dindigul (387 km).
46 : Krishnagiri-Ranipet (132 km).
47 : Salem-Coimbatore-Trichur-Ernakulam-Trivandrum-Kanyakumari (640 km).
48 : Bangalore-Hassan-Mangalore (328 km).
49 : Cochin-Madurai-Dhanushkodi (440 km).
50 : Nasik junction with N.H. 4 near Pune (9192 km).
51 : Paikan-Tura-Dalu (149 km).
52 : Baihata-Charali-Tezpur-Bander-Dewa-North Lakhimpur-Pasighat-Tezu-Sitapani junction with N.H.37 near Saikhoaghat (850 km).
53 : Junction with N.H. 44 near Badarpur-Jirighat-Imphal-Silchar (320 km).
54 : Silchar-Aizawal-Tuipang (560 km).
55 : Siliguri-Darjeeling (77 km).
56 : Lucknow-Varanasi (285 km).

ROAD DISTANCES
(in Kilometres)

EASY RECKONER: Conversion of Kilometres to Miles and Miles to Kilometres (for approximate calculations)

Kilometres	5	10	20	30	40	50	80	100
Miles	3	6	12.5	19	25	31	50	62.5
Miles	5	10	20	30	40	60	80	100
Kilometres	8	16	32	48	64	96	128	160

Distance matrix (km). For each city row the values are distances to the preceding cities in list order: Agra, Ahmedabad, Amritsar, Bangalore, Bhopal, Bhubaneswar, Bombay, Calcutta, Cochin, Darjeeling, Delhi, Gangtok, Guwahati, Hyderabad, Indore, Jaipur, Lucknow, Madras, Madurai, Mysore, Panaji, Patna, Pondicherry, Shillong, Shimla, Srinagar, Trichy, Trivandrum, Udaipur, Varanasi, Visakhapatnam. The final value (0) marks the diagonal.

City	Distances (km)
Ahmedabad	855, 0
Amritsar	646, 1332, 0
Bangalore	1819, 1514, 2465, 0
Bhopal	541, 571, 1187, 1379, 0
Bhubaneswar	1556, 1829, 2202, 1430, 789, 1175, 0
Bombay	1208, 551, 1854, 1033, 789, 1691, 0
Calcutta	1242, 2006, 1888, 1883, 1456, 480, 2081, 0
Cochin	2365, 1832, 3011, 546, 1925, 1894, 1351, 2347, 0
Darjeeling	1371, 2135, 2017, 2557, 1585, 1168, 2384, 688, 3103, 0
Delhi	200, 886, 446, 2019, 741, 1745, 1408, 1442, 2562, 1571, 0
Gangtok	1407, 2171, 2053, 2593, 1621, 1204, 2420, 724, 3139, 93, 1607, 0
Guwahati	1834, 2998, 2480, 3020, 2048, 1631, 2847, 1151, 3566, 627, 2034, 625, 0
Hyderabad	1253, 1220, 1899, 566, 813, 1063, 739, 1516, 1792, 1991, 1453, 2027, 2454, 0
Indore	606, 384, 1252, 1369, 187, 1275, 602, 1643, 1772, 2257, 806, 2293, 1808, 803, 0
Jaipur	230, 625, 702, 2049, 735, 1775, 1176, 1472, 2457, 261, 1601, 1637, 2064, 1483, 800, 0
Lucknow	369, 1133, 945, 1900, 703, 1266, 1370, 963, 2446, 669, 569, 1047, 1510, 1334, 768, 599, 0
Madras	1957, 1848, 2603, 334, 1517, 1225, 1367, 1678, 669, 2366, 2157, 2402, 2829, 704, 1617, 1911, 2187, 2038, 0
Madurai	2251, 1946, 2897, 432, 1811, 1686, 1469, 2139, 363, 769, 2457, 2728, 3296, 998, 1911, 2481, 2332, 461, 0
Mysore	1954, 1649, 2600, 135, 1514, 1694, 1168, 2147, 588, 2692, 2154, 2728, 3155, 707, 2035, 2184, 469, 403, 0
Panaji	1704, 1063, 2350, 570, 1285, 582, 2114, 769, 2703, 1904, 2739, 3166, 712, 1098, 1688, 1866, 904, 984, 645, 0
Patna	811, 1575, 1457, 1997, 1025, 560, 1824, 598, 2543, 363, 1011, 560, 1023, 1432, 1212, 1041, 523, 2429, 2132, 2143, 0
Pondicherry	2219, 1817, 2765, 303, 1679, 1387, 1336, 1840, 2528, 2319, 2564, 2991, 866, 1779, 2349, 2200, 162, 340, 438, 873, 2272, 0
Shillong	1934, 2698, 2580, 3120, 2148, 1731, 2947, 1251, 3666, 727, 2134, 100, 2554, 2235, 2929, 3390, 3255, 3266, 3091, 0
Shimla	568, 1254, 342, 2387, 1109, 2113, 1776, 1610, 2933, 1939, 368, 1975, 2402, 1821, 1174, 867, 2525, 2819, 2522, 2279, 2687, 2502, 0
Srinagar	1091, 1777, 519, 2916, 1632, 2636, 2299, 2133, 3456, 2462, 891, 2498, 2925, 2344, 1697, 1390, 3048, 3342, 3045, 2795, 1902, 3210, 3025, 787, 0
Trichy	2188, 1883, 2834, 369, 1748, 1544, 1402, 1997, 379, 2685, 2388, 3014, 935, 1848, 2418, 2269, 319, 340, 939, 198, 3248, 3279, 0
Trivandrum	2580, 2049, 3226, 761, 2140, 2015, 1568, 2468, 217, 3156, 2780, 3192, 3619, 1327, 2084, 2674, 2418, 2661, 1390, 340, 986, 2758, 669, 3719, 471, 0
Udaipur	604, 251, 1081, 1765, 765, 1940, 802, 1755, 2083, 1884, 635, 1920, 2347, 1471, 635, 374, 882, 2099, 1900, 1314, 366, 2068, 2247, 1003, 3148, 3671, 2134, 2300, 0
Varanasi	565, 1329, 1211, 1763, 791, 980, 1590, 677, 2309, 806, 765, 842, 1269, 1197, 978, 795, 286, 1901, 2195, 2197, 1898, 246, 1324, 2366, 1133, 1656, 2524, 2134, 1078, 0
Visakhapatnam	1661, 1857, 2307, 1004, 1221, 426, 879, 1468, 1567, 1861, 1603, 2030, 637, 1321, 1891, 1742, 799, 1139, 1235, 1311, 961, 2063, 1369, 2130, 2229, 2742, 1118, 1589, 2108, 1379, 0

INDIAN AIRWAYS

The Mahabharata and the Ramayana speak a number of times about some sort of an aircraft (Vimana). The Asvins had their sky-strips (antariksha). The Maruts (sons of Vyu, the wind god) are credited with having flying horses. It may be considered a fantasy, but travelling in air finds place in almost all Hindu epics.

The first service carrying mail from London was operated by Puss Moth and flown from Karachi to Bombay. The inaugural commercial air service between Britain and India was flown by De Havill in 66 Hercules, specially designed for Imperial Airways Overseas services. This special flight was operated by Imperial Airways on 30th December 1929 from London to Delhi. Passengers included Sir Samuel Hoare - later Lord Templewood—the then Secretary of State for Air, and Lady Templewood. After arrival, the aircraft was named City of Delhi by Lady Irwin, wife of the Viceroy. Altogether this flight made 29 stops during 12 days it took between London and Delhi.

No revenue passengers were carried on the first few flights after the inauguration of air link between India and Britain due to flying time of 56 hours and 40 minutes. The air service came to close on 29th December 1931. In 1932, came the major breakthrough in the strengthening of air link between U.K. and India with the Tata Sons Ltd. launching a Karachi-Ahmedabad-Mumbai-Madras mail service to extend the Imperial Airways of London to Karachi services. An Indian Trans Continental Airways was then founded to operate the trans India route in association with Imperial Airways.

Thereafter the Delhi Flying Club ceased operating the Karachi-Delhi mail services. The Indian Trans Continental Airways and Imperial Airways began the Karachi-Calcutta service in 1933. In September the eastern terminal became Rangoon and in November Singapore. In 1934 and 1935 another major breakthrough was affected when the once a week frequency was gradually raised to twice-a-week. By 1938 the U.K. to Karachi flying time was reduced just to two and a half days as compared to seven days earlier.

CURRENT AIRLINE STRUCTURE OF INDIA

The civil aviation sector has three main functional divisions-regulatory, infrastructural and operational. On the operational side, Indian Airlines, Alliance Air (Subsidiary of Indian Airlines), private scheduled airlines and air taxis provide domestic air services and Air India provides international air services. Pawan Hans Helicopters Limited provides helicopter services to ONGC in its shore operations and to inaccessible areas and difficult terrains. Indian Airlines operations also extend to the neighbouring countries, South-East Asia and West Asia. Vayudoot Limited was merged with Indian Airlines. India has been a member of International Civil Aviation Organisation and is also on the Council of ICAO since its inception.

The Government has ended the monopoly of the Indian Airlines and Air India on the scheduled operations by repealing the Air Corporation Act 1953. A new policy on domestic air transport service was approved in April 1997 according to which barriers to entry and exit from this sector have been removed; choice of aircraft type and size has been left to the operator; entry of serious entrepreneurs only has been ensured; and equity from foreign airlines, directly or indirectly, in this sector has been prohibited.

The existing policy on air taxi services providing for a route dispersal plan to ensure operation of a minimum number of services in the north-eastern region Andman and Nicobar Islands, Laskhadweep and Jammu & Kashmir has been retained.

TOURIST CHARTER FLIGHTS

The charter flights bringing foreign tourists to the country are now allowed to operate to Goa, Agra, Varanasi, Jaipur and Bangalore in addition to the international airports. The minimum payment to the Indian tour operator by the foreign charter operators is US$ 400 per

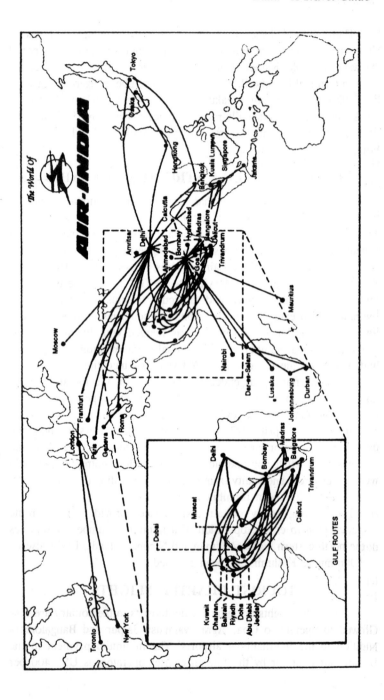

person, effective from 1ˢᵗ April 1998. However for tourists from SAARC countries and Mynamar, the amount to be paid is 50% of the aforesaid amount.

AIR INDIA : In July 1946 Tata Airlines were converted into a public limited company under the name Air India. In 1953 under the Air Corporation Act, it was declared as India's International Airline. India has bilateral air services with 90 countries as on 1 January 1998. It operates services to USA.,Europe, the Russian Confederation, the Gulf, West Asia, East Asia, Far East and Africa. Air India owes a fleet of 26 aircrafts. It also has joint-venture services with three foreign carriers and 'Block space' and 'Code Share Arrangements' with other foreign airlines to enable it to enhance its network with its limited aircraft fleet. During 1997-98 Air India carried 2.93 million passengers as against 2.91 million in 1996-97.

INDIAN AIRLINES : Is the major domestic air carrier of the country. It also provides services to 14 neighbouring countries, viz.,Pakistan, Maldives, Bangladesh, Nepal, Kuwait, Thailand, Sri Lanka, Malaysia,Mynamar Singapore, U.A.E., Oman, Qatar and Baharain. Its operations cover 72 destinations including 16 abroad.

To serve the nation, public interest and for promotion of tourism it offers concessional fares as follows :

Armed Forces : 50% discount on basic fare on all domestic sector.

Senior Citizens : (65 years) 50% discount on basic fare on all domestic sectors.

Student Domestic : 50% discount on basic fare is permitted to travel on any of the domestic sectors.

Student International : 25% discount on all international fares as well as connecting domestic flights.

Blind Persons : 50% discount on fare including fuel s/c on domestic services.

Cancer Patients : 50% discount on fare including fuel s/c on domestic and Indo-Nepal sectors.

Port Blair : A discount of Rs.50/- on the one way fare, when at least 2 members of a family travel together from Madras/Calcutta to Port Blair and Calcutta/Carnicobar or vice versa.

Gorkha Personnel of Indian Defence Forces : 40% discount to Gorkha Personnel in the active service of Indian Defence forces on Indo/Nepal sector.

Common Interest Groups : 10% discount is offered to groups of 10 or more adults travelling together on international sectors as well as connecting domestic services.

Employees of Govt.of India Foreign Missions : 40% discount on round fare on international sectors.

Ships Crew : 25% discount is available on all sectors against US$ fare. In case of group travel - minimum 20 passengers, 44 to 45% discount available.

Airline / IATA Employee : 50% discount on the normal US$ fare.

Youth : 25% discount on US$ tariff on domestic an: Indo Nepal sectors.

Tour Conductors : A tour conductor accompanying at least a group of 10 tourists is permitted at half the normal fare and for 15 or more tourists is allowed to travel free.

Discover India Fare : US% 500 for 15 days; US% 750 for 21 days. Allows unlimited travel with certain routing restrictions on domestic sectors of Indian Airlines.

India Wonderfare : US$ 300, travel for a week within a week, Port Blair not included.

Indian Airlines Approved Agents : Concessional passages to recognised agents

Invalid passengers / Stretcher Case : On all journeys on Indian Airlines domestic as well as international sectors in economy class, the normal adult fare corresponding to the actual number of seats removed to accommodate the stretcher

War Disabled Persons : 50% concession on domestic fare including fuel surcharge.

War Widows : 50% concession on air fares as applicable to Armed Forces personnel.

Promotional Fares SAARC : 20% for individual passengers and 30% for group travel within SAARC countries when three countries are included in the itinerary

Personnel of GREF : 50% concession in air fares to personnel of General Reserve Engineering Force, on the same terms as applicable to Armed forces.

Bravery Award Winners : A concession of 50% is extended to ex-Armed Forces personnel who are recipients of highest bravery awards of level I and II.

Disabled Persons : Suffering from Locomotor disability 50% discount on domestic sectors.

PAWAN HANS HELICOPTERS LIMITED : This is a government-owned helicopter company. It has been providing helicopter support services to the petroleum sector including ONGC, Oil India Limited and Hardy Exploration at Chennai. Apart from this, it also provides services to certain State governments and public sector undertakings and in the north-eastern States i.e., Arunachal Pradesh.

DISTANCES FROM THE AIRPORT TO THE CITY

Agra 7 km; Ahemdabad 10 km; Amritsar 11 km; Aurangabad 10 km; Bagdogza 14 km; Bangalore 13 km; Belgaum 14 km; Bhavnagar 5 km; Bhopal 11 km; Bhubaneshwar 4 km; Mumbai 26 km; Calcutta 16 km; Chandigarh 11 km; Jaipur 15 km; Jodhpur 5 km; Jorhat 6 km; Keshod 3 km; Khujaroho 5 km; Leh 8 km; Lucknow 15 km; Madurai 12 km; Chennai 16 km; Nagpur 10 km; Patna 7 km; Porbandar 4 km; Port Blair 4 km; Cochin 6 km; Coimbatore 23 km; Dabolin (Goo) 30 km; Delhi 13 km; Gorakhpur 7 km; Guwahati 22 km; Gwalior 12 km; Indore 9 km; Jabalpur 15 km; Pune 8 km; Srinagar 14 km; Trichy 8 km; Thiruvananthapuram 7 km; Udaipur 24 km; Varanasi 22 km; Visakhapatnam 14 km.

THE INDIAN RAILWAYS

East India company can be considered to be pioneer of the Indian Railways and Lord Dalhausi for laying the foundation of rail transport in India. In 1853 the Great Indian Peninsula Co. built the first line of 33.6 km from Mumbai to Thana. New lines were opened thereafter and by 1900 the permanent way covered 3396,031 km. In 1947 when India became independent, the length covered was 543,760 km.

Currently the Indian Railway is the second largest railway system in the world under the single management and also the biggest employer in the world. The railway in India provides the principal mode of transportation for freight and passenger. It brings together people from the farthest corners of the country and makes possible the conduct of business, sightseeing, pilgrimage and education. It has played a vital role in the economic, industrial and social development of the country.

Indian railway has 62,545 kilometers of tracks laid between 6,984 stations and over 11,000 locomotives. It is also second biggest electrified railway system in the world after Russsia; 29% of total track kilometre is electrified.

There are three systems operating in the country, they are Broad Guage (1,676 mm) 41,791 km; Meter Guage (1,000 mm) 17, 044 km. Narrow Guage (762 mm and 610 mm) 3,710 km.

TOURIST
RAIL ROUTES

TRACTION

Steam locomotives run on coal. Steam locomotives are not in operation as the entire system is envisaged to be dieselised or electrified.
Diesel locomotives run on diesel and were introduced in 1957.
Electric locomotives were introduced in 1929
Indian Railway has nine administrative zones :

ZONE	HEAD QUARTERS	DATE CREATED	LENGTH IN KM	STATES PASSING THROUGH
Central Railway	Chattrapati Shivaji Terminus	5-11- 51	7076	Maharashtra, Karnataka, Haryana, U.P., Rajasthan, M.P
Eastern Railway	Calcutta	1-8-55	4303	Bihar, M.P., U.P., West Bengal
Northern Railway	New Delhi	14-4-52	11,023	Gujarat, Haryana, Punjab, Rajasthan, H.P., J&K., U.P., Delhi, Chandigarh
North-Eastern Railway	Gorakhpur	14-4-52	5165	Bihar, U.P., Assam
North-East Frontier	Maligaon - Gauwahati	15-1-58	3858	Nagaland, Tripura, West Bengal
Southern Railway	Chennai	14-4-51	7009	Kerala, A.P., T.N., Karnataka
South-Central Railway	Secunderabad	2-10-66	7218	A.P., M.P., Goa, Karnataka, T.N., Maharashtra
South-Eastern Railway	Calcutta	1-8-55	7161	A.P., M.P., W.B., Bihar, Orissa
Western Railway	Churchgate	5-11-51	9845	Maharashtra, Rajasthan, Gujarat, Haryana, M.P, UP

Indian railway provides variety of choices and incentives to promote tourism.

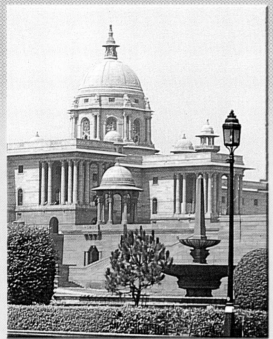

The British laid the foundations of India's new imperial capital, New Delhi, with Edward Lutyens designing its majestic Indo-Saracenic architecture - a city of gardens, pools and impressive buildings.

Safdarjung's Tomb is a monument that is typical of the memorials built to rulers and important noblemen.

Top left: Mahatma Gandhi's riverside memorial, Raj Ghat is a simple samadhi to one of the great leaders of the 20th century.

The Jama Masjid, in close proximity of the Red Fort, is one of the world's largest mosques, and is built in the classic tradition with domes and minarets and a huge courtyard.

Bottom: Gurudwara Bangla Sahib is one of the most important shrines of worship for the capital's Sikh community.

▲   *India Gate.*

◀   *The Quwwat-ul-Islam (might of Islam) mosque in the Qutab complex was made using the columns and blocks of an earlier Hindu temple.*

▼ *Red Fort built by the Mughals.*

Amber overlooks the waters of Maotha lake that offered it its water supply as well as a protective barrier.

Bottom left picture: The ornate entrances to different apartments are decorated with paintings, and have doors in relief.

The palace in Jaipur formed the centre of the city that was built by Sawai Jai Singh II when he decided to shift his capital here from Amber, and all its trappings were truly royal.

Many corridors and balconies that formed the inner part of Hawa Mahal.

A panoramic view of Maotha lake from the ramparts of Amber Fort.

The fascinating Albert Hall Central Museum in the Ram Niwas Public Gardens has been designed by Sir Swinton Jacob in the Indo-Saracenic style.

A home exquisitely carved with the mason's chisel, an art that is still practiced in centres such as Barmer (above).

A martial race, the men of Rajasthan nurture their moustaches - sometimes to excess.

Women bathe in the holy tank of Pushkar in a ritual that is centuries old and then offer their prayers at the Brahma temple, one of several hundred that line its banks.

The typical
architecture
of the
Rajput kingdoms
included influences
that were Mughal,
and later British.
Top to bottom:
Apartments
within
the fortifications
of the
fort in Nagaur,
a cenotaph
to honour
the memory
of past heroes;
a pleasure resort
of the maharanas
of Udaipur.

Rajasthan abounds in
wildlife sanctuaries, preserves
that were once used for
hunting, and are now parks
where from the tiger to deer,
painted strokes and other
avian species can be spotted.

*Though
the memorial was
built by
an emperor,
the Taj Mahal
touches the heart
of every person
who
comes close to it,
a reminder that
love is
immortal
and everlasting.*

The architecture of
the Taj Mahal
may have been
supervised by
Shah Jahan,
but some of the
keenest minds and
sharpest intellects
from around
the world participated
in its
final making.

*The Taj Mahal can be glimpsed
from Agra Fort; it was probably
from here that its builder
had his last
view from his apartment where
he was imprisoned by his son.*

*From these apartments,
Mumtaz Mahal must
have gazed across
the banks of the Yamuna,
little realising that
her tomb would be built
on the same spot.*

*Built along
the banks of the
Yamuna,
the Taj Mahal
is surrounded by
gardens, reminiscent
of the tradition
of paradise
in Tartar folklore.*

Women in their typical Kullu caps, Himachal Pradesh.

Bottom:
Meadows ideal for trekkers, Himachl Pradesh.

Exquisite craftsmanship, Khajuraho.

The magnificent Indian tiger.

Swaying palms at Kovalam beach, Kovalam.

Sea and sand, Lakshadweep.

Golden Temple, Amritsar.

Stately spires of Konark Temple, Orissa.

In the footsteps of the Buddha, Sarnath.

The famous Meenakshi Temple, Madurai.

HIGH SPEED TRAINS

RAJDHANI EXPRESS : Rajdhani Express trains were introduced in 1969 and they operate at the speed of 130 km per hour.

Rajdhani Express runs from Delhi to Howrah, Mumbai, Bangalore Bhubaneshwar, Thiruvananthapuram, Guwahati, Patna, Chennai, Secunderabad, Jammu Tavi, Ahmedabad and back to Delhi.

SHATABDI EXPRESS : Shatabdi Express trains were introduced in 1988 and they operate at the speed of 140 km per hour.

Shatabdi Express runs from Delhi to Bhopal, Lucknow, Kalka, Chandigarh,Dehradun, Amritsar, Ajmer and back to Delhi. Other routes on which Shatabdi Express operates are Chennai to Mysore and back; Chennai to Tirupati and back; Mumbai to Ahmedabad and back; Mumbai to Pune and back. Howrah to Bokaro city and back; Howrah to Rourkela and back; Chennai to Coimbatore and back; Rajahmundry to Secunderabad and back.

A ROYAL TREAT
THE PALACE - ON - WHEELS

Refer Rajasthan chapter for detailed information.

THE ROYAL ORIENT

Refer Gujarat chapter for detailed information.

SHIVALIK DELUXE

This train has only one stop—Barog between Delhi and Shimla, the journey time is 4 hours and 45 minutes. The amenity fittings match the modern times. Wall to wall carpet, wide glass windows, reversible cushioned chairs, improved toilet facilities, cabin for couple, table for meal, tube lights, music system, micro phones for communication with the guard to name just a few. With a sitting capacity of 120 it connects the Howrah-Kalka Mail. Breakfast between Delhi-Shimla and dinner between Simla-Delhi is served on the train.

SHIVALIK PALACE (TOURIST COACH)

For an exciting and charming journey for the elite class tourists between Kalka and Shimla, the Shivalik Palace has on board catering with an exclusive range of kitchen ware. Special features include— decorative lights, musical cordless bell music system, variety of indoor games, magazines and books, most ultra-modern fittings in bathroom, artificial decorative plant, dinning table with beautiful cushioned chair, folding beds etc. Train is meant normally for a party of six persons. Meals are provided on board as well as two retiring rooms at Shimla for one day.

FAIRY QUEEN

Fairy Queen comes out of the Treasure Chest of the Indian Railways. Built in the year 1855, this 143-year-old pristine beauty, now comes alive. The oldest working steam locomotive in the world kept at the National Rail Museum, runs once again taking 50 discerning passengers on an unforgettable two-day trip from Delhi to Alwar on selected days. The train consists of First Class chair car and pantry car, all majestically hauled by the fabled Fairy Queen. The two-day trip includes departure from Delhi Cantt. Railway station at 1000 hrs.

On day 1 - reaching Alwar at 1600 hrs. The night halt is in Star Hotel at Sariska near Alwar from where the tourists are taken around the Tiger Sanctuary the next morning. The night at Sariska is full of entertainment with ethnic artists only for the travellers.

THE JOY RIDE UP THE HILLS

THE TOY TRAINS OF INDIA

SHIMLA : The toy train journey from Kalka to Shimla is entrancing with 107 tunnels and lofty arched bridges. The dazzling view and the stops at the picturesque stations along the way add to the experience.

Shimla is connected by a broad guage line up to Kalka. From Kalka to Shimla—THE TOY TRAIN covers 96 km of track in six hours.

UDHAGAMANDALAM (OOTY) : At a speed of 33 km. per hour, this TOY TRAIN treks across plains, plantations and forest clad hills. The 16 tunnels and tall girder bridges on the way, along with the breathtaking view, make this toy journey to Ooty, something not to be missed.

Ooty is connected by a narrow guage line from Mettupalayam which serves as the railhead for mainline trains.

DARJEELING : The most famous of the little trains, is the one linking the town of New Jalpaiguri in the plains to the lovely hill station of Darjeeling. The 86 km Darjeeling line allows the traveller an uninterrupted view of the breathtaking scenery of the Himalayas.

New Jalpaiguri, the starting point of the hill station to Darjeeling, has direct connection to Calcutta Guwahati and other places.

MATHERAN : The 77-year-old line, connecting Neral to Matheran, is the main way to reach the tiny hill resort, close to Mumbai. As the little train wheezes up into the clear mountain air, one can view the scenic vista of hills and plains below.

The toy train to Matheran commences from Neral (on Mumbai - Pune line). The journey takes about one and a half hours. The toy train runs between sunrise and sunset.

INDRAIL PASS

To explore the splendour of multi-faceted India, Indrail passes provide excellent value for money and enhance the charm of holidays for foreign visitors. Indrail pass offers visitors a budget, the facility to travel as they like, over the entire railway system without any route restrictions within the period of validity of the ticket. The Indrail pass holders are not required to pay any reservation fee and the superfast charges for the journey. The passes are available for a duration ranging from 1,7,15,21,30,60 to 90 days and are also available for half day, two days and four days. This new facility will offer economies of scale to visitors arriving by International flights and visiting India for only one or two days for connecting destinations.

One can contact the nearest Government of India Tourist office for further information and brochure.

IMPORTANT FACTS OF INDIAN RAILWAYS

First Train in India (also in Asia)	April 16,1853 between 1st and Thane 32 km
First Electric train in India	Deccan Queen, introduced in 1929 between Kalyan and Thane
Number of trains running per day	About 11,275
Number of railway stations	6985

SCENIC SOJOURN—THE KONKAN RAILWAY

A breathtaking journey, traversing the beautiful Konkan Railway is a 760 kilometre long adventure on rails. It is the largest railway project undertaken by the Indian Railway in the current century. The railway line traverses through some of the most formidable terrain ever encountered in the history of railway construction. It is the first time that a major transport infrastructure project in the country has been completed on the B.O.T.(Build, Operate and Transfer) concept. This project will not only be a trend-setter in terms of B.O.T. principle but also in adoption of frontline technologies in several years of railway construction and working.

The construction of this project commenced on 15th October 1990 and was completed and commissioned for both goods and passenger traffic on 26th January 1998.

The 760 kilometer long railway project involves construction of 179 major bridges, 1819 minor bridges, 92 tunnels (aggregate length 84 km) and 89 million cu.m. earthwork in cutting and embankments.

The project involves bridging of deep valleys as well as wide perennial rivers. The longest bridge on the project is across river Sharavati near Honnavar and is 2.065 km in length. The tallest viaduct is across Panval Nandi near Ratnagiri in Maharashtra State with a height of 64 meter (210 ft) which is the tallest bridge in Indian sub-continent.

Tunnelling is another important activity on this project involving construction of 92 tunnels totalling a length of 84 kilometers. It is for the first time in India that tunnelling works of this magnitude was carried out in a short time frame of less than seven years. The longest tunnel on the project is 6.50 km at Karbude near Ratnagiri and this is the longest railway tunnel in this part of the world.

Modern track structure with 52 kg long welded rails laid on prestressed concrete monoblock sleepers was adopted on the entire route. The points and crossings used for switching trains from one track to another were laid on concrete sleepers instead of wooden sleepers. This has saved the country in terms of avoidance of deforestation.

Despite the formidable terrain conditions through which the alignment passess minimum radius of curvature of 1250 m and a ruling gradient of 1 in 150 (Compensated), has been adopted in order to facilitate a speed potential of 160 kmph and smooth movement of heavy haul freight trains.

Out of 59 stations on the Konkan Railways, the important ones are Veer, Khed Chiplun, Ratnagiri, Rajapur road, Kankavali, Sawantwadi, Thivim, Karmali Verna, Madgaon, Karwar Kumta, Bhatkal, Kundaoura, Udipi and Surathkal.

TOURISM AND KONKAN RAILWAY

Konkan railway traverses through picturesque region of the west coast of India. Despite its scenic beauty it has not been fully exploited to its true potential, due to non-availabiliy of proper mass-transport system. Konkan railway will now open up areas hitherto unknown to tourist like Ratnagiri, Singhdurga and Karwar district which have plenty of unexplored beaches and other tourist locations. In an offer to make the region more accessible to tourists, important surface trains like Delhi - Trivandrum Rajdhani Express are being diverted over the Konkan Railway. In addition a Shatabdi Railway has been proposed between Mumbai - Madgaon which will traverse the distance in about 8 hours.

REDUCTION IN DISTANCE

	Distance as per present route in km	Distance as per new route in km	Savings in kms
Mangalore - Mumbai	2041	914	1127
Mangalore - Ahmedabad	2653	1358	1295
Mangalore - Delhi	3033	2249	784
Cochin - Mumbai	1849	1336	513

REDUCTION IN TRAVEL TIME

	Present time in hours	Expected time in hours	Savings in time in hours
Mangalore - Mumbai	41	15	26
Mumbai - Cochin	36	24	12
Mumbai - Goa	20	10	10

INDIAN WATERWAYS AND PORTS

Nature has gifted India 6100 km coastline and fertile inland river system.

Known from earliest times in India, seal from find spot of Mohenjodaro, Indus Valley Civilisation is engraved with two-masted ship; Rig Veda has references to ships; naval expeditions, merchants praying to sea before starting   (sea) enterprises; Varuna (sea god) said to have known sea paths over which ships went; Vijaya (king) went to Sri Lanka by taking horses and elephants (56-48 B.C.) crossing of the sea being depicted in an Ajanta fresco. Under Chandragupta Maurya, ship building was a flourishing industry with a controller of ship-building and commissioner of ports, convoys of ships being built for making sea voyages. During Mughal times shipping and internal navigation had a department of its own. Under Akbar big ships and boats were built.Nicoli Conti who visited India (15th century AD) says the Indian built ships were longer than the Italian ones.

Calicut was the greatest shipbuilding centre and executed orders from other countries as well. Indian ship-building gradually declined with the coming of Europeans. Since Independence shipping industry has expanded significantly.

INLAND WATER SYSTEM

Inland water transportation also plays important means of communication for common man.

India's vast river system offers the possibility of transport that is not only expensive but also environment friendly.Unfortunately suitable steps have not been taken for its development.

Three national waterways have been declared to be functional now. In 1986 the Allahabad-Haldia stretch (1,620 km) of Ganga Bhagirathi-Hooghly river system was inaugurated as National. Waterways number I. Two years later the Sadiya-Dhubri (Bangladesh border)stretch (891km) of the Brahmputra was declared as National Waterways number II. In 1993, the Kollam-Kottapuram (168 km), Champakara canal (14km), Udyogmandal canal (23km), stretch on the west coast canal, were declared as National Waterways number III.

Three more waterways systems are being developed. One is in the Sunderbans (191km), to provide a steamer route between Sagar and Raimangal at the Bangladesh border. The second is between Cherla and Rajamundhry (208km) along with delta canals, on the Godavari. The third are the waterways in Goa on the Mandovi river (41km), Zurai (64km) and the Cumberjua canal system (17km).

PORTS IN INDIA

The history of Indian ports is as old as our civilisation.

About 1,000 BC, from Ophir (Saphir or Sopara), a port on the west-coast near Mumbai certain goods were taken for Hiram, King of Tyre in his ships. About 25 BC, Bharakachha (Barygaza or Broach)in the first half of the 1st century AD, Muzuris (Cranganore), Nylkynda and Baraka (both in the Pandyan country) and later half of same century, the Deccan and Southern Indian ports of Poduca (Pondicherry), Saptanea (Madras), and Masalia (Masulipatam) Pukar (coast of Orissa) and Tamarlipti (Tamluk at mouth of Ganga) were well known and traded with Greece, Rome, West Asia and Gulf countries. Kalyani was chief port of Andhra kings (225 B.C, to 225 A.D.). Puhar was the greatest Chola port at the mouth of Kaveri and Mamallapuram was ancient and important Pallava port (deserted by 9th century). Palura (coast of Orissa) In the 17th c. Calicut and Cochin were important ports trading with Europe Iran and other Gulf countries. Masulipatnam, Pulicat, Nagapattinam, Madras Satgoan and Sripur (in Bengal) were ports trading with East & East Indies.

PRESENT PORTS

There are 11 major ports (West Coast - 6; East coast - 5) apart from 139 minor working ports which are directly under the Government of India administration

SEA PORT	SEA	FEATURES
Mumbai	Arabian Sea	Natural and biggest port, handles one fifth of the total traffic
Calcutta	Bay of Bengal	Situated on Hooghly river, biggest terminal port of South Asia
Cochin	Arabian Sea	Largest natural harbour

SEA PORT	SEA	FEATURES
Kandla	Arabian sea— Gulf of Kutch	Tidel port
Madras	Indian Ocean— Bay of Bengal	Oldest port, artificial harbour and the largest
Mormugoa	Arabian Sea	Second largest and an important naval station
Mangalore	Arabian Sea	A tidal port
Tuticorin	Indian Ocean	Shallow port
Visakhapatnam	Bay of Bengal	Deepest protected port, has a big unit and major naval base at the tip of the Indian peninsula
Paradeep	Bay of Bengal	Newly opened port declared as major port in 1966
	Arabian Sea	Newly constructed port

There are four major Shipyards : Garden Reach Shipbuilders & Engineering Ltd. Calcutta; Mazagon Dock Ltd. Mumbai; Hindustan Shipyard Ltd., Visakhapatnam; Cochin Shipyard, Cochin. In addition there are 32 small shipping yards in private sectors.

There are three training institutions at TS Rajendra, Marine Engineering College and Lal Bahadur Shastri Nautical and Engineering College—all in Mumbai.

ANDHRA PRADESH

ANDHRA PRADESH
AT A GLANCE

AREA : 2,75,068 Sq.km

CAPITAL : Hyderabad

BOUNDARIES : East - Bay of Bengal; West and South-West - Karnataka; South - Tamil Nadu; North-East - Orissa.

LANGUAGE : Telugu and Urdu.

ROADS : National highways passing through Hyderabad constitute 2,949 km and State highways, including roads taken over by the districts and Zilla Praja Parishad, cover 43,763 km. There are 1 03,971 km of district roads in the State.

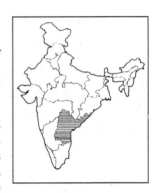

AIRPORTS : Hyderabad, Tirupati Vijayawada Visakhapatnam International flights are operated from Hyderabad to Kuwait, Muscat, Sharjah and Jeddah.

MUSEUMS

Hyderabad : Salar Jung Museum, Archaeological Museum, Khajana Buildings Museum, Yelleshwaram Museum, Prince Azmatajah Museum.

Nagarjunakonda : Archaeological Museum.

Tirupati : Sri Venkateshwara University Museum.

HILL STATIONS OF THE STATE

NAME	ALTITUDE	CONVENIENT RAILHEAD
Horsley Hills	1265 m.	Madanapalli Road – 29 km

PILGRIM CENTRES (A : Air; R : Rail)

Ahobilam : Nine forms of Lord Narasimham; A – Tirupati – 272 km, R – Nadyal – 74 km.

Bhadrachalam : Temple of Ramchandra; A – Vijaywada - 241 km, R – Bhadrachalam Ramchandra Road – 40 km.

Kalahasti : Kalahasteswara worshipped as a Vayu Lingam; A and R - Tirupati 27 km.

Kolanupaka : Jain temple of Mahavira; A and R - Hyderabad 60 km.

Mantralayam : The "jeeva samadhi"of Mantralayam Saint Raghavendraswamy Bellary 112 km; A - Mantralayam Road - 14 km

Puttaparthi : Satya Sai Baba's Prashanti Nilayam; A - Bangalore160 km, R - Penukonda 29km

Simhachalam : Hill temple of Narasimhaswamy; A and R - Visakhapatnam 16km

Srisailam : Sri Mallikarjunaswamy One of the Jyortirlingams; A - Hyderabad 232 km, R - Markapur road 85 km

Tirupati : Shrine of Lord Venkateswara; A and R - Tirupati

Vijayawada Kanaka : Durga temple; A and R - Vijaywada

Yadagiri Gutta : Narasimha temple - believed to cure diseases; A - Hyderabad 70 km, R - Raigir 4 km

Andhra Pradesh is northernmost State of South India and the fifth largest State in India. Nagarjunasagar, a 380 sq.km reservoir and a 124 meter high dam across the river Krishna is the world's tallest masonry dam; Salar Jung Museum, world's largest one man collection, is a rich repository of antiques and artifacts from all over the world, Borra caves near Visakhapatnam are believed to be a million years old, Nehru Zoological park is South Asia's First Lion Safari, Tirumala Tirupati is world's richest temple, Charminar. Arc of Triumph of the east, eastern ghats rail route from Visakhapatnam to Anantgiris is one of the highest broad guage tracks in the world, all are incredible sights.

HISTORY

The earliest mention of Andhras is in Aitereya Brahmana (2000 BC). It indicates that the Andhras, originally an Aryan race living in North India migrated to the south of the Vindhyas and later mixed with non-Aryans. Regular history of Andhra Desa, according to historians begins with 236 BC, the year of Ashoka's death.

During the following centuries, Satavahanas, Sakas, Ikshvakus, Eastern Chalukyas and Kakatiyas ruled the Telugu country. In the 13th century, the Kakatiyas, with their capital of Warrangal dominated Andhra Desa. The Tughlaks never cared to annex the Kakatiyan dominions and four local kingdoms arose out of the old Kakatiya empire.

One of these kingdoms was Vijaynagar. The Vijaynagar empire stood as a bulwark against Muslim expansionism for more than 200 years. Vijaynagar had to contend with Muslim Sultanates in the north time and again. Sometimes Vijaynagar joined one sultan against another.

These tactics finally led to a grand alliance of the sultanates of Ahmednagar, Bijapur and Golconda against Vijaynagar. On 23rd January 1565 the Deccan sultans humbled the mighty Vijaynagar army at the battle of Taloikota.

The Qutb Shahis of Golconda laid the foundation of the modern city of Hyderabad. Emperor Aurangzeb routed the Qutb Shahis and appointed Asaf Jah, as the governor of Deccan. As the Mughal empire tottered under Aurenzeb's successors, the Asaf Jahis made themselves independent rulers under the title of Nizam. The Nizams became involved in the Anglo-French wars in Deccan and had finally to enter into a subsidiary alliance with the British in 1800.

After independence, the Telugu speaking areas were separated from the composite Madras State and a new Andhra State came into being on 1st October 1953. With the passing of the State Reorganisation Act, 1959, there was a merger of Hyderabad State and Andhra State and Andhra Pradesh came into being.

HYDERABAD

Hyderabad, the capital of the Andhra Pradesh, situated on the banks of the river Musi, is known as the Istambul of India. The history of city dates back to the time of the Kakatiya rulers of Warangal (13th century). In the 14th century the Qutab Shahi dynasty laid the foundation of Hyderabad city. Later, the Nizams proclaimed their independence from the Mughals. Mohammed Qutub Shah, the fifth king of Golconda fell in love with Bhagmathi and founded the city of Bhagyanagra in1591. Later he renamed the city as Hyderabad. The last Nizam was considered to be the richest man in India.

PLACES OF INTEREST

CHAR MINAR : Called the Arc de Triomphe of the East, stands in the centre of the city. Built as the legend goes, by the fifth King of the dynasty Mohamed Quli Qutb Shah in honour of his Hindu wife Bhagmati who lived in Chiham village located in the surrounding, its central structure soars to a height of 180 feet.

MECCA MASJID : The largest Masjid of South India, it lies 100 yards south west of Charminar. Its construction was started by King Abdullah Qutub Shah in 1614 AD but it was completed by Aurangzeb in 1687. It is very impressive mosque with lofty colonnades and entrance arches made of single slabs of granite. On one side is an enclosure where the Asaf Jahi rulers lie buried.

GOLCONDA FORT : The name originates from the Telugu words 'Golla and Konda' Sheperd's hill after the neighbouring Warangal.

A clap under the canopy of the Fateh Darwaza can be heard at the far away summit palace. Famous KOHINOOR DIAMOND of the British Crown was mined from this area. Famous features of Golconda Fort include its system of acoustic palaces, water supply system and the famous Rahban cannon - one of those used during the last seize of Golconda to whom the fort ultimately fell.

QUTUB SHAHI TOMBS : Close to Golconda Fort are the tombs of the seven Qutub Shahi rulers amidst the Ibrahim bagh. The tombs are domed structures built in a square base surrounded by pointed arches and well laid gardens.

BIRLA TEMPLE : Sri Venkateswara temple or the Kala Pahad temple is built with 2000 tones of white marble—blend of the Khajuraho and Bodhgaya of North India and Raj Gopuram and Garudalaya of South India architecture.

BIRLA PLANETARIUM : It is India's most modern planetarium and first of its kind in the country.

PUBLIC GARDENS : These are gardens with some outstanding specimens of Asaf Jahi architecture; Ajanta Pavilion - with life size replicas of the world famous Ajanta frescoes, ornate Jubilee Hall - containing the Nizam's own collection of rare artifacts.

HUSSAIN SAGAR : Constructed in 1562 AD the lake divides Secunderabad from Hyderabad. It also provides boating facilities. Later 33 statues of historical personage of Andhra Desa were placed along the bund of the lake. The 16 meter tall, 350 tonne monolith colossus statue of Lord Buddha is placed on the rock of Gibraltor in the middle of the lake.

OSMANIA UNIVERSITY : Founded in 1917 at the suggestion of Sir Akbar Hydri, it is a fine piece of architecture. Walls are decorated with flowered jali work with marble inlay on them.

NEHRU ZOOLOGICAL PARK : Sprawling across 300 lush green acres, it is the biggest zoo in India with 250 species.

HOW TO REACH

AIR : Hyderabad is connected by air with Ahmedabad, Bhubaneshwar, Calcutta, Chennai, Delhi, Mumbai, Pune, Nagpur, Tirupati and Visakhapatnam.

RAIL : Hyderabad / Secunderabad are connected by rail with major cities.

ROAD : Hyderabad is also well-connected by National Highways.

Local Transport : Metered Taxis, auto-rikshaws and all types of tourist vehicles are easily available.

DISTANCES FROM HYDERABAD

Aurangabad 539 km; Badami 657 km; Bangalore 590 km; Visakhapatnam 667 km; Chennai 671 km; Goa 698 km; Mumbai 713 km.

HOTEL ACCOMMODATION (STD CODE 040)

— The Krishna Oberoi (5 Star), Road No. 1, Banjara Hills
  PH 3392323; FAX 3393979,

— Welcomegroup Grand Kakatiya Hotel and Towers, Begumpet
  PH 331 0132; FAX 3309945

— Holiday Inn Krishna (5 Star), Road No. 1, Banjara Hills
  PH 339 3939; FAX 339 2684

— Taj Residency (5 Star), Road No. 1, Banjara Hills
  PH 3399999; FAX 339 2218
  E Mail : trcha-ryd@tajgroup.sprint.rpg.ems.vsnl.net.in

— Hotel Bhaskar palace (4 Star), Road no 1, Banjara Hills
  PH 3301523; FAX 3304036

— Ramada Hotel Manohar (4 Star), adjacent to Airport Exit
  Road, Begumpet. PH 040 819917; FAX 819801, 818 936

— Viceroy : (4 Star) 1-3-1036/3/1 Opp Hussain Sagar Lake tank
  Bund Road. PH 753 8383; FAX 753 8797 / 753 0674

— Ashoka (3 Star) 6-1-70, Lakdi-ka-pul
  PH 230 105; FAX 230 105

— Asrani International Hotel (3 Star), 1-7-179, M.G.Road
  PH 842267; FAX 846 903

— Hotel Basera(3 Star), 9-1-167/68, S.D. Road
  PH 770 3200; FAX 770 4745

- The Central Court Hotel (3 Star) 6-1-71, Lakdi-ka-pul
  PH 233 262, FAX 232 737
- Hotel Golkonda(3 Star)10-1-124, Masab Tank
  PH 332 0202; FAX 332 0404
- Hotel Java International (2 Star), P.O. Box No. 264, Abids
  PH 475 2929; FAX 475 3919
- Hotel Nagarjuna(2 Star) 3-6-356/58, Basheer Bagh
  PH 322 0201; FAX 322 6789
- Hotel Rajdhani (1 Star) 15-1-503 Siddiamber Bazar
  PH 040 590650
- Hotel Ambassador, 1-7-27 S.D.Road. PH 843 760, 844 882

CONDUCTED TOURS

The Andhra Pradesh Tourism Department offers following conducted tours :

(1) Nagarjunasagar Tour (Daily)
(2) Tirupati Tour Departure on Friday and Return on Monday morning
(3) Srisailam tour Departure on Sarurday and return on Sunday evening
(4) Mantralayam Tour Departure on Saturday and return on Sunday
(5) South India Tour (14 Days)
(6) Shirdi Tour Departure on Wednesday and return on Friday morning
(7) One day pilgrim Tour
(8) Heritage Tour of Lesser known monuments (Daily)
(9) Hampi, Goa and Bijapur Tour Departure on every 1st and 2nd Saturday and return on Thursday evening
(10) Aurangabad Tour Departure every 1st and 3rd Monday and return on Friday morning
(11) Hyderabad Local City Tour Daily
(12) Deccan by Dusk - Hyderabad half day Tour (Daily)
(13) Krishna Cruise Departure 1st and 3rd Saturday and return on Sunday evening

For Detailed information contact

- Andhra Pradesh Tourism, 5th and 11th Floor, Gagan Vihar, M.J.Road, Hyderabad 500 001.
  PH 040 501519, 501520; FAX 040 473 2700

EXCURSIONS

SHILPARAMAM : Craft village set up at Madhapur beyond Jubilee hills of Hyderabad.

YADAGIRIGUTTA : (Shrine of the Lord of Light) Situated on the hillock near Hyderabad in Nagalconda district, three forms of Lord Narasimha are manifested here as Gandhabherunda, Yogananda and Jwala. The reigning deity Laxmi Narayanaswamy is enshrined at a height of 178 m.the majestic five storey gopuram and the Vaikunta Dwaram are impressive.

NACHARAM : Close to Hyderabad in Medak district, it has an ancient Laxmi Narasimha Swamy temple. The Andhra Pradesh Tourism Department runs a tourist complex here.

DECCAN PRE-HISTORIC ROCKS : Geologist date the grey granite rocks here at approximately 2500 million years—the only one in Asia.

MEDAK CHURCH : (100 km) Built on an immense scale in solid white granite, the Gothic structure is one of the best and largest in the country. It can accommodate as many as 5000 people.

NAGARJUNASAGAR - NAGARJUNAKONDA : (150 km) Built across the river Krishna, it is the world's tallest masonary dam. Further ahead stands a pylon bearing image of second century Mahayana Buddhist sage Nagarjunacharya.

The reservoir has submerged three historical sites : Dhyankataka, capital of Andhra's first dynasty Satvahanas (200 BC); Vijayapuri, capital of the second dynasty— Ikshavakus, and a great complex of Buddhist heritage—a university,  chaityas, monastries, arena, ashwamedha altar, royal baths, drainage system and nine stupa-like structures made of bricks on a wheel-shaped ground plan.

The Mahachaitya yielded a body relic of the Buddha. The excavations (dating from the early stone age) have been reassembled on an island 11 km upstream and are called Nagarjunakonda.

Down from the dam are the Ethipothala waterfalls.

SHAMIRPET : (27 km) An Andhra Pradesh tourist complex is located in the vicinity of the man-made Jawahar Lake.

OSMANSAGAR LAKE : (27 km) It was built by constructing a dam on the river Musi in 1920 by Mir Osman Ali Khan and planned by Mokshagundam Visweswarayya for water supply. The place offers excellent picnic spot with well laid gardens.

KOLANUPAK : (80 km) It was the second capital town of Kalyani Chalukyas during 11ᵗʰ century and as a religious center of Jains.Several historic monuments, temples and sculptures from 10ᵗʰ and 11ᵗʰ century exist here.

KONDAPUR : (90 km) It is known as the 'TAXAXILA OF THE SOUTH' and is referred to as the 'TOWN OF MOUNDS'. Remains of the vast Buddhist complex, buildings, coins of gold silver, copper and lead have been excavated here over the years.

WARANGAL

WARANGAL - KAZIPET - HANAMKONDA : A cluster of three towns it presents images of the awe-inspiring Kakatiya splendour. The birth place of saint-poet Pothana, author of the Telugu classic 'Bhagwatam', Warangal was founded by Kakatiya ruler Prodaraja and remained the Kakatiya capital during 12ᵗʰ and 13ᵗʰ centuries. Marco Polo had visited the Warangal Fort and was fascinated by its riches. Its four inner gates have become the signature of Kakatiya architecture.

PLACES OF INTEREST

THOUSAND PILLAR TEMPLE : The 1000-pillar temple on Hanamkonda hill, built in Chalukyan style is dedicated to Lord Shiva, Lord Vishnu and Surya (Sun). Built during the reign of Rudra Deva in 1163 AD as a gratitude for being victorious in a battle, it has 300 pillared mandapa, rock cut elephants guarding the entrance and an 1.8 m exquisitely carved Nandi in the front and scenes from epics adorn the ceilings.

WARANGAL FORT : It was built during 13ᵗʰ century by Kakatiya king Ganapathi Deva and his daughter Rudramma. The remains of four huge stone gateways, similar to those of Sanchi and several exquisite pieces of sculpture can be seen.

HOW TO REACH

AIR : Nearest Airport Hyderabad 157 kms.

RAIL : Warangal is connected by rail with Ahmedabad, Delhi, Chennai, Howrah, Bhubaneshwar, Hyderabad, Bhopal and Tirupati.

ROAD : Warangal is connected by road with Hyderabad, Vijayawada, Karimnagar, Khammam   and other cities.

HOTEL ACCOMMODATION (STD CODE 08712)

— Hotel Ashok (2 Star)
— Hotel Ekasila; Hotel Radhika; Hotel Annapurna; Hotel Jaya; Hotel Chariot

For local tours and tourism information contact :

— Tourist Information Officer, Regional Tourist Information Bureau, Tourist Rest House, Kazipet, Warangal, PH 76201

EXCURSIONS FROM WARANGAL

BHADRAKALI TEMPLE : Situated on a hilltop between Hanumankonda and Warangal, it is noted for its stone image of the Goddess Kali here shown in a sitting posture. She is depicted with eight arms and carries a weapon in each hand.

PALAMPET : (50 km) Here exists the glorious Ramappa shrines constructed in 1213 AD referred to as the brightest star in the galaxy of medieval temples of Deccan. Constructed in pink sandstone the ornamented bands, floral motifs and an array of dancers, musicians and goddesses in stone are unbelievably beautiful.

BHADRACHALAM : (in Khammam district) The city is famous for Sri Seetha Ramachandraswamy temple where all 48 forms of Lord Vishnu have been depicted.

KALESAI : Known as Kashi of the South it is famous for Mukteshwara temple which has two lingams (Phallus) —one for Lord Shiva and another for Lord Yama, the God of Death, each guarded by an umbrella of seven hooded stone cobras.

RAMAPPA TEMPLE : (70 km) Ramappa or Ramalimgeswara temple, a magnificent monument dating back to 1213 AD is an archaeological wonder and the best contribution to South Indian temple architecture. The temple was built on behalf of king, Kakati by  Ganapathi Deva who was a great patron of art and learning.

VIJAYWADA

The city is the heart of Andhra Pradesh and is historically a cultural, political and educational centre.

The Vijaywada region is renowned for pickles. As Legend has it Arjuna of the epic Mahabharata, had prayed on the top of Indrakali hill and had obtained blessings from Lord Shiva for the victory in the war. The name Vijaywada is derived from this divine blessing for 'vijaya' (victory). Two thousand years old city, it is known as Bezwada, named after Goddess Kanakadurga, locally called Vijaya. The site abounds in caves and temples with inscriptions dating from the first  century. The Kanakadurga temple is set on the Indrakali Hill. A temple of Lord Maleswara is also within the city. It is said that Adi Sankara had visited this temple and installed a Srichakra here. The Chienese traveller Hieun Tsang had also visited Vijaywada. The Victoria museum has a colossal Buddha statue carved in black granite on a nearby hill. The Hazratbal mosque has a sacred relic of Prophet Mohammed. The Gandhi Stupa 15.8 m high, stands on Gandhi hill which was formerly known as Orr Hill.

The Mogalarajapuram caves have three cave temples dating back to 5th century AD containing idols of Lord Nataraja, Vinayaka and others. The Ardha Nari Murthy found here is considered the only one of its kind in South India. The other famous caves are the Undavalli caves carved in the 7th C. A huge monolithic Vishnu, in lying position is a magnificent sight at the caves. The renowned temple of Lord Narasimha, one of the nine Avatars of Vishnu, is located on the hillock at Mangalagiri, 12km south of Vijaywada. The unique feature of this temple, according to the devotees, is that the deity accepts only half the quantity of the Panakam offered, irrespective of the quantity.

Many Jain and Buddhist relics are also found at GUDIVADA, 45 km from Vijaywada. Another unique site here are the 99 low mounds with remains of Buddhist stupas which has been declared a national monument.

HOW TO REACH

AIR : Vijaywada is connected by air with Hyderabad and Visakhapatnam.

RAIL : Vijaywada is connected by rail with all major cities of the country.

ROAD : Vijaywada is well-connected by road with Madras, Hyderabad, Vizag and Nellore.

HOTEL ACCOMMODATION (STD CODE 0866)

- Hotel Ila Puram(3Star), Besant Road, Gandhi Nagar
  PH 571 282; FAX 575 251
- Hotel Kandhari International(3 Star) Bunder Road, Labbipet,
  PH 471 010
- Hotel Krishna Residency (3 Star),Rajagopalachari Street,
  Governorpet. PH 75302, 74709, 731 97; FAX 643 73
- Hotel Mamata (3 Star), Eluru Road
  PH 571 251; FAX 574 343
- Hotel Raj Tower (3 Star), Eluru Road. PH 61 310, 11
- Hotel Manorama (2 Star), 27-38-61, M.G.Road
  PH 572 626; FAX 575619
- Sree Lakshmi Vilas Modern Cafe, Besant Road, Governorpet
  PH 572525
- A.P. Tourism operates pleasure boating from Krishna Veni
  Motel.

EXCURSIONS

KODANPALLI : (16 km) Production centre for the famous
Kodonpalli toys, made with a light wood called 'Poniki'.

KUCHIPUDI : (60 km) Birth palce of Siddendra Yogi - originator
of the famous Kuchipudi dance.

AMRAVATI : (66 km)The first and foremost site of Buddhist
inheritance lies on the south bank of the Krishna river. It is famed for
its Buddhist influence that attained glorious heights during the
Satavahana reign.The remnants of Buddhist cult can be seen in the many
magnificent carvings, chaityas, viharas, murals, sculptured panels which
are considered even today as some of the greatest works on Indian art.

TIRUPATI - TIRUMALA

Tirupati, at the foothills of Tirumala, is the abode of Lord
Venkateswara one of the most venerated shrines in India. One of the
oldest temples, it was patronised by Pallavas, Cholas, Pandyas and
Vijayanagara kings. This place is also mentioned in the Sastras, Puranas
and the Sthalamahattyas (ancient Hindu epics). The range of the
Tirumala hills, according to the Puranas, represents the body of the
serpent Adisesha on which Lord Vishnu—protector of the world—rests.
The seven hills represent the seven heads of the serpent. The main
temple is a magnificent example of Indian temple architecture. The
shrine is dedicated to Lord Vishnu in the form of Varahaswami. The

splendid Vimana over the sanctum sanatorium is plated with gold, as Dhwajasthambam or temple flag. The Varahaswami temple, situated near the Venkateshwara temple, is said to be more ancient.

Other famous shrines in Tirupati town include the Shri Govindarajaswami temple and the sacred Kapila Theertham Tank, where Lord Shiva is said to have appeared before the Sage Kapila. The Temple of Goddess Alivelumanga, the divine consort of Lord Venkateswara, is at Tiruchanur. Another temple dedicated to this goddess is in Sri Mangapuram, 12 km from Tirupati. Chandragiri Fort, stronghold of the Vijaynagar empire, is 11 km from Tirupati. It is built on a huge rock,  56 meter high and dates back to 1000 AD. Within its walls lie the remains of ancient palaces and temples.

The Tripuati Temple is the world's richest temple. Shops around it remain open day and night.

HOW TO REACH

AIR : Tirupati is connected by air with Hyderabad, Chennai and Bangalore

RAIL : Tirupati is connected by rail with Hubli, Hyderabad, Chennai, Kolhapur, Mumbai, Puri, Tiruchirapalli, Varanasi and Vijaywada.

ROAD : Tirupati is linked by regular bus services with important cities like Hyderabad, Bangalore, Madras, Vijaywada and Chittor. Pre-paid taxi services are available from Tirupati to Tirumala.

Regular buses and taxis are also available from Chennai.

CONDUCTED TOURS

— Local Alaya Darshan (Daily)
— Madras conducted Tour (Daily)
For detailed information contact :
— Asst. manager, Transport Unit, APTTDC Stall No 12
— APSRTC Commercial Complex.
  PH 517 501 / 25602
Or, Officer, Regional Tourist Information Bureau,
  Near TTD 3rd Choultry.
  PH 245306

HOTEL ACCOMMODATION (STD CODE 08574)

- Guestline Hotels and Resorts (3 Star),14-37, Karakambdi Road, Akarampalli. PH 28 336, 28 800, 28 868; FAX 27774
- Hotel Mayura (3 Star), 209, T. P.Area PH 25 925, 25251; FAX 25911
- Bhimas Deluxe Hotel (2 Star), 34-38, G.Car street PH 25521; FAX 25471
- Hotel Bhimas Paradise, 33-37, Renugunta Road PH 25 747, 25 200; FAX 25 568

EXCURSIONS

CHANDRAGIRI FORT : (11km) Stronghold of the Vijaynagar empire this fort was built on a huge rock, 56 m. high in 1000 AD. Ruins of palaces and temples stand as mute witnesses of their once glorious era.

LEEPAKSHI : Easily accessible from Tirupati, this religious centre has some of the finest temple architecture and paintings.The famous Veerabhadra temple is built in the Vijayanagara style. As per local legend, Lord Shiva and Parvati were married in this temple at portion called Kalyan Mandapa.

PUTTUPARTHI : A small village shot into international fame as abode of Bhagwan shri Satya Sai Baba. Domestic and foreign visitors seeking spiritual solace come to Prashanti Nilayam throughout the year.

SRI KALAHASTI : (36km),This town has India's only temple dedicated to Vayudeva, the wind god. The Swamamukhi river turns north and touches the feet of the temple. Another famous temple is a Shiva temple Sri Kalahasteeswara built in the 12th century AD by the Chola king Rajarajendran.

VISAKHAPATNAM

This port is the headquarters of the Eastern Command of the Indian Navy and is the most modern shipyard. An industrial town it is surrounded by densely wooded hills and watered valleys. A 174 m high cliff, called Dolphin's Nose, rises above the sea and is capped by one of the most powerful light houses of east of Suez, it can signal upto 64 km into the sea.

The city was named after the god of valour, Visakha. Once a small fishing village, it formed a part of the Kalinga empire under Emperor Ashoka in 260 BC passing successively from the Andhra king Vengi to the Pallavas, Cholas and Gangas. In the 15th century it became a part of the Vijayanagara empire and was annexed to the British empire subsequently.

PLACES OF INTEREST

HINDUSTAN SHIPYARD : It is the nation's biggest ship building yard.

ANDHRA UNIVERSITY : The massive structure building of the Andhra University on the uplands of Visakhapatnam was opened in 1926. The three hillocks, a mountain on the eastern ghats, was cut into three and they house the following places of worship;

The Ross Hill : The highest mountain named after Mr. Ross, the local authority who built a house in 1864. This was converted into Roman Catholic Chapel and named Our Lady of the Sacred Heart.

Darga Konda : There is a mosque and a shrine of a Muslim sage Iashaque Madina who was revered for his prophecies.

Sri Venkateswara Konda : The temple was built by Captain Blackmoor in 1886, according to Telugu inscriptions.

HOW TO REACH

AIR : Visakhapatnam is connected by air with Hyderabad, Bhubaneshwar and Calcutta.

RAIL : Visakhpatnam is connected by rail with major cities of India.

ROAD : Being an important port town, Visakhpatnam is connected by road with all major cities.

HOTEL ACCOMMODATION (STD CODE 0891)

— The Park (5Star),Beach Road,
  PH 554488, 555185; FAX 554 181
— Dolphin Hotels Ltd(4 Star), Dabagarden
  PH 567000; FAX 567 555
— Hotel Daspalla (3 Star), Suryabagh
  PH 564825; FAX 562 043
— Green Park (3 Star) Waltair Main Road,
  PH 564 444; FAX 563 763

— Hotel Meghalaya (2 Star),Asilmetta Junction
   PH 555 141-45; FAX 555 824
— Welcomegroup Grand Bay, Beach Road
   PH 560101; FAX 550691

SRISAILAM

Srisailam, is a site of 12 meter long Srisailam dam on the banks of the Krishna river. On the south bank, in the Nallamalai forest on a 457 meter high hill is the Bhramramba Mallikarjunaswamy temple. It is one of the 12 Jyotirlingas, the most sacred and divine Phallus representing Lord Shiva. It is the seat of 18 leading Shaktis, revelation of the female power superior to all others represented by Parvati, the divine consort of Lord Shiva, here as Mahakali in her manifestation as Bharamarambha. The temple structure narrates in stone episodes from Ramayana and Mahabharata.

HOW TO REACH

AIR : Nearest airport Hyderabad 237 kms.

RAIL : The nearest railhead is Nandyal on Guntur-Hubli line 158 km.

ROAD : Srisailam is well-connected by road with all important towns.

MAHANANDI

One of the Nava Nandis in the country, it is situated in the thick forests at Nallamalai hills in the Nandyal taluka of Kurnool district. The temple here is dedicated to Sri.Mahanandisware Swamy in the form of Linga (Phallus). The outstanding feature in Mahanandi temple is the crystalline water which flows throughout the year from five perennial springs. About 1000 acres of Banana plantations are irrigated with these springs alone.

HOW TO REACH

AIR : Nearest airport Hyderabad 320 km; Tirupati 290 km.

RAIL : Nearest railhead Nandyal 16 km.

ROAD : Mahanandi is connected by road with Nandyal town situated at a distance of 16 km.

BHADRACHALAM

Bhadrachalam is Famous for the temple of Sree Seetaramachandra Swamy. On Ramnavami festival the people conregate here from all over the state as also from other parts of the country to witness the holy 'Kalyana Mahotsavam'—the marriage ceremony of Rama and Sita. The Puranic and historic facts relate that Lord Rama long after he shed his mortal coils manifested himself before Maharishi Bhadra whom he promised 'moksha'. That is why the village is named after Bhadra as Bhadrachalam. Some of the jewels like Kalikiturai, Pachala Pathakam, Chitaku Pathakam presented to Sita by Ramdasas are still preserved in the temple and they can be seen now.

HOW TO REACH

AIR : Nearest airport Vijaywada 201 kms.

RAIL : Nearest railhead Kothagudem 40 kms.

ROAD : Bhadrachalam is connected by road with Vijaywada, Khammam, Hyderabad, Machilipatnam. Telani, Kakinada and Nalgonda.

FESTIVALS

JANUARY—VISAKHA UTSAV : At Visakhapatnam, from third Friday to Sunday of every January Visakha Utsav is celebrated to bring together the kaleidoscope of brilliant hues that constitute Visakhapatnam district. Besides, Makar Sankranti is celebrated for three days that marks the reaping of harvest and is also known for kites flying.

FEBRUARY—DECCAN FESTIVAL : Deccan festival is celebrated to highlight Hyderabad's Art, crafts, culture and cuisine. Cultural programmes are arranged during the festival in Hyderabad. A pearl and bangle fair displays creations in lustrous pearls and multi-hued bangles that are local specialities. A food feast serves the best of Hyderabad's famed cuisine to visitors.

MARCH—MAHASHIVRATRI : It is celebrated at Kalahasteeswara temple at Kalahasti and the Bhraramaramba-Mallikarjunaswamy temple at Srisailam. The temple festival Chandana Yatra in March –April in Simhachalam is a time to pay homage to the reigning deity Narasimha who is covered with Chandanam (sandel paste). Pilgrims gather to view the idol smeared and decorated in all glory.

OCTOBER—RAYALASEEMA FOOD AND DANCE FESTIVAL : The Rayalaseema Food and dance festival in October is organised to highlight the art and cuisine of Rayalaseema area, Tirupati and Chittoor district.

DECEMBER—LUMBINI FESTIVAL : The Lumbini festival is organised to celebrate the Buddhist heritage of Andhra Pradesh from second Friday to Sunday of every December.

Besides Moharrum and Ramzan are also celebrated. After a period of fasting special prayers are offered on the Idd day. The Muslim prepare a special dish for the Idd with milk and dates which is called "Shir Khurma". Muslims in the twin cities of Hyderabad and Secunderabad celebrate "Bakrid" in the traditional manner by offering prayers in the mosques and with the sacrifice of goats.

BIHAR

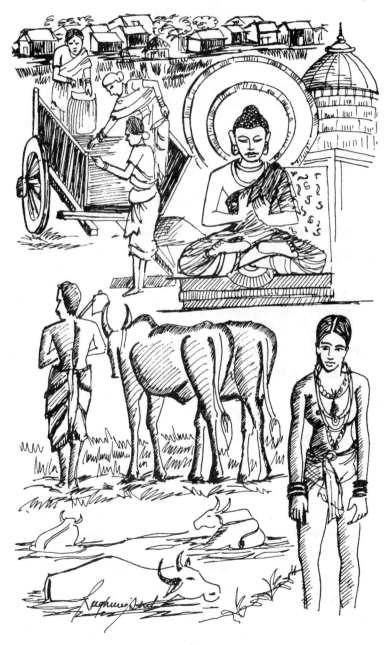

BIHAR
AT A GLANCE

AREA : 1,73,877 sq.km
CAPITAL : Patna
BOUNDARIES : East - West Bengal
West - Uttar Pradesh, Madhya Pradesh.

LANGUAGE : Hindi
ROADS : Up to March 1995, Bihar
had 19,095 km of metalled road including
2,118 km of national highways, 4,192 km
of State highways and 12,785 km of other
PWD roads.
AIRPORTS : Patna, Ranchi, Gaya and Jamshedpur

IMPORTANT MUSEUMS

Bodh Gaya and Gaya : Archaeological Museum - Bodh Gaya;
Gaya Museum Gaya
Nalanda : Archaeological Museum
Patna : Patna Museum

IMPORTANT HILL RESORTS

Hazaribagh (621 m) Railhead – Hazaribagh Road 29 km.
Ranchi (658 m) railhead - Ranchi

PILGRIM CENTRES (A : Air, R : Rail)

Baidyanath Dham - Deogarh : Baidyanath (Shiva temple); A/R
– Patna 29 km.
Bodhagaya : Most holy centre for Buddhists; A/R Gaya 15 km.
Gaya : Hindu pilgrims offer oblations to their deceased ancestors;
A/R – Gaya.
Maner : Tomb of Sufi saint Hazrat Maneri; A/R – Patna 29 km.
Pawanpuri : Place where Mahavira attained Nirvana; A - Patna
90 km, R – Pawanpuri Rd.
Parasnath Hill : 20 Jain Tirthankaras attained Nirvana here; A -
Dhanbad 66 km; R – Gomoh 28 km.
Rajgir : Vishwa Shanti Stupa and Jain Temples; A – Patna; R –
Rajgir.

Sitamarhi : Janaki Kund—the spot where the infant Sita was found by King Janak A - Patna133 km; R Sitamarhi.

Vaishali : Birthplace of Mahavira, also associated with the Lord Buddha; A - Patna 55 km, R - Hajipur 35 km – Muzzafarpur 37 km.

Bihar—the name is in fact a corrupt form of the word "VIHARA" which means a Buddhist monastery. Patliputra, a Kingdom was, centuries before the birth of Christ, known for its graciousness, richness patronage of fine arts and was a major centre of international studies. Today the State has incredible range of mineral resources and is the largest producer of the coal in India.

HISTORY

Bihar has a very ancient glorious and colourful history. Several of its cities are very ancient having mythological background and finds mention in the Vedas and Puranas. Bihar was the main scene of activities of Buddha and 24 Jain Tirthankaras. Great rulers of the State before the Christian era were Bimbisar Udayin who founded the city of Patliputra,Chandragupta Maurya and Emperor Ashoka under whom Magadha and its capital Patliputra became famous all over the world. With the death of Ashoka, its fortunes declined. However, under the Gupta emperors, it regained its lost glories. During the medieval period, the Muslim invaders made in-roads here. The first to conquer Bihar was Mohammed-bin-Bakhtiar Khaliji. The Khalijis were followed by the Tughluqs and then Mughals.Taking advantage of the disintegration of the Mughal empire the British established their footholds in Bihar with the battle of Plassey in 1757.Through successive battles and annexations, the British consolidated their position till 1911. Bihar formed part of the Bengal Presidency when on 12 December 1911, a separate province of Bihar and Orissa was created. In 1936 Bihar was made a separate province.

PATNA

History and heritage of capital city of Patna goes back to more than two millennium years. Patna had been the regal seat of governance for successive kingdoms each ruler was ascended in power, gave his capital a new name—Kusumpur, Pushapapura, Patliputra, Azeemabad but now being called Patna. A continuos history ranging from 8-7 century BC to present times a record claimed by very few cities in the world. From 6th century BC to 6th century AD Ajatshatru, second in the line of

Magadha kings, built a small fort at Pataligram at the confluence of the Ganga and Sone rivers. This later became the famous Mauryan metropolis of Pataliputra and was ruled by Chandragupta Maurya and his grandson Ashoka who became immortal for the spread of Buddhism. Other emperors who ruled from Pataliputra were the Gupta and the Pala Kings, Sher Shah Suri (16th C.) and Azimush Shan (18th C.), grandson of the Mughal Emperor Aurangzab who renamed it Azeemabad. Today, Patna is an important business centre of eastern India and also the gateway to the Buddhist and Jain Pilgrim centres of Vaishali, Rajgir, Nalanda, Bodhgaya and Pawanpuri.

PLACES OF INTEREST

KUMRAHAR : Archaeological findings in this area have established Patna's claim over a thousand years of political glory from 600 BC to 600 AD and then again from 16th C. onwards, spanning the rule of several dynasties. The only remains found are the remnants of a huge Mauryan hall supported by 80 sandstone pillars dating back to 400-300 BC.

GOLGARH : Alarmed by the famine of 1770 AD, Captain John Garstin built this huge granary for the British army in 1786 AD. The massive structure is 29 m high and the walls are 3.6 m wide at the base. The stairway winding around this monument offers a magnificent panoramic view of the city and the Ganga flowing nearby.

HAR MANDIR TAKHT : Guru Gobind Singh, the tenth Guru of the Sikhs, was born here in 1660AD. The Har Mandir Takht, one of the four sacred shrines of the Sikhs, stands at this holy site. The original temple was built by Maharaja Ranjit Singh and contains belongings of the Guru and Sikh holy texts.

MARTY'S MEMORIAL : A memorial to seven freedom fighters who sacrifice their lives in the Quit India Movement of August 1942, it is a modern sculpture facing the Secretariat where they were shot dead in their attempt to hoist the national flag.

PATHAR KI MASJID : Adjacent to Har Mandir Sahib, on the banks of the Ganga this beautiful mosque was built by Parwez Shah, son of Jahangir, when he was the governor of Bihar. It is also called Saif Khan's mosque, Chimmi Ghat mosque and Sangi Masjid.

SHER SHAH SURI MASJID : Sher Shah Suri built this mosque in 1545AD to commemorate his reign.Built in Afghan architectural style, it is one of the many beautiful mosques in Bihar.

KHUDA BAKSH ORIENTAL LIBRARY : A magnificent one-man collection of rare Arabic and Persian manuscripts, Rajput and Mughal paintings, assortment of old and new books from the university of Cordoba, Spain. It is one of the national libraries of India now.

SADAQAT ASHRAM : It is the headquarters of Bihar Vidyapeeth,a national university. India's first President Dr.Rajendra Prasad lived here. It contains a small museum displaying his belongings.

MANER : About 29 km from Patna, Bari Dargah, is the cenotaph of the Sufi Saint Hazrat Makhodoom Yahiya Maner. The tomb of his disciple Shah Daulat is also here. It is an important pilgrimage centre for the Muslims during the annual urs.

AGAM KUAN : Agam Kuan is one of the most important early historic archaeological remains in Patna associated with the Mauryan Emperor Ashok.

JALAN MUSEUM : Constructed at the site of Sher Shah's fort, it preserves a rich private collection of jade, Chinese paintings and silver filigree work of the Mughal period. The museum can be visited only with prior permission, since it is a private collection.

PATNA MUSEUM : It contains metal and stone sculptures of the Maurya and Gupta periods, terracotta figures and archaeological finds from sites in Bihar. Among its prized exhibits is a 16 km long fossilized tree.

HOW TO REACH

AIR : Patna is connected by air with Ahmedabad, Delhi, Mumbai, Calcutta, Lucknow and Ranchi.

RAIL : Patna is connected by rail with major cities.

ROAD : Patna is the entry point to visit Buddhist cities and is connected with major cities and towns of Bihar and Uttar Pradesh.

DISTANCES FROM PATNA

Gaya - 92 km; Bodhgaya 104 km; Nalanda - 89km; Rajgir 102 km; Vaishali 54 km; Muzzafarpur 72 km; Raxaul 206 km; Ranchi 326 km; Sasaram 152 km and Dhanbad 322km.

Daily sightseeing tours of the city and trips to the historic sites of Nalanda, Rajgir, Pawanpuri Gaya-Bodhgaya, Maner andVaishali are arranged during the tourist season by BSTDC.

For detailed information please contact :
— Bihar State Tourism Development Corporation, Tourist Bhawan, Beer Chand Patel Marg.
  PH 225 411, 222 2622; FAX 236 218
— Tourist Information Centre, Frazer Road, PH 225 295
— Tourist Information Centre Railway Station and Airport

HOTEL ACCOMMODATION (STD CODE (0612)

— Maurya Patna (5 Star), South Gandhi Maidan
  PH 222 061- 68;F 222 2069
— Hotel Chanakya (3 Star),Birchand Patel Marg
  PH 220 590/96; FAX 220 598
— Hotel Republic (3 Star), Exhibition Road
  PH 655 021/24; FAX 655 024
— Patliputra Ashok : (3 Star), Bir Chand Patel Marg
  PH 226270; FAX 223467
— Hotel President (2 Star), Off Fraser Road
  PH 220 600-05; FAX 224 455
— Marwari Awas Griha, Fraser Road
  PH 220 626-34; FAX 220 943
— Hotel Satkar International, Fraser Road
  PH 220 551-55; FAX 220 556

EXCURSION

Gaya (92 km). Gaya is one of the most important pilgrim centre for the Hindus since times immemorial. It is believed that a Hindu will reach heaven if his post-cremation rites are performed under the celebrated 'Akshayobat' or immortal banyan tree standing in the courtyard of Vishnupad temple. Believed to be built on the footsteps of Lord Vishnu, the grand temple was renovated by a Ahalyabai, queen of Indore.

BUDDHIST CIRCUIT

BODHGAYA

Serene and quiet this tiny little village, holiest among the Buddhist religious centres is Bodhgaya. It was here that the quest of Prince Siddharth was fulfilled after years of quest for the ultimate truth, the supreme enlightenment and he became 'THE BUDDHA', the enlightened one. Thus, in away, Buddhism was born under the Peepal

Tree here. The tree still appears to radiate an aura of abiding serenity, spiritual solitude and peace. It is believed that the original Bodhi tree sprang up on the day of Buddha's birth. The Prince had been wandering in search of supreme peace for six years, but it was at Bodhgaya where his mission was achieved. Lying in sylvan solitude this sacred place is situated on the banks of Niranjana river (modern Falgu). It is 13 km from Gaya.

PLACES OF INTEREST

THE BODHI TREE : The present Bodhi Tree is supposed to be the fifth in succession of the original tree under which the Buddha had attained enlightenment.

MAHABODHINI TEMPLE : The Mahabodhini temple stands east to the Bodhi Tree. Its basement is 48 square feet and it rises in the form of a slender Pyramid till it reaches its neck which is cylindrical in shape. The total height of the temple is 170 feet and on the top of it are Chatras which symbolise sovereignty of religion. Inside the temple in the main sanctum, on an altar, is a colossal image of the Buddha in a sitting posture touching the earth by his right hand. In this posture the Buddha is believed to have accomplished the supreme enlightenment. The statue is in black stone but guilded by the devotees. The entire courtyard of the temple is studded with a large number of varieties of stupas—votive, decorative and memorative. These stupas are of all sizes built during the past 2500 years. Most of them are extremely elegant in structural beauty.

VAJRASANA : Vajrasana, the seat of stability. The Buddha is supposed to have sat in meditation gazing east under the Bodhi tree where the Vajrasana, the stone platform, is kept.

THE ANCIENT RAILINGS : The ancient railings which surround the temples are of the first century BC and are very interesting monuments.

CHANKARAMANA : This marks the sacred spot of the Buddha's meditative perambulations during the third week after the pious enlightenment. It is believed that where the Buddha put his feet lotus had sprang up.

ANIMESHLOCHANA : It is believed that the Buddha spent one week here looking towards the great Mahabodhini Tree out of gratitude, without tinkling eyelids.

RATNAGAR : The Buddha is said to have spent one week here where, it is believed five colours had sprang out of his body.

LOTUS TANK : The sacred tank where it is believed the Buddha had spent a week.

HOW TO REACH

AIR : Nearest airport Patna (112 km)
RAIL : Nearest railhead Gaya (16 km)
ROAD : Bodhgaya is connected by road with Gaya, 16 km. to the Delhi-Calcutta highway junction (on Grand Trunk Road). The Bihar State Tourism Development Corporation operates daily deluxe coach service to and from Bodhgaya from its headquarters.

TOURIST INFORMATION OFFICE

Tourist Information Centre, Gaya Railway Station and at tourist mini market in Bodhgaya.

HOTEL ACCOMMODATION (STD CODE 0631)

— Hotel Bodhgaya Ashok, Bodhgaya
PH 400 790-91; FAX 400 788/89
— Hotel Siddharth Vihar and Hotel Buddha Vihar near temple,
PH 400 445.

RAJGIR

Rajgir is located in a verdant valley surrounded by rocky hills. An aerial ropeway provides the link with a hill top stupa "Peace Pagoda" built by the Japanese. On one of the hills is the cave of Saptaparni where the first Buddhist Council was held. Hot water springs here have curative properties and are sacred to the Hindus. Rajgir is 10 km south of Nalanda, sacred to the memory of the founder of both Buddhism and Jainism as the Buddha lived here in the sixth century BC. He used to meditate and preach on the "Hill of the Vultures". Mahavira was born here in 567 BC and  spent fourteen years. It was in Rajgriha that Lord Buddha delivered some of his famous sermons and had converted king Bimbisara 'of the Magadha empire and countless others to his creed. Once a great city, Rajgir is just a village today but vestiges of a legendary and historical past remain, like the cyclopean wall that encircles the town and the marks engraved in rock that local folklore ascribes to Lord Krishna's chariot. This legend like many others, associated Rajgir to that distinct time when the stirring events recorded in the epic Mahabharata were being enacted.

PLACES OF INTEREST

AMARAVANA OR JIVAKA'S MANGO GARDEN : Site of the Royal Physician's dispensary where Lord Buddha was once brought to have a wound dressed by Jivaka, the royal physician, during the reign of Ajatashatru and Bhimbisara.

VENUVANA : Site of the monastery Venuvana Vihar built by King Bimbisara for Lord Buddha to reside. This was the king's first offering to Lord Buddha.

AJATSHATRU'S FORT : Built by Ajatashatru (6th century BC), the king of Magadha during the Buddha's time, the 6.5 sq. metre stupa in it is also believed to have been built by him.

BIMBISARA'S JAIL : King Bimbisara was imprisoned here by his impatient son and heir, Ajatshatru. The captive king chose this site for his incarceration because from here he could see Lord Buddha climbing up to his mountain retreat atop the Griddakuta hill. One gets clear view of the Japanese Pagoda, stupa of peace, built on the top of the hill from here.

SWARNA BHANDAR : Two cave chambers were hollowed here out of a single massive rock one of which is believed to have been the guard room. The rear wall has two straight vertical lines and one horizontal line cut into the rock. Thus 'doorway' is supposed to be used by king Bimbisara. Treasury Inscriptions in the Sankhalipi or shell script, etched on the walls and so far undeciphered, are believed to give the clue to how to open the doorway. The treasure, according to folklore, is still intact. The second chamber bears a few traces of seated and standing guards into the outer wall.

THE CYCLOPEAN WALL : Once 40 km long, it encircled the ancient Rajgir. Built of massive undressed stone carefully fitted together, the wall is one of few important Mauryan stone structures ever to have been found. Traces of the wall still subsist, particularly at the exit of Rajgir to Gaya.

GRIDDAKUTA OR VULTURE'S PEAK : This was the place where Lord Buddha had put in motion his second wheel of law and for three months every year during the rainy season had preached many inspiring sermons to his disciples. The Buddha Sangha of Japan have constructed a massive modern stupa, the Shanti Stupa (Peace Pagoda), at the top of the hill in commemoration.

JAIN TEMPLES : On the hill crests around Rajgir, far in the distances one can see about 26 Jain temples. They are difficult to approach for the untrained, but make exciting trekking for those who can.

HOT SPRINGS : At the top of the Vaibhava hill, a staircase leads up to the various temples. Separated bathing places have been organised for men and women and the water comes through spouts from Saptdhara, the seven streams  believed to find their source behind the "Saptaparni Cave", up in the hills. The hottest of the spring is the Brahmakund with a temperature of 45^0C.

PIPPALA CAVE : Above the hot springs on the Vaibhava hill, is a rectangular stone sculpted by the forces of nature which appears to have been used as a watch tower. Since it later became the resort of pious hermits, it is also called Pippala cave and is popularly known as "Jarasandh Ki Baithak" after the name of the king Jarasandh, a contemporary of Lord Krishna described in the epic Mahabharata.

Other archaeological sites include the Karanada Tank where Lord Buddha used to bathe; the Maniyar Math that dates from 1st century AD; the Maraka Kukshi were the still unborn Ajatshatru was cursed for patricide; the Rannbhumi where Bhima and Jarasandh had fought a duel to the finish described in the Mahabharata.

HOW TO REACH

AIR : Nearest airport Patna (107 km)

RAIL : The nearest railhead on Delhi-Howrah main line is Bakhtiyarpur, 54 km which through the loop line connects Rajgir

ROAD : Rajgir is connected by road with Patna, Gaya, Delhi and Calcutta.

Bihar State Tourism Development Corporation organises trips for Rajgir, Nalanda etc. from its headquarters at Tourist Bhawan, Beer Chand Patel Marg, Patna, PH 225411/222622; FAX 236218

HOTEL ACCOMMODATION (STD CODE 061192)

There are a number of moderately priced hotels in the town. Tourist can stay at any of the three Tourist Bungalows of the BSTDC. PH 06119 5273 or 06119 53231

The Centaur Hokke Hotel, Nalanda, Rajgir, PH 06119 5245; FAX 06119 5231.

EXCURSIONS

SWARAJPUR-BARAGAON : (18 km) The lake with temple of Surya is a pilgrim destination twice a year in 'Vaisakha' and in 'Kartika' month during the Chhath Puja or Sun worship.

KUNDALPUR : (18 km) The Digambar sect of the Jains believe that Lord Mahavira was born at this place. A Jain temple and two lotus lakes—the Dirga Pushkarni and Pandava Pushkarni mark the spot.

PAWANPURI (35 km). It is a great pilgrimage centre of the Jains. Lord Mahavira the 24th Teerthankara, had delivered his last sermon here prior to his 'Mahaparinirvana' (death) and was cremated here. Jalamandir and Samosharan are two beautiful temples to be visited here.

BIHAR SHARIF : (25 km) This little town on the top of a craggy rock, attracts thousands of pilgrims of all religions who visit the tomb of Makhdum Shah Sharif-ud-din, a Muslim saint of 14th century. Bihar Sharif was once the capital of the Muslim governors of Bihar between the 13th and the 16th centuries when the city was an active cultural centre and an important seat of Muslim thought and learning.

NALANDA

Nalanda has a very ancient history. Lord Vardhamana Mahavira and Lord Buddha had frequently visited it in the 6th century BC. It is also supposed to be the birth place of Sariputra, one of the chief disciples of Lord Buddha.

Hieun Tsang, the Chinese traveller of the seventh century, says, that according to tradition the place owned its name to a Naga saint of the same name who resided in a tank here. But he thinks it more probable that Lord Buddha, in one of his previous births as Bodhistawa, became a king with his capital at this place and that his liberality won for him and his capital the name Nalanda or "Charity without intermission". The third theory about the name of the place is that it derived its name from 'Nalam' plus 'DO'. Nalam means lotus which is a symbol of knowledge and 'DO' means give. The place had many ponds full of

lotuses. The place subsequently came to be called Nalanda and later on Nalanda.

The University of Nalanda was founded in the 5th century BC by the Gupta emperors and recorded as the world's earliest university. There were thousands of students and teachers. The courses of study included scriptures of Buddhism (both mahanayana and Hinayana schools), Vedas, Hetu Vidya (Logic), Shabda Vaidya (grammer), Chikitsa Viadya (medicine), politics, philosophy etc. The University received royal patronage of the emperor Harshavardhana of Kannauj and also Pala kings. It was a great centre of learning and students from foreign countries were also attracted to this university. Nalanda acquired a celebrity spread all over the east as a centre of Buddhist theology and educational activities. Its importance as a monastic university continued until the end of the 12th century. The ruins extend over a large area and represent only a part of the extensive establishment.

PLACES OF INTEREST

THE NALANDA UNIVERSITY ARCHAEOLOGICAL COMPLEX : The total area of excavation is 14 hectares. All the edifices are of red brick and the gardens beautiful. The buildings are divided by a central walkway that goes south to north, the monasteries or 'Viharas' are to the east of this central alley and the temples of 'Chaiyas' to the west. The Vihara I is perhaps the most interesting one with its cells on two steps lead upto what must have been a dais for the gurus, the teachers, to address the students. A small chapel still retains a half-broken statue of Lord Buddha.

The enormous pyramidal mass of the temple No. 3 is impressive and from its top one commands a splendid view of the entire area. It is surrounded by smaller stupas, many of which are studded with small and big statues of Lord Buddha in various poses.

THE NALANDA ARCHAEOLOGICAL MUSEUM : Just opposite to the entrance to the ruins of the university, it has a small but beautiful collection of undamaged statues of Lord Buddha that were found during excavation in the area. Two enormous terracotta jars of the first century stand intact behind the museum in a shaded enclosure. The collection includes copper plates and stone inscriptions, coins, pottery and samples of burnt rice (12th century AD).

HOW TO REACH

AIR : Nearest airport Patna (93 km)

RAIL : The nearest railhead on Delhi-Howrah main line is Bakhtiyarpur, 38km., through the loop line connects Nalanda.

ROAD : Nalanda is connected by road to Patna, Rajgir, Gaya, Delhi and Calcutta

VAISHALI

Vaishali has a past that pre-dates recorded history. It is believed that the town derives its name from king Vishal whose heroic deeds are narrated in the Hindu epic Ramayana. However the history records that around the time Patliputra was the centre of political activity in the Gangetic plains, Vaishali became the centre of trade. Lying on the north bank of the Ganga it was the seat of the republic of Vajji. Vaihshali is credited with being India's first and the world's finest republic to have a duly elected assembly of representatives and an efficient administration in those ancient days.

Lord Buddha had visited Vaishali and announced his approaching 'Mahaparinirvana' (death). And a hundred years later the second Budddhist council was held here. According to one belief, the 24th Jain Tirthankar, Lord Mahavira was born at Vaishali. The Chinese travellers Fa-Hien and Hieun Tsang had also visited Vaishali in the early 5th and 7th century BC respectively and had written about the city in their memoirs.

PLACES OF INTEREST

ASHOKA PILLAR : The Lion Pillar at Kolhua, was built by Emperor Ashoka. It is made of a highly polished single piece of red sandstone, surrounded by a bell shaped capital, 18.3m.high. A life size figure of a lion is placed on top of the pillar. There is also a small tank known as Ramkund.

BAWAN POKHAR TEMPLE : Built during the Pala period it stands on the northern bank of a tank known as Bawan Pokhar and enshrines beautiful images of several Hindu gods.

BUDDHA STUPA I : The exterior of this stupa which is now in a dilapidated condition has a plain surface. One-eighth of the sacred ashes of Lord Buddha were enshrined here in a stone casket.

BUDDHA STUPA II : Excavations at this site in 1958 led to the discovery of another casket containing the ashes of Lord Buddha.

RAJA VILAS KA GARH : A huge mound with a circumference of about one kilometre and walls nearly 2 meter high with a 43 meter wide moot around them, is said to be the ancient parliament house. Over seven thousand representatives of the federal assembly used to gather here to legislate and discuss the problems in the pre-Christian era.

KUNDPUR (4 km) It is believed that the 24th Jain Tirthankar, Lord Mahavira was born here over 2550 years ago and had spent first 22 years of his life.

CORONATION TANK : Coronation tank, orginially called Abhishek Pushkarni, its water was believed to be sacred in the old days and all of Vaishali's elected representatives were anointed here before their swearing in ceremony.

HOW TO REACH

AIR : Nearest airpcrt Patna (56 km)
RAIL : Hajipur on the North-Eastern railway (35 km)
ROAD : Vishali is well-connected by road with Patna (56 km),
Muzzaffarpur (36 km) and Hajipur (35 km)

CHOTANAGPUR

Chotanagpur offers an ideal escape from the present-day civilisation. The Chotanagpur plateau is a region of great unevenness and consists of a succession of plateaus, hills and valleys. Most of the plateau has an elevation exceeding 1,000 feet. In the heart of Chotanagpur are two plateaus—Hazaribagh and Ranchi.

Anthropologists would make us believe that Chotanagpur region must have witnessed the transformation of Homo Erectus to Homo Sapiens. Their claim is based on the findings of hand axes and blades that are littered hare in the region of Pathalgarwa. The discovery of Harrappan pottery in Hazaribagh has further strengthened its claim to antiquity. Thirty different tribes of Bihar are spread over the Chotanagpur plateau.

HAZARIBAGH

Meaning a thousand gardens,Hazaribagh is a famous health hill resort situated at a height of 2,019 ft.above sea level.The Hazaribagh plateau has on its eastern margin, Parasnath—the highest hill in Bihar, rising to a height of 4,480 feet. According to Jain tradition, 23 out of 24 Tirthankaras (including Parsvanatha) are believed to have attained salvation on the Sammetasikhara of the Parasnath hills. Both the Swetambar and Digambar Jains have beautiful temples here on the hill. The Hazaribag lake in the vicinity is a beautiful site to visit. Hazaribagh Wildilfe Sanctuary nestles in the low hilly terrain. Hazaribagh perhaps holds more Sambhars than any other area of comparable size. The 111 km roads in the sanctuary take motorists to the remotest corners and to many towers, strategically located and offers excellent opportunities for viewing the wilds during the best months of October to April. The sanctuary is surrounded by habitations of tribals. Accommodation in the sanctuary is available at Tourist Bungalow and the Forest Rest House.

EXCURSIONS

TILAIYA DAM : (55 km) This dam, situated across Barakar river offers a breath-taking sight.

URWAN : Few kilometres from Tilaiya Dam is the Bihar State Tourism Development's tourist complex at Urwan where one can consider spending some time by the side of the dam enjoying boating and other water sports. Interested tourists can follow the main road and drive to Hari Har Dham at Bagodar which is famous for the 52 feet high Shiv Ling (Phallus) which took 30 years to complete and is believed to be the tallest in the world.

KONAR DAM : (51 km) There is another Dam—Konar at this site.

HOW TO REACH

AIR : Nearest airport Ranchi (93 km)

RAIL : Nearest railhead Ranchi on Howrah-Delhi route.

RANCHI

Once the summer capital of Bihar, Ranchi is well-known for its scenic beauty water falls barren rocks and hillocks. It has several industrial complexes. It is also an important place for the study of tribal ways of life and it offers an ideal opportunity to those interested in anthropology.

PLACES OF INTEREST

RANCHI HILL AND RANCHI LAKE : The landmark of Ranchi is a hill bearing a temple of Lord Shiva on the summit with a lake at its foot, known as Ranchi Lake. One can have a panoramic view of the town and the surroundings from the top of the hill.

TAGORE HILL : Rabindranath Tagore is believed to have written a part of his famous Gitanjali here. Ram Krishna Ashram is alos situated at the foot of the hill.

KANKEDAM AND JAGANNATH TEMPLE : Kankedam is a popular picnic spot few kilometers from the dam. About 10 km from Ranchi is the 17th century Jagannath Temple where the annual Rath Yatra is held in the month of June/July.

HOW TO REACH

AIR : Ranchi is connected by air with Patna, Calcutta and New Delhi.

RAIL : Ranchi is connected by direct trains with Gorakhpur, Howrah, Chennai and Bhubaneshwar.

ROAD : There are regular bus services from Ranchi to all important places of the state. BSTDC runs its daily coaches from Patna to Ranchi and back.

HOTEL ACCOMMODATION (STD CODE 0657)

— Hotel Yuvraj Palace (4 Star), Doranda
  PH 500 326/27; FAX 500 328
— Hotel Arya (3 Star) H.B. Road, Lalpur
  PH 204 000, 205 000; FAX 202 222
— Hotel Chinar (3 Star) Main Road
  PH 207 780, 304 327; FAX 202 451
— Hotel Yuvraj (2 Star) Doranda
  PH 300513, 300 513, 300 358

DELHI
AT A GLANCE

AREA : 1438 sq. km.
CAPITAL : Delhi.
LANGUAGES : Hindi, Punjabi and Urdu.

MUSEUMS : Delhi Museum, National Museum, National Children's Museum, Crafts Museum, Gandhi Smarak Sangrahalaya, Gandhi Smriti Museum, Nehru Memorial Museum, National Museum of Natural History, National Philatelic Museum, Rail Transport Museum, Red Fort Museum and International Dolls Museum.

AIRPORT : Indira Gandhi International Airport and Palam Airport.

Sprawling on the banks of the Yamuna river—Delhi, the Capital of India—combines in its folds the ancient with the modern. Amidst the fast spiralling skyscrapers, the remnants of a bygone time in the form of monuments stand as silent reminders to the region's ancient history.

HISTORY

History of Delhi dates back to the Mahabharata period and much earlier as this was the site of the ancient Indraprastha. The city of Delhi was founded in the 11th century by a Rajput chieftain of Tomara clan. Chauhans had obtained possession of the city from the Tomars. Prithvi Raj, the Chauhan ruler of Ajmer and Delhi made the city of Delhi famous by his heroic valour and romantic adventures. Delhi under Prithvi Raj and Kanauj under Jai Chand were the principal kingdoms of North India at that time.

The invasion of India by Muhammed Ghori was beaten back by Prithvi Raj in the first Battle of Taran in **1191 AD**. Next year Ghori came back to avenge his defeat and in the second Battle of Taran in **1192 AD**, the Rajput army was routed. Prithvi Raj was captured and put to death. Delhi thus passed into the hands of Muslim rulers for six centuries. Delhi was here after ruled by a series of Muslim dynasties, the Qutub Shahis Khiljis; Tughluqs; Sayyids and Lodis, each of whom built forts, tombs and palaces of different artistic styles.

After the 1857 the mutiny by Indian troops the British deposed the titular Emperor Bahadur Shah. They formally annexed Delhi in 1912 and transferred the capital of British India from Calcutta to Delhi. A New capital was designed by Edwin Lutyens and Herbert Baker, English architect.

New Delhi—a city of imposing dimensions was laid out by the side of the old city by the British Indian Government. Independent India has retained this historic capital.

PLACES OF INTEREST

QUTUB MINAR : The tallest stone tower in India was started by Qutb-ud-din Aibak as a memorial of victory and also as an accessory to the adjoining mosque to call the faithful to prayers. The minar is taping tower of five tiers 72.5 metres high. The attached Quwwat-ul-Islam Mosque was erected pulling down 27 Hindu and Jain temples and using their columns. The iron pillar originally a standard of Lord Vishnu, is now in the courtyard of the mosque.

TUGHLUQABAD : Ghyyas-ud-din Tughluq's Delhi (14th century AD), it is noted for remains of some palaces and his tomb.

SHAMSI TALAB AND JAHAZ MAHAL : Site of an important festival, the water reservoir and the Chhatri were built in 1230 AD.

HAUZ KHAS AND DEER PARK : Feroz Shah's tomb is located here. The water reservoir built by Allauddin Khilji, after which the place is named, no longer exists.

SAFDARJUNG'S TOMB : Built in the 18th century AD by Nawab Shuja-ud-Daulah (1753-54 AD) it is a fine example of later Mughal architecture.

RASHTRAPATI BHAWAN : Standing on Raisina Hill, it was built by the British as the residence of the Viceroy of India and now is the official residence of the President of India. This massive building is surrounded by 330 acre of land.

INDIA GATE : The 42-meter high arch was raised as a memorial to soldiers who laid their lives in the Second World War. It is now a monument to the unknown soldier.

JANTAR MANTAR : The unique observatory with masonry instruments was designed by astronomer king—Sawai Jai Singh of Jaipur in 1724 AD.

LAKSHMI NARAYAN TEMPLE : Built in the Orissan style, the temple is a fine example of modern Indian temple architecture.

RED FORT : Built with red sand stone by the great Mughal

- Centaur Hotel : (5 Star Deluxe), Indira Gandhi International Airport. PH 3296660, 5452233; FAX 565 2256
- Hyatt Regency : (5 Star Deluxe) Bhikaji Cama Place, M.G.Marg. PH 6181234; FAX 6186633, 6196437
- Le Meridien : (5 Star Deluxe) 8 Windsor Place, Janapath. PH 3710101; FAX 3714545
- New Delhi Hilton : (5 Star Deluxe) Barakhamba Avenue, Connaught Place. PH 332 0101; FAX 3325335, 3316163
- The Oberoi : (5 Star Deluxe) Dr. Zakir Hussain Marg. PH 4363030; FAX 4360484
- Best Western Surya Hotel : (5 Star Deluxe) New Friend's Colony. PH 6835070 FAX : 6835070
- The Taj Mahal Hotel : (5 Star Deluxe) No. 1 Mansingh Road. PH 6110202; FAX 3017299
- Taj Palace Hotel : (5 Star Deluxe) Sardar Patel Marg, Diplomatic Enclave. PH 6110202; FAX 6884848, 6110808
- Hotel Vasant Continental : (5 Star Deluxe) Vasant Vihar. PH 6148800; FAX 6148900, 6145959
- Welcomegroup Maurya Sheraton : Diplomatic Enclave. PH 6112233; FAX 6113333
- The Claridges : (5 Star) 12, Aurangzeb Road. PH 3010211; FAX 3010625
- Hotel Imperial : (5 Star) Janapath. PH 3341234, FAX 3342255, 3368141
- The Park : (5 Star) 15, Parliament Street. PH 373373; FAX 3732025
- Royal Park : (5 Star) Nehru Place. PH 6223344; FAX 6224288
- Qutub : (5 Star) Shaheed Jeet Singh Marg. PH 6521234; FAX 6960828
- Hotel Samrat : (5 Star) 20-B, Chanakyapuri. PH 6110606; FAX 6887047
- Hotel Siddharth : (5 Star) 3, Rajendra Place. PH 5712501; FAX 5781016
- The Ambassador Hotel : (4 Star) Sujan Singh Park. PH 4632600; FAX 5632252, 4638219
- The Connaught : (4 Star) 37, Shahid Bhagat Singh Marg. PH 3364225; FAX 3340757
- Hotel Hans Plaza : (4 Star) 15, Barakhamba Road. PH 3316868, FAX 3314830
- Hotel Diplomat : (4 Star) 9, Sardar Patel Marg. PH 3010204; FAX 3018605

— Hotel Janapath : (4 Star) Janapath.
  PH 3340070; FAX 3347083, 3368618
— Hotel Kanishka : (4 Star) 19, Ashok Road.
  PH 3344422; FAX 3368242
— Hotel Marina : (4 Star) G-59, Connaught Circus.
  PH 3324658; FAX 3328609
— Narula's Hotel : (4 Star) L-Block Connaught Circus.
  PH 3322419; FAX 3324669
— Hotel Oberoi Maidens : (4 Star) 7, Sham Nath Marg.
  PH 2525464; FAX 2915134
— Hotel Rajdoot Pvt. Ltd (4 Star) Mathura Road.
  PH 4699583; FAX 4647442
— Hotel Broadway (4 Star) 4/5A Asaf Ali Road.
  PH 3273821; FAX 3269966
— Lodhi Hotel : (3 Star) Lala Lajpat Rai Marg.
  PH 4362422; FAX 4360883
— HotelRanjit : (3 Star) Maharaja Ranjit Singh Road.
  PH 3231256; FAX 3233166
— Hotel Vikram : (3 Star) Ring Road, Lajpat Nagar.
  PH 6432422; FAX 6435657
— York Hotel : (3 Star) K-10, Connaught Circus.
  PH 3323769; FAX 33252419
— Hotel Flora : (2 Star) Dayanand Road, Daryaganj.
  PH 3273634; FAX 3280887
— Hotel Oasis : (2 Star) HD-8, Pitam Pura.
  PH 7246869; FAX 7434665
— YMCA Tourist Hostel : (2 Star) Jai Singh Road.
  PH 3746667; FAX 3746032
  Hotel Fifty Five : (1 Star)H55 Connaught Circus.
  PH 3321244; FAX 3320769
— Hotel Inn : (1 Star) F-33, Connaught Circus.
  PH 3310431; FAX 3313628
— Ashok Yatri Niwas : 19 Ashok Road,
  PH 3344511; FAX 3368153
— Centre Point : 13 K.G.Marg. PH 3326715; FAX 3329138
— Hotel Jukaso Down Town : L-1, Connaught Circus.
  PH 3324451; FAX 3324448
— India International Centre : Lodhi Estate. Ph 4619431
— YWCA : Ashok Road. PH 3360133
— YMCA Tourist Hostel : Jai Singh Road. PH 3361847

— MANALI/CHANDIGARH (5 Nights / 6 Days)
  Delhi/Bilaspur/Manali/Chandigarh and back to Delhi
— SHIMLA/MANALI/DHARAMSHALA/DALHOUSIE
  (8 Nights / 9Days)
  Delhi/Shimla/Manali/Rohtang pass/Snow Point/Manali/
  palampur/Dharamshala/Dalhousie and back to Delhi
— VAISHNODEVI (3 Nights / 4 Days)
  Delhi/Jammu/Katra/Bhawan and back to Delhi
— MUSSOORIE/RISHIKESH/HARIDWAR (3 Nights / 4 Days)
  Delhi / Mussoorie/ Kempty falls / Dhanolti/ Rishikesh /
  Haridwar and back to Delhi

TOURS TO PILGRIMAGE SITES

— BADRINATH (4 Nights / 5 Days)
  Delhi/Rishikesh/Srinagar/Badrinath/Srinagar/Haridwar and
  back to Delhi.
— KEDARNATH/BADRINATH (7 Nights / 8 days)
— Delhi/Haridwar/Rishikesh/Gaurikund/Kedarnath/Nandprayag/
  Pipalkoti /Badrinath and back to Delhi.
— CHARDHAM YATRA (13 Nights/14 Days)
  Delhi/Rishikesh/Barkot/syani Chatti/Yamunotri/Janki Bal
  Chatti/Hanuman Chatti/Uttarkashi/Gangotri/Gaurikund/
  Kedarnath/Nandpyrayag/Piplkoti/Badrinath/Haridwar and back
  to Delhi.
— YAMUNOTRI/GANGOTRI (7 Nights / 8 Days)
  Delhi/Rishikesh/Barkot/Syani Chatti/Hanuman Chatti/
  Yamunotri/Janki Bai Chatti / Uttarkashi/Gangotri/Rishikesh/
  Haridwar and back to Delhi.

For further details contact :
— Delhi Tourism and Transportation Development Corporation
  Ltd., Central Reservation Office, Coffee Home 1, Baba
  Kharaksingh Marg (Opp Hanuman temple), New Delhi 110001.
  PH 3365358/3363607; FAX 3367322

FESTIVALS

All Festivals of all religions are celebrated in Delhi so much so
that some tourism festivals have become regular annual events. Delhi
Tourism Development Corporation organizes International Kite festival—
flying festival, Roshnara festival, Shalimar festival, Qutub festival,
Winter Carnival, Garden Tourism and Mango festival every year.

GOA

Raghuvir Shah

1541 and rebuilt in 1619); **JAMA MASJID** (built in mid 18th century); **MAHALAXMI TEMPLE** are some other places of interest.

On the eastern promontory, beyond the hill, is the **ST.THOME** quarter with its traditional 18th and19th century houses. Other places of interest are **MINT** and **SEBASTIAN CHAPEL**.

MIRAMAR, DONA PAULA and **VAINGUINIM** are three beaches near Panaji.

OLD GOA – VELHA GOA
(SPIRITUAL HEART OF PORTUGUESE GOA)

PLACES OF INTEREST

Old Goa has a melancholy beauty, a city of Baroque churches, now revived by a steady flow of tourists and the great pilgrimage to the tomb of ST.FRANCIS XAVIER in the magnificent Cathedral of BOM JESUS. The road to Old Goa from Panaji passes over the causeway built by the then Viceroy. At the end of the causeway is the attractive preserved village of 'RIBANDAR' or 'ROYAL HARBOUR', possibly named after the arrival of the Vijaynagar King in the 14th century AD. The old houses along the road still conjure up an image of the 17th century Goa. Old Goa owes its origin as Portuguese capital to Alfonso de Albuquerque, and some of its early ecclesiastical development to St.Francis Xavier who was here in the mid 16th century. Before the Portuguese arrival, it was the second capital of the Bijapur kingdom.

CHURCH OF OUR LADY OF HELP : Originally built in 1565 AD it gives thanks to the safe arrival of a Portuguese vessel after a fierce storm at the sea.

The HOLY HILL has number of churches. The CHAPEL OF OUR LADY OF THE ROSARY (1526) belongs to the earliest period of church building, the architectural style that evolved borrowed from Iberian decoration, but also included many local naturalistic motifs as well as Islamic elements, seen on marble cenotaph owing to the Hindu and Muslim craftsmen employed. The church here has a two storey entrance, a single tower and low flanking turrets. Behind it is the ROYAL CHAPEL OF ST ANTHONY (1543), the national saint of Portugal and TOWER OF AUGUSTINE. Further on it is the CONVENT OF ST MONICA and CHURCH AND CONVENT OF ST JOHN OF GOD. The other places of interest are HOUSE FOR JESUIT

FATHER, MODERN ART GALLERY, the St. CATHERINE (the largest church in old Goa built by the Dominicans between 1562-1623 AD in a Tuscan style), PALACE OF INQUISITION, the CHURCH AND CONVENT OF ASSIS, ARCHAEOLOGICAL MUSEUM, the VICEROY' S ARCH, CHURCH OF ST CAJETAN and GATE OF THE FORTRESS OF THE ADIL SHAH.

THE BASILICA OF BOM JESUS (1594) : The world-renowned church contains the body of St.Francis Xavier, a former pupil of soldier –turned –saint, Ignatius Loyola, the founder of the Order of Jesuits. St. Francis Xavier remains the principal spiritual treasure of the territory. The Jesuits began work on their own church in 1594. By 1605 it was finished and consecrated. In 1613 the body of St.Francis was brought there from the Clooege of ST Paul. It was moved into the church in 1624 and its present chapel in 1655 where it has remained ever since. St Francis was canonized by Pope Gregory XV in 1622 and in 1964 Pope Pius XIIraised the church to a minor basilica. The Order of Jesuits was suppressed in 1759 and its property confiscated by the State. The church was, however allowed to continue services.

MAPUSA

Mapusa stands on a long ridge which runs east-west, fertile agricultural land occupying the flat valley floor right up to the edge of the town. Mapusa is known for beautiful gardens and houses. Main places of interest are ST JEROME'S CHRUCH, CHURCH OF OUR LADY OF MIRACLES. MARKET on FRIDAY is interesting to wander around and observe local activity. Plenty of buses ply between Panaji to Mapusa covering a distance of 13km.

NORTH GOA

Goa beaches are among the best in the world. CALANGUTE and CANDOLIM are the two beaches at a distance of the 15km from Panaji. Once Calangute was the paradise of the Hippies. BAGA beach is 2km north of Calangute and is a favourite tourist spot.

FORT AGUADA : The Fort, built in 1612, at a distance of 19km from Panaji at the mouth of Mandovi river had the first lighthouse in Asia equipped with a room for ammunition, barracks and a church. It was a place of strength and power. It houses a jail today. Agua means water in Portuguese. It is said that once this place had seven fountains and the ships used to halt here for collecting sweet water.

CHHAPORA : Chhapora beach is shaded with beautiful coconut tree groves.Three kilometer north is VAGATOR BEACH. ANJUNA BEACH is on the north of the Baga. Every Wednesday sellers sell numerous old and new items of both foreign and domestic origin in the FLEA MARKET at Anjuna beach. ARAMBOL is the latest sea beach, it is three hours journey from Mapusa. MOYEM LAKE is located 32km from Panaji amidst hills.

SOUTH GOA

PONDA : Ponda is surrounded by hills on all sides ad has many Hindu temples.

MANGESH TEMPLE : The 400-year-old Mangeshi temple is the most famous temple. A unique feature of this temple is multi-storied lamp tower. The famous singer, Lata Mangeshkar's ancestral home is located in this Mangesh village.

Apart from Mnagesh temple, the other temples are Shri Shanta Durga, Shri Ramnath, Shri Mahalsa, Shri Gopal Ganapati, Shri Nagesh, Shri Saptakoteshwara and Shri Mahalakshmi. All these temples escaped the fury of the Portuguese who destroyed all other temples at Bardez.

MADGAON OR MARGAON

Madgaon is the commercial capital of Goa, capital of the Salcete province. It is well connected by rail and road.Madgaon is famous for its well maintained gardens and beautiful houses.The houses are built on Latin American pattern and look-wise resemble Mexico. The king of the beaches the COLVA BEACH is loacted at a distance of 6 km from Madgaon (40 km from Panaji).BENAULIM BEACH is 2 km south of Colva. Other important beaches are VARCA BEACH and BETUL BEACH

VASCO Da GAMA

Vasco is 31 km from Panaji. The only airport of Goa is located at the fringe of the Vasco city. Frequent buses are available from Panaji to Vasco.

TEREKHOL FORT

Terekhol Fort is on the north west side of Goa situated within the green and hilly valley in between Terekhol river and Arabian Sea. The fort was built by the Marathas at the beginning of the

18th century later on but was captured by the Portuguese in 1745. In 1794, for a brief spell, it was occupied by the Marathas.In 1825, the people revolted against the then Goanese Governor General D Barnado Peres De Silver, but the revolt was a short lived one. Then again in 1954, the freedom struggle gained momentum in Terekhol. They were joined by the foot march column protesters from all over India. Its leadership was given by Shri Tridib Chowdhury of Bengal. The death of the Satyagrahis in 1955 hastened the independance. The Therekhol Fort is the mute spectator of this independence struggle. Regular buses ply from Panaji

DUDHSAGAR WATERFALL

The waterfall is 10 km from Kolem railway station, 60kms east of Panaji. It falls from a height of 603 meters. The colour of the water is milky white thus named Dudhsagr or ocean of milk.

MAHABIR WILDLIFE SANCTUARY : It is the biggest sanctuary of Goa and is spread over 240 sq. km of forest land and is a heaven for bird watchers.

BONDLA WILDLIFE SANCTUARY : 55 km from Panaji, this sanctuary is located at a height of about 3000 feet on the slopes of the western hilly range. There is a natural botanical garden where a deer sanctuary and a zoo have been established. Rangado river flows on to the east of this forest and Madhel on its north. Bondla forest nests bison, wild beer, deer, leopard, varoius types of serpents and birds. On to its way, the only mosque Safa Shahouri Masjid built by Ali Adilshah in 1560 can be seen at Ponda.

HOW TO REACH

AIR : Goa is connected by air with Bangalore, Chennai, Cochin, Delhi, Mumbai, Pune and Thiruvananthapuram.

Goa is also connected by Chartered flights with various countries such as U.K., Switzerland, Germany, Belgium and Netherlands.

RAIL : Goa is connected conveniently by Konkan Railway with major cities of Maharashtra, Karnataka and Kerala through coastal route.

ROAD : Goa is connected by road with Maharashtra and Karnataka. There are regular luxury and regular bus services to Mumbai, Pune, Kolhapur, Miraj, Bangalore, Mangalore, Hubli, Belgaum, Mysore and many other places.

DISTANCES FROM PANAJI

Aurangabad 699 km; Ahmedabad 1138 km; Hyderabad 757 km; Trivandrum 1046 km; Kolhapur 229 km; Satara 363 km; Mumbai 594 km; Pune 473 km; Karwar 103 km; Mangalore 371 km; Hospet 314 km; Londa 106 km; Hubli 184 km and Mangalore 592 km.

CONDUCTED TOURS

TOURS OPERATED BY THE GOA TOURISM DEVELOPMENT CORPORATION
— North Goa Tour (9.30 AM to 6 PM) Ex - Panaji
— South Goa Tour (9.30 AM to 6 PM) Ex - Panaji
— Village Darshan Tour (10.00 AM to 4 PM) Ex - Panaji
— North Goa Darshan (9.30 AM to 6 PM) Ex – Margaon/ Colva/Vasco
— North Goa Tour (9.30 AM to 6 PM) Ex – Mapusa/Calangute
— South Goa Tour (8.30 AM to 8 PM) Ex – Mapusa/Calangute
— Traditional Tour (9.30 AM to 6 PM) Ex – Margao/Colva/ Vasco
— Dudhsagar Special (10 AM to 6 PM) Ex – Panaji
— Tiracol Fort Special (10 AM to 6 PM) Ex – Panaji/Mapusa
— Beach Special (3 AM to 7 PM) Ex – Panaji/Calangute

PACKAGE TOURS

— Saptalokeshwar Special Tour (5 Nights / 6 Days)
— Goa Beach Special (5 Nights / 6 Days)
— Traditional North/South Goa (3 Nights / 4 Days)

RIVER CRUISES organised by GTDC

— Sunset Cruise – Dep 6 PM (one hour)
— Sundown Cruise – Dep 7.15 PM (one hour)
— Full Moon Cruise / Special Cruise Dep 8.30 PM /Arr 10.30PM

For Further Details Contact
— Goa Tourism Development Corporation, Trionora Apartments, DR. Alvares Costa Rd., Panaji, Goa 403 001 PH 0832 226515, 226728, 224132; FAX 0832 223926

HOTEL ACCOMMODATION

— Cidade De Goa Beach Resort : (5 Star Deluxe) Vainguinim Beach, Goa-403 004. PH 0832 221133; FAX 0832 223303

— Fort Aguada Beach Resort : (5 Star Deluxe) Sinquwrim Bardez, Goa-403 591.
PH 0832 276201/10; FAX 0832 276045/277410
— Four Seasons Leela Beach (5 Star Deluxe) Mobor, Cavelossim, Goa-403 731. PH 0834 746352
— Goa Renaissance Resort : (5 Star Deluxe) Colva Beach, Varca Village, Salcette.
PH 0834 745208-13; FAX 0834 745225
— Holiday Inn Resort; (5 Star) Cavelossim, Mobor Beach, Salcete, Goa-403 731.
PH 0834 746303–09; FAX 0834 746333
— Sarovar Park Plaza Resort : (5 Star) P.O. Bogmalo, Goa-403806. PH 0834 513291; FAX 0834 512510
— Hotel La Paz Garden : (3 Star) Swantantra Path, Vaso da Gama, Goa. PH 0834 51212-26; FAX 0834 513302
— Hotel Mondovi : (3 Star) P.B.No 164, D.B. Bandodkar Marg, Panaji, Goa-403 001.
PH 0832 226270–73; FAX 0832 225451
— Nanu Resort : (3 Star) Betalbatim Beach, Goa-403 713.
PH 0834 733029, 734950-53; FAX 0834 734428, 737919
— Hotel Nova Goa : (3 Star) Dr.Atmaram Borkar Road, Goa-403 001. PH 0832 226231-7; FAX 0832 224958
— Hotel Prainha : (2 Star) Dona Paula, Goa-403 004.
PH 0832 334162, 225917; FAX 229959
— Ronil Beach Resort L (2 Star) Baga-Calangute Beach, Goa-403 516. PH 0832 276009, 276101; FAX 0832 296068
— Hotel Delmon : (1 Star) Caetano De Albuquerque Road, Panaji. PH 0832 225616, 226846; FAX 0832 223527

FESTIVALS

JANUARY : Reis Magos Zatra to celebrate the Feast of the three kings on January 6 to commemorate the visit to infant Christ.

FEB/MARCH : The Carnival is a joyous 3-day festival celebrated all over Goa. There is a lot of music and dancin and masquerades and processions are led by the legendary king Momo

APRIL : The Lairai Jatra in April where the highlight is the fire-walking spectacle in the early morning.

OCT/NOV : Diwali is celebrated by the Hindus.

Jatras or temple processions are held in various parts of the year at the temples of Sri Shanta Durga – Ponda (JAN); Shri Hanuman – Panaji (JAN); Shri Mangeshi – Ponda (JAN/FEB)

Mardol (FEB); also the Narve Jatra, Bichlim (SEPT); Dindi at Margaon (SEPT); Nageshi Jatra (NOV); Shri Datta Jayanti (DEC).

DECEMBER : Feast of St.Francis Xavier, Old Goa; X'Mas all over Goa.

The most famous celebration of Goa is the exposition of Saint Francis Xavier's relics once in ten years.

GUJARAT

GUJARAT
AT A GLANCE

AREA : 1,96,024 Sq.km
CAPITAL : Gandhinagar
BOUNDARIES : East - Madhya
Pradesh; West - Arabian Sea; North and
North East - Rajasthan; South -
Maharashtra.
LANGUAGE : Gujarati
ROADS : The State has approximately
72,165 km of roads.The finest expressway
of the nation is under construction
between Ahmedabad and Vadodara.

AIRPORTS : Ahmedabad, Baroda, Jamnagar Bhuj, Keshod,
Rajkot, Kandla, Bhavnagar and Surat.

IMPORTANT MUSEUMS

Ahmedabad : Gandhi Memorial Museum - Sabarmati Ashram;
Calico Museum of Textiles; Shreyas Folk Museum; Tribal Research
and Training Institute Museum – Gujarat Vidyapith; Vechaar Utensil
Museum; N.C.Mehta Collection of Rare Miniatures.

Baroda : Maharaja Fatehsingh Museum – Laxmi Vilas Palace;
Museum and Picture Gallery; Archaeological Museum – Sayajirao
University

Somnath : Somnath Temple Museum (46 km. from Gir)

IMPORTANT HILL RESORT

Saputara (873 m) Railhead – Nasik 82 km.

PILGRIM CENTRES (A : Air; R : Rail)

Ambaji : Dedicated to Durga, Goddess of Shakti ; A - Ahmedabad
200 km, R - Palanpur 40 km.

Bahucharaji : A shrine of the Mother Goddess; A - Ahmedabad
111km, R – Mehsana 32 km.

Balaram : Shrine of Balaram Mahadev; A – Ahmedabad 160 km,
R – Palanpur 17 km.

Dakor : The original image of Lord Krishna from Dwarka is here;
A - Vadodara 80 km, R - Dakor.

Dwarka : One of the four main Hindu dhamas (pilgrimage centers), was the seat of the Kingdom of Lord Krishna during the Mahabharata; A-Jamnagar 145 km, R - Dwaraka

Junagarh : On Girnar hill are the marble shrines sacred to Jains; A - Keshod 36 km, R-Junagarh.

Khumbariya : Important Jain pilgrim centre; A - Ahmedabad 198 km, R - Palanpur 65 km.

Mahudi : Jain Centre, A - Ahmedabad 73 km; R - Mehsana 44 km.

Miradatar : Important Muslim pilgrim centre; A - Ahmedabad 98 km; R - Mehsana 20 km.

Palitana : There are 863 Jain temples on Shatrunjaya hill; A - Bhavnagar 62 km, R - Palitana.

Pavagadh : Temple of Mahakali on hilltop. Noted for Pavagadh fair; A and R - Vadodara 51km.

Shamlaji : One of the principal Vaishnav shrines of Gujarat; A - Ahmedabad 126 km, R - Himmatgarh 48 km.

Somnath : One of the 12 Jyortirling shrines. Nearby are Bhalka Tirth and Dehotsarga believed to be the place where Lord Krishna ended his earthly existence and body; A - Keshod 47 km, R - Veraval 5 km.

Taranga Hill : Important Jain pilgrim centre; A - Ahmedabad 138 km, R - Mehsana 60 km

Udwada : The holy flame brought by the Parsis from Persia in the 8th century AD still burns here; A - Mumbai 213 km, R - Daman 20 km and Udwada.

Virpur : Jalaram Temple, A and R - Rajkot 54 km.

The State of Gujarat occupies the northern extremity of the western sea-board of India. The State is renowned for its beaches, holy temples, historic cities replete with immense architectural wealth and wildlife sanctuaries. The fascinating handicrafts, mouth-watering cuisine and colourful lifestyle of the people of Gujarat, are renowned all over the country. The hardwork and civilised approach of the people of Gujarat are evident in every walk of life.

HISTORY

Over a long period, Gujarat has been the abode of a number of races—settlers as well as conqueres—and amalgamated their cultures into its very own. It is believed that Lord Krishna had left Mathura to settle on the west coast of Saurashtra, which later came to be known as Dwarka, the gateway. Being a coastal State, Gujarat has had contacts with the Western trading world since Greco - Roman times. In fact, in Lothal a civilization dating back to 3000 BC has been excavated which bears testimony of the State. Later the Aryans from Central Asia found it a good entry point. It saw various kingdoms— Mauryans, Guptas Pratiharas and others. It was with Chalukyas (Solanki) that Gujarat witnessed progress and prosperity.After the golden age of Gupta's, Gujarat successively came under the Rajput kings, the Muslim Sultans, the Mughals and finally under the British Raj, which however, excluded Saurashtra and its 202 princely States.

Before Independence, the present territories of Gujarat used to be in two parts—the British and the princely territories. With the recognition of the State, the Union of the State of Saurastra and the Union Territory of Kutch along with the former British Gujarat, became a part of the bilingual State of Bombay. The present state of Gujarat came into being on May 1, 1960.

AHMEDABAD

Founded in 1411AD by Ahmed Shah, Ahmedabad was at one time considered to be India's finest city. Associated with Mahatama Gandhi, the Apostle of peace and non-violence, whose simple Ashram on the banks of the Sabarmati river is now a site of national pilgrimage.

Renowned as a great textile and commercial centre and as 'MANCHESTER OF INDIA' today it is the second largest prosperous and thriving city in western India.

PLACES OF INTEREST

JUMMA MASJID : Built in 1423 AD by Sultan Ahmed Shah's slave—Siddi Sayed, it is a magnificent structure with 15 domes supported on 260 pillars and has some excellent examples of filigree work. Two minarets are so designed that if one is shaken, the other trembles as well.

SIDDI SAYED MOSQUE : This also built in honour by Sidi Sayyed is example of the finest filigree work in stone.

BHADRA FORT OR WALLED CITY : Spread over 45 acres its construction was started in 1411 AD. It houses the Bhadrakali temple which was built by the Marathas when they captured it. Within the fort numerous havelis—traditional mansions of Gujaratis—line the alleys and squares, their ornate, carved woodwork forming an almost antique facade. The Tran Darwaza, a trite arched gateway was originally meant for use only by royalty. It is one of the dozen arched gateways providing access to Bhadra Fort.

HATHEESINGH JAIN TEMPLE : Built outside Delhi Gate in 1850 AD by a rich Jain merchant, the Hatheesingh temple is the best known of Ahmedabad's many ornate Jain temples. Built of pure white marble and embellished with intricate and elaborate carvings,the temple is dedicated to the 15th Jain apostle—Dharamanath. The temple is said to have derived its architectural inspiration from famous Dilwara temple of Mount Abu.

RANI RUPMATI MOSQUE : The Queen's Mosque in Mirzapur, built between 1430 and 1440 AD, is more representative of the pattern of mosque building in 15th century. Three domes stand on twelve pillars each, with the central part so raised as to let in natural light without direct sunshine.

KANKARIA LAKE : A man-made lake constructed by Sultan Qutab-ud-din almost 500 years ago is still a popular recreational spot. Originally called Houj-e-Qutab, the lake is surrounded by artistically landscaped gardens and terraced slopes.

GANDHI ASHRAM, SABARMATI : Mahatama Gandhi set up his first Ashram here in 1915. It was the nerve centre of India's freedom movement. He had begun his famous Dandi March from here in 1930 AD. It is now a national monument and preserved as it was in Gandhi's life-time. The Gandhi Memorial Centre, Liabrary and a son-et-lumiere show gives a glimpse of the life and work of Gandhiji.

THE SHAKING MINARETS : The shaking minarets of Sidi Bashir's Mosque are unique in that when one is shaken, the other vibrates too in sympathy. An architectural marvel, this mysterious provision was made for protection against earthquakes.

THREE GATES : The triple-arched gateway was built by Sultan Ahmed Shah to serve as the royal entrance to the Maidan Shah or the Royal Square.

CALICO TEXTILE MUSEUM : Appropriately for a city that owes its prosperity to three threads "Cotton, Silk and Gold". Ahmedabad has one of the finest textile museums in the world. Housed in one of the Gujarat's famous carved-wooden havelis, the museum displays a magnificent collection of rare textiles that dates back to 17th century. There is also an excellent reference library on textiles.

HOW TO REACH

AIR : Ahmedabad is connected by air with Mumbai, Bhuj, Chennai, Delhi, Rajkot, Vadodara and Bangalore.

RAIL : Ahmedabad is connected directly by rail with all major cities.

Ahmedabad is connected by Shatabdi Express with Mumbai, the timings are as follows :

— 2009 Mumbai D 0625 Hrs / Ahmedabad A 1312 Hrs (Except Friday).
— 2010 Ahmedabad D 1445 Hrs / Mumbai A 2145 Hrs (Except Friday).
— Ahmedabad/New Delhi Swarna Jayanti Rajdhani Express.
— 2958 (Tuesday, Thursday and Saturday) New Delhi D 1440 Hrs / Ahmedabad A 0545 Hrs.
— Rt Ahmedabad D 1710 Hrs / New Delhi A 0750 Hrs.

ROAD : Ahmedabad is connected by road with all major cities. Regular bus services are available from Mumbai, Indore, Mt.Abu and all centres in Gujarat. All types of tourist vehicles are easily available.

DISTANCES FROM AHMEDABAD

Lothal 76 km; Dakor 92 km; Vadodara 113km; Surat 255 km; Vapi 364 km; Daman 376 km; Mumbai 510 km; Nal Sarovar 64 km; Rajkot 216 km; Jamnagar 302 km; Junagarh 315 km; Porbundar 412 km Somnath 404 km; Sasangir 442 km; Bhavnagar 207 km; Palitana 215 km; Kandla 350 km Dwarka 450 km; Mehsana 76 km; Medhora 106 km; Ambaji 177 km; Abu Road 200 km; Udaipur 251 km; Diu 438 km; Indore 407 km; Bhopal 571 km; Delhi 886 km and Calcutta 2006 km.

CONDUCTED TOURS

Tours Operated by Gujarat Tourism :
Half-day city tour

SAURASHTRA DARSHAN TOUR (FIVE DAYS)

ITINERARY

DAY 1 : Ahmedabad - Dwarka enroute visit Rajkot and, Jamnagar - night stay at Dwarka Tourist Bungalow.

DAY 2 : Dwarka - Porbander enroute visit Bet - Dwarka, Dwarka, Harshad Mata and Porbander - night stay at Toram Tourist Bungalow, Porbander.

DAY 3 : Porbander - Junagarh enroute visit Somnath, Sasan Gir - night stay at Hotel Junagarh.

DAY 4 : Junagarh - Palitana enroute visit Junagarh, Virpur, Palitana - night stay at Hotel Sumeru.

DAY 5 : Palitana - Ahmedabad enroute visit Jain temple atop Shatrunjaya Hills Lothal and back to Ahmedabad.

The tour leaves Ahmedabad every Friday at 6 a.m. and returns by 8.80 p.m. on Tuesday.

NORTH GUJARAT AND RAJASTHAN TOUR (FIVE DAYS)

ITINERARY

DAY 1 : Ahmedabad - Udaipur enroute visit Shamlaji, Kesariaji, night stay at Udaipur.

DAY 2 : Udaipur - visit Chittorgarh and return to Udaipur for night stay.

DAY 3 : Udaipur - Mount Abu enroute visit Haldighati, Nathadwara, Charbhuja, Ranakpur night stay at Mt.Abu.

DAY 4 : Mt Abu and the adjoining places, night stay at Mt. Abu.

DAY 5 : Mt.Abu - Back to Ahmedabad enroute visit Ambaji, Kumbharia, Modhera, Bahucharaji.

The Tour leaves Ahmedabad on 2nd and 4th Saturday at 6 a.m. and returns at 8.00 p.m. on the following Wednesday.

KUTCH TOUR 5 DAYS

ITINERARY

DAY 1 : Ahmedabad - Bhuj enroute visit Morvi. Night stay at Bhuj.

DAY 2 : Full day visit Anjar, Bhadreshwar, Mandvi and Kera. Night stay at Bhuj.

DAY 3 : Full day visit mata-no- Madh, Narayan sarovar and Koteshwar - night stay at Bhuj.

DAY 4 : Full day visit Bhirandiyara, Khavda, Hodko and Dhordo - night stay at Bhuj.

DAY 5 : Local sightseeing and return to Ahmedabad.

The Tour leaves Ahmedabad on 2nd and 4th Saturday at 6 a.m. and returns at 8 p.m. on the following Wednesday.

For detailed information contact :

— GUJARAT TOURISM, Nigam Bhawan, Sector 16, Gandhinagar, PH 225 23, 226 45; FAX 221 89

Or H.K.House, Opp Bata Showroom, Ashram Road PH 6589172, 658217; FAX 6582183

ON THE TRAIL OF THE MAHATAMA

"Generations to come, it may be, will scarce believe that such a one as this ever in flesh and blood, walked upon the earth".

—ALBERT EINSTEIN

Mohandas was the name given to the youngest child of Karamchand and Putlibai Gandhi, a highly respectable and prominent family of Porbandar. Mohandas was a product of the Alfred High School in Rajkot. After completing his school at Rajkot, he joined Shamaldas College at Bhavnagar. In 1888 he sailed for London to study law and returned in 1891 to start practice in Bombay and Rajkot.

Gandhiji left India for South Africa to take up a job as a legal advisor. However, destiny had charted a different course for him. His

sensitive mind repelled the subhuman treatment meted out to the Indians and the Black natives of South Africa by the British. He decided to protest against and launched a Satyagraha. It was then that Satyagraha became his novel method of peaceful agitation.

On his return from South Africa to India, Gandhiji immediately plunged himself into the freedom struggle setting up a satyagraha ashram in Kochrab, a suburb in Ahmedabad. The ashram was later shifted to Sabarmati in 1917. It was from here that the Mahatama and his followers led various satyagrahas the most notable being the historic Dandi March in 1930, a journey that ultimately culminated into the end of the British rule.

Gandhi was the man who stirred to action millions of people and unfettered the shackles of the British Empire.

Ahmedabad, Porbandar, Rajkot and Bhavnagar are the cities associated with the father of the nation as he came to be known after Independence.

HOTEL ACCOMMODATION AT AHMEDABAD (STD CODE 079)

— Hotel Trident (5 Star), Airport Cross Road, Hansol
   PH 286 4444, 286 9999 FAX 286 4454
— Cama Hotels Ltd.(4 Star),Khanpur Road
   PH 550 5281 - 89; FAX 550 5285
— Inder Residency (4 Star),Opp.Gujarat College, Ellisbridge
   PH 656 5222; FAX 656 0407
— Shalin Suits (4 Star), Gujarat College, Cross Road, Ellisbridge
   PH 642 6967; FAX 656 0022
— Holiday Inn (3 Star), Near Nehru Bridge
   PH 550 5505; FAX 550 5501
— Hotel Nest(3 Star), 37,Sardar Patel Nagar, B/H Navrangpura Telephone Exchange, Navrangpura
   PH 656 2211, 642 6255; FAX 642 6259
— Rivera Hotel, Khanpur Road
   PH 550 4201, 550 5220; FAX 550 2327

ROYAL ORIENT ITINERARY

DAY 1 WED DEP From Delhi Cantonment Railway Station 1500
                  Evening Tea/Dinner on board
DAY 2 THU ARR At Chittaurgarh Railway station 0530
                  Visit Chittaurgarh Fort 0630
                  DEP For Udaipur, Breakfast on board 0900
                  ARR At Udaipur, On arrival transfer to hotel 1215

			For lunch. Post lunch local sightseeing	
		DEP	For Mehsana. Dinner on board	1750
DAY 3	FRI	DEP	For Mehsana. Breakfast on board	0415
		ARR	At Mehsana	0645
			Visit Sun Temple at Medhora	
			Visit Ran-ki-vav and Patola	
			Weaving centre at Patan	
		DEP	For Ahmedabad	1115
		ARR	At Ahmedabad	1245
			On arrival transfer to hotel for lunch	
			Sightseeing at Ahmedabad, Adalaj	
			Step well, Gandhi Ashram, Calico	
			Museum of Textiles, Sidi Sayyad mosque	
			Dinner on board	
		DEP	For Sasangir	
DAY 4	SAT	ARR	At Sasangir	0800
			Breakfast on board. Visit Lion Sanctuary	
			Optional sightseeing of Somnath temple	
		DEP	For Delwada	1115
		ARR	At Delwada	
			Visit Ahmedpur Mandvi Beach	
			Excursion to Diu Fort and St.Paul Church	1430
		DEP	For Palitana. Dinner on Board	
DAY 5	SUN		Breakfast on board	
		ARR	At Palitana. Visit 863 Jain Temples	
			Atop Shatrunjaya Hills	0745
		DEP	For Sarkhrej. Lunch on board	1200
		ARR	At Sarkhej, Visit Vishalla Village	1745
			Dinner at hotel	
		DEP	For Udaipur	2230
DAY 6	MON		Breakfast on board	
		ARR	At Udaipur.	
			Visit Ranakpur Jain Temple.	
			Lunch at the hotel	
			Post lunch return to Udaipur	
		DEP	For Jaipur. Dinner on board	2000
DAY 7	TUE		Breakfast on board	
		ARR	At Jaipur. Visit Amer Fort	0750
			Elephant ride via Hawa Mahal	
			Post lunch visit City Palace and Jantar Mantar	
		DEP	For Delhi, Dinner on board	2155
DAY 8	WED	ARR	At Delhi Cantonment	

EXCURSIONS FROM AHMEDABAD

ADALAJ STEP WELL : (17 km)The step well at the village of Adalaj is another spot worth visiting. Adalaj Vav is richly carved with every pillar and wall surface covered with leaves and flowers, birds and fishes and friezes of ornamental designs.

INDRODA NATURE PARK : (23 km) It is a beautifully developed park, where man and nature has matched very well.This park is basically a 'Nature education and Nature Awareness Centre' managed by Gujarat Ecological Education and research Foundation. During winter hundreds of varieties of birds visit the park.There is also an estuary - few varieties of birds are kept in cages.

GANDHINAGAR : (25 km) It is the new capital city of Gujarat built in 1960, on the banks of the Sabarmati river after the bifurcation of the old Bombay State into Maharashtra and Gujarat. Gandhinagar presents the spacious well-organised look of an architecturally integrated city.

THOL WILDLIFE SANCTUARY : (42km) There is a small lake called Thol Lake and this sanctuary is allotted 7 sq. km area. There are agricultural farms around the lake and pelicans, painted stroks, sarus cranes, flamingoes and ducks and black ibis are found here.

NAL SAROVAR BIRD SANCTUARY : (65 km) The lake at the sanctuary extends over a vast low-lying stretch which serves as a catchment area for the monsoon rain and provides a perfect habitat for resident birds as well as a huge number of species that  migrate here starting from November to February. Winter migrants from the North include the rosy pelicans, the flamingos, the white storks brahminy ducks and herons.

LOTHAL : (80 km) A civilisation dating back to Harrappan times has been unearthed here. Excavations have revealed a 3000 BC port city with dockyards, street houses and an underground drainage system.

MODHERA : (104 km) It has a beautiful sun temple built by the Solanki dynasty. Every inch of the edifice both inside and outside are magnificently carved with gods and goddesses, birds, beasts and flowers.

SIDDHPUR : (115 km) Situated on the bank of the Saraswati river it is famous as a pilgrimage centre for the Hindus. Apart from Rudra

Mahalaya, Bindu Sarovar Kapilashram, Govind Mahadev temple there are havelis of Vora community wherein marvellous carvings and glass paintings could be seen.

SHAMLAJI : (126 km) One of the principal Vaishnava shrines in the State, it is well-known for its temple carvings.

PATAN : (130 km) Patan city was founded during the 9th century Originally known as Anhilwad Patan the city is famous for its architectural wonders built during the era of the Solanki dynasty. The Rani Udaymati vav or stepwell and the Sahastraling lake are some of the architectural wonders here. Patan is also known for the delicate wood carving and important weaving centre for the geometrically patterned Patola Sarees.

PALANPUR : (144 km) A former princely State ruled by the nawabs. City has the sacred temple of Balaram Mahadev situated at about 12 km from Palanpur in Banaskantha district.

BALARAM-AMBAJI WILDLIFE SANCTUARY : (225 km) Sloth Bear, panther, nilgai four-horned antelope and a wide variety of birds can be watched here.

VADODRA (BARODA)

Vadodara, Gujarat's cultural capital, has a long tradition of music, fine arts and education. The former capital of Gaikwads, this city has many palaces, museums and spacious gardens. The Fine Arts School at the university here is well-known for having given rise to a prominent style of contemporary paintings—'THE BARODA SCHOOL'.

PLACES OF INTEREST

NAZARBAGH PALACE : Built in the old classical style, the palace was used on ceremonial occasions by the Gaekwads. It now houses the royal family heirlooms.

KIRTI MANDIR : The family vault of the Gaekwad rulers. It is decorated with murals by the famous Indian artist, Nandlal Bose.

MAHARAJA FATEH SINGH MUSEUM : This is the royal collection of art treasures of old masters like Raphael, Titian and Murillo as well as modern western and Indian paintings, Graeco-Roman exhibits, Chinese and Japanese art and a large collection of contemporary Indian art.

MAKARPURA PALACE : A beautiful palace designed in the

Italian style, the Makarpura palace is now used as a training school of the Indian Air Force.

PRATAP VILAS PALACE AT LALBAGH : Built as the residence of the royal family, the Pratap Vilas is an extravagant and flamboyant building in the Indo-Saracenic style. The palace houses a remarkable collection of old armoury and sculptures in bronze, marble and terracotta.

VADODARA MUSEUM AND PICTURE GALLERY : Founded by the Gaekwad in 1894, it has impressive collections on art and archaeology, natural history, geology and ethnology. The adjoining Art Gallery has a great collection of European old masters : Veronese, Giordano, Zurbaran, some Flemish and Dutch school paintings; Turner and Constable; a collection of Mughal miniatures and valuable palm-leaf manuscripts of Buddhist and Jain origin.

TAMBEKARWADA : It is famous for its wall paintings.

HOW TO RECAH

AIR : Baroda is connected by air with Ahmedabad, Delhi and Mumbai.

RAIL : Baroda is on main route between Mumbai and Delhi and is therefore connected directly to major cities.

ROAD : State transport buses and private luxury coaches connect Baroda with various centres of Gujarat and Mumbai.All types of tourist vehicles are easily available on hire.

For city tours and tourism information contact :

— Tourism Corporation of Gujarat Limited, Narmada Bhawan, C block, Indira Avenue, Vadodara
  PH 427 489; TELEFAX 431 297

HOTEL ACCOMMODATION (STD CODE 0265)

— Welcomegroup Vadodara (5 Star), R.C.Dutt Road
  PH 330 033; FAX 330 050
— Express Hotels Private Ltd. (4 Star), R.C. Dutta Road
  PH 330 750, 330 960; FAX 330 980
— Express Alkapuri (3 Star), 18/19, Alkapuri
  PH 337 899, 337 966; FAX 330 980
— Hotel Surya (3 Star), Sayajigunj
  PH 363 366; FAX 363 338
— Hotel Yuvraj (3 Star), Near Central S.T. Depot, Station Road. PH 795 252, 794 785; FAX 794 439

- Hotel Utsav (2 Star), Navrang Complex Compound, Prof. Manekrao Road. PH 435 859,434 871; FAX 425 567
- Hotel Tulsi (1 Star), Opp. Rosary High School, Pratap Gunj PH 795 330 /32; FAX 795 331
- Rajdhani Hotel, Shivaji Road, Dandya Bazar PH 438 383; FAX 438 384

EXCURSIONS

ANAND : (35 km) One of the most successful examples of a cooperative venture in the country.

CHAMPANER : (47 km), The town of Champaner was subjugated by Sultan Mehmud Begara in 1484 and made it his capital. Champaner lies at the foot of Pavagadh Fort. The ruins of its mosques and palaces reflected in the lake are some of the most picturesque ones in India.

PAVAGADH FORT : (49 km) The hill of Pavagadh rises from Champaner in three stages. The plateau at an altitude of 1471ft.is known as Machi Haveli. It is known as the birth place of Gujarat's famous musician Baiju, who preceded Tansen.

BHARUCH : (70 km) It is an ancient town with a 2000-year history. On a hilltop is a fort which overlooks the Narmada river.

DAKOR : (94 km) Dakor is the temple town sacred to Lord Krishna. His image said to be the original from Dwarka, was brought here by a devotee and installed in the temple of Ranchodrai.

SURAT

Since the earliest times, the ancient port of Surat has been renowned for its fine silks and exquisite brocades and its trade in spices. Surat has been one of the most prosperous of Indian cities in the 17th and 18th century. The East India Company established its first warehouse in Surat in 1612. And it was at Surat that Sir Thomas Roe landed when he came as King Jame's ambassador to the court of the Emperor Jehangir. In Mughal times, Surat was the main port from which pilgrims sailed to Mecca.

Today Surat is more known for diamond cutting and polishing industry.

HOW TO REACH

RAIL : Surat is on Mumbai-Ahmedabad-Delhi broad guage line and is connected directly to major cities.

ROAD : State transport buses and private luxury coaches connect Surat with various cities of Gujarat and Mumbai.

HOTEL ACCOMMODATION (STD CODE 0261)

— Holiday Inn (5 Star), Near Bharti Park, Ambica Niketan, Athwa Lines. PH 226 565; FAX 227 294
— Hotel Yuvraj (3 Star),7/278 A/13, Gulambaba Mill Compound
  PH 413 001; FAX 413 007
— Hotel Rohit International, Moti Ragahvji Mill Compound, Unapani Road. PH 433 993/ 94

PLACES OF INTEREST

THE OLD FORT : Built by Muhammed Tughlak in the 14th century as a defence fortification against the Bhils.

SARDAR PATEL MUSEUM : Nearly 100 years old museum has 10,000 specimens of arts and crafts.

RANGUPAVAN : An open air theatre with 18 metres by 10.5 metres stage and a capacity of around 4,000 spectators is one of the biggest in the country.

The ancient Dutch gardens, the Dutch cemetery and makaipul, the ancient original port from where the ships sailed to other parts of the world are other attractions.

EXCURSION

DUMAS : (16 km) It is an excellent health resort which overlooks the Arabian Sea. There are number of cottages available for visitors to stay and relax.

HAJIRA : (28 km) The pleasant Hajira beach is fringed by feathery casurina trees and has a comfortable holiday home for visitors.Hajira has two wells with water rich in iron and sulphur.

BARDOLI : (34 km) Gandhiji had launched a farmer's satyagraha, known as the Bardoli satyagraha in 1921-22 under the leadership of Sardar Vallabhbhai Patel. Swaraj Ashram at Bardoli has become a place of pilgrimage now.

UBHARAT : (42 km) Ubharat is known for a fine, sandy beach with a backdrop of shady palm groves.

DANDI : (50 km) Along the coastline of Gujarat lies Dandi where the story of salt was scripted with the famous Dandi march Satyagraha, in 1930 led by Mahatama Gandhi.

UNAI : (64 km) Unai finds reference in the puranic literature and is believed to have been created by Lord Rama by shooting an arrow in the ground.Unai also has hot springs. Unai has a major multipurpose irrigation project of Gujarat. The storage of water at the dam site is nearly as large as that of Bhakra Nangal Dam in Punjab.

TITHAL : (108 km) It is a beautiful sandy beach and has palm-sheltered cottages.

SAPUTARA HILL RESORT (164 km) from Surat)Gujarat's picturesque hill station is arched on a plateau in the Dang forest area of the Sahyadari Range.At an altitude of about 1000m., it has a cool bracing climate, the highest temperature even in the summer months not exceeding 28^0 c. Sapurata means the Abode of Serpents. A snake image on the banks of the Sarpagana river is worshipped by the Adivasis on festivals like Holi.

Saputara has been developed as a planned hill resort with all necessary amenities like hotels, parks, swimming pools, boat club, theatres and a museum to ensure an enjoyable holiday in the cool of the hill. Excursions from Saputara can be made to the wild life sanctuary in the Mahal Baripara forest, 60 kms and the Gira waterfalls 52 km away from the resort.

The thick forest around Saputara is dotted with Adivasi tribal villages and their unique dance is of great interest to visitors.

BHAVNAGAR

Once the capital of the princely state, Bhavnagar was founded in 1743 AD and is now a flourishing ports on the gulf of Khambat. For tourist it is the convenient base for visits to the town of Palitana and the sacred hill of Shatunjaya.

PLACES OF INTEREST

GAURISHANKAR LAKE : A beautiful picnic spot. There is also a well-laid-out park.

TAKHTESHWAR TEMPLE : Situated on a hill, the site provides panoramic view.

LOCK GATE : The first of its kind in Gujarat. The sea water here is impound by the lock gates to keep ships afloat during low tide, which could be seen with special permission.

HOW TO REACH

AIR : Bhavnagar is connected by air with Surat and Mumbai.
RAIL : Bhavnagar is connected by rail directly with Mumbai, Ahmedabad, Rajkot and Veraval.
ROAD : State transport buses and luxury coaches connect Bhavnagar with various cities of Gujarat.

HOTEL ACCOMMODATION (0278)

— Nilambagh Palace Hotel(Heritage), Nilambagh
  PH 412 431, 429 323; FAX 428 072
— Blue Hill Hotel (3 Star), Opp. Pill Garden
  PH 426 951-54; FAX 427 313
— Hotel Apollo (2 Star), Opposite central bus station
  PH 425 251; FAX 412 440
— Hotel White Rose, Nilambagh. PH 541 0221; FAX 413 403

EXCURSION

PALITANA : Palitana lies 56 km from Bhavnagar at the foot of the Shatrunjaya Hill with the Shatrunjaya river flowing to its south. The sacred hill rises in a crescendo of magnificent temples—863 in all—that soar in marble splendour to the top of the hill. The temples were built over an impressive span of 900 years with each generation of pilgrims making its contribution to the Shatrunjaya. The 600-metre climb to Shatrunjaya is usually made on foot. Dolis or lift-chairs are also available for the ascent.

RAJKOT

Rajkot was once the capital of the princely state of Saurashtra. Today it is best known as the town where Mahatma Gandhi spent the early years of his life when his father was a Diwan to the king of Saurashtra.

PLACES OF INTEREST

KABA GANDHI NO DELO : Gandhiji's ancestral home which now houses the Gandhi Smriti—a permanent exhibition.
WATSON MUSEUM AND LIBRARY : Located in the pleasant Jubilee Garden the museum is a good introduction to Saurashtra's cultural heritage.
LAL PARI LAKE AND RANDERDA : A picturesque picnic spot, 5 km from Rajkot.

THE RAJKUMAR COLLEGE : As early as in 1870 AD, the State had become known for its Rajkumar Colllege, built for the education of the princes of the Indian States.

RASTRIYA SHALA : It was founded by Mahatma Gandhi and is a centre of Patola weaving.

JAGAT MANDIR : It is a beautiful temple of Shri Ramkrishna Paramhansa. It is made of red stones.

HOW TO REACH

AIR : Rajkot is connected by air with Mumbai

RAIL : Rajkot is a junction on the Western Railway. Viramgaon-Okha meter guage line. Rajkot is connected directly with Mumbai, Ahmedabad, Gandhidham, Porbandar, Coimbatore, Secunderabad Howrah and Puri.

ROAD : State transport buses and private luxury coaches connect Rajkot with various cities of Gujarat and Mumbai.

HOTEL ACCOMMODATION (STD CODE 0281)

- Hotel Kavery (3 Star), Near GEB Kanak Road
  PH 239331; FAX 231 107
- Hotel Aditya : Opp Rajshri Talkies, Bhupendra Road
  PH 220044; FAX 229 901
- The Galaxy Hotel, Jawahar Road
  PH 222 904, 222909; FAX 227 053
- Jayson Hotel Private Ltd., Canal Road
  PH 228 451, 226 404; FAX 234 371 224 455
- Hotel Samrat International, 37, Karan Para
  PH 222 269, 222 275; FAX 232 274

JUNAGADH

An ancient fortified city rich in myth and legend, Junagarh lies at the foot of Girnar Hills and takes its name from the 'old fort' which circles the medieval town. The antiquities of Junagarh dates back to times of   Emperor Ashoka (250 BC). There are 14 rock edicts  cut into a great rock outside the city of that period.

PLACES OF INTEREST OF JUNAGADH

UPAR KOT OR UPPER FORT : Famous for its inaccessibility the Upar Kot or Upper Fort is girdled by a wall that is, in some places, over 20m high. An ornate entrance gateway now lies in ruins.A mosque still stands in a state of preservation. A Nilamtope (canon) was acquired by the Nawab of Junagadh from a Turkish Sultan. There are also two step-wells, Jami Masjid and Buddhist caves in the fort premises.

ASHOKA'S ROCK EDICTS : On the way to Girnar, 14 rock edicts of Emperor Ashoka can be seen inscribed on a great boulder. The inscriptions are in Brahmi script in Pali language and dates back to 250 BC.

DAMODAR KUND : A sacred tank marks the ascent to the Girnar temples.

CHORWAD BEACH : 66 km from Junagarh and 23 km from the fishing centre of Veraval, Chorwad is a delightful resort on the sunny coast of Gujarat. About 125 km from the coastline from Chorwad is the Ahmedpur Mandvi. This beach is remarkably unspoilt and pleasantly cool even during the hot summer months.

MAQBARA : The mausoleums of the Nawabs, the traditional rulers of Junagarh.

HOW TO REACH

AIR : Nearest airport Keshod 40 km.

RAIL : Nearest railhead Chorwad 66 km on Ahmedabad -Veraval line.

ROAD : State transport buses and private luxury coaches connect Junagadh with various cities of Gujarat.

EXCURSIONS

TEMPLES OF GIRNAR : Girnar, is most sacred to the Jains, rises to a height of more than 600 meters. Its five peaks crowned by 16 carved and sculptured marble shrines adorn this famous hilltop temple city.

SASANGIR FOREST AND SANCTUARY (54 km) Sasangir sanctuary provides refuge to the rare species of the Asiatic Lion. The sanctuary covers an area of 500 square miles of dry open scrubland where the lions roam freely. They can be seen on guided jeep tours through the jungles.

SOMNATH : (79 km) The legendary shore temple of Somnath is one of the 12 most sacred JYOTIRLINGAMS (PHALLUS) of Lord Shiva in India. According to Hindu mythology Somnath is as old as the creation built by none other than the Moon God Himself. The temple derives its name from Somraj, the Moon god, who originally said to have built this temple out of gold. Mehmud of Gazni having heard of its fabulous treasure had raided it in 1026 AD and carried away thousdands of camel-loads of jewels and gold.

PORBANDAR : (145 km) South of Dwarka, on the western coast, Porbandar is a picturesque old sea port associated with the birth of Mahatama Gandhi. Kirti Mandir Memorial contains the little room where the Mahatma was born. Por bandar has a pleasant beach with beach villas.

TULSI SHYAM HOT SORINGS : (165 km) In the heart of the Gir forests is the scenic spot of Tulsi shyam with hot springs.

KUTCH

Kutch is   fascinating as its remoteness has kept it separate from the country. Kandla a major sea-port of the country with its single point-mooring facilities, happens to be the only free trade zone of India. Kutch produces some of Gujarat's most exquisite crafts like embroidery, tie die fabrics enamelled silverware and other handicrafts.The great and little Rann of Kutch are the breeding grounds of Flamingo, Pelican and Avocet and the home of the rare Indian wild ass.

BHUJ

The gateway city to Kutch, Bhuj is the most important town of Kutch area. Kutch Museum formerly called the Fergusson Museum, built in 1877 AD, is the oldest museum in the State and has an exquisite collection of exhibits including a picture gallery, anthropological and archaeological sections displaying   textiles, weapons, musical instruments and stuffed animals. Bhuj has old gateways and palaces with intricately carved wooden pavilions and numerous Hindu temples, the colourful tribals and lively bazars, Ayanamahal, Cenotaphs Lakes and Old Palace are the important places worth a visit.

HOW TO REACH

AIR : Nearest airport Bhuj / Kandla.

RAIL : Bhuj is connected by train with Ahmedabad on meter guage line and with Mumbai on broad guage line.

ROAD : State transport and private luxury coaches connect Bhuj various cities of Gujarat.

EXCURSIONS

KERA : Kera has a 10th century Shiva temple.

MANDVI : Mandvi founded in 1581AD has a fortification with 25 bastions. The place is known for being the centre production of country crafts. The Rukmavati bridge built in 1883 AD. is the longest existing one of its kind. Mandvi is also well-known for its beautiful sea beach and the Vijayvillas Palace built in 1935 AD.

NARAYAN SAROVAR : Narayan Sarovar, 210 km from Bhuj, is one of the five lakes of the Hindus. Koteshwar, at a short distance from Narayan Sarovar is an ancient place of pilgrimage.

PURNESHWAR : (35 km)Town has 9th /10th century AD temple raised on a high plinth and has some fine sculptures on display.

JAMNAGAR

Founded in 1540 AD, Jamnagar has been the abode of the Jains— the Jadeja Rajput rulers of Nawanagar, and has been the capital of their State. It is renowned for pearl fisheries, a naval base and a certain type of tie-and-dye fabricks.

PLACES OF INTEREST

SOLARIUM : The Ranjit Institute of Poly-Radio Therapy is a slowly revolving tower providing sun light throughout the dya. It is open to visitors after working hours.

LAKHOTA FORT AND KOTHA BASTION : Lakhota Fort is Jamnagar's museum and its terraces disply sculpture spanning a period from 9th to18th century AD. The Kotha Bastion is Jamnagar's arsenal. One of its most interesting sights is an old well, the water of which can be drawn by blowing into a small hole on the floor.

HOW TO REACH

AIR : Jamnagar is connected by air with Mumbai and Bhuj.

RAIL : Jamnagar is connected by rail directly with Mumbai, Porbundar, Ahmedabad, Howrah and Puri.

ROAD : State transport buses and private luxury coaches connect Jamnagar with various cities of Gujarat.

EXCURSION

DWARKA : (145 km) Dwarka lies on the northern tip of the Saurastra peninsula at the confluence of the Gomati river and the Arabian sea. Legend has it that Lord Krishna along with his elder brother Balaram and thousands of followers crossed the Indian peninsula from Mathura and established his kingdom here. Dwarkadhish temple or Jagat Mandir, is over 1400 years old, profusely carved and has five storeys supported by 60 columns rendered in traditional Hindu style. The Janmastami celebration here, to commemorate Lord Krishna's birth, attract devotees from all over the world. Dwarka is also important because the great Indian reformer, Adi Shankaracharya, set up the SHARDA PEETH - one of the four seats in the country propagating Hinduism after the 8th century.

Situated at 17kms from Dwaraka, Nagesjwar Mahadev and Gopi Talav Tirth are two sites of religious significance.

SOMNATH

One of the most sacred and renowned Hindi pilgrimage centres being one of the 12 Jyortirlingas of Lord Shiva. This city has seen a tumultuous history—having been plundered more than once for its legendary wealth and having been resurrected every time by its  devotees. The temple derives its name from Somraj, the Moon God, who is originally said to have built this temple out of gold. However, the present temple resurrected and rebuilt as late as 1950 reflects little of its original magnificence.

MOUNT GIRNAR

One of the most sacred pilgrimage centres for the Jains there are 16 marble temples atop the 1,118 metre high Mount Girnar. Visitors have to ascend 10,000 stone steps which begin near the Damodar Kund. The largest and oldest temple, dedicated to Neminath, the 22nd Jain Tirthnkar, was built in 12th century AD. On the summit stands the temple of Amba Mata and on the adjoining hill of Datar is a Muslim shrine dedicated to Jaiamal Shah Pir.

PALITANA

The architectural grandeur of many of the 863 Jain temples at Palitana has few parallels. Located at the 600 meters high Shetrunjay Hills, this cluster of temples executed in marble has a wide variety of exquisite stone workmanship—wholly dedicated to Jain saints and deities. The oldest temple here was built over 1,000 years ago and is dedicated to Lord Adinath—the first Jain tirthankar. The most famous, however is the Chaumukha Temple which houses a four-faced image of Adinath.

UDAVADA AND NAVSARI

These two places are important centres for the Parsi community. Udvada is home to the oldest Parsi sacred fire in India. It is said that the fire was brought here from Persia. Udavada and Navsari can be reached by rail from Mumbai.

AHMEDPUR MANDVI AND DIU

Close by the sea and with the option of entertaining oneself gazing on the beach, swimming or enjoying a veritable host of watersports facilities the Samudra Beach Resort at Ahmedpur Mandvi is the ideal place for holidays. Across from the resort is Diu which can be visited by ferry or by bridge connecting the mainland. Ahmedpur Mandvi has one of the country's finest beaches and is increasingly becoming more popular.

FESTIVALS

JANUARY—INTERNATIONAL KITE FESTIVAL : Kite flying is a special event in Ahmedabad held on Makar Sankranti day, the beginning of the northerly journey of the Sun. Ahmedabad is as its colourful best as kites of all colours, patterns and dimensions soar into the sky. Special kites with little paper lamps fill the night sky with a myriad flickering lights. Special Gujarati cuisine, exhibitions of handicrafts and folk art enhance the spirit.

KUTCH UTSAV : This three-day organised package in February combines the journey to lovely destinations with evenings filled with the choicest food, dance, music and craft from Kutch is an unforgettable experience.

JULY—RATHYATRA : A massive procession is taken out from the Jagannath Temple at Ahmedabad amjdst the chanting of Vedic hymns with the idols of Hindu deities—Lord Krishna, Lord Balram and Subhadra their only sister, placed in the main temple chariot.

SEPTEMBER—TARNETAR MELA : Tarnetar fair is an exceedingly colourful gathering of the rural men and women. There is a heady mixture of Gujarati folk dance and music and lovely handcrafted umbrellas for two days in every September. The fair coincides with the festival at the Trineteshwar Temple celebrating the wedding of the legendary Mahabharata hero Arjuna with Draupadi. The fair is a kind of a market for the local tribals – Kolis, Bharwads and Rabaris. The wonderful Tarnetar "Chhatris" – umbrellas with intricate embroidery are the special attraction of the fair.

NAVRATRI : This is a nine-day festival in dedication to Goddess Amba held from the first day of Ashvin. It is the most important and colourful festival of Gujarat also, as in any other part of India, when different forms of the Mother Goddess are worshipped. People dance the garba and dandiya 'ras' (dance by men and women together) throughout the night in all their traditional finery. Garba competitions are also held on the occasion.

HARYANA

HARYANA
AT A GLANCE

AREA : 44,212 sq. km.
CAPITAL : Chandigarh
BOUNDARIES : East - Uttar Pradesh;
North West - Punjab : North - Himachal
Pradesh : South - Rajasthan.
LANGUAGES : Hindi and Punjabi.
ROADS : In Haryana all villages stand
connected with metalled roads. The length
of roads in the State today is 22,756 km.
AIRPORTS : Chandigarh; Hisar; Jind
and karnal.

Haryana, was once part of Punjab and was separated in 1966 to
be made an independent State.The hard working people made it self-
supporting in a short time through agriculture.

"THE GREEN LAND". Department of tourism and state started
gaining importance in modern tourism promoting adventure tourism in
big way and Hayrana Tourism repeatedly won awards from P.A.T.A.
and T.A.A.I.

HISTORY

Haryana has a proud history going back to the Vedic Age. The State
was the home of the legendary Bharata dynasty which has given the
name Bharat to India. Haryana finds mention in the great epic of
Mahabharata. Kurukshetra, the scene of the epic battle between the
Kauravas and the Pandavas, is situated in Haryana. The State continued
to play a leading part in the history of India, till the advent of the Muslim
and the rise of Delhi as the imperial capital of India. Thereafter,
Haryana functioned as an adjunct to Delhi and practically remained
anonymous till the first war of India's Independence in 1857. When the
rebellion was crushed and the British administration was re-established,
the Nawabs of Jhajjar and Bahadurgarh, Raja of Ballabgarh and Rao
Tula of Rewari of the Haryana region were deprived of their
territories.Their territories were either merged with the British
territories or handed to the rulers of Patiala, Nabha and Jind. Haryana
thus became a part of Punjab province. With the reorganisation of
Punjab on November 1, 1966, Haryana was made a full-fledged
independent State.

Haryana lies on the crossroads of North India. All main routes to Delhi go through this State which has taken advantage of this fact and built hotels, motels and restaurants on the Delhi-Agra; Delhi-Jaipur; Delhi-Amritsar and Delhi-Fazilka highways. Tourist complexes built by the State have been named after birds in view of the rich bird life of the region.

CONDUCTED TOURS

Full Day tour from Delhi covering Panipat, Kurukshetra, Jyotisar and Karna Lake.

Full Day tour to Hodal, Bhadkal and Surajkund (Saturdays).

Contact Haryana Government Tourist Bureau, PH 332 4911.

PLACES OF INTEREST

BADKAL LAKE : Location –32 km from Delhi; Dist.Faridabad. The lake complex came into existence in 1973 in the vast 203 acre area. PH 0129-218731-33.

DABCHICK (HODAL) : Location 92km from Delhi; Dist. Faridabad. The complex covers 13 acres and is soon to provide fast food facilities for travellers on the Delhi-Agra national highway. PH 01276-55555, 55625.

KARNA LAKE (UCHANA) : Location 124 km from Delhi; Dist. Karnal. Karna lake came into existence in 1972 and covers 17 acres. Karnal lake is providing restaurant, bar, conference hall along with luxury cottages for the family. PH 0184 255264, 24249.

MAGPIE (FARIDABAD) : Location 30 km from Delhi; Dist. Faridabad. Magpie has new accommodation wings with a modern convention centre coming up here shortly. PH 0129 288083, 290404.

SARAS (SAMDAMA LAKE) : Location 64 km from Delhi; Dist. Gurgaon. This lake is deep and nearly 8 km in length on the other end is the Saras Tourist complex. It lies in the heart of Haryana. The surrounding hill sides invite the rock climbers. The vast water stretch is popular for canoeing and kayaking, cycling, tented accommodation and indoor games. PH 01249-8352.

SOHNA : Location 56 km from Delhi; Dist,Gurgaon. Situated in the picturesque setting of Aravalli Hills, its landscape attracts dancing peacocks. PH 01249-2256.

SKYLARK (PANIPAT) : Location 92 km from Delhi; Dist. Panipat. PH 017242-21051

YADAVINDRA GARDENS (PINJORE) : Location 22 km from Chandigarh. These are mughal gardens with soothing waterways and fountains. The niches and green patches play up the pattern of mughal tradition. The gardens  were built by Nawab Fidai Khan, the Governor of the province in the 17th century AD.

Toady the gardens are the most popular of holiday retreats.

PH 01733-66177, 67759, 67877.

SURAJKUND : Location 8km from South Delhi; Dist Faridabad. Surajkund gets its name from an ancient amphi theatre structure : like a sun moving westward. An architectural specimen that has been built by the Raja Suraj Pal,  a chieftain from Tomar dynasty that ruled during the 10th century AD. A famous Surajkund Mela is held here every year.

PH 0129 275357.

HIMACHAL PRADESH

HIMACHAL PRADESH
AT A GLANCE

AREA : 55,673 sq. km.

CAPITAL : Shimla

BOUNDARIES : East - Tibet Uttar Pradesh; West and South - Punjab and Haryana; North - Jammu and Kashmir, Jubbarhatti (Shimla).

LANGUAGE : Hindi, Pahari.

ROADS : Himachal Pradesh has now a road length of 20,276 km and 7,652 villages have been connected with motorable roads.

AIRPORTS : Bhuntar (Kullu Valley), Gaggal (Kangra), Jubbarhatti (Shimla). Work on airstrips at Banikhet in Chamba district is in ogress. The State government has set up 12 helipads in different parts.

IMPORTANT MUSEUMS

Shimla : Himachal State Museum

IMPORTANT HILL RESORTS

Name	Altitude (m)	Important railhead
Chail	2150	Shimla 45 km
Chamba	996	Pathankot 118 km
Dalhousie	2039	Pathankot 80 km
Dharamshala	1250 to 1982	Pathankot 90 km, Kangra 17
Kasauli	1927	kalka 34 km
Kulu	1219	Pathankot 285
Manali	1982	
Shimla	2202	Shimla

IMPORTANT PILGRIM CENTRES (A : Air; R : Rail)

Baijnath : Old Shiva temple built by the Pandavas, has a Jyotirlinga (Vaidyanath); A — Kulu 150 km, R — Paprola — 5 km.

Baba Balak Nath : Cave Shrine; A — Chandigarh 220 km, R — Nangal 100 km.

Chamba : Katasan Devi temple, Laxmi Narayan temple; A — Jammu 240 km, R — Pathankot 130 km.

Chamunda Devi Dadh : Temple of Goddess Chamunda Devi; A — Jammu 200 km, R — Nagrota 12 km.

Jwalamukhi : The Flaming Goddess represented by a shining flame; A — Chandigarh 225 km, R — Ranital 24 km.

Kulu : Raghunathji Temple, very important during Dussehra; A — Bhuntar, R — Jogindar Nagar.

Manikaran : Important centre for Hindus and Sikhs; A — Bhuntar.

Naina Devi : Temple of the eyes of the Goddess; A — Chandigarh 100 km, R — Kiratpur 30 km.

Poanta Sahib : Associated with Guru Gobind Singh; R — Dehradun 45 km.

Renuka Lake : Associated with Lord Parsurama, an encarnation of Lord Vishnu and immortality of Renuka; R — Dehradun 90 km.

Saharan : Bhimakali (Durga temple); A and R — Shimla 170 km

Tarna Temple, Mandi : Temple of Kali; A — Bhuntar 70 km, R — Joginder Nagar 60 km.

Triloknath : Marble figure of Bodhistava Avalokiteshwara — In Pattan Valley, it is reached from Keylong.

Trilokpur : Temple of Goddess Mahamaya Balasundari; A — Jammu 170 km, R — Nurpur 30 km.

The mountain state of Himachal Pradesh is incredibly beautiful with its lush green valleys, fierce rocky ravine nines, flowering meadows and the mysterious snow-clad mountains. Himachal Pradesh people are simple, lively and good natured. Life moves at a serene pace in the state, far from the travails of the modern age. The simple rhythm, revolving around the tending fields, flocks and orchards, is punctuated by the celebration of festivals and fairs that bring alive colourful traditions of music and dance. For the visitors there are exquisite locations for a relaxing holiday and marvelous opportunities for trekking, mountaineering, white river rafting, para sailing and angling.

HISTORY

The earliest known inhabitants of the region were tribals called Dasas. Later Aryans came and they assimilated three tribes. In the later centuries, the hill chieftains accepted the suzerainty of the Mauryan empire, the Kushans, the Guptas and Kanuaj rulers. During the Mughal period, the Rajas of the hill State made some mutually agreed arrangements which governed their relations. In the 19th century, Ranjit Singh of Punjab annexed many of the States. When the British came, they defeated Gorkhas and entered into treaties with some Rajas and annexed the kingdom of others. This situation persisted till 1947. After independence, 30 princely States of the area were united and the present Himachal Pradesh was formed on April 15, 1948. With the reorganisation of Punjab on November 1, 1966 certain areas belonging to it were also included in Himachal Pradesh. On January 25, 1971 Himachal Pradesh was made a full-fledged State.

SHIMLA

Shimla, capital of the State, came into prominence nearly a century ago as the summer capital of the British Raj. Shimla is named after its patron goddess Shamla Devi, a manifestation of Kali.

Shimla's salubrious climate, easy accessibility and numerous attractions have made it one of the most popular hill station in northern India. The splendid views of the snow clad ranges of the Himalayas, fine walk through oaks and flowering rhododendron, enchanting resorts with easy reach, golf at Naldehra, skiing at Kufri and Narkanda, make Shimla attractive throughout the year

PLACES OF INTEREST

THE MALL : A busy shopping area with old colonial buildings, souvenir shops and restaurants. At the top end of the Mall is Scandal Point, a large open square with a view of the town - a favourite rendezvous for visitors and the local people. Overlooking it is the elegant Christ Church with its fine stained glass windows.

VICEREGAL LODGE : Housed in the Gothic splendour of the Viceregal Lodge is the India Institute of Advanced studies, India's premier academy for higher research.

HIMACHAL STATE MUSEUM : It has collection of Pahari miniatures, stone sculptures, local handicrafts, textiles and embroidery.

JAKHOO HILLS : (2,438 Mts) Highest point of Shimla offers superb view of town and surroundings. At the top is an old Hanuman temple.

SANJAULI : (2,257 m) A serene location with delightful walks, Sanjauli is ideal for tranquil weekends. There are fine vistas and the light of Shimla and Chail can be seen twinkling at night. On the other side, Mashobra and Naldehra are visible.

CHADWICK FALLS : It is a 67 meter waterfall, cascading into a deep gorge.

ANNANDALE ; THE GLEN; SUMMER HILLS; SAANJAUPI; PROSPECT HILLS are some other places of tourist interest which are popular as picnic spots.

HOW TO REACH

AIR : Shimla is connected by air with Delhi, Chandigarh and Kullu.

RAIL : Shimla is linked by a narrow guage line to Kalka which is connected to Delhi, Calcutta and Amritsar by broad guage.

ROAD : Shimla is well connected by road to most towns in Punjab and Haryana. It is linked by Bus and coach to Delhi and Chandigarh.

HPTDC operates coaches within and outside the State. Regular long distance services are operated on the route : Delhi — Manali — Delhi; Delhi — Shimla — Delhi; Shimla — Manali — Shimla; Manali — Dharamshala — Manali.

Many private transport operators also operate luxury coaches from Delhi to many places in Himachal Pradesh.

DISTANCES FROM SHIMLA

Delhi 368 km; Chandigarh 117 km; Mandi 150 km; Kullu 220 km; Manali 260 km; Kalka 90 km; Dehradun 243 km; Haridwar 310 km; Kasauli 80 km; Vilaspur 81 km; Dharmshala 293 km and Ambala 151 km.

LOCAL SIGHT SEEING TOURS

(1) Full day : Shimla — Kufri — Chini Bungalow — Naldehra — Mashobra and back to Shimla.
(2) Full day : Shimla — fagu — Theog — Matiana — Narkanda and back to Shimla.
(3) Shimla — Kufri — Chini Bungalow — Chail — Kiari Bungalow and back.
(4) Shimla — Naldehra — Tattapani and back.
(5) Shimla — Naldehra — Mashobra — Kurfi — Nature park — Chail and back.

HPTDC conducts special package tours to Leh and Kaza during May to September. *For detailed information contact :*
— HPTDC Ltd., Marketing Office, the Mall
  PH 252 561 ; FAX 252 557
Or The Director, Department of Tourism and Civil Aviation, Government of Himachal Pradesh, Block 28, SDA Complex, Kasumpti, Shimla 171 009.
  PH 0177 225864/225 924; FAX 017 225864/225 926

HOTEL ACCOMMODATION (STD CODE 0177)

— Hotel Oberoi Clarks (4 Star), The Mall
  PH 250 010, FAX 251 015
— Hotel Cecil (5 Star), D1 Chaura Maidan, Ambedkar Chowk, The Mall. PH 204 484, FAX 211 024
— Shilon Resort (Fortune Resort) (5 Star), Kufri-Chail Road, Shilon Bagh P.O. Mundaghat
  PH 0177 483 344; FAX 0177 483 362
— Hotel Asia the Dawn (4 Star) Kachi Ghati, Tara Devi
  PH 231162-65; FAX 231 007
— Hotel Gables (3 Star), Mashorba
  PH 280171-75; FAX 280 174
— Himland Hotel East (3 Star), Circular Road
  PH 224312; FAX 224436
— Kufri Holiday Resort, P.O.Box 57.
  PH 280 300; FAX 280 344

— Hotel Amber, Opp UCO Bank, Ram Bazar
PH 254 774; FAX 258 764
— Hotel Crystal Palace, Metropole, Cottage Estate, Circular
Road. PH 257 588, 257 589; FAX 202 634.
— Hotel Holiday Home. PH 258 889/90; FAX 201 705

EXCURSIONS

MASHOBRA : (2,149 m) Noted for its apple orchard and thick woods of oak and pine. It is a sylvan retreat for pretty walk and a picnic spot.

CRAIGNANO : (3 km) This spot has delightful flower-filled garden.

KUFRI : (16 km) Situated at an altitude of 2,622 meters, it is a noted venue for summer and winter sports. A sparkling winter sports festival is held here each year in February.

FAGU : (22 km) Situated at an altitude of 2,509 meters, it is a vantage point with panoramic views of the ranges and valleys. Fagu has a rest house and a tourist bungalow overlooking the Gir Valley.

NALDEHRA : (23 km) Site for scenic beauty, nine hole golf ground - with its springy turf crown of Deodar it was laid out at the instance of the Viceroy, Lord Curzon.

SOLAN : (48 km) It is located in an agricultural area where a variety of vegetables and mashrooms are grown. Solan has a number of picturesque spots ideal for walks and picnics. Solan is also known for its famous brewery which was set up in 1835. KAROL TIBBA and METEOL are pretty spots while KOTLA NALLAH with its stream, the SAPROON SPRING and the HAPPY VALLEY are delightful locations for rambles. MAREOG, GAURA and KARKANU on the Giri river, all within a 20 km radius are excellent for a spot of angling. BAROG, 5 km from Solan, was an important stop on the railway line in the early part of the century. The hill train halted for an hour here, while the travellers indulged in a lavish lunch. HPTDC runs a Tourist Bungalow at Solan and Hotel Pinewood at Barog.

TATTAPANI : (52 km) A place of hot sulphur springs, it is noted for their invigorating and curative effects.

NARKANDA : (64 km) Situated at an altitude of 2,707 meters, this place is a famous skiing resort. It has a choice of slopes ranging from a beginners run and a slalom slop, to sharper descents for the experienced skiers.

KASAULI : (73 km) Located 1927 m above sea level-forest of pines, oak and the crisp mountain air are incentives for picnics here. Monkey point, the highest point offers a panorama of green hills, the distant plains and the Sutlej river tracing a silvery trail through the scene. SANWAR - 5.6 km is famous for its public school. SABATHU 28 km from Kasauli is situated at an altitude of an 1,437 meters. It has an old Gurkha fort built in the early 19th century.

HATKOI : (104 km) Situated at an altitude of 1,100 meters, this place is noted for its historic temple dedicated to Goddess Durga. About 11 km beyond hatkoi is ROHRU on the Pabbar river, an excellent spot for angling and fishing pools. Enroute to Hatkoi — KOTKHAI is a village located among apple orchards and fine traditional architecture. JUBBAL, once the capital of a princely State has a impressive palace.

RAMPUR : (140 km) Rampur was once the capital of the princely State of Bushair and a major centre on the old trade route into Tibet. The scenic village of Saharan with its fascinating Bhimkali temple is on this road beyond Rampur.

NAHAN : (142 km) A historic town pleasantly located on a ridge of the Shivalik hills, has an outlook ever green forests and valleys with the Churdhat Peak. This little town with a salubrious climate has gardens, temples and three popular walking circuits — the Villa round, Military round and the Hospital round. Nahan's royal affiliation and the remains of old capital, Sirmuri Tal, are to be seen in the sculptures that has been preserved at Circuit House. Nahan is also famous for its Bewan Dwadeshi festival held every year in September.

SAKETI : 14 km from Nahan is Shivalik Fossil Park, a site where huge 85 million years old fiberglass models of prehistoric animals are placed.

RENUKA : 45 km from Nahan has a temple dedicated to the immortal Renuka and her son Parsurama and a tiny wildlife sanctuary. According to the legend, sage Jamadagni, incensed with his wife Renuka for her wrong demeanor, had ordered his son Parsurama to cut off her head. The obedient son obeyed his father and the sage, pleased with his son's compliance, grated him a boon. Parsurama requested his father to use his spiritual powers and restore life to his slain mother and also to ensure her immortality. Around the lake is a wildlife sanctuary, home of a variety of birds, deer, jungle fowl and black pheasant. Facilities are available for boating at the lake.

PAONTA SAHIB : (142 km) A town where Guru Gobind Singh wrote a major part of the Dassam Granth. The story goes that the place acquired its name after the Guru had lost an ornament known as Paonta worn on the foot and thus came into existence an important place of pilgrimage for the Sikhs. It is said that the Yamuna flows without a ripple here because the guru calmed its turbulent water. There are also temples dedicated to Lord Rama and Lord Krishna.

CHAIL : (170 km) Chail was once the summer resort of the Maharaja of Patiala. Located on a wooded spur, Chail (2150 m) overlooks the Sutlej Valley. Shimla and Kasauli are also visible and at night their twinkling lights seem part of the starlit sky. The palace of Maharaja built in the late 19th century is now a holiday resort. Chail has fine tennis and squash courts. There are excellent sports along the Gaura river with opportunities for anglers to tangle with Himalayan mahaseer. Chail has also the highest cricket ground in the world — 2250 m. above sea level.

KUFRI : A long and enjoyable drive through lush forests and quaint villages takes one to small but thoroughly popular hill station of Kufri. Its main attractions are the nature park and the exciting trek that leads to the divine Mahasu peak. Several trek routes lead out of Chail up to the Choor peak to Shimla. During winters, skiing is possible at Narkanda. The Giri river at Gaura, 29 km away, is ideal for fishing — buffs.

KINNUR : (200 km) District of Kinnaur, where the icy waters of the Sutlej river and its tributaries have carved deep gorges through the high ranges, the landscape varies from the lush green orchards of picturesque Sangla Valley to the stark magnificence of the Hangrang valley. Kinnur Kailash peak — revered by the Kinnauris as the abode of Lord Shiva is located within massive snow-clad mountain ranges. Kinnur is linked by road to Shimla. Buses, jeeps and taxis are available from Shimla and Rampur.

KULLU

Kullu, located on the banks of the Beas river was once known as Kulanthpitha — the end of the habitable world. Beyond its perimeter loomed the magnificent Himalayas, and by the Beas sprawled the 'Silver Valley' Kullu came to be accessible only after independence. Kullu is famous for Dussehra festival. Decorated palanquins and processions convey gods and goddesses from temples all over the valley of Kullu, to pay homage to the reigning deity,

Raghunathji. A mela springs up during the festival which is celebrated with a great deal of singing, dancing and festivity.

PLACES OF INTEREST

RAGHUNATH TEMPLE : In the 17th century, Raja Jagat Singh of Kullu is said to have committed a wrong deed, to atone for which, he sent courtier to Ayodhya for a statue of Lord Raghunath — Lord Rama. He built this temple to house the image, and the shrine became popular ever since. The Kullu valley is the meeting point of several trek routes, mainly those from Chanderkhani Pass to Malana, over the Jalori Pass or Bashleo Pass to Shimla and over the Pin Parvati Pass to Sarahan. The magnificent Beas also offers ample opportunities for some exciting white river rafting.

HOW TO REACH

AIR : Kullu is connected by air with Chandigarh and Delhi.

RAIL : Nearest railhead Jogindernagar 95 km.

ROAD : Kullu is well-connected by road with Delhi and Chandigarh. Luxury buses ply from Delhi and Shimla to Kullu.

HOTEL ACCOMMODATION (STD CODE 01902)

— Apple Valley Resorts (4 Star) Village Mohal
  PH 66266-66271; FAX 24116
— Span Resorts (4 Star) Kullu-Manali Highway, P.O. Katrain 175129, Kulu. PH 40138, 40140; FAX 01902 40140
— Sagar Resorts, Opp Tourist Bungalow, Near Circuit House. PH 52553 FAX 01092 52552
— Hotel Sarvari (Operated by HPTDC) PH 01902 2471
— Hotel Silvermoon (Operated by HPTDC) PH 01902 2488

EXCURSIONS

BIJLI MAHADEV TEMPLE : (8 km) The temple tower, a 20 m rod on top, attracts lightning from the clouds which shatters the stone linga (Phallus) in the sanctum. The remarkable feature of the shrine is a high pole or staff that periodically draws lightning, which shatters the 'Shivlinga' and scorches the building. Butter is then anointed by the priest to put the shattered 'linga' back into shape.

RAISON : (13 km) Situated at an altitude of an 1,433 meters, this is a starting point for a number of interesting walks and treks.

KATRAIN : (19 km) Situated at an altitude of an 1,463 meters, it is the widest part of the valley. There is an excellent fishing spot here and a trout hatchery nearby. At a distance of 5 km from the town is a gracious house set in a flower-filled garden. The art gallery in the house displays the works of the famous painter Prof. Nicholas Roerich.

NAGGAR : (24 km) Situated at an altitude of 1,768 meters across a bridge at Patki Kuhl, the town high above the valley—has an old castle. Once the capital of Kullu, the town has a marvellous medieval building, built of a rough stone around a courtyard with a tiny temple in its central courtyard.

MANIKARAN : (45 km) Situated at an altitude of 1,737 meters, high up under the snowy peaks of the Parvati valley are the hot springs at Manikaran. It derives its name from a legend according to which Parvati, lost her earrings—Manikarana—and recovered them at the site from which sulphur spring arises. Manikaran, is a place of pilgrimage for the Hindus and Sikhs both as there is a temple and a gurudwara. It is also a good spot for trout fishing. There are also trek routes that lead to Pulga, Khirganga and Mantalai. HPTDC runs hotel Parvati.

MANDI : (59 km) Mandi, at the lower end of the Beas valley, 760 meters above sea level, 400 years old town is located on an old trade route into Tibet. Mandi is famous for its beautifully sculpted stone temples of Panchvaktra, Ardhanarinateshwar, Triloknath and Bhutnath. Jnajheli, an unspoilt village, is located at 67 km from Mandi. REWALSAR 25 km away from the Mandi has a lake with its curious floating islands of reed. It is believed that the Buddhist sage and teacher Padmasambhava had departed for Tibet from Rewalsar to spread the message of Lord Buddha. Buddhist pilgrims come every year to the ancient Nyingmapa monastery on the bank of the lake. There is a temple and gurudwara by the lake side held sacred by the Hindus and the Sikhs both. BILASPUR overlooking the vast Govind Sagar reservoir of the Bhakra Dam, is on the main highway between Chandigarh and Mandi. GOVIND SAGAR, the biggest man-made lake of Himachal offers wide facilities of water sport and angling 57 km from Bilaspur situated at an altitude of 914 meters, is the famous shrine of NAINA DEVI. A colourful fair—Shravana Astami Mela—is held here every year.

MANALI

Situated at the northern end of the Kullu Valley, Manali has
spectacular views of snow capped
peaks and wooded slopes along the
banks of the Beas. It is the main
holiday destination in the entire
valley.

The Manali market is crowded
with myriad of interesting shops
selling Tibetian carpets and crafts.
Manali, is a popular base for
trekking and mountaineering in
summer and skiing in winter.

HOW TO REACH

AIR : Nearest airport Bhuntar (50 km) connected with Delhi and
Chandigarh.

RAIL : Nearest railhead Chandigarh 285 km; Pathankot 285 km.

ROAD : Manali is connected by road with Kullu, Delhi and
Chandigarh. Regular bus services are available from these places.

The Mountaineering Institute in Manali organises skiing, rock
climbing and mountaineering courses. The common trek routes lead
out from Manali to Leh, Bhrigu Lake, Chandratal and Spiti. For
fishing enthusiasts, Katrain, Raison, Kasol, Larji and Nagar are some
of the ideal places for trout.

LOCAL SIGHT-SEEING TOURS

One Day Rohtang Tour : Manali — Nehru Kund — Marhi —
Rohtang Pass

One Day Naggar Tour : Manali — Solang — Jagatsukh —
Naggar — Manali

One Day Manikaran Tour : Manali — Arvati Valley —
Manikaran — Kullu — Mandi

One Day Jalori Pass Tour : Manali — Kullu — Aut-Shoja-Jalori
Pass — Manali

HPTDC operates special Manali-Leh tour during July-August.
For detailed information contact
—   HPTDC LTD., Marketing Office, The Mall, Manali,
     Dist Kullu. PH 01902 53531 ; FAX 01902 52325

HOTEL ACCOMMODATION (STD CODE 01902)

— Ambassador Resort, Sunny Side, Chandiyari
  PH 52235/8; FAX 52173
— Banon Resorts, New Hope Orchards. PH 52490, FAX 52378
— The Conifer, P. O. Box 38, Near Log Huts
  PH 52434/39; FAX 52434
— John Banon's Orchards. PH 52335; FAX 52392
  Legrand, National Highway, Near Manali Barrier
  PH 53165; FAX 53166
— Hotel Manali Ashok (3 Star). PH 531039; FAX 53108/9
— The Manali Inn : Rangree Manali. PH 53550-4; FAX 52582
— Manali Resorts. PH 52274; FAX 52174
— Sterling Himalayan Continental. PH 53011/12; FAX 52494

EXCURSIONS

HADIMBA TEMPLE : The ancient temple built like a pagoda, its lintel and door frame have intricately carved wood. It was built by Maharaja Bahadur Singh in 1553 and enshrines the footprints of the Goddess Hadimba - wife of Bhima. It later became the patron goddess of the Kullu royal family.

A colourful festival is held here in May every year.

MANU TEMPLE : Just near the Hadimba temple flows the Manalsu river, that culminates in the main Beas river. Across the Manalsu river is the original village of Manali, that houses the ancient temple of Sage Manu. Manali itself is named after Manu, who is said to have dwelt here.

VASHIST SPRINGS : (3 km) Situated at an altitude of 1982 m above sea level, these are the sulphur springs at Vashist.

JAGSTSUKH : (6 km) Once the capital of Kullu, it has the earliest surviving stone temple of the 8th century is dedicated to Lord Shiva and Sandhya Gayatri.

ARJUN GUFA : (5 km) Legend has it that it was here that Arjun had practised austerities to get the Parshupata Ashtra, the sacred weapon from Lord Indra.

NEHRU KUND : (6 km) A spring of cold and clear water along the road to the Rohtang Pass.

SOLANG VALLEY : (14 km) It presents marvellous views of the snow-capped peaks and glaciers. It is a popular winter resort for skiing in winter.

Replete with terrific picnic spots, the amazing ski slopes here are full of hectic activities in January — February.

KOTHI : (12 km) It is a picturesque spot and a convenient camping site. The P.W.D. rest house has a panoramic view of the magnificent mountain scape. Close-by flows the Beas river through a deep chasm.

ROHTANG PASS : (51 km) Located at a height of 3980 m, the pass served a crucial trade route and a starting point for visits to the Lahaul and Spiti valleys. The Manali-Leh road is one of the highest highways in the world. The pass is open for just four months in a year—from June to October, when the snow melts.

BEAS KUND : It is the origin of the Beas river. The river gets its name from the great sage Vyas, who believed to have meditated here.

GRAMPHU : (67 km) A junction on the Manali-Leh highway where a road branches off to go to Kunzam pass and Sipti.

LAHAUL : (115 km) Situated at an altitude of 3980 meters, Lahul is a entry point to the district of Lahul-Spiti. The Manali-Leh Road, one of the highest motorable roads in the world, crosses the subdivision linking Keylong, its headquarters, to Manali. Lahaul, curious mixture of Buddhism and Hinduism has fine gompas and temples. **KOKSAR** is the coldest place in Lahul district. **KARDANG** 5 km away has the largest monastery in the area. It has barrel size prayer drums that the monks turn during their perambulations. Paintings, ancient weapons, musical instruments and large life-size statues of Lord Buddha and the Bodhisattavas can be seen in this monastery. **SHASHUR**, another monastery situated opposite Kardang monastery is approached by a steep and difficult track. At the confluence of the Chandra and Bhaga rivers, 8 kms short of Keylong **TANDI** has a monastery called Guru Ghantal monastery. **KEYLONG** the district headquarters of Lahaul (3350 m above sea level) is located in the heart of the district. A number of gompas are located in the vicinity of Keylong. **UDAIPUR** town, 59 km from Keylong and located in the Pattan Valley is a starting point for a number of exciting treks to Chamba, Kistwar and Padam. It has a rest house and camping sites Mrikula Devi Temple built in the 15th century by the ruler of Chamba and dedicated to Mahishasurmardini has exquisite wood carvings. **SURAJ TAL** 65 km from Keylong, this emerald lake is the source of the Bhaga river. **BARA LACHA PASS,** 73 km from Keylong is the base for treks to the Chandra Tal lake in Leh. **SARUCHU** is last point on the Himachal Pradesh—Ladakh border. **LAKE CHANDRA TAL** is a high altitude lake, approachable through the Kumzam Pass which links Lahaul and Sipti. **BATAL** in the southern Lahul is a base for treks to Lake Chandra Tal and beyond to the Bara Lacha Pass on the Manali-Leh Road.

Foreign tourists are required to obtain interline / protected area permits issued by :

(a) Special Commissioner (Tourism) Govt. of Himachal Pradesh, New Delhi

(b) Resident Commissioner, Govt. of Himachal Pradesh, New Delhi

(c) Director General of Police, Himachal Pradesh, Shimla.

SPITI

Spiti is linked by road with Shimla and Manali. A high altitude cold desert, Spiti is out of the land of fairy tales and fantasies. Small village of box-like houses along the river valleys, it is blanketed with snow and temperature falls below zero except during the three months of summer. Sipti is influenced by Buddhism and nearly 30 monasteries guard a rich cultural heritage. **SUMOD** is entry point into Sipti from Kinnur district. **TABO**, close to Sumod has a thousand year old Tabo Gompa, established by the legendary Rinchen Tsangpo. This Gompa is considered important next to the Tholing Gompa in Tibet and has priceless collection of manuscripts and thangkas. **SHCHICHILING** 50 km from Sumado is famous for Dhankar Monastery built on a high rugged hillside and has interesting murals and stuccos.

ATTERGU, a small village along the N.H.22 has another important Gompa at Kungri. **KUNZAM PASS** (4,590 m) is the other entry point into Sipti traversing through Lahul. **KAZA** is noted for its historic Kyi Gompa. Established in the 14th century AD, it has breathtaking murals and valuable collection of 'Kangyur' —ancient Buddhist texts. Over 200 monks reside at Kyi.

DHARAMSHALA

Is the main hill station in the Kangra valley. A fertile, undulating valley, lying between the gentle Shaivalik hills and the foothills of the mighty Dhauladhars— 'The white mountains' rising 400 m above sea level, a valley noted for the beauty of its scenery—lush terraces, wooded hills, manicured tea gardens and sparkling streams, commands a splendid view of the surrounding country.

PLACES OF INTEREST

MACLEODGANJ : It is a charming Tibetan settlement with bustling bazars that sells carpets, handicrafts and delicious Tibetan food. A giant prayer wheel ornaments the main street and in the monastery a serene statue of Lord Buddha presides over the gentle chanting of the monks. The Dalai Lama resides in Macleodganj, which is now a major centre of Tibetan culture. It has a school for Tibetan studies with rare manuscripts and ancient texts besides the Tibetan Institute for the Performing Arts and a handicraft centre.

ST. JOHN IN THE WILDERNESS : A stone church with delicate stained glass windows and memorial to Lord Elgin. Other places of interest are **TRIUND DHARAMKOT** and **KARERI** famous for its scenic beauty, **KUNAL PATHRI** - a rock temple of local goddess; **MACHHRIAL** - beautiful waterfalls; **TATWANI** - hot springs.

CHAMUNDA DEVI TEMPLE - A temple surrounded by glorious mountains.

HOW TO REACH

(District Kangra—Dharamshala, Kangra and Palampur)

AIR : Nearest airport—Kangra 12 km

RAIL : Nearest railhead Kangra on narrow guage line (18 km), Pathankot on broad guage line (90 km).

ROAD : Dharamshala is connected by road with Delhi, Chandigarh, Kullu, Shimla and Chamba.

HOTEL ACCOMMODATION (STD CODE 01902)

Hotel Dhauladhar, Hotel Bhagsu, Yatri Niwas are the hotels operated by HPTDC.

For reservation contact :

HPTDC Ltd., Marketing Office, Kotwal Bazar, Dharamshala, Dist. Kangra, Ph. 01892 24928; FAX 01902 24212

EXCURSIONS

KANGRA : (17 km) Kangra town in the Kangra valley was once the capital of a powerful hill State noted for its beautiful temples and artistic heritage. During the rule of Raja Sansar Chand (1775-1823), the arts flourished, fine miniatures of the Kangra school and murals commissioned by him are still to be seen in the palaces and temples. **BARJESHWARI TEMPLE** is dedicated to Bajreshwari Devi, known once for its legendary wealth. This temple was subject to successive depredations by invaders from the north. Mohammed of Ghazni is known to have departed from here with a King's ransom in gold, silver and jewels in 1009 AD. **KANGRA FORT** the ruins of which are located

on a strategic height overlooking the Ban Ganga and Manijhi rivers. **JWALAMUKHI**, 30 km from Kangra town is an important pilgrim place. The temple with its gilded dome has the eternally burning flame issuing form a hollow in the rock considered the manifestation of the goddess. **NADAN** 48 km from Kangra is a former capital of King Sansar Chand and has fine murals. It is an ideal spot for a quiet holiday.

TRILOKPUR : (41 km) Here is a natural cave temple dedicated to Lord Shiva.

MASRUR : (40 km) Here is a temple carved of monolithic rocks in the style of the Kailash temple at Ellora, belonging to 8th century AD.

PALAMPUR : (52 km) The town surrounded by tea gardens, forests of pine and deodar, is located at 35 km from Kangra. It provides opportunities for angling in the Bundla river and hang-gliding, para-gliding at Bir-Billing. **BIR BILLING** surrounded by tea gardens, is an ideal landing ground for hang/para-gilders. **BIR** has an Buddhist monastery. Fine Tibetan handicrafts are also produced here. **BILLING,** up in the hills, 14 km from Bir with an area of 200 km (or more) for an high altitude and cross country flying, is one of the best aerosport sites in the world. **ALHILAL**, very close to Palampur, was once the summer retreat of the Dogra rulers of Jammu. The Taragarh Palace at Alhilal is now a splendid hotel.

NURPUR (66 km) The ruined fort and Krishna temple are noted for fine wood carvings. Nurpur which was named after the Mughal Empress Nurjehan, is famous for its fine Pashmina shawls and textiles.

DALHOUSIE

Standing at the foot of the spectacular Dhauladhar range of the Himalayas, sprawled over five hills—Kathlog, Portrevn, Moti Tibba (formerly known as Tehra), Bakrota and Balun, Dalhousie is noted for the magnificence of its scenery. A resort that still exudes an old worldly charm, Dalhousie has retained much of the British Raj style. The British Governor General, Lord Dalhousie, had visited this area and ever since it has been named after him. Set amidst the thickly wooded hills, clothed in deodar and pine, Dalhousie has marvellous forest trails and picnic spots with splendid vistas over the Chamba Valley.

PLACES OF INTEREST

SUBHASH BAOLI : One gets panoramic views of the snow-capped mountains around from here.

SATDHARA : Sparkling springs, rich in mica and other minerals are noted for their medicinal properties. Panjpulla is another pretty spot beyond Satdhara, where the water from a natural tank flows under five little bridges.

BAKROTA HILLS, KALATOPE, DHANIKUND are popular picnic resorts with natural beauty.

BARA PATHAR : En route to Kalatope there is a temple of Bhulwani Matha in Ahla village.

HOW TO REACH

AIR : Nearest airport Gaggal in Kangra 135 km.
RAIL : Nearest railhead Pathankot 80 km.

HOTEL ACCOMMODATION (STD CODE 18982)

— Hotel Grand View : (2 Star) The Mall.
   PH 42623; FAX 42123
— Alps Holiday Resort, Khaijar Road
   PH 01899 42714; FAX 42480
— Hotel Mount View, Bus Stand.
   PH 42120, 42127; FAX 42556
— Hotel Taj Palace, Gandhi Chowk.
   PH 42406, FAX 232227

CHAMBA

The serene town of Chamba lies on the bank of the Ravi river. An erstwhile princely State, it was the capital of the former rulers of Chamba. It was founded in 920 AD by Raja Sahil Varma who had named it after his daughter Champavati. Isolated in this valley by the high ranges, Chamba developed its own style of architecture and art.

Much of this heritage has been preserved and Chamba is known for its exquisite miniatures and handicrafts.

PLACES OF INTEREST

LAKSHMINARAYAN TEMPLE : This is one of the group of six ancient temples carved in stone with tall vimanas. Dedicated to both Lord Shiva and Lord Vishnu they were built around the 8th century AD. The oldest Lakshminarayan temple is richly ornamented.

BHURI SINGH MUSEUM : There is a collection of fine miniatures form Knagra, Basholi and Chamba schools of paintings in it.

CHAUGAN : It is the centre of all cultural activities.

HARI RAI TEMPLE : This 11th century temple has an exquisite bronze images of the Chaturmurti, the four armed Vishnu, enshrined in the sanctum.

CHAMUNDA DEVI TEMPLE : Located at Chaugan it is dedicated to Goddess Chamunda Devi and is embellished with fine wood carvings.

KATASAN DEVI TEMPLE (30 km) A popular place of pilgrimage.

SAHO : (20 km) Situated on a high plateau on the banks of the Sal river, Saho is famous for the temple Chandrashekhar—Lord Shiva, with his moon crown.

SAROL, JHAMWAR, SALOONI are some other places that provide breathtaking views and are picnic destinations.

HOW TO REACH

AIR : Nearest Airport Kangra (Gaggal) 180 km.

RAIL : Nearest railhead Pathankot 122 km.

Geographical diversity offers a whole range of adventure activities such as golf trekking, heli-skiing, skiing, camping, ice-skating, para gliding, angling, water and river sports, mountain cycling, vehicle safaris, mountaineering and rock climbing. HPTDC has explored new treks in Kinnur and Spiti areas which were till now a forbidden land for tourists but has now been opened for the adventurous people.

TREKKING

A range of options for trekking are available from the very exotic to soft treks for the year round. Some of the major trekking trails are

(a) The northern districts of Lahaul-Spiti and Kinnur as well as Pangi subdivision of Chamba. Trekking altitudes even go upto 5000 m. The Sangla Valley Trek in Kinnur and Grand Himalayan Trek in Lahul are more popular routes.

(b) The Parvati Valley in Kullu District offers some exotic routes for seasoned trekkers. The popular routes include the one across the Pin-Parvati Pass into the Chandra Valley of Lahul as well as treks across the high passes of the Pir-Panjal range.

(c) These treks are only possible during the months of summer and autumn.

TREKKING INFORMATION

Trekking package start and terminate at Shimla.

Good health is essential for varying climatic conditions of high altitude.

Insurance for sickness and accident is must. A doctor must be consulted before taking on the trekking package.

For Reservation and information contact :

— HPTDC Marketing Offices, The Mall, Shimla
    PH 0177 252 561, 258 302; FAX 0177 252 557

Or HPTDC offices at Manali, Dharamshala, New Delhi, Ahmedabad, Calcutta, Chandigarh, Bangalore, Mumbai and Chennai.

KINNER KAILASH PARIKRAMA TREK; 8 DAYS TREKKING PACKAGE

4 DAYS BY BUS - 4 DAYS BY TREK

Mount Kinner Kailash a magestic mountain (6050 m) has religious significance of huge "SHIVALINGAM" the representative of Lord Shiva. This mountain changes colours several times a day with change of weather conditions. The circuit around the whole range attracts many trekkers and pilgrims every year. The Parikrama begins from Kalpa via Thangi, Charang and Chhitkul and terminates at Kalpa via Sangla valley.

ITINERARY

DAY 1 : Shimla to kalpa (2960 m) 244 km.
          Drive through Narkanda-Rampur-Saharan-Kalpa.

DAY 2 : Kalpa to Thangi (2966 m) by bus via
Powari-Ribba-Jangi then diversion to Thangi

DAY 3 : Thangi to Lambar (2760 m) 12 km. The treak is
descending alongwith Thangi Nallah.

DAY 4 : Lambar to Charang (3510 m) 12 km trek through
different terrain via Surting.

DAY 5 : Charang to Lalanti (4420 m) 8 km. Lalanti is a beautiful
place with varities of flowers all around.

DAY 6 : Lalanti to Base Camp (5000 M) 6 km. The base camp
is a nice place for camping with glaciered water falls.

DAY 7 : La Base Camp to Chitkul (3450 m) 9 km. After crossing
the Lalanti pass (5000 m) a continuous descending
upto Chitkul a beautiful place situated on the left bank
of Bapsa river. Chitkul to Sangla (2689 m) 26 km by
bus.

DAY 8 : Sangla to Shimla (273 km) by Bus.

BHABA-PIN VALLEY TREK : 10 DAYS TREKKING

5 DAYS BY BUS AND 5 DAYS TREKKING

The trek starts from Kafnoo (Bhava Nagar) in district Kinnaur
through lush green medows and grazing fields on the bank of river
Bhaba and extends to valley of monastries i.e. Sipti Division of
district Lahul Sipti through the picturesque land, high passes,
glaciers, wide pastures full of medicinal herbs and seasonal flowers.
Geologically and archaeologically, Sipti valley is a living museum.
The barren rock mountains are devoid of any vegetation due to
erosion by wind, sun and snow over thousands of years.

THE TREK STARTS FROM THE BASE CAMP AT KAFNOO
ITINERARY

DAY 1 : Shimla to Sarahan (2165 m) 175 km.
Sarahan is a charming station famous for Bhimakali
Temple.

DAY 2 : Sarahan to Kanfoo 52 km by bus via Jeori-Wangtu and
then diversion to Kanfoo.

DAY 3 : Kanfoo to Mulling 12 km. A gradual descending trek
enrout green pastures.

DAY 4 : Mulling to Tesa Pasture 10 km. The trek through the
green pasture of Kaza.

DAY 5 : Tesa to Baldur 12 km. The trek upto Bhava pass
(4000 m) and then steep descending upto Baldur.

DAY 6 : Baldur to Mud 11 km. A moderate trek through the green pastures.

DAY 7 : Mud to Gulling 12 km Gradual trek along the side of Pin river, famous for Himalayan wildlife.

DAY 8 : Gulling to Kaza 30 km. One has the option to trek along the bank of Pin river upto Change or reach Kaza by bus.

DAY 9 : Kaza to Sarahan by bus Drive through Tabo the oldest monastery of Spiti and Kaurik, Pooh and Kalpa.

DAY 10 : 175 km by bus via Rampur, Narkanda, Kurfi and reach Shimla.

For further details and reservation contact :
— Himachal Tourism, The Mall, Shimla
  PH 252561, 258302; FAX 252557

A WINTER PARADISE (OCTOBER TO MARCH)

SHIMLA SOJOURN 5 NIGHTS AND 6 DAYS

Delhi-Chandigarh-Chail-Shimla-Arki-Nalagarh-Chandigarh-Patiala-Delhi.

SHIMLA SOJOURN

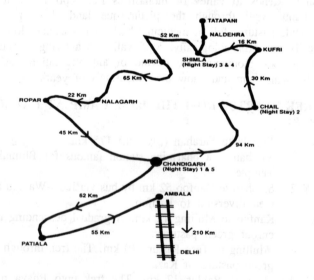

Sketch map not to scale

SUTLEJ BEAS TRAIL 7 DAYS AND 7 NIGHTS

Delhi-Chandigarh-Chail-Shimla-Manali-Nalagarh-Patiala-Delhi.

SUTLEJ BEAS TRAIL

Sketch map not to scale

THE HERITAGE TRAIL 8 DAYS AND 8 NIGHTS

Delhi-Patiala-Nalagarh-Meleodganj-Palampur-Manali-Bilaspur-Shimla-Chail-Chandigarh-Delhi.

THE HERITAGE TRAIL

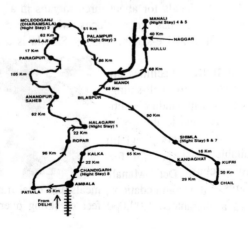

THE HIMALAYAN SPECTRUM 9 DAYS AND 9 NIGHTS

Delhi-Chandigarh-Chail-Shimla-Manali-Palampur-Meleodganj-Delhousie-Madhopur-Pathankot-Delhi.

THE HIMALAYAN SPECTRUM

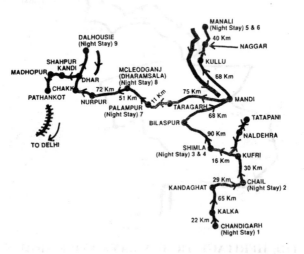

The season starts from middle of December. Manali and Narkanda are the most popular resorts in Himachal. The Solangs Nallah slopes at Manali allow ski-runs of upto 30 km. Great slopes are available at Narkanda for about three months in a year. Rohtang Pass beyond Manali has good slopes which permit skiing till July/August. A natural ice-skating rink at Shimla is also popular in winter.

HELI SKIING : Facilities are available at Manali for heli-skiing. Helicopters fitted with landing equipment ferry ski-runners to the top of the slopes in areas where a ski lift is not available. Packages for foreign tourists include Delhi-Manali-Delhi air-fares, all accommodations, meals and local transportation in Manali, and a guaranteed 1,00,000 feet of skiing over a seven day period.

RIVER RAFTING : Beas and the Chandra river in Lahaul are used for river running. There are regular runs between Shamshi and Aut and the Beas. This 20 km stretch has exciting white water and class 3 rapids. The Chandra river flowing through the exotic  mountain scape of Lahaul is another interesting area for river rafting.

FISHING : Trout, mahaseer, katla and rohu are the major game fishes in Himachal Pradesh. Trout is found in Rohru (Pabbar river) in the Shimla district, Sangla (Baspa river) in Kinnur and in the Sainj river in the Kullu Valley. Trout seeding areas are at Patli Kuhl. Katrain in the Kullu Valley and Barot in the Mandi district fill the Beas river with trout. Further downstream, the Beas offers excellent opportunities for mahaseer fishing. The Deragopipur, region of the Beas is also an excellent area for mahaseer. The Sutlej and Govind Sagar reservoir of the Bhakra Dam are home to the Rohu and Katla and offer excellent fishing.

HANG-GLIDING : The spectacular Dhauladhar range extending for 150 km and rising to a height of 4000 m from the valleys provide the best launching pads for the exciting sport of hang-gliding and para-sailing. Bir-Billing in Kangra district is one of the most promising areas for this sport and is being further developed for the same.

MOUNTAINEERING : The state of Himachal is traversed by four major ranges of the Himalayas. The peaks of the inner Himalayas and the Pir Panjal range over 6000 m high. The Lahaul and Manali regions are also promising. The Mulkila group and the peaks of the Chandra Bhaga are still unconquered. Challenging peaks are also to be found near the Bara Shigri glacier in Lahaul and at the headwaters of the Paravati river.

For further information contact :
— Golf, Camping and skiing—HPTDC, The Mall, Shimla-171001
  PH 0177-252561/258302; FAX 0177 252 557
— Heli Skiing—Himachal Helicopter Skiing, 55/56, The Mall, Shimla 171 001. Telefax : 0177 258 995
Or GI M.G. Bhawan, 7, Local Shopping Centre, Madangir, New Delhi 110 162. PH 698 3358/59, FAX 698 3357.

— Mountaineering, trekking, rock climbing and skiing - Directorate of Mountaineering and Allied sports, Aleo, Manali-175 131.

Or Indian Institute of Skiing and Mountaineering, C-1, Hutments, Dalhousie Road, New Delhi-110 011 PH 301 6179; FAX 301 1518.

— Director of Mountaineering and Allied Sports, Regional Water Centre, Pong Dam—176 501, Dist. Kangra.

— Regional Mountaineering Centre, Dharamsala—176 219.

— Regional Mountaineering Sub-Centre, Bharmaur—176 315, Dist. Chamba.

— Regional Mountaineering Sub-Centre, Jispa—175 132, Dist. Lahaul-Spiti.

— Angling—Chief Warden Fisheries, Bilaspur—174 001 PH 0796 2396.

Himachal Pradesh has a necklace of Buddhist monasteries etched across its landscape. Some gompas go back to the time when Buddhism was a shadowless sapling in the region.

TRACING THE MONASTERIES-12 DAYS AND 13 NIGHTS

The itinerary starts from Shimla and ends at Mc.Leodganj, the residence of His Highness the Dalai Lama.

Day 1 : Visit two newly built monasteries; the Geluk-pa sect Himalayan Buddhism has one at Sanjauli and the Nyingma-pa one at Kasumpti.

Day 2 : Leave for Kinnaur's Baspa valley, en route visit small 19th century Buddha temple at Rampur and the Drug-pa temple at Kilba (95 km from Rampur) on the left bank of the Sutlej river. Stay in the Baspa valley rest house or tented accommodation in the night.

Day 3 : Leave for Recong Peo (2290 mt., 38 km from Sangla village) after visiting the Baspa valley's four small Buddhist temples in the villages of Sapni, Barua, Sangla and Batseri. Recong Peo has a recently build Gompa where His Holiness, the Dalai Lama had conducted a 'Kalchakra' ceremony in 1992. Halt at Recong peo and Kalpa—rest house or tented accomodation for night stay.

Day 4 : Leave for Nako (107 km). Visit four Buddhist temples with stucco images and murals at Yaughhang. Stay at Nako rest house during the night.

Day 5 : Leave for Tabo (65 km) founded in 996 AD. by the great Teacher Rinchensgopo. Tabo is renowned for its breath-taking murals and stucco images and is often called "Ajanta of the Himalayas". There are several caves adorned with frescoes and contemporary structures, the old section has 9 temples, 23 chartens, a monk's chamber and a nun's chamber. Spend the night at the rest house.

Day 6 : Leave for Kaza (47 km) Enroute visit Dhankar gampa—a repository of Buddhist scriptures in the Bhoti script. Make night stay at rest houses/tented accommodation.

Day 7 : Based at Kaza, visit the Ki monastery as well as the Hikim, Komic and Langia monasteries. Make night stay at rest house Kaza.

Day 8 : Leave early for Keylong (188 km), en route visit gompas at Damphug, Chakur, Labrang, Jagdang, Shashin, Khangsar, Gondhia, Teling, Dalang and Ganjang. Make night stay at Keylong rest house or hostels.

Day 9 : Visit gompas at Guru Ghantal, Kardang, Shashur, Tayul, Gemur. Night stay at Keylong.

Day 10 : Leave for Manali (115 km) travel over Rohtang pass and visit the four recently built monasteries. Night stay at Manali guest house.

Day 11 : Leave for Rewalsar (132 km). Accommodation at Rewalsar rest house or hotel.

Day 12 : Leave for McLeodganj (160 km), enroute visit the recently built monasteries at Bir and Tashijong. Night stay at McLeodganj.

Day 13 : Visit McLeodganj.

FAIRS AND FESTIVALS

FEBRUARY—Winter Carnival : At the peak of the skiing season this impressive festival is held at Manali. **Basant Panchmi :** A festival heralding the onset of spring. There is festivity in the air and colourful kites fill the skies.

MARCH—Holi : This festival is a riot of colour and gaiety. Thousands of devotees throng the shrine of Paonta Sahib on the banks of the Yamuna river. Holi celebrations at the historic town of Sujanpur Tira are celebrated with song, dance and festivities.

APRIL : A seasonal festival is celebrated all over the State with colourful fairs, dancing, wrestling and archery contests. At Paonta Sahib, devotees gather and hymns are chanted throughout the day. At the lakes of Rewalsar and Prashar near Mandi and at Tattapani, purifying dips are taken on this auspicious occasion.

MAY : The river festival at Kullu and the summer festival at Dharamsala are two exciting events in Himachal. The season for hang gliding at Billing, near Kangra, begins and it is the time for Hang Gliding Rally. Summer festivals held at Shimla, Dharamsala and Dalhousie are memorable events. A variety of programmes add to the summer season. These include folk dances, mushairs as (recitation of Urdu poetry by poets), fairs, sport tournaments, golf and flower shows.

OCTOBER : October is marked by the spectacular Kullu Dussehra. The presiding deity of Lord Raghunath and gaiety, music and colour are part of the festival. The Mountaineering Institute organises the All India Water Sports Regatta at the Pong Dam during this month. The other major fair is held near the Jwalamukhi Temple in Kangra. At Kilar and Panai (in Pangi Valley), in Chamba, the Phool Yatra, another remarkable neighbourhood festival is celebrated and the Dehant Nag is worshipped.

DECEMBER : The most important event of this month is Ice Skating Carnival which is held in Shimla. Fancy Dress and other competitions, and the grand finale of a torchlight tattoo make it a marvellous occasion. Christmas celebrations mark the end of this festive month and churches in Shimla and Dalhousie resound with the sonorous chimes of bells.

JAMMU AND KASHMIR

JAMMU AND KASHMIR
AT A GLANCE

AREA : 2,22,236 Sq. km.
CAPITAL : Srinagar (Summer)
Jammu (Winter).
BOUNDARIES : East and North
East - China; West - Pakistan; North East
- Afhganistan; South - Himachal Pradesh
and Punjab.
LANGUAGES : Kashmiri, Dongri,
Punjabi, Urdu and Pahari.
ROADS : The road length of the
state is 13,540 km.

AIRPORTS : Srinagar : Jammu and Leh.

MUSEUMS

Jammu : Dongra Art Gallery
Srinagar : Sri Pratap Singh Government Museum

HILL RESORTS

Gulmarg (2730 m) Railhead – Jammu Tavi 305 km
Leh (3514 m) Railhead – Jammu Tavi 739 km
Pahalgam (2130 m) Railhead – Jammu Tavi 305 km
Srinagar (1586 m) Railhead – Jammu Tavi 305 km

PILGRIM CENTRES (A : Air; R : Rail)

Amarnath : An ice Shiva Lingam which waxes and wanes with
the moon; A - Srinagar 141 km, R Jammu Tavi 401.

Asrari Sharief : Shrines of Shah Asar-ud-din Sahib;
A and R Jammu.

Charari Sharief : Ziarat of Shaikh Nur-ud-din popularly known
as Nunda Rishi; A – Srinagar 28 km; R – Jammu 305 km.

Hazratbal Dargah : The sacred hair of Prophet Mohammed is
enshrined here A – Srinagar.

Khir Bhawani : Marble temple of Rangeya Devi; A – Srinagar
27 km.

Leh : Buddhist monastery associated with Guru Padmasambhava;
A Leh; R Jammu 739 km.

Shahdra Sharief : Tomb of Saint Pir Ghulam Shah; A and R Jammu.

Srinagar : Shankaracharya Temple built around 200 BC; A – Srinagar, R - Jammu 305 km.

Sudhmahadev : Ancient Shiva temple visited on full moon night in Sawan month; A and R Jammu 120 km.

Vaishno Devi : Cave shrine of Goddess Vaishno Devi (14 km trek from Katra); A and R Jammu 62 km.

Ziarat Babareshi : Tomb of saint Baba Payam-ud-din (5km from Gulmarg); A Srinagar 61 km. R – Jammu 361 km.

Valley of Kashmir : set in the lap of the Himalayas towering to 18,000 feet with the sinuous Jhelum river cutting across in coils and curves forming the highway and the main source of sustenance. This fertile land has over centuries enticed people from all over the world to behold its legendary beauty. Indeed no other place on earth has more widely been referred to as **"PARADISE"**.

HISTORY

Jammu has been mentioned in the Mahabharata. According to a legend which is even mentioned in Rajatarangini and Nilmat Purana Kashmir was once a large lake. Kashyap Rishi had drained off the water making it an abode.

Emperor Ashoka introduced Buddhism to Kashmir in the 3rd century BC which was later strengthened by Kanishka. Huns got the control of the valley in the early 6th century. The valley regained freedom in 530AD but soon came under the rule of the Ujjain empire. After the decline of the Vikramaditya the valley had its own rulers. There was a synthesis of Hindu and Buddhist cultures. Lalitaditya (697 – 738 AD) was most famous Hindu ruler who extended his kingdom up to Bengal in the east, Konkan in the south and Turkistan in the north. Islam came into Kashmir in the 13th and 14th centuries. Zain-ul-Abedin (1420 – 70 AD) was the most famous Muslim ruler who came to Kashmir when the Hindu king Sinha Dev reigned there before Tatar invasion. Later Charaks Haider Shah, son of Zain-ul-Abedin, continued to rule till 1596 AD when Akbar conquered Kashmir. In 1752 AD, Kashmir passed on from the feeble control of the Mughal emperor of the time to Ahmed Shah Abdali of Afghanistan. The Valley was ruled by the Pathans for 67 years.

The land of Jammu was divided into 22 hill participants. Raja Maldev, one of the Dogra rulers conquered many to consolidate the kingdom. Raja Ranjit Dev ruled over Jammu from 1733 to 1782 AD.

His successors were weak and thus Maharaja Ranjit Singh annexed the territory to Punjab. He later handed over Jammu to Raja Gulab Singh, a scion of the Dogra family. The State was governed by the Dogra rulers till 1947 when Maharaja Hari Singh signed the Instrument of Accession in favour of the Indian Union on October 26, 1947.

SRINAGAR

Srinagar is located in the heart of the Kashmir Valley, and is spread on both sides of the Jhelum river. Kalahana, author of 'Rajtaragini'

states that Srinagar was founded by Emperor Asoka in 3rd century BC. The present Srinagar was founded by Pravarasena II. Hiuen Tsang, the Chinese traveller had visited it in 631 AD. Lalitaditya Mukhtapida was the most illustrious ruler of the Hindu period which ended in 1339 AD. King Zain-ul-Abidin (1420-70AD), who was popularly known as 'Badshah' was a great patron of Sanskrit. Akbar captured the valley and endowed Srinagar with beautiful mosques and gardens. The Sikhs overthrew the last Muslim ruler during the reign of Maharaja Ranjit Singh in 1819. In 1846 the Dogras secured the sovereignty of Kashmir from the British under the Treaty of Amritsar, and in 1947 the State became a part of the Indian Union.

Today, Srinagar is a pleasure resort for tourists. It is a unique city because of its lakes – the Dal, the Nagin and the Anchar which provide delightful houseboat holiday.

PLACES OF INTEREST

PATHER MASJID : This stone mosque built by Nur Jehan is located in the heart of the city. It is reserved for prayers Shia Muslims.

SHAH HAMDAN MOSQUE : One of the oldest in the city it has fine paper work on its walls and ceilings.

JAMIA MASJID : Originally built by Sikandar Lodi in 1400 AD and enlarged by his son Zain-ul-Abidin it is a typical example of Indo-Saracenic architecture.

NAGIN LAKE : The jewel in the ring, the smallest but most lovely part of Dal Lake, its deep blue waters, encircled by a ring of green trees. Water skiing and swimming facilities are available. Most houseboats on the Nagin and the Jhelum are situated on the banks of the lake and can be accessed directly from land with the help of a shikara, while all those on the Dal Lake require a shikara to reach them.

DAL LAKE : It is the largest lake spread over 18 sq. km and is divided by causeways in four parts— Gagribal, Lokutdal Boddal and Nagin. Lokutdal and Boddal each have an island in the centre called Rup lank and Sona Lank respectively.

A shikara ride is one of the most soothing and relaxing aspects of a holiday in Kashmir. It can be an hour long ride to see the various sights of the lake, a shopping by shikara visiting handicraft shops within the periphery of the lake or a whole day trip to visit important city landmarks.

MUGHAL GARDENS : Kashmir was a favourite of the Mughal emperors who visited it often. They planted gardens with terraces and flowing water courses.

CHASHMA SHAHI : The smallest of Srinagar's Mughal Gardens, built in terraces with a spring of cool, refreshing digestive water, at a height above the city. The original garden was laid out by Shah Jehan in 1632 AD.

NISHAT BAGH : It was designed in 1633 AD by Asaf Khan, brother of Nur Jehan. It commands a magnificent view of the lake and the snow-capped Pir Panjal mountain range. Largest of the gardens, it has several terraces, a central water course and a majestic site between the Dal Lake and Zabarwan hills.

SHALIMAR BAGH : Built by Emperor Jehangir for his wife Nur Jehan, the garden is 539 by 182 meters and has four terraces. A canal lined with polished stone and supplied water from Harwan runs through the middle of the garden. The fourth terrace was once served for royal ladies. I.T.D.C. runs a Son-et-Lumiere show from May to October.

HAZRATBAL : Across the Dal Lake near Shalimar is the mosque of Hazratbal, made of marble with a dome and a minaret. It is the only one of its kind architecturally in Kashmir. This shrine has a special sanctity because a sacred hair of Prophet Mohammad is preserved here and displayed to public on special occasions.

HARWAN : These are the remains of ancient ornamented, tile pavements of Buddhist period. The tiles indicate the dresses of the people, such as loose trousers, Turkoman caps or close fitting turbans and large ear-rings which reveal a Central Asian influence.

PARI MAHAL : Once a Buddhist monastery, it was converted into a school of astrology by Dara Shikoh, Emperor Shah Jenah's eldest son. This ancient monument is connected to Chashmashahi by road.

SHANKARACHARYA TEMPLE : Located on a hill one thousand feet above the city, it is also known as Takht-i-Sulaiman. The philosopher sage Shankaracharya had stayed at this site when he had visited Kashmir ten centuries ago to revive Sanatan Dharma. The present structure is said to have been built by an unknown Hindu devotee during the reign of Emperor Jehangir. The temple offers a magnificent view of the valley.

HOW TO REACH

AIR : Srinagar is connected by air to Delhi, Amritsar, Jammu, Chandigarh, Leh, Ahmedabad and Mumbai. The Jammu and Kashmir tourism operates Westland Helicopter services with a capacity of 10 to 15 people on following routes :
(1)   City round (15 minutes).
(2)   Srinagar to Pahelgaom and back.
(3)   Srinagar to Gulmarg and back.

RAIL : Nearest railway station Jammu Tavi 305 km.

ROAD : Srinagar is connected by road to Jammu and Leh.

Jammu and Kashmir Tourism operates mini, luxury, super-deluxe, 'A' and 'B' class buses between Jammu and Srinagar.

Halting and overnight stay facilities between Jammu and Srinagar are available at the - Jajjar Kotli – tourist bungalow; Kud – tourist bungalow, Dormitory; Patnitop – huts, tourist bungalow, youth hostel; Batote – huts, tourist bungalow and dormotory; Ramban – tourist bungalow; Banihal – tourist bungalow and Dormitory; Qazigund – tourist bungalow.

DISTANCES FROM SRINAGAR

Jammu Tavi 293 km; Amarnath 142 km; Delhi 876 km; Aharbal 51 km; Leh 434 km; Yousmargh 47 km; Sonmarg 81 km; Gulmarg 46 km; Katra 285 km; Pahalgaon 94 km.

CONDUCTED TOURS

J & K RTC runs several sightseeing services. Timings tours vary with the season.

For further information contact :
— Tourist Reception Centre, Maulana Azad Road and Sherwani Road, Srinagar. PH 72698.
— J & K Tourism Development Corporation
— Tourist Reception Centre. PH 76107, 72644

HOTEL ACCOMMODATION (STD CODE 0194)

— Hotel Oberoi Palace, Boulevard (4 Star Deluxe) PH 71241 – 6
— Centaur Lake View Hotel : (5 Star Deluxe) P.O.Box 221 PH 475 631/34; FAX 471 877
— Broadway Hotel, Maulana Azad Road PH 75621,22,23
— Metro Hotel and Hotel Boulevard. PH 77089
— Hotel Tramboo Continental. PH 73914, 71718
— Asia Brown Hotel. PH 73856, 73844
— Hotel Sabena. PH 78046
— Khazir Trabels (P) Ltd (2 Star) Dalgate PH 478 256, 477 126
— Ahdoo's Hotel Pvt Ltd. Residency Road PH 472 593, 471 904; FAX 455 251

HOUSEBOATS

Houseboats are peculiar to Srinagar and perhaps the most memorable accommodation available. There are over 1000 houseboats moored on the banks of the Jhelum river, the Dal Lake and the Nagin Lake. They are known for their comfort and have been categorised into Deluxe, A, B, C and D categories. Meals are generally included in the tariff.

Names of the Houseboats :
— Hotel Shangrila. PH 72422
— Hotel Zamrud. PH 72563, 73614 / 15

— Meena Bazar Group of Houseboats. PH 74044, 77662
— M.S. Baktoo Group of Houseboat. PH 78698, 79612/13
— Welcome Group Gurkha Houseboat. PH 75229

EXCURSIONS

GANDERBAL : (19 km) Situated on the banks of Sindh, it offers excellent camping and mooring sites.

BURZAHOM : (24 km) The excavations at Burzahom have revealed settlements dating back to 2600 BC.

AVANTIPUR : (29 km) It is famous for the ruins of the ancient temple believed to have been built in honour of Lord Shiva by Avanti Verma in the 9th century AD. Accommodation is available at tourist huts and bungalows.

CHARAT SHARIFF : (30 km) It is on the road to Yusmarg and the "zairat" or shrine of the famous patron saint of Kashmir, Sheikh Noor-ud-Din, popularly known as Nunda Rishi is here.

MANASBAL : (32 km - 1560 meters) It is a panoramic lake laden with flowering lotus plants during summer and is a birdwatchers' paradise. Accommodation is available at tourist huts.

DACHINGAM NATIONAL PARK : (32 km – 2400 metres) Originally a royal game preserve, this sanctuary is now protected and provides shelter to the Himalayan black bear, brown bear, musk deer and the hangul or Kashmir stag. Permits to enter the sanctuary can be obtained from chief wildlife warden – Tourist Reception centre.

YUSMARG : (47km - 2377 meters) It is located in a small open valley in the Pir Panjal range surrounded by pines and firs. Accommodation is available at tourist bungalows, dormitories. Ponies can be hired from local tourist offices.

AHARBAL : (51km - 2400 meters) It is famous for an impressive waterfall formed by Veshav river, falling from a height of 24.4 meters.

ACHBAL : (58 km via Anantnag - 1677 Meters) Once the pleasure retreat of Empress Nur Jehan, it has fine gardens in Mughal style and trout hatchery.

WULAR LAKE : (60km - 1580 meters) Largest fresh water lake in India, is an important hydrographic system of Kashmir and acts as a flood reservoir.

MATTAN : (61km) Located on Pahalgam road, the spring in Mattan has a Shiva temple. Accommodation is available at tourist sarai.

MARTAND : (64km) Martand has the most impressive ancient ruins in Kashmir. Devoted to Sun God Surya, the Martand temple was built by Lalitaditya Mukhtapida in 7th–8th centuries AD. Accommodation is available at a Tourist Sarai.

KOKERANG : (70 km - 2020 meters) It is famous for curative properties of its springs. It also has a botanical garden with a variety of roses. Accommodation is available at tourist huts and bungalows.

VERTANG : (80 km - 1876 Meters) The spring here is reported to be the chief source of the Jhelum river. Further to the east lies the remains of a pavilion and baths built during the Mughal period. Accommodation is available at tourist bungalows.

DASKUM : (85km - 2513 meters) It is the forest retreat girdled by mountains. Accommodation is available at tourist bungalows

SPORTS ACTIVITIES

GOLF : Kashmir government runs 18 holes Golf club, located at Maulana Azad Road. Temporary membership is available from the Secretary.

FISHING : Rivers and streams are stocked with trout fish. Fishing permits can be obtained from the Director of Fisheries, Tourist Reception Centre, PH 72862.

TREKKING : A set of trekking map is available with the Tourist Reception Centre and Jand K tourism offices giving details on routes. Trekking equipment can be hired from the Department of Tourism, Tourist Reception Centre.

WATER SPORTS : Water sports Institute on Nagin Lake offers a variety of facilities like water-skiing, boating, swimming etc.

GULMARG

Gulmarg is rated as one of the matchless hill resorts in the world. Gulmarg is the valley, lush and green, located in the uplands of Jammu and Kashmir. The summer and autumn months provide excellent opportunities for excursions. All around are snow-capped mountains, and on clear day one can see all the way to Nanga Parbat, in one direction and Srinagar to another. Gulmarg also has one of the world's highest green golf course, there are golf sets on hire and temporary memberships, including one-day memberships.

PLACES OF INTEREST

ALPATHER LAKE : It is a icy water lake which remains frozen till the middle of June.

KHILANMARG : Carpeted with flowers in summer, this uphill journey from Gulmarg offers an unrivalled spectacle of the peaks and wide spreading waters of Wular and other lakes.

NINGAL NALLAH : This stream flows from the snow-bed and springs near Alhawat and Alpather and cuts through picturesque pine forests.

ZIARAT OF BABARESHI : A Muslim shrine, the 'ziarat' or tomb is of baba Payam-u-Din, a noted Muslim saint who lived here during the Mughal rule. Both Hindu and Muslims make offerings here.

HOW TO REACH

AIR : Jammu and Kashmir department runs a helicopter service from Srinagar depending upon demand.

RAIL : Nearest railway station Jammu

ROAD : Gulmarg is connected by road from Srinagar (56km). In winter the buses operate up to Tanmarg (7 km from Gulmarg) and the remaining distance is covered by Jeep. Tourist taxis are also available between Srinagar and Gulmarg.

Local Tourist Office : Tourist Office, Club Building, Gulmarg PH 239

HOTEL ACCOMMODATION (STD CODE 01953)

— Highlands Park Hotel, PH 207, 230
— Hill Top, PH 277, 245
— Hotel Ornate Woodlands, PH 68

SPORT ACTIVITIES

In winter Gulmarg becomes country's premier skiing resort. One can hire snow boots, mufflers, woollen socks, windproof jackets and caps.

Some of the best slopes in the country for beginners and intermediates are available. The largest Ski run in Gulmarg is provided by the Gondola Cable Car which allows a ski run of 2213 metres.

French ski lifts are operated by J and K Department of Tourism on three different slopes.

TREKKING : Well defined trekking routes are :
— Gulmarg – Khilanmarg – Apharwat (1 Day return).
— Gulmarg – Danvas - Teijan – Tosha Maidan (3 Days).

GOLF : 18-hole golf course maintained by J and K Tourism, membership is available from local tourist office. A limited supply of golfing equipment is available for hire.

SLEDGING : A flat wooden board is taken up the hill-top and, without a navigator, allowed to slide downhill.

SKIING : Some of the best slopes in the country for beginners and intermediates are available at Gulmarg. Skiing equipment is available for hire from the ski shops, PH 289

SKI LIFTS : French ski lifts are operated by J and K Department of Tourism on three different slopes.

PAHALGAM

Pahalgam is an idyllic resort, located on the banks of river Lidder and Sheshnag. It is the base for several treks in the region and for the annual pilgrimage to the cave shrine of Amarnath. The surroundings are ideal and allow for relaxation and leisure in the true spirit of traditional hill resort.

PLACES OF INTEREST

AMARNTH : (47 km - 3962 meters) The shrine of Amarnath is believed to be the abode of Lord Shiva. An stalagmite formed by water dripping through the limestone roof of the cave, has formed in the shape of a natural 'lingam' (Phallus). The lingam waxes and wanes with the moon. Each year in the month of Sawan, several thousands of pilgrims start on a journey on the cave from Pahalgam to make obeisance on the full-moon day.

Chandanwari from Pahalgam is the starting point for the Amarnath Yatra. Road from Pahalgam to Chandanwari is fairly flat terrain and can be covered by car. From Chandanwari onwards the trek becomes much steeper, being accessible on foot or by pony about 11 km from Chandanwari is the mountain lake of Sheshnag after which 13 km away is the last stop Panchtarni. The Amarnath cave is 6 km from there. The State government makes extensive arrangements every year for the successful completion of the pilgrimage registering each year over 1,00,000 pilgrims, registering pony owners and dandiwalas, providing camps en route and ensuring safe comfortable and speedy progress of the pilgrims. If one visits Amarnath in other than the Yatra period, one can take a pony ride up to Sheshnag lake, returning late the same evening.

Accommodation : Camp at Zoijpal or rest house and pilgrim shelters at Wawjan.

BALSARA : A glen in the pine and fir forest commanding a charming view of the valley, about 152 meters up on the mountainside.

KOLAHOL GLACIER : (2408 meters) 36 kilometers from Pahalgam to Aru pony track. The path winds through woods to the meadow of Aru. There the river disappears and reappears after about 27 meters.

MAMLESVARA : Small ancient stone temple consecrated to Shiva Mamesvara. The temple was built before 12th century AD.

TARSAR LAKE : 35 kilometer via Aru and Lidderwatt, the lake has beautiful surroundings.

MAMAL : This village has a Shiva temple considered to be Kashmir's oldest existing temple dating back to the 8th century AD.

HOW TO REACH

AIR : Jammu and Kashmir department of tourism runs a helicopter service from Srinagar depending upon the demand.

RAIL : Nearest railway station Jammu.

ROAD : Pahalgan is connected by all-weather road to Srinagar. JandK SRTC runs deluxe and ordinary bus services from Tourist Reception Centre, Srinagar. Ponies and Porters can be arranged through local Tourist office, PH 24.

HOTEL ACCOMMODATION (STD CODE 0191)

— Pahalgam Hotel (3 Star) PH 26, 52
— Hotel Woodstock, PH 27

SPORT ACTIVITIES

GOLF : The Government Club has a 9-hole golf course which can be used by tourists. Golf sets can be hired. PH 51.

FISHING : Lidder River offers excellent fishing beats for brown trout. The fishing season stretches from April to September. Permits are issued for a maximum of three days at a time on first come first serve basis. Fishing equipment can be hired in Srinagar. Contact the Directorate of Fisheries, Tourist Reception centre, Srinagar, PH 72862.

TREKKING : Some well-known routes are

— Pahalgam-Chandanwari-Sheshnag-panchtarni-Amarnath Cave Temple-Sonmarg (7 days)
— Pahalgam-Chandanwari-Sheshnag-Rangamarg-Humpet-kanital-Lonivilad-Panikhar-Kargil (9 Days)

Trekking equipment can be hired from the local Tourist office or at the Tourist Reception Centre Srinagar.

SONMARG

Legend has it that a well in the vale has been bestowed with water which is further bestowed by mystical qualities of turning everything into eternal riches - gold. Sonmarg derives its name from it. It literally stands for 'MEADOWS OF GOLD'. The blooming valley has been chiselled over the ages by the mighty Indus river.Major trekking routes begin from here. Two lakes—Gadsar and Satsar are on the periphery of Sonmarg.

Sonmarg is sheer scenic splendour. The very way—metalled road snakes through massive mountains laden with forests and firs. After a breathtaking journey of 27 km from Srinagar, one goes over the Indus river at Wayil. Onwards, the valley opens up to a meadow. Kangan and Gund are two important halts en route. The mountain range here is Harmukg and serves as the ideal foreground to an all pervasive backdrop of blue Himalayas. The road takes an incline before slapping into Sonmarg proper. The valley is ringed by mountains scaling 5,300 metres in height. The river meanders across the valley and abounds in trout and masheer an angler's delight. Major Trekking routes begin at Sonmarg. In a sharp and joyous contrast to the green meadow land Sonmarg has a string of shimmering waterfalls and the Thaijwas Glacier. Two lakes ' Gadsar and Satsar' are on the periphery of Sonmarg.

HOW TO REACH

AIR : Jammu and Kashmir department of Tourism operates helicopter services from Srinagar. Contact Tourist Reception Centre, Srinagar for possibility of service to Sonmarg.

RAIL : Nearest railway station Jammu

ROAD : Sonmarg is connected by road to Srinagar 87 km.

JandK SRTC runs deluxe and ordinary bus services from Tourist Reception Centre, Srinagar, PH 72689

Ponies and porters can be arranged through the local Tourist Office.

HOTEL ACCOMMODATION (STD CODE 0191)

Tourist huts, tourist bungalows, rest houses. For reservation and enquiries, contact : Tourist Reception Centre, Srinagar, PH 77303, 77305, 73648

LADAKH

Ladakh means a land of passes. Viewed from high above its surface, Ladakh appears a vast monotony of three colours; the brown of the earth, the white of the snow and the black dark shadows in the valleys. Leh, 434 km from Sringar and at a height of 3521 meters on the Karakoram range, is the district headquarters of Ladakh.

Ladakh's early history is woven into its mythology. The great Chinese wanderer Fa-Hien travelled its folds as far back as 399 AD. Ladakh is renowned for its Buddhist monasteries which are dotted all over the sparsely populated countryside, each richly decorated with paintings and virtually a storehouse of ancient religious manuscripts.

PLACES OF INTEREST

LEH PALACE : Built in the 16th century by Singay Namgiyal, the palace stands like a sentinel overlooking the town. Inside there are old wall paintings depicting the life of the Buddha.

NAMGYAL TSEMO : Soaring above the valley-crags, the monastery dominates both the palace and the town, exhibiting in a manner the supremacy of the spiritual king. The monastery houses a guilded statue of the Buddha, painted scroll, ancient manuscripts and wall paintings.

LEH MOSQUE : Built by Deldan Namgyal in the mid-17th century AD, a tribute to his Muslim mother, the Leh mosque is an exquisite work of Turko - Iranian architecture.

GOMPA TSEMO : One of the royal monastries, located near the palace it is known for its two storied statue of Chamb Buddha in a sitting posture.

HOW TO REACH

AIR : Leh is connected by air to Srinagar, Delhi and Chandigarh.

RAIL : Nearest railway station Jammu 690 km.

ROAD : Leh is connected by road to Srinagar. Road communication between Srinagar and Leh is closed   from October to May. J and K SRTC runs regular super deluxe, A and B class bus service to Leh from Srinagar. Taxis, Jeeps and Jongas can be hired for local and

out station journeys. Contact Tourist officer for hiring mules and ponies.
Foreigner's Regional Registration Office – Suprintendent of Police
– Leh.

HOTEL ACCOMMODATION (STD CODE 01982)

— A CLASS HOTELS : Lingzi – PH 20; Gal-dan Continental
Shambala. PH 67
— Tsemola PH 94; Hotel Kang-Lha-Chan- Larimo PH 101;
Kangri. PH 51
— Indus PH 166; Ladakh Sari Stock. PH 181
— B CLASS : Himalaya PH 104; Choskor-Tibet PH 149; Bijoo
PH 131
— Yak-Tail PH 118; Lung-se-Jung. PH 193
For reservation contact Assistant Director of Tourism - Leh *Or*
J and K Department of Tourism, Tourist Office – Leh, PH 97

SPORT ACTIVITIES

Mountaineering,
trekking, white river
rafting, Heli Skiing all
have unlimited scope. For
mountaineering, the
Zanskar range and the
Ladakh range offer some
of the finest challenges
anywhere. A list of peaks,
their climbing charges and schedules for reservation is available with
the Indian Mountaineering Foundation, Benito Juarez Marg, New Delhi
110 021

TREKKING

The Markha Valley trek

Spituk to Zinghchen, 12 km; Zingchen to Yurutse, 13 km; Yurutse
to Sku (via Kandala 4,800 metres), 14 km; Sku to Markha, 12 km;
Markha to Hankar, 11 km; Hankar to Nimaling, 10 km; Nimaling to
Shang Sumdo (via Kongmarula 5,030 metres) 14 km; Shang Sumdo
to Martselang, 10 km; Martselang to Hemis, 6 km.

(1) The Padam-Manali Trek

Padam to Raru 22 km; Raru to Cha 23 km; Cha to Tasta 25 km;
Tasta to Kargiah, 26 km; Kargiah to Lakhang Pulu, 24 km; Lakhang
Pulu to Zanskar Sumdo (via Shingkula 5,100 metres), 25 km; Zanskar
Sumdo to Darcha Sumdo, 25 km.

(2) The Padam-Kishtwar Trek

Padam to Tungri, 12 km; Tungri to Ating, 12 km; Ating to Huttra, 24 km; Huttra to Buswas, 17 km, Buswas to Machail, 27 km, Galar to Kishtwar, 32 km.

(3) The Lamayuru-Spadum Trek

Lamayrur to Fanjila, 24 km; Fanjila to Hanupata, 23 km; Hanupata to Photoksar 20 km; Photoksar to Base of Singila, 18 km; Base of Singila to Skumpata (via Singila 5,000 metres), 19 km; Skumpata to Lingshet, 9 km; Lingshet to Omangschu (via Hanumala 4,700 metres), 28 km; Omangschu to Pido (Parpela 4,700 metres), 18 km; Pidmo to Rinam, 17 km; Rinam to Spadum, 16 km.

(4) The Likir-Nurla Trek

Main Road to Likir Gompa, 5 km; Likir Gompat to Yanghthang, 9 km; Yangthang to Hemis Sukpachen, 10 km; Hemis Sukpachen to Temisgam, 11 km; Temisgam to Nurla, 8 km.

EXCURSIONS

SPITUK MONASTERY : (9km) Five hundred years old, this monastery has some prized thangkas and huge statues of goddess Kali, whose faces are unveiled once every year. This chamber also contains an ancient collection of masks. Enormous statues of Goddess kali are exhibited once in the year on occasion of the annual festival which falls in January.

STAKHANA MONASTERY : The monastery consists of old thangkas from 10th century.

From the top a splendid view of the Indus, Thinksey Monastery and surroundings can be seen.

MONASTERY : (15 km) This is the summer palace of the erstwhile rulers of Leh, surrounded by picturesque gardens. Built in 1620 AD., the palace has the largest victory stupa, topped with pure gold. There is a spectacular double storied statue of Buddha Sayamunni in a sitting posture. Wrought of copper and brass, gilded with gold and silver and studded with precious gems, it leaves the onlooker stunned with bewilderment.

THIKSEY MONASTERY : (19 km) Enroute to Hemis is this 15th century monastery. It has twelve storeys and consists of eight temples and about 250 residents Lamas. The chambers are full of statues, stupas, thangkas, ancient swords and Tantric wall paintings.

SHEY PALACE AND HEMIS HIGH ALTITUDE NATIONAL PARK : (35 km) This 600 sq.km area is home to some of the most exotic and rare flora and faunal species, many of which are on the endangered list.

HEMIS GOMPA : (43 km) Situated in a side ravine off the main Indus valley the monastery contains gold statues and stupas decorated with precious stones. It has superb collection of thangkas, including the largest which is exhibited once in twelve years. Every June a colourful festival, marking the birthday of Guru Padmasambhava is held here. Masked dancers with slow steps and loud music are supported to fight away the demons.

LIRIK GOMPA : (61 km) Lirik Gompa contains a number of enormous clay statues of the Buddha in different forms. Founded during the 12th century, Lirik was the first royal monastery to be established in Ladakh under direct Tibetan infulence.

ALCHIGOMPA : (66 km) This monastery consists of six temples which contains a chorten, seated Buddha and exquisite paintings. Over 10 centuries old, profusely painted walls depict the events of Buddha's life, lamas and musicians.

CHOGLAMSAR : A place full of flowers and plants which grow fantastically at such high altitudes. Polo and golf grounds offer adventurers a rare opportunity of such sporting activities. From Chogalmsar to the summer palace, it is an exhilarating journey through beautiful trees.

LAMAYURU : (125 km) On Leh-Srinagar road, this is the oldest known monastery of the region dating back to the 10th century. It has fascinating caves carved out of the mountain. Some rooms are richly furnished with carpets, Tibetan tables, prized thangkas and butter -lamps can be seen.

SAMKAR GOMPA : The only monastery built on valley level, it is the seat of the yellow sect of the Buddhists. It has a formidable collection of miniature statues of pure gold and number of wall paintings. This is the modern monastery with eletricity, yet it is an ancient edifice which has a huge statue of eleven heads and 100 hands, a form of Avalokiteshwara Another statue of Chanzeri with 1,000 eyes, 1,000 arms and 1,000 legs is a gorgeous representation of a Buddhist deity.

SPORTS ACTIVITIES

Ladakh is paradise for adventure sports; mountaineering, trekking, white-river rafting /canoeing. A list of peaks, their climbing charges and schudule for reservations is available with the Indian Mountaineering Foundation, Benito Juarez Marg, New Delhi 110 021, PH 671211.

TREKKING : Well known treks around Leh
— Leh-Lamayuru-Wanla-Ursi-Tar La-Mangyur-Saspol-Leh (7 Days)
— Padam-Tongde-Zangla-Cher Cher La –Chup-Cha-Shang Kong-Ma Kurma Sumdo-Nari Narsa-Lang Tan-Hankar Nima-Linh-Shakdo-Hemis (9/11 Day)

Trekking equipment can be hired from the Leh Toursit Office on nominal charges.

FESTIVALS

HEMIS : (June) A colourful festival is held to commemorate the birth of Guru Padmasambhava who is believed to have fought with demons for the safety of the local people. Mask dances are organised and stalls are put up selling handicrafts and other wares.

LADAKH FESTIVAL : (August) It is organised by the District Tourist Office.

KARGIL

Kargil, 204 km from Srinagar, on the high way to Leh, is the second most important town of the Ladakh region. All J & K SRTC buses running between Srinagar and Leh make a night's halt here.

PLACES OF INTEREST

DRASS : A small township, 57 km short of Kargil on Srinagar-Leh highway is reputed to be the second coldest inhabited place in the world. Its inhabitants are of the Dard stock—an Indo Aryan race—believed to have originally come form Central Asia.

SURU VALLEY : This is a fertile valley of immense beauty occupied by a population of Tibeto-Dard desent. The farthest part of the valley consists of a picturesque alluvial pan towered over by the lofty Nun (7,135m) and Kun (7,035m) massif. Kartse village near Sankoo has a seven meter high rock sculpture of Maitreya, which is the remnant of the ancient Indian Buddhist influence. Panikhar is the approach base for mountaineering expeditions to Nun Kun and many treks.

RANGDUM : This is an isolated amphitheatre-like valley which lies 130 km from Kargil. It has a 17th century monastery perphed atop a central hillock

MULKBEKH : Situated 45 km east of Kargil on the road to Leh, Mulbeks is a 9-metre high rock sculpture of Maitreya. Percjed atop a rocky cliff, the Mulbekh monastery dominates the valley.

ZANSKAR : Zanskar is the remotest and most isolated valley of Ladakh. It has a number of interesting monasteries and monuments. A number of highly adventurous trek routes criss-cross the valley connecting Manali and Kishtwar with Leh and the Indus valley.

KARSHA : The largest and wealthiest of all monasteries in Zanskar, which dates back to the 16ᵗʰ century. Karsha can be reached on foot in two hours from Padum.

BURDAN : 12 km from Padum this monastery houses an interesting collection of idols and stupas.

PHUGTAL : It is one of the two rare monastries of Zanskar.

ZONG KHUL : This cave monastery, situated on the Padum-Kishtwar route is built around two caves in the sheer rock-face of a gorge.

Kargil also serves as a base for trekking expeditions.

HOW TO REACH

Kargil is approachable by road on the Leh-Srinagar highway. All buses running between Srinagar and Leh make a night's halt here.

Kargil is the second most important town of the Ladakh region and an important base for exploring the surrounding areas and for forays into the Zanskar region.

JAMMU

Amongst the three regions of Jammu and Kashmir State, Jammu, perhaps, offers the widest diversity of terrain and beauty. In its undulating plains and lower hills of the south to its fierce heights of Kishtwar to the north-east, one is witness to its history, arts, religions and an abundance of natural beauty. The entire region is pocketed with lakes and valleys. The foundation of the settlement of Jammu is attributed to King Jambulochan of the 9ᵗʰ century BC when, as the legend goes, he saw a tiger and a goat together drinking at the same pool. At this auspicious spot he constructed a fort, believed to be the present Bahu Fort. Little is known of its subsequent history. Till 1730 AD, it remained under Dogra rule of Raja Dhruv Deva. Dogra rulers moved their capital to present site across the river Tawi and Jammu became an important centre for arts and culture, now renowned as the Pahari school. Religion too, played an important part in its development. So beautifully evidenced in its various shrines and temples spread throughout the region.

HOW TO REACH

AIR : Jammu is connected by air to Delhi, Chandigarh, Amritsar and Srinagar

RAIL : Jammu is connected by rail to Ahmedabad, Chennai, Delhi, Howrah, Jodhpur, Lucknow Mangalore, Mumbai and Pune.

ROAD : Jammu is connected by good all-weather roads to all parts of the country. In addition to the J and K State Road Transport Corporation, tourist agencies in various places in North India operate all types of coaches to Jammu.

Tourist Information Centres :
— Toursit Reception Centre, J and K Department of Tourism, Veer Marg. PH 48172
— J and K Tourism Development Corporation, Veer Marg. PH 5421

HOTEL ACCOMMODATION

— Asia Jammu Tavi, National Highway, PH 43930
— Hotel Jammu Askok, Ram Nagar, PH 43127, 43864
— Vardan Hotel, J.P.Chowk, PH 43212
— Premiere Hotel, veer Marg, PH 43234, 43436
— Mansar Hotel, Denis Gate, PH 46161
— Samrat Hotel, Near Central Bus Stand, PH 47402
— Jagan Lodge, Raghunath Bazar, PH 43243
— Regal Lodge, Raghunath Bazar, PH 42295, 46598
— Airlines Lodge, 209 Canal Road, PH 42910
— Broadway Lodge, Below Gumat, PH 43636

PLACES OF INTEREST

PEER KHOH : A Shivlingam formed naturally in a cave, neither its antiquity or cause is known, and legend has it that the cave leads underground out of the country.

PEER BABA : On the back side of the civil airport is the famous Dargah of the Muslim saint Peer Ali Shah. On Thursdays, Hindu and Sikh devotees vastly outnumber their Muslim brethren at the shrine.

RANBIRESHWAR TEMPLE : Built by Maharaja Ranbir Singh in 1883 AD it is dedicated to Lord Shiva. There are twelve Shiva Lingams of crystal measuring from 15 cm to 38 cm and galleries with thousands of Shiva lingams fixed on stone slab. Later another temple was built in its campus by his wife, Rani Bandral, in 1888 AD. It is dedicated to Lord Rama. The temple is renowned for its depiction of the Ram Lila and Krishna Lila in Paintings.

RAGAHNATH TEMPLE : Situated in the heart of the city and surrounded by a group of other temples, this temple dedicated to Lord Rama is outstanding and unique in northern India. Work on the temple was started by Maharaja Gulab Singh, founder of the present city, in 1835 AD and was completed by his son Maharaja Ranbir Singh in 1860 AD. The inner walls of the main temple are covered with gold sheet on three sides. There are many galleries with lakhs of saligrams. The surrounding temples are dedicated to various gods and goddesses connected with the epic of Ramayana.

RANBIR CANAL : The canal branches off from the Chenab river at Akhnoor, 32 km away. Its waters are ice cold throughout the year. Its banks serve as good view points and walkways.

BAHU FORT : Situated on a rock face on the left bank of the

Tawi river, this is perhaps the oldest fort and edifice in the city. It was constructed originally by Raja Bahulochan over 3,000 years ago. The existing fort was more recently improved and built by the Dogra rulers. There is a temple dedicated to goddess Kali inside the court.

BAGHE BAHU : These extensive gardens, laid around the Bahu Fort provides a pleasant view of the city.

MAHAMAYA TEMPLE AND CITY FOREST : On the bypass road behind Bahu Fort, the city forest surrounds the ancient Mahamaya temple overlooking the Tawi river. A small garden surrounded by woods provides the best view of the city.

MUBARAK MANDI PALACE : The oldest building in the palace complex dates to 1824 AD. The architecture is a blend of Rajasthani, Mughal and even Baroque European influences. The most stunning segment is the Sheesh Mahal, the pink hall now houses the Dogra Art Museum which has miniature paintings of the various hill schools.

EXCURSIONS

AKHNOOR : (32 km) It is a picnic spot situated on the bank of the Chenab river.

PURMANDAL : (39 km) It is a sacred place for the Hindus. Most Shiva lingams that are believed to have been automatically arisen following the rise of Devika are in and around Purmandal, towards the south-east of Jammu. It is sometimes referred to as Chotta Kashi

SURINSAR LAKE : (42 km) It is a picturesque spot with lake surrounded by wooded hills. Accommodation is available in tourist bungalows of J and K Tourism.

KATRA : (50 km) This small town serves as the base camp for visiting the famous shrine of Vaishnodeviji in the Trikuta hills. The shrine is approchable on foot along a 12km long well laid foot path. Accommodation is available in tourist bungalows / yatrikas and a number of private lodges besides dharamshalas.

VAISHNO DEVI : (62 km) A venerated Hindu shrine. There are regular bus services upto Katra (48 km), the remaining distance has to be covered on foot or by pony.

MANSAR LAKE : (80 km) A beautiful lake fringed by forest-covered hills.

RAMNAGAR : (102 km) Ramnagar is known for its murals in the Pahari style.

KUD : (106 km) At 1,738 meters on the Jammu-Srinagar highway, this is another resort. Private accommodation and huts/tourist bungalows of J and K Tourism are available.

BATOTE : (113 km) At 1,560 meters on the Jammu -Srinagar highway, it is a health resort. This resort straddles the forested slopes of the Patnitop mountain ranges. Accommodation is available in huts and tourist bungalows of the J and K Tourism.

PATNITOP : (112 km) The peaceful resort is located at 2,024 meters on the Jammu-Srinagar highway. It is enveloped by thickly wooded forests and is perched on a lovely plateau offering unusual lush green picnic spots.Private accommodation and huts/tourist bungalows of J and K Tourism are available.

SUDH MAHADEV : (120 km) A holy spot near Patnitop, pilgrims visit this place on the full moon night of Sawan and worship a 'Trishul' and a 'mace' supposedly belonging to Bhima. Here Devak stream originates and disappears into its bed after flowing down a few kilometres. Short of Sudh-kund is Gauri Kund, the legendary spring where Goddess Parvati used to bathe before commencing her daily prayers at Sudh Mahadev. This springs came to be named after her as 'Gauri Kund'.Few kilometres further from Sudh Mahadev is Matalai surrounded by lush deodar forests at an altitude of over 2000 metres. It is believed that Lord Shiva had got married to Goddess Parvati here. Accommodation is available at pilgrim centres of J and K Tourism.

SANSAR : (129 km) It is 19 km from Patnitop. Slightly away from national highway, it looks as though it has been scooped out of the earth in the shape of a cup, fringed by gigantic conifers.Accommodation is available in huts/tourist bungalows and dormitory of J and K Tourism.

RAMBAN : (148 km) An important halting station on Jammu-Srinagar highway.

KISHTWAR HIGH ALTITUDE NATIONAL PARK : (248 km) This unique national park is home to some rare animals and bird species.

FESTIVALS

APRIL—BAISAKHI : This day marks the end of winter. Gardens are in full bloom.

It is basically a harvest festival. Numerous fairs are organised and people come in thousands to celebrate the beginning of the harvest

Lohri : Makar Sankranti heralds the onset of spring. Thousands take a dip in the holy rivers. 'Yagnas' are performed almost in every house and temple. In rular areas, customs require boys to go around asking for gifts from newly-weds. A special "CHAHHA" dance is held on this occasion.

Bahu Mela : A major festival is held at the Kali temple in Bahu Fort (Jammu) twice a year.

Purmandal Mela : On Shivratri, the town is transformed for three days as people celebrate the marriage of Lord Shiva to Goddess Parvati here.

Mansar Food and Craft Mela : This mela is organised by J and K Tourism during Baisakhi every year. Held at picturesque Mansar Lake it is a three day celebration of the local crafts and cuisine where people from adjoining States also take part.

KARNATAKA

KARNATAKA
AT A GLANCE

AREA : 1,91,791 Sq. km.

CAPITAL : Bangalore

BOUNDARIES : East - Andhra Pradesh West - Goa and the Arabian Sea; South - Kerala and Karnataka; North - Maharashtra.

LANGUAGE : Kannada

ROADS : Karnataka had 1,37,520 km (1996-97) of motorable roads including 1,997 km of national highways. The

surfaced road length with 87,000 km constituted 65% of the total road length.

AIRPORTS : Bangalore, Mangalore, Hubli and Belgaum.

IMPORTANT MUSEUMS

Bangalore : Government Museum – Cubbon Park; Karnataka Government Museum and Venkatappa Art Gallery; Visvesvarayya Industrial and Techonological Museum

Bijapur : Archaeological Museum

Halebid : Archaeological Museum

Hampi : Archaeological Museum

Mysore : Sri Chamarajendra Art Gallery - Jagan Mohan Palace; Museum of Art and Archaeology – University of Mysore; Folklore Museum – University of Mysore

Srirangapatnam : Tipu Sultan Museum

HILL RESORTS

Kemmanagudi (1434m) Railhead- Terikere 38 km

Madikere (1170m) Railhead – Mysore 120 km

Nandi Hills (1479m) Railhead Bangalore 60 km

PILGRIM CENTRES (A : Air; R : Rail)

Bijapur : Ibrahim Rauza, tomb of Ibrahim Adil Shah; A - Belgaum 205 km, R - Bijapur.

Dharmasthala : Temple of Manjunatha (Shiva), Gomateswara statue and Jain centre; A – Mangalore – 75 km, R – Subramanya 35 km.

Devarayanadadurga : Temples of Narasimha at the top and at the foot of a hill; A – Bangalore 79 km, R Tumkur -12 km.

Gokarna : Called Dakshina Kashi, there is a Shiva temple with Atmalinga worshipped by Ravana. A - Goa 160 km, R - Hubli 110km

Kaiwara : Temple dedicated to the Pandavas; A and R Bangalore - 79 km.

Melkote : There is a Vishnu temple atop Yadavagiri hill. It is noted for Vairamundi festival in March-April; A – Bangalore 188 km, R - Srirangapatnam 30 km.

Mysore : Chamundeswari temple on the top of Chamundi hill; A – Bangalore 140km, R – Mysore.

Pattadakal : Sangameswara temple; A – Belgaum 192 km, R - Badami 33 km.

Shivanga : Temple dedicated to Gangadhara and Honna Devi; A - Bangalore 60 km, R- Tumkur 22 km.

Soundatti : Temple of Renuka or Yellamma; A - Belgaum 90 km, R - Dharwar 41 km.

Sringeri : Spot on the banks of Tunga river where Adi Shankaracharya established the first math; A - Mangaloe 152 km, R - Shimoga 140 km.

Talakaveri : Source of Kaveri river, 44 km from Medikere; A – Bangalore, R - Mysore 167 km.

Udipi : Krishna Temple and seat of the eight mathas founded by Madhvacharya; A and R - Mangalore 58 km.

Whitefield : Satya Sai Baba Ashram; A and R – Bangalore 16 km.

Karnataka is a land of fragrance—fragrance of enchanting perfume of sandal and agarbathis, the aroma of fresh roasted coffee beans, the

heady fragrance of the Mysore Mallige and thousands of roses blossoming. Ancient sculptured temples, magnificent palaces, ornate buildings and colourful festivals blend beautifully with the evergreen forests, golden beaches, orange groves and garden cities to form this exquisite land.

HISTORY

The name Karnataka is derived from Karunadu, literally lofty land. The history of Karnataka dates back to the period of epics. The capital of Bali and Sugreeva, 'Monkey Kings' of the Ramayana is said to have been Hampi in the Bellary district.

In the 4th century BC., a local dynasty Satavahana came to power and his dynasty's rule lasted nearly 300 years. With the disintegration of the Satavahana dynasty, the Kadambas came to power in the north, and the Gangas in the south of the State. The gigantic monolithic statue of Gomateswara is considered to be the monument of the Ganga period. The Chalukyas of Badami (500 to 735 AD) ruled over a wider area, from the Narmada to the Kaveri from the days of Pulikeshi II (609 to 642 AD) who had even defeated Harshvardhana of Kannauj. This dynasty created fine monuments at Badami, Aihole and Pattadakal, both structural and rock-cut. Aihole has been one of the cradles of temple architecture in the country. The Rastrakatas (753-973 AD) of Malkhed who succeeded them levied tribute on the rulers of Kannauj successively in the so-called Age of 'Imperial Kannauj'. Kannada literature developed in this period. Outstanding Jain scholars of India lived in their court. The Chalukyas of Kalyana ((973 to 1189 AD) and their feudatories, the Hoysalas of Halebidu built fine temples, encouraged literature and fine arts. Noted jurist Vijnaneshwara (work - Mitakshara) lived at Kalyana. The great religious leader Basaveshwara was a minister at Kalyana. Vijaynagar empire (1136 to 1646 AD) fostered indigenous traditions and encouraged arts religion and literature in Sanskrit, Kannada, Telugu and Tamil. Overseas trade flourished. The Bahamani Sultans(Capital -Gulbarga, later Bidar and Bijapur)Adilshahis raised fine Indo-Saranic bulidings and encouraged Urdu and Persian literature. Advent of the Portuguese resulted in the introduction of new crops (tobacco, chillies, potato etc.). After the fall of Peshwa (1818 AD) and Tipu (1799 AD) Karnataka came under the British.

After independence, the new united Mysore State was created in 1956 and was renamed Karnataka in 1973 AD.

SOUTHERN SPLENDOUR

BANGALORE

Bangalore, the 'GARDEN CITY OF INDIA' and capital of the State (1000 m above sea level) was founded in 1537 AD by a Vijaynagar chieftan Kempe Gowda. The legend goes that the King Veera Ballala of Vijaynagara once lost his way while hunting in a forest. Hung ry and tired, he came upon a lone hut in the thick of forest where he met an old woman. When he asked for food she gave him some baked beans (Benda Kalu in Kannada). To the King this humble meal tasted better than those served in his palace. To commemorate the incident, he

called the place 'BENDA KALU OORU' (place of baked beans) and this in time transformed into Bangalore. In the 18th century it was the stronghold of Haider Ali and Tipu Sultan. Today it is the fifth largest city of India and country's main industrial city which includes industries like aircraft, telephones, eletronics etc.

PLACES OF INTEREST

BULL TEMPLE : At Basavanagudi is one of the oldest temple, typical of the Dravidian style of architecture. Built by Kempe Gowda, the Nandi, the sacred bull, carved out of a single boulder, is 6.1 meter long and 4.6 meter high.

CUBBON PARK : This beautiful 300 acre park built in 1864 has the public library and the museum.

GANGADHARESWARA CAVE TEMPLE : Built by Kempe Gowda, this temple with four remarkable monolithic pillars, is dedicated to Lord Shiva.It also has a rare idol of Agni, God of Fire.

JUMMA MASJID : Oldest mosque built by Nughal Killedar, was damaged by cannon fire during the third Mysore war and renovated in 1836.

ST. MARY'S CATHEDRAL : Built by French missionary in 1882 AD it is a grand Basillica with an impressive tower and typically gothic pointed arches.

THE FORT : Built initially in 1537 by Kempe Gowda as a crude mud structure, it was rebuilt by Hyder Ali in 1761. In this fort Hyder

Ali had imprisoned David Baird along with a number of British army officers. The fort has well preserved Ganapati temple within its precincts and the temple on the outer wall carries exquisite carvings of Sri Krishna playing his flute and inside, there is a fine statue of Lord Ganesh which still attracts devotees. Near the fort is Tipu's palace, begun by Hyder Ali and completed by Tipu Sultan in 1791. It resembles Daria Daulat Palace of Srirangapatnam.

VIDHANA SOUDHA : This is an imposing granite structure with a total plinth area of over 5,00,000 sq.ft and houses the secretariat, the State legislature and several government offices.The huge carved doors of the cabinet are made of pure sandalwood.

VENKATARAMANSWAMY TEMPLE : Temple near Tipu's Palace was built by Chikka Deva Raja Wodeyar nearly 300 years ago, in the typical Dravidian style.

DURGAH OF HAZRAT TAWAKKAL MASTAN SHAH SUHARAWARDI : Situated in the heart of Cottonpet this Muslim saint's shrine has been associated with the Hindu festival of 'KANGRA'. The famous Kangra procession, while passing through the city, visits the 'Durgah' of the sufi saint Tawakkal Mastan whose tomb attracts thousands of both Muslims and non-Muslims.

HOW TO REACH

AIR : Bangalore is connected by air with Ahmedabad, Calcutta,Chennai, Cochin, Coimbatore, Delhi, Goa, Hyderabad, Mangalore, Mumbai, Pune and Thiruvananthapuram.

RAIL : Bangalore is connected by rail with cities all over India. Bangalore is connected by Rajdhani Express with Delhi.

Rajdhani timings : (A : Arrival, D : Departure)
— 2430 Rajdhani Exp (Monday, Tuesday, Saturday) H. Nizamuddin 2050 / Bangalore A 0635
— Rt 2429 (Monday, Wednesday, Thursday) Bangalore 1835 / A H.Nizamuddin 0505

Bangalore – Mysore Timings
— 6206 Tipu Exp D Bangalore 1445 / A Mysore 1650
— Rt 6205 D Mysore 1120 / A Bangalore 1345
— 6216 Chamundi Exp D Bangalore 1815 / A Mysore 2110
— Rt 6215 D Mysore 0645 / A Bangalore 0940

ROAD : Bangalore is connected by road with national highways throughout the country

All types of tourist buses are easily available on hire. Karnataka

State Transport and many private bus operators run buses from Bangalore to many centres of the State and also to the neighbouring States.

ROAD DISTANCES FROM BANGALORE

Aihole 510 km; Hassan 187 km; Belur 221 km; Badami 499 km; Bijapur 579 km; Jog falls 377 km; Mangalore 347 km; Mysore 139 km; Sravanbelgola 155 km; Halebid 226 km; Hampi 350 km; Nandi Hills 60 km; Somnathpur 121 km; Ooty 297km;Madras 331 km; Hyderabad 562 km; Panjim 540 km; Pondicherry 303 km; Tirupati 260.

CONDUCTED TOURS

KSTDC operates following conducted tours from Bangalore
1. Bangalore Sightseeing Tour
2. Mysore sightseeing Tour
3. Belur, Halebid, Sravanbelgola
4. Tirupathi, Mangapura
5. Mysore, Sravanbelgola, Ooty, Nanjangud
6. Matralaya, Tungabhadra Dam, Hampi
7. North Karnataka
8. Goa, Gokarna
9. South Canara Tour
10. Bannerghatta, Mathuyalamaduvu
11. Nandi Hills, Muddenahalli
12. Shivasamuram, Somnathpur, Ranhanthittu
13. Hogenkal Falls, Krishnagiri Dam
14. Nagarhole, Mercara, Nisargadhama
15. Jog Falls
16. Dharmstala

For detailed information contact :
— Maurya Central Reservation - KSTDC, 10/4 Kasturba Road, Queen's Circle. Bangalore 560 001, PH 221 2901/02/03
Or KSTDC counters at :
— Badami House (Central Reservation Counter), N.R. Square PH 227 5883 / 227 5869; FAX 223 8016

HOTEL ACCOMMODATION (STD CODE 080)

— Taj West End (5 Star Deluxe), Race Course PH 2255055; FAX 220 0010, 220 4575
— The Oberoi : (5 Star Deluxe), 37-39 M.G.Road PH 558 5858; FAX 558 5960

— Welcome Group Windsor Manor Shereton and Towers : (5
  Star Deluxe), 25 Sankey Road. PH 226 9898; FAX 226 4941
— Hotel Ashok (5 Star), Kumara Krupa, High Grounds
  PH 226 9462, FAX 225 0033
— Le Meridien (5 Star), No 28, Sankey Road
  PH 226 2233; FAX 267676, 226 2050
— Taj Residency, (5 Star), 41/3 Mahatma Gandhi Road
  PH 5584444; FAX 558 4748
— Gateway Hotel on Residency Road (4 Star), No 66, Residency
  Road. PH 558 4545
— Ramanashree Comforts (3 Star), No1, Raja Ram Mohan Roy
  Road. PH 222 5152
— The Central Park : (3 Star). PH 558 4242; FAX 558 8594
— Harsha Hotel and Convention Centre (2 Star), No11, Park
  Road. PH 286 5566
— Kamat Yatri Nivas (2 Star), No 4, 1st cross, Gandhinagar.
  PH 226 0088; FAX 228 1070
— Nilgiris Nest (2 Star), 171Brigade Road
  PH 558 8401, 558 8702; FAX 558 5348
— Woodlands Hotel Pvt.Ltd. (2 Star), No 5 RajaRammohan Roy
  Road. PH 222 5111
— Hotel Ajantha (1 Star), 22-A, Mahatama Gandhi Road.
  PH 5584321; FAX 558 4780
— Hotel Guestline, Plot No 1and2, KIADB Industrail Area
  PH 420 430

EXCURSIONS

VASANTHAPUR : (13 km) This town has an ancient temple said
to have been built by Cholas of Sri.Vasantha Vallabharayaswamy.It has
a beautiful image of God which is 5 feet long. Legend has it that sage
Mandavya once disappeared from his ashram situated on the banks of
the Ganga. He was found meditating in a cave in Vasantpur. The devotees
believe that Rishi Mandavya could not attend the marriage ceremony
of Lord Venkatapathy and Padmavathi in time. Therefore the Rishi
desired that the Divine Couple solemnise the remaining rites at his
ashram. They agreed to oblige the sage. Since the God and the Goddess
had celebrated their marriage here, the pilgrim centre is a popular
wedding place.

WHITEFIELD : (16 km) The ashram of Sai Baba is situated
adjacent to Whitefield railway station and attracts devotees from all over
India and the world.

HESSARGHATTA LAKE : (27 km) An artificial lake spread over 1,000 acres it provides facilities for sailing. A livestock breeding and poultry centre has been established here as part of the Indo-Danish dairy project.

RAMOHALLI : (28 km—a deviation on the Mysore road) This picnic spot has the fabled big Banyan tree, spread over 4 acres with an impressive girth and vertical roots.

DEVANAHALLI : (35 km) The birthplace of Tipu sultan it has a monument in his memory. The town also has a fort and an old mosque. The Venugopal temple built in Dravidian style has scenes from the Ramayana carved on the outer walls.

MUTHYALA MADUVU : (45 km) Picnic spot with an enchanting waterfall and a small temple.

MAGADI : (45 km) The birth place of Kempe Gowda, the founder of Bangalore, there are several temples in this town. The Cholas had founded this historical city in 1139 AD.

RAMANGANGA : (48 km) Besides being a famous film shooting spot, the legend has that Lord Rama Sita and Lakshmana had halted on the Ramadeva Betta while going on Vanvas. There is a temple with the idols of the three. Besides, the temple has a huge pond called 'Lakshmana Teertha'. There is also another temple dedicated to Parvati with a linga facing Nandi. It is also famous as the biggest silk production centre in the country and for exquisite pottery.

SHIVANGA : (56 km) A well-known pilgrim centre it is located on a hill with four faces rising to a height of 4,599 feet. Gangadhareshwar, Honnadevi temple and the cave spring of Patal Ganga are revered greatly.

NANDI HILLS : (60 km) It is a popular hill resort with delightful climate. Tipu Sultan's Palace, the Gandhi Nilaya, the Nehru House and the Yoganandeeswara Temple are the other attractions. The Pennar, the Palar and the Arkavati rivers originate in these hills.

SAVANDURG : (60 km) Also known as Magadi hills, it has the beautifully painted temple of Ugra Narasimha. The nearby Veerbhadra Temple is massive stony structure built by Kempe Gowda. Between these two temples is the tomb of Sayyed Ghulam Hussain Shah Qadri, a Muslim saint.

DEVARAYANADURGA : (79 km) Dedicated to Ugra Narasimha this temple is situated at a height of 3,940 feet on Devarayanadurga hill. Namada Chilume, natural springs, are at the foot of the hill.

MEKEDATU : (98 km) It is an enchanting picnic spot. At the sangam of Arkavathi and Cauvery rivers is a temple dedicated to Lord Sangameshwara.

THE BHAVANI SHANKAR TEMPLE : Located in the vicinity at Vasanthapur this temple has a Linga and an idol of Goddess Bhavani. It is said that Shivaji, the warrior king of Maharashtra had camped here and worshipped the Goddess.

HASSAN - SHRAVANBELGOLA - BELUR - HALEBID

HASSAN

194 km from Bangalore and well-connected by road and rail to Bangalore, Mysore and Mangalore this calm and peaceful town is a convenient base to visit Shravanbelgola, Belur and Halebid. Hasanamba temple has a presiding deity of the town.

HOW TO REACH

AIR : Nearest airport – Mangalore

RAIL : Nearest railhead – Hassan

ROAD : KSTDC and many private tour operators run package tours. All types of tourist vehicles are easily available from Hassan.

HOTEL ACCOMMODATION (STD CODE 08172)

— Hotel Hassan Ashok (1 Star), Bangalore-Mangalore Road
   PH 68731-36; FAX 67154 ,

— Hotel Suvarna Regency, Suvarna Arcade, B.N. Road
   PH 66 774, 64 006; FAX 638 22

SHRAVANBELGOLA

51 km south-east of Hassan and 160 km from Bangalore, this is the most important Jain pilgrimage centre. The name of the place translated as naked ascetic (Sravana) and white pond (belgola), is known for the greatest monument of Jain art. The colossal statue of Gomateswara (17 meter high) situated on the summit of Indragiri hill is one of the two giant sculptures in the world after the colossus of Ramses II in Egypt. Chamundaraya, General under the King Rachmalla,

had commissioned the carving of this huge statue during the 10th c. The Jain muni Bhadrabahu is said to accompany Emperor Chandragupta to this place in 300 BC. Thousands of devotees congregate here to perform the 'Mahamastakabhisheka'. A spectacular ceremony - held once in 12 years - when the 1000 year old statue is anointed with milk, curd, ghee, saffron and gold coins. The next Mahamastakabhisheka will be held in 2005 AD.

BELUR

Belur is 38 km from Hassan and 222 km from Bangalore. It is styled as Dakshina Varanasi or Southern Benaras. The sanctity of the town is due to Channakeshava temple, one of the finest example of Hoyasala architecture. Built by the Hoyasala King Vishnuvardhana in 117 AD to commemorate his conversion from Jaina faith to Vaishnava, it took 103 years to complete. The facade of the temple is filled with intricate sculptures and frizzes—with no portion left blank. Elephants, episodes from the epics, sensuous dancers—they are all there—awe-inspiring in their intricate workmanship. Inside are hand-lathe-turned filigreed pillars. The Veeranarayana temple and the smaller shrines are well worth a visit.

HALEBID

27 km north-west of Hassan and 17 km east of Belur is Halebid. This old city was the site of the ancient capital city of Dwarasamudra of the wealthy Hoyasalas. The splendour of the city is attested by its architectural monuments which still rank among the masterpieces of the Hindu art. The Hoysaleswara temple dating back to the 12th century is outstanding for its wealth of sculptural details. The walls of the Hoysaleswara temple are covered with an endless variety of goddesses, animals, birds and dancing girls. Yet no two facets of the temple are same. Temple—guarded by the sacred Nandi Bull—was never completed despite 86 years of labour.

MYSORE

Mysore, the 'SANDALWOOD CITY', once the residence and capital of the Wodeyars is located at 770 m above sea level and 140 km from Bangalore. The Mahabharata refers to this city as 'Mahisamati' in connection with an expedition of the Pandava Prince Sahadeva. The great king Ashoka sent a missionary in the 3rd century BC to preachthe religion of Buddha. Raja Raja Deva, a Chola Prince ruled over Mysore in the 9th century AD. Gangas were ruling this territory between 1003 and 1022 AD. The Cholas, Hoysalas, Vijaynagara and Mysore kings ruled over it in succession.

PLACES OF INTEREST

THE MYSORE PALACE : Once the residence of the Wodeyars, it is one of the largest of its kind in India.Built in Indo-Saracenic style, it is mainly a three storyed tower crowned by a gilded dome. It consists of great courtyard, the marraige pavilion, the Durbar hall, the armoury, the music and drawing rooms, a carved silver door, a solid gold throne and a gallery of exquisite paintings.

SRI JAYACHAMARAJENDRA ART GALLERY : It is a palace transformed into an art gallery with paintings dating from 1875 AD. The collection includes paintings by Ravi Varma, the Russian Svetoslav Roerich and the traditional Mysore gold leaf style of painting.

RAILWAY MUSEUM : Behind the city railway station is an interesting museum pertaining to Railways.

LALITHA MAHAL PALACE : The summer palace of the royal family it stands at the highest point commanding panoramic view of the city which has been now converted into a five-star hotel.

MYSORE ZOO : It owes its origin to his Highness, Sri Chamaraja Wodeyar Bahadur. The very extensive grounds are beautifully laid out and rare animals bred in captivity.

ST. PHILOMENA'S CHURCH : Built in the Gothic style, it is one of the largest churches in the country and has beautiful stained glass windows. A beautiful image of Philomena placed in an underground chamber is worth paying a visit.

The city has a number of temples such as Varahaswamy temple, one of the Hoysala type of architecture, Parsanna krishnaswamy temple founded in 1825 by Krishnaraja Wodeyar III Trineswara temple with a Dravedian structure and Laxminarayan Swamy temple.

HOW TO REACH

AIR : Nearest airport – Bangalore 139 km.

RAIL : Mysore is connected by rail with major cities of the State. Mysore is connected with Chennai by Shatabdi Express, Timings;
- 2008 Mysore/Chennai Exp D Mysore 1410 Hrs; A Chennai 21125 Hrs, Return 2007Chennai/Mysore Exp D Chennai 0600 Hrs; A Mysore 1300 Hrs(Except Tuesday)

ROAD : Mysore is connected by road to all important cities of Karnataka, Tamil Nadu and Kerala. Regular bus services and tourist taxis are available from Banaglore.

For local tours contact :
— KSTDC Transport Wing, C/O Maurya Yatri Niwas, 2, JLB Road, Mysore. PH 23652.

HOTEL ACCOMMODATION (STD CODE 0821)
— Lalitha Mahal Palace Hotel (5 Star)
 PH 571 265; FAX 571 770
— Ramanashree Comforts Ltd. (3 Star), L-43/A, B.N. Road
 PH 522 202; FAX 565 781
— The Viceroy (3 Star), Rajendra Enterprises, Sri Harsha Rd
 PH 424 001; FAX 433 391
— Hotel Metropole (2 Star), 5, Jhansi Lakshmibai Road
 PH 420 681; FAX 420 854
— Hotel Dasaprakash (1 Star), Gandhi House. PH 24 444
— Hotel Krishnarajsagar (1 Star), P.O. Krishnarajsagar
 PH 57322-26; FAX 420 854
— Quality Inn Southern Star, 13/14 Vinobha Road
 PH 438 141; FAX 421 689

EXCURSIONS

CHAMUNDI HILLS : (13 km) It takes its name from the goddess Kali or Chamundi, the consort of Shiva, who is worshipped in a Chamundeswari temple dated to 13th century on a summit dedicated to the patron goddess of the royal family. Halfway up is the sacred Nandi Bull, 4.8 m monolith—a colossal figure of Nandi—worshipped by the Maharaja.

SRIRANGAPATNAM : (14 km) The  island fortress that was once the capital of the warrior kings Hyder Ali and his son Tipu Sultan, the tiger of Mysore. Tipu's summer palace, Daria Daulat, built in 1784, was his favourite retreat. It is now a museum and tells eloquently of his valour and his losing battle against British expansion. It has ornate and beautiful frescoes. The temple of Lord Srirangapatnam is said to have been built by the Chieftain Thirumalaiah in 894 AD.

RANGANATHITTU : (19 km) This bird sanctuary is an abode for migratory birds like Stock, White Ibis, Little Egret, Partridges, wild duck, spon bill peafowl, pond heron. June to September is the best season to witness the birds.

KRISHNARAJENDRA DAM AND BRINDAVAN GARDENS : (19 km) A dam was constructed across the Kaveri river during the reign of his Highness Shri Krishnaraja Wodeyar Bahadur. The dam was built keeping in view the need for a constant supply of water for electric installation at Shivanasamundram which was put in 1902. A pleasant garden called Brindavan is raised adjacent to dam and has swirling fountains dancing to rhythm of soft music—the colourful fairy lights.

NANJANGUD : (22 km) Important pilgrim centre it has famous temple dedicated to Nanjundeswara built in Dravidian style with a lofty Gopuram. This spacious temple is 385 x 160 ft. and supported by 147 columns. The temple's car festival and procession is held towards the end of March.

SOMNATHPUR : (38 km) Town has 13th century. Hoysala temple with an image of Venugopal standing about 62 ft. high in the south cell, Vishnu image in the west and Janardhana image in the north. The exterior walls of the temple are frescoed with episodes from the epics.

TALKAD : (45 km) This is an ancient town buried under centuries of sand. A dravidin style Vidyeswara temple is visible above the ground. Once in a 12 years during the Panchalinga Darshana the town awakes to fairs and festivities.

MELKOT : (50 km) A celebrated sacred town built on Yadugiri hills, where the great exponent of Visistadvaita philosophy Ramanuja lived.The Chellapillai temple dedicated to Krishna and Narasimha is known for its Vairamundi festival in March and April. Melkot is also known for handlooms.

BANDIPUR : (80 km) Bandipur sanctuary on Mysore-Ooty road has an area of 185 Sq. km. One can see several wild animals such as bisons, elephants, tigers, panthers from watchtowers.

CAUVERY FISHING CAMP : (82 km) This fishing camp at Bhimeshwari is a paradise for anglers with the rich mahseer found in abundance.

SHIVASAMUDRAM : (85 km) The 'SEA OF SHIVA' where Cauvery branches into two streams each descending to a depth of 200 ft., these falls are best during the monsoon months. 1.5 km away is the Asia's first hydro-eletric project, set up in 1905.

BILIGIRIRANGA'S HILL : (114 km) A range of hills, the place derives its name from the temple of Biligirirangaswamy, a shrine of great antiquity. Situated at the height of 5091 ft Biligrirangana Betta is a pleasant hill station. There is also a wildlife camp here run by the Forest Department.

THE WESTERN GHATS OF KARNATAKA — MADIKERI, CHIKMAGALUR AND SHIMOGA

MERCARA - MADIKERI

252 km from Bangalore and 120 km west of Mysore lies Mercara, the district headquarters of Coorg known as "The Scotland of India". Mercara has enchanted the visitors with its misty hills, lush forests, coffee plantations, undulating streets and breath-taking views. It is also a trekker's delight with lovely mountain trails.Coorg district is in the south-west of Karnataka bordering with Kerala.

PLACES OF INTEREST

THE FORT : The fort houses the palace which was built in 1812 by king Lingaraja II. The palace now houses the government offices. Two life size elephants made out of mortar are located inside the fort.

RAJA'S SEAT : The Kodava Kings used to spend their evenings here witnessing the panoramic view of the meandering roads going down the western ghats.

SRI OMKARESHWARA TEMPLE : Situated to the west of the fort lies Shiva temple built in 1820 is a mixture of Islamic and Gothic styles.

HOW TO REACH

AIRPORT : Bangalore 252 km.

ROAD : Mercara is connected by road to Mysore and Bangalore. Tourist taxis coaches operated by State transport and private coach operators are easily available.

EXCURSIONS

ABBEY FALLS : (8 km) This waterfall created by Medikeri stream is a beautiful picnic spot.

BHAGAMANDALA : (30 km) It is the meeting place of the Cauvery, the Kanike and the Suiyothi rivers. Bagandeshwara temple built in the multi roofed Kerala style resembles the temples of Nepal. It is also an important bee keeping centre.

TALACAUVERY : (48 km) The source of the Cauvery river, it is the sacred pilgrim centre among the Kodavas. On October 17th every year the river rises in the form of a bubbling spring. It is believed that a bath on this day is auspicious.

CHIKMANGLUR

The district takes its name from the headquarter town of Chikmanglur which literally means youngest daughter's town. The Chikmanglur district is full of scenic surprises —hills, valleys, streams and snow-white coffee blossoms. It is also trekker's territory.

PLACES OF INTEREST

ISHWARA TEMPLE : It has a 1.22 meter high idol installed by King Janmejaya.

LODANDARAMA TEMPLE : This temple is a synthesis of Hoysala and Dravidian style of architecture.

HOW TO REACH

AIR : Nearest airport – Mangalore.

ROAD : Regular bus services are available from Bangalore, Mysore and Mangalore.

EXCURSIONS

KEMMANGUDI : (54 km) An ideal retreat of solitude and natural beauty, located in Baba-Budan range. Placed at a height of 4,702 ft.above sea level, Kemmangundi has a bracing climate, mineral-enriched water and a tranquil verdant mountains cape. The two waterfalls—Kalahasti and Hebbe are ideal picnic spots. BABABUDAN MOUNTAINS, 30 km from Kemmangundi, are the loftiest range of hills with a stupendous ridge. The Dattatreya Peetha here is a well known pilgrimage shrine both for the Hindus and the Muslims.

KUDREMUKH : (95 km) Literally means 'Horse face'. The deep valleys and steep precipices of this hill station have great natural beauty. It is also known as 'the Mining Giant of Asia' and is famous for Iron.

SRINGERI : (98 km) This well-known pilgrim centre is situated on the banks of Tunga river. Adishankara, exponent of the Advaita philosophy had founded this monastry. The chief attraction being the 12 zodiac pillars in the Vidya Shankara temple, which are so arranged that the Sun's rays fall on the particular pillar corresponding to the month.

SHIMOGA

The town Shimoga, on the banks of the Tunga river, lies about 274 km. south-west of Bangalore was the stronghold of the Keladi Nayakas during 16th century AD.

PLACES OF INTEREST

CHURCH OF THE SACRED HEART OF JESUS : This imposing structure, built in the Roman and Gothic styles of architecture, has beautiful stained glass panels.

THE GOVERNMENT MUSEUM : The museum displays palm leaf manuscripts, coins, copper plates and statues made in the Hoyasala style. An interesting exhibit is 18.29 meter long ancient accounts book.

THE SHIMOGA FORT : Though the fort is largely in ruins, the recently renovated Seetharamanjaneya shrine is an excellent example of the elegance of Hoysala workmanship.

HOW TO REACH

AIR : Mangalore 200 km.

RAIL : Shimoga is connected by rail to Bangalore, Mysore and Hubli.

ROAD : Shimoga is connected by road to all important cities of the State.

EXCURSIONS

TAVAREKOPPA : (10 km) The forest department has set up the Shettyhally Lion safari here.

BHADRAVATI : (18 km) This industrial town, the 'Steel Town', is situated on the banks of the Bhadra river. The 13th century Lakshminarasimha temple, belonging to the Hoysala period, is found in the centre of the old town.

AGUMBE : (70 km) Situated at 826 meters above sea level, it is known for its fascinating sunset, the best during the month of November.

JOG FALLS : (88 km) The highest waterfall in India, the river Sharavathi, flowing over a rocky bed, reaches a steep chasm of 292 meters and leaps down in four distinct falls; Raja - Rani - Rocket and Roarer presenting a view of extreme grandeur. The Mahatama Gandhi Hydro-eletric Power Station is functional here. The Sharavathi Valley Wildlife Sanctuary is located at 40 km form Sagar town.

MANDAGADDE BIRD SANCTUARY : This natural bird sanctuary is located on the banks of the Tunga river. Every year, flocks of migratory birds take shelter on the leafless trees found here.

GAJANUR : There is an elephant camp and a dam is being constructed across the river Tunga.

COASTAL CHARM OF KARNATAKA —
MANGALORE AND KARWAR

MANGALORE

357 km from Bangalore, this town is located near the back waters formed by converging the Netravathi and the Gurpur rivers. Mangalore city derives its name from the presiding deity Mangaladevi the goddess of fortune. The city has acquired importance due to completion of the new port.

Main places of interest are the 10th century Mangala Devi temple, Kadri temple, St. Aloysious College Chapel, Mangalore Harbour, Light House and the Government museum.

HOW TO REACH

AIR : Mangalore is connected by air to Bangalore, Chennai and Mumbai.

RAIL : Mangalore is connected by rail to Trivandrum, Mumbai and Madgaon.

ROAD : Mangalore is connected by road to Goa, Cochin, Bangalore and Mumbai. Many private coach operators run buses from Mumbai, Bangalore, Goa, Chennai and from many other towns.

EXCURSIONS

ULLAL : (12 km) The Ullal Jamma Masjid is a famous pilgrim centre for the Muslims.

MOODABIDIRE : (35 km) The place here is considered as the holy Kashi of the Jains. There are 18 Jain temples here, the oldest of which is the Chandranatha temple with 1000 pillars.

KARKALA : (50 km) A Jain centre it has a 15th century 12.8 m high monolith of Gomateswara.

UDIPI : (58 km) The town is sacred to the devotees of Lord Krishna and where the Saint Madhwacharya lived and preached 700 years ago. The famous Masala Dosai has its origin here. About 5 km from Udipi at Manipal, there are several professional colleges of which Kasturba Medical College is the most outstanding institution.

MALPE : (66 km) Town near Manipal is noted for its beautiful beach.

DHARMASTALA : (75 km) Town is surrounded on all sides by the river Netravathi. The Majunatha temple here is a famous pilgrim centre. A monolithic statue of Bahubali has recently been installed here.

KOLLUR : (147 km) The famous temple of goddess Mookambika is located here on top of the Kodacgadri hill.

KARWAR

520 kms north west of Bangalore Karwar has one of the most beautiful beaches in the country which is said to have inspired Tagore to pen his first drama. The drive of 160 km from Hubli takes one through hills and valleys covered with dense tropical jungles and plenty of wildlife. The Kalindi river flows through the town into Arabian Sea. Motor launches are available for boating up to the Kali river. Karwar is also known for its fine muslin. The muslin industry was started in 1638 by Sir Willam Counten who had opened a factory here.

HOW TO REACH

AIR : Nearest airport – Mangalore

ROAD : Karwar is connected by road to Goa, Belgaum, Hubli, Dharwar, Mangalore and Mysore.

EXCURSIONS

DANDELI : (40 km) An industrial township, it is surrounded by abundance of forest and mineral wealth. This forest region is famous for its paper, plywood, teakwood and ferro-manganese factories. The Dandeli forest is famous and has a wild life sanctuary.

GOKARNA : (56 km) The Mahabaleshwar temple here is considered to be next to the Vishwanatha temple of Varanasi in north India.Yana, a place 60 km from here, is a centre for learning Sanskrit.

BHATKAL : (135 km) This ancient historical port town has temples of Vijayanagra times and many interesting Jain monuments. 16 kms away is the scenic place of MURDESHWAR—the temple here attracts a lot of devotees and tourists. The Pigeon island is off Murdeshwar coast. The beaches at Gokarna Bhatkal and Murdeshwar are undiscovered and thankfully unspoilt.

BANAVASI : (140 km) Situated on the left bank of the river Varada, it was once the capital of the Kadambas.The main attraction here is the Madhukeshvara temple, the ruins of the Buddhist stupa and the Veerabhadra temple. Several idols and Jain icons are found here.

THE NORTHERN NOSTALGIA
HOSPET- HAMPI-CHITRADURGA-BIJAPUR
BADAMI-AIHOLE-PATTADAKAL

HOSPET

330 km from Bangalore lies Hospet. Its tourist importance lies in its proximity to Hampi, the site of the medieval Vijaynagara empire

situated about 13 km from Hampi. Tungabhadra Dam here harnesses the sweet waters of Tungabhadra river.

HOW TO REACH

AIR : Nearest airport – Bangalore 352 km.

RAIL : Nearest rail station–Hospet. Main Guntakal railway station is only 100 km from Hospet Guntakal falls on main route trains running from Delhi and Mumbai towards South direction.

ROAD : Hospet is connected by road with major towns of Karnataka. Local transport, all types of tourist vehicles are easily available from Hospet to Hampi.

HAMPI

Hampi, Vijaynagara—was once the capital of the largest Hindu empires in the Indian history. Founded by the Telugu princes Harihara and Bukka in 1336, it reached the height of its glory under Krishnadevaraya (1509-29) when it controlled the whole of peninsula, except for a string of commercial principalities along the Malbar coast. Hampi had trade connections with international markets. Hindu, Muslim and Jain religions were practiced. The Brahmins were a privileged class. Sati (burning of the wife on husband's pyre) and Devdasi system (temple prostitution) were common and widely practised. Brahmini inscriptions discovered on the site date the first settlement here back to the 1st century AD and suggest that there was a Buddhist centre nearby. The empire came to a sudden end after the battle of Talikota when the city was ransacked by the confederacy of the Deccan Sultans.

A world heritage centre, Hampi is the most beautiful and evocative of all ruins in Karnataka. The erstwhile capital of the Vijayanagara kingdom, Hampi is full of delightful surprises like the King's Balance where Kings were weighed against grain, gold or money which was then distributed amongst the poor, the Queen's bath with its arched corridors projecting balconies and lotus-shaped fountains that once sprouted perfumed water, the two storied Lotus Mahal with recessed archways, the huge Elephant Stables, the Splendid Vithala temple with its 'Musical pillars' and the stone chariot, the Vrupaksha Temple, still used for worship, Ugra Narasimha, the 6.7 m tall monolith and the Pushkarini the Mahanavami Dibba .

Once-powerful Vijaynagara empire was compared to Rome by the Portuguese traveller Paes.

CHITRADURGA

Chitradurga is situated on an umbrella-shaped lofty hill and in the valley of the Vedavati river, with the Tungabhadra flowing in the north-west. History dates back to the period of epic Ramayana and Mahabharata. The district was part of the Satvahanas, the Kadambas, Rashtrakutas, Hoysalas, Vijaynagar and later Hyder Ali. The fort built in parts, by the Palegars, Hyder Ali and Tipu Sultan has seven series of enclosure walls. Many ancient temples can also be found inside the fort Harihar, a town located 78 km has the temple of Harihareshwara built in the Hoysala style. Hosdurga town (63) km has the remnants of a hill which was erected by Chikkanna Nayaka, a Palegar of Chitradurga. Molakalmuru was a fortified town of the Kadambas. Situated nearby is a temple, a large reservior and a rock which produces a chain of echoes. The town is also known for its silk weaving industry.

HOW TO REACH

AIR : Nearest airport Bangalore 167 km.

ROAD : There are regular buses available from Bangalore and Mysore.

BIJAPUR

Bijapur, a medieval Muslim walled city, 530 km north-west of Bangalore, is characterised by domes and minarets. Its founder called it Vijayapura or Bijapur, the city of victory. Bijapur capital of the Adil Shahi kings, experienced a great deal of architectural activity under the Adil Shahi dynasty between 10th and 11th centuries. The Adil Shahis encouraged building activities to such an extent that Bijapur itself has over 50 mosques, more than 20 tombs and a number of palaces.

PLACES OF INTEREST

GOL GUMBAZ : It Contains the mausoleum tomb of Mahammed Adil Shah (1626 -56 AD), the seventh ruler of dynasty, and is the fourth largest dome in the world. This has the floor area of 1700 sq.m, a height of 51 m.and diameter  37 m. The walls are three meter thick. The interior of the dome, mysteriously unsupported, has a whispering gallery, where the sound returns to the listener nine times. Even the tick of the watch or the rustle of paper can be heard across a distance of 37m in the whispering gallery.

GAGAN MAHAL : Royal Palace constructed by Ali Adil Shah I in 1561. There are three magnificent arches, the central one being the widest. The ground floor was the Durbar Hall and the first floor is the private residence of the royal family.

ASAR MAHAL : Constructed by Muhammad Adil Shah in 1646 to serve as a hall for justice. The Mahal contains some relics of prophet Mohammed.

THE FORT : Built by Yusuf Adil Shah I, the fort is six and a quarter mile long, with deep moats all around and five massive gates.

JUMMA MASJID : Built between 1557 and 1686, it is still used for worship. It is believed to be one of the first mosques in India and holds an exquisite copy of the Koran written in gold letters.

IBRAHIM ROZA : It was probably the inspiration for Agra's Taj Mahal. It is a delicately designed structure.

MALLIK-E-MAIDAN : An enormous cannon, 14 feet-long and weighing 55 ton, it is one of the largest bell metal guns in the world. A unique feature is that it is always cool, even under blazing sun and when tapped gently it tinkles softy like a bell. It was cast in 1549 AD by Mohammed Bin Hasan Rumi, a Turkish officer. It was brought to Bijapur as a trophy of war and was set up here with the help of 100 elephants, 400 oxen and hundreds of men.

HOW TO REACH

AIR : Nearest airport – Belgaum 192 km.

ROAD : Bijapur is conected by road to Bangalore and Belgaum.

BADAMI, AIHOLE AND PATTADAKAL
BADAMI

Standing close to each other (within 13 km radius) these temple towns represent Chalukyan architecture at its best.

Badami was the capital of the Chalukyas in the 6th and 7th centuries and is noted for 4 rock caves excavated in the sand stone cliff. The important carvings at the caves are an eight armed dancing Shiva and a two handed Ganesha. The second cave has Vaishnavite influence with panel of Thrivikrama and Bhuvaraha. On the ceiling are carvings of Anantha Shayana, Brahma, Vishnu, Shiva and Ashtadikpalas. The third cave is the largest and has carvings pertaining to both Shaivite and Vaishnavite themes. Panels of Thrivikrama, Narasimha, Shankaracharya, Bhuvarna, Anantha Shayana and Harihara are engraved in vigorous style. In the fourth cave of Jains there is a image of Mahavira. The place is also known for the earliest group of Chalukyan structural temples. Badami Fort, on top of a hill, encloses large granaries, a treasury and a watch tower. The famed Malegitti Shivalaya temple set on the summit is built with stones joined together with mortar.

AIHOLE

Known as Ayyavvole in inscriptions, it was the earliest capital of the Chalukyas. The cradle of Indian temple architecture has 125 temples - intricately carved, rich in details. The oldest temple, the Lad Khan, dates back to 5th century AD. There are 70 temples in this group. The Durga temple is noted for its sculpture. The Meguti temple is built of 630 small stone blocks. The Arvanaphadi cave has some beautiful carvings.

PATTADAKAL

Located on the banks of the Malaprabha, 29 km from Badami, Pattadakal functioned as a royal commemorative site and a place for coronation ceremonies. The town was well known even in the 1st century AD. when Ptolemy referred to it as Petrigal. It reached its pinnacle of glory under the Chalukya kings from 7th to 9th centuries. The queen Lokamahadevi and Trailokyamahadevi brought sculptors from Kanchipuram and created fantasies in stone. Pattadakal is unique in having temple architecture of the northern Nagara and southern Dravida style.The oldest temple is Sanghameswara temple. The Mallikarjuna temple has pillars depicting the birth and life of Krishna. The largest Virupaksha temple has sculptures and panels depicting scenes from the epics, the Ramayana and Mahabharata. The Padmanatha temple in the northern style has impressive carvings on pillars and on the ceiling.

Archaeological Survey of India maintains a gallery in the temple.

BADAMI

Badami is a convenient base to visit Aihole and Pattadakal. Buses, tourist taxis are easily available from Badami to these places.

AIR : Nearest airport : Belgaum 192 kms.

ROAD : Badami is connected by road to Bangalore, Bagalkot and Bijapur.

RAIL : Nearest railway station is Bagalkot on Hubli Sholapur line.

BELGAUM

HOW TO REACH

AIRPORT : Nearest airport – Belgaum.

RAILWAY : Belgaum is connected by rail to New Delhi, Hyderabad, Bangalore and Mysore.

ROADS : Belgaum is connected by road to major cities, towns of Karnataka, Maharastra and Goa.

This was once the capital of Rattas, chieftains of Soundatti in the 12th and 13th centuries. Today it is a modern cantonment town. The ancient fort, oval shaped stone structure encloses an area about 40 hectare and has two gates. Mahatama Gandhi was once imprisoned here.

EXCURSIONS

GOKAK FALLS : (80 km) The river Ghatprabha plunges into a rocky bed 170 feet below in the picturesque Gokak Valley. Traces of ruined temples can be found on the banks of the river.

SOUNDATTI-YELLAMMA TEMPLE : 80 km from Belgaum, Yellamma (Renuka) was Lord Parshurama's mother and wife of Rishi Jamadagni. Nearby is a well 'Jogal Bhavi' with healing powers, which is always thronged by people with skin diseases. Malaprabha dam is located 3 km away.

KITTUR : (44 km) A place of historic importance. The queen of Kittur bravely resisted the imposition of British rule in 1824. The Basava temple here, contains inscriptions on stone, belonging to the 12th century.

FESTIVALS

JANUARY : Pattadakal dance Festival : Pattadakal, ancient capital of the Chalukya's celebrates dance festival against the backdrop of the temples.

OCT AND NOV—Dussehra : Mysore – the city of palaces celebrates the ten days Dussehra in royal style. The Mysore palace is illuminated with a myriad lights. Majestic processions, a torch light parade and dance and musical events enliven the tranquil city on this occasion.

NOVEMBER—Hampi Festival : The magnificent ruined city of Hampi, once the capital of Vijaynagara Empire, comes alive once again during this lively festival of dance and music, held in the first week of November.

KERALA

KERALA
AT A GLANCE

AREA : 38,863 sq. km.

CAPITAL : Thiruvananthapuram.

BOUNDARIES : East and South East - Tamil Nadu, West and South West - Arabian Sea, North and North East - Karnataka.

LANGUAGE : Malayalam.

ROADS : The length of roads in the state is 1,42,000 km. The national highways that pass through the State are NH17, NH 47 and NH 49.

AIRPORTS : Cochin, Kozhikode and Thiruvananthapuram.

IMPORTANT MUSEUMS

Cochin : Hill Palace Museum - Tripunithura; Parishath Thamburan Museum.

Trichur : Archaeological Museum.

Thiruvananthapuram : Napier Museum and Sri Chitra Art Gallery.

HILL RESORTS

Name	Altitude	Convenient Railhead
Munar	1524 m	Idikki – 56 km
Ponmudi	912 m	Thiruvananthapuram – 61 km

PILGRIM CENTRES (A : Air; R : Rail)

Alwaye : Shivlinga on Sandbank; A - Cochin 21 km, R - Alwaye

Ambalapuzha : Famous Sri Krishna Temple with image of divine origin; A - Cochin 76 km, R - Alleppey 10 km.

Aranmula : Parthasarathi Temple. The snake –boat race is associated with this temple; A – Cochin 122 km, R – Chengannur – 10 km.

Arthungal : St.Andrew's France Church; A and R - Cochin 35 km.

Baranaganam : Mortal remains of Sister Alphonsa; A - Cochin 85 km, R - Kottayam 30 km.

Beemapalli, Trivandrum : Tomb of Beema Beevi and son Chandrakudam. Muslim festival held here. A and R Thiruvananthapuram.

Chengannur : Temple of Goddess Bhagavati; A – Cochin 89 km, R – Chengannur.

Chottanikara : Devi temple where the goddess is worshipped in three forms; A and R Cochin - 25 km.

Cranganore (Kodungallore) : Hindu, Christian and Muslim pilgrim attractions; A and R Cochin – 32 km.

Ettumanoor : Temple of Lord Shiva, known for holy lamp, Valia Vilakku; A - Cochin 65 km, R - Kottayam 11 km.

Guruvayoor : Famed ancient shrine of Sri Krishna; A - Cochin 109 km, R - Trichur 32 km.

Irinjalakuda : The only temple in India to Bharata, brother of Lord Rama; A - Cochin 57 km, R – Irinjalakuda – 8 km.

Kalady : Birthplace of Adi Shankaracharya; A Cochin 45 km, R Alwaye 24 km.

Kottayam : Mahadeva temple with swayambhu Shivalinga; A - Cochin 76 km, R - Kottayam.

Kozencherry : Maramon Convention held here; A - Cohin112km, R Chengannur - 30 km.

Malappuram : Noted for Nercha Muslim festival; A - Cochin 165 km, R - Tirur 28 km.

Malayattoor : Church of St.Thomas famed for annual festival; A - Cochin 47 km, R - Alwaye 24 km.

Omallur : Manjanikkara Church with tomb of Patriarch of Antioch; A - Cochin 139 km, Chengannur 44 km.

Sabarimala : Temple of Sri Ayyappa. Reached by a trek through the jungle from Pampa; A Cochin - 214 km, R Chengannur - 88 km.

Trichur : Temple of Shiva as Vedakkunathan. Famous for Pooram festival; A - Cochin - 80 km, R - Trichur.

Triprayar : Sri Rama temple; A - Cochin 70 km, R - Trichur 25 km.

Tripunithura : Temple of Vishnu; A - Cochin 13 km, R - Tripunithura.

Thiruvananthapuram : Sri Padmanabhaswamy temple; A and R - Thiruvananthapuram.

Vagomon : Kurisumala Ashram, Christian centre; A - Cochin 107 km, R - Ettumanoor - 35 km.

Vaikam : The Shiva image here assumes three forms during the day; A and R Cochin 40 km.

Varkala : Jarardanswamy temple. Also Samadhi of Sri Narayana Guru; A - Thiruvananthapuram - 55 km, R - Varkala.

Kerala is an exotic mixture of nature's very best.The high ranges of western ghats on the east, the Arabian Sea on the west, emerald paddy fields, virgin forests and backwaters make Kerala traveller's paradise. Kerala is also called 'A SPICE GARDEN OF INDIA'.

HISTORY

Legends, myths and archaeological findings combine to provide interesting evidence regarding the early history of Kerala.

The most popular legend is that Kerala was raised from the depths of the ocean. Parsurama, one of the Avatars of Vishnu had waged an unique series of vengeful war on the Kshatriyas. A time came, when Parsurama was struck by remorse at the wanton annihilation he had wrought. He offered severe penance atop the mountain. In a mood of profound atonement the sage threw his mighty axe into the distant ocean. Waves foamed and frothed as a crescent-shaped stretch of land extending from Gokarnam to Kanyakumari surfaced from the depth of the sea.

The recorded history of Kerala dates back to 3rd century BC on Ashoka's rock edict. Later constant wars between Cheras, Cholas, Pandyas and Pallavas culminated in 1120 AD into the breaking-up of Kerala into many petty kingdoms. These kingdoms were ruled by the Thampurans or chiefs under whom Kerala attained its most brilliant period in history. The Thampurans were succeeded by the Zamorins of Kozikode during whose reign the Portuguese set foot in Kerala.

The phoenicians in 1200 BC were the pioneer in the sea trade with Kerala. In 1000 BC King Soloman's ships visited 'Ophix' (the modern Puvar, south on Thiruvananthapuram) to trade in ivory, apes, sandalwood and peacocks. The fame of Kerala spices brought the Romans in 30 AD followed soon after by the Greeks. The spice trade also brought Vasco da Gama to Kozikode in 1498 who paved the way for a fresh wave of trading history with the Europeans. Traders from the Malayan peninsula, the Philippines, Java and Sumatra also visited the ports of Kerala. Gold was traded by these countries from the east and the west for spices, ivory and sandalwood.

The rulers of Kerala and the Zamorins of Kozikode gave these traders all facilities and permitted them to settle down on Kerala soil. The Portuguese gained trading rights in 1516 followed by the Dutch merchants who obtained a stronghold in 1602. But the Portuguese were forced out of the area by 1663 and in 1795 the Dutch too had to move out as the British traders had become the strongest power in India by that time and had established their supremacy.

In 1956 the present state of Kerala was formed comprising the Malayalam speaking tracts of South India.

THIRUVANANTHAPURAM

Thiruvananthapuram is the gateway to one of the most beautiful State in India. City opens the gate to a world of beaches, mountains, backwaters, wildlife sanctuaries and islands. The city is named after the holy serpant, the thousand headed Anantha built over seven hills. As early as 1000 BC this southern tip of India was in frequent trade contact with foreign civilisations, especially from the West Asian region. Cotton, fabrics, spices, ivory and hordes of other goods were exported from its ports. This contact has manifested in the co-existance of diverse religions and culture in the State.

PLACES OF INTEREST

SRI PADMANABHASWAMY TEMPLE : This is an ancient temple dedicated to Lord Vishnu. The deity is depicted in a reclining position resting on the holy serpent Anantha. The profusely carved seven-storey mandapam is a fine example of South Indian

sculpture. The temple was rebuilt by Raja Marthanda Verma in 1733. Only Hindus are allowed inside the temple and dress regulations are strictly followed.

KUTHIRAMALIKA MUSEUM : Located near Sree Padmanabhaswamy temple, Thampanoor, the building itself is unique in its Kerala architecture.

NAPIER MUSEUM : It has a fine collection of Kerala bronzes, ornaments and costumes and a model of 'tharawad', a traditional Nair family home.

SREE CHITHIRA ART GALLERY : Situated in the Napier Museum ground it has a collection of paintings by Raja Ravi Verma and Roerich, copies of Rajput, Mughal and Tanjore school of art and paintings and Ajanta Caves. There are also works of art from China, Bali, Tibet and Japan.

ZOO : It is situated near the Napier Museum and is one of the best Zoos in South India.

SCIENCE AND TECHNOLOGICAL MUSEUM : This museum exhibits scores of items highlighting science and technology.

ARUVIKKARA : It is both a pilgrim centre and a picnic spot. On the banks of the Karamana river, this spot houses a Bhagavathy temple with a waterfall nearby. A stream with fishes which comes up to be fed by visitors is another attraction.

HOW TO REACH

AIR : Thiruvananthapuram is connected by air with Bangalore, Chennai, Delhi and Mumbai. Thiruvananthapuram International Airport has over 30 air links with convenient connections to Colombo, Maldive Islands and West Asia.

RAIL : Thiruvananthapuram is connected by trains with major cities.

— Rajdhani Express operates between Thiruvananthapuram and New Delhi
— 2432 H.Nizamuddin (Wednesday-Thursday) D 1100 / A Thiruvananthapuram 0610
— Rt 2431 Thiruvananthapuram (Friday and Saturday) D 1915/ A H. Nizamuddin 1350

ROAD : Thiruvananthapuram is connected by good roads with all parts of the South India.

IMPORTANT ROAD DISTANCES FROM THIRUVANANTHAPURAM

— Kanyakumari 87 km, Cochin 223 km, Periyar 220 km, Madurai 320 km.

CONDUCTED TOURS

Conducted tours are operated by the Kerala Tourism Development Corporation Ltd.
— Full-Day Thiruvananthapuram City Tour
— Half-Day City Tour (Except Wednesday)
— Full-Day Kanyakumari Tour
— Full-Day Ponmudi
— Three-Day Munar (Departure on Wednesday, Friday and Saturday)
— Two-Day Thekkady (Periyar Wildlife Sanctuary, Every Saturday except last Saturday)
— Three-Day Kodaikanal (Last Saturday of every month)
— Full-Day Courtllam Water falls
— Seven-Day Karnataka Bangalore, Malampuzha, Ooty, Mysore and Madurai (Second Saturday of every month)
— Four-Day Rameshwaram, Suchidram, Kanyakumari, Tiruchendur, Rameswaram and Madurai(Every Thursday)
— Sabarimala Lord Ayyappa Temple (Last day of every Malayalam month and everyday during Mandala Pooja and Makaravilakku season)
For further details and reservation, contact :
— Kerala Tourism Development Corporation Ltd., Adjacent to Hotel Chaithram (Near Railway and Bus Terminals) Subramaniam Road, Thampanoor, Thiruvananthapuram - 695 001
PH 330 031

HOTEL ACCOMMODATION (STO CODE 0471)

— The South park (4 Star), M.G.Road
PH 333 333; FAX 331 1861
— Hotel Horizon (3 Star), Aristo Road
PH 326 688; FAX 324 444
— Hotel Luciya Continental (3 star), East Fort
PH 463 443; FAX 463 347

- Mascot Hotel (3 star), Palayam
  PH 318 990; FAX 317 745
- Hotel Pankaj (3 Star), PO. Box No. 110
  PH 464 815, 464 815; FAX 465 020
- Jas Hotel(1 Star), P.O. Box No 431, Thycaud
  PH 324 881; FAX 324 443
- Hotel Amtitha Private Ltd., Thycaud
  PH 323 091; PH 324977
- Hotel Geeth, Pulimoodu Junction, Near G.P.O.
  PH 471 987; FAX 460 278
- Surya Samudra Beach Garden, Pulinkudi, Mullur P.O. Box
  PH 481 413; FAX 481 124

YOGA CENTRES

- Ashok Beach Resort, Kovalam; PH 480 101
- Shilpa Health Club, Mascot Hotel; PH 438 990
- Institute of Yogic Culture, Vazhuthacaud; PH 60408
- Sivananda Yoga Centre – West Fort; PH 451 776

AYURVEDIC MESSAGE CENTRES

- Ayurvedic College, M.G.Road; PH 74 823
- Kottakkal Arya Vaidya Sala,

EXCURSIONS

VELI TOURIST VILLAGE : (9 km) Located by the side of the sea it is a beautiful lake separated by a bund. This spot has a attractive landscape, gardens and wading pools. There is a floating bridge and a restaurant. This location is excellent for water sports and provides facilities for boating - row speed safari and pedal boats, water scooters and hovercraft. Few kilometres away from Veli tourist village is Akkulam lake which has one of the biggest Children's park of Kerala. One can travel by boat cruises from Veli to this place.

KOVALAM : (16 km) This is one of the best beaches in India. It also ranks amongst one of the loveliest beaches in the world. It is a sheltered bay and is endowed with unusual natural beauty. It offers facilities for safe bathing, yoga,  ayurvedic massage, water sport facilities etc. A wide range of accommodation is dished up along the shores of Kovalam.

ARUVIKKARA : (16 km) This pilgrim centre is situated on the banks of Karamana. It also has an ancient temple dedicated to Goddess Bhagavati, built on a rock on the right bank of the river.

ARUVIPPURAM : (24 km) This place has small Shiva temple built by Sree Narayana Guru and attracts a large number of worshippers during the Shivaratri festival. There is a small waterfall here and the place derives its name from this waterfall.

NEYYAR DAM : (32 km) This is a popular picnic spot which has a lake and a dam. Facilities for boating are provided in the reservoir. There is a crocodile farm and a lion safari park. Sivananda Yoga Vedantha Dhanvathari Ashram is located nearby.

SARKARA CHIRAINKEEZHU : (40 km) The Bhagawati temple here celebrates the annual festival 'Bharani' during March/April every year. The 'Kaliyoottu' in this temple is performed one month before Bharani Utsavam.

VARKALA : (51 kms North of Thiruvananthapuram and 37 kms South of Quilon) This place is known for its Vishnu shrine dedicated to Lord Janardhana. This ancient temple is believed to be 2000 years old. The Sivagiri Muttu situated at an elevation, 3 km east of Janardhana temple, is held sacred by Hindu pilgrims. This was built in 1904 by the great Hindu reformist Sree Narayan Guru. Varkala is also a beautiful seaside resort with mineral water springs. The sea shore is called 'Papanasm' and hundreds of Hindu devotees perform 'Vavu Bali' on full moon days of Malayalam month of Karkidakam.

PADMANABHAPURAM : (54 km) This is the 'Teak Edifice' of yesteryears from where Maharaja Marthanda Verma had ruled the Travancore State. Set in a scenic surrounding along the Thiruvananthapuram-Kanyakumari route, this palace was in use from 1550 - 1790 and has carvings and murals from 17th and 18th centuries.

AGASTHYAKOODAM : (61 km) This is a prominent peak in Sahyadri ranges and is conspicuous for its height and isolation when seen from a distance. This peak can be approached on foot from Bonacadu.

QUILON (KOLLAM) : (72 km) Quilon is an old sea port on the banks of Ashtamundi lake. Quilon has maintained a commercial reputation from ancient times. Phoenicians, Persians, Arabs, Greeks, Romans and Chinese traded with this port. There are some historic remains and a number of temples built in the traditional ornate architecture. This town is also the gateway point to the magnificent backwaters of Kerala.

THANGNASERRY : 5 km from Quilon this town has ancient Churches built in the 18th century.

THIRUMULLAVARAM is a beautiful beach outside the town.

MAYYANAD : 10 km from Quilon is noted for its shrines and temples. There are nine temples and the most important is one of the Umayanallor dedicated to Lord Subramanya. The shrine is said to have been constructed by Sree Sankaracharya. There are frequent buses from Quilon to Mayyanad.

PATHANAMTHIATTA : (119 km) Pathanamthiatta, a hilly terrain of pristine beauty, is popular as the headquarters of pilgrim worship of Kerala. More than 50% of the total area of this simple land of temples, rivers, mountain ranges and coconut groves is covered by forests. This little district is frequented by visitors from India and abroad often for its water fiestas,religious shrines and cultural training centre.Charalkunnu is a picturesque hill station of this district offering a panoramic view of the nearby valley. A camp house on the hill provides comfortable lodging.

CALICUT

Calicut is the town where the first European, Vasco-de-Gama, had landed at Kappad in 1498. Later the Dutch, the French and the British dominated the area. Today it is one of the important ports on the west coast of India and still maintains its commercial traditions.

PLACES OF INTEREST

BEYPORE : It is a fishing harbour and a site for boat building industry.

PAZHASSI RAJA MUSEUM : This Museum houses copies of ancient mural paintings, antique bronzes and old coins. The museum also houses paintings of Raja Ravi Verma and a section dedicated to personal belongings of India's first Defence Minister, the late V.K. Krishna Menon.

LOK ANARKAVU TEMPLE : Believed to be 1500 years old it is dedicated to Goddess Durga. The candid murals and carvings on the temple walls are worth-seeing. Two other temples dedicated to Lord Vishnu and Lord Shiva are also located adjacent to this temple.

KAPPAD : 16 km from Calicut it is a historical beach where Vasco-de-Gama had landed on May 20, 1498 with 170 sailors.

C.V.N. KALARI CENTRE : Kerala's martial art performing centre.

HOW TO REACH

AIR : Calicut is connected by air with Chennai, Coimbatore, Delhi and Mumbai.

RAIL : Calicut is connected by rail with major cities of India.

ROAD : Calicut is connected by road with all major cities of the State.

HOTEL ACCOMMODATION (STD CODE 0495)

— Hotel Malbar Palace (4 Star), Manuelsons Junction, G.H.Road
   PH 721 511; FAX 721 794
— Paramount Tower (2 Star), P.O.Box No 204, Town Hall Road,
   PH 722 651; FAX 721 639
— Sea Queen Hotel (2 Star) Beach Road
   PH 366 804; FAX 365 854
— Kappad Beach Resort, Kappad, Chemancherry
   PH 0496 683 760, FAX 0496 683 706
— Taj Residency, P.T.Usha Road, Calicut. PH 765 354

EXCURSIONS

PERUVANNAMUZHI DAM : (60 km) There is also a Crocodile farm and a bird sanctuary.

MALAPPURAM : (50 km) This place is a military headquarters from ancient times. Thali temple (Perinthalmanna) is an important pilgrim centre dedicated to Goddess Durga. Pazhayangadi Mosque associated with the Muslim saint Muhammed Shah is also located here.

CANNANORE : (92 km) This important historical centre was the capital of North Kolathiri Rajas for many centuries. It was once a premier port of ancient Kerala. It came into importance with the arrival of the Portuguese in the 15th century. Morco Polo has referred to this place as a great Emporia of spice trade. ST.ANGELES FORT is built by the first Portuguese viceroy in 1505 and since then it is an important military station in Malabar.

ZHIMALA : 50 km from Cannanore is an cluster of hills. There is a cave at the foot of the hills and a mosque further up on the hill. The place is also known for its medicinal herbs.

PARASSINIKADAVU : (18 km) It is an important pilgrim centre of Kerala and has the only temple where 'Theyyam', a form of folk ritual dance, is performed daily. There is also a snake park near the temple.

TELLICHERY : (60 km) There is an 18th century fort besides a church built by German Scholar, Dr.Hermen Gundert in 1889 AD. The East India Company had established its settlement on Malabar Coast here in 1683. The Mahe trading centre established by the French in the 17th century is located nearby.

SULTHAN BATTERY : (98 km) This place was known as Ganapathivattam, the fields of Ganapathi. There are two caves 16 km from Sulthan Battery famous as one of the earliest centres of human habitat. There is Chethalayam waterfall 12 km away and 29 km away is the Panamara, the ruins of an historic fort.

COCHIN

The Queen of the Arabian Sea—one of the finest natural harbours on the Arabian Coast of India. Cochin has been a port of call for foreign traders from very early times. From time immemorial Arabs, Dutch, Chinese, British, Portuguese sea sailors followed the sea route to Cochin and left their unprint on the town.

PLACES OF INTEREST

DUTCH PALACE : Built by the Portuguese and presented to the Raja of Cochin in 1555 it was renovated by the Dutch during their short regime. The palace is well-known for its mural paintings which covers a wide range of themes from the Puthra kameshiyajam to Rama's return to Ayodhya after vanquishing king Ravana of Lanka. In the central courtyard of the palace is the temple dedicated to Pazhayanur Bhagvati. In the coronation hall are displayed the dresses and palanquins used by the rulers of Kochi.

KOONAN KURISHU SHRINE : This small chapel in which the Koonal Cross stands is situated in the heart of the busy commercial centre of Mattancherry. It was in the name of this cross that the famous oath of 'Koonan Kurishu' had taken place on January 3, 1653.

JEWISH SYNAGOUGE : Built in 1568, this building was destroyed by the Portuguese in 1662 and rebuilt by the Dutch two years later. Scrolls of the old Testaments and a number of copper plates inscribed in the Hebrew script are preserved here.

GUNDU ISLAND : The smallest island around Kochi, Gundu Island has a coir factory where coir is made into a rope manually and carpets are manufactured by hand operated looms. This island can be reached from Vyapeen only by boat.

FORT COCHI : Lies 10 km from Ernakulam.

ST. FRANCIS CHURCH : The oldest church constructed by the

Europeans in India. This protestant church was originally built by the Portuguese in 1510. Vasco-de-Gama, who died in 1524, was buried here. Fourteen years later his mortal remains were transferred to Portugal.

DUTCH CEMETRY : Lies at a short distance from St.Francis church near the entrance to the beach.

SANTA CURZ BASILICA : This Roman Catholic church has some very beautiful paintings on the ceiling.

CHINESE FISHING NETS : At the entrance of Kochi harbour, these nets are a fascinating sight. They can be seen all along the backwaters of Kerala. They were first brought to Kerala by the Chienese traders from Kublai Khan's court.

WILLINGTON ISLANDS : This is a man-made island created from the materials dug while deepening the Kochi Port. There are frequent ferry and bus services from Ernakulam. The harbour, airport and railway terminus are located here.

BOLGATTY ISLANDS : This is a beautiful island lying close to Ernakulam. Built by the Dutch in 1744, Bolgatty palace is situated here. A former residence of the British resident of Kochi, is now a hotel.

SHIVA TEMPLE, ERNAKULAM : Situated in the centre of the town the annual festival in the temple is conducted for eight days in January. A cultural festival is also held on the occasion.

MANGALAVANA : Located in the heart of the town, thousands of species of birds both migrant and resident, are found here.

PARIKSHITH THAMPURAN MUSEUM : Collection of 19th century oil paintings. old coins, stone sculptures, temple models, copies of murals etc.are displayed here.

MUSEUM OF KERALA HISTORY : Located at Edappally and the only of its kind, history of Kerala is exhibited and narrated with the help of light and sound here.

HILL PALACE MUSEUM : This is the largest archaeological museum of Kerala where sculptures, rare coins, old weapons, manuscripts and memorabilia from the Kochi royal family exhibited.

HOW TO REACH

AIR : Cochin is connected by air with Aggati, Bangalore, Chennai, Delhi, Goa and Mumbai.

RAIL : Cochin is connected by rail with major cities of India.

ROAD : Cochin is connected by road with various cities of South India.

CONDUCTED TOURS

Conducted Tours are operated by Kerala Tourism Development Corporation Ltd.

Cochin sight seeing boat tour : Daily two tours from Dealord Jetty, Ernakulam, first tour : 9 a.m.to 12.30 p.m.; second tour : 2 p.m. to 5.30 p.m. Village-backwater-canal tour on country boat. Only the State Government agency operates tours in Cochin with experienced and trained guides.

Daily two Tours from K.T.D.C.Office

COACH TOURS

— 2-Day Cochin-Thekkady Tour (Every Saturday and return on Sunday)
— Full-Day Cochin-Athirappally and Vazhachal tour
— Cochin city tour (In and around Cochin)

For further details and reservations contact :

— K.T.D.C. TOURIST Reception Centre, Shanmugham Road, Ernakulam, Kochi 682 199. PH 353 234; FAX 382 011

HOTEL ACCOMMODATION (STD CODE 0484)

— Taj Malbar : (5 Star Deluxe), Willington Island
  PH 666 811, 668 010; FAX 668 297
— The Avenue Regent : (4Star), 39/1796 ABC, M.G. Road
  PH 372 660/1;FAX 370 129
— Taj Residency: (4 Star) Marine Drive, Ernakulam
  PH 371 471; FAX 371 481
— Hotel Quality Inn Presidency (4 Star), Ernakulam
  PH 394 300; FAX 393 222
— Hotel Abad Plaza (3 Star), M.G. Road
  PH 381 122, 361 595; FAX 370 729
— Casino Hotel (3 Star), P.B. No 585, Willington Islands
  PH 668 221/421; FAX 668 001
— Hill Top Resort:(3 Star) Joymat Nagar Edathala
  PH 680 279; FAX 680 490
— Sealord Hotel : (3 Star) Shanmugham Rd
  PH 382 473; FAX 370 135
— Bharat Hotel (2 Star), P.B. No 2357, Durbar Hall Road
  PH 353 501; FAX 370 502
— Hotel Luciya (1 Star), Stadium Road
  PH 381 177,382 471; FAX 361 524

- Hotel Sangeetha (1Star),Chitoor Road, Near Railway Station PH 368 487, 368 417; FAX 368 261
- Woodlands (1 Star), Woodlands Junction, M.G. Road, Ernakulam. PH 382 051;FAX 382 080
- Hotel Blue Nile, Opp KSTDC Bus Stand PH 355 277 FAX 367 838

EXCURSIONS

ALWAYE : (20 km) This place is the most important industrial centre of Kerala.

CHENNAMANGALAM : (42 km) It was the seat of Paliath Achan, the hereditary prime minister of the earstwhile state of Cochin from 1632 to 1809 and one of the chief centres of the Jews. In the vicinity of the Jewish colony once stood the famous Vaipinkotta Seminary built in the 16th century by the Portuguese. The remains of the seminary are still visible. There is an old Syrian Catholic Church near the ruins of the seminary established in 1201. Kottayil Kovilakam, the seat of the Kshatriya chieftains of yore is also situated near the temple. An ancient Kunnathahalli temple and a temple of Gowda Saraswatha Brahmins are here.

KALADY : (48 km) The birth place of Shankaracharya, the great 8th century philosopher is situated on the banks of the Periyar river. Shankaracharya had revived the 'Sanatan' (i.e. since the beginning of the time) Hindu Dharma which was eclipsed by Buddhism and Jainism and highlighted the religious unity of India by establishing four Hindu religious centres in four corners of the country. A person of amazing genius he had revived the special intellectual kind of Hinduism. There are two shrines dedicated to his memory—Sree Saradamba and Sree Shankara temple—built in 1910 AD by Jagadguru Sree Sachithananda Shiva Abhinava Narsimha Barathi Swamigal of Sringeri Saradapitha. There is also Sree Adi Sankara Keerthi Stambha Mandapam. Important events in Sree Sankara's life are depicted on the inside wall of the Sthoopam on the top of the floor of the mandapam. Nearby is the crocodile ghat where Sree sankaracharya had taken to sanyasa (relinquishment of all wordly ties and attachments). According to legend, it was here that a crocodile had caught hold of him and when his mother Aryamba permitted him to accept sanyasa the crocodile disappeared.

MALAYATTUR : 8 km from Kalady is a Christian pilgrim centre believed to have been blessed by the apostle of Christ St.Thomas. The

church atop a hill was established in 900.KALLIL BHAGAVATHY
TEMPLE, 22 away from the town has a Jain temple cut from a huge
rock. One has to climb 120 steps to reach the temple.

KODUNGALLUR : 50 km from Kalady, this was the premier sea
port on India's west coast. It was the capital of Cheraman Perumals.
It was believed that St.Thomas, the Apostle of Jesus, who came to India
in 52 AD had landed at Kottappuram near Kodungallur. Cherman Juma
Musjid, the first mosque in India is situated at kilometres away from
this town. It was built in 629 AD. An ancient Portuguese Fort and
Thiruvanchikulam temple are also situated here. The Bharani festival
during March/April in the Kali Bahgavati temple attracts thousands of
Hindu pilgrims.

ALLEPPY : (64 km) Known as the Venice of the East, this town
is situated on the Vembanad Lake, the longest lake in India. The large
net work of canals provides Alleppy its life line. It has a long sandy
beach. A major tourist attraction is the Nehru Trophy boat race
organised on the second Saturday of August every year. Alleppy is also
famous for the manufacture of coir yarn, coir matts and mattings. A
boat journey through the canals and back waters is a delightful
experience. Alleppy is connected by water transport with Kollam,
Kottayam, Chengnacherry and Chenganur.AMBALAPUZHA, a town
14 km from Alleppy has Sreekrishna temple built in typical Kerala style.
ARTHUNKAL, 22km away is known for the famous St. Andrews
Church established by the Portuguese missionaries in 1951. The famous
'Arthunkal Perunnal', is held in January every year in connection with
the feast of St.Sebastian.

KOTTAYAM : (76 km) Kottayam is a prominent commercial centre
with palm fringed backwaters on the west and the scenic western ghats
to the east.This was the capital of the Thekkumkur Rajas before the
annexation of the kingdom by Marthandavarma. The existence of ancient
religious shrines of different communities in close proximity is proof
of the glorious tradition of religious tolerance of its people.
THIRUNAKKARA SHIVA TEMPLE, built in the indigenous Kerala
style, the dancing hall here is one of the best in the State and the temple
also has a wealth of paintings on its walls. The main festival, Phalguna
Utsav is celebrated during March. ST. MARY'S CHURCH
(VALLAPALLY) believed to have been built in 1515, is famous for the
Persian cross and Phalvi inscriptions. ST.MARY'S CHRUCH
(CHERIYAPALLY) has exquisite murals and paintings of Biblical and
non-Biblical themes. MANNANAM, 8 km away, is an important centre

for Christians. St. Joseph's monastery here is an old institution and associated with Fr.Kuriskose Elisas of Chavars (1805-71). KUMARKONAM BIRD SANCTUARY is situated 12 km away on the eastern banks of Vembanad lake and sprawls over 14 acres of land. It is an ideal place for backwater cruises. ETTUMANOOR near the Kottayam has a Shiva temple—a good specimen of Kerala temple architecture. Its centre shrine is circular with copper plates and a stupa of copper built at the top. There are exquisite mural paintings and sculptures inside the temple. There is a mural art centre near the temple which is preserved by the state archaeological Department. The annual festival of the temple falls in February-March which lasts for 10 days.

THRISSUR : (80 km) The cultural capital of Kerala has played significant role since ancient times. It was a former capital of the Cochin State and was ruled by the Zamorin and later by Tipu Sultan in the second half of the 18th century.

In 1790 Raja Rama Varma popularly known as Sakthan Thampuran ascended the throne of Cochin and created the present town of Trichur.The famous Pooram festival is celebrated at VEDAKKUMNATHAN TEMPLE every year during April/May.This ancient temple has many wall paintings and historically important pieces of art. TOWN HALL of the city is an imposing building with a picture Gallery of mural paintings. There is an archaeological museum on town hall road. At ARATTUPUZHA POORAM a festival is held in April/ May. The image of the deities from 41 neighbouring temples are brought in a procession to this village during the festival. GURUVAYOOR (29 km) is a place sacred for Sree Krishna temple known as 'Guruvayoorappam'. As the legend goes, the temple is the creation of Guru, the preceptor of the Vayu Deva, the Lord of Winds. Entry is restricted to Hindus only. A 10-Day Utsav is celebrate every February/ March. CHERUTHURUTHY (32 km) away is a site for Kathakali training centre. A music and dance academy was founded here by the famous poet, the late Vallothol Narayan Menon. 80 km from Trichur is PALGHAT, the granary of the State of Kerala. TIPU'S FORT here dates back to 1766 AD. constructed by Hyder Ali of Mysore. TEMPLE KALPATHI, dedicated to Lord Shiva is believed to be built in 1425 AD. There is also an ancient Jain temple at Jainamedu built by Jain guru Inchanna Satur 500 years ago in the name of sage Chandranataswami.

IDUKKI : (132 km) Sprawling over an area of 5061 Sq. km, this district is marked by undulating hills and valleys. The name Idukki is derived from the name 'Idukku' meaning a narrow gorge. The high ranges vary in altitude from 2500 feet above sea level to more than 5000 feet. Idukki has at present about 1,500 Sq. km of reserved forest which is rich in flora and fauna. The famous arch dam here is constructed across the Periyar river between two huge granite hills. Idukki with its many streams, wooded valleys and hills, is a beautiful place to visit any time of year. Frequent buses are available from Cochin, Thekkady and Thodupuzha.

MUNNAR : (136 km) Munnar is a beautiful station on the western ghats at about 1,600 meters above sea level. The town is situated at the confluence of the three mountain streams of Mudrapuzha, Nallathanni and Kundala. There are lakes, reservoirs, green forests and several tea estates.Anamudi, the highest peak in South India is nearby. There is a wildlife sanctuary in the Eravikulam-Rajamala area. Chinnar wildlife sanctuary is close to Eravikulam National Park

This is a protected area in Kerala with semi-arid and dry deciduous shrub forests the preferred habitat of the starred Tortoise. Munnar was the summer resort of the British government in the South. MATTUPETTY town,13 km away has the Indo-Swiss dairy farm. About 100 varieties of high yielding cattle are reared here. A few yards away from the farms is the beautiful lake on dam which is a beautiful picnic spot. The vast stretch of Kandala tea plantations offer a stunning view of Munar.MARAYOOR relics of the New stone age civilisation have been unearthed 40 km away from Munar.

SABARIMALA : (210 km) A well-known pilgrim centre, Sabrimala lies 191 km north of Thiruvananthapuram and 210 km from Cochin. The holy shrine dedicated to Lord Ayyappa is situated at 914 metres above sea level amidst dense forests in the rugged terrains of the Western Ghats. The festivals which are celebrated here are the Mandala Pooja, Makara Vilakku and Vishnu Vilakku. Vehicles go only upto Pampa and the temple which is situated at 5 km from Pampa, can be reached only by trekking.

WYNAD

Wyand situated at a height of 700 to 2,100 meters above sea level has unique geographical position. It is surrounded by Nilgiries and bounded by Tamil Nadu and Karnataka. In ancient times it was ruled by the Rajas of the Veda tribe and later came under the control of the Pazhassi Rajas of Kottayam's royal dynasty, Tipu sultan of Mysore and the British. This district has the highest concentration of tribals in Kerala. KALPETTA, famous Anathanthaswami Jain temple is situated at Puliyarmala near Kalpetta. It is the headquarters of Wynad district. About 14 km west of Kalpetta lies CHEMBRA PEAK situated at 2100 meters above sea level and is ideal for trekking. POOKOT LAKE, is the beautiful natural fresh water lake surrounded by evergreen forests and wooded hills. There is a fresh water aquarium with wide varieties of fishes. THE GLASS TEMPLE OF KOOTTAMUNDA is located 20 kms away on the slop of 'Vellarimala' dedicated to Parswanatha Swami, third thirthankara of the Jain faith.

LAKKADI is a place of great scenic beauty with picturesque hills, streams and luxuriant vegetation, one of the highest location in Wynad and gets the second highest degree of rainfall in the world. Three km from here is Pookate lake, the natural fresh water lake, very deep and wide, and is one of the rare reservoirs of water in Wynad, surrounded on all sides by meadows and hills.

KASARGOD

Northernmost district of Kerala, it is situated on the sea coast 420 km from Cochin and 50 km from Mangalore. There is a fort at CHANDRAGIRI built in the 17th century by Sivappa Nayaka of Bedanore who established his authority over the area and built a chain of forts. A mosque is situated nearby and there is an ancient Kizhur State temple. GOVINDA PAI MEMORIAL of the great Patriarch of Kannda literature is situated at Manjeswaram. There are also 15 mosques at Manjeswaram.

MADIYANKULAM TEMPLE : Temple dedicated to Goddess Bhadrakali is situated near Kanjangad in Hosdurg. BEKAL, 16 km from Kasargod, is one of the most beautiful beaches in Kerala. Fort at Bekal is of great historical and Archaeological interest and is one of the largest and best preserved one in Kerala.

PERIYAR NATIONAL PARK : Periyar is one of India's most picturesque national parks. It has a picturesque lake at the heart of the sanctuary. Formed with the building of a dam in 1895, this resevior meanders around the contours of the wooded hills, providing a perennial source of water for the local wildlife. Though one of India's 16 tiger reserves, Periyar is best known for its large population of elephants. Among the unusual species found at Periyar are the flying lizards and the flying snakes. Lake attracts varieties of birds. Boats are the only means of exploring Periyar. Nearest airport to reach the sanctuary is Madurai (145 km), Cochin (190 km) railhead - Kottayam (114 km)

For accommodation and additional information :
— Wildlife Preservation Officer, Thekkady, Idukki – Kerala.

FESTIVALS

JANUARY—THE GREAT ELEPHANT MARCH : This festival takes place in some of Kerala's major towns—Thrissur, Alappuzha and Thrivananthapuram. While caparisoned elephants go out in procession, boat races on the backwaters and cultural events lend colour to the festivities.

KERALA VILLAGE FAIR : (Kovalam) Every year mid-January is the time for cultural events. The traditional thatch houses are decorated during the 10-day long festival and are the venue for folk dances, music and festivities.

MAY—POORAM : The colourful Pooram festival is held in Thrissur at its fine Vadakkumnathan temple. Processions of beautifully caparisoned elephants provide a magnificent spectacle. The festival is rounded off at night by dazzling firework displays.

AUGUST—ONAM : Onam coincides with the harvest season and is an occasion of spontaneous revelry. Onam celebrates the home coming of Mahabali, the legendary king, who had ruled over Kerala in the mythological age of plenty but was sent down to infernal regions by Lord Vishnu in the form of Vamana. The decorating of houses with carpets of flowers, a sumptuous lunch and songs in praise of the golden reign of Mahabali, mark the 10-day long festivities. A major attraction of Onam celebrations are the famed snake boat races along the backwaters at Champakulam, Arbnmula and Kottayam.

NHERU TROPHY BOAT RACE : Alappuzha is famous for its annual boat race conducted in the Punnamada held on the second Saturday of August every year. The long elegant snakeboats, with crews of over hundred men vying to win the coveted trophy, attract spectators from all over.

AYURVEDA —AN ATTRACTION FOR TOURIST

Popularity of Ayurveda is turning out to be an important cause for a tourism boom in Kerala. Kerala iS the only state which practices this system of medicine with absolute dedication.

Around 600 BC in India a new system of medicine evolved. A system that in addition to treating an ailment, stressed on its prevention. A system that came to be called Ayurveda. This tradition of heath and care was followed by the Dravidians and Aryans alike and has been practiced ever since. In the 5th century, there are historical references of some sort of a crude system of healing prevalent in Kerala. Marco Polo in the 13th century had observed good traditional practitioners and astrologists in Kerala. Ashtavaidyans, the traditional healers of Kerala, used to practice Vagbhandan's remedies and his followers, Indu and Geggdan are believed to have stayed in Kerala and were instrumental in propagating the Ayurveda system of healing. It is also believed that Indu, who wrote Sasilekha, a preface for Ayurveda, belonged to Kerala.

Today, Ayurveda is an indispensable branch of medicine—a complete naturalistic system that depends on the diagnosis of your body's humours —vata, pitta and kapha—to achieve the right balance. Ayurveda believes in the treatment of not just the affected part but the individual as a whole making. The practice is presently both a mixture of Vagabhadan's remedies and traditionally proved methods of healing practiced by an ancient families.

Unique health holiday opportunity from Kerala Tourism is based on Ayurveda the time-tested, ancient Indian system of medicine. Ayurveda offers two kinds of holiday options, Rejuvenative and Therapeutic.

REJUVENATIVE PROGRAMMES

Rejuvenation Theory - Rassayana Chikitsa : It tones up the skin and rejuvenates and strengthens all the tissues so as to achieve ideal health and longevity. It also increases 'Ojas' (primary vitality) and improves 'Satva' (mental clarity) and thereby increases the resistance power of the body. It includes head and face massage with medicated oils and herbal oil or powder by hand and foot, intake of rejuvenative medicines and medicated steam bath. Herbal baths are also used.

Body Immunisation and Longevity Treatment - Kayakalpa Chikitsa : Prime treatment for retarding the ageing process, arresting the degeneration of body cells and immunisation of the system it includes intake of Rasayana (special Ayurvedic medicines and diet) and comprehensive body care programmes. The treatment proves most effective if undertaken before the age of 50.

Body Sudation - Sweda Karma : Medicated steam baths eliminate impurities from the body, improve the tone and complexion of the skin, reduce fat and are recommended for certain rheumatic diseases, particularly for pain. Precious herbs and herbal leaves are boiled and the setam is passed over the entire body fro 10 to 20 minutes daily. Hand massage with herbal oils or herbal powder improves body circulation and tones up the muscles.

Mental and Physical Well Being - Meditation and Yoga : Mental and physical exercises meant to isolate the ego from the body and the mind- designed to hone your concentration, improve health and help attain peace of mind through eight stages of training :

(1) Disciplined behaviour (yama); (2) Self-purification(niyama); (3) Bodily postures such as the lotus position (asana); (4) Control of breathing (pranayama); (5) Control of the senses (pratyahara); (6) Fixing of the mind on a chosen object (dharana); (7) Meditation (dhyana); (8) Samadhi—a state of being where you experience absolute tranquility and well-being.

Beauty Care : Herbal face pack, herbal oil, intake herbal tea etc. improve complexion and beautifies the body.

Body Slimming : Medicated herbal powder and medicated herbal oil massages, an Ayurvedic diet of herbal juices etc.are part of the programme.

Overall Fitness - Panchakarma Treatment : A five fold treatment for mental and physical well being - tunes the body, organs, mind, breath, nerves and purifies the blood.

THERAPEUTIC PROGRAMMES

Treatment for chronic headache, insomnia, mental tension, hysteria, hallucination and insanity - Dhara : Herbal oils, medicated milk or decoctions are poured on the forehead/whole body in a special manner.

Variations include Oordhwanga Dhara (good for diseases of eyes, ears and skin), Takra Dhara (for those suffering from memory loss, severe headache or insanity) and Sarvanga Dhara (for both head and body).

Treatment to alleviate osteoarthritis, leukemina etc. - Snehapanam : Medicated ghee is given internally in a gradually increased quantity for specific periods.

Treatment for spondilosis, rheumatic diseases like arthritis, paralysis, hemiplegia, nervous weakness and nervous disorders - Pizhichil : Lukewarm herbal oil is applied with fresh linen all over the body by trained masseurs in a rhythmic manner for one to two hours daily for 7 to 21 days.

Treatment for diseases like hemiplegia, paralysis, obesity and certain rheumatic ailments -Udvarthanam : Therapeutic massage with herbal powders.

Treatment for musculoskeletal ailments due to trauma or accidents - Marma Chikitsa : Treatment that works on the extremely sensitive vital points of the body (the 107 marmas).

Treatment for nasal ailments - Nasyam : Inhalation of medicated herbal preparations, decoction of oils, ghee etc. to eliminate the morbid factors from the head and neck area.

Treatment for ear ailment - Karnapooranam : Medicated oils are applied to the ear for 5 to 10 minutes daily to clean as well as treat specific ailments.

Preventing cataract and strengthening vision - Tharpanam : A treatment for the eys effective in preventing cataract and strengthening the optic nerve.

Treatment for wasting of muscles, all types of rheumatism, sports injuries, pain in joints, emaciation of the body or parts of the body and certain kinds of skin diseases.

Nijavarakizhi : The whole body is made to perspire by the external application of medicated rice packs in the form of boluses i.e. clod or lump of earth tied in muslin bags.

Treatment for dryness of nostrils, mouth and throat, severe haedaches, facial paralysis and burning sensation in the head - Sirovasti : Lukewarm herbal oils are poured into a leather cap fitted on the head for specific duration as per physician's recommendation.

REJUVENATION PROGRAMME OPERATORS
APPROVED BY KERALA TOURISM

— Ayurvedic Health Spa, Kappad Beach Resort, Calicut
   TEFAX 683 706
— Aranya Niwas, Thekkady. PH 220 23; FAX 220 82
— Kottakkal Arya Vaidyasala, P.O. Kottakkal, Malappuram
   PH 742 216; FAX 742 572
— Shilpa Health Club, Mascot Hotel, Trivandrum
   PH 438 990; FAX 437 745
— Hotel Samudra, Kovalam. PH 480 089; FAX 480 242
— Kovalam Ashok Beach Resort, Kovalam
   PH 480 101; FAX 481 522

MADHYA PRADESH

MADHYA PRADESH
AT A GLANCE

AREA : 4,43,446 sq. km.

CAPITAL : Bhopal

BOUNDARIES : East - Orissa and Bihar, West - Rajasthan and Gujarat; North - Uttar Pradesh; South - Maharashtra and Andhra Pradesh.

LANGUAGE : Hindi

ROADS : Total length of roads in the State was 97,343 km in 1995-96 including 76,614km of metalled roads.

AIRPORTS : Bhopal, Indore, Jabalpur, Khajuraho, Raipur and Gwalior.

MUSEUMS

Bhopal : State Museum
Gwalior : Archaeological Museum – Gajari Mahal
Indore : Central Museum
Khajuraho : Archaeological Museum; Dhubela Museum (64 km from Khajuraho)
Sanchi : Archaeological Museum
Ujjain : Vikram University Museum

HILL RESORT

Pachmarchi (1067 m) Piparia 47 km.

PILGRIM CENTRES (A : Air; R : Rail)

Amarkantak : Source of the Narmada; A – Jabalpur – 246 km, R – Pendra Road – 17 km.

Bawanganja : Jain pilgrim centre, it has a 22 m high statue in the rock face; A – Indore 170 km, R – Barwani – 10 km.

Chitrakoot : Place of 11 years of Rama's stay during his 14-year exile from Ayodhya. Also the ashram of Sage Atri ans Sati Anasuya; A – Khajuraho 175 km, R – Chitrakoot 11 km.

Indore : Jain Kabch Mandir; A and R – Indore.

Maheshwar : The ancient Mahishamati mentioned in the Ramayana and the Mahabharata. It has many temples on the banks of the Narmada; A – Indore 91 km, R – Barwaha – 39 km.

Muktagiri : Has 52 Jain temples; A – Bhopal 220 km, R – Betul 97 km.

Omkareshwar : An island shaped like the sacred symbol Om. Has one of the 12 Jyotirlinga Shrines; A Indore – 77 km, R – Omkareshwar Road 97 km.

Sanchi : Ancient Buddhist centre with a new Buddhist Vihara; A - Bhopal 46 km, R – Sanchi.

Sheorinarayan : The annual fair held during Magh Purnima attracts pilgrims; A – Raipur 140 km, R – Akaltara – 55 km.

Ujjain : One of the ancient cities of India. The Mahakaleshwar temple has one of the 12 Jyotirlingas; A Indore – 53 km, R – Ujjain.

This biggest State is situated in the centre of the country. Except for the valleys of the Narmada and the Tapi rivers, M.P. consists of a plateau with a mean elevation of 1600 ft.above sea level, interspersed with the mountains of the Vindhyachal and the Satpura ranges. Madhya Pradesh is the site of one of the world's earliest and most developed civilizations.There are over 1800 magnificent monuments bearing to the glory that was this land of Malwa.

HISTORY

Emperor Ashok had first of all ruled over Ujjain. A sizeable portion of Central India was part of the Gupta empire (300-500AD). The Muslims came into Central India in the beginning of the 11th century. First of all Mahmud of Ghazni came over here and then Mohammad Gauri who incorporated some parts of Central India into his ruling territory of Delhi. Central India was also part of the Mughal empire. During the period between the beginning of the influence of the Marathas and the death of Madhoji Scindia in 1794, Marathas were on the rise in Central India but later on the small States started coming into existence which helped the perpetuation of British power in the country. Queen Ahilyabai Holkar of Indore, the Gaud Maharani Kamala Devi and Queen Durgawati were some women rulers whose names have been written in an indelible ink in the Indian history for their outstanding rule. After independence Madhya Pradesh came into being in November 1956.

Madhya Pradesh has the largest population of scheduled tribes of all States and a high proportion of Schedule Castes, together they constitute nearly one third of the population.

BHOPAL

Bhopal, capital of Madhya Pradesh, is a fascinating amalgam of scenic beauty, historicity and modern urban planning. Bhopal was founded by Raja Bhoja in the 11th century. The founder of the existing city was an Afghan soldier, Dost Mohammed (1708-1740 AD), fleeing Delhi. Bhopal was then ruled by a series of Nawabs and in succession by powerful Begums from 1819 AD to 1926 AD.

PLACES OF INTEREST

TAJ-UL-MASJID : Said to be the largest in the country, the construction of this mosque was started by Shah Jehan Begum (1868 to 1901AD) but was left incomplete due to her death and construction work could be resumed in 1971 AD only. The most striking features of the mosque are the impressive main hall with its inter-arched roof, broad facade, spacious courtyard and smooth marble floors. A three-day Ijtima congregation held here annually draws people from all over the country.

MOTI MASJID : Built by Sikandar Jahan, daughter of Kudesia Begum in 1860 AD, its architecture resembles Delhi's Jama Masjid.

SHAUKAT MAHAL AND SARDAR MANZIL : Situated in the heart of the walled city, it is an architectural curiosity. Its mixture of styles, in occidental idioms, sets it apart from the predominantly Islamic architecture of the area. It was designed by a Frenchman, said to be a descendant of an offshoot of the Bourbon kings of France.

BHARAT BHAVAN : Centre for the performing and visual arts it houses a museum of arts, art gallery, a workshop for fine arts and libraries of Indian poetry, classical and folk music.

TRIBAL HABITAT : An open air exhibition of tribal house types located on Shamla Hills, the Tribal Habitat is a presentation of actual size dwelling houses typical of contemporary tribal cultures in various States of India. The surroundings have been reconstructed to match some of the interesting environmental features of tribal villages.

CHOWK : In the heart of the old city the chowk is lined with old mosques and havelis, reminders of a bygone princely lifestyle shops here are treasure troves of traditional Bhopali crafts.

GOVERNMENT ARCHAEOLOGICAL MUSEUM : A fine collection of sculpture is on display here from various parts of Madhya Pradesh.

GANDHI BHAWAN : Housed here is an exhibition of Mahatama Gandhi's photographs and a Gandhi museum.

UPPER AND LOWER LAKES : Trips by sail, paddle and motor boats are available here.

VAN VIHAR : This safari park is located on a hill adjacent to the upper lake with an area of 445 hectares. In these natural surroundings, wildlife watchers can view a variety of herbivorous and carnivorous species.

HOW TO REACH

AIR : Bhopal is connected by air with Delhi, Gwalior, Indore and Mumbai

RAIL : Bhopal is on Mumabi-Delhi and Delhi-Chennai main line.

2002 Shatabadi Exp			2001 Shatabdi Exp	
06:00	D	New Delhi	A	22:40
07:55	A	Agra Cantt	D	20:18
08:00	D		A	20:10
09:15	A	Gwalior	D	19:00
09:18	D		A	18:55
10:24	A	Jhansi	D	17:55
10:32	D		A	17:47
14:00	A	Bhopal	D	14:40

ROAD : Regular bus services connect Bhopal with Indore, Mandu, Ujjain, Khajuraho, Pachmarhi, Gwalior, Sanchi, Jabalpur and Shivpuri.

DISTANCES FROM BHOPAL

Sanchi 47 km; Ujjain 188 km; Mandu 285 km; Indore 186 km; Gwalior 428 km; Kanha 537 km; Jabalpur 295 km; Shivpuri 311 km; Panchamarhi 210 km; Amarkantak 575 km; Chitrakoot 559; Khajuraho 387 km; Jhansi 402 km; Agra 541 km; Delhi 741 km and Allhabad 680.

CONDUCTED TOURS

Madhya Pradesh State Tourism Development Corporation operates following tours :

FROM MUMBAI

ENCHANTING FORTNIGHT (13 nights and 14 days) : Mumbai – Satna – Khajuraho – Bandavgarh – Jabalpur – Panchamarhi – Bhopal – Ujjain – Mandu – Omkareshwar – Mandu – Indore.

MYSTICAL MANDU (Three nights and four days) : Mumbai – Ujjain – Maheshwar – Mandu – Indore.

DOWN MEMORY LANE (six nights and seven days) : Mumbai – Khajuraho – Orcha – Shivpuri – Gwalior.

DIVINE MOMENTS (Six nights and seven days) : Mumbai – Chitrakoot – Khajuraho – Bandavgarh – Jabalpur.

CALL THE WILD (Six nights and seven days) : Mumbai – Jabalpur – Bandavgarh – Kanha – Jabalpur.

KIPLING COUNTRY (Seven nights and eight days) : Mumbai – Panchmarhi – Kanha – Jabalpur.

FROM AHMEDABAD

SYLVAN RETRET (Seven nights and eight days) : Ahmedabad -- Bhopal (By train) onwards by surface Pachmarhi – Jabalpur – Marble Rocks – Kanha and back to Ahmedabad via Jabalpur by train.

MALWA TO SATPURA (Seven Nights and eight days) : Ahmedabad – Ujjain (By train) onwards by surface Mandu – Bhopal – Bhimbekta – Panchmarhi – Bhopal and back to Ahmedabad by train

DOWN MEMORY LANE (Five nights and Six days) : Ahmedabad – Bhopal (By train) onwards by surface Shivpuri – Khajuraho – Satna and back to Ahmedabad by train.

TEMPLES 'N' TIGERS (Seven nights and eight days) : Ahmedabad – Bhopal (By train) onwards by surface Jabalpur – Marbel Rocks – Amarkantak – Bandhavgarh – Khajuraho – Satna and back to Ahmedabad by train.

FROM CALCUTTA

MAGICAL FORTNIGHT (14 nights and 15 days) : Calcutta-Satna (By train) onwards by surface Khajuraho – Gwalior – Shivpuri – Ujjain – Mandu – Indore – Bhopal – Sanchi – Panchmarhi – Jabalpur – Marble Rocks and back to Calcutta by train.

TEMPLES 'N' TIGERS (Six nights and seven Days) : Calcutta – Satna (By train) Chitrakoot, Bandhavgarh – Amarkantak – Jabalpur – Marble Rock and back to Calcutta by train

DOWN MEMORY LANE (Six nights and seven days) : Calcutta – Gwalior (By train) onward by surface Shivpuri – Orchha – Khajuraho and bach to Calcutta by train

CALL OF THE WILD (Six nights and seven days) : Calcutta – Satna (By train) onwards by surface to Bandhavgarh – Kanha – Jabalpur – Marble Rocks and back to Calcutta by train.

SATPURA TO MALWA (Seven nights and eight days) : Calcutta – Piparia (By train) onwards by surface Pachmarhi – Bhopal – Sanchi – Mandu – Ujjain – Omkareshwar and back to Calcutta by train.

For detailed information contact :
— M.P.S.T.D.C. Ltd., Hotel Palash, near T.T.Nagar, Bhopal. PH 553 006, 553 076

HOTEL ACCOMMODATION (STD CODE 0217)

— Jehan Numa Palace Hotel (Heritage B Classic) 157, Shamla Hill. PH 540 100 FAX 540 720
— The Residency (4 Star) 208, Zone1, M.P. Nagar PH 556 001-06; FAX 557 637
— Hotel Amar Palace (3 star) 209, Zone1, M.P. Nagar PH 557 127/28; FAX 575 308
— Hotel Lake View Ashok (3 Star) Shamla Hills PH 541 600-10; FAX 541 606/07
— Hotel Mayur (2 Star) Berasia Road. PH 536 711, 536 643
— Hotel Panchanan, New Market, T.T. Nagar PH 551 647; FAX 552 384

EXCURSIONS

ISLAMNAGAR : (16km) Islamnagar is a place of Bhopal's Afghan rulers and was built by Dost Mohammed Khan. Gardens, palaces of Hindu-Muslim style and the Rani Mahal are worth seeing.

Other monuments to see here are the hamam of Chaman Mahal and the double storyed Rani Mahal.

BHOJPUR : (28km) Founded by the legendary Parmara king of Dhar, Raja Bhoja (1010-53 AD) has remains of its magnificent Shiva temple and cyclopean dam. The Bhojeshwar temple here is known as Somnath of the east.

BHIMBEKTA : (40km) This is a rocky terrain of dense forests and craggy cliffs. Over 700 rock shelters were recently discovered here. In vivid panoramic detail paintings in over 500 caves depict the life of the prehistoric cave-dwellers, making the Bhimabekta group an archaeological treasure, an invaluable chronicle in the history of man.

UDAYPUR : (90 km) Udaypur has the colossal Neelantheshwara temple of the 11th century. The crowning beauty of this temple lies in its well proportioned and gracefully designed spire or shikara and delicately carved medallions adorning its sides.

SANCHI

Sanchi is known for its stupas, monasteries, temples and pillars stretching from the 3rd century BC to 12th century AD.

Carved with stories of the Buddha's past and present lives and with incidents from the subsequent history of Buddhism, the gateways are the finest specimen of early classical art which formed the seedbed for the entire vocabulary of later Indian art. .

Archaeological museum houses stone sculptures in Indian art from the 3rd to 1st century BC.

PLACES OF INTEREST

GREAT STUPA NO. 1 : The oldest stone structure in India, 36.5 m in diameter and 16.4 m high, and with a massive hemispherical dome, the stupa stands in eternal majesty, the paved procession path around it worn smooth by centuries of pilgrims.

THE FOUR GATEWAYS : The Buddha, according to the tenets of early Buddhist art, is portrayed in symbols; the lotus representing his birth, the tree his enlightenment, the wheel, derived from the title of his first sermon, the footprints and throne symbolising his presence. These are carved with inspired intensity and considered the finest of all Buddhist toranas and counter-balance the massive solidity of the stupa they encircle.

THE EASTERN GATEWAY : Depicts the seven incarnations of the Buddha.

THE NORTHERN GATEWAY : Crowned by a wheel of law, it depicts the miracles associated with the Buddha as told in the jatakas.

THE SOUTHERN GATEWAY : The birth of Gautama is revealed in a series of dramatically rich carvings.

STUPA NO. 2 : This stupa stands at the very edge of the hill and its most striking feature is the stone balustrade that rings it.

STUPA NO. 3 : The relics of Sariputta and Mahamogallena, two of the Buddha's earlier disciples, were found in its inmost chamber.

THE ASHOKA PILLAR : One of the finest examples of the architecture of Ashokan period this pillar is known for its exquisite structural balance.

THE BUDDHIST VIHARA : The sacred relics of the Satdhara stupa, a few km away from Sanchi, have been enshrined in a glass casket on a platform in the inner sanctum of this modern monastery.

THE GREAT BOWL : Carved out of one block of stone, this mammoth bowl contained the food that was distributed among the monks of Sanchi.

THE GUPAT TEMPLE : This 5th century temple now lies in ruins.

THE MUSEUM : The Archaeological survey of India maintains a site museum. On display mainly is the lion capital of the Ashokarr pillar and metal objects used by the monks, discovered during excavations at Sanchi.

HOW TO REACH

AIR : Nearest airport – Bhopal (46 km via Diwanganj and 78 km via Raisen)

RAIL : Convenient railhead is Vidisha (10 km). Sanchi lies on the Jhansi-Itarsi section of the Central Railway.

ROAD : Regular bus service connects Sanchi with Bhopal, Indore, Sagar, Gwalior, Vidisha and Raisen besides other places.

HOTEL ACCOMMODATION

— Travellers Lodge (MPT), Tourist Cafeteria (MPT), P.W.D. resthouse, Buddhist resthouse

EXCURSIONS

VIDISHA : (10 km) Situated in the fork of the Betwa and Beas rivers, Vidisha was a bustling town from 5th to 16th centuries under the Sungas, Nagas, Satvahanas and Guptas. The nearby monuments like the 2nd century BC Heliodorus pillar, the 5th century AD Udayagiri caves, the Lohangi hill monuments in Vidisha are situated within a radius of 10 km of Sanchi.

UDAYGIRI CAVES : (13 km) Udaygiri caves were produced during the regin of Chandragupta II (382-401). The caves have all distinct features that gave Gupta art its unique vitality, vigour and richness of expression. The beautifully moulded capitals, the treatment of the intercumilation the design of the entrance gateway and the system of continuing the architrave as a string course around the structure.

GYARASPUR : (40 km North East of Sanchi) Important place of the medieval period, now lies in ruins, where one can see temples called Athkhamba (Eight pillars) and Chaukhamba (four pillars) belonging to the 9th and 10th centuries AD.

GWALIOR

In legend Gwalior's history goes back to multitude of reigning dynasties of the great Rajput clans of the Pratiharas, Kachwas and Tomars who have left indelible etchings of their rule in this city of palaces, temples and monuments. The magnificent mementoes of a glorious past have been preserved with care giving Gwalior a unique and timeless appeal. In the 8th century AD its chieftain Suraj Sen was cured of leprosy by a hermit saint, Gwalipa in gratitude he named the city after his name.

PLACES OF INTEREST

THE FORT : Fort has been the scene of momentous events : imprisonments, battles and Jauhars.Fort contains several interesting temples and ruined palaces. Its dramatic and colourful history dates back to over 1000 years.

Rising 100 meters above the town, the fort hill is about 3 km in length. A steep road winds upwards to the Fort, flanked by the Jain tirthankaras, carved into the rock faces. The magnificent outer walls of the fort still stand, two miles in length and 35 feet high, bearing witness to its reputation for  being one of the most invincible forts of India. Its width varies from nearly 1 km to less than 200 meters. The walls, which encircle almost the entire hilltop, are 10 meter high and imposingly solid. The imposing structure inspired the Emperor Babur to describe it as 'the pearl amongst the fortress of Hindu,.

GUJARI MAHAL : Within the fort is the 15th century Gujari Mahal, a monument to the love of Raja Mansingh Tomar for the intrepid Mriganayani, a tribal Gujar Queen.The archaeological museum located within this Mahal houses rare antiquities, Hindu and Jain sculptures,some of them dating back to the 1st century AD.

MAN MANDIR PALACE : Once a grand music hall it was built by Raja Man Singh during 1486 AD and 1517 AD for the royal ladies of the palace to learn music from the great masters of the day. A superbly mounted Son-et-Lumiere here brings it all alive every evening.

SURAJ KUND : Though the major portion of the fort was built in the 15th century reference to this gigantic complex can be traced back to 425 AD. Older than the city is the Suraj Kund within the fort walls, the original pond where Suraj Sen was cured by saint Gwalipa.

TELI KA MANDIR AND SAS BAHU KA MANDIR : Within the fort complex is the 9th century Teli Ka Mandir, towering 100 ft. high it is a Pratihara Vishnu temple with the roof in Dravidian style while the decorations bear the Indo-Aryan characteristics of northern India. A Garuda tops the 95 meter high doorway.Sas Bahu ka Mandir is also dedicated to Lord Vishnu. Originally known as the 'Sahasrabahu' temple, this is probably the most ancient structure within the fort walls, built by Mahipala, the kachchwah King, in the early 11th century AD.

GURUDWARA DATA BANDHI CHHOD : Built in the memory of Guru Hargobind Saheb the sixth Sikh Guru, who was imprisoned here by Emperor Jehangir for over two years.

JAI VILAS PALACE AND MUSEUM : 35 rooms from the current residence of the Scindia family (Jai Vilas Palace) have been turned into Jivaji Rao Scindia Museum.

TANSEN'S TOMB : A pillar of Hindustani classical music, TANSEN, one of the NINE JEWELS of Akbar's court lies buried in Gwalior.Tomb is part of Gwalior's living cultural heritage and is a venue for the annual music festival in November / December.

GHAUS MOHAMMED'S TOMB : The sandstone mausoleum of the Afghan prince, Ghaus Mohammed, is also designed on early Mughal lines. Particularly exquisite are the screens which use the pierced stone technique as delicate as lace.

MEMORIALS : The earliest freedom fighters, Tatya Tope and the indomitable Rani of Jhansi, are commemorated in memorials in Gwalior.

HOW TO REACH

AIR : Gwalior is connected by air with Delhi, Bhopal, Indore and Mumbai

RAIL : Gwalior is on Central Railway's main line between Delhi, Mumbai and Chennai.

Taj Express and Shatabdi Express connect Gwalior with Delhi and Agra.

ROAD : There are regular bus services from Agra, Mathrua, Jaipur, Delhi, Lucknow, Bhopal, Chanderi, Indore, Jhansi, Khajuraho, Rewa, Ujjain and Shivpuri.

TOURIST INFORMATION OFFICE

— Hotel Tansen, 6 Gandhi Road
  PH 340 370, 342 606; FAX 340 371
— Tourist Office, Railway Station, PH 345 370

HOTEL ACCOMMODATION (STD CODE 0751)

— Welcomegroup Usha Kiran (Heritage), Jayendraganj, Lashkar
  PH 323 993 FAX 321 103
— Hotel Gwalior Regency, Link Road
  PH 340 670-74; FAX 343 520
— Hotel Shelter, Padav. PH 326 209/10; FAX 326 212
— Hotel Tansen, 6A, Gandhi Road
  PH 340 370, 342 606; FAX 340 371
— Hotel Vivek Continental Pvt.Ltd.
  PH 329 016, 427 017; FAX 429 878

EXCURSION

SHIVPURI : (101 km) Shivpuri was the summer capital of the Scindia rulers of Gwalior. Earlier, its dense forests were the hunting grounds of the Mughal emperors. A Shivpuri National Park for rare wildlife and avifauna, has transformed a royal past into a vibrant, hopeful present. This park is opened throughout the year. The artificial lake Chandpata is winter home for migratory geese, pochard pintail teal, mallard and gadwall. The Scindia family has built beautiful Chhatris in a Mughal garden, synthesising the architectural idioms of Hindu and Islamic styles with their shikhara-type spires and Rajput and Mughal Pavilions.

Madhav Vilas palace standing upon a natural eminence, the elongated rosepink summer palace of Scindia, a fine example of colonial architecture is remarkable for its marble floors, iron columns, terraces and Ganapati mandap. Deep within the forests of the Park, on its highest point, is the turreted George Castle built by Jiyaji Rao Scindia. Edging the forests of the Madhav National Park is the Sakhya Sager lake, habitat of a variety of reptiles. On the shores of the lake and connected to it by a broad pier is a boat club, an airy, delicate structure with glass panels. Bhadaiya kund is a picnic spot. A natural spring, the water here is rich in minerals, supposedly of a curative nature.

UJJAIN

Ujjain is among one of India's most sacred and holy cities whose origin can be traced to the age of Upanishads and Puranas wherein it is described as Avantika. Legend has it that the King Shiva commemorated his victory over the demon ruler of Tripuri by changing the name of his capital Ujjayini—one who conquers with ease.As early as the time of the Aryan settlers,Ujjain seems to have acquired importance. By the 6th century BC Avanti with its capital Ujjayini, is mentioned in Buddhist literature as one of four great powers along with Vatsa, Kosala and Magadha.The names of Kalidasa and Ujjayini are linked together in the Indian traditions. It is in Meghdoot, a poem of little over hundred verses describing the anguish of a yaksha, separated from his beloved by a curse, sending a message to her in the city of Alaka through a rain cloude from his exile in Ramanagri (now identified as Ramtek near Negpur) that Kalidasa's love of Ujjayini finds full expression. The poet describes the imaginary passage of the cloud over Ujjayini and it is almost as if it is loath to move. Today, Ujjain abounds in temples hoary old traditions attached to each one of them.

PLACES OF INTEREST

MAHAKALESHWARA TEMPLE : The presiding deity of time, Lord Shiva in all his splendour, reigns eternal in Ujjain. The divine lingam (phallus) is one of the 12 Jyotirlingas in India and is believed to be Swayambhu, deriving its shakti or power from within itself. Another unique feature of this majestic shrine is the idol which faces the south, a positioning upheld by trantric traditions and found only in Maheshwara along the 12 Jyotirlingas. The idol of Omakareshwara Shiva is consecrated in the sanctum above the Mahakal shrine and the images of Ganesha, Parvati and Kartikeya and Shiva's bull steed Nandi. Annual fair is held at Mahashivratri every year.

BHARTRIHARI CAVES : According to the legend, these caves near the Gadkalika temple are where the great scholar poet Bhartrihari, who is said to have been the step-brother of Vikramaditya, lived and medicated after renouncing the worldly life. His famous works,Shringarshatak, Vairagyashatak and Nitishatak are known for the exquisite use of the Sanskrit metre.

Bade Ganeshji ka Mandir, Harsiddhi temple (temple of godess Annapurna) Kal Bhairava temple (temple has exquisite paintings in Malwa style), Gola Mandir (Built by Bayajabai Shinde, in Maratha architect), Navagraha mandir (Temple dedicated to nine planets)are some other famous temples of the city.

KALIDEH PALACE : It is believed that there was once a majestic Sun temple at this site. The Avanti-Mahatmya of the Skanda Purana has recorded a description of the Sun temple and two tanks—the Surya Kunda and the Brahma Kunda. People from nearby villages have a ritual dip in the Surya Kunda even today. Remains of the old temples are found scattered all over this area.

Present palace was built by Mahumad Khilji in 1458AD.The story goes that the tanks were constructed all around to keep the temperature very low by Sultan Nasiruddin Khilji, the Sultan of Malwa in the 16th century because he was in the habit of taking mercury which is hot. The central dome is in Persian architectural style and inscription records the visits of Emperor Akbar and Emperor Jahangir to this place. The palace was broken down in the time of Pindaris and was restored by Madhav Rao Scindia in 1920 to its present glory. The Sun temple was also restored by the family.

BADE GANESHJI KA MANDIR : This temple enshrines a huge artistic sculpture of Lord Ganesh, son of Shiva.

CHINTAMAN GANESH : The Ganesh idol enshrined here is supposed to be swayambhu—born of itself. Riddhi and Siddhi, the consorts of Ganesh, are seated on either side of Ganesh.

SIDDHAVAT : According to one tradition, Parvati is believed to have performed penance here. It used to be a place of worship for the followers of the Natha sect. The enormous banyan tree on the banks of Shipra has been vested with the same religious sanctity as the Akashyat in Prayag and Gaya Vanshivat of Vridavan and the Panchavata of Nasik.

THE CEDHA SHALA (OBESRVATORY) : According to Indian astronomers, the Tropic of Cancer is supposed to pass through Ujjain. It is also the first meridian longitude of the Hindu geographers.The observatory existing today was built by Raja Jai Singh (1686-1743AD), who was a great scholar. He translated the works of Ptolemy and Euclid into Sanskrit from Arabic Astronomical studies are conducted through the Department of Education.

PANCHAKROSHI YATRA : This yatra takes place in the month of Vaisakha which is believed, according to the Padma Purana, to be an auspicious month of Avantika. Skanda Purana attaches great religious sanctity to a five-day stay at Ujjain in the month of Vaisakha which is probably related to the five-day Panchakroshi yatra. Thousnad of people join it here every year.

Harisiddhi temple, Gopal Mandir, Vikram Kirti Mandir,navgraha Mandir Mangalnath temple, Gadkalika temple are some other temples to be visited.

HOW TO REACH

AIR : Nearest airport – Indore (53 km)
RAIL : Ujjain has direct connections with Ahmedabad, Lucknow, Varanasi, Delhi, Jammu Tavi, Chennai, Durg and Howrah.
ROAD : There are convenient buses available from Indore.

HOTEL ACCOMMODATION (STD CODE 0734)

— Hotel Ashrya, 77,Cewis Road. PH 555 886, 561 265
— Hotel Shipra, Univeristy Road, Near Madho Club
    PH 551495/96.

OMKARESHWARA

A holy island, shaped like the sacred Hindu symbol 'OM'. Here the Narmada and the Kaveri rivers meet and the pilgrims gather at the confluence in large numbers to pay obeisance before the Jyotirlinga (one of the 12 Jyotirlingas) at the temple of Shri Omkar Mandhata.

PLACES OF INTEREST

SHRI OMKAR MANDHATA : This temple, situated on an island, is made of soft stone with intricately carved frizes. Encircling the shrine are verandahs with columns which are richly carved.

SIDDHNATH TEMPLE : Built in the tradition of early medieval Brahmanic architecture it has a unique frize of elephants carved upon a stone slab at its outer perimeter.

24 AVATARS : A group of Hindu and Jain temples displaying architectural expertise in each structure.

SATMATRIKA TEMPLE : A group of 10th century temple situated 6 km from the city.

KAJAL RANI CAVES : Nine kilometer from the city from here one can get an uninterrupted view of the gentle undulating landscape.

HOW TO REACH

AIR : Nearest airport – Indore (77 km).
RAIL : Nearest railhead - Omkareshwar Road on the Ratlam-Khandwa section of the Western Railway.
ROAD : Regular bus services are available from Indore, Ujjain, Khandawa and Omkareshwar.

HOTEL ACCOMMODATION

- Holkar Guest House
- Forest and P W D guest House

A number of Dharamshalas offer accommodation with basic amenities.

MAHESHWAR

An ages old temple town on the bank of the Narmada river, is mentioned in the Puranas, Ramayana and Mahabharata when it was Mahishamati, capital of King Kartaviryarjuna. Having been revived to its ancient glory by Rani Ahilyabai of Indore, the town with its temple and fortress stands in serene dignity.

PLACES OF INTEREST

RAGADDI AND RAJWADA : Located within the fort complex is a life size statue of Rani Ahilyabai seated on throne. Other fascinating relics and heirlooms of the Holkar dynasty can be seen in the rooms which are open to the public.

GHATS : Along the Narmada river are the Peshwa Fanase and Ahilya Ghats. A flight of step lead down to the river, often crowded with pilgrims.

TEMPLES : Meheswar's temples stand high with spires reaching out to the sky. Their balconies and carved doorways are a sight to behold. Temples to visit are Kaleshwara, Rajarajeshwara, Vithaleshwara and Ahileshwar temples.

MAHESHWARI SAREES : Introduced into Maheshwar 250 years ago by Rani Ahilyabai, the sarees are renowned throughout India. Woven mostly in cotton the 'palu' is distinctive with five strips, three coloured and two white alternating running along its with hand reversible border, known as Bugdi.

HOW TO REACH

AIR : Nearest airport – Indore (91 km).

RAIL : Nearest railheads are Barwaha (39 km), Khandawa (110 km), Indore (91km) on Western Railway.

ROAD : Regular buses are available from Barwah, Khandawa, Dhar and Dhamnod.

CHITRAKOOT

Chitrakoot is the HILL OF MANY WONDERS of the Vindhyas. A city with more than legendary significance, it was the abode of Lord Ram and Sita for eleven year when in exile, the place where Sage Atri and Sati Anusuya meditated, the divine spot saw the incarnations of Brahma, Vishnu and Mahesh. This holy city is dotted with innumerable temples and shrines today.

RAMGHAT : The ghats that line the banks of the river Mandakini river reveal a constantly moving and changing kaleidoscope of religious activity. The evening "ARATI"is a unique experience for visitors.

KADAMGIRI : The original Chitrakoot, is a place of prime religious significance. A forested hill, it is skirted all along its base by a chain of temples and is venerated today, as the holy embodiment of Rama. The Bharat Milap temple is located here, marking the spot where Bharat is said to have met Rama to persuade him to return to Ayodhya.

JANAKI KUND : Upstream from Ramghat in the idyllic pastrol setting Sita is believed to bathe in its crystal-clear water during the years of her exile with Rama.

SATI ANUSUYA : It was at this place where Atri Muni, his wife Anusuya and their three sons (who were the incarnations of Brhma, Vishnu and Mahesh), are said to have medicated.

GUPTA GODAVARI : 18 km from the town by road is a pair of caves, one high and wide with an entrance through which one can barely pass, and the other, long and narrow with a stream of water running along its base.

HANUMAN DHARA : Located on a rock-face several hundred feet up a steep hillside is a spring said to have been created by Rama to assuage Hanumana when he returned after setting Lanka on fire.

HOW TO REACH

AIR : Nearest airport – Allahabad (128 km).

RAIL : Nearest railhead – Karvi (8 km).

ROAD : Regular bus services are available from all major towns in the state.

ORCHHA

Orchha's grandeur has been captured in stone, frozen in time; a rich legacy to the ages. For this medieval city, the hand of time has rested lightly and the palaces and temples built by its Bundela rulers in the 16th and 17th centuries retain much of their pristine perfection. Set along Betwa river, the site of Orcha was chosen by the Bundela Chief Raja  Rudra Pratap (1501-31AD) for his capital. Orcha contains three palaces each built by succeeding Maharajas.

PLACES OF INTEREST

Orchha's fort complex, approached by a multi-arched bridge, has three palaces set in an open quadrangle. The most spectacular of these are :

JEHANGIR MAHAL : Built by Raja Bir Singh Ju Deo in the 17th centuries to commemorate the visit of Emperor Jehangir to Orchha. Its strong lines are counterbalanced by delicate chattris.

RAJ MAHAL : This was built by Madhukar Shah, the deeply religious predecessor of Bir Singh Ju Deo. The plain exteriors, crowned by Chattris, give way to interiors with exquisite murals, boldly colourful on a variety of religious themes.

POETS AND MUISCIANS : Rai Praveen was the beautiful paramour of Raja Indramani (1672-76AD) and was sent to Delhi on the orders of Emperor Akbar who was captivated by her. She so impressed the great Mughal with the purity of her love for Raja Indramani that he sent her back to Orchha. The palace built for her is a low, two-storied brick structure, designed to match the height of the trees in the surroundings, beautifully landscaped gardens of ANAND MAHAL, with its octagonal flower beds and elaborate water supply system. Skillfully carved niches allow light into the mahal which has a main hall and smaller chambers.

RAM RAJA TEMPLE : Madhukar Shah's wife once had a dream that she should install the idol of Lord Rama at Orchha, which she brought from Ayodhya. It was kept in the palace, now known as the Ram Raja temple which is the only temple where Rama is worshipped as king.

CHATURBHUJ TEMPLE : Built upon a massive stone platform and reached by a steep flight of steps the temple was specially constructed to enshrine the image of Lord Rama that remained in the Ram Raja Temple.Lotus emblems and other symbols of religious significance provide the delicate exterior ornamentation.

DINMAN HARDAUL'S PALACE : Hardaul was a son of Bir Singh Ju Deo who died to prove his innocence over an affair with the wife of his elder brother, Jujhar who had doubts on his relationship with her. This saintly prince was, after his martyrdom, worshipped as a god, and even today the villages of Bundelkhand contain platform-like shrines where Hardaul is worshipped.

The walled Phool Bagh is a cool summer retreat. Orchha also has a series of impressive temples, dating back to 17th century. The soaring spires of Ram Raja Temple and the well preserved Lakshmi Narayan Temple are especially worth a look. Fourteen beautiful Chattris or memorials are lined up on the Kanchan Ghat of the Betwa river.

HOW TO REACH

RAIL : Nearest railhead – Jhansi (16 km). Jhansi is on the Delhi-Mumbai and Chennai main lines.

ROAD : Orcha lies on the Jhansi-Khajuraho road. Regular buses are available from Jhansi.

HOTEL ACCOMMODATION

— Hotel Sheesh Mahal, Betwa Cottage
— The Orcha Resort
— Hotel Mansarovar
— Hotel Palaki Mahal
— Sattar Yatri Niwas

For local tours and reservations at MPT Hotels contact :

— Central Reservations, Marketing Division, M.P.S.T.D.C. Ltd., 4th floor, Gangotri, T.T. Nagar, Bhopal 462003. PH 552340/42/43, FAX 552384

KHAJURAHO
ETERNAL EXPRESSIONS OF LOVE

The temples of Khajuraho are India's unique gift to the world, representing, as they do, a paean to life, love, to joy—perfect in execution and sublime in expression. Life in every form and mood, has been captured in stone, testifying not only to the craftman's artistry but also to the extraordinary breadth of vision of the Chandela Rajputs under whose rule the temples were conceived and constructed.

Khajuraho temples were built by Chandelas,(a dynasty which survived for five centuries before falling to the onslaught of Islam), in a short span of hundred years from 950 - 1050 AD in a truly inspired burst of creativity. Of the 85 original only 22 which have survived today, constitute one of world's great artistic wonders.

The temples are superb examples of Indo-Aryan architecture, the sculptures shows innumerable aspects of the Indian life 1000 years ago—Gods and Godesses, warriors and musicians, real and mythological figures and animals.

WESTERN GROUP OF TEMPLES

KANDARIYA MAHADEO : The largest temple soars 31 m high, dedicated to Lord Shiva, the sanctum enshrines a lingam. The main shrine is exquisitely carved and features, in delicate details, Gods, Goddesses, celestial maidens and lovers.

CHAUNSAT YOGINI : The only granite temple and the earliest surviving shrine of the group (900 AD), is dedicated to Kali. Only 35 of the original 65 shrines remain today.

CHITRAGUPTA TEMPLE : Facing eastwards to the rising sun, the temple is dedicated to the Sun God Surya. The image of the deity in the inner sanctum is particularly imposing : five feet high and driving a horse-drawn chariot. The group scenes depict royal processions, hunting scenes of the Chandela courts.

VISHWANATH TEMPLE : A three headed image of Brahma is enshrined in this temple. The approach is equally impressive, with lions flanking the northern and elephants the southern steps that lead up to it. A Nandi bull faces the shrine. LAKSHMANA TEMPLE : The lintel over the entrance of this beautiful Vaishnavite temple shows the trinity of Brahma, Vishnu and Shiva, with Lakshmi, Vishnu's consort. The finely carved sanctum has a three-headed idol of Vishnu's incarnations, Narasimha and Varaha.

MATENGESWARA TEMPLE : One of the oldest temple, is dedicated to Lord Shiva and has an eight feet high lingam.

EASTERN GROUP OF TEMPLES

The temples in this group can be subdivided into two one being a cluster of Jain temples and another scattered through the small village. Outside the Jain temple enclosure a Jain museum has recently been constructed with a circular gallery housing statues of 24 Tirthankaras.

PARSVANATH TEMPLE : This is the largest in this group. It is said that this temple was initially dedicated to Adinath but the statue was replaced by that of Parsvanath in 1860 AD.

GHANTAI TEMPLE : This Jain temple has a frieze which depicts the 16 dreams of Mahavira's mother and a Jain goddess on a winged Garuda.

ADINAH TEMPLE : Dedicated to the Jain saint Adinath the temple is lavishly embellished with sculpted figures, including Yakshis.

The three Hindu temples of the group are the Brahma containing a four-faced linga; the Vamana, which is adorned on its outer walls with carvings of Apsaras in a variety of sensuous attitudes; and the Javari, with a richly carved gateway and exterior sculptors.

SOUTHERN GROUP

This group comprises only two temples. A track running south from Jain enclosures reaches the first called DULADEO TEMPLE. It is among the latest built temples at Khajuraho, more accurate, finer and equally graceful, with figures of Mithuna (sexual intercourse) and Women in various poses. The other temple is CHATURBHUJ TEMPLE which has a three meter image of Vishnu.

The sculptures and statues have their own terminology :

Apsara - havenly nymph, beautiful dancing women.

Mithuna – Kahjuraho's most famous image, sensuously carved and erotic.

Salabhanjika - female figure with tree, which together act as supporting brackets in the inner chambers of the temple.

Sardula - a mythical beast part lion, part some other animal or even human.

HOW TO REACH

AIR : Khajuraho is connected by air with Delhi, Agra and Varanasi.

RAIL : Nearest railheads are Harpalpur (94km),Mahoba (61km), Jhnasi (172 km) and Satna (117km)

ROAD : Regular buses are available from Satna, Harpalpur, Jhansi and Mahoba

TOURIST INFORMATION OFFICE

— Chandela Culture Centre. PH 44051; FAX 42330

HOTEL ACCOMMODATION (STD CODE 0786)

— Hotel Chandela (5 Star Deluxe), Dist. Chhatarpur
  PH 42355-65; FAX 42366
— Hotel Jass Oberoi (5 Star), By Pass Road
  PH 42344, 42376/7; FAX 42345
— Hotel Khajuraho Ashok (3 Star).
  PH 42024, 42042; FAX 42239
— Hotel Clarks Bundela. PH 42386/7; FAX 42385
— Hotel Jhankar, Airport Road
  PH 42063, 42194; FAX 42330

JABALPUR

'A MARBLE CITY' rise to hundred feet on either side of Narmada.

PLACES OF INTEREST

MARBLE ROCKS : Boating facilities are available from November to May and while boating by moonlight is a thrilling experience, the marble rocks have recently been floodlit adding a new dimensions to their splendour.

DHUDSAGAR FALL : The Narmada, making its way through the marble rocks narrows down as Dhudsagar or the smoke cascade.

CHUSATH YOGINI TEMPLE : Dedicated to goddess Durga, this 10th century temple has exquisitely carved stone figures of deities belonging to the Kalchuri period.

HOW TO REACH

AIR : Nearest airport – Jabalpur.

RAIL : Jabalpur is on main route between Mumabi and Howrah.

KANHA NATIONAL PARK

Kanha is India's Eden. No other sanctuary in the country offers the density of wildlife found in this park.often called 'tiger land', Kanha is located in a horse shoe shaped valley, bound by two distinct spurs which rim the valley with sheer cliffs and large plateau. A favourite hunting ground at the time of the British Raj, Kanha was notified as a sanctuary in 1955 and upgraded to a national park in 1976, Kanha covers 1,945 Sq.km of hills, plateaus and grassland. It supports 22 species of mammals in the central park land and the adjoining plateaus. Vegetation at Kanha also varies between the sal dominated meadows and plateaus with rich forests of bija, haldu, dhaora and bamboo.

HOW TO REACH

AIR : Nearest airport – Jabalpur 160 km.

RAIL : Nearest railhead – Kandla 65 km.

HOTEL ACCOMMODATION

— Forest Rest Houses at Kisli, Mukki, Supkar and Garhi, Kanha Safari Lodge Mukki, kipling camp.

PANCHAMARHI

Panchamarhi's natural glory lies in green, nature's own colour. Complementing the magnificence of nature are the works of man, for Panchamarhi is also a archaeological treasure house. Caves shelters in the Mahadeo hills contain an astonishing wealth of rock paintings. The bulk of these have been placed in the 500 - 800 AD, but the earliest paintings are an estimating 10,000 years old. The valley, ravines and maze of gorges, sculpted in red sandstone by the wind and weather, add their own colouring to this palette of shades, and cascading waterfalls flash silver in the sun shine.

PLACES OF INTEREST

PRIYADARSHINI POINT : This point marks the place from where Panchamarhi was discovered. In 1857AD, Captain Forsyth, a Bengal Lancer, approached the plateau at the head of a column of troops. At this point, he first glimpsed the extraordinary beauty of this saucer shaped Panchamarhi.

HANDI KHOH : Most impressive ravine has a 300 feet high

precipice and dramatically steep sides. A solitary place, with water flowing far below with an incessant murmuring sound, Handi Khoh's over changing crags shelter gigantic, undisturbed, bee hives.

APSARA VIHAR : A lovely little bathing pool is an ideal picnic spot for families.

RAJAT PRAPAT : The big fall close to Apsara vihar.

MAHADEO : Regarded as holy for countless generations, Mahadeo hill has a shrine with an idol of Lord Shiva and an impressive Shivling. On the east side of the hills is an excellent cave shelter with paintings.

CHOTTA MAHADEO : Revered as a sacred spot, this is a narrow point in the valley with rocks overhanging a stream and a small spring from which water cascades down.

JATA SHANKAR : A sacred cave under a mass of loose boulders in which the Jambu Dwip stream has its source. A rocky formation of this place resembles the meted locks of Lord Shiva.

DHOOPGARH : the highest point in the Satpura range.

PANDAVCAVE : Five ancient dwellings excavated in the sandstone rock in a low hill. Panchamarhi derives its name from these caves which, as the legend goes, once provided sanctuary to the five Pandav brothers. These caves are now protected monuments.

There are many picnic spots and waterfalls around the area.

HOW TO REACH

AIR : Nearest airport - Bhopal (195 km)

RAIL : Nearest railhead is Pipariya (47 km) on the Mumbai-Howrah main line via Allahabad.

ROAD : Regular bus services are available form Bhopal, Hoshangabad, Nagpur Pipariya and Chindwara. M.P. Tourism operates coach services between Bhopal and Panchamarhi.

HOTEL ACCOMMODATION

M.P. Tourism operates eight accommodation units which cater to the requirements of all income groups. Holiday homes and D.I. bungalows are also available for budget travellers.

MANDU

Emperor Jehangir who journeyed all the way from Delhi to spend time here wrote : 'I know of no place so pleasant in climate and so pretty in scenery as Mandu during the rains'. A fine example of Indo-Islamic architecture, Mandu is a romance in stone echoing joyous life and the love tales of poet-prince Baz Bahadur for the beautiful Rani Roopmati. The balladeers of Malwa continue to sing of the royal romance. According to a legend Rani Rupmati's lyrical voice can still be heard across the Narmada.

Mandu situated at an altitude of 2000 ft. was originally the fort capital of the Parmar rulers of Malwa. Towards the end of the 13th century, it became the pleasure resort of the Sultans of Malwa who renamed it Shahidabad or the city of Joy.

Enclosed by 45 kms of parapets and walls, it can be entered by 12 gates, the most important among these being the Delhi Darwaza, the main entrance of this fortress city.

PLACES OF INTEREST

JAHAZ MAHAL : A 120 meter. long double-storied pleasure palace, built between two lakes Munji Talao and Kanpur Talao, resembles a ship. This was said to have been built by Sultan Ghiyas-ud-din Khilji for his large harem of 15,000 women. With its large balconies and open pavilions the Jahaz Mahal is a remarkable creation in stone.

HINDOLA MAHAL : The 'Swinging palace' gets its name from the leaning walls of the palace that resemble a swing and dates back to the time of Ghiyas-ud-Din.

HOSHANG SHAH'S TOMB : Retains the masculinity and majesty of the Afghan ruler and is one of the finest example of Afghan architecture. It has a beautiful dome, marble lattice work, porticos, courts and towers. Emperor Shahjahan is said to have sent his master craftsmen to study it before starting the Taj Mahal.

JAMI MASJID : Built on the lines of the great mosque of Damascus this grand mosque stands on a high ground with a porch protruding in the centre. In the background too there are similar domes filling up the space.

ASHARFI MAHAL : This 'PALACE OF GOLD COINS' opposite the Jami Masjid was built by Mahmud Khilji. Intended to be a 'MADARASSA' or an institution for boys its class rooms still remain intact.

REWA KUND : Today respected as a sacred spot this is a reservoir built with an aqueduct to provide water to the Palace of Rani Roopmati.

BAZ BAHADUR PALACE : The 6th century palace with a wide courtyard is encircled by halls and high terraces.

ROOPMATI'S PAVILION : The Pavilion was originally built as an army observation post. From its hilltop perch, this graceful structure with its two pavilions was a retreat of the lovely queen, from where she could see Baz Bahadur's Palace and the Narmada flowing far below.

NILKANTHA : On the edge of a gorge is the shrine of Lord Shiva inside an Islamic palace. This palace was constructed by the Mughal Governor for Emperor Akbar's Hindu wife.

ECHO POINT : A call from here reverberates many times clearly among the temple ruins and caves of Mandu.

SUNSET POINT : In front of the caves it affords a panoramic view of the surrounding counrtyside.

HOW TO REACH

AIR : Nearest airport – Indore 100 km

RAIL : Convenient railheads are Ratlam (124km) and Indore 99 km on Western Railway line.

ROAD : Regular buses are available for Indore and major cities/of the State.

BANDHAVGARH NATIONAL PARK

Bandhavgarh is situated in Shahdol district amongst outlying hills of the Vindhyan range. The Tiger population at Bandavgarh is the densest in India and have perhaps the best chance in the world of seeing this elusive cat. Bandhavgarh is densely populated with other species : the great Gaur or Indian Bison can be seen with ease as they come onto the meadows to graze at dusk, sambar and barking deer are a common sight, Nilgai are to be seen in the more open area of the park. There are also many species of birds to be seen in the park.

FESTIVALS

KHAJURAHO DANCE FESTIVAL : Every year in March these splendid temples come alive during the week-long festival of classical dances.

The tribal people of Bastar celebrate Dussehra exhibiting their unity and faith. Another important tribal festival is Bhagoriya in Jhabua marked by traditional gaiety and enthusiasm. Shivratri as celebrated in Khajuraho, Bhojpur, Panchamarhi and Ujjain and Ramnavmi festival in Chitrakoot and Orchha have uniqueness of devotion imbued with tradition. Festivals of Orchha, Malwa and Panchamarhi bring to the fore, repertoire of culture and art, Tansen Music festival of Maihar and Kalidas Samaroh of Ujjain make Madhya Pradesh cynosure of art lovers.

MAHARASHTRA

MAHARASHTRA
AT A GLANCE

AREA : 3,07,690 Sq. km.
CAPITAL : Mumbai
BOUNDARIES : East and North - Madhya Pradesh.
LANGUAGE : Marathi
ROADS : Total length of roads in the State is 1,87,575 km consisting of 2,958km of national highways, 32,359 km of State highways, 41,081km of district roads, 41,043km of other district roads and 70,134 km of village roads.

AIRPORTS : Maharashtra has a total of 24 air fields and airports 17 of which are under the control of Maharashtra Government, four under the International Airport Authority or The Airport Authority of India and the remaining three are managed by the Ministry of Defence.

The airports under the control of the State Government are : Amravati, Baramati, Chandrapur, Dhule, Gondia, Jalgaon, Karad, Kolhapur, Kinwat, Latur, Nanded, Osmanabad, Phaltan, Ratnagiri, Sangli, Sholapur and Yatmal.

MUSEUMS

Mumbai : Prince of Wales Museum; Mani Bhavan – Gandhi Memorial; Jehangir Nicholson Museum of Modern Art; Victoria and Albert Museum; Nehru Science Museum
Nagpur : Central Museum
Pune : Raja Kelkar Museum; Maratha History Museum – Deccan College; Bharat Itihasa Samsodhak Mandal Museum

HILL RESORTS

Lonavala-Khandala : (625 m) Railhead – Lonavala
Mahabaleshwar : (1372 m) Railhead -Pune 120km
Matheran : (803 m) Railhead – Matheran
Panhala : (831 m) Railhead – Kolhapur 18 km

PILGRIM CENTRES (A : Air; R : Rail)

Ashtavinayak Temples : 8 places where 'Swayambhu' (self-formed) figures of Sri Ganesh are found.

Madh : A – Pune 80 km, R – Khandala 20 km.

Morgaon : A – Pune 85 km, R – Jejuri 17 km.

Pali : A – Pune 111 km, R – Khopoli 38 km.

Ranjangaon : A and R – Pune 53 km.

Siddhatek : A – Pune 99 km, R – Daund 20 km.

Theur : A and R – Pune 25 km.

Leniyadri : A and R – Pune 90 km.

Ojhar : A and R – Pune 75 km.

Audumbar : Temple of Dattatraya and Brahmanand Swami Math; A– Belgaum 183km, R – Bhilwadi 6 km.

Aundha Nagnath : believed to be the first (adya) of the 12 Jyotirlingas shrines; A – Aurangabad 210 km, R – Chondi 21 km.

Bahubali : A Jain pilgrim centre with a huge figure of Bahubali; A – Belgaum 143 km, R – Halkanangale 11 km – Kolhapur 32 km.

Battis Shirala : Important during Nagapanchami festival; A– Belgaum 150 km,R – Sangli 73 km.

Bhimashankar : One of the 12 Jyotirlinga shrines; A and R – Pune 95 km.

Dehu : Birthplace of Saint-poet Tukaram; A – Pune 34 km, R – Dehu Road.

Ganapatipule : Has an ancient temple of Sri Ganapati built on a rock; A and R – Ratnagiri 50.

Ganeshpuri : Swami Muktanand Ashram; A – Mumbai 88 km, R – Bassein Road 29 km.

Jejuri : Temple of Khandoba; A – Pune 38 km, R – Jejuri.

Maheshmal : Fair held at the Girija Bhavani temple on Chaitra Poornima day; A and R – Aurangabad 40 km.

Nasik : One of the Hindu sacred cities. The Sinhastha fair is held here once in 12 years. Trimbakeshwar on hilltop has a Jyotirlinga shrine; A and R - Nasik 8 km.

Pandharpur : Temple of Vithoba and Rukmani; A – Pune 204 km, R – Kurduwadi 57 km.

Parli Vaijnath : One of the Jyotirling shrines; A – Nanded 120 km, R – Parli Vaijnath.

Shirdi : Renowed for its association with the mystic saint Sai Baba; A – Nasik 86 km, R – Kopargaon 18 km.

Srikshetra Mahuli : Pilgrim centre at the confluence of the Krishna and the Venna rivers; A – Pune 112 km, R – Satara 6 km.

Srikshetra Mahur : Birthplace of Sri Dattatreya; A – Nagpur 225 km, R Kinwat 45 km.

Titwala : Ancient temple of Ganapati; A – Mumbai 75 km, R – Titwala.

Tuljapur : Goddess Tulja Bhawani presented a Sword to Chhatrapati Shivaji here; A – Aurangabad – 257 km, R – Sholapur 40 km.

Maharashtra, the great land as the name itself suggests, has great diversity of riches to offer to the tourists. Overlooking the vast expanses of the Arabian Sea on one side. Maharashtra is a strong blend of very tradiational and very contemporary, each co-existing with the other with surprising ease.

HISTORY

The first well-known rulers of Maharashtra were the Satvahanas (230 BC to 225 AD) who were the founders of the Maharashtra and have left a plethora of literary, epigraphic, artistic and archaeological evidence. Then came the Vakatakas who established a pan-Indian empire. Under them Maharashtra witnessed an all-sided development in the fields of learning, arts and religion. Some of the Ajanta caves and fresco paintings reached high-level mark during their rule. After the Vakatakas and after a brief interlude of the Kalachuri dynasty, the most important rulers were the Chalukyas followed by the Rashtrakutas and the Yadavas apart from the Shilaharas on the coast. The Yadavas, with Marathi as their court language, extended their authority over parts of the Deccan.

While the Bahamani rule brought a degree of cohesion to the land and its culture a uniquely homogeneous evaluation of Maharashtra as an entity became a reality under the able leadership of Shivaji. With the rise of Shivaji, Maharashtra entered a new phase in history. Shivaji welded the Marathas into a powerful nation and become the rulers. The Peshwas who succeeded Shivaji built up a Maratha empire which extended from Gwalior in the north to Tanjore in the south. The Maratha power received a set back at Panipat in 1761 AD when the Afghan ruler Ahmed Shah Abdali routed the Maratha forces. They recovered only to confront the British power and were decisively defeated in 1818 AD. After this defeat Maharashtra settled down as part of the Bombay Presidency under the British administration till Indepen dence in 1947.

The administrative evolution of the State of Maharashtra is the outcome of the linguistic re-organisation of the States in India, effected on May 1, 1960. The State was formed by bringing together all contiguous Marathi-speaking areas.

MUMBAI

Mumbai is home to people of all Indian creeds and cultures, a fascinating city, throbbing with life and for many people 'GATEWAY TO INDIA'. Mumbai is a group of seven islands (Colaba, Mahim Mazgaon, Parel, Worli, Girgaum and Dongri) whose inhabitants, the Kolis have given the city its Indian name Mumbai, after their Goddess, Mother Mumba Aai.The early Hindu rulers were conquered by Sultans of Gujarat who were later superseded by the Portuguese.The British, who followed, received these seven islands as a dowry when Charles II married Catherine of Braganza. The British in turn leased them to East India Company. A far sighted President of the company, the real founder of the present city, was Gerald Aungier. He invited Hindu and Parsi merchants from Gujarat to come to Bombay and develop it, giving them all help and city never looked back.

PLACES OF INTEREST

GATEWAY OF INDIA : Was the principal port when the visitors came to India by ship. It commemorates the visit of King George V and Queen Marry to India in 1911 and was officially opened in 1924. Nearby is COLABA—the shopping paradise and SASSOON DOCK— the unloading centre of fish.

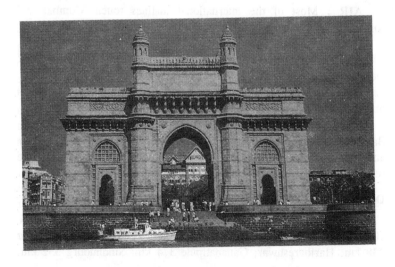

HANGING GARDENS AND KAMALA NEHRU PARK ON MALABAR HILL : The former is built over Mumbai's reservoir. From the Kamala Nehru park, situated opposite there gardens, one can get a panoramic view of the picturesque Marine Drive.

THE QUEENS NECKLACE : As lights on Marine Drive are called, they are a great attraction after sunset.

HAJI ALI TOMB AND MOSQUE : It can be reached by a long causeway which can be crossed at low tide.

MANI BHAWAN : (GANDHI MEMORIAL) There is the house where Mahatma Gandhi stayed on his early visit to the city. Scenes of Gandhi's life in photographs and models are displayed here.

PRINCE OF WALES MUSEUM : One of the leading museums of the country

JUHU BEACH : This beach have rows of beach hotels on the sea front.

KANHERI CAVES : There are 109 Buddhist caves dating from 2nd to 9th centuries. out of which number 3, the great Chaitya cave, is most beautiful.

ELEPHANTA CAVES : Elephanta is the glorious abode of Shiva. He reigns supreme here. An-hour journey by launch takes you to the cave temple of Elephanta caves, dedicated to Lord Shiva, built in the 7th century. Elephanta festival of music and dance is celebrated every year on the backdrops of the caves.

HOW TO REACH

AIR : Most of the international airlines touch Mumbai and connect it with major cities of the world.

Domestic airlies connect Mumbai with all parts of India.

RAIL : Mumbai is connected with all major cities and towns of the country by rail.

ROAD : Mumbai is connected by good motorable roads with all major tourist centres all over India.

There are regular bus services to Goa, Ahmedabad, Aruangabad, Bangalore, Belgaum, Bhavnagar, Hyderabad, Mangalore, Udaipur and many other places . The State Transport operates regular and semi-luxury buses to all towns as well as villages within the State.

DISTANCES FROM MUMBAI

Aurangabad 388 km; Nasik 188 km; Shirdi 278 km; Matherab 104 km; Karla 104 km; Pune 170 km; Mahad 177 km; Mahabaleshwar 238 km; Harihareshwar; Ganapatipule 374 km; Sindhudurg 532 km.

There is a daily service by ship between Mumbai and Goa (Except during monsoon).

All types of tourist vehicles are easily available on hire.

CONDUCTED TOURS

M.T.D.C. operates following conducted tours :
AT MUMBAI : Half-day city tour (Morning and Afternoon)— Daily except Monday.

Shirdi round tour (Only on Wednesday and Saturday)
AT AURANGABAD : Full-day Ajanta tour (Daily)
Full-day Ellora and city tour (Daily)
Half-day Paithan tour (Afternoon - Daily)
AT KOLHAPUR : Full-day Karveer Darshan (Daily)
Full-day Datta Darshan (Every Thursday)
AT PUNE : Half-day city tour (Morning and Afternoon)
Full-day Mahabaleshwar round tour (Daily)
Contact M.T.D.C. for further details.

— Maharashtra Tourism Development Corporation Ltd. Opp. L.I.C. building, Madame Cama Road
  PH 202 6713 / 202 2762 / 202 7784

HOTEL ACCOMMODATION (STD CODE 022)

— Hotel Centaur Juhu Beach,Juhu tara Road
  PH 611 3040; FAX 611 6343
— Leela Kempinski (5 Star Deluxe), Sahar
  PH 836 3636; FAX 836 0606
— The Oberoi (5 Star deluxe), Nariman Point
  PH 203 5757; FAX 204 1505
— The Oberoi Towers (5 Star Deluxe) Nariman Point
  PH 202 4343; FAX 204 3282,204 505
— The Retreat (5 Star Deluxe) Erangal Beach, Madh Marve Road, Malad (West). PH 882 5335, 882 0150; FAX 882 5171
— The Taj Mahal Hotel (5 Star Deluxe) Apollo Bunder
  PH202 3366 : FAX 287 2711
— Centaur Airport (5 Star) Mumbai
  PH 611 6660; Fax 611 3535
— Holiday Inn (5 Star) Balraj Sahani Marg, Juhu Beach
  PH 620 4444; FAX 620 4452,670 1710
— The President Hotel (5 Star) 90, Cuffe Parade
  PH 215 0808; FAX 215 1201

- Ramada Hotel Palm Grove (5 Star) Juhu Beach
  PH 611 2323; FAX 611 3682
- The Resort (5 Star) 11, Madh Marve Road, Aksa Beach,
  Malad (West). PH 882 0992, 882 0471; FAX 882 0738
- Hotel Sea Princes (5 Star) Juhu Tara Road, Juhu
  PH 617 5857, 611 7600; FAX 611 3973
- Sun-N-Sand Hotel Private Ltd., 39, Juhu Tara Road
  PH 620 1811, 620 4821 FAX 620 2170
- The Ambassador (4 Star) Churchgate Extension, off Marine
  Drive. PH 204 1131; FAX 204 0004
- Hotel Bawa International (4 Star) 352,Linking Road, Khar
  (West). PH 649 4416; FAX 604 0137
- Hotel Guestline (4 Star) 462, AB Nair Marg, Juhu
  PH 625 2222,620 4331; FAX 620 2821
- Fariyas Hotel (4 Star) 25, off Aurthur Bubder Road, Colaba
  PH 204 2911; FAX 283 4992
- Hotel Horizon Pvt.Ltd.(4 Star) 37,Juhu Beach
  PH611 7979; FAX 611 6715
- Hotel Midtown Pritam (4 Star) 20-B, Pritam Estate, Dadar
  PH 414 5555; FAX 414 3388
- Ritz Hotel Pvt.Ltd. (4 Star) 5, T.Tata Road, Churchgate
  PH 285 0500; FAX 285 0494
- Sands Hotel Pvt. Ltd (4 Star) 39/2 Juhu Beach
  PH 6204512, 6204521; FAX 620 5268
- West End (4 Star) 45, New Marine Lines
  PH 2039121, 205 7506; FAX 205 7506
- Hotel Airlink (3 Star) Plot No 75, Off, Nehru Road, Near
  Santacruz Airport. PH 618 4220, 618 3575; FAX 610 5186
- Hotel Airport Kohinoor Pvt. Ltd.(3 Star) Opp. J.N. Nagar,
  Andheri-Kural Road Andheri (East).
  PH 820 9999; FAX 838 2434
- Hotel Accord (2 Star) 32. J. Nehru Road, Santacruz (East)
  PH 611 0560-62; FAX 611 7808
- Chateau Windsor Hotel (2 Star) Next to Hotel Ambassador,
  86 Veer Nariman Road, Churchgate
  PH 204 3376; FAX 202 6459
- Hotel Diplomat (2 Star) 24-26 B.K. Boman Behram Marg,
  Apollo Bunder. PH 202 1661; FAX 283000
- Garden Hotel (2 Star) 42, Garden Road, Colaba
  PH 284 1476, 284 1700; FAX 204 4290

EXCURSIONS

MARVE - MANORI - GORAI : These are the popular spots of Mumbai's fun lovers. Marve is a lovely little fishing village. It has some beautiful bungalows. Low hills along the beach offer extraordinary views of sunrise and sunset. Gorai and Manori, a little further away, are more crowded with travellers and are famous for all night beach parties.

BASSEIN : Bassin used to be a place for ship-building in the beginning of the 17ᵗʰ century. It was here that the Marathas besieged the Portuguese in 1739 AD. The ruins of the Portuguese Fort still stand almost hidden by bruswood and palm groves.An hour from Bassein are the Vajreshwari temple and Akoli hot springs and Ganeshpuri with the Sadgurunatyanand Maharaj Samadhi Mandir.

About 10 km from here lies The NALASOPARA VILLAGE, the capital of the Konkan from 1500 BC to 1300 AD. Many Buddhist relics were discovered here. Nalasopara is believed to have been Gautama Buddha's birthplace in a previous life.

MANDAWA - KIHIM : Easily accessible by ferry from Mumbai, Kihim near Mandawa is a beautiful, untrodden beach. On a clear day one can enjoy a long breathtaking view right up to The Gateway of India.

TITWALA : (75 km) A pilgrim spot sacred twice over - for its Mahaganesha temple and the temple of Shri Vithoba. Another fascinating temple is the one at Ambarnath, dating back to 11ᵗʰ century. built in the 'Hemadpanti' style. Titwala can be reached by local trains from Mumbai.

MURUD - JANGIRA : (165 km) This place is easily accessible by road from Mumbai. Formerly the capital town of the Siddis of Janjira, who built here their palaces, lying in ruins battered on all the four sides by the sea waves, its strong 40 ft. high walls are still standing intact. This is the only impregnable fort on the 720 km Maharashtra coastline. Murud is today popular for its alluring beach, whispering caesarean coconut and betal palms and an ancient fort. On a hillock is the shrine of Lord Dattatrya, the three heads representing Brahma, Vishnu and Maheshwara. The 300 year old fort of Jangira is an architectural marvel, once upon a time considered to be impregnable.

SHRIWARDHAN - HARIHARESHWAR : (200 km) These places are easily accessible by road from Mumbai. The State transport as well as private buses ply regularly from Mumbai.Gentle winds, soft sands and inciting waters makes Shriwardhan and Harihareshwar irresistible to beach lovers. The adventurers can even take a small boat to the north side of the bay and explore the land of 'Peshwas' where they originally resided. The town Harihareshwar is known for tranquil and picturesque beach and is also famous for the temple of Harihareshwar. Private as well as state transport operated buses are easily available from Mumbai and Pune.

VELNESHWAR : (370 km) Around Konkan area (Accessible by road), North of Shastri river lies the idyllic village of Valneshwar. The quiet coconut-fringed beach offers an ideal opportunity for swimming. There is an old Shiva temple in the environs which is often frequented by pilgrims. Mahashivratri fair is held once a year in March. Private as well as State transport operated buses are easily available from Mumbai and Pune.

GANPATIPULE : (375 km) Around Konkan area (Accessible by road) this sun-kissed beach and lush green of Ganpatipule inevitably draws tourist back, year after year. The added attraction is a 400 year old temple which houses the Swayambhoo Ganapati. Privates as well as State transport buses are easily available from Mumbai and Pune.

VIAJYDURG SINDHUDURG : (510 km from Mumbai) Once naval bases, Viajydurg and Sindhudurg bear testimony to Maharashtra's martial supremacy during Shivaji's reign. Vijaydurg or fort of victory was strengthened around 17th century. by Shivaji to whom it owes its finest features—the triple line of walls, the numerous towers and the massive interior buildings.

VENGURLA-MALVAN : (514 km from Mumbai) Further south to Sindhudurg lies Vengurla with its long stretch of white sands and hills covered by cashew, coconut, jackfruit and mango groves. The town has two well-known temples Shri Devi Satelri and Rameshwar Mandir.

KARNALA BIRD SANCTUARY : (60 km) This small bird sanctuary is located just outside near new Mumbai, Panvel on Mumbai-Goa highway. In winter, Karnala is visited by several migratory birds, mostly woodland species which come in from their breeding grounds in Himalayas. Some travel shorter distances from peninsular India and from there to the nearby western ghats. Established as a sanctuary in the year 1971 the sanctuary houses 140 species.

LONAVALA-KANDALA-KARLA : Lonaval–khandala are charming hills on the western slopes of the Sahyadri hills and lie in between Mumbai and Pune, easily approachable by road from both the places being 200 km away. Its clean crisp air greets you as you wind your way up the steep ghats, leaving the humidity, heat and dust behind.

Both Lonavala and Khandala offer breathtaking views of cascading waterfalls during the monsoon and the surrounding mountains of the plains spread out to the horizon far below.

Karla, 12 km from Lonavala boasts one of the best-preserved caves dating back to 160 BC. The construction of this cave temple started during the Hinayana period of Buddhism. Regular bus services are available from Mumbai and Pune. Accommodation is available for the visitors at MTD guest house.

MATHERAN : (100 km) An easy escape from Mumbai offers a well deserved holiday. Travelling to Matheran by a tiny narrow guage toy train, one of the last mini trains in the world, from Mumbai via Neral is an experience by itself. This 'Car free' eco-friendly hill station situated at 803 meters above sea level offers salubrious climate, an unpolluted atmosphere with no vehicular traffic. Matheran offers fascinating landscapes through thickets and woods. The Heart Point offers beautiful view of Mumbai at night. The Porcupine Point and Louise Point, Chaelotte Lake with panthers, Caves and Paymaster Park are places of interest in Matheran. The main bazzar offers a variety of items such as cane and leather articles, hats, chappals etc. A wide range of accommodation is available.

MAHABALESHWAR : (320 km) The summer capital of Bombay Presidency during the days of the British, it is a mountain top plateau often covered with a light morning mist. Elphinstone, Babbington, Bombay, Kate's and numerous other points offer panoramic views of the plains below. Short distance away are Chinaman's and Dhobi, Lingamala waterfalls. Veena Lake, the focal point of Mahabaleshwar has boating and fishing facilities. About 24 km from Mahabaleshwar is FORT PRATAPGAD, Shivaji's most impressive fort perched on the summit of the hill, was built to control three strategic passes— Rodtondi, Poladpr and Par. PANCHGANI or 'FIVE HILLS' is on the way to Mahabaleshwar. It has the Raj stamp all over it which is evident in the architecture of the old British buildings, the Parsi bungalows and the boarding schools that have been around for over a country. It is a delight to canter through the thickly wooded walkways to explore the area, catching glimpses of the Krishna river winding its way through the ravines, hundreds of metres below. Kamalgad fort is easily accessible on foot or on horseback.

DAHANU and BORDI : (145 km) Dahanu is approachable conveniently by train or by road. Dahanu is a quite seaside town with a sprawling, uncluttered beach. The Dahanu-Bordi stretch is 17 km long. This once barren land thrived under Irani settlers, an earthy people. Dahanu is lined with fruit orchards and is famous for its CHIKOOS. Easily Accessible from Dahanu is UDWADA—the

'MECCA OF THE PARSIS'—with a large beautiful temple which houses their sacred fire. It is an amazing fact but this holy fire has been kept burning for almost 1000 years.

AURANGABAD-AJANTA-ELLORA
AURANGABAD

The present city of Aurangabad was founded by Malik Ambar, Prime Minister of Murtaza Nizam Shah II, in 1610 AD around khirki village. Aurangzeb renamed it Aurangabad.

Maurya rule marked the arrival of the Buddism in Maharashtra. The caves at Ajanta and Pitalkhora were excavated during the Satvahana period in the 2nd century. Pratishthana, now known as Paithan, became an important centre of trade around the same time. During the Chalukya reign, Buddhism continued to flourish. This resulted in several 'Viharas' (Monasteries) and 'Chaityas' (chapels) being excavated at Aurangabad, Ajanta and Ellora. In the later years the Rastrakutas built several temples, the most significant being the KAILASA TEMPLE—an unrivaled example of Indian architecture.

PLACES OF INTEREST

AURANGABAD CAVES : Hidden in the hills just outside the city are a cluster of caves probably excavated in the early 6th century. There are Tantric influences evident in the iconography and architectural designs of the caves. Some of the Chaitya halls here are constructed on a Mandala plan for circumambulation (walking around) of the Buddha depicted here seated on an intricately carved throne. There are nine caves which are mainly viharas. The most interesting among these are caves no 3 and 7. The former is supported on 12 highly ornate columns and has sculptures depicting scenes from the legendary 'Jataka tales'. Cave no 7 with its detailed figures of bejewelled women also has a dominating sculpture of a 'Bodhisattva' praying for deliverance.

BIBI-KA-MAQBARA : From Persia had come the idea of an arched alcove surmounted by a welling dome which developed its own individual character in India— subsequently seen at its height of perfection in the Taj in Agra. Bibi-ka-maqbara, the tomb of Begum Rabia Durani, wife of Emperor

THE BEWITCHING BREATH
OF A 2000 YEAR OLD CIVILIZATION.

Aurangabad. A city packed with history and culture, its colourful past with rich and vibrant tradition make for a truly unforgettable visit. The majestic effulgence of Bibi ka Maqbara, the 2000-year-old World Heritage Monuments - Ajanta and Ellora, the artistic grace of Khultabad, Daulatabad, Pitalkhora, the mystical aura of Paithan and the wondrous 50,000 year old meteorite impact, Lonar crater.

And Hotel President Park, the super luxury resort sprawled over an area of lush greenery, adds joy to this city of mystery. Elegant decor, breathtaking expanse and superb hospitality - President Park is everything you would expect from a luxury hotel. And more. Whatever you need from a holiday or a business trip, Hotel President Park is the place to be. Come to where life is.

Aurangzeb, is a pleasing example of the same idea. It was built by her son in tribute to his beloved mother.

PAN CHAKKI : An intriguing water mill, was built by Malik Ambar in 1695 AD. In 1634 AD, a Sufi saint who was much revered by Aurangzeb was buried here. The gardens and fish tanks serve as his memorial. Ingenious engineers channelled and brought down  water from a spring on a hill some distance away to generate energy to turn the large grinding stones which served as a flour mill in the times gone by.

EXCURSIONS

DAULATABAD : (13 km) The fortress known as 'Devgiri' was built in the 12th century by Bhillama, king of the Yadav dynasty. Centuries later, the Hindu fortress was elevated to an imperial capital of the Muslim Sultanate of Muhammad-bin-Tughlaq, who had shifted here with Delhi's entire population leaving behind not even the only one lame beggar.

One of the world's best preserved forts of medieval times, surviving virtually unaltered, Daulatabad yet displays many internal contrivances that made it invincible. A series of secret, quizzical subterranean passages lie coiled like a python amidst the fort. KHULADABAD, few km away from Daulatabad, has the tomb of Aurangzeb.

BANI BEGUM GARDENS : (24 km) built in various styles, equipped with massive domes, fountains and fluted pillars it has a tomb of Bani Begum, the consort of one of Aurangzeb's son.

GHRINESHWAR : (30 km) One of the twelve 'Jyortirlingas' of India, built by Rani Ahilyabai Holkar, a Maratha princes, is the most superb example of medieval temple architecture.

LONAR CRATER : This crater ranks as the third largest crater in the world. 170 km from Aurangabad, the Lonar Crater was formed by a meteorite impact about 50,000 years ago. The meteor is believed to have been buried 600 mts. below the Crater level. Within the depression a saline lake has formed, sanctuary to many a myriad birds. Water in the lake is brackish and has given birth to a new life form (*a unique blue-green algae*), a scientific mystery. A four-room lodging house has been built by the state government near the crater. Meals and water arrangements have to be organised from Aurangabad.

PAITHAN : (56 km) Ancient capital of Satvahanas is now renowned for its Paithani silk Sarees with exquisite Zari borders. Centuries ago, the famous Marathi poet - saint Eknath lived here. Jayakwadi dam is located here. A variety of resident and migratory birds can be sighted here.

AUNDHA NAGNATH : (200 km) It is a pligrim centre of great significance since it is considered to be the first (adya) of the 12 Jyortirlingas in the country. Apart from this honour, the temple of Nagnath has exquisite carvings.

TUAJAPUR : (257 km) It is famous for the temple of Tulja Bhawani (Goddess Durga). It is said that before venturing a military expedition, Shivaji always came here to seek her blessings.

HOW TO REACH

AIR : Aurangabad is connected by air with Delhi, Jaipur, Mumbai and Udaipur

RAIL : Aurangabad is connected directly by rail with Mumbai and Secundarabad.

ROAD : Aurangabad is a convenient base to visit Ajanta and Ellora caves. There are regular buses available from Mumbai, Pune, Kolhapur and many towns in Maharashtra. M.T.D.C.operates conducted tours from Mumbai to Aurangabad, Ajanta and Ellora.

TOURIST INFORMATION OFFICES

— Holiday Resort, Station Road : Information and Booking counter at Aurangabad Airport

HOTEL ACCOMMODATION (STD CODE 0240)

— Hotel President Park : R - 7/2 Chikhalthana, Airport Road
  PH 486 201 (10 Lines); FAX 484 823.
  E-mail : hpp@bom4.vsnl.net.in;
  Internet : www.presidenthotels.com
— Hotel Ambassador Ajanta (5 Star), Jalna Road, CODCO
  PH 485 211-13; FAX 484 367.
— Taj Residency (5 Star), 8-N-12, CIDCO
  PH 381106-10; FAX 381 053.
— Welcomegroup Rama International (5 Star), R-3 Chikhalthana
  PH 485 441; FAX 484 768.
— Hotel Aurangabad Ashok (2 Star), D. R. Rajendra Prasad
  Marg. PH 332 492/3; FAX 331 328.
— Hotel Amarpreet, Pandit Nehru Marg, Jalna Road
  PH 332 521/2; FAX 334 326.

AJANTA

Early in the 19th century a party of British officers scrambling over the thickly wooded slopes of the Sahyadri hills discovered these caves buried under debris and screened by foilage. 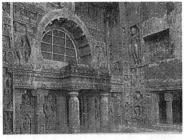 Strung out in a sweeping horseshoe shape in an inner fold of the hills, the caves were a secluded retreat for Buddhist monastic orders and yet offered easy access to the trade routes that swung past here to the coast. With little more than hammer and chisel but with a deep faith inspiring them, these simple monks excavated chaityas, chapels for prayer and viharas, monasteries where they lived and taught and carried out ritual performances. The 29 caves at Ajanta, some unfinished, span a period of 800 years and contain numerous images of Lord Buddha. They depict the story of Buddhism, spanning the period from 200 BC to 650 BC.

Cave 1 houses some of the most well-preserved wall paintings which include two great Boddhisattvas, Padmapani and Avaloketeshwara. Cave 2, 16 and 17 also contain amazing paintings, while caves 1, 4, 17, 19, 24 and 26 boasts of some of the most divine sculptures. The flying Apsara of cave 17 and the image of Buddha preaching in cave 17, are a couple of unforgettable works of art.

In their range of times and treatment the paintings of Ajanta are a panorama of life in ancient India.

LISTING OF CAVES

PHASE 1 : 2nd century BC to 1st century BC - Cave 9 and 10 : Chaitya Halls or shrines. Caves 12 and 13 : Viharas or monasteries

PHASE II : 5th century AD to 6th century AD - Caves 19,26 and 29 : Chaitya Halls or shrines

Caves 1-7, 11,14-18, 20-25, 27 and 28 : Viharas or monasteries

UNFINISHED CAVES :3, 5, 8, 23-25, 28 and 29.

ELLORA

The cave temples and monasteries at Ellora, excavated out of the vertical face of an escarpment, are 26 km north of Aurangabad. Extending in a linear arrangement, the 34 caves contain Buddhist

Chaityas, or halls of worship, and Viharas, or monasteries, Hindu and Jain temples. Spanning a period of about 600 years between the 5ᵗʰ and 11ᵗʰ centuries. AD., the earliest excavation here is of the Dhumar Lena (Cave 29). The sculpture in the Buddhist caves accurately convey the nobility, grace and serenity inherent in the Buddha. Caves 6 and 10 houses images from the Buddhist and Hindu faith, under the same roof, the latter dedicated to Vashwakarma, the patron saint of Indian craftsmen. The Vishvakarma cave is both a Chaitya and a Vihara, with a seated Buddha placed in the stupa. Its two-storied structure sports

a colourful pageant of dwarfs, dancing and making music. The Kailasa temple in cave 16 is an architectural wonder, the entire structure having been carved out of a monolith, the process taking over a century to finish. This mountain-abode of Lord Shiva is in all probability, the world's largest monolith, the gateway, pavilion, assembly hall sanctum and tower, all hewn out of a single rock.

The Jain caves are about a mile away from the Kailasa temple, amongst which cave 32, houses a beautiful shrine adorned with fine carvings of a lotus flower on the roof, and a yakshini on a lion under a mango tree, while cave 32 and 34 contain grand statues of Parasnath. The other Jain caves sport the images of Tirthankaras and one of them, also has a figure of Mahavira.

LISTING OF CAVES

BUDDHIST CAVES : Caves 1 to 12 at the southern end, 5th century to 7th Century AD.

HINDU CAVES : Caves 13 to 29 in the middle, 8th century to 10th Century AD.

JAIN CAVES : Caves 30 to 34 at the northern end, 9th century to 11th century AD.

KOLHAPUR

Kolhapur is located on the Panchganga river nestling along the Sahyadi ranges surrounded by hillocks and fortresses. Woven around the temple of Goddess Mahalakshmi built in the 9ᵗʰ century. There is a fable which recalls the Puranic past.  Some verses in the Puranas suggest that the city is spiritually vibrant as Lord Mahadeva, dwells here in the form of water, Lord Vishnu in the form of rocks, goddesses in the form of trees and seers in the form of sand.

Chatrapati Shahu Maharaja's reign lent a progressive spirit to the city and the King extended his patronage to arts like theatre, music, painting sculptures, wrestling and crafts like tanning and Jewellery making.

PLACES OF INTEREST

THE MAHALAKSHMI TEMPLE : This exquisitely carved temple invites millions of pilgrims from all over India. The temple has artistically sculpted structures and houses the temples of deities like Kashi Vishweshwar, Kartikswami, Sheshashayi, Siddhivinayak Mahaswaraswati, Mahakali, Shree Datta and Shree Ram.In the 7th century AD. the Chalukya ruler Karandev initiated the construction of this temple and later in the 9th century, the Shilahara Yadavas beautified it further.

THE NEW PALACE—SHREE CHHATRAPATI SHAHU MUSEUM : A royal palace partly converted into museum houses rare paintings and artefacts used by the royal family. Royal weapons and a tableau depicting the court life of the past create an aristocratic ambience.

THE TOWN HALL MUSEUM : Antiques found during the excavations at Bramhapuri, old sculptures, filigree work in sandalwood and ivory, old coins and paintings of master artists of the region are displayed here.

THE OLD PALACE : Located behind the temple of Mahalakshmi, this magnificent structure has an impressive marquee with filigree work in stone. It houses a temple of goddess Bhawani.

BINKHAMBI GANESH MANDIR : Students of architecture will enjoy visiting this place as this unique temple does not have any pillar.

RANKALA LAKE : This wide and spacious lake is so called because at its centre is the temple of 'Rankabhairav'.

HOW TO REACH

AIR : Nearest airport-Kolhapur.

RAIL : Kolhapur is connected by rail directly with Nagpur, Mumbai and Tirupati.

ROAD : Kolhapur is well-connected by buses operated by State Transport. Private transporters operate luxury, semi-luxury and ordinary buses to and fro Mumbai Pune, Aurangabad, Goa, Nasik and many other cities in the state.

A wide range of accommodation is available for the visitors.

TOURIST INFORMATION OFFICE

M.T.D.C., Kedar Complex, Station Road, Kolhapur.

FORTS AROUND KOLHAPUR

The forts of Maharashtra have played a vital role in Maratha history. They provide glimpses into the life of charismatic Shivaji Maharaj.. Panhala, Vishalgad, Bhudargarh, Paargad and Sindhudurg are the forts which can be visited from Kolhapur.

EXCURSIONS

NARASIMHA WADI : (45 km) This is a holy place on the confluence of the Krishna and the Panchganga rivers and is renowned for the holy 'Padukas'(wooden slippers) of Shree Dattaguru (an incarnation of Brahma, Vishnu and Mahesh) Shree Narasimha Saraswati who was an incarnation of Shree Dattaguru lived here for 12 years.

JYOTIBA : Situated at a height of 3100 feet above sea level, this holy place nestles in the mountains near Wadi Ratnagiri 17 km north west of Kolhapur and is supposed to be the place of incarnation of the three gods —Brahma, Vishnu and Mahesh at the ashram of seer Jamadgni. A mammoth colourful fair takes place on the full moon night of Chaitra and Vaishakh.

BAHUBALI OF KUMBHOJGIRI : (27 km) This holy place revered by the Hindus as well as the Jain devotees who pay respects to the 28 feet tall marble statue of Shree Bahubali and visit the temples of 24 teerthankaras. A temple of Durgamata on the hill also attracts devotees.

KHIDRAPUR, AN AESTHETE'S DREAM : The artistic temple of Kopeshwar (Mahadev) at Khidrapur is a treasure house of beautifully carved sculptures and a rare architectural marvel. The entire temple rests on a 'Gajapeeth'. There is a semi-circular platform resting on the back of 92 carved stone elephants on which the temple is built.

THE GIROLI TOURIST PARK : Tropical flora and fauna, the wild cry of the colourful peacock, the chirp of the forest birds and then a well planned tour covering a visit to Panhala, Jyotiba, Warnanagar and carvings of Pohale, make holiday experience complete.

DAJIPUR SANCTUARY : The evergreen tropical forest of Dajipur has a profusion of thick foliage and sprawling trees and abounds in medicinal herbs. The weather is extremely cool as the place is 1200 meters above sea level. Heavy monsoon showers account for a thick forest and ever flowing springs and brooks. The animals are in abundance too and the sanctuary offers a visual feast for animals and bird watchers.

RAMTEERTH : 85 km away is a scenic picnic spot in Ajra taluka, with an ancient temple, a river, an old coffee plantation and an orchard. According to a fable the place is so named because Lord Ram had stayed here during his 'Vanvas'.

AMBOLI : In the southern ranges of the Sahyadri Hills, Amboli is the last mountain resort before the coastal plains begin. Quiet and isolated Amboli is perfect for those who really want to get away from the hustle and bustle of city life.

NASIK

Nasik is a bustling township with an interesting blend of the ancient and the modern. Mythology has it that Lord Rama, had made Nasik his temporary abode during the 14 years of his exile. The renowned poets Valmiki, Kalidas and Bhavbhooti have paid rich tributes to Nasik in their works. Nasik has always been the epic centre of commerce and trade. Ptolemy, the famous philosopher has made a mention of Naski in 150 BC, leading researchers to believe that it was probably the country's largest market place. From 1487 AD this prosperous province came under the rule of the Mughals and was known as Gulchnabad. Emperor Akbar lived in Nasik and has written extensively about it in Ein-e-Akbari. During the reign of Chhatrapati Shivaji, Nasik was known as the 'LAND OF THE BRAVE'.

PLACES OF INTEREST

RAMKUND : This holy tank is 27 m by 12 m and was built in 1696 by Chitrarao Khatarkar. It is believed that Ram and Sita used to bathe in this tank during their exile. Every Hindu wishes his ashes to be immersed here so as to attain 'MOKSHA'.

MUKTIDHAM TEMPLE : Built in white marble, the 18 chapters of the Geeta are written on the walls here.

COIN MUSEUM : The Indian Institute of Research in Numismatic Studies, the only one of its kind in Asia, established in 1980, has maintained extensive archives or photographs of coins.

KALARAM TEMPLE : Built in 1794, this temple is 70 feet high and was built with black stones from the mines of Ramsej hill. Temple is surrounded by many small temples and the main temple is dedicated to Rama, Sita and Lakshmana.

ANDAVLENI : Located on the Trivasmi hill, these caves are built by Jain kings 2000 years ago. There are some 24 caves that were home to Jain saints. Inside the caves one can see icons of Buddha, Bodhistava, Jain Tirthankar, Vrishabdeo Veer Manibhadraji and Ambikadevi.

HOW TO REACH

AIR : Nearest airport-Nasik.

RAIL : Nasik is connected by rail with all major cities of the country.

ROAD : Regular bus services, private as well as state transport, are available from Mumbai, Pune, Kolhapur and many parts of the State. One can travel by share-a-taxi also from Mumabi.

TOURIST OFFICE

— M.T.D.C., T/1, Golf club, Old Agra Road. PH 70059

HOTEL ACCOMMODATION (STD CODE 0253)

— Hotel Panchavati (430,vakilwad)
  PH575 771-73; FAX 571 823
— Hotel Panchavati Elite Inn Pvt. Ltd., Trimbak Road, near Vinod Auto. PH 579 031/32; FAX579214
— Wasan's Inn (2 Star),Near Kalika Mandir, Old Agra Road, Nasik 422 002.
— Hotel Panchavati Yatri (1 Star), 430, Vakilwadi
  PH 572 290-92; FAX 572 293/571 823

EXCURSIONS

SHIRDI : (122 km) Abode of Sai Baba of Shirdi, popularly known as 'the Child of God'. Sai Baba preached tolerance towards all religions and the message of universal brotherhood. Thursday holy to Sai Baba, is marked by special 'pujas and darshans'.

TRIMAKESHWAR : (36 km) It is the place of one of the main out of 12 Jyortirlingas and source of Godavari river. According to legend, Gautam rishi had performed 'Tapasya' to Lord Shiva on the Brahmgiri hill which rises high above the temple. Lord Shiva blessed him and allowed him to bring the sacred rivers Gautami, Gamga and Godavari from the heavens down to earth. Gautam Rishi checked the flowing waters of Godavari by making a 'Varta from Kusha' thereby creating the 'kushavarta Teertha'. Here devotees take a dip and purify themselves before entering the temple. Sivratri is celebrated with great pomp and gaiety.

SAPTASHRINGI DEVI TEMPLE : (55 km) At Wani is the temple of goddess Saptshringi. 'sapta means seven and Shring means pinnacle'. The goddess is supposed to be self-manifested. Also known as the goddess possessing 18 weapons  in 18 hands, she is positioned as if ready to fight the demons.

NANDURMADHMESHWAR : (60 km) A paradise for bird lovers and watchers it is called Maharashtra's Bharatpur. A bird sanctuary has been developed here since 1950.

JAWAHAR : (80 km) One of the few tribal kingdoms, Jawahar is famous for the vibrant Warli paintings. Jai vilas, the palace of tribal lords and the relics of Bhupatgad are worth a visit. The scenic beauty of the Dadar Kopra falls, the enchanting Hanuman and Sun set points, Jawahar is known as Mahabaleshwar of the district.Nearby is Shirpamal, where Shivaji Maharaj had camped on his way to Surat.

TORANMAL : Tucked away in the Satpura mountains at an altitude of 1461 metre, Toranmal is one of the most peaceful place. Yashwant Lake and seetha Khali temple are main attractions.

PUNE

Pune was home for a long time to the Maratha leader Shivaji.It later became capital of the Peshwas. The British capture the city after the battle of Koregaon in 1818 AD.

One of the city's most famous residents was the self proclaimed Guru, Bhagwan Rajneesh, later known as Osho. Although he died in 1990, the ashram he had set up in Pune still attracts thousands of devotees, sightseers, curious onlookers despite lot of controversy.

PLACES OF INTEREST

KASTURBA SAMADHI IN THE AGA KHAN'S PALACE : A marble memorial to Kasturba who died when she and Mahatma Gandhi were imprisoned here.

PARVATI HILL : 108 steps lead to this historical temple where from one can get a panoramic view of the city. The palace was burned down in 1828 AD. Where it once stood, there are pleasant gardens now.

SHANWARWADA : Once the palace of Peshwa rulers now only the fortified walls remain.

SHINDE'S CHATTRI : A memorial to Mahadji Shinde.

BHANDARKAR ORIENTAL RESEARCH INSTITUTE : Which has a museum displaying 20,000 manuscripts.

RAJA KELKAR MUSEUM : It is a private museum, the fruit of one man's passion for collecting the unusal, the antique and the artistic. There are collection of the 17th century miniatures, of musical instruments, antique pottery and unusual betel-nut-cutters and brass padlocks. Another tiny Tribal Museum is close to railway station.

In the 18th century, Mahadji Scindia, one of the ruling Maratha princes, built a small Shiva temple in Pune. Generations later, one of his descendant's built an annexe in the memory of Mahadji. Close by is the mausoleum of the prince, known as Samadhi.

PATALESHWAR TEMPLE : In the centre of the town is an 18th century rock-cut temple and on a hill nearby is one of the most popular temples dedicated to Goddess Parvati.

HOW TO REACH

AIR : Pune is connected by air with Bangalore, Mumbai, Delhi and Madras

RAIL : Pune is connected by rail directly with major cities of the country.

Pune is conveniently connected with Mumbai by Superfast trains

MUMBAI - PUNE - MUMBAI

	1021/1022 Indrayani Exp	1007/1008 Deccan Exp	2027/2028 Shatabdi Exp	1025/1026 Pragati Exp	2123/2124 Deccan Queen
	D : A	D : A	D : A	D : A	D : A
Mumbai	0540:2205	0635:1945	0640:2055	1620:1130	710:1040
Lonavala	0815 :1917	0955:1623	0905:1824	1857:0842	1930:0810
Pune	0925 :1820	1115: 1515	1005:1735	2005:0745	2035:0715

EXCURSIONS

PANSHET : (45 km) Set in an idyllic location between Panshet Dam and Varasgaon Dam Panshet offers you a holiday options–there are water sports organised by MTDC.

RAIGAD : (126 km) Shivaji's impregnable capital, the place where he was crowned and where he died. Besides the fort is his Samadhi and the remains of his palace.

Shivaji, on advice of his long-estranged father had built his capital city (in the 14th century), forsaking Rajgad with its narrow summit plateau. And it was here, in 1674 AD that he had crowned himself Chatrapati, with the help of a venerated priest from Varanasi.For six years upto his death Raigad remained the capital of the Marathas,its broad gates and magnificent monuments earning it the grudging compliment from the British as 'Gibraltar of the East'.

SINHGAD : (25 km)Sinhgad is associated with Shivaji's general, Tanaji Malasure. He launched a dare-devil attack armed with ingenuity and an aguana (ghorpad), to recapture the fort for Shivaji, through a surprise attack by scaling its steep face—a sheer precipice of 3,000 feet.In the ensuing battle Tanaji valiantly laid down his life but captured the fort.

A grieving Shivaji is known to have said "GAD AALA PAN SINH GELA"(The fort's won. but the lion's gone)Whereupon the fort got its name "Sinh"(lion)gad(fort)." Bal Gangadhar 'Lokmanya' Tilak, who declared 'Swaraj is my birthright' has a bungalow atop here. Gandhiji is said to have asked for water from Sinhgad's DevTaka, whenever he was imprisoned at Pune.

TORNA : (35 km) This was first captured by Shivaji during the monsoons of 1646 AD at the age of 15. According to legend during the rebuilding of the fort he had found hidden treasure.He reputedly used this fortune to build a new fort on the crest of an adjoining hill - this was Raigad. Raigad was the headqaurter of Shivaji. On March 5, 1666, Shivaji escaped from custody in Agra and six months later, on September 12, 1666, he returned to this fort.

PURANDER : (40 km) This place is believed to have been built by Lord Indra, king of the Heavens, himself. Standing at a height of 4000 feet above sea level, out of which, 1200 feet have to be climbed, the uppermost terrace has two 12th centuries temples, Purvaresh and Narayanesvar. It has a lower fort Vijragad to the east.

MAHARASHTRA ON A PILGRIM TRAIL

Maharashtra has a long tradition of tolerance and symbiotic interaction with different religious faiths. Maharashtra imbibed the cultural and religious influences of the northern Aryans and southern Dravidians. Thus both vaishnavism and Shaivism flourished in the region.

Shaivism extended its ambit to the worship of Ganesha, son of Shiva.In fact the elephant headed god is one of the most popular deities worshipped by the people here.

ASHTAVINAKYAKA

A pilgrimage to the Ashtavinayaka or eight important Ganapati shrines ensures for the pilgrims everlasting bliss. Glorified as swayambhu or self-appeared each of the eight idols has a distinctive feature. The foremost shrine is Mayureshwar at Morgaon about 64 km from Pune.

It was built in the14th century by Morya Gosavi who installed it at Chinchwad. Closely associated with Morgaon is the Chintamani Ganpati at Theur where Morya Gosavi believed to have attained siddhi (knowledge). The temple was built by his son Chintamani Dev to commemorate the event.

At Ranjangaon the deity is known as Mahaganapati because of the size of the statue. It has ten trunks and twenty arms. It is believed that Mahaganapati was hidden to prevent its destruction from non-believers.Thousands of devotees visit the place during the Bhadrapada festival.Sri Siddhi Vinayak in Ahmednagar district is also a spiritual destination where Morya Gosavi had done penance. But the main temple was constructed by Ahilyabai Holkar.

Built in 1833 AD the temple at Ozhar is famous for its garland of lights.Its golden dome was gifted by Bajirao Peshwa's younger brother Chimaji Appa. Here Ganesha is worshipped in his incarnation as 'Vigneshwara' or' the remover of obstacles'.Situated on a hill, on the banks of the Kukdi river at Lenyadri this temple has 283 steps, symbolising the devotion that unites the devotee with the deity. According to folklore, it was here that Parvati spent time in prayer and penance and gave birth to Ganapati.

Named after Ballal at Pali, Ganapati is known as Ballaleshwar. He is said to have appeared at this spot.the wooden temple was so constructed that the rays of the sun fall directly on the deity from the two equinoxes of the temple. The temple was constructed in 1770 AD by Nana Phadnis.

SAIBABA

The Saibaba of Shirdi has attracted many followers from different sects and religions across the country. Known to be an incarnation of Guru Pattareya he attained samadhi on Dussehra in 1918 AD.

PANDHARPUR

Pandharpur, situated on the shores of the Chandrabhaga river in the Sholapur district is supposed to be the spiritual capital of Maharashtra.The Ashadi fair held at Pandharpur has thrived and is the silver thread running through the entire history of Maharashtra.

Pundalika, when honoured by the visit of Lord Krishna, had prayed for his eternal presence there and therefore the temple is dedicated to Lord Krishna. The temple complex is very old and was first renovated in 83 AD.

The tradition of royal worship and the ratha yatra begun in 1810 and is still carried out on Ashad and Kartik Ekadashi days.

FESTIVALS

ELEPHANTA FESTIVAL : This festival is held across Mumbai harbour on the Elephnata island near Elephanta caves. This feast of music and dance, celebrated under the stars transforms the entire Island into a large auditorium.

MARCH—ELLORA FESTIVAL : Every December a festival of dance and music is organised here with the caves forming a splendid backdrop.

AUG/SEPT.—GANESH CHATURTHI : This day is dedicated to the Lord Ganesha, the elephant-headed god of all good beginning and success. Held annually, this fair is a 10 day-long event. The images of Lord Ganesha are installed and worshipped and on the last day are taken in a procession to be immersed in the river or the Sea. The sea front of Mumbai is packed with people to witness the emersion.

GANESH FESTIVAL : Ganesh festival is dedicated to Lord Ganesha—the harbour of good fortune and success. This cultural feast is held at Pune with classical dance and music performances.

NORTH-EASTERN STATES

1. ARUNACHAL PRADESH

AREA : 83, 743 sq. km

CAPITAL : Itanagar

BOUNDARIES : East - China and Mynamar; West - Bhutan; South - Assam; North - China.

LANGUAGES : Several tribal dialects—Monpa, Miji, Aka, Apatani, Tagin, Khamti, Nocte, Wanch etc.

ROADS : Arunachal Pradesh has 330 km of national highway.

Arunachal Pradesh,one of the most sparsely populated State of the country is home to a complex mix of communities. Its people are friendly, colourful and simple. Once described as the 'Hidden Land', Arunachal Pradesh has now opened its doors to outsiders. Its rich flora ranges from rhododendrons to orchids. Its verdant forests, turbulent streams, lofty mountains and snow-clad peaks make it a

ARUNACHAL PRADESH

unique place offering the tourists numerous opportunities for rafting, hiking and mountaineering.

Its inhabitants belong to Mongoloid and Tibeto - Burmese tribes, the main ones being the Apatanis, the Kamptis, the Padmad and the Miris —most are Buddhists

In Arunachal dance is a way of life. The dances incorporate steps from martial arts of Adis, Wnagchos and Nicte tribes.

Entry to all places of Arunachal Pradesh is from Assam. Important railway stations are Rangapara, Lakhimpur north, Dibrugarh, Tinsukhia and Naharkatia - all are in Assam. The nearest airports are Guwahati, Tezpur, Jorhat and Dibrugarh - all in Assam. Taxis are easily available at all tourist centres. Three wheelers are available at Naharlagun and Pasighat.

HISTORY

The North East Frontier Agency (NEFA) now Arunachal Pradesh has practically no written records relating to the history of this area other than some oral literature and a number of historical ruins lying in the foothills along the territory. As a result of subsequent explorations and excavations a good number of historical ruins dating approximately to the early Christian era have been brought to light. These historical evidences speak that the area was not only known but inhabited by people having close relations with the rest of the country lying specially to the West. From the extensive ruins it can be presumed that the whole of the north bank of Brahmaputra up to the foothills was inhabited by people who were advanced politically, culturally and in various other aspects.

ITANAGAR

Capital of Arunachal Pradesh, it is a beautiful historic city, known as the 'land of Dawnlit mountains' and has been identified with Mayapur, a city of the 14th or 15th century AD. Places of interest are Itanagar fort; Buddhist monastery; Jawaharlal Nehru Memorial Museum; Zoo; Craft centre and Polo park at Naharlagun. Boating facilities are available on Ganga lake. City is ideal for trekking, hiking, boating and canoeing in the Ganga river and angling in the Dikrong river.

HOW TO REACH

AIR : Nearest airport-Tezpur.

RAIL : Nearest railhead is Harmuti which can be reached by Arunachal Express from New Bangaigaon.

ROAD : By bus or car from Tezpur, north Lakhimpur and Banderdewa.

HOTEL ACCOMMODATION (STD CODE 03781)

— Circuit House—for reservation contact Addl. Deputy Commissioner, Naharlagun, PH 4325.
— Field Hostel—for reservation contact Chief engineer, Zone-1, PWD. PH 2427
— Hotel Donyi Polo Ashok. PH 2626/27, 2630/31

Names of the few private hotels : Youth Hostel, Naharagun; Hotel Arunachal Subansiri; Hotel Bomdila; Hotel Itanagar; Hotel Sangrila; Hotel Horn Bill, Naharlagun; Hotel Lakshim, Naharagun; Hotel Alena, Naharagun.

ZIRO

Ziro is the headquarters of lower Subansiri district.

PLACES OF INTEREST :

Tarin fish dam, a heigh altitude fish farm. Pine and Bamboo groves, villages and the indigenous method of rice cultivation there besides craft centre are also worth a visit.

HOW TO REACH

AIR : Nearest airport-Tezpur.

RAIL : Nearest railhead is north Lahkimpur which can be reached by Arunachal Express from New Bongaigaon.

ROAD : By bus from Itanagar / Naharlagun and from north Lakhimpur.

HOTEL ACCOMMODATION (STD CODE 01682)

Circuit House; Inspection Bungalows—for reservation contact Deputy Commissioner. PH 255, 325, 233

TAWANG

City Tawang is the headquarters of Tawang district. Situated at the towering height of 1000 meters, the city houses the 350 years old famous Buddhist Monastery—Tawang Monastery locally called Gompa. City craft center produces very fine woollen carpets of colorful designs and masks.

HOW TO REACH

AIR : Nearest airport-Tezpur.

RAIL : Rangapara by Arunachal Express from New Bongaigaon.

ROAD : By bus from Bomdila.

HOTEL ACCOMMODATION (STD CODE 06182)

Circuit House-cum-Inspection Bungalow—for reservation contact Deputy Commissioner, Tawang, PH 221, 222.

Hotel Shangrila and Hotel Nichu are the two hotels in the town.

TIPI

Tipi has a rich collection of more than 500 species of orchids. They are available for sale by banks of the Kameng river. Tipi is also ideal for rafting and angling in the Kameng river.

HOW TO REACH

AIR : Nearest airport-Tezpur.

RAIL : Rangapara by Arunachal Express from New Bongaigaon.

ROAD : By bus or car from Tezpur.

HOTEL ACCOMMODATION

Forest Inspection Bungalow—for reservation contact Divisional forest officer, Bhalukpong.

BOMDILA

A scenic hill station, the headquarters of West Kameng river. Craft centre and is known for, producing very fine colorful designs and masks. The district also houses some Buddhists monasteries.

RUPA

A beautiful hill town, 18 km on way to Bhalukpong from Bomdila by the Tenga river is an ideal picnic spot.

HOW TO REACH

AIR : Nearest airport-Tezpur.
RAIL : Rangapara by Arunachal Express from New Bongaigoan.
ROAD : By bus or car from Tezpur.

HOTEL ACCOMMODATION (STD CODE 06182)

Tourist Lodge and Circuit House—for reservation contact Deputy commissioner, Bomdila, PH 221, 222.
Hotel La and Hotel Sweet are two private hotels in the town.

BHALUKPONG

Historical place for the Aka tribe. Also a picnic spot.
PARSURAMKUNDA : The legendary place where sage Parsurama is believed to have washed away his sins. A divine pilgrim centre, it overflows with devotees on Makar Sankranti day, when people take a holy dip in the kund.

HOW TO REACH

AIR : Nearest airport-Tezpur.
RAIL : Rangapara by Arunachal Express from New Boingaigaon.
ROAD : By bus or car from Tezpur.

HOTEL ACCOMMODATION

Bhalukpong Inspection Bungalow—for reservation contact Extra assistant commissioner, Bhalukpong Assam Tourist Lodge.

DIRANG

Dirang is a sub-divisional headquarters in West Kameng district. The district houses Apple Orchards and sheep breeding farms. A few kilometers from Dirang are hot springs where people go far a holy dip to wash away their sins and diseases.

HOW TO REACH

AIR : Nearest airport-Tezpur.
RAIL : Rangapara by Arunachal Express from New Bongaigoan.
ROAD : By bus from Bomdila.

HOTEL ACCOMMODATION

Inspection Bungalow and Anchal Lodge—For reservation contact Extra Assistant Commissioner, Dirang.

DAPORIJO

Daporijo is the headquarters of the upper Subansiri district situated on the right bank of the Subansir river. There is a beautiful cave few kilometers away from the town Angling is possible in the Subansiri river.

HOW TO REACH

AIR : Nearest airport-Tezpur.
RAIL : North Lakhimpur and Silapathar by Arunachal Express from New Bongaigaon.
ROAD : By bus from Itanagar via Ziro and from Likabali in west Siang district.

HOTEL ACCOMMODATION (STD CODE 06182)

Circuit House and Inspection Bungalow—for reservation contact Deputy commissioner, Daporijo, PH 223, 224.

ALONG

Along is the headquarters of the east Siang district situated on the south bank of Siyom river. The town is ideal for trekking, hiking and angling in the Siyom river.

Mithun and Jersey cross-breeding farm at Kamki, b 25 km away from Along village, is also worth a visit.

HOW TO REACH

AIR : Tezpur.
RAIL : Silapathar by Arunachal Express from New Bongaigaon.
ROAD : By bus or car from Likabali and Pasighat.

HOTEL ACCOMMODATION (STD CODE 06182)

Circuit House and Inspection Bungalow—for reservation contact Deputy Commissioner, Along, PH 221, 220.

PASIGHAT

Pasighat is the headquarters of the east Siang district situated on the right bank of Siang river. Siang is the name of the Brahmaputra river in Arunachal Pradesh the town is ideal for river rafting, boating and angling in Siang river. Lali wildlife sanctuary can be visited from this place.

HOW TO REACH

AIR : Nearest airport-Dibrugarh.

RAIL : Nearest railhead-Murkongselek.

ROAD : By bus or car from Itanagar, north Lakhimpur and by ferry from Dibrugarh to Oiramghat and from Oiramghat to Pasighat.

HOTEL ACCOMMODATION (STD CODE 06182)

Circuit House and Inspection Bungalow—for reservation contact Deputy Commissioner, Pasighat, PH 340, 320, 222.

Hotel Siang, Hotel Arun, Hotel Sangoo, Arunachal Samadhi Guest Hosue are other hotels available in the town.

MALINITHAN

Malinithan, situated at Likabali, is the headquarters of sub-division of west-Siang district. Ruins of a temple belonging to 14th and 15th centuries have been excavated here. The ruins include sculptures of Indra and Airavata; Surya and Nandi bull, akashi Ganga waterfalls are 5 km away from Malinithan where people take a bath to wash away sins.

HOW TO REACH

AIR : Nearest airport-Tezpur.

RAIL : Silapathar by Arunachal Express from New Bongaigaon.

ROAD : By bus or car from Silapathar.

HOTEL ACCOMMODATION

Inspection Bungalow—for reservation contact Sub-divisional officer, Likabali.

TEZU

Tezu, headquarters of Lohit district is ideal for trekking and hiking, river rafting and angling in the Lohit river.

HOW TO REACH

AIR : Nearest airport-Dibrugarh.

RAIL : Nearest railhead-Tinsukhia.

ROAD : By bus from Tinsukhia via Namsai and by ferry from Dhalaghat to Sadia and by bus from Sadia.

HOTEL ACCOMMODATION (STD CODE 06182)

Circuit House—for reservation contact Deputy commissioner, Tezu, PH 221, 222.

MIAO

Miao is the headquarters of Miao sub-division. Tibetan refugee settlement here produces woollen carpets of various designs. Oil drilling at Kharsang, plywood and veneer mills and Namdapha National Park are few kilometres away from Miao. Trekking, hiking and angling is possible in Noadihing river.

HOW TO REACH

AIR : Nearest airprot-Dibrugarh.

RAIL : Nearest railway station-Margherita by local passenger train from Tinsukia.

ROAD : by Jeep or by Gypsy from Margherita, Assam.

HOTEL ACCOMMODATION

Inspection Bungalow—for reservation contact Extra Assistant Commissioner, Miao Tourist lodge.

FESTIVALS

Festivals are the mirror of the people's culture. Some important festivals of the State are Solung and Mopin of the Adis, Lossar of the Monpas and the Sherdukpens, Boori-boot of the Hill Miris, Dree of the Apatanis, Si-Donyi of the Tagnis, Reh of the Idu-Mishmis, Nyokum of the Nishings and Chalo loku of the Noctes etc. Animal sacrifice are a common ritual in most of the festivals, particularly among the non-Buddhist tribes. The religious rites and the sacrifices are generally performed by the priests assisted by some select male members.

ASSAM

ASSAM
AT A GLANCE

AREA : 78, 439 sq. km

CAPITAL : Dispur

BOUNDARIES : East - Nagaland; West - West Bengal and Bangladesh; South and South - East - Tripura, Mizoram, Manipur, North and North - East - Arunachal Pradesh and Bhutan; South-West - Meghalaya.

LANGUAGE : Assamese and Bangla.

ROADS : In 1993-94 the total length of roads in Assam was 32,154 km which includes 2,033 km National Highway, 2,080 km of State Highways and 20,081 km of other PWD roads.

AIRPORTS : Guwahati, Tezpur, Jorhat, Dibrugarh, Lakhimpur Silchar.

MUSEUMS

Guwahati : Anthropological Museum - Guwahati University; Assam State Museum; Assam Forest Museum and Assam Government Cottage Industries Museum.

PLIGRIM CENTRES (A : Air; R : Rail)

Guwahati : Kamakhya temple - centre of Tantrik worship; A and R - Guwahati.

Peacock Islands : Umananda temple noted for Shivratri festival; A and R Guwahati.

Hajo : It has important Hindu, Muslim and Buddhist shrines; A and R Guwahati 24 km.

Sibsagar : It has several temples, mosques and Buddhist and Shakta shrines; A - Jorhat - 55 km; R - Simalugiri - 19 km.

Assam, aptly described as the SHANGRILA in the North-Eastern India is the gateway to the North-East. The word ASSAM is derived from the Sanskrit word "ASOMA" meaning peerless. Nestling in the foothills of the Himalayas Assam is known as the land of blue hills and red rivers. Assam is synonymous with tea but exotic wildlife reserves are the principal attractions for it is the home of India's rare one-horned rhinoceros.

HISTORY

Assam has a rich legacy of culture and civilization. The State is the homeland of different races of men : Austric, Mongolian, Dravidian and Aryan that came to dwell in her hills and valleys at different times since remote antiquity. Assam has developed a composite culture of variegated colour.

During the epic period Assam was known as 'Kamrupa'. Guwahati is an ancient town whose history goes back to the puranic days. The city known as 'Pragjyotishpur' (place of eastern astronomy) was said to have been founded by Narkasur who is mentioned in Puranas and epics. His son Bhagadatta had led a large elephant force to the battlefield of Kurukshetra and had fallen fighting on the side of the Kauravas, according to the Mahabharata.

The earliest epigraphic reference to the kingdom of Kamrupa is found in Allahabad Pillar inscription of Samudragupta. Hiuen Sang, the Chienese scholar pilgrim who visited Kamrupa in about 783 AD, on an invitation of its monarch Kumar Bhaskar Varman, left a record of the kingdom he called Kamolupa. Kamrupa also figured in the writings of the Arab historian Alberuni in 11th century.

The advent of the Ahomas across the eastern hills in 1228 AD changed the course of Assam's history. The Ahomas defeated the local Karchari, Chutia and Moran kings and ruled Assam nearly for six centuries.

The Burmese entered through eastern borders and overrun the territory. The British appeared in 1826 and defeated the Burmese in several battles. With the Treaty of Yan Dabo in 1826 the Burmese vacated Assam leaving the British in possession. The conquered territory was placed under the administration of an agent to the Governor-General. In 1832 Cachar was annexed to Assam and Jaintia hills were made part of it in 1835. In 1874, a separate province of Assam under a Chief Commissioner was created with Shillong as capital.

On the partition of Bengal in 1905 Assam was united with the eastern districts of Bengal. From 1912, the chief commissionership of Assam was revived and in 1921 a Governorship was created.

The Muslim district of Sylhet emerged with the formation of East Bengal (Bangladesh at present) after partition of India in 1947.

Dewanagiri in north Kamrupa was ceded to Bhutan in 1951. In 1948, the North East Frontier Agency was separated from Assam for security reasons. In 1963 Nagaland, and in 1972 Meghalaya and in 1987 Mizoram emerged out of Assam as full-fledged States.

GUWAHATI

Situated on the banks of the Brahmputra river, Guwahati is the gateway to the north-eastern India. Guwahati—said to be a the legendary Pragijyotishpur or city of eastern light—is a, busy and crowded city as per its name—Guwa meaning areca nut and Hat meaning market or market for areca nuts.

HOW TO REACH

AIR : Guwahati is the principal airport in north-east India and is connected with Calcutta, New Delhi, Bagdogra, Agartala, Imphal, and Dibrugarh.

RAIL : Guwahati is well-connected by trains with Calcutta, New Delhi, Mumbai, Chennai, Bangalore, Cochin and Thiruvananthapuram. Timings of Rajdhani train between Delhi and Guwahati.

Delhi - Guwahati
— 2436 Rajdhani Exp D Delhi 1245 Hrs (M.F.); A Guwahati 2030;
— 2435 Rajdhani Exp D Guwahati 0600 Hrs ((W.Su.); A Delhi 1430 Hrs

ROADS : A network of National Highways and other roads connect all the important cities of Assam. The Assam State Transport Corporation operates buses to all towns and capitals of the neighbouring States. Tourist vehicles are easily available on hire.

ROAD DISTANCES FROM GUWAHATI : Agartala 597 km Aizwal 538 km; Cherapunjee 154 km; Dimapur 280 km; Dibrugarh 445 km Diphu 269 km; Darang 100 km; Darjeeling 587 km; Gangtok 624 km;Haflong 355 km; Itanagar 420 km; Imphal 487 km; Jorhat 314 km;Kaziranga 217 km; Kohima 342 km; Kalimpong 582 km; Lumding 221 km; Manas 176 km; Sibsagar 369 km; Silchar 398 km; Shillong 100 km; Siliguari 513 km; Tezpur 181 km; Thimpu 549 km; Twang 532 km; Zero 480 km.

CONDUCTED TOURS

The Directorate of Tourism operates the following package tours for visitors :

(1) Kaziranga 2 Days : Departure on Monday, Thursday, Saturday and Sunday
(2) Manas 2 Days : Departure on Friday
(3) Full-day city tour of Guwahati
(4) Full-day Shillong : Departure on Wednesday and Sunday
(5) Full-day Hajo, Sualkuchi and Madan Kamdev
(6) Sibsagar 2 Days : Departure every 2nd and 4th Saturday
For Detailed Information contact :
Directorate of Tourism, Assam, Station Road, GUWAHATI 781 001. PH 27102, 31022 and 24475

HOTEL ACCOMMODATION (STD CODE 0361)

— Hotel Dynasty (4 Star),Rehman Building,Lakhotia S.S.Road
  PH 510 496-99;FAX 522 112
— Hotel Raj Mahal 1 (4 Star),A.T.Road,Paltan Bazar
  PH 522 478- 83; FAX 521 59
— Hotel Brahmputra Ashok (3 Star), Mahatma Gandhi Road
  PH 541 064/5; FAX 540 870
— Hotel Nandan (3 Star), G.S.Road, Paltan Road
  PH 540 855, 521 476; FAX 542 634
— Hotel Samrat (2 Star), A.T.Road, Santipur. PH 541 657
— Hotel Kuber International,Hern Baruna Road, Fanzy Bazar
  PH 514 353; FAX 541 465
— Hotel Nav-Alka, S.R.C.B. Road, Fancy Bazar
  PH 541 070, 541 080.

PLACES OF INTEREST IN AND AROUND GUWAHATI

THE STATE MUSEUM : Has a rare collection of old sculptures and artefacts of ancient times.

KAMAKHYA and BHUBANESHWARI TEMPLES : (10 km) These temples honour the Mother Goddess **Kamakhya, the essence** of female energy. Kamakhya is one of the 51 Hindu 'Pithas' where as per the mythology the genital organ of the 'SATI' i.e. Parvati— the eternal wife of Lord Shiva— had fallen down after death in one of her incarnations. It is considered as one of the most important centres of tantrik and shakti cult.

SOALKUCHI : (32 km from Guwahati) It is Famous for Assamese silk-Muga and Pat. One can see here the silk begining its journey from the cocoon stage to its unravelling and then to loom and finally as sarees or the traditional 'Mekhala Chandor', the two pieces saree, which women wear on festive occasions.

HAJO : (32 km from Guwahati) The epitome of national integration where Hayagriba temple, sacred to both Hindus and Buddhists co-exists in perfect harmony with Islamic holy place Poa-Mecca.

MADAN KAMDEV : (35 km from Guwahati) It is an archaeological site where erotic sculptures and other stone carvings abound.

CHANDUBI : (64 km from Guwahati) A natural lagoon and a fine picnic spot.

DARANGA : (81 km from Guwahati) Famous for its Bhutia Fair during winters held annually from November to March.

BATADRAWA : (134 km from Guwahati) It is the Birth place of Shri Sankar Deva, famous Vaishnava Saint and is 14 km from Nagoan.

BHAIRABKUNDA : (137 km from Guwahati) A beautiful picnic spot on the border of Arunachal Pradesh and Bhutan.

BARPETA : (140 km from Guwahati) It is Famous for its Vaishnava Monastery containing the shrine of Shri Madhav Dev, successor to the Vaishnava reformer Shri Sankar Deva.

DHUBRI : (287 km from Guwahati) A Sikh Gurudwara is situated on the south east corner of Dhubri town established by the 9th Guru Teg Bahadur during the Mughal invasion of Assam.

HAFLONG : (383 km from Guwahati) The only hill station in Assam,it is the district headquarter of North Cachar Hills district. Besides the Haflong Lake one should visit Jatinga, famous for migratory birds during the months from August to November where ornithologists gather to study the bird's strange reaction to light in the night. 47 km from Haflong on the banks of the river Mahur is Maibong, once flourished as the capital of Dimasa, The Kachri Kingdom. The stone house and a temple of Kachri king can be seen at Maibong.

TINSUKHIA : (483 km from Guwahati) An important commercial centre especially for plywood.

DIBRUGARH : (445 km from Guwahati) A lovely riverside town in Upper Assam is important for tea production.

TEZPUR

Known as Sonitpur in mythology it conjures up the image of the romantic legend of Usha and Aniruhda, son of Lord Krishna. The ruins of Anigarh, where this immortal romance blossomed in the post-Mahabharata era still bear mute testimony to this legend. Few kilometers from Tezpur lies 'Da – Parbatia' finest and oldest specimen of sculptures which date back to 5th and 6th centuries. Other architectural remains include the 'Agnigarh' and 'Bamuni hills', the 'Bhairavi' and 'Bamuni hills', the 'Bhairavi' and 'Mahabhairab' temples and the twin tanks of 'Bar Pukhuri' and 'Padum Pukhuri'. 'Bhaluk -pung' - 60 kilometers from Tezpur has hot springs and huge orchid gardens. Bhaluk - Pung is a favourite angling spot and a gateway to Bomdila and Tawang in Arunachal Pradesh. About 50 km from Tezpur, off the road to Arunachal Pradesh, lies 'Eco camp', a unique experiment by the Assam Anglers Association and the State Forest Department. Visitors can do river rafting guided by experts.

The 'Nameri National Park' sprawls over from Assam into Arunachal Pradesh. The best way of travelling here is on elephants. There are no roads inside the park. The thick jungle, with patches of swamp, is home to variety of animals and birds.

HOW TO RECAH

AIR : Nearest airport-Saloni.

RAIL : Nearest railhead-Rangapara 26 km.

RAOD : Tezpur is connected by road with Guwahati 189 km.

SIBSAGAR

Sibsagar was the capital of the mighty Ahomas who ruled Assam for more than 600 years before the advent of the British rule. The town literally means the Ocean of Shiva. The Shiva temple with its golden dome is believed to be among the tallest Hindu temples in India. About six kilometers lies seven storied palace, three of which are below the ground level - known as Talatar Ghar and the rest above - known as Kareng Ghar. Rang Ghar is a two storied oval - shaped pavilion, from which Ahom royalties used to watch elephant fights and other sporting events. It was built by king Pramatta Singha (1744-1751 AD). Gargaon, the principal town of the Ahoms, lies 13 kilometers east of Sibsagar. The old palace was destroyed and the present seven storied was rebuilt around 1762 AD by king Rajeshwar Singha. The Jaysagar tank was built by King Rudra Singha in 1967. On its bank are three temples - Joydol, Shivdol and Devidol. Eight kilometers from Sibsagar is the Rudrasagar tank built by king Lakshmi Singha in 1773. Twenty eight kilometers east of Sibsagar is Charaideo, original capital of the Ahom kings is famous for numerous Amaidams or burial vaults of the members of the royalty. About 22 kilometers from Sibsagaar at Saraguri stands Ajan Pir Dargah Sarif who was the first Muslim saint to compose Azirik in

Assamese language. On the day of his Urs thousands of devotees gather here to pay homage to this great Muslim reformer.

HOW TO REACH

AIR : Nearest airport-Jorhat 55 km.

RAIL : Nearest railhead-Simluguri 16 km.

ROAD : One has to travel by the State Transport bus or by private vehicle from Guwahati.

HOTEL ACCOMMODATION :

Tourist Lodge. For booking contact Toursit Information Officer; Or Circuit and Dak Bungalows under the Dy.Commissioner. There are some moderate hotels like Picolo, Kareng and Priya Bramhputra.

TOURIST INFORMATION OFFICE

Tourist Information Officer, Sibsagar. PH 03772 2394

MAJULI

Majuli, situated in the midst of the Brahmputra river, is a centre of Vaishnavite culture with a number of Satras (Monastries). This is the largest riverine town in the world. The river provides the backdrop for the historic "Moni kanchan Sanjog" between Assam's pioneeer Vaishnavite saints Shankardeva and his disciple Madhabdeva in 15th century. Ever since that meeting of the great minds and the subsequent establishment of "Satras" that followed, Majuli emerged as the carving glory of Vaishnavite culture in Assam.

Majuli is dominated by the Mishing tribe which came down from the hills of Arunachal Pradesh many years ago and is among the only tribal riverine community in the Assam valley. Their handlooms are exquisite, particularly the colourful MIRIZEN shawls and blankets which can be used as wall hangings or even as bedcovers.

Multifaceted in its attractions, Majuli unfolds a variety of interest to the tourist—rare migratory birds, traditional handicrafts and pottery, ethnic culture and dance forms and sports.

Majuli can be reached by three main routes—Jorhat Nimatighat from Jorhat, Dhokuakhana from Dhemaji and Luitkhabolughat from North Lakhimpur. Besides these there are many ghats with single machine boats on both banks of the Brahmaputra.

DHUBRI : A Sikh Gurudwara is situated on the south-east corner of Dhubri town established by the ninth Guru Teg Bahadur during the Mughal invasion of Assam.

HOW TO REACH

AIR : Nearest Airport Jorhat.
RAIL : Nearest railhead Jorhat.

HOTEL ACCOMMODATION (STD CODE 0376)

— Circuit House at Garamuth—For reservation contact SDO (Civil) Majuli PH 03775 424/5
— P.W.D. (Kamalabari)—For reservation contact Executive Engineer P.W.D.building
— A Guest House at Kalambari Satra—For reservation contact head priest of the Satra.

WILDLIFE SANCTUARY

KAZIRANGA NATIONAL PARK

Kaziranga National Park, the oldest in Assam lies partly in Golaghat district and partly in the Nagaon district of Assam. In covers an area of 430 sq. km. It is the best home of the great Indian one-horned rhinoceros. The landscape of Kaziranga is of sheer forest, tall elephant grass, rugged reeds, marshes and shallow pools. The park was first established in 1908 as a reserve forest with only about a dozen rhinos and was declared a National Park in 1974. Apart from great one-horned Rhinos, tigers are there in sizable numbers, other attractions are wild buffalo, magnificent swamp deer, hog deer, wild boar, hoolok gibbon, capped langur and ratel.

Mihimukh is the starting area for the park and elephants can be hired from here to enter the sanctuary.

HOW TO REACH

AIR and RAIL : Jorhat 94 km. Kaziranga is 217 from Guwahati.

Conducted tours to Kazirangaare organised by Tourism Department on every Sunday, Monday, Wednesday, Thursday and Saturday. For detailed information contact : Tourist Information Officer, Station road, Guwahati, TELEFAX - 547 102

HOTEL ACCOMMODATION :

Forest rest house and bungalows are available in the park area. Kaziranga Forest Lodhe is also available with air-conditioned rooms, bar restaurant and other facilities.

MANAS NATIONAL PARK

The only Tiger project in Assam Manas is one of the most magnificent national Park situated on the bank of the Manas river with the nack drop of Sub-Himalayan hills. It is well known as one of the world heritage sites, its unique combination of scenic beauty and rare wealth of wildlife. Apart from tiger, the rarest species of hispid animals—Pigmy Hog and Golden langur—are found here.

HOW TO REACH

AIR : Nearest airport-Guwahati 176 km.

RAIL : Nearest railhead-Barpeta 136 km.

HOTEL ACCOMMODATION

The Tourism Department has two tourist lodges—one at Barpeta Road and the other at Bansbari. For reservation contact Tourist Information Officer, Barpeta Road, PH 03666 32749. The State Forest Department has two bungalows at Mathanguri inside the Forest. There is no catering facilities hence the tourists have to carry their own foodstaff from Barpeta Road to be cooked by the Chefs of Forest Department. For reservation contact The Field Director, Manas Tiger Project, P.O.Barpets Road.

FESTIVALS

The culture of Assam is a rich tapestry woven with multicoloured yarns of heritage of all races that inhabit her.Assam has an exclusive range of colourful featival. Bihu is the chief festival celebrated on three occasions Rangali Bihu or Bohag Bihu marks the advent of the cropping season and it also ushers in the Assamese New Year. Bhogali Bihu or Nagh Bihu is the harvest festival and Kati Bihu or Kangali Bihu marking the coming of autumn is a simple affair.

AMBUBASI MELA : This mela is held every year during monsoon at Kamkhya temple Guwahati.This mela is associated with the legend of menstrual cycle of the Goddess Kamakhya. This is a purely ritual Tantric cult and practice. During Ambubasi the temple remains closed for three as the Goddess menstruales. Inside the temple is the 'Devi Kuavs'. One can see the vaginal image covered with a red piece of cloth. This temple is shrouded with mystery. The blood-stained clothes of these three days are kept in high esteem by the Hindu pilgrims coming from all over the country.

JONBEEL MELA : This spectacular mela is held every year during winter at Jonbeel of Jagiroad. On the occasion of the mela a big bazar is held here where Tiwa, Karbi, Khasi and Jaintia tribes excahnge their products with local people in Barter system. Before the mela they perform fire worship for the well-being of the mankind.

BAISHAGU : It is celebrated by the Boro kacharis in the month of baishak as spring celebration at the advent of the new year.

RONGKER AND CHOMANGKAN : Rongker and Chomangkan are the two most important festivals of the Karbis. Rongker is basically a spring time festival and is performed at the beginning of the new year. Chomangkan, dedicated to the dead, is primarily a death ceremony and is celebrated, to remember and honour ones ancestors.

Vaishnavites observe birth and death anniversaries of prominent Vaishnava saints through day-long singing of hymns and staging of Bhaonas (theatrical performances in traditional style). Sivaratri Mela at Umanand and other places near Siva temple, Durga Puja, Diwali Dol-Jatra, Idd, Christmas, Ashokastami Mela, Paushamela, Parasueam Mela are other religious festivals.

SUGGESTED NORTH EAST ITINERARY

DAY	TIMINGS	ITINERARY	OVER NIGHT
1	am	Arrive Guwahati by air	
	pm	City tour of Guwahati	Guwahati
2	Full Day	In and around Guwahati	"
3		Depart for Manipur by air	Manipur
4	Full Day	In and around manipur	"
5	am	Depart by car for Imphal	Kohima
6	Full Day	In and around Kohima	"
7	am	Depart by air for Guwahati	
	pm	and proceed by road for Itanagar	Itanagar
8	Full Day	In and around Itanagar visit Bomdila and Tawang	"
9	am	Depart by Car for Shillong	Shillong
10	Full Day	In and around Shillong	"
11	am	Depart by car for Silchar	Silchar
	pm	City Tour of Silchar	
12	am	Depart by car for Aizwal	Aizwal
13	Full Day	City Tour of Aizwal	
14		Depart by air End of the tour	

MANIPUR

MANIPUR
AT A GLANCE

AREA : 22, 327 sq. km.

CAPITAL : Imphal

BOUNDARIES : East and South - Mynamar; West - Assam; South-East - Mizoram; North - Nagaland

LANGUAGES : Manipuri and English.

ROADS : National highways No 39 and 53 pass through Manipur for a distance of 437.67 km. The State has 5,816 km of roads both metalled and unmetalled as on March 31, 1993.

AIRPORT : Imphal

Manipur literally means a 'A JEWELLED LAND' — a land of blue green hills, cascading rapids, carpets of flowers and unwinding rivers. Manipur lies in the easternmost corner of India, a veritable paradise on earth, Rich with tradition, this oval shaped valley is surrounded by an aura of mystery.

Polo is said to have originated here. Songol Kangiej (Manipur Polo) is the chief sport in the State even today.

HISTORY

Not much of recorded history of Manipur is available. According to historians, Pakhangba ascended the throne of one of the seven main principalities in 33 AD and founded a long dynasty which ruled Manipur till 1891 AD.

Manipur came under the British rule in 1891 AD and later it was merged in the Indian Union as part 'C' State on October 15, 1949. In 1950-51 an advisory form of government was introduced. In 1957 this was replaced by a Territorial Council of 30 elected and two nominated members.

Later in 1963 a Legislative Assembly of 30 elected and three nominated members was established under the Union Territories Act, 1963. The status of the administrator was raised from Chief Commissioner to Lt. Governor on December 19, 1969.

Manipur attained full-fledged Statehood on January 21, 1972.

IMPHAL

Imphal, the capital of Manipur, is a bustling mini-metropolis situated at a height of 790 m above sea level.

HOW TO REACH

AIR : Nearest airport-Imphal connected with Dimapur, Silchar and Calcutta.

RAIL : Nearest railhead Dimapur 225 km.

ROAD : Imphal is connected by road with Guwahati and Silchar.

HOTEL ACCOMMODATION (STD CODE 03852)

— Hotel Imphal run by the Tourism Department
PH 220 459 / 223 250; FAX 222 629
— Anand Continental. PH 223 433
— Hotel Excellency. PH 223 231
— Hotel Prince. PH 220 587
— Hotel White Palace. PH 220 599

There are Tourist Homes at Moirang, Sendra, Phubala, Kahngiam and Churachandpur managed by the Department of Tourism, Government of Manipur.

CONDUCTED TOURS

Regular conducted tours are organised by Manipur Tourism, covering Shree Govindjee Temple, Bishru Temple, Phubala Tourist Home, INA memorial at Moirang, Keibul, Lamjao Natoional Park and Sendra Tourist Home (Lake Side) - Sundays only.

For detailed information contact :

— Tourist Officer, Department of Tourism, Imphal. PH 224603
Or Reception Counter, Tourism Department, Imphal Airport

PLACES OF INTEREST IN AND AROUND IMPHAL

SRI GOVINDAJEE : This temple adjoining the palace of the former rulers of Manipur, is a historic centre for Vaishnavites. It is a simple and beautiful structure with twin gold domes, a paved court and a large raised congregation hall. The presiding deity in the centre is flanked by shrines of Balaram and Krishna on one side and Jagannath on the other.

KHWAIRAMBAND BAZAR : The market is very special because all the stall-holders are women. Not far from here, is a street where beautiful furniture and cane baskets are sold. Other smaller markets are Singaimei, Kongba, Lamlong, Kwakeithel, Heirangoithong, Trea keithel and Naoremthong.

MANIPUR STATE MUSEUM : This interesting museum near the Polo ground houses Manipur's tribal heritage and a collection of portraits of Manipur's former rulers. Interesting items are costumes, arms and weapons, relics and historical documents.

WAR CEMETERIES : The British and the Indian Army cemeteries commemorating those who died in the Second War are serene and well-maintained with little stone markers and bronze plaques recording the glorious sacrifice of the heroes. These graves are maintained by the Commonwealth War Graves Commission.

SAHEED MINAR : This tall tower at Bir Tikendrajit park in the capital commemorates the indomitable spirit of Manipuri martyrs who sacrificed their lives while fighting against the British in 1891 AD.

MANIPUR ZOOLOGICAL GARDEN : (6 km) West of Imphal is the Zoological Garden at Iroishemba on the Imphal Kanchup Road. The graceful brow - antlered deer, one of the rarest species in the world, can be seen here in sylvan surroundings.

LANGTHABAL : (8km) Overlooking the Manipur University, amidst jack fruit and pine trees are the relics of an old historic palace, well planned temples and ceremonial houses.

KHNOGHAMPAT ORCHIDARUM : (12km) More than 110 varieties of orchids, including several rare species are grown here. Peak season is from April to May.

BISHNUPUR : (27km) The single - celled conical roofed temple of Lord Vishnu here was built in 1467 in Chi nese style design. The town is also known for its stoneware production.

KAINA : (29km) A beautiful hillock and a sacred place of Hindus.

PHUBALA : (40km) A charming island on a little island, on the western fringes of the Loktak lake to the south of Imphal. It is joined to the mainland by a low causeway.

MOIRANG : (45km) Here is the ancient temple of the pre - Hindu deity, Lord Thangiing. It was in Moirang that the flag of the Indian National Army was first hoisted on Indian soil by Netaji Subhash Chandra Bose. The INA museum here contains letters, photographs badges of ranks and other articles associated with the movement.

It is also a centre of Meitei folk culture where every summer colourful 'Lai Haroaba' dance is traditionally performed in honour of the presiding pre-Hindu deity Thangling.

LOKTAK LAKE AND SENDRA ISLAND : (48km) A huge and beautiful stretch of water. From the tourist bungalow set atop Sendra Island one can get a bird's eye view of the lake and life around it. Gaze at the fishermen as they cast their nets, rare fish farms using nets as floating walls or as they build houses on islands of floating weeds.

The Sendra Tourist Home with an attached Cafeteria in the middle of the lake is an ideal tourist spot.

UKHRUL : (83km) The district headquarter, a hill station east of Imphal bears a gay and festive appearance during Christmas. It is also famous for a peculiar type of land lily, the Siroi, grown on the Siroi hills. One can take excursion to the Siroi hills and Kangkhui lime caves.

KEIBUL LAMJAO NATIONAL PARK : 53 km from Imphal on the fringes of the Laktak Lake this is the best natural habitat of the marsh dwelling Brow-Antlered Deer. Previously an area for Water Fowl Shoots it became a sanctuary in 1954.

Brow-Antlered Deer were spotted, one of the most localized and endangered mammal in the world.

FESTIVALS

Important festivals of the State are Dol-Jatra, Lai Haraoba, Heikru Hitongba Rasa Leela, Cheiraoba, Ningol Chak-Kouba, Rath-Jatra, Kut, Lui-Ngai-Ni,Gang-Ngai, Idul-Fitre and Christmas.

MANIPURI DANCE

Legends say that the discovery of Manipur is the result of the delight the gods took in dancing still practised today this dance is marked by graceful and restrained movements and delicate hand gestures, known as Manipuri. Manipur is a mosaic of traditions and cultural patterns, best represented by its dance forms. The "Lai-Haraoba", a traditional stylised dance is a ritual dance for appeasing gods and goddesses. The Lai-Haraoba festival is generally celebrated between April and May after the harvest season. The Rass songs and dances express the "Leelas"of Lord Krishna as a child with the Gopis of Brindavan and depict their yearning for communion with the Lord. The tribal dances of Manipur are the expression of love, creativity and aestheticism of the tribal people of the State. Manipuris were earlier recognised as skilful warriors and still practice the arts of wrestling, sword fighting and martial arts.

MEGHALAYA

MEGHALAYA
AT A GLANCE

AREA : 22, 429 sq. km

CAPITAL : Shillong

BOUNDARIES : East and North – Assam; West and South – Bangladesh.

LANGUAGES : Khasi, Garo and English.

ROADS : Three national highways pass through Meghalaya for a distance of 456.54 km. The State had 6,707 km of both surfaced and unsurfaced road in 1996-97.

AIRPORT : Umaroi near Shillong (35 km).

Meghalaya or 'ABODE OF CLOUDS', gifted with ample scenic beauty and abundant vegetation, it presents a panorama of lush rolling hills, heather—covered slopes, breathtaking beautiful waterfalls, mountain springs, moving mists, silent lakes and multitude of flora and fauna.

HISTORY

Meghalaya was created as an autonomous State within the State of Assam on April 2, 1970. The full-fledged State of Meghalaya came into existence on January 21, 1972. It is now divided into seven administrative districts. They are Jantia Hills; East Garo Hills; West Garo Hills; East Khasi Hills; West Khasi Hills; Ri Bhoi and South Garo Hills districts.

These are predominantly inhabited by the Khasis, the Jaintias and the Garos. These tribal communities are the descendants of very ancient people having distinctive traits and ethnic origin. The Khasi Hills and Jaintia which form the central and eastern parts of the Meghalaya is a plateau with rolling grassland hills and river valleys. The southern face of this plateau is marked by deep gorges and abrupt slopes at the foot of which a narrow strip of plain land runs along the international border with Bangladesh.

KHASI HILLS

SHILLONG

Shillong, the capital of Meghalaya, is situated in the centre of a high plateau within Khasi hills. It has been called 'the Scotland

of the South' because of its elevation 1496 m above sea level. The highest peak in the State is the Shillong peak 1965 m. Nokrek in the Garo hill district is the next peak. Shillong is one of the best known hill resorts in India. It derives its name from the deity Shyllong whose dwelling place is said to be on the Shyllong Peak over the township.

HOW TO REACH

AIR : Nearest airport-Guwahati 104 km.

RAIL : Nearest railhead-Guwahati.

ROAD : Regular bus service run by the Meghalaya Transport Corporation ply between Guwahati and Shilllong every hour. Private buses ply daily from Guwahati and Shillong.

Tourist Taxis with the capacity of five passengers ply daily from Guwahati to Shillong.

HOTEL ACCOMMODATION (STD CODE 0364)

— Hotel Pinewood Ashok. PH 223 116 / 223 765
— Hotel Alpine Continental (3Star), Thana, Quinton Road PH 220 991; FAX 220 996
— Hotel PoloTowers (3 Star), Oakland Road, Polo Grounds PH 222 340-2; FAX 220090
— Orchid Hotel, Polo Road. PH 224 933
— Orchid Lake Resort, Umiam, Barapani. PH 73258
— Orchid Lodge, Tura. PH 22568
— Hotel Centre Point, Police Bazar. PH 225 210 / 220 480
— Pegasus Crown, Police Bazar. PH 220 667 / 220 669
— Hotel Magnum, Police Bazar. PH 227 797/8

CONDUCTED TOURS

The Meghalaya Tourism Development Corporation operates following conducted tours :

Local Sight Seeing : Elephant Falls, Shillong Peak, Don Bosco, Lady Hydari Park,Wards Lake, Golf Links and Orchid Lake Resort.

Cherreapunjee : Mawsmai Falls and Caves, Cherra bazar, Noh kali Kai Falls, Ram Krishna Mission and Thangkharang Park.

For further information contact :

— Directorate of Tourism, Government Of Meghalaya, MTC Building, Shillong. PH 226 054

Or Meghalaya Tourism Corporation, Orchid Horel, Polo Ground, Shillong. PH 224 933

PLACES OF INTEREST IN AND AROUND SHILLONG

WARD'S LAKE : In the heart of Shillong it is a 100 years old man made lake where boating facilities are available.

LADY HYDARI PARK : A colourful park with nurseries and horticultural wealth.Crinoline waterfalls are situated close to the park. This place also has the Shillong's only swimming pool.

FIVE WATERFALLS : Sweet, Beadon, Bishop, Elephant and Crinoline falls, each with a character of their own.

STATE AND TRIBAL MUSEUM : It Brings to life the art and culture of the tribes of the Meghalaya.

SAINT PAUL'S CATHEDRAL : One of the region's oldest places of Christian worship.

18 HOLE GOLF COURSE : Lush green golf course set amidst beautifully landscaped gardens, it is the second largest in Asia. It is termed as 'Gleneagle of the East' at the United State Golf Association Library.

BOTANICAL GARDENS : A secluded but captivating spot with a plethora of indigenous and exotic plants is located below the Ward's Lake.

SHILLONG PEAK : (10km) An ideal picnic park, situated at 1965 metres above sea level, offers a panoramic view of the scenic countryside and is also the highest point in the state.

UMIAM LAKE : (17km) A water sport complex with facilities of sailing, water skiing and to bogganing (i.e. moving down swiftly on a light sledlike vehicle. Adjacent to it lies Lum Nehru Park, an ideal picnic spot.

SOHPETBNENG PEAK : (20km) Situated at 1343 metres above

sea level this place is regarded as sacred by the Hynniewtrep people and is set amidst a beautiful scenic view against the backdrop of a sacred forest.

This 'Navel of Heaven' as per Khasi mythology is a heavenly peak which offers to fill the spiritual void and emptiness of those seeking solace and peace of mind.

MAWSYNRAM : (55 km) Recently it has recorded as receiving the highest rainfall in the world even more than Cherrapunjee. A picturesque cave with a giant stalagmite in a shape of a Shivalinga, called locally as 'Mawjymbuin' makes this place a Hindu pilgrim centre.

THADLASKEIN LAKE : (56 km) According to legend it was dug with the ends of bows by members of 290 clans under U Sajiar Niangli, a rebel general of a Jantia Raja, to commemorate the great exodus of the clans, now mainly settled in the Ri Bhoi and West Khasi Hills districts. Today, it is a beautiful spot for outing, boating and picnickers. Meghalaya Tourism has a Tourist Bungalow here and the reservations for the same can be made at Shillong itself.

CHERRAPUNJEE : (56 km) Situated in one of the heaviest rain-belts in the world, this town with roaring waterfalls is also famous for its limestone cave and orange honey.

Centre of Khasi culture and literature, it also has the oldest Presbyterian church and an establishment of the Ramakrishna Mission.

JAKREM : (64 km) A popular health resort with hot sulphur springs which are supposed to have medicated virtues.

JOWAI : (64 km) Headquarters of the Jaintia Hills district and the biggest town nearest to Shillong it is circled by the majestic Myntdu river. The circuit house can be booked through Deputy Commissioner, Jowai. It is connected by an excellent, all weather road, the Shillong-Silchar highway. State Transport, and private buses and taxis are easily available.

DAWKI : (96 km) An excellent picnic spot with silver streams and deep waters. Eight kilometres from Dawki one can visit the ruins of the royal bath of the Jaintiapur Kings. A further 2 kms. away is the Syndai cave. It is a border town which gives a glimpse of Bangladesh. The colourful annual boat race during spring at the Umgot river is an added attraction.

RANIKOR : (140 km) Popular spot for angling with an abundance of carp and other fresh water fish.

MAIRANG : (40 km) Capital of Nongkhlaw State. Home of the legendary Tirot Sing Sylem (Raja of Nongkhlaw), who spearheaded a war against the British invaders to defend the territorial integrity and cultural identity of the Hynniewrtrep people. He raised the battle-cry on April 4, 1829, but was finally captured and died in capativity in Dhaka on July 17, 1835.

GARO HILLS

Homeland of the Garos, who originally inhabited Torua, a province in Tibet. Garo hills is known for its abundance of wildlife. Two mountain ranges—the Arabella range and the Tura range—pass through the Garo hills forming the great Balpakram Valley in between. The headquarters town of Tura is 323 km via Guwahati at an altitude of 657 metres. The highest point is Nokrek Peak with elevation of 1,412 metres.

Tura has a picturesque landscape of hills against a backdrop of low-lying plains with the mighty Brahmputra river making sweeping curves as it flows towards Bangladesh. A sunset view can be best seen from Tura Peak at 1,400 metre and its summit can be reached by a five kilometres trek.

PLACES TO VISIT IN AND AROUND TURA

BALPAKRAM : A Natioanl Wildlife Park, it is about 167 km from Tura and is known as the abode of perpetual winds. It is believed that here, the spirits of the dead dwell temporarily before embarking on the final journey.

RONGRENGIRI : Located 79 km from Tura it is a historic place where the Garos fought their final battle against the British.

NAPHAK LAKE : Located 112 km from Tura it ideal for fishing and bird watching with the Simsang river flowing nearby.

SIJU CAVES : The famous limestone caves of Siju are located near Naphak Lake and the Simsang Game Preserve. The formation of stalagmites and stalactites in these caves resemble those of the blue Grotto in Isle of Capri.

WILLIAMNAGAR : (308 km) Headquarters of the east Garo Hills District it is situated on the banks of the Simsang river.

JAINTIA HILLS

Jowai, headquarters of the Jaintia hills district is situated 64 km away from Shillong along the Shillong-Silchar national highway. A picturesque town circled by the majestic Mybtdu river.

PLACES OF INTEREST IN AND AROUND JOWAI

NARTIANG : (65km from Shillong) It was the summer capital of the Jaintia kings of Sutanga State. Huge monoliths form the striking landmark of the village said to be erected by U Mar Phalyngki, known as the Goliath of the Jaintia hills. The Nartiang Menhir measures 27 feet in height above the ground, 6 feet in breadth and 2 feet 6 inches in thickness. The monoliths represent the megalithic culture of the Hynniewtrep people. Nartiang also has a 550 years old Durga temple where there is an evidence human sacrifice once being offered regularly. Nartiang's other attraction is to be found off the small road that runs amid forest, streams and hills in a quiet and shaded glean.

SYNDAL : This village is noted with a number of caves and caverns, used as hide-outs during war times between Jaintia kings and foreign intruders.

NONGKHYLLEM SANCTUARY : Established in 1981, this sanctuary has a good range of species including Binturong, Clouded Leopard, Golden Cat and Leopard Cat.

FESTIVALS

Ka Pamblang Nongkrem popularly known as Nongkrem dance is one of the most important festivals of the Khasis. It is a five-day religious festival held annually at Smit village, 11 km from Shillong, the headquarters of 'syiem' (chief) of Khyrim. The festival is held as a thanks-giving ceremony to God Almighty for the harvest and to pray for peace and prosperity. Shad Sukmynsiem is another important festival of the Khasis.

It means 'Dance of the Joyful Heart' and is also a thanks-giving dance. Maidens dressed in traditional fineries and men folk in colourful costumes participate in the dance to the accompaniment of drums and flute. It is held in Shillong sometime during the second week of April every year and lasts for three days.

Behdiengkhlam, the most important festival of the Jaintias, is celebrated annually at Jowai in Jaintia hills during the month of July. **Wangala,** one of the most important festivals of the Garos, is held during October-November and lasts for a week. This festival is observed to honour and offer sacrifices to their greatest God called Saljong (Sungod). The occasion is initiated, right in the field by a simple but impressive ceremony known as Rugula. After that the ceremony of incense burning known as Sasta Soa is celebrated. This is performed inside the house of the chief of the village. On this occasion people, young and old, boys and girls in their colourful costumes with feathered headgear dance to the tunes of music played on long oval shaped drums.

MIZORAM

MIZORAM
AT A GLANCE

AREA : 21, 081 sq. km

CAPITAL : Aizwal

BOUNDARIES : East and South - Mynamar; West - Bangladesh; North West - Tripura.

LANGUAGES : Mizo and English.

ROADS : Total road length in the state is 4,787 km. National highway no. 54 links Tripura to the southern most districts of Mizoram to Silchar town in Assam on the border of Mizoram.

AIRPORT : Dimapur

The word AMIZO 'means highlander'. Mizoram's traditional rulers were the famous sailors who ruled as chiefs having rights over land and life. As rulers of an agricultural economy each chief had in his court an agricultural expert who was well acquainted with the secrets of the forests.

The Mizos are a very musical people who consider singing the best form of relaxation after a hard day's work. Traditional Mizo society nurtured itself on a unique code of behaviour based on a philosophy called 'Tlawmngaihna' or selflessness. Traits of this can still be seen today.

HISTORY

Mizoram is a mountainous region which became the 23rd State of the Indian Union in February 1987. It was one of the districts of Assam till 1972 when it became Union Territory. After being annexed by the British in 1891, for the first few years Lushai Hills in the north remained under Assam while the southern half remained under Bengal. Both these parts were amalgamated in 1898 into one district called Lushai Hills District under the Chief Commissioner of Assam. With the implementation of the North Eastern Reorganisation Act in 1972, Mizoram became Union Territory and as a sequel to the signing of the historic memorandum of settlement between the Government of India and Mizo National Front in 1986 it was granted statehood on February 20, 1987.

The origin of the Mizo is not known. The Mizos came under the influence of the British missionaries in 19th century and now most of them are Christians. Mizo language has no script of its own. The missionaries introduced the Roman script for Mizo language and formal education.

AIZWAL

Aizwal stands out like a citadel over the valleys of Mizoram. The valleys like the north-east are hot and wet during the summer but up in the hills it is pleasant and cool. To the south of Aizwal is the idyllic town of Lungki set in a beautiful forested area. In between Aizwal and Lungki is the Serchhip village. Travellers stop here to enjoy the market place where traditional objects, fruits and local vegetables are sold.

HOW TO REACH

AIR : Aizwal is connected by air with Calcutta and Guwahati.

RAIL : Nearest railhead-Silchar 180 km.

ROAD : The bus journey from Silchar to Aizwal usually takes about six hours. The Mizoram State Transport buses ply between Aizwal and Silchar daily. The Mizoram State transport besides running passenger services on 33 routes including two-inter State services to Silchar in Assam and Shillong also provides goods carriages on hire therefore and also functions as Railway Out Agency for Silchar railway station in Cachar district of Assam.

Apart from the State-run MST, a number of private firms-Capital Travels, Blue Hills Travels operate daily deluxe services between Aizwal and Guwahati via different routes.

HOTEL ACCOMMODATION (STD CODE 0389)

Mizoram and Aizwal offers very comfortable and affordable accommodation for all types of tourists. The State Tourist Department has many beautifully constructed tourist lodges which offer lodging and boarding at nominal rates.

For booking contact
— Joint Director of Tourism, Aizwal 796001, Mizoram
  PH 0389 21226/ 27/28
— Tourist Lodge, Chaltlang. PH 0389 20206 / 21083
— Tourist Home, Luangmual. PH 0389 32263
— State Guest House. PH 0389 20131 / 32

— Ritz Hotel, Bara Bazar, near 1st A.R.Ground
  PH 0389 23358/26247
— Ahimsa Hotel, Zarkwat. PH 0389 20914
— Hotel Sangchia, Zarkawat. PH 0389 20914
— Chawlhna Hotel, Zakawat. PH 0389 20108

PLACES OF INTEREST IN AND AROUND AIZWAL

MIZORAM STATE MUSEUM : Houses a rare and exquisite collection of artefacts of the State.

BARA BAZAR : Main shopping area where a variety of goods ranging from handicrafts to utility items can be found.

DINGDI ART GALLERY : It has a large collection of artistic masterpieces of Mizoram.

DURLANG HILLS : The northernmost part of Aizwal

BUNG : (15 km) A beautiful hilltop picnic spot towards the airfield.

PAIKHI : (16 km) Quiet and enchanting picnic and recreational spot.

TAMDIL : (85 km) A natural lake near Saitual village is in the midst of cool virgin forest that offers an ideal picnic spot for tourists. It has boating facilities for the tourists and accommodation is available at the Tourist Lodge Saitual—only 7 km away.

DUMOOR LAKE : (110 km) Deep green island dot for the panorama of transparent waters. Feel the thrill of motorboat or float aimlessly in a country boat.

BHUBANESHWARI TEMPLE : (110 km) The temple has been immortalised by Rabindranath Tagore's famous play Visarjan and Rajarshi. Built by Maharaja Govinda Manikya, the temple is situated on the right bank of the Gunti river at Udaipur.

VANTAWNG : (137 km) Largest and highest waterfall of Mizoram. The fall is 750 ft. high surrounded by a lush green tropical forest filled with bamboo groves.

UNAKOTI : (180 km) Along a serpentine carpeted road Unakoti Tirtha is a holy place for pilgrims. Magnificent rock figures and stone images dating to 12th century are found here. There is also an image of Lord Shiva holding a conch in the left hand, a position seldom found elsewhere. It is the largest bas relief sculpture in India.

CHAMPHAI : (204km) A sub - divisional headquarter town on the Burma border, it offers a cool climate and a stunning view of hills of Burma. Accommodation is available at Tourist Lodge and holiday home. PH 03881 2015.

LUNGLEI : (235km) A district headquarters town of south Mizoram, has great natural beauty, cool pleasant climate and peaceful atmosphere make Lunglei, a beautiful hill station of the south. Accommodation is available at tourist lodge, Zotlang, Lunglei. PH 0372 21365.

DAMPA SANCTUARY : Established in 1976 at the north - west tip of the sanctuary it is covered with bamboos, while the rest is mostly semi-evergreen forest. Swamp deer inhabit the lower areas. Tiger, Leopard, elephant and hoolock gibbon are among the mammal species seen here. Nearest town Phaileng :10 km.

Accommodation is available in Government rest house.

FESTIVALS

Mizos are basically agriculturists practising what is known as "Jhum cultivation'. All their activities revolve around this cultivation and their festivals are also connected with such agricultural operations. Among many festivals, Chapchar Kut or Spring festival is the most popular festival, celebrated after completion of their most arduous task of jungle clearing for 'Jhum' operations. On this day, people of all ages, young and old, men and women, dressed in their respective colourful costumes and head-gears, assemble and perform various folkdances, sing traditional songs accompanied by the beating sound of drums, gongs and cymbals.

NAGALAND

NAGALAND
AT A GLANCE

AREA : 16, 579 sq. km
CAPITAL : Kohima
BOUNDARIES : East - Mynamar; West North and North west - Assam.
LANGUAGES : Naga, Assamese, Konyak Lotha.
ROADS : Road network consists of national, State and district roads with total length of 9,351 km.
AIRPORT : Dimapur

Nagaland is a land of fascinating folklore, with 16 tribes and sub-tribes who have their own languages and dialects. They are said

to belong to the Indo - Mongoloid stock, a race whose presence was first noted 10 centuries before Christ. Sanskrit literature describes them as Kiratas or hillmen living on nature's gifts, warlike and having formidable weapons. The ceremonial dress of each tribe is quite fascinating, and people are fond of seasonal songs, solo, duet and choric. Each tribe is proud of the distinguishing colours and patterns woven in their shawls. It is only in Nagaland that one can see the multicoloured spears, ceremonial daos, bracelets, chest plates and head dress of coloured bamboos. The First building at the entrance of a typical Naga village is known as Morung or boy's dormitory. It is also used for storing the weapons and displaying trophies and prizes of war. The villages are generally situated on the hill tops and ridges protected by stone walls. The Nagas are wonderful musicians, singers and dancers, with a great sense of rhythm which dominates traditional and contemporary music.

HISTORY

Like other inhabitants of the north eastern region, the Nagas too have their share of legend and folklore regarding their origin and evolution through the ages. Nagas are basically tribal people and every tribe had its own effective system of self governance since times immemorial. In the 12th and 13th centuries gradual contact with the Ahomas of present-day Assam was established but this did not have any significant impact on the traditional Naga way of life

However, in the 19th century the British appeared on the scene and ultimately the area was brought under British administration.

After Independence this territory was made a centrally administered area in 1957 controlled by the Governor of Assam. It was known as the Naga hills Tuensang area. This failed to quell popular aspirations and unrest began. Hence in 1961 this was renamed and given the status of State of the Indian Union which was formally inaugurated on December 1, 1963.

KOHIMA

The State capital, Kohima is less than three hours drive from Dimapur. It is a hill station situated at an altitude of 1,495 m. above sea level, known the world over for halting the Japanese tide during the second World War.

HOW TO REACH

AIR : Dimapur is the only airport connected with Delhi and Calcutta.

RAIL : Dimapur is on the main line of the North-Eastern Frontier Railway.

ROAD : Buses of the Nagaland State Transport ply regularly from Dimapur to Guwahati and Shillong.

PLACES OF INTEREST IN AND AROUND KOHIMA

WAR CEMETRY : A symbolic memorial raised as citation for the supreme sacrifices made by the officers and men during the Second World War. A bronze plaque with a suitable epitaph that makes one reflect on the freedom that we take for grated supports each grave.

MUSEUM : The State treasure trove having a rare collection of articles which depicts the tradition and history of the Naga tribes. The basement of the museum has birds and animals of North-Eastern hill States.

CATHOLIC CATHEDRAL : The Catholic Cathedral at Aradura hill is an important landmark in Kohima for it is one of the biggest cathedral in the whole North-East and houses the biggest cross in India made of wood.

ZOOLOGICAL PARK : (15 km) Situated at an altitude of 3,043 meters above sea level it is a famous spot for scaling and trekking.

KHANOMA : (20 km) A village having its unique story of courage and valour reflected in its surroundings. The terraced fields which produce 20 types of paddy at different elevations, present a beautiful view. The Khanoma gate relates the story of the British infiltration into Naga Hills.

DZUKOU VALLEY : (30 km) One of the best trekking spots in the north-east region is situated at an altitude of 2,438.4 metres above sea level, behind Japfu peak. The entire valley is over-shadowed with a type of tough bamboo brush which makes the place appear like a mowed lawn. White and Yellow lilies and numerous other flowers adorn the valley in summers while rhododendrons ornament the hills surrounding the valley.

DIMAPUR : (74 km) Situated at an altitude of 195 meters above sea level, it is the gateway to Nagaland and the commercial centre of the State. Dimapur is the only airport in Nagaland. Dimapur is well-connected with the neighbouring States by National Highway 39.

WOKHA : (80 km) The sitting place for colourful shawls for men and women.

MOKOKCHUNG : (160 km) A cultural centre of the Ao Nagas and beautiful town at 1,325 meters above sea level.

ZUNHEBOTO : (150 km) The home of the Semas, a martial tribe with sensational ceremonial war dresses.

JAPFU PEAK : (15 km) A perfect spot for scaling and trekking. An altitude of 3,043 metres above sea level, the peak offers an excellent view of Kohima town and distant, snow-clad Himalayan peaks.

FAKIM SANCTUARY : This small sanctuary in the eastern hills close to the Burma border was established in 1983. The park rises almost 300 meters and receives heavy rainfall in June-July. Tiger and hoolock gibbo are among the animals seen here. Along the bird life, the tragopan pheasant is a delight to sight. Nearest town - Kiphire 98 km.

ITANAGAR : Two kilometers from Kohima lies Itanagar sanctuary with elephant population of above 250 in numbers.

PULIEBADZE SANCTUARY : Established in 1979, on a small area of forest about 9 sq. km on the edge of Kohima tragopan and kaleej pheasant are among the many fascinating hill and forest birds seen here.

TRIPURA

TRIPURA
AT A GLANCE

AREA : 10,486 sq. km.

CAPITAL : Agartala

BOUNDARIES : East - Assam and Mezereum; West, North and South - Bangladesh.

LANGUAGES : Bengali, Manipuri and Tripuri.

ROADS : Roads in Tripura are categorised as National Highway 334 km, major district roads 545 km, other district roads 1,519 km and village roads 3,642 km.

AIRPORT : Agartala.

Tripura, second smallest State of India, with its forests and lakes represents a delicate fusion of the styles and culture of the hills and plains. Its rich and varied culture, its handlooms and handicrafts which are exquisite in colour and excellent in design and craftsmanship, are a temptation to the visitor.

Tripura is inhabited by various ethnic groups with the cultural heritage of one community differing from another yet they have mingled into a single whole giving birth to a unique cultural genre.

HISTORY

History of Tripura dates back to the Mahabharata, the Puranas and pillar inscriptions of Emperor Ashoka. There are no historical records available of Tripura except Rajmala which is the chronicle of the kings of the riling family of Tripura. According to it, rulers were known by the surname "Fa, meaning father".

There is a reference of rulers of Bengal helping the Tripura kings in the 14th century. Kings of Tripura had to face frequent Mughal invasions with varying successes. They defeated the sultans of Bengal in several battles.

The nineteenth century marked the beginning of the modern era in Tripura when King Maharaja Birchandra Kishore Manikya Bahadur modelled his administrative set-up on the British India pattern and introduced several reforms. His successors ruled over Tripura till October 19, 1949 when it was annexed to Indian Union.

After Independence it became a part 'C' State and with the re-organisation of States in 1956 it became a centrally administered territory. In 1972, this territory attained the status of a full-fledged State along with Manipur and Meghalaya.

AGARTALA

The capital is surrounded by hills on three sides. The present site of Agartala was chosen by Maharaja Krishna Kishore Manikya Bahadur who shifted the capital from old Agartala.

HOW TO REACH

AIR : Agartala is connected by regular flights with Delhi, Calcutta and Guwahati.

RAIL : Agartala is connected by N.F.Railway via Guwahati. The nearest railhead is Kumarghat 140 km from Agartala.

ROAD : The State capital is also connected with Dhaka, capital of Bangladesh, by road.

A wide net work of bus services link Agartala with several destinations. Unmetered taxis, auto rikshwas and city bus services are available from Agartala Airport.

HOTEL ACCOMMODATION (STD CODE 0381)

- Hotel Rajdhani, PH 22 3837 / 6312;
- Hotel Radha International
  PH 22 4530 / 2615
- Royal Guest House. PH 22 5652 / 5539
- Hotel Haven. PH 22 5737/3159
- Hotel Amber. PH 22 3587
- Tripura Guest House. PH 22 7994

- Deep Guest House. PH 22 7482
- Hotel Minakshi. PH 22 3430 / 5810

CONDUCTED TOURS

One Day Tours :
- Agartala-Sepahijala-Matabari-Bhuvanesweri Temple-Agartala
- Agartala-Sepahijala-Neermahal-Agartala
- Agartala-Matabari-Neermahal-Agartala
- Agartala-Kamalsagar-Sepahijala-Agartala
- Agartala-Kamalsagar-Neermahal-Agartala
- Udaipur-Neermahal-Sepahijala-Udaipur
- Udaipur-Kamalasagar-Agartala-Udaipur

1 Night and 2 Days
- Agartala-Sepahijala-Matabari-Neermahal-Kamalasagr-Agartala

2 Nights and 3 Days
- Agartala-Jampuri-Agartala
- Agartala-Unakoti-Jampui-Agartala

PACKAGE TOURS

3 Nights and 4 Days
- From Calcutta : Calcutta - Agartala-Neermahal-Udaipur-Sepahijala-Arkaneer-Kamalsagar-Agartala-Calcutta

5 Nights and 6 Days
- From Calcutta : Calcutta -Agartala-Kumarghat-Jampui-Unakoti-Agartala-Calcutta

6 Nights and 7 Days
- From Calcutta : Calcutta-Agartala-Jampui Hills-Unakoti-Agartala-Calcutta (Nov/Dec)

7 Nights and 8 Days
- From Culcutta : Calcutta-Agartala-Neermahal-Udaipur-Sepahijala-Arkaneer-kamalasagar-Agartala-Jampui Hills-Unakoti-Agartala-Calcutta

For Detailed Information Contact :
- Department of Information, Cultural Affairs and Tourism, Swet Mahal, Palace Compound, Agartala 799 001, PH 0381 22 5930; FAX 0381 224 688 and Tourist Information Offices at :
- Calcutta; Tourist Information centre, Tripura Bhawan, 1 Pretoria Street, Calcutta 700071
  PH 033 242 5703; FAX 033 242 6842
- Delhi; Tripura Bhawan, Chanakyapuri, Kautilya Marg, New Delhi 110 001. PH 011 301 4607; FAX 011 379 3827
- Guwahati; Tripura Bhawan, G.S.Road, Ulubari, Guwahati 781007. PH 036 528 761

PLACES OF INTEREST IN AND AROUND AGARTALA

TEMPLE OF LORD JAGANNATHA : This orange coloured temple rises from an octagonal base. Every pillar of the octagon is crowned by a square pyramidal cone. Built in the 19th century it is dedicated to the Lord of Universe.

UJJAYANATA PALACE : At the heart of the town stands the royal palace which was built by the philanthropist Maharaja Bikram Singh in 1901. A fine example of Indo - Saracenic architecture, this white sprawling palace with its colite structure is surrounded by lush Mughal Gardens. The carved Chinese Room, tiled floors and doors are strikingly magnificent.

KAMLA SAGAR : KALI TEMPLE : (27 km) The temple of Goddess Kali is atop a hillock. A big lake was excavated by Maharaja Dhanya Manikya in the late 15th century in front of the temple enhancing its beauty. It is situated just besides the Bangladesh Border.

BRAHMAKUNDA : (48 km) It is famous for its colourful fair held every year in April and November. The tea gardens on the way are a major tourist attractions.

NEERMAHAL : (53 km) The Palace built in 1930 by Maharaja Bir Bikram Kishore Manikya as summer resort is an combination of assimilation between Hindu and Muslim architecture and is a spectacular edifice in the centre of the Rudrasagar Lake. Well-laid gardens and flood lighting add colour to its beauty.

TRIPURA SUNDARI TEMPLE : (57 km) Situated on a hill-top at Udaipur it was built by the former Maharaja, Dhanya Manikya in 1501 AD. The temple is one of the '51 Pithas' recorded in the Hindu Puranas. It consists of a square type sanctum of the typical Bengali hut type. The lake in front of the temple adds to its beauty. During Diwali people from different communities assemble here.

DEOTAMURA : (70 km) Famous for its panels of rock carvings on the steep mountain walls on the back of the Gomati river. It dates back to 15th and 16th centuries.

CHABIMURA PILAK : (100 km) Its main attraction is its archaeological remains of the 8th and 9th centuries. Number of terracotta plaques, sealing with stupa and stone images of Avolokitesvara including the image of Narasimhan have been found there which date backs to Buddhist period.

DUMOOR LAKE : (110 km) Deep green 48 islands in the midst of the lake dot the panorama of transparent waters.Migratory birds, water sport facilities including boating facilities and variety of wildlife is an additional attraction.

BHUBANESHWARI TEMPLE : (110 km) The temple has been immortalized by Rabindranath Tagore's famous play Visarjan and Rajarshi. Built by Maharaja Govinda Manikya, the temple is situated on the right bank of the river Gumti at Udaipur.

UNAKOTI : (180 km) Along a serpentine carpeted road is Unakoti Tirtha—a holy place for thousands of pilgrims. The Unakoti means one less than a crore i.e. 99,99,999. Magnificent rock figures and stone images of 12th century are found here. There is also an image of Lord Shiva, holding a conch in the left hand, a position seldom found elsewhere. It is the largest Bas relief sculpture in India.

JAMPUI HILLS : (250 km) Situated at an altitude of 3000 feet above sea level, it is famous for scenic beauty and is an orange and orchid growing area.

SEPAHIJALA WILDLIFE SANCTUARY : About 30 km away fromAgartala the sanctuary covers an area of 18.53 sq. km and has a rich collection of wildlife, particularly birds and primates. Zoo, botanical garden, lake elephant joy ride and the scenic beauty including rubber and coffee plantation attracts the visitors.

FESTIVALS

Kharchi Puja : The fourteen Gods are worshiped every year in the month of July for seven days which is popularly known as Kharchi Puja. Large number of pilgrims, both tribal and non-tribal from different parts assemble there to pray.

Garia Puja : The tribals of Tripura perform Garia Puja for seven days and on the seventh day of the month of Baisakhi when they dance in movement.

Dewali Festival : This festival is observed at Tripura Sundari temple in Udaipur. A big colourful fair followed by cultural programme is held during the festival.

Pous Sankranti Mela : This mela at Tirthamukh attracts devotees even from the neighbouring States. Thousand of people, tribal and non-tribal assemble every year on the occasion of Uttarayana Sankranti (On 14th January) at this place to take a holi dip in the Gomati river at Tirtha Mukh.

Ashokastami Festival : An important festival of the State followed by a big fair popularly known as 'Ashokastami Fair' is held at Unakoti Tirtha at Kailashahar Sub-Division every year in March-April.

Orange and Tourism Festival : Orange and Tourism festival is organised every year in Jampui hill in November during the orage season. Jampui is the only hill station in Tripura where large number of oranges are grown.

Boat Race : Colourful boat race is organised by the Information, Cultural Affairs and Tourism Department every year at Rudrasagar Lake.

ORISSA

ORISSA
AT A GLANCE

AREA : 1,55,707 Sq. km

CAPITAL : Bhubaneshwar

BOUNDARIES : East : Bay Of Bengal; West - Madhya Pradesh; North - Bihar; North - East - West Bengal; South - Andhra Pradesh.

LANGUAGE : Oriya

ROADS : The length of different categories of roads : 1,625 km National Highway; 67 km Express Highways, 4,360 km State Highways, 14,160 km village roads, 20,426 km panchayat samiti roads, 1,39,968 km grampanchayat roads, 7,030 km forest road and 10,280 km municipal roads.

AIRPORT : Bhubaneshwar is connected by air with Delhi, Calcutta, Chennai and Hyderabad. There are 17 air strips and 17 helipads at different places in the State.

MUSEUMS

Bhubaneshwar : Orissa State Museum.
Konarak : Archaeological Museum.

PILGRIM CENTRES (A : Air; R : Rail)

Atri : Hatakeswar temple and curative springs.
A - Bhubaneshwar 42 km, R -Khurda Rd 22 km.
Aradi : Akhandalmani Temple on the banks of the Vaitarani river.
A - Buhbaneshwar 210 km, R - Bhadrak - 52 km.
Banki : Charchika Chamundi Temple with Tantrik rites.
A and R - Bhubaneshwar 64 km.
Banpur : Ancient temple of Goddess Bhagavati.
A - Bhubaneshwar 105 km, R- Balugaon 8 km.
Bhubaneshwar : Temple of Goddess Bhagavati.
A and R - Bhubaneshwar.
Chhatia : Chhatiabata, temple of Jagannath.
A - Bhubaneshwar 59 km, R - Cuttak 30 km.
Cuttak : Sacred Muslim shrine of Quadam-i-Rasool.
A - Bhubaneshwar 29 km, R - Cuttak.
Dhauli : Buddhist Peace Pagoda on the site of the Kalinga War.
A and R - Bhubaneshwar 8 km.
Dhavaleswar : Shiva temple on an island in the Mahanadi river.
A - Bhubaneshwar 66 km, R - Cuttak 37 km.
Ghatagaon : Shrine of Goddess Tarini.
A - Bhubaneshwar 185 km, R - Jaipur-Keonjhar Rd 64 km.
Gupteswar : Known as Gupta Kedar, it has a cave shrine of Lord Shiva.
A - Visahkapatnam 220 km from Jeypore, R - Jeypore 58 km.
Harisankar : Temple of Hari and Sankar.
A - Bhubaneshwar 408 km, R- Harisankar Road - 43 km.
Jaipur : Vaitarani Tirtha and shrine of Goddess Viraja (Durga).
A-Bhubaneshwar 121 km, R-Cuttak 92 km.
Joranda : Samadhi of Mahima Gosain, founder of Mahima cult.
A - Bhubaneshwar 123 km, R - Dhenkanal -- 24 km.
Kakatpur : Temple of Goddess mangala.
A and R - Bhubaneshwar 61 km.
Kalijai : Temple of Kalijai (Shakti) on an island in Chilka Lake.
A - Bhubaneshwar 108 km, R - Balugaon 12 km.
Kantilo : Nilamadhab Temple on the banks of the Mahanadi river.
A - Bhubaneshwar 100 km, R - Khurda 70 km.

Kapilas : Temple of Dhenkanal Shiva.
  A – Bhubaneshwar 125 km, R – Dhenkanal –26 km.
Kendrapara : Tulasi Kshetra, A – Bhubaneshwar 94 km.
  R – Cuttak 65 km.
Khiching : Temple of Goddess Kichakeswari.
  A – Bhubaneshwar 65 km, R – Bangiriposi 110 km.
Konarak : Sun-Temple, A – Bhubaneshwar 65 km.
  R – Puri 35 km.
Puri : One of the four 'Dhams' has the temple of Lord Jagannath
famed for the annual Rath Yatra.
  A – Bhubaneshwar 62 km, R – Puri.
Remuna : Kirachora Gopinath Temple, centre of Vaishnav culture.
  A – Bhubaneshwar – 223 km, R – Balasore 9 km.
Sakshigopal : Temple of Sri Krishna.
  A – Bhubaneshwar 42 km, R – Puri 19 km.
Sambalpur : Temple of Goddess Samaleswari.
  A - Bhubaneshwar 321 km, R – Sambalpur.

One of India's best cultural centres Orissa presents a vibrant open
air museum where the lingering mists of its ancient past mingle easily
with the sunlight of its dynamic present. Today, Orissa's cultural
heritage emerges as an almost sublime synthesis of harmony and
stimulating creativity.The very stone speak of its unique history, its
waterways spin yarns of its maritime acivities with far-off lands, its
magnificent old temples and shrines reverberate with the spiritual
energy that permeates the very fabric of everyday life amongst her
people.

HISTORY

Orissa, the land of Oriyas, was known as Kalinga in ancient days.
In 286 BC Ashoka, the Mauryan Emperor, had sent a powerful army
to conquer Kalinga which offered stubborn resistance. Kalinga was
subdued but the carnage which followed struck Ashoka with remorse.
After the death of Ashoka, Kalinga regained its independence. In the
2nd century BC it became a powerful country under Kharavela. With
the death of Kharavela, Orissa passed into obscurity. In the 4th century
AD Samudragupta invaded Orissa and overcame the resistance offered
by five of its kings. Later Orissa came under the sway of King
Sasanka. After Sasanka's death, Harsha Vardhan, King of Ujjain,
conquered Orissa.

The period from 7th to 13th century AD was the most creative one for Orissa when it became the hub of state craft, commerce, art and architecture and development of important pilgrim centres under royal patronage. The Chienese scholar Huen Tsang had visited Orissa in 638 AD and reported the existence of hundreds of monastries. Some ruins can be seen at Lalitgiri temples even today.

Orissa had its own independent dynasty of rulers (Ganga dynasty) in the seventh century AD. In 795 AD Mahasivagupta Yagati II ascended the throne and with him began the most brilliant epoch in the history of Orissa. He united Kalinga, Kangda, Utkal and Koshala in the imperial tradition of Kharavela. Under kings of the Ganga dynasty, Orissa continued to flourish. Narashingha Dev of this dynasty is reputed to have built the unique Sun temple of Konarak. From 14th century Orissa was ruled successively by five Muslim kings till 1572 when Akbar annexed it into Mughal empire. After the decline of the Mughal empire the Marathas occupied Orissa. They continued to hold it till the British took over in 1803.

BHUBANESHWAR

Bhubaneshwar stands in a region which harbours a rich historical and cultural heritage. Many civilisations flourished on this rich soil, tangible remains of some are still visible in and around the city. A temple city, it literally means 'The abode of the terrestrial lord'. The history stretches at least 2,200 years in the past. On Dhauli hill, in the 3rd century BC, a bloody battle was fought to subdue the defiant and prosperous kingdom of Kalinga which made Emperor Ashoka forsake arms for ever and choose the path of peace and amity - the path of the Buddha. It is believed that at one time, the city boasted 7000 temples of which only 500 remain today.

PLACES OF INTEREST

LINGARAJA TEMPLE : (11th C.) This is the largest conglomerate of shrines with nearly 180 spires, depicting the culmination of the Orissan style of architecture. The temple is 147 feet high and was built by Lalatendu Keshari of Somavamsi dynasty in 617-657 AD. The Natamandap and Bhogamandap, were later added to the temple over different historical periods. The spire of the temple is devoted to.Lord Shiva. Entry to non-Hindus is limited to a viewing gallery.

PARSURAMESWARA TEMPLE : (7th C.) Built in 650 AD it is the city's oldest surviving temple. Dedicated to Lord Shiva it has some of the best sculptural examples of Orissan craftsmen, depicted in friezes, lattice windows and busts of Shiva. There are images of Lord Vishnu, Yama, Surya and seven Mother Goddesses in the temple.

MUKTESHWARA TEMPLE (10th C.) One of the most delightful expression of the Kalinga school of architecture is the luminous beauty of the Mukteshwara temple. Often called the 'Gem of Orissan Architecture' it has some of the most ornate carvings and renditions of stories from the Panchatantra. It also shows an excellent combination of Hindu, Buddhist and Jain features. A 'Torana', an arched gateway is a unique feature of this temple. The temple is dedicated to Lord Shiva. Mukteshwara is carved with figures of ascetics in various poses of meditation. A dip in a sacred pond to the east of the temple is supposed to be a cure for infertility.

RAJARANI TEMPLE : (11th C.) This temple is an elegant example of finesse in temple architecture and is particularly interesting as it has no deity. The name of this temple is supposed to be derived from the redgold sand used – Rajarani being the local name for the stone. The sensuous beauty of the female form and the filigree sweetness of flowers and fruits are enhanced by the artist's dexterity.

VAITAL TEMPLE (8th C) An example of Khakara school of architecture, an offshoot of the Kalinga school, dedicated to the Goddess Chamunda (Kapali) it is said to have been the centre of Tantric worship. The Goddess can be seen in the murky depths of the inner sanctum, enthroned upon a corpse. It is the first of the temples to depict erotic sculptures.

BRAMESHWAR (1050 C) The temple has sculptural panels.

BHASKARESHWAR TEMPLE : The first example of the Orissan architecture dating back to perhaps the 7th century AD can be seen at Lakshaneswar and Bhakteshwar temples. This is a peculiar temple where the Shiva Linga is two–storey–high and the worship is done both on the ground floor as well as the first floor.

JAGANNATH TEMPLE : The Jagannath temple in Puri is one of the four most sacred places (Dhams) of worship for the Hindus. The reigning deity who holds the devotees in intense religious fervour is Jagannath, the Lord of the Universe, incarnation of VISHNU or SRI KRISHNA, with his sister Subhadra and brother Balabhadra. In his 12th century abode Lord Jagannath holds sway not only over Puri but the entire State. The 65 metre conical tower slashes the skies with its Vishnu Wheel and flag punctuating its glorious ascent. The exquisite pillar with its Aruna head, at the entrance, once rested at the Konark Sun temple. The lavish scale of devotion, the mammoth rituals of His rebirth, the monumental movement of His odyssey amongst His devotees – on His annual trip to the Gundicha Ghar during Rath Yatra – are symbols of the enormous importance He held and how greatly devotees are in His thrall. The Rath Yatra has, over the centuries, become synonymous with Orissa. Over 20,000 people are known to be dependent for their livelihood on the temple activities.

KHANDGIRI AND UDAYAGIRI : Huge residential blocks for the Jain monks were carved out of the rocks at Khandgiri and Udayagiri in the 1st century BC in the city of Bhubaneshwar. These caves were also an excel-  lent canvas for detailing the various achievements of king Kharvela's reign.There are about 18 rock-hewn apartments at 'Udaygiri alone with Hathi Gumpha or Elephant cave, bearing the well-known inscriptions of the King. Both the King and his queen appear to have been great patrons of the arts. In keeping with this patronage, the Queen's cave is elaborately embellished with sculptural friezes and carvings of historical scenes and dancers in a variety of poses. The Ganesha Gumpha is well worth a visit. Khandgiri has also about 15 caves.

HOW TO REACH

AIR : Bhubaneshwar is connected by air with Delhi, Calcutta, Visakhapatnam, Hyderabad and Chennai.

RAIL : Bhubaneshwar is connected by rail to Howrah, Chennai, Guwahati, Trivandrum, Hyderabad, New Delhi, Rourkela, Puri and Mumbai.

ROAD : Bhubaneshwar is connected by all with all cities weather motorable roads within the State and also the neighbouring States.

There are regular bus services to Puri, Calcuatta, Visakhapatnam etc.

ROAD DISTANCES FROM BHUBANESHWAR

Puri 56 km : Konarak 64 km; Gopalpur on Sea 184 km; Chilka 94 km; Cuttack 37 km; Sambalpur 321 km; Visakhapatnam 426 km.

HOTEL ACCOMMODATION (STD CODE 0674)

—   The Oberoi : (5 Star Deluxe) Post : R.R.L. CB- 1 Nayapalli
    PH 440890-7, FAX 440 898
—   The Kenilworth : (4 Star) 86/A, Gautam Nagar
    PH 433600/1/2//; FAX411561
—   Hotel Swosti Pvt. Ltd : (4 Star), 103 Jagannath, Unit 3
    PH 518256, 504179; FAX 507524, 518261
—   Hotel Sishmo : (4 Star) 86/A - 1 Gautam Nagar
    PH 433600-05; FAX433351
—   Hotel Keshri : (3 Star) 113,Station Square
    PH 501095, 508593; FAX 511553
—   Hotel Kalinga Ashok : (3 Star) Gautam Nagar
    PH 431055/6; FAX 432001
—   Hotel Siddharth : (3 Star) A/19, Cuttack Road
    PH 475981/2, FAX 475985
—   Safari International, PH 480550/02
—   Meghdoot, PH 405802

CONDUCTED TOURS

Tour of Bhubaneshwar, Kandgiri-Udaygiri, Dauli, Nandan Kanan and Museum – Full Day
Puri and Konarak – Full Day
Chilka Lake – Full Day
For further details contact :
—   Government of Orissa Tourist Office
—   Jayadev Marg – Bhubaneshwar, PH 431299
—   Tourist Counter at railway station
    PH 404715; at Airport PH 404006
—   Government of India Tourist Office, B-21, B.J.B. Nagar
    PH 432203

SAMPLE ITINERARY

TEMPLE, BEACHES and WILDLIFE (6 NIGHTS and 7 DAYS)
DAY 1 : Visit Bhubaneshwar temples, monuments and Nandankanan Zoo
DAY 2 : Same as above.
DAY 3 : Depart for Puri enroute visit Konarak.

DAY 4 : Excursions to Jagannath temple
DAY 5 : Visit Raghurajpur artist's village, Balighai beach
DAY 6 : Visit Satpara-on-Chikla and Brahmgiri
DAY 7 : Return to Bhubaneshwar

SCENERY, SHOPPING and WILDLIFE (6 NIGHTS and 7 DAYS)
DAY 1 : Visit temples and monuments
DAY 2 : Excursion to Cuttack and Nandankanan
DAY 3 : Drive to Sambalpur, visit weavers at Manibandhan and Nuapatna, Dhokra casting at Sadeiberini near Dhenkanal
DAY 4 : Visit textile shops in Sambalpur and weaver's village in the region
DAY 5 : Visit – Hirakund Dam. P.M. – Visit Ushakothi Wildlife Sanctuary
DAY 6 : Return to Bhubaneshwar enroute visit Bolangir – to see weavers in Sonepur area.
DAY 7 : Excursion to Pipli applique village from Bhubaneshwar

EXCURSIONS

YOGINI TEMPLES : On the outskirts of Bhubaneshwar is Hirapur village with its Hypaethral temple of sixty four Yoginis one of the two of such distinguished temples in Orissa and four in India. It has beautiful Yogini images. The second one is located at Ranipur - Jhariwal with a plethora of other temples - 104 km from Balangir.

DHAULI ROCK (8 km) The Dhauli hills, on the bank of the Daga river, stands in mute testimony to the epoch - making Kalinga war fought in the 3rd century BC. The rock cut edicts, topped by a sculpted elephant (the universal symbol of Buddhism) perpetuate the cult of gentleness, peace and justice. Further up the hill the Peace Pagoda, built by the Japan Buddha Sangha and the Kalinga Nippon Buddha Sangha, in the 70s stands as a lustrous beacon beaming out its message of peace.

Another set of edicts carved out by the same emperor at Jaugada, is still intact only 35 km from Behrampur in Ganjam district.

BALADEVAJEW TEMPLE (95 km) Known to the pilgrims as 'Tulsi Kshetra', Kendrapara houses the temple of Lord Baladeva. The rites and rituals of Lord Jagannath at puri are generally followed here.

CHILKA LAKE (110 km) A carpet of Emeralds. Chilka is India's biggest inland lake. Spread over 1,100 sq.km. stretching across the length of the three districts of Puri, Khurda and Ganjam, it joins up with the Bay of Bengal through a narrow mouth, forming an enormous lagoon of brackish water.

Due to the availability of animal and vegetables and safe nesting sites, it is the wintering home of a large number of migratory birds which come here in flocks in early November and stay till March. Innumerable birds from Siberia and other northern latitudes migrate here. Within the lake the temple of Kalijai, the presiding deity of this area is located on a tiny island. Cruise boats are provided at Barkul and Rambha by O.T.D.C.

Accommodation : Toursit lodges and rest houses are available at Barkul, Rambah, Balugaon,

GOPALPUR ON SEA (150 km) This famous beach resort is about three and half hour drive from Bhubaneshwar. This was developed during British times to create an atmosphere of complete relaxation, since it was not possible to avoid totally the Pilgrim crowd at Puri. This place still has a British atmosphere with country cottages dotting around. It is located between the sea and the beautiful backwaters and has been a seaside resort of choice of the discriminating. The nearby beach at Aryapalli is also worth visiting.

TATAPANI (60 km FROM GOPALPUR ON SEA) This place is known for its sulphur springs and has a tourist lodge ' Pantha Niwas'. The hot spring water is piped into baths of the Pantha Niwas where the tourists can have the luxury of the Roman style bath with all the curative and invigorating properties of the mineral water.

NANDAN KANAN : It is the complex of low hill lakes and woods. The sanctuaries' star attraction is the lion and white tiger Safari. The park has facilities picnicking and boating. On the way there is Ekamra Kanan, the largest centre in India. A large variety of roses is seen here.

SIMLIPAL NATIONAL PARK : (350 km) One of the earliest to be taken under Project Tiger, it is located in the forest belt of northern Orissa. Once the hunting preserve of the Maharajas of Mayurbhanj, the park is set in an expanse of fine sal forests. Twelve rivers cut across the attractive terrain and there are innumerable waterfalls. Covering an area of 2,750 sq. km has been declared in 1973 as one of the nine Tiger project reserves in India. Rich in wild life, it is home to tigers, panthers, gaur bison, antelopes, sambar, spotted mouse and more than 223 species of birds.

The nearest railhead is Jamshedpur – 140 km, accommodation is available at forest rest houses.

KONARAK

The epic in stone (13th century AD), this temple was built on the sea front with water lashing its walls but now the sea has receded and the temple is a little away from the beach. The temple stands upon its enormous 24 intricately carved wheels. The walls of this magnificent ruin have exquisite sculptures covering many aspects of life.  Scenes of love and war, trade and court transactions, hunting, catching elephants, sages teaching, childbirth, dancers and mythical figures, all vie for attention on the panels and niches of this immortal work of art. The temple conceived as a chariot hauling the Sun God, across the heavens by the might of seven splendidly carved horses caught in the mute symphony of stone, lies in partial ruins. The Natamandira, a separate enclosure, is still intact. The temple was built by King Narasimha of the Ganga dynasty in the 13th century AD. The Sun God's chariot also represents the seven days of the week and the 24 hours of the day in its concept.

This temple was once the Black Pagoda to maritime visitors to Orissa in ancient times. The temple museum of the Archaeological Survey of India has some rare collection of sculptures from the ruins of the main temple. Today the temple is protected by UNESCO as a World heritage site.

HOW TO REACH

AIR : Nearest airport : Bhubaneshwar 65 km

RAIL : Nearest railhead Bhubaneshwar

ROAD : Konarak is connected by road to Bhubaneshwar and major cities of the State. Public and tourist bus services and taxis are available.

HOTEL ACCOMMODATION (STD CODE 06758)

— Yatri Niwas of State Tourism. PH 35820
— Panthanivas. PH 35831
— Travellers Lodge of State Tourism. PH 35823
— Inspection Bungalow of P.W.D. PH 35834

LOCAL TOURIST OFFICE

— O.T.D.C., Hotel Yatri Niwas. PH 35821

EXCURSIONS

RAMACHANDI : (8 km) Temple of Goddess Ramachandi, meeting place of the Kushabhadra river with sea.

BALESHWAR : (20 km) Has shaiva shrine and sea beach.

BALAGHAI : (25 km) Has sea beach and sea Turtle Research centre.

KURUMA : (8 km) An excavated Buddhist site.

KAKATAPUR : (25 km) It has a temple with the shrine of Goddess Mangala on the Prachi river.

CHAURASI : (35 km) It has a temple of Barahi, a typical order of temple architecture.

KONARAK BEACH : Ideal site for sun bathing it is three kilometers away from the temple. One can see local fishing fleet at work.

PIPLI : On the way to Konarak, Pipli is famous for its exquisite appliqué work of Oriya culture. It is also the home of the most colourful and original awnings rooflike cover, canopies, garden and beach umbrellas, shoulder and hand bags.

PURI

Puri, the hallowed seat of the Hindu religion, is one of the four Dhams of India, home of Lord Jagannath, Subhadra and Balabhadra. Puri is also a cultural capital of the State. This ancient town has dual personality - the old town is characterised by lofty temple shrines and the new with a long chain of golden beach. Adi Shankaracharya (8ᵗʰ C.) had established one of the four 'Maths' here. Puri, famous for its golden beaches, is ideal for swimming and surfing.

PLACES OF INTEREST

JAGANNATH TEMPLE : Life in Puri revolves around the temple of Lord Jagannath.

Temple of the Lord of Universe was built in the 12ᵗʰ century during the reign of King Chodaganga Deva to commemorate the shifting of his capital from south to central Orissa. The 65 meter high temple has the richness of Kilinga style of architecture.

Comprising four chambers surrounded by a 6 metre high wall the temple has got 6,000 people in its service for serving 'Mahaprasad' to thousands of pilgrims daily. There are many other smaller shrines also. Anand Bazar, one of the biggest food market in the world, is also situated within the temples precinets.

The Gundicha Ghar, is a smaller shrine and the annual Rath Yatra comes here for a weeklong sojourn. Over 20,000 people are known to be dependent for their livelihood on the temple activities.

Among the anciant monuments still intact and in use are Indradyumna tank, temple of Sakshi Gopal and the 13ᵗʰ century Atharnala bridge.

Puri has excellent sea beach and has number of good hotels.

HOW TO REACH

AIR : Nearest airport–Bhubaneshwar

ROAD : Puri is approachable by road from Bhubaneshwar 62 kms.

All weather motorable roads connect Puri to different parts of the state and that of the neighbouring States. Regular bus services operate between Puri and Calcutta, Raipur, Ranchi, Visakhapatnam and Durgapur.

RAIL : Puri is well linked by super fast trains to Calcutta.

EXCURSIONS

RAGHURAJPUR (10km) It is the artist's village famous for its Chitra paintings. The paintings are done on specially prepared cotton cloth which is coated with a mixture of gum and chalk and polished before natural colours are applied. The Patta Chitra art is originally inspired by religious themes as these Pattas were affixed to the sheltering screen behind which Lord Jagannatha, Balabhadra and Subhadra rested.

CUTTACK

Cuttack was the capital of Orissa in the medieval times. The city lies surrounded by the Kathajuri rivers and the Mahanadi. The ancient stone embankment on the Kathajuri river, built in the 11th century by a king of the Kesari dynasty to protect the town from floods, is an engineering marvel. Kodam Rasul, a muslim shrine contains some holy relics of Prophet Mohammad. About 65 kilometres away are the RATANGIRI, LALITGIRI and UDAIGIRI caves wherein in ancient times a Buddhist centre of learning was flourished.

HOW TO REACH

AIR : Nearest airport–Bhubaneshwar 110 km.

RAIL : Cuttack is connected by rail to Agra, Calcutta, Delhi, Guwahati, Hyderabad, Gaya, Madras, Puri, Trivandrum, Varanasi, Visakhapatnam and Mumbai.

ROAD : Cuttack is conncted by road to Bhubaneshwar and major cities of the State.

LALITGIRI : Dating back to the 2nd century BC. Lalitgiri could be considered as one of the earliest Buddhist establishment in the world. A series of brick pagodas, stone porches, prayer halls and Buddhist images have surfaced at Lalitgiri recantly.

RATANGIRI : It is said that Ratangiri and Udaigiri were nucleus of Tantric Buddhist and it was from here that Buddhism spread to other parts of India and the world. Ratangiri finds have been the richest in terms of cultural treasures—two large monasteries, a huge stupa, Buddhist shrines and numerous sculptures are witness to the strong influence of Buddhism in this region. The site also yielded a rich crop of antiquities. A large head of Buddha found on the top of the hill indicates the colossal nature of the original images.

UDAYAGIRI : The largest Buddhist site in Orissa Udayagiri caves (5 km from Ratangiri) contain two spurs forming a sloping terrace which is covered with extensive archaeological remains. At the foot of the hill, there is a colossal image of Lokesvara holding a large lotus. Two separate inscriptions are found incised on it. The peak of the hills contains broken pieces of sculptures and the ruins of ancient structures. Two four armed images of Jatamukuta Lokesvara are also seen on this hill. A little to the south this image a colossal Buddha sitting in Bhumisparsa Mudra can be seen carved in several pieces of stone.

LINGUDI : Situated in Salipur village of Jatinagar district of Orissa, Lingudi is a hillock where inexhaustible hoards of rare rock cut Buddhist monuments such as stupas, Dyani Buddha in variegated postures, Buddhisattava Avalikitesvara and other feminine Vajrayagna Buddhist divinities like Tara, Prajnaparmita and the dilapidated remains of an imposing brick-built central stupa as well as quadrangular monastries indicating that it was an emporium of the Mahayana and Vajrayana sects of Buddhism are found recently.

FESTIVALS

APRIL—CHITRA PARBA : The festival commences on April 11 every year and continues for three days concluding on 'Mahavisuba Sankranti Day' at Baripada.

JULY—The RATH YATRA : The Rath Yatra has, over centuries, become synonymous with Orissa. The image of Jagannath, his brother Balabhadra and sister Subhadra are brought out of the temple and are carried in a huge beautiful caparisoned multi-wheeled chariot to another temple about three kilometres away. After nine days stay' there is a return trip to the main temple. The chariots are pulled by thousands of devotees who congregate on the occasion.

DECEMBER—KONARAK DANCE FESTIVAL : One of the most splendiferous venues for an evening of dance is the Amphitheatre located at the backdrop of the fabulous Sun temple at Konarak. It is the site for one of the most spectacular dance festival in India every year. The ancient stones come alive with the light footwork and tinkle of ankle bells of the country's foremost classical dancers.

DHANU YATRA : Dhanu Yatra relating to the episode of Lord Krishna's visit to Mathura to witness the ceremony of 'Bow' is colourful one served at Baragarh. The town of Baragarh becomes Mathura, the Jira river becomes Yamuna and the Amapali village on the other bank becomes Gopa (Gokul). Different acts of the puranic description are performed at their right place and the spectators move from place to place with the actors to see their performance.

PUNJAB

PUNJAB
AT A GLANCE

AREA : 50,362 sq. km.
CAPITAL : Chandigarh
BOUNDARIES : East - Haryana; West - Pakistan; North - Jammu and Kashmir, North-East -Himachal Pradesh; South - Rajasthan and Haryana.
LANGUAGE : Punjabi

ROADS : The road length in Punjab is 39,950km out of which provincial roads are 38,962km while National Highways are 988km. All village of the State have been linked with metalled road.

AIRPORTS : *International* - Amritsar; *Domestic* - Chandigarh. There are three Civil Aviation Clubs at Bhatinda, Ludhiana and Patiala.

MUSEUMS

Amritsar : Central Sikh Museum – Golden Temple
Chandigarh : Government Museum and Art gallery

PILGRIM CENTRES (A : Air; R : Rail)

Amritsar : Golden Temple, the most important shrine of the Sikhs, Durgiana Mandir, Temple of Durga, A and R – Amritsar.

Anandpur Sahib : Place where Guru Gobind Singh, the tenth Guru, had formed the Khalsa Panth. Site of Hola Mahalla festival, A – Chandigarh 68 km, R – Anandpur Sahib.

Baba Bakala : Gurudwara dedicated to Guru Teg Bahadur A and R - Amritsar.

Gobindwal Sahib : Samadhi of Guru Angad Devji, A and R – Amritsar 30 km.

Ram Tirath : Birth place of Lav and Kush, sons of Lord Rama born in exile after their mother was abandoned. A and R – Amritsar 10 km

Taran Taran : Gurudwara in memory of Guru Ramdas A– Amritsar 22 km, R Taran Taran

Sirhind : Fatehgarh Sahib Gurudwara where Guru Gobind Singh's sons were martyred.
Rauza of Hazrat Mujadad-ud-din- Altaf Shaikh Ahmed Farooqui A – Chandigarh 40 km, R - Sirhind.

Punjab is a State of traditional hospitality proud heritage and captivating grandeur. This rich abundant region with its fun–loving people offers so many visual–spiritual and culinary–delights to the tourists.

HISTORY

Ancient Punjab, the land of the Vedas, Indus Valley Civilisation, Taxila University, of milk and honey, arts and artefacts, rich agriculture formed a part of the Persian Empire in 522 BC when king Darius had occupied it. In 322 BC Alexander had entered India through Punjab.

The word Punjab is made of two Persian words 'Panj and Aab'– Panj means five and Aab means water. This name was probably given to the land of five rivers by the Persians. In later years it saw the rise and fall of the Mauryans, Dactrians, Greeks, Sakas, Kushans and Guptas.

The medieval Punjab saw the supremacy of the Muslims. Ghazani was followed by the Ghori, the slave–kings, the Khiljis, the Tughlaks land, the Lodhis and family the Mughals. Fifteenth and sixteenth centuries mark a period of watershed in the history of Punjab. Through the teachings of Guru Nanak Bhakti Movement *i.e.* the cult of religious faith in God received a great impetus. Prima facie, Sikhism was a socio-religious movement which was more interested in fighting evils in religion and society.It was Guru Gobind Singh, the tenth Guru, who transformed the Sikhs into the 'Khalsa'. They rise to challenge tyranny and after centuries of servitude established a human Punjabi Raj based on secularism, and patriotism. But soon after his death, the entire edifice collapsed on account of internal intrigues and British mechanisation. After two abortive Anglo-Sikh wars, Punjab was finally annexed to the British empire in 1849.

Punjab was constituted as a separate province of India in 1937. With the partition of India Punjab was divided between India and Pakistan as East Punjab and West Punjab.

AMRITSAR

The home of the world famous Golden Temple, founded by Guru Ramdas, the fourth Guru of the Sikhs, in 1579 and completed by Guru Arjun Dev who also enshrined in it the holy book of his successor Sikhs the Guru Granth Sahib. In 1803, the renowned Maharaja Ranjit Singh, covered the lower half of the temple with marble and the upper half was encrusted later with pure gold leaf which has given the name Golden Temple. The interiors of the temple, decorated with inlay work using semi-precious stones present a delicate floral pattern. Akal the Takht or the eternal throne was established by the sixth Guru, Guru

Hargobind. It is the seat of the supreme head of the Sikh religious authority. The birth place of Lav and Kush—the sons of Lord Rama of the epic of Ramayana is located nearby Amritsar is the most important seat of Sikh history and culture, trade centre and also the gateway for travellers coming to India on the overland route through Pakistan.

PLACES OF INTEREST

Besides the Golden Temple. Durgian Mandir, a 16th century white marble temple with a golden dome and silver portals, is a place of pilgrimage for the Hindus.

JALLIANWALLA BAGH : A memorial where even 2000 people, all unarmed, who had gathered there on April 13, 1919 to protest against the Rowlatt Act, were massacred by the notorious English General Dawyer and his man who stood at the only enterence and fired till the last bullet with them. The park is enclosed by a high wall and is surrounded by houses. More than 300 man and woman with children in arms had jumped into a well in it to protect themselves from bullets and died. The walls still bear the bullet marks.

BABA ATAL RAI TOWER : In memory of the 9-year old son of Guru Hargobind, who martyred himself.

HOW TO REACH

AIR : Amritsar is connected by air with Delhi and Chandigarh.

RAIL : Amritsar is connected by rail with Bhopal, Delhi, Howrah, Jaipur, Lahore, Lucknow, Mumbai, Nanded, Patna, Tatanagar and Vadodara.

It is also connected with Lahore (Pakistan) via Attari Border.

ROAD : Amritsar is connected by road with all major cities of Punjab, Haryana and Himchal Pradesh.

ROAD DISTANCES

Wagah (India Pakistan Border) – 29 km; Jammu – 216 km; Chandigarh -240 km; Delhi 435 km

HOTEL ACCOMMODATION (STD CODE 0183)

— Hotel Mohan International : (4 Star) Albert Road
  PH 227 801; FAX 226 520
— Hotel Ritz Plaza : (3 star) 45, The Mall
  PH 226 606, 401295; FAX 226 657
— Hotel Suncity Towers : 84/15-2 Queen's Road
  PH 229 636/7;FAX221 117

— Hotel Astoria : 1-Queen's Road
  PH 566 414, 401 122; FAX 564 443
— Grand Hotel : Queen's Road
  PH 562 424, 562 977; FAX 229 677

ANANDPUR SAHIB - THE CITY OF BLISS

With a backdrop of Naina Devi Hill, Anandpur Sahib has a number of historical Gurudwaras. It was here that the 10th Guru of Sikhs, Guru Gobind Singh, had given the new form of baptism and called the Sikhs, thus baptised, Khalsa. On the day following Holi devotess flock to Anandpur Sahib to participate in Hola Mohalla celebrations re-enacting the past Sikh battles with ancient arms and weapons. Hola Mohalla, most colourful and the only of its type is an annual event.

FEROZEPORE

Ferozpore is an ancient city situated close to the present Pakistan Border. The city's strategic position has witnessed many military expeditions – during the first Anglo-Sikh war in 1845 it was due to the negligence of the British commander at Ferozepore that the Khalsas were able to cross the Sutlej unopposed. When Lord Hardings declared war on the Sikhs, the first battle was fought at Mudki, 32 km south-west of Ferozepore. In 1838, Ferozepore was the centre from where the British troops proceeded to Kabul during the first Anglo-Afghan war. Bhagat Singh and his associates, Rajguru and Sukhdev, had their final resting place on the banks of the Sutlej river in Ferozepore where they were cramated. The Saragarhi Gurudwara had commemorat the sacrifice of 21 Sikh soldiers who perished at Saragarhi in Balochistan. On September 12 every year people gather here to pay tribute to there heroic soldiers and celebrate the Saragarhi Day.

(CHANDIGARH— REFER UNION TERRITORY)

JALANDHAR - SPORTS CITY OF INDIA

Jalandhar was the capital of the Hindu Kingdom in the days gone by. In 185 BC the city defined the north–west boundary of Pushyamitra Sunga's kingdom. Jalandhar also finds mentione in accounts of King Harsha Vardhan's reign which began in 606 AD. During the 9th century Jalandhar was known as Trigarta kingdom. Jalandhar continued to flourish under the Mughals and played a prominent role in the freedom struggle. Monuments in and around the city include 800 years old Imam Nasir Mausoleum, Devi Tala the four centuries old Jama Masjid, the fort at Phillaur which once served as Maharaja Ranjit Singh's line of defence against the British, a Shiv Mandir which dates back to the Lodhi era and the Gurudwara of Kartarpur built by Guru Arjun Devji in 1656.

LUDHIANA—MANCHESTER OF INDIA

Ludhiana is famous in the world for its hosiery goods. Woollen garments made here are sold in the prestigious shopping centres from Moscow to Montreal and Bangkok to London and New York. The famous Punjab Agricultural University patterned after the Land Grant College of America is situated on the outskirts of the city. During the freedom struggle with British, many leaders emerged from Ludhiana - the prominent were Lala Lajpat Rai, Baba Santa Singh and Maulana Habibur Rehman.

SANGHOL—THE KUSHANAS REDISCOVERED

Sanghol located in Ludhiana district figures prominently in the archaeological atlas of India. Excavations at the site have yielded coins and seals related to Nomadic rulers. Toramana and Mahiragula belonged to Central Asia. A Buddhist stupa was excavated in 1968. Again in February 1985 a rich treasure of 117 beautiful carved stone slabs, pillars, crossbars, figures and figurines were excavated by the experts of the Directorate of Archaeology, Punjab. Scholars have related them to the Kushan sculptures of the Mathura school of the 1st and 2nd centuries AD. These treasures have since been displayed to art lovers and historians in the museum at Sanghol.

SIRHIND—THE MUGHAL LEGACY

Standing amidst the ruins of beautiful mosques and tombs, Sirhind was an important city during the Mughal period. It was here in the ancient Sirhind Fort built by Firoze Tughlak that the two young sons of Guru Gobind Singh were bricked alive when they refused to embrace Islam. Fateh Sahib Gurudwara marks the spot of incident. Closely is the Rauza of Hazrat Mujadadud -din Altaf Sheikh Ahmed Farooque regarded by many Muslims to be only second to Prophet Mohammed. Urs in August and Jor Mela in December every year attract thousands.

FESTIVALS

APRIL—BAISAKHI : Baisakhi festival synchronizes with the Rabi harvesting season and is being celebrated since times immemorial in Punjab. The fair at Dam Dama Sahib (Talwandi Saboo in Bhatinda district) has a history of 250 years. It is held for three days. Baisakhi is a very special day for the Sikhs as it was on this day that Guru Gobind Singh had founded the Khalsa Panth. Baisakhi celebrations are spectacular. Robust revelry and feasting mark the celebrations and dancers perform vigorous Bhangara to the rhythmic beat of the drums.

RAJASTHAN

RAJASTHAN
AT A GLANCE

AREA : 342, 238 sq. km
CAPITAL : Jaipur
BOUNDARIES : East - Madhya
Pradesh; West - Pakistan; North-west-
Uttar Pradesh; North - Haryana and
Punjab; South- Gujarat.
LANGUAGES : Hindi and Rajasthani.
ROADS : Total length of roads was
74,947 km as in March 1998.
AIRPORTS : Jaipur, Jodhpur, Kota,
Jaisalmer and Udaipur.

MUSEUMS

Ajmer : The Rajputana Museum and the Government Museum
Amber : Archaeological Museum
Bharatpur : Government Museum
Bikaner : Government Museum
Jaipur : Maharaja Sawai Jai Singh II Museum – City Palace,
Government Museum and Museum of Indology
Jodhpur : Sardar Museum and Metrangarh Fort Museum
Udaipur : City Palace Museum, Archaeological Museum,
Government Museum and Manuscript Library

HILL RESORT

Mount Abu (1105 m), Railhead – Abu Road 27 km

IMPORTANT PILGRIM CENTRES (A : Air; R : Rail)

Ajmer : Tomb of Sufi Saint Khwaja Moinuddin Chisti; A – Jaipur
138 km, R - Ajmer.
Alwar : Bhanda Sagar Jain Temple; A Jaipur 148 km, R – Alwar.
Bikaner : Bhanda Sagar Jain Temple; A – Jodhpur 240 km, R
Bikaner.
Chittorgarh : Meera and Kumbha Shyam temples and Kalika Mata
Temple; A – Udaipur 98 km, R Chittor.
Deshnoke : Karnimata (Durga) temple; A – Jodhpur 240 km, R
Bikaner 32 km.

Eklingji : Shiva Temple with black marble icon; A and R Udaipur - 22 km.

Jaipur : Govind Devji (temple of Sri Krishna); **Galtaji** : Sun temple and holy a pond. A and R - Jaipur.

Jaisalmer : Jain temples of Rikhabdevji and Sambhavnathji; A - Jodhpur 285 km, R - Jaisalmer.

Jodhpur : Mahamandir (Shiva Temple); A and R Jodhpur.

Kankroli : Dwarkadish temple of the Vallabhacharya sect; A and R - Udaipur.

Kolayat : Temple of Kapil Muni, Venue of Kolayatji fair; A - Jodhpur 240 km, R - Bikaner.

Mount Abu : Dilwara Jain temples, Adhar Devi (Arbuda Devi) temple, Gaumukh temple; A - Udaipur 185 km, R - Abu Road 27 km.

Nagda : Sasbahu and Adbutji temples (Hindu and Jain); A and R Udaipur 23 km.

Nathdwara : Temple of Lord Krishna as Sri Nathji; A and R Udaipur

Pushkar : Brahma Temple A - Jaipur 138 km, R - Ajmer 11 km.

Ranakpur : Jain temples, A and R - Udaipur - 90 km.

Rishabdeoji : Temple of Rishabdeo, Jain tirthankara; A and R Udaipur 65 km.

Udaipur : Jagdish temple of Vishnu as Jagannath; A and R Udaipur.

Rajasthan or Rajputana of the old-days, the land of chivalrous brave and people with a warlike lifestyle around whom grew the most amazing legends of romance, heroism and sacrifice; the land endowed with invincible forts, magnificent palaces and havelis. The cities of Rajasthan still retain the medieval touch keeping alive the timeless traditions in their rich art and crafts.

The state represents an unusual diversity in all its forms - people, culture, customs, costumes and cuisine.

HISTORY

Rajasthan was known as Rajputana or the home of Rajputs, a martial community who ruled over this area for centuries.

History of Rajasthan dates back to the pre-historic times. From 3000 to 1000 BC it had a culture akin to that of the Indus valley civilisation. It were the Chauhans who dominated the Rajput affairs from 7th century and by 12th century they had become an imperial power. After the Chauhans it was the Guhilots of Mewar who controlled the destiny of the warring tribes. Besides Mewar other States, also historically prominent, were Marwar, Jaipur, Bundi, Kota, Bharatpur and Alwar. The other small states were only the off-shoots of these. All these States had accepted the British Treaty of Subordinate Alliance in 1818 as it protected the interests of the princes. It naturally left the people discontented.

After the revolt of 1857, the people united themselves under the leadership of Mahatama Gandhi to contribute to the freedom movement. With the introduction of provincial autonomy in 1935 in British India agitation for civil liberties and political rights became stronger in Rajasthan. The process of uniting the scattered States commenced from 1948 to 1956 when the States Reorganisation Act was promulgated.

First came the Matsya Union (1948) consisting of a fraction of the States. Slowly and gradually other States merged with this union. By 1949, major States like Bikaner, Jaipur, Jodhpur and Jaisalmer had joined this Union making it an united State of greater Rajasthan.

Ultimately in 1958 the present State of Rajasthan formally came into being with the Ajmer State, the Abu Road Taluka and Sunel Tappa joining it.

JAIPUR

Capital of Rajasthan has earned universal renown as the "Pink City".

Jaipur, meaning the 'city of victory', was founded in 1727 by the astronomer king Sawai Jai Singh of Kachhawaha clan, and designed by architect Vidyadhar Bhattacharya in accordance with the principles of town planning set down in the 'Shilpa Shastra' – an epochal treatise on the Hindu architecture.

Attractive monuments, comfortable hotels, gardens and excursions nearby places and shopping makes the Pink City a memorable one.

PLACES OF INTEREST

THE CITY PALACE : The City Palace complex is a historic

landmark with its numerous out buildings, courtyards, impressive gateways and temples. Two elephants carved in marble guard the entrance, occupying one-seventh of the walled city area. The palace houses the seven-storied Chandra Mahal, Mubarak Mahal, the Diwan-e-Am and Diwani-e-Khas. The museum houses a rare collection of arms, carpets, costumes, paintings and royal paraphernalia.

A notable exhibit is a pair of pure silver containers which are the largest single pieces of silver in the world.

JANTAR MANTAR : One of the astronomer king Jai Singh's five remarkable observatories (the others being in Delhi, Ujjain, Varanasi and Mathura), represents the high points of medieval Indian astronomy. It is a collection of complex astronomical instruments chiselled out of stone-most of which continue to provide fairly accurate information to this day.

HAWA MAHAL : Built in 1799 by Maharaja Sawai Pratap Singh, this is a remarkable structure which overlooks one of the main streets and also provides some excellent views of the city.The multi-niched five-storey high balconies of the complex were built to provide adequate vantage position behind delicate stone-carved jali screens to the palace women for watching the royal procession through the bazar below.

GOVIND DEVJI TEMPLE : Dedicated to Lord Krishna, the temple is shaped like a Mukut, which adorns the Lord's head. The image in the form of Govind Devji, originally installed in a temple of Vrindavan, was reinstalled here by Sawai Jai Singh II as his family deity.

SWARGASHULI/ISAR LAT : The tower dominating the skyline on the western side of Tripolia Bazar, the largest structure of Jaipur was built by Sawai Ishwari Singh in 1749 to commemorate an important victory.

RAM NIWAS BAGH (GARDENS) : This is a lush spacious garden with a zoo an aviary (i.e. a large enclosure for birds), a green house, a museum and a popular sport ground. Built during the reign of Sawai Ram Singh in 1868 as a famine relief project, the majestic Albert Hall Museum opened in 1887 AD displays a rich collection of paintings, carpets, ivory, stone and metal sculptures and other objects besides an Egyptian mummy of a priestess. The Bagh also houses one of the oldest zoos in the country.

MAHARANI KI CHATTRI : The traditional site where the last rites of royal ladies were performed. It has a number of cenotaphs some of which are still in very good condition.

GAITOR : Located in the foothills of the Nahargarh hills, this is the funeral ground of the rulers of the Jaipur, there are some fine cenotaphs with intricately carved marble columns and lattices.

JAL MAHAL : A palace amidst the Man Sagar lake was built for royal duck shooting parties.

A KANAK VRINDAVAN : A newly restored temple and a popular picnic spot.

GALTAJI : Old pilgrim centre with several pavilions, natural springs and a Sun temple.

SISODIA PALACE, GARDENS AND VIDYADHAR GARDENS : These are well-laid out garden houses with several galleries, pavilions and murals depicting the scenes from the life of Lord Krishna which are a visual delight.

THE GARLAND OF FORTS

NAHARGARH : Meaning the Tigar fort it was built in 1734 AD and provides some stunning views of the city. A royal retreat for the Maharanis, it was also used as a treasury for many years.

JAIGARH : The Fort of Victory built in 1726 by Sawai Jai Singh, the world's largest cannon on wheels is located here. Also of interest is the intricate water supply and storage system which is considered a marvel of planning. The fort has its own museum.

AMER : Amer is a fascinating blend of Hindu and Muslim architecture. Built in the 16th century by Raja Man Singh, it sprawls on the hillside. Built in red sandstone and white marble, the palace complex has some very interesting apartments. Jai Mandir, Sheesh mahal, Sukh niwas and Ganesh pol are some of the prominent areas of interest. The old township at foothills with its cobbled streets and ruins of havelis provides an old world atmosphere.

HOW TO REACH

AIR : Jaipur is connected by air to Delhi, Ahmedabad, Aurangabad, Calcutta, Jodhpur, Mumbai and Udaipur.

RAIL : Jaipur is connected by rail to Delhi, Mumbai, Ahmedabad, Indore, Agra, Lucknow, Varanasi, Amritsar and all important cities of Rajasthan.

Jaipur is connected with Delhi by Shatabdi Express

Delhi – Jaipur Shatabdi Express (Train operates between Delhi and Ajmer)

— 2015 (Except Sunday) Delhi D 0615 Hrs; Jaipur A 1030 Hrs
— Rt 2016(Except Sundays) Jaipur D 1755; Delhi A 2215

Jaipur-Bikaner Inter-city Express
— 2468 (Daily) Jaipur D 1520 Hrs; Bikaner A 2215
— Rt (Daily) 2467 D Bikaner 0500; A Jaipur 1155
Jaipur-Jodhpur Inter-city Express
— 2465 (Daily) Jaipur D 1730 Hrs; Jodhpur A 2245
— Rt 2466 (Daily) D Jodhpur 0545; A Jaipur 1035
Refer Agra for timings between Agra and Jaipur

ROADS : Delhi, Jaipur and Agra is known as the Golden Triangle and as such it is well-connected by road. Rajasthan Roadways and many private bus operators run regular service of A/c and deluxe coaches from Delhi to Jaipur and many other cities of the Rajasthan.

DISTANCES FROM JAIPUR

Delhi 259 km; Agra 228 km; Bharatpur 176 km; Sariska 108 km; Ajmer 132 km; Chittore 320 km; Udaipur 407 km; Jodhpur 343 km; Jaisalmer 654 km; Bikaner 321 km; Sawaimadhopur 157 km; Ahmedabad 664 km.

PALACE ON WHEELS

Palace on Wheels is a legendary palace on wheels providing a week-long cruise recreating the ambience of the glorious past through the heart of Rajasthan.

The train departs on every Wednesday from New Delhi. There are four coupes in each coach, with wall to wall carpeting, a lounge car with a well stocked bar and two restaurant cars, the Maharaja and Maharani serving Continental, Indian and Rajasthani cuisine.

ITINERARY

DAY 1	2245	Departure from Delhi
		Dinner on board
DAY 2	0830	Welcome to Pink City by Caparisoned elephants and strains of shehnai.
		Lunch at Rambagh Palace
		City tour of Jaipur
	2210	Dinner on board and departure

DAY 3	0730	Arrive and visit Chittorgarh and proceed to Udaipur.
		City tour of Udaipur
	2200	Dinner on board and departure
DAY 4	0630	Arrive at Sawaimadhopur and Visit Ranthambore National Park.
DAY 5	0900	Arrive at Jaisalmer and visit havelis and Palaces. Dinner under the stars with rhythm of Rajasthani music drifts into the night
DAY 6	0900	Arrive at Jodhpur and city tour of Jodhpur. Lunch at Umaid Bhawan palace.
	1545	Departure and overnight on board.
DAY 7	0715	Arrive at Bharatpur and visit Ghana National Park, proceed to Agra for lunch at Taj View. After lunch visit the TAJ MAHAL and city tour of Agra.
	2000	Departure and overnight on board.
DAY 8	0630	Arrive at Delhi.
		END OF THE JOURNEY

CONDUCTED TOURS

OPERATED BY RTDC LTD., from Delhi

Tour No. 1 : Golden Triangle (3 Days) Every Friday, Delhi-Silliserh-Sariska-Jaipur-Bharatpur-Fatehpur Sikri-Agra-Delhi.

Tour No. 2 : Hawa Mahal (3 Days) Every Tuesday, Delhi-Agra-Fatehpur Sikri-Bharatpur-Deeg-Sariska-Jaipur-Delhi.

Tour No. 3 : Mewar Package (6 Days) Every Saturday, Delhi – Jaipur-Chittorgarh-Udaipur-Ranakpur-Ajmer-Pushkar-Delhi.

Tour No. 4 : Desert Circuit (7 Days) Every Monday, Delhi-Bikaner-Jaisalmer-Jodhpur-Ajmer-Pushkar-Delhi.

Tour No. 5 : Rajasthan Package (15 Days) Every 1st and 3rd Thursday, Delhi-Bikaner-Jaisalmer-Jodhpur-Mount Abu-Ranakpur-Haldighati-Nathdwara-Udaipur-Chittor-Ajmer-Pushkar-Jaipur-Bharatpur-Sariska-Delhi.

Tour No. 6 : Wildlife Tour Every Thursday on demand, Delhi-Sariska-Ranthambhor-Bharatpur-Delhi.

For detailed information contact :

—   Department of Tourism, Art and Culture, Government of Rajasthan, Jaipur.

—   Government Hostel Campus, Paryan Bhawan, MI Road, Jaipur PH 365256, FAX 376362

— RTDC Ltd. Bikaner House, Pandara Road, New Delhi 110011
  PH 338 3837, 338 9525; FAX 338 2823

HOTEL ACCOMMODATION (STD CODE 0141)

— Rambagh Palace : (5 Star Deluxe) Bhawani Singh Road
  PH 381 919; FAX 381 098
— Hotel Jai Mahal Palace :(5 Star Deluxe) Jacob Road, Civil
  Lines. PH 371 616 : FAX 365 237
— Welcomegroup Rajputana Palace Shereton : (5 Star Deluxe)
  Palace Road. PH 360 011; FAX 367 848
— Clarks Amer : (5 Star) Jawaharlal Nehru Marg
  PH 550 616; FAX 550 013
— Hotel Mansingh : (5 Star) Sansar Chandra Road
  PH 378 771; FAX 377 582
— Hotel Jaipur Palace :(5 Star) Tonk Road
  PH 512 961-64; FAX 512 966
— Bissau Palace : (Heritage) O/S Chandpole, Near Saroj
  Cinema. PH 304 371, FAX 512 966
— Narain Niwas Palace Hotel (Heritage) Narain Singh Road,
  Kanota Bagh. PH 563 448, 561 291; FAX 561 045
— Holiday Inn Jaipur : (3 Star) Amer Road
  PH 609 000; FAX 609 090
— Hotel Kanchan Deep; (3 Star) 17, Vanasttaho Marg
  PH 364 500; FAX 364 518
— Hotel Aditya :(2 Star) 2, Bhawani Singh Road
  PH 381 720/ 26 FAX 381730
— Hotel Broadway : (2 Star) Agra Road
  PH 488 44-47; FAX 491 96
— Hotel Arya Niwas : (1Star) Behind Amber Towers, Sansar
  Chandra Road. PH 368 524, 372 456; FAX 364 376
— Choki Dhani, 12th Mile, Tonk Road, Via Vatika
  PH 382 034; FAX 381 888

EXCURSIONS

SANGANER : (12 km) It has an exquisitely carved Jain temple.
The town is an important centre of crafts industry and produces one
of the finest hand printed textiles from units of block and screen
paintings.

JAISINGHPURA : (12 km) One of the settlements of the Meena
tribe, it has also an imposing fort, a Jain temple and a step-well in
a picturesque location.

RAMGARH LAKE : (32 km) An huge artificial lake created by constructing a high bund amidst tree covered hills. Beside there is a temple of Jamuna Mata and the ruins of a fort.

BAGRU : (35 km) It is noted for printed handloom industry.

SAMODE : (40 km) It has the old palace which is renovated and rebuilt provides decorated and painted examples of Rajput haveli architecture.

MADHOGARH TUNGA: (40 km) An historic battle between Jaipur forces and Marathas was fought at Tunga fort. Madhogarh nestles amidst orchards.

BAIRATH : (86 km) An important historical place with the excavated remains of a circular Buddhist temple - unique in Rajasthan and the earliest known temples in India. The town also has the relics and structure of Mauryan, Maghal and Rajput peridos.

SAMBHAR : (94 km) It is the largest inland salt lake in India known for the holy Devayani Tank. The palace and the Naliasar are located nearby.

TONK : (96 km) On the way to Ranthambore this quite little town was ruled by a tribe of Pathans from Afghanistan. Sunheri Kothi's interior is richly ornamented with stained glass mirrors, stucco and gilt. There is a thriving leather and felt industry in Tonk. The Nawabs of Tonk were avid book lovers and collectors. In the nineteenth and early decades of the 20 centuries, they built up a large collection of rare and magnificent manuscripts and books in Arabic and Persian. A few years back Arabic and Persian research institute has been set up here.

ABHNERI : (128 km) Near Bandikui it has the famous temple of Harshad Mata built in 7th and 8th centuries.

RANTHAMBORE : (132 km) Founded in the 11th century, the fort was the stronghold of the Yadav a kings in the 8th century and later the Chauhans from 10th century onwards. The fort faced several attacks, its most valiant ruler was Hammir who faced Allauddin Khilji and refused to bow to the enemy in spite of severe shortage of food and provisions. Thousands of people gather at Ganesh temple in the fort during Ganesh Chaturthi. One interesting aspect is the mail that is sent to Lord Ganesha consisting mainly of wedding invitations, the letters are brought up to the temple in large sacks every day.

Today the town is known for its Ranthambhor National Park. History and natural history blend in right proportion in the Ranthambhor National Park, a famous tiger reserve under the Project Tiger. Here sambar, chital, chinkara, nilgai, wild boar and common langur provide a good spectrum of prey range for the resident tigers and their co-predators—leopard jackal, sloth bear and hyena who also live in the 392 Sq. km of unique habitat of dry deciduous forests.

The park is approachable both by rail (132km) and road (180km) from Jaipur. RTDC castle Jhoomar Baori, Hotel Kamdhenu, Maharaja's Lodge, PWD rest house, railway retiring rooms and several hotels are available on advance notice

AJMER : (135 km) Surrounded by the Aravallies, the city was established in the early 7th century by Ajaipal Chauhan and named Ajaimeru - the invisible hill. The Chauhans dominated the city for many years. Towards the end of the 12th century Prihviraj Chauhan was killed in a battle with Mohammed Ghori and the city came under Delhi Sultanate. Ajmer saw many upheavals until Emperor Akbar came to the throne in 1556 and gave Ajmer the status of a full-fledged province and also made it his base for operations in Rajputana. The Rajputs, the Mughals, the Marathas and the British were all involved on it and left their marks. In 1818 it passed into British empire by accepting the British Treaty of Subordinate Alliance.

Today, Ajmer is a popular pilgrimage centre for the Hindus as well as the Muslims, especially for the Dargah-tomb and the Pushkar Lake where lies the abode of Lord Brahma.

The Dargah, is the final resting place of the great Sufi saint - Khwaja Moinuddin Chisti. The Dargah Sharif, where the saint lies buried, was visited by Akbar. During the URS Several Thousands of Muslim pilgrims from all over the sub-continent visit the shrine. The Dargah has two massive cauldrons which are filled with about 48 and 32 quintals of rice,  dry fruits and condiments respectively and then cooked by professionals who slide down into massive cauldrons for mixing it. The cooked rice is then sold as "TA BARUKH - SANCTIFIED FOOD".

Other places of interest in Ajmer are ADHAI-DIN-KA-JHOPRA, TARAGARH FORT, MUSEUM AND MAYO COLLEGE.

PUSHKAR, 11 km from Ajmer, is sacred to the Hindus. The lake at Pushkar is believed to have been created by Lord Brahma himself and has the same sanctity as Manasarover in Tibet. The lake is situated on the edge of the desert and surrounded by hills from Ajmer by 'Nag

Parvat'. On this mountain the Panchkund and the cave of saint Agystya are located. It is believed that Kalidasa the 4th century poet and playwriter had chosen the setting for his masterpiece 'Abhigyana Shakuntalam'in this forest heritage.no pilgrimage is complete without a visit to Pushkar. There are 400 temples and the lake is circled by 52 ghats built over the years by several kings and nobles. The important temples are dedicated to Lord Brahma, Lord Shiva, Badri Narayan, Varaha, Gayatri and Savitri The important ghats are the Varaha, Brahma and Gau.

Pushkar is also the site for one of the largest CATTLE FAIR AND MELA, and is believed to be the most colourful animal fair in the world. On the full-moon night of Kartik (November) pilgrims take a holy dip in the lake.

Along the banks of the Pushkar lake is the former residence of Raja Mansingh of Amer.

ALWAR : (150 km) Alwar, one of the oldest cities in Rajasthan, was once a part of Matsya Desh. It was here, in the city of Viratnagar, in the court of king Virata that the mighty Pandavas, heroes of the great Indian epic Mahabharata, spent the last year of their 13 years of exile. There are still exist several monuments around Alwar named after the Pandavas. Matsya kingdom was overshadowed by the more influential Mauryan empire and with the passing of the years there were many more upheavals. Alwar today is a busy and growing industrial district - but full of ancient ancient temples, medieval forts and palaces, gardens and a wildlife sanctuary.

BALA QUILA (FORT) : This huge fort with its ramparts stretching 5 km from north to south and 2.6 km from east to west, stands 304 metres above the city and 595 metres above sea level constructed before the rise of the Mughal empire. The fort is a witness to many historical events. CITY PALACE OR VINAY VILAS PALACE, built in the 18th century, it has traces of both Rajput and Mughal style architecture. The palace has its own museum.The ground floor apartments have now been converted into government offices and district court. GOVERNMENT MUSEUM has the finest collection of Mughal and Rajput paintings dating back to the 18th and 19th century and some rare ancient manuscripts in Persian, Arabic Urdu and Sanskrit. VIJAY MANDIR PALACE, 10 from Alwar, this is the royal residence, built by Maharaja Jai Singh in 1819. A splendid temple of Sita Ram here is visited by devotees on the occasion of Ram Navmi. SILISERH LAKE AND PALACE HOTEL, 13 km away, is a popular picnic spot built as a summer retreat. A magnificent royal palace and the hunting lodge, built by Maharaja Vinay Singh in 1845 for his queen Shila stands overlooking the lake which is now converted into hotel. JAI SAMAND LAKE, 37 km, is the largest artificial lake constructed by Maharaja Jai Singh in 1910. It is a popular picnic spot for outing and picnic. VIRATNAGAR, 66 km from Alwar, is one of the oldest historical sites in Rajasthan, edict of King Ashoka the great dating back to the 3rd century. BC was found here. 37 km away is the SARISKA SANCTUARY AND PALACE. The 765.80 Sq. km. thickly wooded reserve is cradled in the picturesque reserve in the valley of Aravellis. Established in 1955 it is an excellent tiger sanctuary under Project Tiger. A marvellous palace was built here by Maharaja Jai Singh in the honour of Duke of Edinburgh during his visit to the sanctuary

BHARATPUR

Bharatpur being close to Uttar Pradesh, its life style was strongly influenced by it, and was dominated by Jats in the 17th century. It is visited mainly for it's bird sanctuary—KEOLADEO NATIONAL PARK. Once the hunting preserve of the princes of Bharatpur, it is one of the finest bird sanctuaries in the world inundated with 400 species of water birds. Exotic migratory birds from Afghanistan, Central Asia, Tibet as well as Siberian cranes from the Arctic grey leg geese from Siberia and barheaded geese from China come here in July/August to spend the winter. The Jat king Suraj Mal had started work on the fort in 1732 - known as LOHAGARH which took 60 years to build. It is called Iron Fort because it remained invincible during attacks by the Britishers. It was able to sustain itself with a powerful resistance due to the ingenious defensive works, conceived and designed by Mahajara Suraj Mal, the founder of Bharatpur in early 18th century. The fort has three palaces within its precincts—Kishori Mahal, Mahal Khas and Kothi Khas. The government museum in the fort houses antiquities from this region. DEEG, 34 km from Bharatpur, is known for its palaces and well preserved gardens. Once the summer resort of the rulers of Bharatpur, it served as the second capital of the region.

Gopal Bhawan overlooking the Gopal Sagar, Nand Bhawan, Krishna Bhawan and the waterworks of the Keshav Bhawan are of interest here. DHOLPUR; it is known country-wide for its locally -quarried red sandstone. Being close to Agra Dholpur witnessed many important battles. Jhor, a village 16 km from Dholpur, was the site of the oldest Mughal garden in the sub-continent. Started by Babar it was discovered in the late 1970s.Mach Kund, a lake surrounded by over a hundred temples, lies a kilometer away and only comes to life once a year.

HOW TO REACH

AIR : Nearest airport : Agra 56 km.

RAIL : Nearest Railhead : Bharatpur.

ROAD : Bharatpur is connected by road with Agra, Delhi, Jaipur and major cities of Rajasthan. Local transport is easily available from Agra.

HOTEL ACCOMMODATION (STD CODE 05644)

— ITDC Bharatpur Forest Lodge
— RTDC Hotel Saras, PH 237 00
— Hotel Pratap Palace, PH 242 45
— Laxman Niwas palace (Heritage), PH 235 23
— Govind Niwas, PH 232 47
— Tourist Information Centre : Hotel Saras, Agra Road PH 22542

MERTA

Merta was founded by Rao Duda, son of Rao Jodha of Jodhpur in the 15th century. Rao Maldeo had erected the fortress, known as Matkot. In the centre of this fortified town is the famous temple of Charbhuja, the tutelary deity of the Mertias, a clan of the Rathores. The medieval mystic poetess princess Meera Bai, born in the Kukri village was associated with this shrine. The famous mosque erected by Aurangzeb on the ruins of a Shiva temple is an imposing edifice and is surrounded by many Hindu shrines. Dudasagar, 'the lake of Duda', and many other small ponds surround the town. Near Vishnusagar is the Ashram of Mauni baba, a focal point for his devotees.

NAGAUR

Nagaur (135 km from Jodhpur) is an impressive town and was granted to Raja Amar Singh Rathore by Mughal Emperor Shah Jehan. The historic Nagaur Fort houses splendid palaces, temples and palatial mansions. Moti Mahal, Badal mahal, Hawa Mahal are splendid palaces within the fort. The courtyard has painted walls, adorned with some exquisite frescoes and lovely murals which are a blend of the Persian and the typical Nagaur Style. Nagaur's temples have decorated walls and entrances, ornate

with beautiful paintings depicting various episodes from the Ramayana and the Mahabharata.

Nagaur is the venue for annual cattle fair held in January-February. During the four day festival, the town is thronged by cows, bullocks, oxen and camels accompanied by turbaned sellers and buyers.Cock and bull fights, camel races folk dances and music enhance the excitement of the fair.

KOTA

The medieval town Kota lies along the eastern bank of the Chambal river.

The Hada chieftain, Rao Deva, had conquered the territory in the 14th century and founded Bundi and Hadoti. Later during the reign of Mughal emperor Jahangir at the beginning of the 17th century, Rao Ratan Singh, the ruler of Bundi, had given his son, Madho Singh, the smaller principality of Kota. In course of time Kota came to be regarded as a hallmark of Rajput power and culture and today is known as the industrial capital of Rajasthan.

Kota is famous for Kota Doria sarees.

HOW TO REACH KOTA

AIR : Nearest airport-Jaipur 245 km.

RAIL : Lying on the Mumbai-Delhi route all major trains including Rajdhani hault at Kota.

ROAD : Kota is connected by road with all major cities and towns of Rajasthan.

HOTEL ACCOMMODATION (STD CODE 0744)

— Uned Bhawan Palace, RTDC Hotel, Chambal. PH. 27695.
— Hotel Priya. PH. 23294, 26853.
— Hotel Payal. PH. 25059, 21440.
— Hotel Marudhar. PH. 25402.

Tourist Information

— Tourist Reception Centre, Hotel Chambal. PH. 327695.

PLACES OF INTEREST

CHAMBAL GARDEN : The lush green gardens at Amer Niwas offer boating facilities.

MAHARAJA MADHO SINGH MUSEUM : Situated in the old palace, it houses a rich collection of Rajput miniature paintings of Kota school, exquisite sculptures, frescoes and other antiques.

JAG MANDIR : An artificial lake Kishore Sagar was constructed in 1346 by Prince Dher Deh of Bundi. Jog Mandir was built in the middle of this lake with ripples of its blue water enchanting the serenity. Near the lake is Keshar Bagh famous for its royal cenotaphs.

HAVELI OF DEVTAJI : Haveli in the middle of the busy market is famous for its beautiful frescoses some rooms of this haveli are full of wall paintings.

KOTA BARRAGE : A part of the irrigation canal system on the Chamba river this beautiful setting is ideal for outing and evening strolls.

OTHER PALACES WORTH VISITING : Kansua Temple with a four-faced Shiva Lingam, Bhitria Kund, Adhar Shila, Budh Singh Bafna haveli and yatayat park.

EXCURSION

Bundi, (36 km) from Kota, is one of the unexplored cities with a rich historical wealth. Bundi and Kota were once a single principality ruled by Hada Chauhans after the death of Prithviraj Chauhan by Sultan Mohammed Ghori in 1193. The Chauhan nobles sought sanctuary in Mewar. Some young warriers ventured on their own, overpowered the Meena and Bhil tribals of the Chambal valley and established a kingdom of Hadoti or Hadavati. Later two branches of the hadas formed two separate States on either side of the Chambal - Kota and Bundi. Bundi nestles in a narrow valley, enclosed by strong walls and fortified by four gateways. In the centre lies a lake. A medieval fortress stands sentinel— a mute witness to history and time. Bundi is famous for its intricate paintings and murals.

PLACES OF INTEREST

TARAGARH OR THE STAR FORT : This white fort on the top of thickly wooded hill has an enormous tank which once supplied the palace with water.

THE PALACE : It was started by Maharao Balwant Singh and is considered to be one of the finest examples of Rajput architecture. Intricately carved bracket pillars and balconies and sculpted elephants are used liberally.

NAWAL SAGAR : Is an artificial lake broken up by islets. A temple of Varuna stands in the middle.

RANIJI-KI-BAORI : A stepped well outside the old city walls has a high arched gate, ornated with excellent carvings on its pillars. The well has a depth of 46 meters and was built by a Rani.

SUKH MAHAL : A summer palace built on Sukh Sagar lake, it is said that an underground tunnel runs from Sukh Mahal to old palace.

PHOOL SAGAR : A palace built in the 20th century in contemporary style.

SIKAR BAGH : Royal hunting lodge.

SHAR BAGH : These are old well-maintained gardens where cenotaphs of the kings and queens of Bundi stand in all their architectural splendor.

EIGHTY FOUR PILLARED CENOTAPH : This remarkably constructed memorial erected by Rao Anirudh has 84 pillars in this single cenotaph along with a Shiva-linga.

JHALWAR (86 km) The princely State of the Jhalas, Jhalwar is located 86 km from Kota. The land of Jhalas was created in 1838AD by separating this area from Kota State by the British. Besides Zallim Singh I, various other enlightened rulers contributed to make Jhalwar a culturally rich State. Not only the city, but the whole district and areas around Jhalwar, are a treasure house of pre-historic cave paintings, formidable forts, forests and exotic wildlife. Jhalwar boasts of rich historic as well as natural wealth.

PLACES OF INTEREST

JHALWAR FORT (Garh palace) : In the centre of the town the fort now houses the Collectorate and other district offices. The Janana Khas of the fort has some exquisite paintings on walls and mirrors.

GOVERNMENT MUSEUM : One of the oldest museum of Rajasthan, it was established in 1915. Paintings, rare manuscripts, idols and exquisite statues of Lakshminarayan, Vishnu, Krishna, Ardanarishvar Natraj and Trimurti are specially noteworthy.

BHAWANI NATYA SHALA : An interesting building constructed in 1921 where Parsi theatre was performed.

SEKAWATI AN OPEN AIR ART GALLERY

It is a large area in north-eastern Rajasthan, spread over Jhunjhunu, Sikar and Churu districts, in its 20 odd towns and villages. Shekawati as a region is known for its exquisite frescoes that adorn the walls and ceilings of the buildings. There is no other region anywhere in the world that has such a large concentration of frescoes. In the 14th century the ruler, Mokal Singh sought the blessings of fakir Sheikh Burhan for a male child and he named his son Shekha in honour of the fakir. Until 1820 frescoes financed by the Rajputs were largely religious and historical events. Towards the end of 19th century Marwaris the business community, found itself in a position of strength. By the beginning of 19th century. East India Company began to levy heavy taxes and Marwaris were forced to leave the region leaving their families behind. They later sent back huge sums of money to their hometown and most of it was spent on the welfare of the community, wells and reservoirs. For the families they built large havelis and had the most intricate frescoes painted in them.The desire to show off spread over from one village to another and the region has now become famous for its frescoes. Majority of the frescoes have themes from mythology, pictures of God, epics and legends.

SIKAR

In the feudal time it was the largest contributor to the Jaipur exchequer. Founded in the late 17th century, the town of Sikar has good examples of frescoes in the Gopinath Raghunath and the Madan Mahal temples and the fort. The Jubilee Hall, Madho Niwas Kothi, Biwani Haveli and Sadhani Haveli are also worth seeing. HARSH NATH TEMPLE, 11 km from Sikar, is a 10th century temple situated on Harsh Nath hills. The ruins of the temple are strewn all over the area.

JEEN MATA TEMPLE, 29 km from Sikar was built thousands years ago.

RAMGARH has the Chhatris with exquisite paintings. Shanti temple of the 'Saturday God' and the Ganga temple at Ramgarh are worth seeing.

JHUNJHUNU

Capital of Shekawati was another stronghold of the Kayamkhani Nawabs till 1730 when Shardul Singh established Hindu rule and his descendants ruled this region till India's Independence. There exist many artistically painted Havelis. Other important places to visit are Badolgarh, Jarawargarh, Mertani Boari, Birdi Chand ka Kuan and Jain temple.

MUKUNDGARH : Mukundgarh fort is now a heritage hotel and the town has many havelis.

BAGAD : Founded by the Nagad Pathans in 15th century it is known as the home of Rungtas and Piramalas.

CHIRWA : Trading town located between Churu and Loharu. There are havelis of Nand Lal Dalmia, Tara Chand Dalmia and Mongal Chand Dalmia.

PILANI : Home of Birla's, it has a large campus of the Birla Institute of Technology and Science.

SURAJGARH AND KAJRA : There is a fort built towards the end of 18ᵗʰ century. **ALSISAR AND MALSISAR.** These towns founded in the late and mid 18ᵗʰ century respectively, have angular type of the frescoes and their different palette are refreshing. One can witness the fort, temples and havelis along the main street at Malsisar.

BISSAU : Founded in the mid 18ᵗʰ century it has Chhatries of its Thakurs and havelis to visit.

MAHANSAR : Founded in the mid 18ᵗʰ century, it is worthwhile to visit the Sone-Chandi-ki-Haveli and the Raghunath Temple, both built by Poddars.

NAWALGARH : Some of the country's leading merchant families come from this little town. Roop Niwas, Saat Haveli, two old forts and a palace are worth visiting.

DUNDLOD : A fort and a palace and the Goenka's Haveli have some fine frescoes.

CHURU

Churu is famous for Kothari Haveli (1915) and Kanhaiya Lal Bagla Haveli (1870) with superb life-size paintings of Dhola Maru, Sassi-Punnu etc. The six-storied high Surana Haveli with more than 1,100 doors and windows and many other havelis with painted rooms and facades.

SALASAR BALAJI : Famous for a sacred temple of Hanumanji.

LACHHMANGARH : It is one of the best forts in this region. There is also imposing Ganeriwala haveli.

MANDAWA : There are many havelis in Madawa notable are the Chokidhani Saraf and Ladia havelies.

FATEHPUR : A very good place to see the combination of Indian and western style frescoes. The Devra, Singhania and Goenka havelis can be seen as also the Jalan and Bhartiya havelies.

RATANGARH : Ratangarh is situated on Agra-Bikaner National Highway and is 52 km from Churu towards Bikaner. The Raja of Bikaner named it Ratangarh in 1820 AD by building a fort on the site of a village. The market of the town is in the shape of a cross giving impression of a planned town. Painted havelis are situated around the clock tower at the main crossing.

SARDARSHAHAR : 46 km from Churu and 150 km from Bikaner, this is the most enchanting town of the desert. The havelis here, besides colourful wall paintings, have some remarkable carved woodwork.

DUDAHWA KHARA : 36 km from Churu towards Rajgarh, it is a big but old historical village situated on enchanting topography of the Thar desert. There are some huge havelis, having excellent architectural designs. This village is ideal for enjoying ruler life and camel safaris.

TAL CHHAPPAR : The natural habitat of blackbuck is 100 km away from Churu. The endangered species of blackbuck and some migratory birds can be seen in this wild life sanctuary. Forests guides are available to take visitors around.

JODHPUR

The former capital of Marwar State, Jodhpur was founded in 1459 AD by Rao Jodha who claimed to be a descendant of lord Rama. The massive fort – Mehrangarh – came first and around it grew the city of Jodhpur protected by a high stone wall with seven gates and countless bastions. A flourishing trading centre of the 16th century, the fortress city of Jodhpur is now the second largest city of Rajasthan. Jodhpur is still one of the leading centres for cattle, and boasts of fine reminders of history - palaces, forts, temples and historical monuments.

PLACES OF INTEREST

MEHRANGARH FORT : Spreading over 5 km on a perpendicular hill and looking down from a height of about 125 meters, the fort appears rugged from outside but houses some of the most intricately adorned palaces with exquisitely carved panels and latticed windows. Moti Mahal, Phool Mahal, Sheesh Mahal Sileh Khana and Daulat Khana should be visited to view the collection of palanquins howdahs, royal cradles, miniatures, musical instruments, costumes and furnitures.

JASWANT THADA : A collection of royal cenotaphs, built in marble, lies very close to the fort. Built in 1899, the cenotaph also houses portraits of the ruler of Jodhpur. It has extremely rare 15cm thick milk white marble slab.

UMAID BHAWAN PALACE : Built in the 20th century, it was meant to be a relief project which gave employment to citizens for 16 years. The palace is presently run as a hotel while a part of it is still retained by the royal family.

GIRDIKOT AND SARDAR MARKET : In the heart of the city are colourful markets throbbing with activity, tiny shops dotting the narrow lanes.

HOW TO REACH

AIR : Jodhpur is connected by air with Delhi, Mumbai, Udaipur and Jaipur.

RAIL : Jodhpur is connected by rail with major cities of the state.

ROAD : Jodhpur is connected by road with all major towns and cities of Rajasthan.

For Tourism details contact : RTDC, Jodhpur Division, Regional Tourist Offfice, RTDC Hotel Ghoomar, High Court Road, PH 45083/ 44010

HOTEL ACCOMMODATION (STD CODE 0291)

— Welcomegroup Umaid Bhawan Palace (5 Star Deluxe)
  PH 33316; FAX 35373
— Ratanda Polo Palace : (4 Star) Residency Road, P.O.Box 63
  PH 31910; FAX 33118
— Hotel Ajit Bhawan : (Heritage) Opp Circuit House
  PH 510418; FAX 637774
— Hotel Karni Bhawan : (Heritage) Defence Lab Road,
  PH 32220 : FAX 33495
— Hotel Adarsh Niwas : (2 Star) Near Adarsh Niwas, Near Railway Station. PH 627 338 : FAX 627 314
— RTDC Hotel Ghoomar
— Hotel Karni Bhawan
— Arun hotel
— Hotel Amenity Inter Continental

For paying guest accommodation, contact Rajasthan Tourist Office.

EXCURSIONS

MANDORE : The ancient capital of Marwar, has 16 gigantic figures carved out of a single rock depicting popular Hindu and folk deities stand there in bright colours, surrounded by gardens.

KAILANA LAKE : 11 km away, it is popular as a picnic spot.

BALSAMAND : (5 km) An artificial but the oldest lake in Asia it was constructed in 1159 AD. This pretty lake has a summer palace on its banks.

OSIAN : (58 km) Here lies the ruins of an ancient city which was the cradle of Rajasthani temple art and which was destroyed by the Muslim invaders and iconoclasts. There are now only 16 Hindu and Jain temples dating from 8th to 11th centuries.

SARDAR SAMAND LAKE AND PALACE : (55 km) A shimmering lake and palace with interesting villages and lively people.

NAGAUR : (135 km) There is an imposing fort with beautiful murals in Nagaur style. The cattle fair here attracts many buyers.

ROHIT FORT : (60 km) The fort has now been converted into a heritage hotel.

SAILA : (74 km) The Shiva temple here has a unique Sabha Mandap with beautifully carved pillars.

BIKANER

The royal walled medieval city dating back to 1486 AD lies on the northern point of the triangle of desert cities. It was established by Prince Bika Rathore and came to be called Bikaner after him. Bika was the eldest son of the founder of the Jodhpur State—Rao Jodha. Bikaner was well-protected from its enemies by the harsh deserts. Bikaner was also a major trade centre as it stood on the ancient caravan route which linked Central Asia and North India with Gujarat seaports. It was thereafter a great centre of trade in the ancient world.

Bikaner stands on a slightly raised ground and is circumscribed by a seven km long embattled wall with five gates. The magnificent forts and palaces, created with delicacy in reddish-pink sandstone, bear testimony to its rich historical and architectural legacy. Undulating lanes, colourful bazars and bright and cheerful folks make Bikaner an interesting place.

PLACES OF INTEREST

JUNAGARH FORT : Started in 1587 AD this fort has never been conquered. The foundation of the fort was laid by Raja Rai Singh. Thirty-seven palaces, pavilions and temples were later added to the original structure by successive rulers and each has been cleverly built to connect with the previous building.  Anup Mahal, Ganga Niwas Durbar hall, Har Mandir, Sheesh Mahal, Karan Mahal, Pool Mahal and Chandra Mahal are some of the areas worth seeing. The museum in the fort houses valuable collection of miniature paintings dating back to several centuries.

LALGARH PALACE : It was designed by Sir Swinton Jacob for Maharaja Ganga Singh almost 90 years ago and has interesting combination of European luxury and oriental fantasy. Important sights are Laxmi Vilas and Shiv Vilas. Major part of the palace has now been turned into a luxury hotel.

GANGA GOLDEN JUBILEE MUSEUM : The museum houses brilliant specimens of Harappan civilisation, the Gupta and Kushan era and sculptures of the late classical time, besides a rich collection of terracotta pottery, carpets, paintings, armoury and coins.

HOW TO REACH

AIR : Nearest Airport Jodhpur 243 kms

RAIL : Bikaner is connected by rail with Delhi, Ahmedabad, Jodhpur, Ambala and Jammu Tavi.

ROAD : Bikaner is connected by road with all cities in the State.

HOTEL ACCOMMODATION (STD CODE 0151)

- Lalgarh Palace : (Heritage)
  PH 523 963, 543 815; FAX 522 253
- Thar Hotel : PBM Hospital Road.
  PH 543 050, FAX 525 150
- Hotel Gajner Palace, Gajner. PH 5039
- Hotel Bhanwar Niwas. PH 61880

RTDC Hotel Dhola Maru, Thar Hotel, Joshi Hotel, Sagar Hotel Deluxe tents with attached baths at Royal Camp on Bikaner-Jaipur highway—for reservation contact Bikaner – PH 27180; Delhi 541 9719

For local sightseeing and further tourism information contact :
RTDC, Tourist Reception Centre, Hotel Dhola Maru, PH 27445

EXCURSIONS

BHANDASAR JAIN TEMPLE : (5 km) Beautiful Jain temple of 16th century dedicated to 23rd Jain Tirthankara Parsvanathji.

CAMEL BREEDING FARM : (8 km) The only of its kind in Asia managed by Central Government. Bikaner's Camel Corps (former Ganga Risala) was a famous fighting force and still maintains its importance in the desert werfare and defence through the Border Security Force.

DEVI KUND : (9 km) It is a royal crematorium with several cenotaphs with decorative Chattris built in memory of the rulers of the Bika dynasty.

DESHNOK'S KARNI MATA TEMPLE : (30 km) Temple devoted to Karni Mata, offers a heaven to rats as they are believed to be incarnated as future bards and considered to be sacred.

KALAYATJI : (50 km) Temple here dedicated to Kapil muni and a site of fair an Kartik month.

JAISALMER

Jaisalmer rises from the heart of the Thar desert like a golden mirage. According to legend, Lord Krishna – the head of the Yadav Clan, foretold Arjuna that a remote descendent of the Yadav Clan would build his kingdom atop the Trikuta Hill.His prophecy was fulfilled in 1156 AD. when Rawal Jaiswal a descendent of the Yadav Clan and a Bhatti Rajput, abandoned his fort at Lodurva and founded a new capital Jaisalmer, perched on the Trikuta Hill. The Bhati Rajputs were feared bandit chiefs who lived off the forced levis on the great caravans that crossed their area en route Delhi. These caravans, laden with precious cargoes of spices and silk brought great wealth to this town. Not only the princes but even the merchants prospered and their riches were displayed in the exquisitely carved and ornamented havelis. Its remote location kept it almost untouched by outside influence and even during the days of the British Raj, Jaisalmer was last to sign the instrument of Agreement with the British. Mughal Emperor Akbar was born in Amarkot, close to Jaisalmer. Jaisalmer today is famous for its carved havelis and Jain Temple.

PLACES OF INTEREST

THE FORT : The golden-hued Jaisalmer Fort 'Sanar Kella' can be seen from miles away. The fort stands almost 100 meters above the city and houses an entire living area within its huge ramparts. It is approached through Ganesh Pol. Suraj Pol, Bhoota Pol, Hava pol are other main entrances which guard the Negh Durbar and Jawahar Mahal. Also in the inner enclosure are a group of Jain temples dating back from 12th to 15th centuries.

MANAK CHOWK AND HAVELIS : These are the centre of main local market activities. From Manak Chowk one can walk into the lanes where the famous carved havelis are to be found. Nathmaji ki Haveli, Patwon ki Haveli, Salim Singh ki Haveli are famous havelis of the city.

HOW TO REACH

AIR : Nearest airport-Jodhpur 285 km.

RAIL : Jaisalmer is connected by rail to Jodhpur.

ROAD : Jaisalmer is connected by road to major cities and towns in Rajasthan.

HOTEL ACCOMMODATION (STD CODE 02992)

— Hotel Dhola Maru : (3 Star) P.O. Box 49
PH 52863; FAX 52761
— Hotel HeritageInn : (3 Star) P.B. Box no 43, Sam Road
PH 52769; FAX 51638
— Himmatgarh Palace : (3 Star) No 1, Ramgarh Road
PH 52002/3 FAX 52005
— Narayan Niwas Palace : (2 Star) Malka Prol
PH 52408; FAX 52101
— Gornabdh Palace Hotel, No 1, Tourist Complex, Sam Road.
PH 51511; FAX 52749

For local sightseeing and further tourism details contact :
— RTDC Tourist Reception Centre, Hotel Station Road
PH 52406
— Tourist Information counter at Railway Station

EXCURSIONS

AMAR SAGAR : (6 km) An enchanting place besides lake, with Mango and other fruit trees. Exquisitely carved Jain temple enhance the aura of the place.

BADA BAGH : (6 km) Surrounded by densely grown trees and on the bank of an artificial lake are the royal cenotophs with ornate carvings on the ceiling and carved images of former rulers on horse back.

MOOL SAGAR : (8 km) A beautiful place for picnic in summer. It is a cool and shady grove which belonged to the former rulers of Jaisalmer.

LUDRUWA : (16 km) It is the ancient capital of Jaisalmer and an important Jain pilgrimage. Toran or the ornate arch at the main entrance of the Jain temple and the splendid carvings here are worthseeing. The replica of the 'Kalpataru' tree is another attraction.

AAKAL : (17 km) It is a fossil park where 180 million years ago stood a forest.

SAM AND DUNES : (42 km) One can get an insight into desert life where Camel rides are possible.

DESERT NATIONAL PARK : (45 km) The Desert National Park with its rolling landscape of sand dunes and scurb covered hills commands a panoramit view.

BARMAR : (153 km) A desert town it is famous for its carved wooden furniture and hand block printing industry.

UDAIPUR

Udaipur, 'VENICE OF THE EAST' known as the City of Lakes, is famous for its marble palaces, beautiful gardens and placid blue lakes,

hemmed in by the lush hills of the Aravalis. Udaipur is the jewel of Mewar—a kingdom ruled by the Sisodia dynasty for 1200 years. The founder, Maharana Udai Singh, was overcome by the misfortune that his old capital Chittorgarh had to face. Repeatedly sacked by the Mughal armies, the fort saw some very fierce battles in 1567, the army of Emperor Akbar sacked the fort and forced Udai Singh to seek refuge in the surrounding Aravelli hills. Udai Singh sought the advice of a holy man and then went building this city on the banks of Pichola Lake.

Of the original eleven gates, only five remain. The Suraj Pol or Sun gate on the eastern side is the main entrance to the city.

PLACES OF INTEREST

CITY PALACE : A majestic architectural marvel towering over the lake on a hill is surrounded by crenallated walls.City Palace is completely white and majestic and is approached through Tripoli gate, built in 1725 AD. The palace has several carved balconies, arches and decorated pillars. Located inside the palace are the Suraj Gokhanda, Bada Mahal, Sheesh Mahal, Bhim Vilas, Chini Chitrashala and Mor

Chowk. The Zenana Mahal, Fatehprakash, Durbar Hall and Shambu Niwas are other places of interest.

JAGDISH TEMPLE : Built in 1651 by Maharaja Jagajti Singh I, this Indo-Aryan temple is the largest and the most beautiful temple of Udaipur with noteworthy sculpted images.

SAHELIYON-KI-BARI : This garden of the maids of honour with numerous fountains brings the unique lifestyle of the royal ladies who once strolled here.

PRATAP MEMORIAL : A bronze statue of Maharan Pratap is placed at Magari overlooking the Fateh Sagar Lake.

FATEH SAGAR : Built by Maharaja Fateh Singh, this elegant lake is surrounded on three sides by hills and palaces, temples, bathing ghats and embankments.

PICHOLA LAKE : The picturesque lake that entranced Maharaja Udai Singh is surrounded by hills, palaces, temples, bathing ghats and embankments. Two island palaces, Jag Mandir and Jag Niwas on the lake are of breathtaking magnificence.

AHAR : The royal centotaphs of the royal Maharanas of Mewar lies here in remains.

SAJJAN NIWAS and its **GULAB BAGH, MACHCHALAYA MAGRA, NATHANI KA MAGRA, DOODH TALAI, SAJJAN GARH PALACE** are some other interesting sights.

HOW TO REACH

AIR : Udaipur is connected by air with Aurangabad, Delhi, Jaipur and Mumbai.

RAIL : Udaipur is connected by rail with Delhi, Ahmedabad and Jaipur.

ROAD : Udaipur is connected by road with all cities and towns in Rajasthan.

HOTEL ACCOMMODATION (STD CODE 0294)

- Lake Palace : (5 Star Deluxe) P.B. Box 5, Pichola lake
  PH 527961; FAX 527974
- Shikarbadi : (4 Star) Govardhan Vilas
  PH 583 200-4; FAX 584 841
- Laxmi Vilas Palace : (Heritage)
  PH 529 711-15; FAX 525 536, 526 273
- Shivniwas Palace : (Heritage) City palace
  PH 528016-19; FAX 528 006

— Hotel Hilltop Palace : (3 Star) 5, Ambavgarh, Fatehsagar
  PH 521 997; FAX 525 106
— Lake Pichola Hotel : (3 Star) Outside Chandpole
  PH 421 197, FAX 410 575
— Heritage Resorts : (3 Star) Lake Bagela, Opp SAS Bahu
  Temple, Nagda, Eklingji
  PH 528 628, 440 382; FAX 527 549
— Hotel Rajdarshan : (3 Star) 18, Pannadhai Marg
  PH 526 601/5;FAX 524 588
— Chandralok Hotel : (2 Star) Saheli Marg. PH 560011
— Hotel Lakend : (2 Star) Alkapuri, Fatehsagar Lake
  PH 521191;FAX 523 898

EXCURSIONS

EKLINGJI : (22 km) This sandstone and marble temple built in
734 AD is a complex of 108 temples enclosed by high walls and is
devoted to the presiding deity of Maharanas of Mewar. The walled
complex encloses an elaborately pillared hall or mandap under a large
pyramidal roof and has four-faced image of Lord Shiva in black marble.

NAGDA : (23 km) Dating back to 6th century AD this ancient sight
is famous for Sas-Bahu Temple (9th/10th C.). Splendid Jain temple of
Adbudji is also located in this area.

HALDIGHATI : (40 km) Historic place where the battle between
Maharana Pratap and Emperor Akbar was fought in 1576 AD. There
is a Chhatri dedicated to the faithful horse of Maharana Pratap 'Chetak'.

NATHDWARA : (48 km) Built in the early 18th century it, is a
renowned centre of pilgrimage for the devotees of Krishna and Vishnu.
It is believed that when the statue of Srinath was being moved to a safer
place to escape the wrath of Emperor Aurangzeb, the wheel of the
chariot carrying this statue got stuck in the mud. Seeing it as a divine
sign that Lord Krishna wished to dwell here, a temple was erected at
this spot and a holy township grew around the temple. The main
Shrinathji temple attracts devotees throughout the year. Cloth painting
or pichhawais are famous.

JAISMAND LAKE : (48 km) Built by Maharana Jai Singh in the
17th century, this is the second largest artificial lake in Asia. There are
also some elegant marble cenotaphs on its banks and a small temple
dedicated to Lord Shiva. On either side of the lake were the summer
palaces built for the Maharanis of that time which today houses
government offices. The lake attracts several species of migratory birds

while the Jaismand wildlife sanctuary is the home of different species of animals.

DUNGARPUR : It was Founded in the early 13th century by Rana Dungar Singh. The Juna Palace and Udai Vilas Palace are the main attractions and the interior have some well-preserved wall paintings.

KUMBALGARH : (84 km) This is the second most important citadel of Mewar after Chittorgarh. Range after range of the Aravallis protect this fortress built by Rana Kumbha in mid 15th century, covering an area of 12 sq. km. This fort fell only once to the army of Akbar and that too because of the water supply of the fort was contaminated by the enemy forces. The fort lies 1,100 meter above sea level and enclosed within its fortified ramparts are palaces, temples, fields, water sources and farms – fully self contained to withstand a long siege.

MOUNT ABU : (185 km) Rajasthan's only hill station and a major pilgrim centre,this holy mountain lies at the southern extremity of the Aravelli. Mount Abu, owing to its good rainfall, has the richest vegetation in Rajasthan, a wide variety of trees and shurbs can be viewed as one drives up to Mount Abu. Abu, according to legend, stands for the son of Himalayas, deriving its name from Arbuda, the powerful serpent who rescued Nandi, the sacred bull of Shiva, from a chasm. Yet another legend explains how the lake at Mt. Abu got its name. It is believed that the gods formed the lake by digging it with their fingernails 'nakh' hence Nakki Lake. Many sages and seers had their retreats on Mt. Abu, most famous being Vashista who is believed to have created four agnikula Rajput clans from a fire-pit by performing a 'yagna' or fire sacrifice, to protect the earth from demons. Till 11th century Mt. Abu was dedicated to Lord Shiva before it became a Jain Pilgrim centre. DILWARA JAIN TEMPLE, built between 11th and 13th centuries and dedicated to Jain Tirtankaras, is famous for its rich and intricate carvings in marble. The Vimal temple is the oldest of these dedicated to the first Tirthankara. Built in 1031 AD, it is a superb example of temple architecture. The central shrine has an image of Rishabdev and large courtyard with 52 small shrines, each housing a beautiful statue of tirthankaras with 48 elegantly carved pillars from the entrance to courtyard. The Lun Vasahi temple, dedicated to 22nd Tirthankara – Neminathji was built in 1231 AD by two brothers – Vastpal and Tejpal, Minister of Raja Vir Dhawal – a ruler of Gujarat – belonging to the Porwal Jain family.

ADHAR DEVI TEMPLE : A beautiful temple chiselled out of a huge rock and flanked by natural cleft is reached by a flight of 360 stairs.

NAKKI LAKE : This lake is studded with little islets, as legend has, it was dug out by gods with their nails. Nowhere in India except in the Himalayas does a lake exist 1200 meters above sea level.

GAUMUKH TEMPLE : Here a little stream flows from the mouth of a marble cow. It was here that the legend of the four Agnikula clans of Rajputs was born. Nearby is the marble image of Nandi who was rescued by the mighty serpent Arbuda.

SUN SET POINT AND HONEYMOON POINT provides a pleasant view of the valley.

SRI RAGHUNATHJI TEMPLE : It is believed that Shri Ramanand, the famous Hindu preacher, placed the image of Shri Raghunathji on this spot in 14th century.

GARDENS AND PARKS : Abu is dotted with beautiful gardens blooming in a riot of colours.

RANAKPUR : (80 km from Udaipur on the way to Mount Abu) In a quite and picturesque valley which runs into the western slopes of the Aravelli hills is a remarkable complex of Jain temples at Ranakpur, one of the five main holy places of the Jain sect. In the 15th century, Rana Kumbha of Mewar gave a large stretch of land in a quiet and picturesque valley, deep in the Aravellis, to the Jains. This area came to be known as Ranakpur. Though over 500 years old the temples here are superbly preserved in a near perfect condition. In the centre is the main temple dedicated to Tirthankara Rishabdeo with a Chaumukha or four faced shrine dedicated to Adinath. The most distinctive features are the 29 halls of the temple which contain 1444 pillars of which not even two are alike everyone being in a different style. Every conceivable surface of the wall pillars and ceilings is carved and every corner and angle is engraved with Jain images. The quadruple image stands in the main sanctuary, which is open on all four sides. Rising in three storeys, it has four subsidiary shrines with a total of 80 'spuies' supported by 420 columns. There are also 24 mandapas and spires.

There are two more Jain temples and temple dedicated to the Sun god.

CHITTORGARH : (112 km) Chittorgarh—pride and glory of Rajasthan—echoes with the tales of romance and valour unique to Rajput tradition. It is more known for Rani Padmini, queen of Rana Bhim Singh whose beauty led the Sultan of Delhi, Allauddin Khilji to attack Chittor in 1303 AD. Legend has it, that Alauddin Khilji desired her and besieged Chittor. Later he offered to return without fighting if the Rana let him see art the image of the queen in a mirror and not her directly. It was agreed and he was allowed to enter the fort and see the reflection of the queen's face in a mirror. But when the Rana accompanied him up to the fort's gate to see him off. Alauddin Khilji resorted to trecherry and arrested him and took him to his camp. He then offered to release the Rana provided the queen agreed to be his wife. History records that Rani Padmani attacked the Sultan's camp and freed the Rana. Later Allauddin vengefully fought and killed every Rajput soldier. In the fierce battle 7,000 Rajput warriors lost their lives and the Maharani with her entire entourage committed 'Jauhar'. Countless tales of Chittor's legendary heroes are still sung by folk musicians all over Rajasthan. Strangely the historic mirror is still intact and can be seen in the fort. It is located on 180 meter high hill, covering 700 acres. Tablets and Chattries bearing testimony to the acts of sacrifice and gallantry lie between several monumental gates. The main gates are Padan Pol, Bhairon Pol, Hanuman Pol and Ram Pol.

RAMA KUMBHA'S PALACE : This historical palace of which only ruins remain today is believed to be one of the underground cellars where Rani Padmini and other women had committed 'Jauhar'. PADMINI'S PALACE, according to legend, was here and her glimpse was shown to Allauddin Khilji, here. It overlooks the pool in which the 'Zenana Mahal' is situated where Padmini had stood when her reflection was shown to the Sultan in a mirror placed in the main hall. MEERA and KUMBHA SHYAM TEMPLE is associated with Meerabai. She was the wife of Rana Bhojraj and is set to have consumed poison sent by the Rana but survived because of Lord Krishna's blessings.

KALIKA MATA MANDIR : A temple of mother Goddess Kali, was originally built as Sun temple in the 8th century and was converted into Kalika Mata temple in the 14th century.

MEERABAI'S TEMPLE : Temple where Meerabai used to worship Lord Krishna.

FESTIVALS

FEBRUARY : DESERT FESTIVAL : A three-day-long extravaganza of colour, music and festivity at the golden city of Jaisalmer. Gair and fire dancers swaying to traditional tunes, a turban-tying competition and a Mr. Desert contest are part of the fun of the occasion. Camel rides and folk dances on sand and dunes are added attraction.

NAGAUR FAIR : Nagaur bustles with life during its annual cattle fair which is one of the largest in the country. Exciting games and races are part of the festivities.

MARCH : ELEPHANT FESTIVAL : A festival where elephants are the centre of attraction. The festival begins with a procession of elephants, camels and horses, followed by lively folk dancers. Elephant races, elephant polo matches and a most interesting tug of war between elephants and men, are all parts of this spectacular event.

APRIL : GANGAUR : The most important local festival in Rajasthan, Gangaur celebrations last for 18 days. It is dedicated to Gauri, a manifestation of goddess Parvati. The festival is celebrated by girls and married women throughout Rajasthan. The images of Gauri are ornamented and offerings are made. This is also an auspicious day for young people to select their life partners. Colourful procession with the town band playing, horses and elaborate palanquins make it a fascinating spectacle.

MEWAR FESTIVAL : An exhilarating welcome to spring, this festival is a visual feast with Rajasthani songs, dances, processions, devotional music and firework displays. It is celebrated in the romantic city of Udaipur during the Gangaur festival. A procession of colourfully attired women carrying images of the goddess Gauri make their way to the Pichola Lake.

MAY : URS – AJMER : The Urs are held every year at the dargah of Sufi Saint Khwaja Moinuddin Chisti, commemorating his symbolic union with god. Pilgrims from all over the world gather to pay homage. Qawalis and poems are presented in the saint's honour.

AUGUST : TEEJ : This swing festival welcomes the advent of the monsoon. Swings are hung from trees and decorated with flowers. Women, colourful and attired, swing on them and sing songs in celebration.

OCTOBER : MARWAR FESTIVAL : The festival celebrates the 'Maand style of folk music – an evolved classical style that describes the romantic life of Rajasthan's rulers. Held during Sharad Purnima, the folk artistes bring alive the legends and folklore of earlier times.

NOVEMBER : PUSHKAR MELA : The tranquil Pushkar is transformed into a spectacular fair ground for 12 days in the month of Kartik. Trading of cattle, camel races and dazzling displays of bangles, brassware, clothes, camel saddles and halters are the major attractions of this colourful event. Devotees come in their thousands to take a ritual dip in the lake on the day of Kartik Purnima and to worship at on the Brahma temple in the world.

DECEMBER : SHILPIGRAM CRAFT MELA : UDAIPUR – Some of the magnificent crafts of Rajasthan displayed at a colourful festival held in Udaipur.

SIKKIM

SIKKIM
AT A GLANCE

AREA : 7,096 Sq. km.
CAPITAL : Gangtok
BOUNDARIES : East - Bhutan;
West - Nepal; South - West Bengal;
North - Tibet.
LANGUAGES : Nepali, Hindi,
Lepca and Bhutani.
ROADS : Gangtok is connected by
road with Darjeeling, Kalimpong, Siliguri
and with all district headquarters within
the State. Road length in the State is
2,383 km.

AIRPORT : Nearest airport-Bagdogra of West Bengal

IMPORTANT HILL RESORT

Gangtok (1547 m) Nearest Railhead –Siliguri 114 km.

PILGRIM CENTRES (A : Air; R : Rail)

Enchey (Gangtok) Festivals held at Buddhist Monastery ; A –
Bagdogra 124 km, R – Siliguri 114 from Gangtok

Rumtek : (24 km from Gangtok) Festival held annually; A –
Bagdogra 124 km, R Siliguri 114 km from Gangtok

Pemayangtse : (137 km from Gangtok) Pilgrim centre attracting
Buddhists for two days dance festival in February ; A – Bagdogra 124
km, R Siliguri 114 from Gangtok

Tashiding Monastery : Buddhist shrine containing sacred pot of
holy water; A – Bagdogra 124 km, R Siliguri 114 km from Gangtok.

Sikkim lies in the heart of the towering eastern Himalayas. Sikkim
has a varied topography with the elevation ranging from 800 feet. Most
of the Sikkim consists of mountainous terrain, interspersed with ravines
and green valleys. Kanchenjunga on the western border with Nepal
dominates the land with its awe inspiring beauty and majesty and its
splendid height of 28028 feet makes it the third highest mountain in
the world. Sikkim boasts of several hundred different kinds of orchids,
the dense forest of Sikkim are an ideal habitat for wild life of which
Yak is the most common animal.

HISTORY

The early history of Sikkim starts in the 13th century with the signing of a Brotherhood Treaty between the Lepcha Chief Thekong-thek and Tibetan Prince Khe-Bhumsa at Kavi in north of Sikkim and the beginning of Namgyal dynasty in Sikkim in 1642. Till the 18th century the inhabitants of Sikkim were Lepchas. In the 18th and 19th centuries a large number of immigrants of Nepalese origin came to Sikkim and they constitute 50% of the total population. With the march of history events also brought a change from monarchy to democracy and Sikkim became an integral part of the Indian Union in 1975.

GANGTOK

Cradled in the manifold splendours of nature, deep within the snow clad Himalayas is the capital of the Sikkim. Gangtok offers a hospitable base to explore the varied wonders of this highland, its picturesque valleys, monasteries, mountains, lakes and trekking trails.

PLACES OF INTEREST

ENCHEY MONASTERY : Built on the site blessed by lama Druptob,a tantric master known for his power of flying. This 200 year old monastery has in its premises images of gods, goddesses and other religious objects.

DIRECTORATE OF HANDICRAFT AND HANDLOOM : Instituted with the aim of promoting and keeping alive the State's traditional arts and crafts.

SIKKIM RESEARCH INSTITUTE OF TIBETOLOGY (SRIT) : The most prestigious of its kind in India—this institute is a treasure trove of vast collection of rare Lepcha, Tibetan and Sanskrit manuscripts, Statues and rare Thankas and has over 200 Buddhist icons and other prized objects of arts. Today, it is a renowned world-wide centre for study of Buddhist philosophy and religion.

SIKKIM TIME CORPORATION LTD. : The first industrial units set up in Sikkim in 1977.

SA-NAGOR-CHOTSHOG-CENTRE : It is a Tibetan refugee monastic institution established in 1961 by His Eminence Luding Khen Rimpoche, Head of Ngorpa, seb-sect of the Sakya Order, with the blessings of H.H. Sakya Trizin and H.H. Dalai Lama.

DO-DRUL-CHORTEN (STUPA) : This was built by the venerable Trulshi Rimpoche, head of the Nyingma order of Tibetan Buddhism in 1945. Inside this stupa, there are complete mandala sets of Dorjee Phurba (Bajra Kilaya), a set of Kan-gyur relics (Holy Books), complete 'Zung' (Mantras) and other religious objects. Around this Chorten, which is one of the most important stupas of the Sikkim, are 108 Mani-Lhakor (Prayer wheels). These prayer wheels are turned by the devout Buddhists while chanting 'Hail to the jewel in the Lotus', to invoke the Boddhisattva. The Chorten is surrounded by Chorten Lakhang and where there are two huge statues of Guru Rimpoche (Guru Padmasambhava).

HOW TO REACH

AIR : Nearest airport-Bagdogra 124 km.

RAIL : Nearest railhead Siliguri (114 km) and New Jalpaiguri (125 km) connecting Howrah, Delhi, Guwahati and Lucknow.

ROAD : Gangtok is connected by road to Darjeeling, Kalimpong and Siliguri. All districts, places within the Sikkim are to be visited by surface transportation. The Sikkim Nationalised Transport (SNT) operate regular buses from Gangtok to all major cities and towns within the State and to North Bengal. Booking facilities are available at Siliguri and Gangtok.

DISTANCES FROM GANGTOK

Kalimpong 67 km; Bagdogra 124 km; 88 km from Darjeeling (direct route) 119 km Darjeeling via Kalimpong, 584 km from Patna; 725 km from Calcutta.

ENTRY FORMALITIES

All foreigners intending to visit Sikkim can avail of 15 day's permit for FIT and Groups for restricted areas i.e. Gangtok, Rumtek, Phodong, Pelling which can be obtained 24 hrs. in advance from all Indian Missions abroad, Sikkim Tourism offices in Delhi, Calcutta, Siliguri and Gantok after furnishing Requisite documents.

PERMITS

Domestic and Foreign tourists require permits to go to Tsomgo and Yumthang. The Superintendent of Police, Check-Post divisions of Sikkim, Police department Gangtok issues permits for Domestic Tourists.For foreigners, the permit is issued by the Tourism Department, Government of Sikkim, Gangtok for a group consisting of not less than four members (all foreigners) and the tour has to be organised by an approved Travel Agency / Tour Operator.

Trekking Permit is available on all working days from Tourism Department, Government of Sikkim, PH 22064, 23425, 25277

To visit sanctuaries contact Chief Wild Life Warden, Forest Secretariat, Deorali – Gangtok.

CONDUCTED TOURS

— Half Day City Tour / Half Day tour to Rumtek Monastery
For detailed information contact –
— Sikkim Tourist Office, Mahatama Gandhi Road, Gangtok
PH 22064/ 23425; FAX (03592)25647

HOTEL ACCOMMODATION (STD CODE 03592)

- Tashi Delek. PH 22991, 22038; FAX 0359 22362
- Nor Khill. PH 23186-7
- Netuk House. PH 22374
- Martam Village Resort. PH 23314
- Hotel Mayur. PH 22752, 22825
- Tibet. PH 22523; FAX 13592 22707
- Central Hotel. PH 22553
- Orchid. PH 22381
- Denzong Inn. PH 22692

TREKKING ROUTES :

(1) Gangtok to Pemayangtse via Rumtek – then to Yaksum, Bakkim and Dzongri
(2) Namchi to Pemayangtse
(3) Pemayangtse to Gangtok - 9 Days
(4) Naya Bazar to Gangtok – 8 Days
Trekking equipment can be hired from Sikkim Tourist Department

EXCURSIONS

TASHI VIEW POINT : One gets bird's eye view of sprawling Gangtok and across the hill Mt. Kanchenjunga and of Mt. Siniolchu, one of the most graceful peaks in the world.

GANESH TOK : (7 km) From this point one gets bird's eye view of sprawling Gangtok town below while across Mt. Kanchenjunga and Mt. Sinilochu loom over the horizon.

HANUMAN TOK : (11 km) Situated above Ganesh Tok a temple of Lord Hanuman where the devotees come and offer prayers.

SARAMSA GARDEN : (14 km) This garden is a home of many exotic orchids and other rare tropical and temperate plants. Established and maintained by the Department of Forest, it is an excellent recreation and picnic spot.

WATER GARDENS : (16 km) Ideal picnic spot for picnic with a small swimming pool for children.

KABI LUNGCHOK : (17 km) The place where the historic Treaty of Brotherhood between the Lepcha Chief Te-Kung-Tek and the Bhutia Chief Khey-Bum-Sar was signed ritually. The spot where the ceremony took place is marked by a memorial stone pillar amidst the cover of dense forest.

RUMTEK DHARMA CHAKRA CENTRE : (24 km) It is a seat of Kagyu order one of the 4 major Tibetan sects. Since the late 1960s, after the arrival of His Holiness the 16th Gyalwa Kramapa, the centre houses some of the world's most unique religious scriptures and religious art objects. Traditional in design, it is almost a replica of the original Kagyu headquarters in Tibet.

FAMBONG LA WILDLIFE SANCTUARY : (25 km) The Sanctuary is home to a large number of wild orchids, rhododenrons etc. The richly forested area is known to be home for various species of wild animals.

TSOMGO LAKE : (40 km) Literally known as the 'Source of the Lake' in Bhutia language, it is about 1 km long, oval in shape, 15 meters deep and is considered sacred by local people. Between May and August it is possible to see a variety of flowers. It is also an ideal habitat for the Red Panda and various species of birds.

NAMCHI : (78 km) Meaning Sky High, this town, HQ of South District situated at an elevation of 5500 ft, is a fast developing tourist destination with all round tourist activities.

PEMAYANGTSE MONASTERY : (137 km) One of the oldest monastery established by Lhatsun Chempo, one of the reverend Lamas to have performed the consecration ceremony of the first Choygal (Religious Monarch) of Sikkim. It was established as a high class monastery for 'Pure Monks'. Inside the Monastery there is a wooden structure depicting the Maha Guru's heavenly peace, which is considered a masterpiece created by late Dungzin Rimpoche.

Accommodation is available at Hotel Mt. Pandim located just across the Monastery on a smaller hill top. For booking contact PH 03593/50756.

TENDONG HILL : Historical place of recluse for Buddhist lamas who spent years in meditation amidst the silent scenic grandeur. Tendong hill is a small flat stretch of land at an altitude of 8,530 ft. Legend says that this hill served the Lepcha Tribes from the ravages of Deluge when the whole world was flooded—legend similar to Noha's Ark of Bible. Even today, the Lepchas perform pujas to pay reverence to the Tendong Hills. The only Tea estate of the State which produces one of the top quality teas in International market is spread out on a gentle hill slope originating this hill.

YUMTHANG : (140 km) At an elevation of 11,800 ft. is a paradise for nature lovers with a fascinating blend of flora and fauna. The valley is also home for Shingbha Rhodondendron Sanctuary with 24 spicies of Rhododendrons. Yumthang "Tsa-Chu" or the hot spring on the left bank of Lachung is immensely popular for its curative properties and healing power.

RABDENTSE RUINS : This was second capital of the erstwhile Kingdom of Sikkim after Yuksom till the year 1814 AD ruins of which can be seen at walkable distance from Pemayangtse Monastery

PLACES OF INTEREST IN WEST SIKKIM

PEMAYANGTSE MONASTERY : Refer excursion from Sikkim

PELLING : Situated at 6,800 ft it is a fast growing urban settlement. Due to tourist influence it has hotels, lodges in and around city. There is a bus service which links Pelling to the West District headquarter town of Gyalshing.

RABDENTSE RUINS : Refer excursions from Sikkim

SANGACHOLING MONASTERY : Situated on a ridge above Pelling and Peymayangste Monastery, one has to spend at least 40 minutes walking up the steep hilly slopes which leads through rich forest covers.

KHECHEOPALRI LAKE : One of the sacred lakes (reachable by motorable road from Pemayangtse) both for the Buddhist and the Hindus. It is believed that birds do not permit even a single leaf to flot on the surface.

YUKSOM : First Capital of Sikkim, where the first Chogyal of the Kingdom was consecrated in 1641 AD by three learned lamas. It is considered as sacred as the evidence of the consecration ceremony is still intact at Norbugang Chorten in the form of stone seats and a footprint of the Head-lama on a stone.

DUBDI MONASTERY : Located on a hill top above Yuksam, it was the first Monastery established soon after the consecration ceremony of the first Chogyal and can be approached by trekking only.

TASHIDING MONASTERY : Located on top of a heart-shaped hill with the back-drop of the sacred Mt. Kanchenjunga. According to Buddhist scriptures Guru Padma Sambhava had blessed the sacred land of Sikkim in the 8th century AD from this spot. The Monastery was built in 18th century AD by Nadak Sempa Chempo, one of three Lamas who had performed the consecration ceremony of first Chogyal. Every year, on the 15th day of the first Tibetan month, the Bhumchu Ceremony is celebrated with devotees coming from far and near to get the blessings of the holy water.

PLACES OF INTEREST IN SOUTH SIKKIM

NAMCHI : Refer excursions from Sikkim.

TENDONG HILL : Refer excursions from Sikkim.

TEMI TEA GARDEN : The only Tea estate producing one of the top quality teas in the International market.

MENAM HILL : Situated at an altitude of 10,300 ft. Kanchenjunga and its surrounding ranges dwarf this richly forested and rugged hill. On a clear sunny day, it is possible to see the plains of Bengal spanning across Kalimpong and Darjeeling hills in the south, right across to the Indo-China border towards the north.

RAVANGLA : At the base of Menam Hill,this is a small township and a transit point to various tourist destinations in South and West Sikikim. The trek to Menam from Ravangla takes about 4 hours and from Menam hill top one has the option to take the gentle trek to Borong village or follow the more treacherous trails taken by the famous British botanist, Sir Joseph Hooker, down to Yangang village.

BORONG : A picturesque village with beautiful landscape, and the hot-spring 'Borong Tsa-Chu', can be reach by motorable road from Ravangla or trek via Menam.

VERSEY : It lies at an elevation of 10,000 ft. and has motorable road access up to Hilley. An easy 4 km trek from there takes one up to the Versey Rhododendron Sanctuary. One can also trek from Soreng or Dentam in West Sikkim. Accommodation is available at "Guras Kunj" trekker's hut.

PLACES OF INTEREST IN NORTH SIKKIM

KABI LUNGCHOK : Refer excursions from Sikkim

PHENSONG MONASTERY : The place is situated on the gentle slop stretching from Kabi to Phodong with perhaps one of the best landscape in the region. The Phensong Monastery, under the Nyingmapa Buddhist Order, was built in 1721 during the time of Jigme Pawo. The annual festival of Chaam is performed on the 28th and 29th day of the tenth month of lunar calender.

PHODONG MONASTERY : One of the six major monasteries in Sikkim this Monastery is located in the north. Four km beyond Phodong is the recently renovated Labrang Monastery, unique in its architectural design.

SINGHIK : The place offers the most spectacular views of Mt.Kanchenjunga

CHUNGTHANG : On the conflunce of Lachen and Lachung Chu and the starting point of the Teesta river, the valley is believed to have been blessed by Guru Rinpoche and one can visit the Holy Guru Lhedo to see the foot and palm prints left behind by the Patron Saint.

LACHUNG : A tourist destination and a monastery is situated on the slope of the mountains

FESTIVALS

Sikkim's population is comprised of the three ethenic communities of the Bhutias, the Lepchas and the Nepalese. Maghey Sankranti, Durga Puja, Laxmi Puja and Chaite Dasai are celebrated by the Nepali community. Panglhabsol, Losoong and Losar are celebrated by the Bhutia community. Namsoong and Tendong Hlo Rum Faat is celebrated by the Lepcha community.

TAMIL NADU

TAMIL NADU
AT A GLANCE

AREA : 1,30,058 Sq. km.

CAPITAL : Chennai

BOUNDARIES : East - Bay of Bengal; West - Kerala; North - Andhra Pradesh; North-West - Karnataka; South - Gulf of Mannar.

LANGUAGE : Tamil

ROADS : The length of road network in Tamil Nadu is nearly 1,70,000 km.

AIRPORT : Tiruchirapally, Coimbattore, Salem

Chennai being the international airport in the southern region is the main centre of airline routes.

MUSEUMS

Chennai : Government Museum and Art Gallery; Fort St.George Museum

Madurai : Temple Museum– Meenakshi Temple; Gandhi Memorial Museum and Government Museum; Palace Museum – Tirumalai Nayak Museum

Tanjore : Saraswati Mahal, Library and Art Gallery; Raja Museum; Temple Museum

Trichy : The Museum

IMPORTANT HILL RESORTS

Name	Altitude	Nearest Railhead
Coonoor	1858 m	Coonoor
Kodaikanal	2133 m	Kodaikanal Road 80 km
Kotagiri	1983 m	Coonoor 21 km
Ooty	2286 m	Udhagamandalam
Yercud	1515 m	Salem 35 km

PILGRIM CENTRES (A : Air; R : Rail)

Chidambaram : Temple where Lord Shiva performed Cosmic Dance as Nataraja; A – Trichy 174 km, R – Chidambaram.

Kanchipuram : One of the seven sacred cities of India and seat of Shankaracharya of Kanchi; A – Chennai 76 km, R – Kanchipuram

Kanyakumari : Temple of the Virgin Goddess. Vivekanand Memorial built on Vivekananda Rock; A – Trhiruvananthapuram 87 km, R Kanyakumari

Kumbakonam : Important Shaivite and Vaishnavite centre; A - Trichy 95 km, R - Kumbakonam

Madurai : Temple of Goddess Meenakshi; A and R Madurai

Nagore : Dargah of saint Hazrat Syed Shahabdul Hameed; A - Trichy 139 km, R - Nagore

Palani : One of the six abodes of Lord Muruga (Subramanya); A – Madurai 122 km, R – Palani

Pondicherry : Seat of Sri Aurobindo Ashram; A- Chennai 160 km, R - Pondicherry

Rameshwaram : Shiva Lingam consecrated by Sri Rama; A - Madurai 152, Rameshwaram

Shantivanam : The Sachitananda Ashram comprises Hindu, Buddhist and Christian traditions; A – Trichy 40 km, R - Kulithalai 2 km

Srirangam : The temple of Sri Ranganatha, famous Vaishnav centre; A and R Trichy 10km

Swamimalai : One of the six abodes of Lord Muruga; A - Madurai 177 km, R Swamimalai

Tiruchendur : One of the six abodes of Lord Muruga; A -Madurai 177 km, R - Tiruchendur

Tirunallar : Saint Peyarchi festival subject to the movement of planet Saturn celebrated every 2½ years; A - Trichy 145 km, R - Karaikal 5 km

Tiruttani : One of the six abodes of Lord Muruga; A - Chennai 84 km, R - Tiruttani

Tiruvannamalai : Shiva temple with a Tejo Lingam (lingam of light) and Shri Ramana Ashram set up by Ramana Maharshi; A - Chennai 188 km, R -Tiruvannamalai

Viatheeswaran Koli : Lord Shiva is worshipped as the great Healer of persons with ailments; A -Trichy 150 km, R -Vaitheeswaran Koli

Velankanni : Catholic Church of Our lady of Velankanni, believed to cure ailments; A Trichy 149 km, R Nagapattinam 12 km.

Tamil Nadu is one of the most ancient regions of India. Civilization flourished in Tamil Nadu long before the beginning of the Christian era. The heart of the Dravidian culture and tradition, home of Classical

dance Bharat Natyam, the visual legacy of the culture of the State is among most satisfying spectacles in India.

HISTORY

Tamil Nadu is one of the most ancient regions in India history of which dates back some 6000 years.

The State represents the nucleus of Dravidian culture in India, which antedated the Aryan culture in India by almost a thousand years. Tamil Nadu was variously ruled by the Cheras, Cholas and Pandyas prior to the Christian era. Karikalan Chola, the greatest of the earlier Chola, ascended the throne at the beginning of this era. He took several measures for the welfare and constructed a barrage across the Kaveri river. Prominent Chola cities were Thanjavur and Kumbakonam. The Pandyas excelled in trade and learning.

A Pandyan king sent an Ambassador to the Roman Emperor Augustus in the first century BC. The Cholas were followed by the Cheras and were powerful on the west coast. Madurai was most important city under them.

The reign of the great temple builders the Pallavas began sometimes during the second quarter of the 4th century AD, and dominated the south for 400 years. Dravidian architecture attained great heights during this period. Some of their major contributions include the beautiful monuments of Mamallapuram, the Kailasnather temple at Kanchpuramand, the Kapaliswarar and Parthasarthy temples at Chennai. The Pallavas continued to hold sway until the 10th century. The end of 11th century once again saw the alternative rule of the Chalukyas, Chola and Pandyas.

In the 13th century, the Pandyas became dominant. Their kingdom was a great centre of international trade. The rise of Vijaynagar Empire spelt the decline of the Pandyas. They were ultimately defeated by Vijaynagar gorces and their territories were annexed to Vijaynagar empire. Later with the disintegration of Vijaynagar empire Tamil Nadu was parcelled out among several petty kings.

The Muslim invasion of South came in 14th century. The Vijaynagar empire held sway until 1564 when it came to an end with a defeat at the hands of the Deccan Sultans in the battle of Talikota. The victorious sultans systematically destroyed the beautiful city of Vijaynagar. The kingdom itself was split into several parts and given to the Nayakas to rule. Of these, the Nayakas of Madurai attained popularity. Tamil Nadu under the Nayakas were peaceful and prosperous. Rulers went out renovating and reconstructing some of the oldest temples remarkable amongst which are the thousand pillar Meenakshi temple at Madurai and Srirangam temple at Tiruchirapally.

With the establishment of East India Company at Madras in 1639, a new chapter was opened in the history of Tamil Nadu. Slowly and steadily the State came under British sway. In 1641 Fort St. George became the headquarters of the East India Company on Coromondal coast.

When India became independent, the old Madras Province comprising Tamil Nadu, Andhra Pradesh and part of Kerala continued as the State of Madras. Agitation for a separate Andhra State compelled the government to bifurcate the State into two different States, Andhra Pradesh to include the Telugu speaking and Madras the Tamil speaking people. On 14th January 1969 Madras State changed its name to Tamil Nadu.

The capital city Madras was renamed Chennai in 1996.

CHENNAI

Chennai, the gateway to the south, represents a culture that's unique to the region. Music, Dance and Drama are an integral part of everyday life.

In 1639 AD Francis Day, a merchant of the East India Company had selected a quaint fishing hamlet called Madraspatnam as a site for settlement. Naturally protected from enemies by the Coovum river in the south, Elambore river in the west and the sea on the east, Madraspatnam was ideal for trading. Some year's

later weavers settled in the area around the fort which was called 'Black Town' by the Britishers after the black skinned natives. By the early 1700s, Chennai became a large city and soon was made the capital of the State and remained as capital till today.

PLACES OF INTEREST

FORT ST. GEORGE : This fort built by the East India Company in 1653 AD is the oldest British tombstone in the country. Inside the fort is St.Mary's Church, the oldest Anglican Church east of Suez Canal. Today, the fort houses the Secretariat and the Legislative Assembly of Tamil Nadu. The museum inside the fort is the repository of rare exhibits of weapons, uniforms, coins, costumes, medals and some other artifacts dating to the British period.

KAPILISWARA TEMPLE : Dedicated to Lord Shiva, this temple has some beautiful sculptures among which are bronze idols of 63 Shaivite saints adorning the outer courtyards. The temple was damaged in 1566 when the Portuguese took over Mylapore. The present temple was rebuilt by the Vijaynagar kings in 16th century. The magnificent 37m.high gopuram depicts many a legend with beautiful carvings. During the Aruvathimoovar festival held in March and April, 63 idols are carried in a procession around the temple.

MARINA BEACH : It is the second longest beach in the world with a length of 11 km in a single stretch. The Acquarium and the swimming pool are situated adjacent to each other on the sea front.

SANTHOME CATHEDRAL : Derives its name from St. Thomas believed to be an apostle of Christ built around 52 AD. The beautiful stain glass windows at the Basilica portrays the story of St.Thomas. The central hall has 14 wooden plaques depicting scenes from the last days of Christ. An old stone cross (called bleading cross) with Sassanian Pehelevi inscriptions can be seen here.

KALAKSHETRA : An internationally renowned academy of music and dance based on an ancient Gurukula style-started by Rukmini Devi Arundale in 1936.

THEOSOPHICAL SOCIETY : It is the world headquarters of Theosophical Society at Adyar.

GUINDY NATIONAL PARK : A sanctuary for the endangered Blackbuck and Spotted Deer. The adjacent Snake Park has a large collection of snakes and other reptiles.

VALLUVAR KOTLAM : Memorial to poet saint Tiruvalluvar is shaped like a temple chariot. The auditorium at Valluvarkotlam is said to be the largest in Asia which can accommodate 4000 people.

SITTARANGAM : Folk and art theatre situated in the Trade Fair complex on Island ground.

KISHINDA PICNIC PARK : Situated near Tambaram, it has an enchanting variety of entertainment facilities including boating in an artificial lake, amusement park, 3 dimension theatre.

HOW TO REACH

AIR : Chennai is an international airport with flight connections to all major parts of the world. Domestic airlines connect Chennai with Ahmedabad, Bangalore, Calicut, Cohin, Coimbatore, Delhi, Goa, Hyderabad, Kozikode Madurai, Mangalore, Mumbai, Port Blair, Pune, Puttuparthy, Tiruchirapalli Thiruvananthapuram and Visakhapatnam.

RAIL : Regular train services connect Chennai directly with all major cities of the country.

Suburban Electric trains run from Beach Station to Tambaram, and from Central to Gummidipoondi and Arakonam.

Chennai is connected by Rajdhani Express with New Delhi, timings:

— 2434 Rajdhani Express (Wed and Fri) D New Delhi 1530 / A Chennai 2005
— Rt 2433 (Fri and Sun) D Chennai 1200 / A New Delhi 1645

Chennai is connected by Shatabdi Express with Mysore, Tirupati and Coimbatore timings :

— 2007 Shatabdi Exp (Except Tues) D Chennai 0600 / A Mysore 1300
— Rt 2008 (Except Tues) D Mysore 1410 / A Chennai 2115
— 2035 Shatabdi Exp (Daily) D Chennai 0545 / A Tirupati 0815
— Rt 2036 (Daily) D Tirupati 1945 / A Chennai 2215
— 2023 Shatabdi Exp (Except Wed) D Chennai 1510 / A Coimbatore 2200
— Rt 2024(Except Wed) D Coimbatore 0725 / A Chennai 1410

ROAD : Chennai, being gateway to the south is connected by excellent roads to all parts of the south. Taxis, Auto-rikshaws and cycle rikshaws are available. All types of tourist vehicles are easily available on hire.

Transport Corporations of the States of Kerala, Karnataka and Andhra Pradesh also operate buses from the bus stand.

SEA : There is a sea line to Andman and Nicobar islands. Booking can be done at the Shipping Corporation of India situated at Rajali Salai, PH 5226873

DISTANCES FROM THE CHENNAI

Bangalore 351 km, Chidambaram 251 km, Cochin 700 km, Coimbatore 497km, Kanyakumari 700 km, Kodaikanal 436 km, Kovalam 760 km, Madurai 447 km, Ooty 565 km, Podicherry 163 km, Rameshwaram 569 km Sabrimala 831 km, Tanjore 321 km, Thekkedy 553 km, Tirupati 152 km, Trichy 319, Trivandrum 764 km, Velankani 328 km, Yercud 363 km.

CONDUCTED TOURS

Tours operated by Tamil Nadu Tourism Development Corporation:
— Half Day Chennai city sightseeing tour (Morning and Evening)
— One day Mammalapuram Tour : One day Pondicherry Tour
— One day Tirupati Tour : Tiruupti tour with one night stay at Tirupati
— One day Sakhti (Deviar Drashan Tour) : One day Thirumal Darshan Tour
— One day Thondainattu Thirupathigal (Vaishnava Temples)Tour
— One day Velankanni Tour : Thiruvannamalai Girivalam Tour
— Arupadai Veedu Tour : 3 Days Navagraha Tour (Nine Planets)
— 4 Days Chozhanattu Thirupathigal Tour (Vaishnava Temple)
— 5 Days Pandiyanattu Thirupathigal Tour (Vaishnava Temple)
— 5 Days arts and architectural Tour : 6 Days South India Tour
— 7 Days Mogambika Tour : 7 Days Goa-Mantralayam Tour
— 8 Days East-West Coast Tour : 8 Days Tamil Nadu Tour
— 8 Days Andhra Tour : 14 Days Puri-Gaya-Kasi-Allahabad Tour
— 12 Days Mumbai-Ajanta-Ellora Tour 14 Days South India Tour
— 14 Days Puri-Gaya-Kasi-Allahabad Tour
— Students Package Tour
For detailed information contact :
— T.N.T.D.C. Ltd., No 04, EVR Salai, Park Town, Chennai - 600 003. PH 582916, 586094; FAX 561 385

Tours Operated by India Tourism Development Corporation
— Chennai Sightseeing Tour - Daily
— Kanchipuram and Mahabalipuram - Daily
— Tirupathi Tour – Daily
— South India Tour (8 days) Departure every Saturday
For detailed information contact :
— I.T.D.C., 154 Anna Salai, Chennai – 600 002 PH 852 4295; FAX 852 2193

HOTEL ACCOMMODATION (STD CODE 044)

— Taj Coromondal (5 Star Deluxe), No 17, M.G. Road
  PH 827 2827; FAX 827 8547
— Connemara Hotel (5 Star), Binny Road
  PH 852 0123; FAX 852 3361
— The Trident (5 Star), 1/24 G.S.T. Road
  PH 234 4747; FAX 234 6699
— Welcomegroup Chola Shereton (5 Star), 10, Cathedral Road.
  PH 828 0101; FAX 827 8779
— Ambassador Pallava (4 Star), 53, Montieth Road, Egmore
  PH 855 4068; FAX 855 4492
— Madras International (4 Star), 693, Mount Road
  PH 852 4111; FAX 852 3412
— Hotel President (4 Star), 16. Dr. Radhakrishnan Salai,
  Mylapore. PH 853 2111; FAX 853 2299
— Savera Hotel (4 Star), DR. Radhakrishnan Road
  PH 827 4700; FAX 827 3475
— Quality Inn Aruna (4 Star), 144, Sterling Road, Nugambakkam.
  PH 825 9090; FAX 825 8282
— Breez Hotel (3 Star) 850, Poonamallee High Road, Kilpauk
  PH 641 3345-37; FAX 641 3301
— Hotel Kanchi (3 Star), Geetha Hotels Pvt. Ltd., 28
  Commander-in-chief. PH 827 1100; FAX 827 2928

EXCURSIONS

CHOLAMANDAL ARTISTS VILLAGE : (20 km) Established in 1966 this place is for exhibition of paintings, sketches, terracotta sculptures, batiks and other crafts.

DAKSHINA CHITRA : (21 km) Art and craft village currently under construction which will house crafts people from Tamil Nadu, Kerala, Karnataka and Andhra Pradesh.It will also have theatres, shops, libraries and archives.

VANDALUR : (35 km) Anna Zoological park spread over an area of 1265 acres is the largest in South Asia, inhabited by various species of mammals, reptiles and birds.

MUTTUKKADU : (36 km) This is a place for backwaters and estuary, Muttukkadu is ideal for rides on motorised boats. Pedel boats are also available here for hire and the place is ideally situated for analging and fishing.

COVELONG : (40 km) Village busy with fishing activities, this village also has fine beach and beach resorts.

CROCODILE PARK : (48 km) Breeding and research caentre for crocodiles has many species of crocodiles and alligators.

PULICAT LAKE : (61 km) One of the largest lagoons in South Asia. It is a major Waterbird sanctuary with migrant shore birds, Flamingos as well as resident birds. A Catamarine ride on a shallow water spread and a visit to a bird sanctuary are two most leisure facilities available here. A Dutch cemetery of 17th century is located on the shore.

Along the East Coast road between Chennai and Mammllapuram, there are amusement parks such as V.G.P., M.G.M. and Little Folks.

MAMMALLAPURAM : (60 km) Situated on the shores of Bay of Bengal, it was once a port of the Pallavas. The Pallava art flourished here from 600 to 749 AD. They have created many marvellous monuments with Sculptural Panels, Caves, Monolithic Rathas and Temples. CAVES—there are nine rock cut cave temples, the Krishna cave is notable for its realistic portrayal. In the MAHISHASURMARDINI CAVE, on one side is a magnificent bas relief of  Lord Vishnu in his cosmic sleep and in contrast on the other side is Goddess Durga fighting a buffalo - headed demon. THE SHORE TEMPLE is one of the oldest temple belonging to the 8th century AD and is a good example of the first phase of structural temples constructed in Dravidian style. It has two shrines facing east and west. ARJUNA'S PENANCE is one of the world's largest and finest stone base-relief (27 meter long and 9 meters high) depicting Arjuna's penance. This huge Whale-back-shaped rock faces the sea, and is split with a fissure in the middle. On the other side are gods semi-gods, men, beasts and birds, earthly and supernatural beings. FIVE RATHAS are five monolithic temples each created in a different style.Thy are known as Panch Pandava Rathas, and the four Rathas are supposed to have scooped out of a single rock formation. The Rathas with their Gopurams, multipillard and sculptured walls and Vimanas were built in Dravidian style in 7th century. Other interesting monuments are Ganesa Ratha, Varaha cave, old light house, Krishna's butter ball etc. Tiger cave, 5 km north of the main complex, was an open air theatre where cultural programmes were held for the benefit of the royal families.

At Government College of Architecture and Sculpture training is given in various branches of temple art and architecture according to 'Silpa Shastra'.

Mahabalipuram is easily accessible from Chennai by local transport, private as well as state government operated coaches, taxis etc. Accommodation is available at various categories of hotels. THIRUAZHUKUNDRAM pilgrim centre, located 14 km away from Mahabalipuram on top of the Vedagiri hills is known for its ancient Shiva temple. Just before noon every day two white kites stop at the temple and are fed by the temple priests. Legend has it that these two birds are actually saints who make a stop to rest at the temple on their flight between Varanasi and Rameshwaram. At the south-east end of the town is a spacious tank whose waters are said to possess curative powers. Once in every twelve years a conch floats in this tank and thousands of devotees flock to bathe in the tank at this auspicious time. VEDANTHANGAL BIRD SANCTUARY is located at 53 km from Mahabalipuram. It is the oldest waterbird sanctuary established in 1858. Many birds like cormorants, egrets grey herons, open billed stork, darters, spoobills, White Ibis, night herons grebes and grey pelicans are found here. Many migratory birds like garganey teals, shovellers, pintails, stilts and sandpipers visit the sanctuary every year. Mammalpur is one of the finest beach resort of India. All types of hotels are available along the sea side.

KANCHIPURAM : (76 km) A City of Thousand Temples, Kanchipuram is one of the seven sacred cities and considered as the second holiest place in India. It was successively the capital of the Pallavas, the Cholas and the Rayas of Vijaynagar. The city was also the seat of learning Shree Sankaracharya, Appar and Siruthonder. The great Buddhist Vhikku Bodhidharna lived and worked here. There are 126 temples in Kanchi and a few more on the outskirts. EKAMBARNATHA TEMPLE, the largest temple dedicated to Lord Shiva, was built originally by Pallavas and later improved by the Cholas and the king of Vijaynagar. The 57 meter high Rajagopuram is one of the tallest in south India. The centre of attraction of this massive temple has the 2500 years old Mango tree which still bears fruit with four different flavours on its four major branches. Krishna Dev Raya constructed outer stone walls of the temple in 1500. KAILASNATHA TEMPLE was constructed in the 8th century and has a beautiful panel depicting Lord Shiva and Parvati during a dance. The Ardhanareeswarar is one of the best sculptural wonder. VAIKUNTA PERUMAL TEMPLE—this Vaishnavite temple dates back to the 8th century and was built by Nandivarman Pallava. Battle scene depicting Pallava Valour are carved on the panels surrounding the main hall. VARADRAJA TEMPLE—the 100 pillared hall of this temple stands testimony to the artistry of the sculptors of Vijaynagar. The annual Garudotsavam festival (May- June) is very colourful and draws thousands of devotees.KAMAKSHI AMMAN TEMPLE dedicated to the goddess Kamakshi (Parvati) is one of the three holy places of Sakthi worship in India and was built by the Cholas in the 14th century.

Kanchipuram is also known for its thriving handloom industry. The silk weavers settled here 400 years ago and today it is known to be the producer of best silk sarees. TIRUTTANI, 42 km from Kanchipuram, has a temple which is one of the six abodes of Lord Subramanya. Situated on a hilltop, the temple is accessible by road as well as the 365 steps on the hill which are said to represent 365 days of the year.The Karthikai festival in December attracts lots of tourists. VELLORE, 64 km from Kanchipuram has the fort which is one of the best example of defence architecture in this part of the country. The strong bastions of the fort defended the Vijaynagar kings until their defeat in 1565. Tipu Sultan held the fort for some years before he was defeated. His family was imprisoned here and their tombs now lie to the west of the fort.

TIRUVANAMALAI, 96km from Pondicherry situated at the foot hills, has over 100 temples. Siva-Parvathy temple of Arunachaleswara is said to be the largest in India. During the Karthigai deepam festival celebrated in Nov-Dec, a huge fair is lit atop the hill and devotees flock to the temple and to the Ashram of the saint Sri Ramana Maharshi, which is 3 km from the temple. GINGEE (SENJI) 37 km from Tiruvannamalai, 150 km south-east of Chennai in south Arcot district, is famous for 700-year-old fort constructed during the period of Vijaynagar empire. There are four temples within the fort among which the Venkataramana temple is the largest. PICHAVARAM, 75 km from Pondicherry, is famous for Mangrove forests which could be seen with backwaters criss crossing the entire forest area. Boating facilities are available at the site. Pondicherry is easily accessible from Chennai by local transport, private as well as State government-operated coaches, taxis etc. Accommodation is available at various categories of hotels.

MADURAI

More than 2500 years old ancient city, situated on the banks of the river Vaigai Madurai is believed to have been built by the Pandyan King Kulasekara. Legend has it that drops of Maduram (nectar) fell from Lord Shiva's locks when he came to bless its people for constructing a temple for him. Madurai's history can be divided into four periods, beginning over 2000 years ago, when it was the capital of the Pandyan Kings. Apart from a brief period it fell to the Cholas, Madurai remain with Pandyan till the decline of the empire. The 200 year old reign of the Nayakas marked the golden era when art, architecture and learning scaled new heights.

PLACES OF INTEREST

MEENAKSHI TEMPLE : City's main attraction is the 2000 years old famous Meenakshi temple in the heart of the old town—a splendid example of Dravidian architecture. The present temple was designed in 1560 by Vishwanatha Nayak and subsequently built during the reign of Tirumalai Nayak. There are four entrances to the temple with an area of six hectares. Each of its 12 towers has the height of 45 to 50 meters. The Potrama Raikulam or the Golden Lotus Tank is the place where the Tamil literacy society, called Sangam used to meet to decide the merits of the work presented to them. The manuscripts that sank were dismissed while those that floated were considered great. The temple museum has 985 richly carved pillars and each one surpasses the other in beauty.

TIRUMALAI NAYAK MAHAL : This Indo-Saracenic building was constructed in 1523 and was originally four times as large as today. Sound and light show on the life of the Tirumalai Nayak and the story of the Silapathikaram are conduced daily.

GANDHI MUSEUM : The 300-year-old palace now converted into Museum has a picture gallery,a library of personal memorables of the Mahatama Gandhi and an exhibit of South Indian handicrafts and village industries.

VANDIYUR MARIAMMAN TEPPAKULAM : This enormous temple tank is fed by water from the Vaigai river.The tank has a mandapam at the centre enshrining Lord Vigneshwara. A colourful float festival is held in this tank every year on Thaipoosam day. (Jan-Feb)

HOW TO REACH

AIR : Madurai is connected by air with Chennai, Trichy and Mumbai.

RAIL : Madurai is an important railway junction of Southern Railway and is directly connected with Chennai and various cities of South India.

ROAD : Madurai is connected by road with major cities of the State. The State transport operates coaches from Chennai and many other places.

TOURIST OFFICE

— Tamil Nadu Tourist office is at Hotel Tamil Nadu Complex. West Veli Street PH – 34757.

HOTEL ACCOMMODATION (STD CODE 0452)

— Taj Garden Retreat (Heritage Hotel), Pasumalai Hill PH 601 020; FAX 604 400
— Hotel Madurai Ashok (3 Star), Alagarkoil Road PH 537 531; FAX 537 530
— Hotel Park Plaza (3Star),114-5, West Perumal Maistry Street. PH 742 112; FAX 743 654
— Hotel International, 46, West Perumal Maistry Street PH 741 552/3/4
— Pandyan Hotel, Race Course. PH 537 090; FAX 533 424
— Hotel Sulochana Palace, 96, West Paerumal Maistry Street. PH 741 071/72; FAX 740 627
— Hotel Supreme Pvt. Ltd., 110, West Perumal Maistry Street. PH 743 151; FAX 742 637

EXCURSIONS

THIRUPPARANKUNDRUM : (8 km) This temple is 350 years old. Its innermost shrine is cut on a solid rock.

THIRUMOHUR : (10 km) It has its legendary origin in the distant mythological past when Devas and Asuras churned the ocean to get Amritham (nectar), a sip of which would ensure immortality. When the pot of nectar emerged Lord Vishnu, in the form of beautiful Mohini, took it away. And while the Asuras stood mesmerized by her beauty, Vishnu distributed the nectar among the Devas.

AZHAGAR KOIL : (21 km) It has a temple dedicated to Lord Vishnu. On the festive day, the image of Azhgar is taken in a procession to the river Vaiga to participate in the marriage of Meenakshi and Sundareswara.

VETTANGUDI WATER BIRD SANCTUARY : (55 km) Species of birds found here are cormorants, herons, egrets, spoonbill etc.

VAIGAI DAM : (69 km) A beautiful picnic spot, it looks enchanting when illuminated.

SRIVILLIPUTTUR : (74 km) The Vatapatrasayi temple has one of the most impressive gopurams in the South.

RAMESWARAM : (171 km) Hailed as the Benares of the South, Rameshwaram is an island in the Palk Straits. Legend has it that Sri Rama had sanctified this place by worshipping Lord Shiva.

RAMANATHASWAMY TEMPLE is famous for its impressive corridor with massive sculptured pillars lining it. The corridor of the temple, 197 meters long east-west and 133 meters long south-north is the longest in the country. Each corridor has hundreds of pillars remarkable for their complex design style and rich carvings. The temple has fresh water springs which are believed to have medicinal properties. Different rulers, as it stands today, built the temple at different periods from 12 century AD onwards. THE GANDHAMATHANA PARAVATHAM is a hillock situated to the north of the temple. The two-storey mandapam and an imprint of Lord Rama's feet on a chakra attracts pilgrims. DHANUSKODI, the southernmost tip of the island was completely washed away by the 1964 cyclone. However, still remains intact are the icons of Lord Rama, Sita, Lakshmana, Hanuman and Vibhishana. UTHIRAKOSAMANGAI, 72km from Rameshwaram, has a temple dedicated to Lord Shiva where the deity is carved in emrald. The annual 'Aruthra' festival in December attracts a large number of pilgrims.

TIRUNELVELI : (140 km) Situated on the banks of the river Tamarabarani the small town of Tirunelveli which was once the Pandya province, has a history that goes back to 2000 years. The main attraction is the twin temples of Kanthimati-Nellaipappar dedicated to Parvati and Lord Shiva respectively. Among the interesting sights in the temple are the Golden Lily Tank, the thousand-pillar hall which has some exquisite sculptures and the musical pillars that produce different musical notes when struck. About 13 km from Tirunelveli, a place called Krishnapuram, has a temple dedicated to Lord Vishnu with some beautiful lifesize sculptures carved with great intricacy. Tiruchendur near Tirunelveli, the shore temple here is one of the six abode of Lord Subramanya and the only one of them to be built on unlevelled land. Tiruchedur is believed to be the place where Subramanya had offered victory prayers to his father Lord Shiva after slaying the demon Surapadma. The Skandha Shashti festival is celebrated at this temple in November every year. Ettaiyapuram the birthplace of the legendary poet Subramanya Bharathi is reachable from Tirunelveli.

KODAIKANAL : (120 km) Situated at an altitude of over 700 feet on the Palani hills of the western ghats, Kodaikanal is a beautiful and unspoilt hill station of Tamil Nadu. Kodai has more sunshine than any other Indian hill station. STAR SHAPED 24 hectare lake is set amidst the sylvan serenity of wooded slopes. Boating and angling is possible. THE BYRANT PARK lies near the lake and has 325 species of trees and shrubs. A horticultural show in May is an annual feature that attracts garden lovers. THE KURINJI ANDAVAR TEMPLE in the town enshrines Lord Murugan within its sanctum. GREEN VALLEY view offers some unforgettable spectacles of the hill resort and a beautiful view of the Vaigai Dam. PILLAR ROCKS is a panoramic spot with vertical rock boulders towering over 121 meters. The SHENBAGANUR MUSEUM has an splendid collection of Orchids.

There are also picturesque trek routes in and around Kodai.

One of the world's oldest solar observatories built in 1899 is situated in Kodai.

COURTALLAM : (160 km) Courtllam is situated at an elevation of about 16.7 meters on western ghats. Some of the most important falls in Courtallam are Peraruvi (Main Fall), Chitraruvi (small fall), Shenbaga Devi Falls, Thenaryvi (Honey falls), Aintharuvi (five falls), Puli Aruvi (Tiger fall) Pazhaya Courtallam (Old falls) Puthu Aruvi (new falls) and the Pazhathotta Aruvi(fruit garden fall). These water falls are said to have medicinal properties as they run through a herbs forest. A bath in them has a soothing tonic effect on the entire physical system. The main fall is formed by a sharp three stage drop of about 91 meters high and is flood - lit for bathing at night. THIRUKUTRALANATHAT TEMPLE is dedicated to Lord Shiva and contains inscriptions about the Chola and Pandya Kings. Another temple called CHITRA SABHA dedicated to Lord Natraja is decorated with paintings of rural deities and devotees, puranic stories and religious events. The Chitra Sabha is one of the five Sabhas where Lord Natraja performed the 'Cosmic' Dance.

COIMBATORE

Coimbatore called the 'Manchaster of South India', is famous for its handloom products. It is also known for the manufacture of the centrifugal pump sets and is host of engineering goods.

PLACES OF INTEREST

PERUR TEMPLE : Dedicated to Lord Shiva it was built by Karikola Cholan by the Noyyal river side.

MARUTHAMALAI TEMPLE : Dedicated to Lord Murugan it is located on a hillock 12 km away from Coimbatore. The presiding deity is known as Dhandayuthapani.

V.O.C. PARK : Named after the freedom fighter V.O.Chidambaram the Park has a mini zoo and toy train.

Tamil Nadu Agricultural University and one of the oldest forest college of the country are camped in this city.

HOW TO REACH

AIR : Coimbatore is connected by air with Chennai, Trichy and Mumbai.

RAIL : Coimbatore is connected by air with major cities of the country.

HOTEL ACCOMMODATION (STD CODE 0422)

— Heritage Inn(3 Star),38, Sivaswamy Road, Ramnagar
   PH 231 451; FAX 233 223
— Sree Annapoorna Lodge (3 Star), 75, East Arokiasamy Road,
   R.S. Puram. PH 437 732, 437 621; FAX 437 322;
— Hotel Surya International (3 Star)105, Race Course Road
   PH 217 751-55; FAX 216 110
— Hotel City Tower, P.B.No 2418,Ramnagar
   PH 230 681; FAX 230 103
— Nilgiris Nest, 739-A, Avanashi Road
   PH 217 247, 217 133; FAX 217 131

EXCURSIONS

ANAMALAI OR INDIRA GANDHI WILD LIFE SANCTUARY : (60 km) The biggest sanctuary in Tamil Nadu sprawls over an area of about 958 sq. km. The animals found here are gaur, elephant, tiger, sloth bear, wild boar dog, nilgiri, langur etc. There is a bird watch tower at Kariam Shola, 2 km away from Top slip. The range officer can arrange trekking and hill climbing and elephant rides at the sanctuary. 21 km away from top the slip lies a small waterfall called Monkey falls at Aliyar. A town Amaravathy Nagar has Crocodile breeding centre.

UDHAGAMANDALAM : (100 km) Ooty called the Queen of hill stations is located at the Nilgiri hills at 2240 meters above sea level.BOTANICAL GARDENS were established here in 1847. This 50-acre garden includes a variety of exotic ornamental plants. It is also a venue for the flower show held in May every year. There is a fossil tree trunk which is 20 million years old. ARTIFICIAL LAKE was constructed in 1824 by Mr. John Sullivan, the then Collector of Coimbatore. Row and Motor boats, toy trains are available at the lake. ROSE GARDEN covering an area of 10 acres inside Vijaya Nagar farm has about 1900 varieties of roses. GOVERNMENT MUSEUM has items of tribal objects, ecological details and representative sculptural arts and crafts of Tamil Nadu. DEER PARK houses sambar, chital, and hares besides water birds. THE MUKURTHI PEAK AND MUKURTHI NATIONAL PARK contains viable population of nilgiri tahr. Fascinating feature of the Mukurthi sanctuary is its relationship with the Himalayan flora and fauna. PYKARA, 21 km from Ooty, has Toda settlement well-protected fenced sholas, undisturbed grassy meadows and a rich wildlife habitat.The Pykara Dam and the reservoir attract many tourists. DODABETTA, 10 km from Ooty, lies on the junction of western and eastern ghats, offer beautiful vistas of the Nilgiri hill ranges. There is a telescope house run by the T.T.D.C. AVALANCHI, 28 km from Ooty is a beautiful lake. There are places so dark and dense that even sun light does not penetrate. Uppar Bhavani lies 20 km from Avalanchi, which is the area of undisturbed wildlife habitat.

There are lots of trekking routes. Local tourist office provides more details of the trekking routes. For Trekking in and around Ooty permission has to be obtained from :
   (1)   Wild Life Warden, Mudumalai Wildlife Sanctuary, Mahalingam Buildings Coonoor Roda, Ooty 643 001, PH 440 98
   (2)   District Forest Officer, North and South Division, Ooty 643 001
   (3)   DFO North PH 43968; DFO South 44083
Nilgiri Trekking Association will arrange for the Trekking programmes – Address

Nilgiri Trekking Association, Kavitha Nilayam, State Bank Road, Ooty.

Hang Gliding courses are organised during March to May every year by the department of tourism. Angling, Trout carp and mixed water fishing is possible in various streams and lakes in the Nilgiries. The Assistant Director of Fisheries issues fishing license.

COONOOR : (85 km from Coimbatore) 19 km from Ooty is the second largest hill station of the Nilgiris at an altitude of 1858 metres. At DOLPHIN'S NOSE, 12 km from Coonoor, one can take a glimpses of the Catherine falls. LAMBS'S ROCK, a place 8 km away from the town commands a good view of the Coimbatore plains. LAW'S FALLS and ST. CATHERINE FALLS are two breathtaking falls. SIM'S PARK-CUM-BOTANICAL GARDEN contains many species of the trees not found in Ooty. The annual fruit and vegetable show is held here every May.

Ooty and Coonoor are well-connected with Coimbatore by regular private/state transport operated coaches and taxis. Accommodation is available at various categories of hotels.

THANJAVUR

Thanjavur once the capital of the Chola kings, its origin go back to the beginning of the Christian era. Thajavur rose to glory during the later Chola period from 10th to 14th centuries and became the centre of learning and culture. One of the greatest Chola emperors, Raja Raja (985–1014) was responsible for building the Brihadeshwara temple.  The glorious Choala legacy have left behind not less than 74 temples in and around Thanjuavur itself. Today city known as the 'Rice Bowl' of Tamil Nadu and for its exquisite handicrafts, bronzes and South Indian musical instruments.

PLACES OF INTEREST

BRIHADESHWARA TEMPLE AND FORT : Built by great Chola King in the 10th century it is an outstanding example of Chola architecture and is listed in World heritage. On the top of the apex of 63 metres high, a dome is said to be constructed from a single piece of granite, weighing an estimated 81 tonnes.

The dome was hauled into place along a 6 km earthwork ramp in a manner similar to the one used by the Egyptian Pyramids. Temple has been the sense of continuous worship for over thousand years. Only Hindus are allowed inside.

THAJAVUR PALACE AND MUSEUM : The Palace near the temple is a vast building of masonry built partly by the Nayakas around 1550 and partly by the Marathas. Two of the palace towers, the Armoury and the observation tower are visible from all parts of the city. The palace houses an art gallery, a library and a hall of music.

THE RAJA RAJA CHOLA GALLERY : The gallery has some fine pieces of stone and bronze sculptures from 9th to 12th centuries. Over 30,000 Indian and European manuscripts written on palm leaves and paper are preserved in the Saraswathi Mahal Library.

THE SANGEETA MAHAL is an acoustic marvel, perfectly turned to bring out the best from musical instruments.

HOW TO REACH

AIR : Nearest airport-Trichy 60 km.

RAIL : Thanjavur is connected by rail with all major towns of the country.

ROAD : Thajnavur is connected by road with all major towns of the country.

HOTEL ACCOMMODATION (STD CODE 04362)

- Hotel Parushutam Pvt. Ltd. (3 Star), 55 G.A. Canal Road PH 31 844; FAX 303 18
- Hotel Oriental Towers, 2889, Srinivasam Pillai Road PH 31 467, 30 724; FAX 30 770
- Hotel Sangam (3 Star), Trichy Road PH 34 151, 340 26; FAX 366 95
- Pandiyan Residency, Cutchery Road. PH 312 95
- Hotel Tamil Nadu, 1 Gandhi Road. PH 31 421

EXCURSIONS

THIRUKANDIYUR : (10 km) The town has temple of Brahmasirekandeswarar and Harshavimochana Perumal.

TIRUVAIYARU : (13 km) The famous Panchantheshwara temple here is dedicated to Lord Shiva. The greatest musical festival in the country takes place here annually. The 8-day Thyagaraja Aradhana festival is attended by thousands of ardent fans of classical music.

SWAMIMALAI : (30 km) Situated on a 30 metre high platform, Swamimalai marks the spot where young Subramanya explained to Lord Shiva, the meaning of 'OM' which precedes every Hindu prayer.

DARASURAM : (34 km) The city has the temple, dedicated to Lord Shiva, and built by Rajendra Chola. Darasuram is also a silk weaving centre.

KUMBAKONAM : (36 km) There are four temples dedicated to Sarangapani Kumbeswarar, Nagrswara and the Ramaswamy temples. Mahamagam congregation takes place once in 12 years.

GANGAIKONDACHOLAPURAM : The temple here is almost similar to the temple of Tanjore.

TIRUVARUR : (58 km) This is the hallowed birthplace of the saint Thyagaraja. The temple is visited by pregnant women who take a dip and pray that the unborn child be blessed.

NAGORE : (78 km) An important Muslim pilgrim centre, there is a Dargah of Hazrat Meeras Sultan Syed Shahabudul Hameed. This 500-year-old tomb is topped by a golden dome and flanked by 5 minarets. The tank called 'Peerkulam' is believed to have curative powers and visited by people of various religious faiths.

NAGAPATTINAM : (82 km) This port town has a temple dedicated to Nagraja, the king of serpants. This town is also a convenient base for visiting Velankini and Nagore, two pilgrim centres of two different faiths.

PT. CALIMERE WILDLIFE SANCTUARY : (90 km) Also known as Kodikkarai, this coastal sanctuary is located in a wetland into Palk Strait. It is noted for the vast folk of migratory water fowl, especially flamingos, which congregate here every winter. The best time to visit is between November-January when the tidal mud flats and marshes are covered with teals, shovellers, plovers, sand pipers, shanks, and gulland herons. In the spring, a different set of birds—quils, mynas and barbets are drawn here by the profusion of wild berries. The easiest way to get to Calimere is by bus from Vedaranyam, which is linked by frequent bus service to Nagappattinam, Thanjuvur. Rest house reservation can be made with the forest officer in Thanjavur.

VELENKANNI : (94 km) This is the famous Christian pilgrim centre, the site of the famous Catholic Roman Church of Our Lady of Good Health. People from all religions flock to the Church, many donating gold and silver models of cured body parts. A  major festival is held at the beginning of September.

There are frequent buses from Tanjore, Chennai and many towns of the State.

TIRUNALLAR : (95 km) This is the only temple dedicated to Saneeswaran (Lord of Saturn) and is believed to cure people of their curses and spells of bad luck.

THARANGAMBADI, TRANQUEBAR : (105 km) This coastal town was a Danish settlement from 1624 to 1825. Special tourist interest areas are the two churches and the fort.

CHIDAMBARAM : (106 km) An important pilgrim centre for Shaivites and known for its famous Nataraja temple which was erected in the reign of Vira Chola Raja (927-997 AD). This great temple complex (covering an area of 40 acres)is one of Tamil Nadu's Dravidian architectural highlights. THE NATARAJA TEMPLE has 4 gopurams, the north and the south ones towering 49 metres high. Two of the gopurams are covered with the 108 classical postures of Nataraja - Shiva in his role as the cosmic dancer. Other notable features of the temple are the 1000 pillar hall, the Nritta Sabha court looks like a gigantic chariot. The image of Natraja himself is in the inner sanctorum.

THILLAI KALIAMMAN TEMPLE was also built by the Cholas and is dedicated to Goddess Parvati. It is believed that a trip to Chidambarm is incomplete if both the temples are not visited.

The Natyanjali Dance festival is held for 5 days in February, dancers from all parts of the country perform here. VAITHISVARAN KOIL, 24 km from Chidambaram has a temple dedicated to the 'healer of all diseases'. This is believed to be the place where Lord Shiva treated Angaraka, the ailing god of war. Devotees offer gold and silver replices of organs and pray for good health. POOMPUHAR, 40 km from Chidambaram, the original city was swallowed by sea built over 2000 years ago. Excavations reveal that the city of Puhar was well designed. Today Poompuhar's main attraction are a clean beach and an art gallery. PICHAVARAM, not far from Chidambarm is a tourist spot of an entirely different nature. Enchanting Pichavaram comprises 300 acres of mangrove forests criss-crossed by backwaters. A Marine Research Institute is situated nearby at Parangipettai (Porto Nova), a former Portuguese and Dutch Port. In this eco-paradise, T.T.D.C. provides facilities for watersports. The arignar Anna Tourist complex has cottage, a restaurant, a youth hostle and a boat house.

VEDARANYAM : (115km) Both a centre of pilgrimage and historic interest Vedaranyam is believed to be the place where the lord Shiva and Parvati attired in full bridal finery, appeared before saint Agasthya.

TIRUCHIRAPALLI

Tiruchirapally was the Chola citadel during the Sangam age.

Situated on the banks of the Kaveri river, Trichy was ruled by Chola, Pandya and Pallava Kings - changing hands from time to time. The town and its fort, as it stands today, was built by the Nayakas of Madurai. The Carnatic Wars between the British and the French were fought around this fort. Today, the city is a blend of history and tradition, a pilgrim centre as well as a thriving commercial city.

PLACES OF INTEREST

ROCK FORT TEMPLE : This Vinayaka temple at the top of the hill is 83 metre high and can be reached by climbing 437 steps cut into a tunnel through the rock. The most amazing fact about the rock is that it is one of the oldest in the world - approximately 3800 years old- which makes it as old as the rock of Greenland and older than Himalayas. Halfway up is the Sri Thayumanaswamy temple dedicated to Lord Siva. It has a 100 pillar hall and a Vimana covered with gold. Atop the rock is the Ucchi Pillayar koil, a temple dedicated to Lord Vinayaka Sree Thayumanaswamy. On the southern face of the rock are several beautifully carved rock cut temples of the Pallava period.

JAMBUKESHWARAR TEMPLE : The nearby Jambukeshwara temple is dedicated to Lord Shiva and has seven gopurams. It is built around a Shiva Lingam partly submerged in water that comes from a spring in the sanctum sanctorum.

ST. JOHN'S CHURCH : Trichy also has some interesting Raj-era monuments built in 1812. St.John's church has louver side doors which can be opened to turn the Church in to an airy pavilion.

HOW TO REACH

AIR : Trichy is connected by air with Chennai. Air Lanka operates flights to Colombo from Trichy.

RAIL : Trichy is connected directly by rail with major cities of India.

ROAD : Trichy is connected by road with all parts of the country.

TOURIST OFFICE

— T.N.T.D.C., No 1, Williams Rd., Cantonment, Trichy.

HOTEL ACCOMMODATION (STD CODE 0431)

— Hotel Sangam (4 Star), Collector's Office Road
  PH 414 480; FAX 414779
— Jenney's Residency Pvt.Ltd.(3 Star), 3/14 Macdonald's Road.
  PH 414 414; FAX 414 451
— Femina Hotel, 14-C, Williams Road, Cantonment,
  PH 414 501; FAX 414 615
— Hotel Anand, No 1.Racquet Court Lane
  Ph 415 545; FAX 415 261
— Hotel Royal Southern, Race Couse Road
  PH 421 303-7; FAX 421 307
— Ashbey Hotel, 17-A, Junction Road. PH 460 652/63

EXCURSIONS FROM TIRUCHIRAPALLI

SREERANGAM : (10 km) The Vaishnavite Ranganathaswamy temple and town are set on a 250 hector island in the Cauvery river, connected to the mainland by a bridge. This is a living example of a temple town where all life centres around the temple. This massive temple complex has 21 magnificent gateway doors (gopurams) and 1000 pillared hall with beautiful carvings, all within the 7 walls of the temple town. The 22nd gateway tower which is 236 ft. tall is the tallest temple tower in Asia. The temple complex is very well preserved and has beautiful carvings and painted walls and ceilings.

PUDUKKOTAI : (50 km) A former princely State is one of the most ancient region in the country. Proof of its antiquity is the pre historic dolmens stone circles and megalithic burial sites which have been discovered around the area. The archaeological excavations carried out also reveal that Pudukkottai had a rich cultural heritage that has found a mention in Sangam literature. In the 17th century, it became a princely State and a number of palaces, tanks and canals were constructed by its rulers.

YERCUD—A JEWEL OF SOUTH INDIA

Yercud, a hill station situated on the Shevaroy hills of the eastern ghats, represents a welcome contrast with its cool climate where the temperature never rises above 29°c or dips below 13°c. Coffee and citrus fruits, oranges, bananas pears and jackfruits grow in abundance.

PLACES OF INTEREST are Lake, Ladys' seat, Killiyur falls, Pagoda point, Arthur's seat, Anna park, the Grange Pagoda point, Bear's cave and the Shevaroyan temple.

HOW TO REACH

AIR : Nearest airport-Trichy

RAIL : Nearest railhead – Salem (32km)

ROAD : Yercud is connected by major cities of the State. There are frequent buses to and fro Salem and Yercud.

KANYAKUMARI

The southernmost tip of India, Kanyakumari is the point where three seas meet at the Bay of Bengal—the Arabian sea and the Indian Ocean. On the Chitra Pournima day (full moon day in April)one can witness the Sun and the Moon are face to face at the same horizon.

PLACES OF INTEREST

KANYAKUMARI OR KUMARIAMMAN TEMPLE : The legend behind this temple is as romantic as the place itself. Dedicated to the virgin goddess Kanyakumari (Parvati) who stands guard over the country. The temple is built at the top where the goddesss is believed to have waited for her consort Shiva to come and claim her hand in marriage.

GANDHI MEMORIAL : It has been constructed at the spot where the ashes of Mahatama Gandhi were kept for public view in an urn before a portion was immersed into the three seas.

VIVEKANAND MEMORIAL : This memorial is on a rocky island about 200 metres from the shore line. The memorial has been built on the Vivekanand rock where the great philosopher guide Swami Vivekananda went into meditation that transformed him into one of the most charismatic spiritual leaders of this century. There is a ferry service every half an hour.

GUGANATHASWAMY TEMPLE : This 100 year old temple is said to have been built by Raja Raja Cholan.

HOW TO REACH

AIR : Nearest airport – Thiruvananthapuram 80 km.

RAIL : Kanyakumari is connected by rail with Chennai, New Delhi, Tirunelvi and Thiruvananthapuram.

ROAD : Kanyakumari is connected by road to all major cities of South India.

There are regular bus services from Chennai, Madurai, Trichy, Coimbatore Ooty, Thiruvananthapuram and many other centres of the State.

HOTEL ACCOMMODATION (STD CODE 04652)

— Kerala House, Beach Road, PH 71229
— Govt.Guest House, Beach Road, PH 71226
— Vivekanand Accommodation Unit, PH 71250/1
— Tourist Lodge Dormitory, New Lodge, Cape Road PH71279
— Devsthanam Cottages, PH 71223

EXCURSIONS

VATTAKOTTAI FORT (6 km) It is an 18th century fort visited by tourists.

SUCHIDRAM : (13 km) It has a temple dedicated to deity who is a representation of the combined forces of Shiva, Vishnu and Brahma. Musical pillars and a huge 18 feet Hanuman statue are proof of the artistic skill of the time. Inscriptions said to be of the 9th century are found in the temple.

NAGERCOIL : (20 km) The town has the famous Nagaraja temple,

Nagaraja is the presiding deity and the images of Lord Shiva and Lord Vishnu are also enshrined here. The entrance to the temple resembles Chinese architecture of Budha Viharas and the pillars of the temple contains images of Mahavira and Paraswanatha, the Jain Tirthnkaras.

UDAYAGIRI FORT : (34 km) This fort was built during the reign of Sri Marthanda Varma (1729-1758).

PADMANABHAPURAM : (45 km) The capital of Travancore until 133 AD, Padmanabhapuram is known for the fort which encloses a palace which has some important art relics.

MUDUMALAI SANCTUARY

The hilly terrain of the Western ghats, clothed in dense mixed and moist deciduous forests, make Mudumalai (the ancient hills) a most attractive wildlife reserve. The Mysore-Ooty highway runs through the park, following the course of the Moyar River, which separates Mudumalai and Bandipur.With the elevations varying from 1,150 feet to 4,100 feet, the terrain at Mudumalai comprises hills, valleys, ravines, flats, watercourses and swamps. The wild elephant, gaur, deer and primates like the bonnet macaque and langurs all inhabit the park.

Riding elephants are the best means of transportation at Mudumalai and animals can also be watched from machans which are strategically located near water holes and salt licks. Nearest airport : Coimbatore, Rail : Ootacamund. For additional information contact – Wildlife Warden, Mahalingam Building, Coonoor Road, Ooty – 643 001. Tamil Nadu.

ADVENTURE TRAILS IN TAMIL NADU
TREKKING

UDHAGAMANDALAM : Offers several trek routes which vary in distance, altitude and terrian. There is a base camp at parson's valley, from where one can start trekking to various points within western ghats. The down hill of western ghats on the north-end ends with meeting the extension of eastern ghats, where the sprawling Mudumalai Sanctuary lies which opens vistas for adventure tourists.

Some suggested trekking trails are –

— Udhaganmangalam – Parson's valley – Mukkuthi Lake – Pandiar Hills – Pyakar Hills – Madumalai Sanctuary.
— Parson's Valley – Mukkurthi Lake – Western Catchment – Bangaiappal – Upper Bhavani
— Parson's Valley – Partimund – Emerald – Avalachi – Kolaribetta – Western Catchment II or III – Mukurthi Peak – Mukuruthi Dam - Pykara – Udhagamandalam

Trekking is also possible at ANAMALAI HILLS. Top slip, at an altitude of 740 MSL has all the amenities needed for a naturalist. Some important places to be visited are Monkey Falls Aliyar, the Crocodile Breeding Centre at Amaravathi, Grass Hills, Attakatti, Mirar, Kullipatti, Manompally, Chinnar, Varagaliar, Manjampatty etc. Topslip is 35kms from Pollachi for the road and rail head and Coimbatore has the nearest Airport.

KADAIKANAL : Located on the Palani Hills, an off-shoot of the Western Ghat mountain ranges, Kodaikanal is a spectacular summer resort and ecological paradise of Tamil Nadu. A span of 2068 sq. km of the hills with varied types of forest cover, Kodaikanal offers ideal sites for trekking, hang gliding, angling and golf.

For Trekking through the forests in Tamil Nadu, one has to get prior permission from the Forest Department. Permission can be obtained from :

— The Principal Chief, Conservator of Forests, Panagal Building No. 1, Jennis Road, Saidapet, Chennai 600 015.
   PH 044 434 8059

— The Wildlife Warden, Mahalingam Bulidings, Coonoor Road Udhagamangalam 643 001. PH 0423 44098

— District Forest Officer, Kaodaikanal Division,
   Kodaikanal 624 101. PH 04542 40287

— The Field Director, 'Project Tiger', NGO "A" Colony, Tirunelveli 627 007. PH 0462 552663

— The Wildlife Warden, 178, Meenakarai Salai, Pollachi 642 001.
   PH 04259 25356

AQUA SPORTS

The seas on Coromandel coast are rough and strong and rolling, suitable for surfing, but in places they are rocky. Back waters are there to provide shallow water spreads for wind surfing.

MUTTUKADU, 35 km south of Chennai, is ideal location for wind surfing. T.T.D.C. and other operators provide necessary sails and windsurfing equipment to try surfing on back-waters. Plans to provide, water scooters and other aqua-sports are also on the anvil.

HANG-GLIDING

Though Hang-gliding is not popular in this part of the country, the Chennai Hang Gliders Association is keen on popularising this adventure sport. Now, to train those who are interested in this adventure activities, motorised hang-gliders are being provided by Chennai Hang-Gliders Association. The St. Thomas Mount, an out crop of hillock on the outskirts of Chennai, the hills of Kodaikanal and Udgagamangalam are the best location for Hang-Gliding.

ANGLING

Angling is an interesting pastime for tourists in Tamil Nadu. In the Nilgiris the waters of Mukkurthi Lake and the river, Gurumund river and reservoir, Avalanchi and Emerald river, Peermund, Chambar, Kallundi Streams, Upper Bhavani Reservoir, Billithadakulla river, Bhavani Puzha, Aradha Pezha, Parsons Valley stream and Reservoir, Kings Dhar Stream, Western Catchment Reservoir, Thirupanthurai, Emeri Puzha, Silent Valley streams etc. are fit for trout fishing.

In Kodaikanal hills, trout streams are Pulavachiyar and Konalar. Crap fishing is recommended in Kodai lake. In addition the State's 900 km. long coastal line provides ample marine fishing.

For fishing, licences has to be obtained from the fisheries department. The addresses are

Kodaikanal : Observatory Road, Kodaikanal.

Udhagamangalam : Assistant Director of Fisheries, Fish dale, Udhagamangalam.

FAIRS AND FESTIVALS

JANUARY : PONGAL : Pongal is the harvest festival celebrated for four days commencing from the last day of the Tamil month Margazhi. The sun, earth and the cattle are worshipped by farmers as thanks giving for a bounteous harvest.

Mamallapuram Dance Festival : Music and dance festival is celebrated at Mamallapuram against the backdrop of the Pallava Rock sculptures.

Float Festival, Madurai : On the night of the full moon, ornamented icons of goddess Meenakshi and her consort are taken out in a colourful procession to huge Mariamman Teppakulam. The icons are floated in the tank on a raft decked with flowers and flickering lamps.

A music festival is celebrated every year at Thiruvaiyaru in honour of poet saint Thyagaraja. Musicians from all over India assemble here to take part in the festival.

MARCH : SHIVRATRI : Shivratri is observed as the night, when Lord Shiva dances the 'Tandav'. Fasts and prayers mark the day. This festival is the occasion for a five day long festival of classical dance and music at Chidambaram. The magnificent temple dedicated to Lord Shiva, built a thousand years ago, provides a beautiful backdrop for the event.

Summer festival is held in the hill stations, Ooty, Kodaikanal and Yercud in May every year.

All India Mango festival is held at Krishnagiri during June.

SEPTEMBER : Velankanni annual festival is celebrated for ten days at Velankanni commencing September 7 at the Minor Basilica dedicated to 'Our Lady of Health'.

Annual Music and Dance festival held at Chennai during December/January is world-renowned.

UNION TERRITORIES

ANDMAN AND NICOBAR ISLANDS

AREA : 8,249 sq. km
CAPITAL : Port Blair
LANGUAGES : Bengali, Hindi, Nicobarese, Telegu, Tamil and Malayalam.
AIRPORT : Port Blair

The Andaman and Nicobar Islands, a Union Territory, is situated between 6E and 14E North Latitude and 92E and 94E East Longitude. This group of 572 islands / islets lie in the Bay of Bengal 193 km from Cape Negris in Burma, 1255 km from Calcutta and 1190 km from Chennai. Two principal group of islets are Ritchie's Archipelago and Labyrinth islands. The Nicobar islands are situated to the south of Andmans, 121 km from Little Andman island. There are 36 inhabited islands, including 24 in the Andman and 12 in the Nicobar District.

Two-third population live in Nicobar, while the Andman population is cosmopolite consisting of Indians, Burmese and aboriginal tribes. Almost the entire population of the Nicobar Island is tribal.

The Andman Islands were once called Kala Pani, a penal settlement established by the British in India. It was intended for political prisoners and criminals serving a life sentence. The island gained importance on the arrival of the Europeans in India in 16th century.

HISTORY

The original inhabitants of the islands lived in the forests by hunting and fishing. There are four Negrito tribes, viz, the Great Andmanese, Onge, Jarawa and Sentinalese in the Andman group of islands, and two Mongoloid tribes, viz, Nicobarese and Shompen in the Nicobar group of islands. Among these, the Jarawas and the Sentinalese have not yet learnt the concept of covering their bodies.

The modern history of the Andaman and Nicobar Islands begins with the establishment of a settlement by East India Company in 1789.

Portuguese came first who were followed by the Dutch and the British. However, in 1796 this settlement was abandoned.

Then came the revolt in 1857 in India. Andman offered ready made solution for the rebels. The construction of Cellular jail was taken up in 1896 which was carried out by the convicts. Following the first war of Indian Independence in 1857, the British India Government founded the penal settlement in these islands in 1858, and dreaded criminals from the mainland India which continued till the second World War. During the Second World War, the Japanese forces occupied the Andaman and Nicobar Islands in 1942.

The constitutional reforms of 1935 necessitated a thorough revision of policy in September 1937 the first batch of prisoners left the Andman and by January 1938 all prisoners were realesed. The National flag was first hoisted here in 1943 by the great leader Subhash Chandra Bose. The Second World War and subsequent Japanese occupation from 1942-45 brought the islands a taste of foreign military occupation. After evacuation of the Japanese in 1945, the Islands, a part of India, became free on August 15, 1947. In November 1956, the Andman Nicobar Islands were constituted into a Union Territory administered by the President of India.

PORT BLAIR

PLACES OF INTEREST

The capital was named after Lt. Reginald Blair who conducted survey of the area in 1789 AD until World War II.

THE CELLUR JAIL : The Bastille of India, now a national memorial, where India's freedom fighters were incarcerated by the British in single room cells from where they could not see or communicate with anyone. It has been converted into a museum. It was built in the 18th century facing the sea.

THE CHATHAN SAW MILL where rare species of timber can be seen.

MARINE MUSEUM with 350 species of sea-life.

ANTHROPOLOGICAL MUSEUM

EXCURSIONS

BURMAH NALLA (17 km) where lumber operations are carried out by trained elephants.

MADHUBAN (14 km) where elephants are trained.

SIPPIGHAT FARM (14 km) Agricultural demonstration farm where tropical cash crops and spices are grown.

WANDOOR BEACH (28 km) offers a picturesque landscape and is ideal for swimming. This area has been declared as the Marina National Park.

CHIRIYA TAPU (30 km) This southern tip of South Andmans is also known as Bird Island.

CRUISES AROUND THE HARBOUR

Hope Town, Panighat. Lord Mayo was assassinated by an Afghan convict here.

North Bay, a long and sandy beach.

Viper Island, which used to be the penal settlement before the construction of the Cellur Jail.

Rose Island, administration headquarters during the Raj days. There are many monuments here.

Red Skin, Joly Buoy and Cinque Island. These are picturesque islands offering exotic, coral and marine life. Sandy, virgin beaches and crystal clear waters are ideal for snorkelling, diving and underwater photography.

Boats can be charted for full day.

Sports : Diving, Windsurfing, Fishing, Angling, Water-skiing, Sailing, and Snorkelling.

Equipment for the above are available on hire from the Andman Beach Resort, Corbyn's Cove.

HOW TO REACH

AIR : Indian Airlines connects Port Blair with Calcutta and Chennai.

SHIP : Passenger ships ply between Port Blair and Calcutta, Chennai and Visakhapatnam. (Travel Time 3 days each way)

CONDUCTED TOURS

Half Day Sightseeing Tour of Port Blair.

Wandoor Tour – full day.

Chirya Tapu Tour – full day.

Corbyn's Cove tour (Sundays only) – half day.

For further information contact :

— Directorate of Tourism, PH 20642

HOTEL ACCOMMODATION (STD CODE 03192)

— Welcomegroup Bay Island : (5 Star) Marine Hill
PH 34101/12 : FAX 31555

— Hotel Shompen : (2 Star) 2, Middle Point
    PH 32644, 32360; FAX 32425
— Holiday Resort : (2 Star) Premnagar, Delanipur
    PH 30516; FAX 34331
— Hotel Sinclairs Bay Niew : South Point. PH 31824
— Prresless Resort : Corbny's Cove. PH 33461-4; FAX 33463

Foreign nationals travelling individually are given permission by the Immigration authorities to visit Port Blair municipal area, Jolly Buoy and Cinque Island for a period of 30 days, on arrival at Port Blair.

Permits can also be obtained from Indian missions abroad and the Regional Immigration authorities at Mumbai, Delhi, Calcutta and Chennai.

Foreign nationals in a group of 6 to 20 are allowed to visit Grub, Red Skin, Snob and Boat Islands with prior permission from the Chief Secretary, Andman and Nicobar Administration, Port Blair.

CHANDIGARH

AREA : 114 sq. km.
CAPITAL : Chndigarh
LANGUAGE : Hindi and Punjabi
AIRPORT : Chandigarh

Chandigarh—Union Territory and capital of two States— Haryana and Punjab—is India's most modern and well-planned city, laid by Le Corbusier. Chandigarh—an architect's delight—is a stepping stone to the attractions of the hills of Himachal Pradesh.

The city is named after the Goddess Chandi Devi whose white domed temple stands on the slop of a hill in the north-east of Chandigarh on the edge of the Shivalik hills.

Chandigarh and the area surrounding it were constituted as a Union Territory on November 1, 1966.

PLACES OF INTEREST

THE ROCK GARDEN : It was built by Neckchand Saini with multi-coloured pieces of stones and discarded objects.

THE CAPITAL COMPLEX : It is the administrative hub for two States. The High Court, Legislative Assembly, Secretariat, Open Hand Monument, Geometric Hills and Tower of Shadow are examples of Le Corbusier's genius and are part of Capital complex.

THE ROSE GARDEN : It comprises 30 acres of beautifully landscaped gardens containing 1,600 varieties of roses.

SUKHNA LAKE : It offers sports like boating, yatching, water-skiing and has a cafeteria.

THE CENTRAL BUSINESS DISTRICT : It is the most fashionable area of the city.

YADAVINDRA GARDENS AT PINJORE : 24 km away are these 17th century gardens designed by Nawab Fidal Khan, who was architect to Mughal Emperor Aurangzeb, and are a blend of Mughal and Rajasthani styles Bhima Devi temple is located nearby.

BHAKRA-NANGAL : 116 km away. It is independent India's first major hydel project on the borders of Himachal Pradesh, the first high gravity dam in the world.

HOW TO REACH

AIR : Chandigarh is connected by air with Delhi, Srinagar, Jammu, Leh and Kulu.

RAIL : Chandigarh is connected by train with all major cities of India.

Shatabdi Express operates between Delhi and Chandigarh Timings:
— 2011 (Daily) D New Delhi 0755 / A Chandigarh 1045
— Rt 2012 (Daily) D Chandigarh 1220 / A New Delhi 1530

ROAD : Chandigarh is well-connected by road with Punjab, Himalchal Pradesh and rest of the country.

ROAD DISTANCES

— Amritsar 452 km; Delhi 248 km; Jammu 380 km; Jaipur 507 km; Nainital 586 km; Rishikesh 276 km; Srinagar 666 km.

TOURIST OFFICE

For information on conducted tours, contact Chandigarh Tourism, Sector 17, PH 543839

HOTEL ACCOMMODATION (STD CODE 0172)

— Hotel Mountview : (5Star) Sector 10
   PH 740 544, 743 126; FAX 742 220
— Hotel Piccadily : (4 Star) Sector 22B, Himalaya Marg
   PH 707 521 – 3; FAX 705 692
— Hotel Sunbeam Pvt Ltd (4Star) Udhyog Path, Sector 22B
   PH 708 100 – 8; FAX 708 900
— Hotel Shivalik View. PH 544 651
— The Aroma : (3 Star) Himalaya Marg, Sector 22 C
   PH 700 045 – 48; FAX 700 051
— Maya Palace : (3 Star) S.C.O., Sector 35 B
   PH 600 547; FAX 660 555
— Hotel Park Inn : (3 Star) S.C.O., Sector 35 C,
   PH 660 111, 664 848; FAX 660 110
— Hotel Classic (2 Star) S.C.O., Sector 35 C
   PH 606 092, 604 116 : FAX 663 275
— Hotel Heritage : (2 Star) S.C.O., 468 Sector 35 C
   PH 602 479, 605 909; FAX 601 221

DADRA AND NAGAR HAVELI

AREA : 491 Sq. km
CAPITAL : Silvassa
LANGUAGES : Bhili, Bhilodi, Hindi and Gujarati.

Dadra and Nagar Haveli lie near the west coast surrounded by the State of Gujarat and Maharashtra. It consists of two pockets namely Dadra and Nagar Haveli and these two pockets are intercepted by the territory of Gujarat.

HISTORY

After prolonged skirmishes between the Portuguese and Marathas, on December 17, 1779, the Maratha Government assigned the aggregated revenue of Rs 12,000 in a few villages of this territory to the Portuguese as compensation to ensure their friendship. The Portuguese ruled this territory until its liberation by the people on August 2, 1954. Subsequently, an Administrator carried on the administration for some time. However, the territory was merged with the Indian Union on August 11, 1961 and since then is being administered by the Government of India as a Union Territory through the Administrator. Since liberation of the territory from Portuguese rule a Varishtha Panchayat was working as an advisory body of the administration which was, dissolved in August 1989 and a Pradesh Council for Dadra and Nagar Haveli was announced and subsequently Dadra and Nagar Haveli District Panchayat and eleven village panchayats were constituted as per constitutional amendments at all-India level. Dadra and Nagar Haveli with an area of 491 sq km is surrounded by Gujarat and Maharashtra. It consists of two pockets namely Dadra and Nagar Haveli. There were 72 villages of which one Kothar village is almost uninhabited and has been submerged and four others are partly submerged due to construction of Damanganga Irrigation Project which is a joint venture of Dadra and Nagar Haveli, Daman and Diu and Gujarat.

Dadra and Nagar haveli are still haunted by Portuguese memories. There are beautiful gardens on the banks of the river at Silvassa and Kahnvel. A tourist complex at Kahnvel named 'Van Vihara' has been set up. Van Ganga and Vandhara gardens on the Damanganga river, Bal Udyan, Tadkeshwara temple on sakartod at Brinadavan are other picnic spots of this area.

HOW TO REACH

AIR : Nearest airport Mumabi

RAIL : Nearest railway station is Vapi – 18 km on Mumbai – Ahmedabad route.

ROAD : Located on Mumbai – Ahmedabad highway. All types of vechicles are easily available from Mumbai and Vapi-Surat-Vadodara-Ahmedabad and other important cities of Gujarat.

DAMAN AND DIU

AREA : 112 Sq. km
CAPITAL : Daman
LANGUAGES : Marathi and Gujarati.

Daman, a quaint little settlement, spread over an area of 72 sq. km., is a picturesque port town, and a popular get-away with city dwellers. Situated on the west coast and hugged by the Arabian Sea, Daman has been the home away from home for the Portuguese till its liberation in 1961.

Diu, which makes the other half of the Union Territory of Daman and Diu, is a tiny island measuring less than 40 sq. km., off the west coast near Saurashtra. Diu is perhaps the most exotic destination on the west coast of India.

HISTORY

Daman and Diu along with Goa was a colony held by the Portuguese even after Independence. In 1961, it was made an integral part of India. It was part of the erstwhile Union Territory of Goa. After conferring Statehood on Goa on May 30, 1987, Daman and Diu was made a separate Union Territory. Daman lies about 193 km away from Mumbai. It is bounded on north by Kolak river, on the east by Gujarat on the south by Kolai river and on the west by the Gulf of Cambay. The neighbouring district of Daman is Valsad of Gujarat. Diu is an island connected by two bridges, one near Tad village and the other near Ghoghle village. The neighbouring district of Diu is Junagadh of Gujarat.

PLACES OF INTEREST

IN DAMAN : Devka Beach, there is a popular amusement park on the beach which is illuminated on festive days. At Nani Daman, the Gandhi Park near Daman Jetty, the Nani Daman Fort and the church inside, and the fishing jetty where boats are anchored are worth paying a visit. A Moti Daman, the massive fort, the stately light house, gardens, historic monuments and ancient Gothis churches, are the key places of interest.

The Jampore beach is a favourite with swimming enthusiasts.

IN DIU : The Nagoa beach, one of the best beaches in India, is in the Nagoa hamlet, in the village of Burcharwada, and can be reached from Diu by a 20 minute drive. The sea, at this quite horse-shoe shaped beach, is safe for swimming. The Fort of Diu is an expansive and imposing structure, situated on the extreme coast of the island. The fort commands a magnificent view of the sea and its surrounding areas. Other places of interest are the Fortress of Panikotha, St,Paul's Church, jallandhar-Shrine beach, Gangeshwar temple and Jama Masjid.

HOW TO REACH

AIR : Diu is connected by air with Mumbai

RAIL : Daman – nearest railhead – Vapi on Western railway Mumbai-Delhi route.Diu – nearest railhead – Dalvada.

LAKSHADWEEP

AREA : 32 sq. km
CAPITAL : Kavaratti
LANGUAGE : Malayalam
AIRPORT : Agatti

The tiniest Union Territoray of India, Lakshadweep is an archipelago, consisting of 12 atolls, three reefs and five submerged banks. Out of its 36 islands covering 32 sq. km, only 10 are inhabited namely : Andrott, Amini, Agatti, Bitra, Chetlat, Kadmat, Kalpani, Kavaratti (headquarter) Kitlan and Minicoy. Bitra is the smallest of all islands.

These lie scattered in the Arabian Sea about 280 km to 480 km off the Kerala coast between 8E and 12.3E north and 71E east longitude.

Only five islands are open for tourism—four for domestic tourists and one for foreign tourists.

The Island lies about 220 to 440 km from the coastal city of Cochin.

HISTORY

Not much is known of the early history of these islands. The Islands are supposed to have been inhabited first by the Amini, Kalpeni, Androth, Kavaratti, and Agatti. It was earlier believed that the islanders were originally Hindus and were converted to Islam under the influence of Arab traders sometime in the 14th century. But archaeological evidence recently unearthed indicates that there were Buddhist settlements around sixth or seventh centuries and the earliest Muslim converts or settlers predate the year 139 AH of the Hijra year (eight century) of which date gravestones have recently been discovered in Agatti. This would tend to bear out the local tradition that Islam was brought to the islands by Arab saint Ubaidaulla in 41 AH.

Probably independent till the 16th century, the islanders were driven to seek the assistance of Raja of Chirakkal to help them get rid of the Portuguese attempts to establish dominance. This enabled him to establish his authority and, later, the islands were transferred in jagir to Ali Raja, head of the Moplah community in Cannonore, who later became an independent ruler himself. The Arakkal rule was not popular, and in 1787, Tipu Sultan acceded to the petitions of northern islanders to annex these islands. After the fall of Tipu Sultan, the islands were passed to East India Company but continued to be ruled (de facto) by the rulers of Cannanore till their ultimate annexation by the British in the early 20th century.

In 1956, the islands were constituted into Union Territory in 1956 and since then have been directly administered by the Union Government of India through an administrator. The Laccadives, Minicoy and Aminidivi group of coral islands were renamed as Lakshadweep in 1973.

Lakshdweep islands have in recent years become one of the country's popular destination, surrounded by lagoons and are known for their pristine beauty. Forests abound, the beaches are silver crescents, with the blue sea crystal clear. The coral formations underwater are amazingly colourful gardens and the variety of fish that inhabit these waters is truly exotic.

PLACES OF INTEREST

KAVARATTI : The administrative capital, it is the msot developed of the Island. Fifty two mosques are spread out over the island, the most beautiful being the Ujra Mosque with ornately carved ceilings, said to have been carved from a piece of driftwood. A well within its precincts is believed to contain water having curative powers. Kavaratti also has an aquarium with several colourful species of Fish.There is a glass bottom boat for viewing marine life and an array of remarkable coral formations. Water sports like kayaking, canoeing and snorkelling are available for tourists.

KALPENI : Kalpeni has three uninhabited islands, all surrounded by an immense lagoon of spectacular beauty. Koomel, the gently curving bay where the tourist facilities are located, directly overlooks, Pitti and Thilakkm, two of the islands. Here you can swim, reef walk, snorkel, kayak and sail. Tourists can stay on the island in privately managed huts.

KAFMATH : A fine lagoon of even depth and an endless shoreline, Kadmath is a haven of solitude. The tourist huts are situated some distance away from habitation with only the splash of the waves to break the silence. The feathery network of coconut palms provides a canopy throughout the island. Kadmath is the only island, with lagoons on both the eastern and western sides. An institute for water sports has been set up. Accommodation consists of both A/C and non A/C tourist huts, picturesquely situated amidst the coconut palm groves. The island is becoming increasingly popular for honeymooners.

MINICOY : At 200 km to the south, it is the farthest from the Kavaratti island, but also nearest to the Maldives. Minicoy boasts of a lighthouse built by the British in 1885. Visitors are allowed right to the very top of the lighthouse. The lagoon is one of the largest in Lakshadweep. Minicoy has a fascinating culture, very different from any other islands—the dress, the language, the food are peculiar to this area. It has a cluster of ten villages call Athiris, each presided by a Moopan. Minicoy is renowned for its dances. The lava dance is performed on festive occasions. There is a tuna canning factory – signifying its importance in tuna fishing and boat building activities. Privately managed cottages built on isolated islands are available for tourists.

AGATTI : Agatti has one of the most beautiful lagoons in Lakshadweep. It also has an airport. A virtual gateway to Lakshadweep, a tourist complex has been set up here.

BANGARAM : The tear-drop shaped, uninhabited Bangaram island, is embraced by a halo of creamy sand. Like in all other islands of Lakshadweep, coconut palm groves are uniquitous in Bangaram. There are three uninhabited islands in the same atoll —Tinnakara, Parali-I, Parali-II. All the islands share the same lagoon, an enormous bowl of turquoise blue. The warm, clear and deep waters of the Indian Ocean pose an irresistible invitation to scuba divers. The Bangaram Island resort is fast becoming the by-word among the island—hoppers of the world. Opened only recently to foreign tourists, the resort with its simple but attractive housing, has already become a circled spot in the brochures of tour operators all over. There are attractive package terms for the domestic tourists too.

HOW TO REACH

AIR : Agatti is connected by air with Cochin
SHIP : Vessels ply from Cochin

PONDICHERRY

AREA : 492 sq. km.
CAPITAL : Pondicherry
LANGUAGES : Tamil, Malyalam, English and French.

Pondicherry appears a tiny speck on India's sprawling eastern coast. A vedic association glamourises its past. Sage Agastya is believed to have set up his ashram here in the distant Vedic past. The evidence is sought in the town's ancient name—Vedapuri, and in the nomenclature of the old presiding deity of the area, referred to as 'Vedapurishwara' also known as 'Agastishwara'. Sanskrit scholarship thrived in Vedapuri, assumed to be the seat of a Sanskrit university in the 9th century, a couple of centuries after the decline of learning at Nalanda in Bihar.

HISTORY

In the first century, the Roman traders navigating between the East Indies and the Red Sea had set up a trading post and a settlement here. Fifteen centuries later, in 1673 Pulicherry a small fishermen's village on the Coromandel coast 160 km south of Madras, was acquired by Frenchmen as a trading post for the Frech. The new settlement was called Pucucherry. Two dacades later, it was occupied by the Dutch. Then arrived Dupleix, who thought of Pondicherry in the same terms as Clive thought of Calcutta. For 15 years the British battled with the French enclave. From 1761 to 1816 it was the object of intense internecine rivalry between the British and the French, exchanging hands several times before the French finally occupied it for an uninterrupted spell from 1816 to 1954.

In 1954, Pondicherry, Karaikal, Yanam and Mahe, four widely separated French pockets on the eastern and western coasts of India, returned to mother country, peacefully. Today, Pondicherry is the common haedquaters for karaikal, Yanam and Mahe.

PLACES OF INTEREST

SRI AUROBINDO ASHRAM : Aurobindo Ashram forms the necleus of many activities and trade in Pondicherry. It is a product of Aurobindo's inspirations and Mira Alfassa's earnestness. The main Ashram on Rue de lal marine houses the buildings where Aurobindo and Mirra Alfassa lived and died.

AUROVILLE : Auroville is an experiment in International living where men and women could live in peace and progressive harmony with each other above all creeds, politics and nationalities. It is a developing town 10 km from Pondicherry.

RAJ VILAS : Once the residence of famous Governor Dupliz, this imposing palace is today the official residence of the Lieutenant Governor of Pondichdrry.

THE BEACH : The Pondicherry beach with its 1.5 km long promenade is one of the best place in Pondicherry to have a stroll, a swim or a Sun bath.

THE PONDICHERRY MUSEUM : The Pondicherry museum is a treasure house of antiques with a section on French India which is housed in rooms done in typical French style. It houses specimen from Pallva sculptures to a bed slept in by Dupleix. Also on display are some fine antiques, handicrafts and ornaments.

There are numerous temples and Churches in Pondicherry.

Out of the 350 temples, 75 of are dedicated to Lord Ganesha. The Varadaraja and the Villenour's Thrikakeswarar temples date back to the 12th century.

A large number of churches like the Sacred Heart of Jesus and the Eglis de Notre Dame des Anges are other legacies left behind by the French.

HOW TO REACH

AIR : Nearest airport : Chennia.

RAIL : Nearest railhead : Villupuram.

ROAD : Pondicherry is well-connected by road and major towns of the State. 4 hours drive from Chennai, frequent buses and taxis are easily available.

HOTEL ACCOMMODATION (STD CODE 0413)

— Anandha Inn (P) Ltd. : (3 Star) 154, S.V. Patel Road.

PH. 330711; FAX 331241.
— Pondicherry Ashok : (3 Star) East Coast Road, Kalpet Beach.
  PH. 365160-68; FAX 365140.
— Sea Side Guest House : 14 Goubert Avenue.
  PH 336494; FAX 334447.

EXCURSIONS

OUSSOUDU : (16 km) Picnic resort in pleasant surroundings. Boating in the Chunnambar river near Ariyankuppam is the most enjoyable part of the visit of Pondicherry. Boats, garden umbrellas, chairs etc. can be hired on nominal charges.

TIRUVANNAMALAI : (96 km) Situated at the foothills in Tiruvannamalai is one of the most important Shiva temple in the south. During the Karthigai Deepam festival is celebrated in November or December when a huge fire is lit atop the hill and devotees flock to the temple and to the ashram of the Saint Sri Ramana Maharshi, which is 3 km from the temple. 37 km from Tiruvannamalai is a fort complex constructed during the Vijaynagara empire. There are four temples inside the fort among which the Venkataramana temple is the largest.

UTTAR PRADESH

UTTAR PRADESH
AT A GLANCE

AREA : 2,94,411 Sq. km

CAPITAL : Lucknow

BOUNDARIES : East - Bihar; West - Himachal Pradesh, Haryana and Delhi; South - Rajasthan; North - Tibet; Nort-East-Nepal.

LANGUAGE : Hindi

ROADS : The roads constructed by the end of 1995-96 were 88,200km including 17,940 km Kachha roads. The length of roads in hill areas is 3,335 km and in frontier areas 505 km respectively.

AIRPORTS : Allahabad, Agra, Gorakhpur, Jhansi, Kanpur, Varanasi, Bareilly, Hindon (Ghaziabad), Sarsawa (Saharanpur), Pantnagar (Nainital), Jolly Grant (Dehradun) and Fursatganj (Rae-Bareli).

MUSEUMS

Agra : Taj Mahal Museum – Taj Compound

Allahabad : Allahabad Museum; Kausambi Museum – University of Allahabad

Lucknow : State Museum; Picture Gallery

Mathura : Government Museum

Sarnath : Archaeological Site Museum

Varanasi : Bharat Kala Bhavan – Banaras Hindu University; Departmental Museum – Banaras Hindu University; Maharaja Banaras Vidya Mandir Museum – Ramnagar Fort

HILL RESORTS

Almora (1646m) Railhead – Katgodam 92 km

Chakrata (2138m) Railhead – Dehradun 92 km

Kausani (1890m) Railhead – Katgodam 142 km

Lansdowne(1829m) Railhead – Kotdwra 40 km

Mussoorie (200m) Dehradun 36 km

Nainital (1938m) Railhead – Katgodam 35 km

Pithoragarh (1815m) Railhead – Tanakpur 151 km

Raniket (778m) Railhead – Katgodam 84 km

Tehri (778m) Railhead – Rishikesh 82 km

PILGRIM CENTRES (A : Air; R : Rail)

Allahabad : Meeting place of the three sacred rivers—Triveni Sangam. Kumbha Mela held once in 12 years, A and R Allahabad,
   Ayodhya : Birthplace of Sri Rama, A- Lucknow 115 km, R - Ayodhya.

Badrinath-Kedarnath-Joshimath-Gangotri-Yamunotri-Gomukh-Hemkund-Panchapyrayag important pilgrim spots in the Himalayas. Badrinath is reached by bus, Kedarnath only by a trek. Gangotri and Yamunotri are the places where Ganga and Yamuna rivers originate. Gomukh is the known source of the Ganga -23km trek from Gangotri A - Dehradun 47 from Rishikesh, R - 293 km from Badrinath.

Faizabad : Annual urs at mausoleaum of Muslim saints.
   A - Lucknow 115 km, R - Faizabad

Gorakhpur : Gorakhnath Temple, A and R Gorakhpur.

Hardwar : The 'Gate of God'. The Kumbha Mela held here after every 12 years.
   A - Dehradun 78 km, R - Hardwar

Jaunpur : Tombs of Sharqui rulers of Jaunpur, A and R Varanasi 36 km.

Kushinagar : Spot where the Buddha attained Mahaparinirvana.
   A and R Gorakhpur 53 km.

Mathura : Associated with Sri Krishna's childhood.
   A - Agra 54 km, R - Mathura

Rishikesh : Important centre at the foot of the Himalayas. Has many yoga schools. A - Dehradun 47 km, R - Rishikesh

Sankasia : Spot where the Buddha descended after preaching to his mother in heaven. A - Agra 141 km, R - Pakhna 11 km

Sarnath : Buddhist pilgrim centre where the Buddha preached his first sermon.
   A and R – Varanasi 11 km.

Sravasti : Centre known for one of the miracles of Lord Buddha.
   A Gorakhpur, R Balrampur 29 km.

Varanasi : One of the 4 dhams, the Kashi Vishwanath temple and the Ganga river are important pilgrim attractions A and R Varanasi.

Uttar Pradesh is one of the most fascinating States of India. It has something to offer; hill stations to enjoy the holidays - jungles for hunting - rivers for angling and pilgrim places echoing the glories from the past.

HISTORY

Uttar Pradesh is recognised in the later Vedic age as Brahmanrshi Desa or Mashya Desa. Many great sages of the Vedic times like Bharadwaja, Gautam Yagyavalka, Vasista, Vishwamitra and Valmiki had lived in this area. Several sacred books of the Aryans were also composed here. Two great epics of India the Ramayana and Mahabharata based on the happings in this area.

In the 6th century BC Uttar Pradesh was associated with two new religions - Jainism and Buddhism. It was at Sarnath that Lord Buddha had preached his first sermon and laid the foundation of his order and it was in Kushinagar in U.P. where he had breathed his last. In the post Buddhist period, several centres in U. P. like Ayodhya, Prayag, Varanasi and Mathura became reputed centres of learning.

Sri Sankaracharya the great Hindu reformer, established one of his ashrams at Badrinath in U.P.

In the medieval period, U. P. passed under the Muslim rule and led the way to a new synthesis of Hindu and Islamic cultures, Ramananda and his Muslim disciple Kabir, Tulsidas, Soordas and many other intellectuals contributed to the growth of Hindi and other languages.

Uttar Pradesh preserved its intellectual leadership even under the British administration. The British combined Agra and Oudh into one province and called it United Provinces of Agra and Oudh. The name was shortened to the United Provinces in 1935.

After Independence. In January 1950, United Provinces was renamed as Uttar Pradesh.

LUCKNOW

Lucknow, capital of Uttar Pradesh, extends along the banks of the Gomati river. The creator of Lucknow as it is today was Nawab Asaf-ud- Daulah. The city became a centre of Urdu poetry and reached its acme during the reign of Wajid Ali Shah who was a connoisseur of music and poetry. Today the city is dotted with remnants of its historic past.

Lucknow is also known for its elaborate cuisine and "CHIKANKAARI" on fine cloth.

PLACES OF INTEREST

HUSSAINABAD IMAMBARA : It houses the tombs of Muhammad Ali Shah and his mother amd was built between 1837 AD and 1842 AD. The Imambara has a white dome and numerous turrets and minarets. The walls are decorated with verses in Arabic.

SHAH NAJAF IMAMBARA : Saint Hazrat Ali is burried here.

RESIDENCY : Built for the British Resident in 1780-1800 AD it was the scene of dramatic events during the Mutiny of 1857. The ruins tell the story of British rulers besieged by the rebels.

ASAFI IMAMBARA : Also known as Bara Imambara, built by Nawab Asaf-ud-Daulan 1784 AD it is one of the architectural highlights of the era. The central hall is said to be the largest vaulted chamber in the world.

RUMI DARWAZA : This colossal, ornate gateway is said to be a facsimile of one of the gates of Constantinople. It was built by Nawab Asaf-ud-Daula in to create employment during the terrible famine of 1784 AD.

KAISERBAGH PALACE COMPLEX : The construction of this palace complex was started in 1848 AD by Nawab Wajid Ali Shah and completed in 1850 AD. They were built to create the eighth wonder of the world.

NATIONAL BOTANICAL RESEARCH INSTITUTE : It is located at Sikandarbagh there pitched battles had taken place during the Mutiny of 1857.

HOW TO REACH

AIR : Lucknow is connected by air with Calcutta, Delhi, Patna and Mumbai

RAIL : Lucknow is a major railway junction and connected directly with main cities of the country.

ROAD : Lucknow is connected by road with main cities of the country.

IMPORTANT DISTANCES

Kanpur 77 km; Delhi 497 km; Agra 369 km; Jhansi 301 km; Kahjuraho 320 km; Nainital 407 km; Allahabad 237 km; Varanasi 286 km; Corbett National Park 480 km; Dudhwa National Park 260 km;

Ayodhya 128 km; Patna 532 km; Haridwar 595 km; Calcutta 963 km and Mumbai 1374 km.

CONDUCTED TOURS

(1) City Tour (2) Dudhwa National Park (3) Nawabganj Bird Sanctuary

For further details contact :

— Directorate of U.P. Tourism, Chitrahar Building,3 Newal Kishore Road.
PH 0522 – 228349; FAX 0522 - 114 221776

— Regional Tourist Office, 10 Station Road
PH 0522 - 226205

— Tourist reception Counter, Railway Station, Charbagh, PH 0522 -452533

— PRO, G.M.V.N.,432/4 New Civil Lines
PH 0522 - 387349

— P.R.O., K.M.V.N., 2 Gopal Khera House, Sarojini Naidu Marg. PH 0522 215903

— State Information Bureau, Hazratganj
PH 0522 224728

— Wildlife Information Centre, 17, Rana Pratap Marg
PH 0522 283902

HOTEL ACCOMMODATION (STD CODE 0522)

— Taj Mahal Hotel (5Star Deluxe),Gomati Nagar
PH 393 939; FAX 392 282

— Hotel Clarks Avadh (5 Star), 8, Mahatma Gandhi marg
PH 216 500 - 09; FAX 216 507

— Carlton Hotel pvt.Ltd.(3Star),Shahnaja Road
PH 224 021-4; FAX 229 793.

— Hotel Charan International, 16,Vidhan Sabha Marg
PH 227 219, 227 518; FAX 223 228

— Deep Hotel, 5, Vidhan Sabha Marg
PH 216 441-5; Fax 228 832

— Hotel Deep Avadh, 133/273 Aminabad Road
PH 216 521/2/3/4; FAX 228 832

— Kohinoor Hotel : 6 Station Road
PH 217 693

EXCURSIONS

KUKRAIL RESERVE FOREST : A picnic spot developed by Forest Department, it has a deer park and a crocodile nursery. A variety of birds and deer can be seen in their natural habitat.

NAWANGANJ BIRD SANCTUARY : (43 km)This sanctuary attracts Siberian migratory birds.

NEEMSAR -MISRIKH : (94 km) An important religious centre with the temples of the goddess Lailta, Dadhichi Kund, Vyas Gaddi, Chakratirth and Hanuman Garhi.

AYOHDHYA : (134 km) This holy city and the popular pilgrim centre is situated on the right bank of the Saryu river. It is believed to be the birth place of Lord Rama, the seventh incarnation of Lord Vishnu. The ancient city of Ayodhya according to Ramayana, was founded by Manu, the law-giver of the Hindus. For centuries it was the capital of the descendants of the Surya dynasty of which Lord Rama was the most celebrated King. The story of the epic Ramayana has been immortalised by Valmiki and immensely popularised by the great masses through centuries. Ramkot is the chief sacred place of worship. On 'Ramnavami, this place attracts devotess from India and abroad.

HANUMANGARHI : According to a legend Hanuman lived here in a cave and guarded the Janambhomi or Ramkot. The faithful believed that all their wishes will be granted with a visit to this holy shrine. KANAK BHAWAN is a palace built by Rani Kaikey for Sita and has images of Sri Ram and Sita.SWARG DWAR is a place where, according to mythology, Lord Rama is said to have been cremated. TRETA-KE-THAKUR – a temple where Rama is said to have performed the Ashvamedha Yajnya. NAGESHWARNATH TEMPLE—this temple is said to have been established by Kush, son of Lord Rama.

Main ghats to be visited at Ayodhya are Guptaghat, Rajghat, Lakshmanghat, Janakghat, Suryakund, Vibhishankund, Brahmakund, Daturvan and Vinayakund.

THE RAM VANVAS ROUTE - SAMPLE ITINERARY

DAY 1

Depart from Ayodhya to Allahabad (166 km) enroute visit Faizabad

(7 km) - an important landmark of Avadh culture with many fine monuments; Sultanpur (58 km) - an upcoming industrial town;

Pahphamau (95 km) - an industrial suburb of Allahabad on the Ganga. river and proceed to Allahabad for an overnight stay.

DAY 2

Depart from Allahabad to Chitrakoot (133 km), Morning city tour of Allahabad, visit Sangam-Bharadwaj Ashram - Hanuman and temples on the ghat-Anand Bhawan and proceed to Chitrakoot enroute visit Ghurpur (25km); Shivrajpur (31km); Mau (25 km); Rajpura (23 km); Karwi (11km) and proceed to Chitrakoot for an overnight stay.

DAY 3

Depart from Chitrakoot to Bithur (246 km), enroute visit Kanpur. In afternnoon visit Bithur - see Brahmvarta ghat, the Valmiki Ashram, Dhruv Teela and Luv-Kush temple.Overnight stay at Bithur. End of the tour at Bithur.

AGRA

Agra was the capital of the Mughal empire in the 16th and 17th century and its significance as a political centre ended with the transfer of the capital to Delhi in 1634 AD by Shah Jahan. But its architectural wealth 'TAJ MAHAL' has secured its place on the International Map. Agra is also known for its superb inlay work on marble and soapstone.

PLACES OF INTEREST

TAJ MAHAL : The inimitable poem in white marble, one of the seven modern wonders of the world, the finest expression of love of Emperor Shah Jahan for his queen Mumtaz is located on the banks of the Yamuna river here. The construction of the Taj had commenced in 1631AD and had ended in 1653AD. Workers were gathered from all over the country and from central Asia. About 20,000 people were recruited to translate this dream into reality. The main architect was Isa Khan who was brought from Iran. Taj will remain a symbol of eternal love. Shah Jehan was subsequently buried and reunited finally with his beloved Mumtaz.

AGRA FORT : Built by Emperor Akbar in 1565AD the fort is a masterpiece of design and construction. The fort houses palaces, courts, mosques, baths, gardens and pavilions. Places to visit are—red sandstone Jehangir Mahal built by Akbar for his Hindu queen Jodhabai; Moti Masjid, Diwane-i-Am; Diwane-i-Khas and Musamman Burj where the Emperor Shah Jehan died in imprisonment.

ITMAD-UD-DAULAH'S TOMB : It was built by Empress Noor Jahan, in memory of her father, Ghias-ud-Din Beg in 1622-25AD. This ornate tomb is considered as a precursor of Taj Mahal.

HOW TO REACH

AIR : Agra is connected by air with Delhi, Khajuraho and Varanasi.

RAIL : Agra is connected by rail with all major cities of the country.

Delhi, Agra and Jaipur cities are known as the "GOLDEN TRIANGLE" in the tourism terminology. Agra is well-connected by rail with Delhi. Important trains between Delhi and Agra are :

2180 Taj Express D Delhi 0715 Hrs; A Agra 0945 Hrs.

Retrun 2181 Taj Express D Agra 1700 Hrs; A Delhi 1835 Hrs.

2002 Shatabdi Express D Delhi 0615; A Agra 0810 Hrs.

Return 2003 Shatabdi Express D Agra 2010 Hrs : A Delhi 2225 Hrs.

Agra-Jaipur - 4853 Jodhpur Marudhar Express D Agra 0525Hrs;A Jaipur 1215

Return Jaipur-Agra D Jaipur 1520 Hrs; A Agra 2155 Hrs.

ROAD : Agra is well connected by road with all major cities of the State, Delhi and Haryana. I.T.D.C., D.T.D.C. and many private tour operators operate regular buses to and fro Delhi as well as from Jaipur. Taxis and coaches are easily available.

CONDUCTED TOURS

(1) Full-day tour to Fatehpur Sikri, Taj Mahal and Agra Fort

(2) Half day tour to Fatehpur Sikri

Contact UPTDC at the following address :

— U.P. Government Tourist Office, 64, Taj Road
   PH 360 517

— Government of India Tourist Office, 191, The Mall.
   PH 369 959, 364 439

— U.P. Government Tourist reception Counter, Agra Cantt
   Railway Station. PH 364 439

Similar tours are available from local travel agents also.

HOTEL ACCOMMODATION (0562)

— Welcomegroup Mughal Shereton (5 Star Deluxe)
Fatehabad Road, Taj Ganj
   PH 331 701- 25; FAX 331 730
— Hotel Taj View (5 Star) Taj Ganj, Fatehabad Road
   PH 331 841-59; FAX 331 860
— Hotel Clarks Shiraz (5 Star) 54, Taj Road
   PH 361 421-30; FAX 361 428
— Hotel Mansingh Palace (3 Star) Fatehabad Road
   PH 331771; FAX 330 878
— Hotel Agra Ashok (5 Star) 6/B, Mall Road
   PH 361 223-32; FAX 361 620
— Hotel Howard Park Plaza International : (5 Star)
Fatehabad, Taj Ganj
   PH 391 870 – 78 : FAX 330 408
— The Trident (3 Star) Taj nagri Scheme, Fatehabad Road
   PH 331 818; FAX 331 827
— Hotel Amar (3 Star) Tourist Complex Area,
   Fatehabad Road. PH 331 885; FAX 330 299
— Hotel Atithi (3 Star) Tourist Complex area,
   Fatehabad Road. PH 361 474; FAX 330 878
— Hotel Grand (3 Star) 137, Station Road
   PH 364 014, 364 311; FAX 364 271
— Mayur Tourist Complex, Fatehabad Road
   PH 332 302, 332 310; FAX 332 907
— Agra Deluxe, Tourist Complex Area, Fatehabad Road
   PH 330 110, Fax 331 330

EXCURSIONS

RAM BAGH : (6 km) The earliest example of a Mughal garden was created by Emperor Babar, founder of the dynasty.

SIKANDRA : (12 km) The tomb of Akbar, begun by the Emperor himself and completed by his son Jehangir, the structure is a quaint mixture of Hindu and Islamic art.

CHINI-KA-ROZA : (7 km) The tomb of Allama Afzel Khal Mullah of Shiraz is a memorial to the poet-scholar, who later became the Prime Minister to Emperor Shah Jahan. The surface of the tomb is decorated with glazed tiles.

RADHASWAMY SAMADHI, DAYALBAGH : This highly ornate memorial to the founder of the Radhaswamy sect has been in the making for more than 40 years and is still being worked upon. It is entirely in marble, upon which every manner of ornamentation has been applied.

JAMA MASJID : It is of specific importance due to its assimilation of Iranian architectural elements it was built in 1648 AD by Emperor Shah Jahan's daughter, Jahanara Begum.

MARIYAM'S TOMB : (13 km) It was built for Emperor Akbar's Goan wife, Mariyam in 1611 AD.

SUR SUROVAR (KEETHAM LAKE) : (23 km) This 2.5 sq. km. lake, surrounded by the Surdas Reserve Forest, harbours a rich variety of fish and water-birds and is a popular picnic spot.

FATEHPUR SIKRI : (37 km) This is the first planned city in Indo-Islamic architecture built by Emperor Akbar. According to legend, Emperor Akbar was without a male heir. He made a bare-foot pilgrimage to seek the blessings of Sufi saint Sheikh Salim Chisti who lived here. The saint prophesied the birth of three sons and soonafter was born Prince Salim, later to become Emperor Jehangir. In gratitude Akbar decided to create his imperial residence in Sikri and the new capital Fatehpur Sikri (from 1570- 1586 AD) came into being. The finest monuments within this area are the DIWANI-I-AM; DIWANI-I-KHAS; PASCHI COURT; PRIVATE LIVING LIBRARY; MARIAM'S PALACE; JODHABAI'S PALACE; HAWA MAHAL, BIRBAL'S PALACE; PANCH MAHAL; JAMA MASJID; SALIM CHISTI'S TOMB AND BULAND DARWAZA.

FIROZABAD : (44 km) An important handicraft centre renowned for glassware especially bangles.

BHARATPUR BIRD SANCTUARY : (60 km) Known as Keoladeo National Park, India's renowned waterbird sanctuary, is the winter home of the rare Siberian Crane.

ALIGARH : (82 km) Famous for Muslim University and for being the centre of Islamic studies it is also an important centre for handicrafts and metalware especially locks.

MATHURA AND VRINDAVAN : (62 km) It is traditionally recognised as the capital of the Braj Bhoomi, the land which gave birth to Lord Krishna. Vrindavan is associated with the legend of Lord Krishna. The main places of interest of Mathura are SHRI KRISHNA JANAMBHOOMI - the birthplace of Lord Krishna; DWARKADHEESH TEMPLE - built by Seth Gokul Das of Gwalior in 1814 AD; JAMA MASJID - built in 1661 AD by Abd-un-Nabi Khan; KANS QILA - situated on the banks of Yamuna river, this ruined fort was re-built by Raja Man Singh of Amer. Later Sawai Jai Singh, the founder of Jaipur, built an observatory on the parapet of the fort; GOVERNMENT MUSEUM - houses a fine collection of antiquities belonging to the Mauryan, Sunga, Kushan (finest in the world) and Gupta periods; GITA MANDIR - modern temple embellished with fine paintings and carvings. The entire Bhagwat Gita is inscribed on a pillar called ' Bhagwat Stambha'; MATHURA GHATS : Ghats are of great ritual interest. Main ghats to visit are Visharm, Swami Assikinda, Kali Dah, Govind Keshi etc.

The main places of interest of Vrindavan are : KRISHNA BALRAM TEMPLE built by the International Society for Krishna consciousness, it attracts devotees from all over the world. A Gurukul and a school of yoga are a part of this temple; GOVIND DEV TEMPLE —built in 1590 AD by Raja Mansingh of Amer, this temple is an example of architectural excellence of medieval India; RANGAJI TEMPLE—largest temple built in 1845 AD by Seth Govind Das is an amalgamation of Rajput and South Indian temple architecture.

RADHA BALLABH TEMPLE—built in 1626 AD, is of architectural interest; BANKEY BIHARI TEMPLE - Oldest temple was rebuilt in 1921 AD; SHAHJI TEMPLE - temple built in 1660 AD, known for its architecture, sculpture and marble spiral columns. The Basanti Kamra, decorated with paintings and chandeliers, is in the eastern wing of the temple. GOKUL - 16 km from Mathura is a place where the infant Krishna was reared in secrecy by his foster mother Yashoda. Pilgrim place especially during Janmashtami. GOVARDHAN—26 km from Mathura is a place where according to mythology Lord Krishna lifted and held a cluster of hills knows as Govardhan Parwat on his little finger for several days to protect his friends from the wrath of the God of rain and water i.e. Indra. Atop the Goverdhan hill is a temple built in 1520 AD by Vallabhacharya. BARSANA – 47 km from Mathura is the birthplace of Radha Rani, consort of Lord Krishna. Here four prominent hills are adorned by temples in honour of Radha called Ladliji or the beloved. Prem Sarovar lake is believed to be the first meeting place of Lord Krishna and Radha Barsana is famous for 'Lath-mar' Holi celebration enacted by the residents of Barsana and Nandgaon. In it the woman strike the man playing Holi with bamboo sticks and they protect themselves with a sheild both enjoying their roles. It all ends in merriment and festivities later. NANDGAON – 56 km from Mathura is a home of Nand, Krishna's foster father.

THE KRISHNA LEGEND - SAMPLE ITINERARY

Mathura–Baldeo–Vrindavan–Nandgaon–Barsana–Govardhan–Gokul–
Mathura.

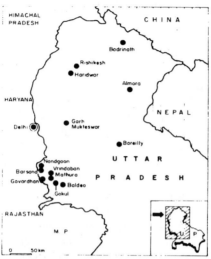

DAY 1

Mathura to Baldeo and back (54 km), enroute visit Mahaban
(18 km) south of Hathsar road, site of child Krishna's youthful episodes,
ruins of the old fortress, Baldeo (9 km) - temple of Dauji, elder brother
of Lord Krishna and return to Mathura.

DAY 2

Mathura to Govardhan (108 km), enroute visit Vrindavan (10km)
stop at Kosi for midway facilities;
Nandgaon (8 km) visit the 12th century temple of Nandji;
Barsana (20 km) visit the temple of Ladliji, Prem Sarovar.
Afternoon visit Govardhan (22 km) visit the 16th century temple,
Mansi Ganga.Overnight at Govardhan at Radha Kund.

DAY 3

Govardhan to Mathura, enroute visit Gokul, village of Lord Krishna
foster mother, Yashodha and return to Mathura.

ALLAHABAD

Allahabad, sacred city of Hinduism was formerly called 'PRAYAG' in commemoration of a sacrifice done by Lord Brahma. According to Hindu mythology for the 'Prakrishta Yagna' Lord Brahma chose a piece of land on the earth on the confluence of the three rivers - the Ganga, the Yamuna and the mytical Saraswati. This confluence is called SANGAM. The Sangam is the venue of many sacred fairs and rituals and attracts thousands of pilgrims throughout the year. Akbar had visited Prayag in 1575 AD and founded a new city by the name Illahabad which has now become Allahabad. The city was an important cantonment during the British Raj and has some beautiful remnants of colonial architecture. In the early 20th century, Allahabad was the foremost centre of learning in the country.

PLACES OF INTEREST

SANGAM : The confluence of the Ganga, the Yamuna and the mytical Saraswati. The waters of the two rivers are of different colours and their meeting point is visible. During Kumbh Mela thousands of devotees gather together for holi dip at the Sangam.

FORT : Built by Emperor Akbar in 1583 AD stands on the banks of the Yamuna, presently used by the army and only a limited area is open to visitors.

HANUMAN TEMPLE : The only temple in India near Sangam where the idol of Lord Hanuman is to be seen in a reclining posture.

ANAND BHAWAN : Home of the Nehru family was donated by Motilal Nehru to the nation in 1930 AD and has been now converted into a family museum.

ALLAHABAD UNIVERSITY : One of the famous universities of the country, it has a sprawling campus graced by fine buildings in Victorian and Islamic architectural styles.

ALLAHABAD MUSEUM : It has a good collection of sculpture, especially of the Gupta era.

PATTHAR GIRJA OR ALL SAINT'S CATHEDRAL : This magnificent cathedral, designed by Sir William Emerson is the finest of Allahabad's many churches dating to colonial times.

HOW TO REACH

AIR : Nearest airport-Lucknow-210 km; Kanpur- 224 km and Varanasi-147 km.

RAIL : Allahabad is the major railway junction and connected directly by mail express and superfast trains with main cities of the country.

ROAD : Allahabad is connected by road with all parts of the country. Local taxis, Rikshaws and tourist vehicles are easily available.

TOURIST INFORMATION OFFICE

— Government of UP Regional Tourist Office, Tourist Bungalow, 35, M.G.Marg, Civil Lines.
  PH 601 873.

HOTEL ACCOMMODATION (STD CODE 0532)

— Hotel Kanha Shyam : (4 Star) Civil Lines.
  PH 420 281/90
— Hotel Allahabad Regency (2 Star) 16, Tashkent Marg
  PH 601 519, 601 735; FAX 600 450
— Presidency (2 Star) 19-Sarojini Naidu Marg
  PH 623 308 : FAX 623 897
— Hotel Samrat,49A/25A, M.G. Marg, Civil Lines
  PH 604 869,604 879; Fax 603 290
— Hotel Yatrik (3 Star), 33, S.P. Marg, Civil Lines
  PH 601713 FAX 601 434

U.P. Tourism celebrates 'The Ganga Water Rally' from Allahabad to Varanasi with the cooperation of Boat club of Varanasi, NCC Naval Wing, Allahabad, and Garhwal Mandal Vikas Nigam.

BUNDELKHAND

Bundelkhand, which emerged from the mists of history during the rule of the mighty Chandelas in the 9th century AD governed the destiny of central India for nearly 300 years. The Bundelas who came to power six centuries later were also to command influence in this region.

Bir Singh Ju Deo (1605-1627 AD) a favourite of the Mughal Emperor Jahangir was a powerful ruler. Centuries later during the 1857 Mutiny against the British Raj, Bundelkhand produced charismatic leader in the Valiant Rani Laxmibai of Jhansi who led her troops into war against the might of the British.

Bundelkhand today is identified with districts of Jhansi, Lalitpur, Jalam, Hamirpur, Banda and Mahoba in Uttar Pradesh and Sagar, Chattarpur, Tikamgarh, Panna and Damoh and parts of Gwalior, Datia, Shivpuri and Chanderi in Madhya Pradesh.

Main cities of Bundelkhand are Jhansi (U.P.), Orcha (M.P.), Shivpuri (M.P), Datia (M.P.), Sonagiri (M.P.), Deogarh (U.P.), Mahoba (U.P.), Chitrakoot (U.P.), Kalpi (U.P.), Kalinjar (U.P.) and Khajuraho (M.P.)

SUGGESTED ITINERARIES FOR BUNDELKHAND

To visit Bundelkhand the convenient itinerary begins in Delhi, from where one can start for Gwalior proceeding to Jhansi-Orcha-Khajuraho-Mahoba-Kalinjar-Chitrakoot-Allahabad and back to Delhi—5 Days.

Jhansi-Matalila-Deogarh-Chanderi-Jhansi—2 Days.

Lucknow-Allahabad-Chitrakoot-mahoba-Khajuraho-Barua-Sagar-Jhansi-Lucknow—5 Days.

JHANSI

Jhansi, the gateway to Bundelkhand, was a stronghold of the Chandela kings but lost its importance after the eclipse of the dynasty in the 11th century. It rose to prominence again in the 17th century under Raja Bir Singh Deo who was a close associate of Mughal Emperor Jahangir. However its greatest claim to fame is its fiery queen Rani Laxmibai who led forces against the British in 1857 AD sacrificing her life to the cause of Indian independence.

Jhansi is ideal base to reach Orcha, Shivpuri, Deogarh and Khajuraho.

PLACES OF INTEREST

JHANSI FORT : The 17th century fort was built by Raja Bir Singh on top of a hill as army stronghold. The fort houses museum with sculptures and provides an insight into Bundelkhand history.

GOVERNMENT MUSEUM : It houses weapons, statues, dresses and photographs of Chandela dynasty.

RANI MAHAL : The palace of Rani Laxmi Bai has now been converted into museum and houses a collection of archaeological remains of the period between 9th and 12th centuries.

HOW TO REACH

AIR : Nearest airport-Gwalior 98 km; Khajuraho 175 km.

RAIL : Jhansi is a junction on Mumbai-Delhi route of Central Railway and is connected with major cities of the country.

ROAD : Jhansi is well-connected by road with the entire country. The city is a gateway to Bundelkhand. All types of tourist vehicles are easily available. Auto-rikshaws operate on a point-to-point basis.

TOURIST INFORMATION OFFICES

— Regional Tourist Office, U.P. Tourism, Hotel Veerangana, Shivpuri Road. PH 442 402
— Tourist Information Centre, Railway Station
— M.P. Tourist Information Centre, Railway Station
PH 442 622

HOTEL ACCOMMODATION (STD CODE 0567)

— Hotel Sita (3 Star), Shivpuri Road, Civil Lines
PH 442956, 444690
— Hotel Chanda : (3 Star) 365/1A Civil Lines
PH 451 281; FAX 450 027
— Jhansi Hotel, Shastri marg,
PH 470 360/74; FAX 470 470
— Prakash Guest House, Civil Lines
PH 443 133, 440 379
— Raj Palace Hotel, Shastri Marg
PH 442 554

EXCURSIONS

BARUA SAGAR : (24 km) Here the Marathas had fought the Bundelas in 1744 AD.

PARICHHA : (25 km) It is a dam built on the Betwa river. Its reservoir is ideal for water sports.

TODI-FATEHPUR : It has a fort covering an area of 5 acres built on a hillock and surrounded by three massive stone walls.

SAMTHAR : (66 km) Formerly called Samshergarh, it was an independent principality under the great Gujar warriors of the 17th and 18th centuries.

ORCHA : (18 km) Refer Madhya Pradesh
SHIVPURI : (101 km) Refer Madhya Pradesh
DATIA : (34 km) Refer Madhya Pradesh
SONAGIRI : (45 km) Refer Madhya Pradesh

DEOGARH

Deogarh is situated on the right bank of the Betwa river at the end of the Lalitpur range of hills. The cliffs, immediately overhanging the bank rise to a height of 300 feet and form a long steep ridge of red sandstone. Deogarh is of great antiquarian, epigraphical and archaeological importance and has figured in the history of the Guptas, the Gujaras – the Pratiharas, the Gondas, the Muslim rulers of Delhi, and Kalpi, the Marathas and the British. The thickly forested hills around Deogarh harbours a variety of wildlife.

PLACES OF INTEREST

DASHAVATAR TEMPLE : This fine Vishnu temple belongs to the Gupta period and is noted for being the first northern Indian temple with shikhara or spire. Only the lower part of the shikhara remains today.

JAIN SHRINES : There are 31 Jain temples of a later date. The site was a Jain centre from the post-Gupat times up to the 17th century. Panels depicting scenes from Jain mythology, Tirthankara images, a Manastambha, Ayagpatta, Sarvato Bhadra pratima and Sahastrakuta are found here.

DEOGARH ARCHAEOLOGICAL MUSEUM : The museum has fine collection of sculptures.

HOW TO REACH

AIR : Nearest airport – Gwalior 235 km

RAIL : Convenient railway station – Lalitpur 33 km

ROAD : Deogarh is connected by regular bus services from Lalitpur and other parts of the State.

HOTEL ACCOMMODATION : Tourist Bungalow and Jain Dharmashala.

EXCURSIONS

CHANDERI : The town is famous for gaossamer Chanderi Sarees. It has also some of the finest examples of Bundela, Rajput and Malwa

Sultanate architecture. A magnificent Mughal fort dominates the skyline of this old interesting town.

BARUA SAGAR : The town situated on the road to Khajuraho, is named after the Barua Sagar Tal, a large lake created about 260 years ago when Raja Udit Singh of Orcha built the embankment. The Barua Sagar fort, picturesque and located at a height, commands an excellent view of the lake and the surroundings landscape.

MAHOBA

Mahoba is the ancient capital of the mighty Chandelas. The Chandelas were great warriors and builders and have left behind an extraordinary legacy. The impregnable hilltop fort and the lakes they created are considered engineering feats and their water management system can still be seen. The lakes include Rahila Sagar built by Rahila (885-905 AD), the Kirat Sagar built by Kirtivarman (1060 – 1100 AD) and the Madan Sagar built by Madan Verma (1128 – 1165 AD). Near Madan Sagar lies the famous granite Shiva temple known as Kakramath, built in the Khaujuraho style of temple architecture. On the island in the lake stands Majhari, the ruins of another Vishnu temple. There is an old Chandela fort known as Quila Mismar, Maniya Devi temple and the Dargah of a Muslim saint from Arabia, who settled in 1252 AD are to be visited in the fort area. Mahoba also has two famous Chandela period tanks Ram Kund and Suraj Kund lined with granite slabs in a reserve pyramid shape. The town is also known for the excellent varieties of paan (betal leaves) which are despatched to all parts of the country.

HOW TO REACH

AIR : Nearest airport – Khajuraho 65 km

RAIL : Mahoba is connected by broad guage rail line with Mumbai, Allahabad, Gwalior, Varansi etc.

ROAD : Mahoba is connected by road with all major cities.

HOTEL ACCOMMODATION (STD CODE 0914)

— Atithi Hotel, Alha Chowk
— Shivam Hotel, near U.P. Roadways bus stand
— Paras Hotel, near Udal Chowk. PH 4181
— Trishul Hotel, near Khank Bazar
— Tourist Bungalow, Khajuraho Road, Mahoba. PH 4108

CHITRAKOOT

Chitrakoot is closely associated with the epic Ramayana. It is a "HILL OF THE WONDERS", hallowed centre of pilgrimage. It is believed to be the place where Lord Rama and Sita spent their 13 of the14 years of exile and where Sage Atri and Sati Anusuya meditated, the divine spot which saw incarnations of Brahma, Vishnu and Mahesh. The holy town is set on the banks of the Mandakini river. Ram ghat on the banks of the Mandakini river is the centre of ritual activity and is most frequently visited. The "ARATI" performed in the evening is  particularly beautiful. Ganesh bagh 11 km from Chitrakoot has an exquisitely carved Shiva temple. A residential palace and a seven storied baoli built during the reign of the Peshwa Vinayak Rao lies in ruins nearby. Bharat Koop (18 km) is believed to contain the holy waters of the sacred rivers brought by Bharat to celebrate the Coronation ceremony of Lord Rama.

Gupta Godavari, 19 km from Chitrakoot is the place where it is believed that Lord Rama and his brother Lakshman held court in the cave which has two natural thronelike rocks. 13 km away is the place called Sati Anasuya where Atri Muni, his wife Anusuya and their three sons (the three incarnations of Brahma, Vishnu and Mahesh) are said to have meditated. It is believed that Lord Rama and Sita used to sit and enjoy scenic beauty on Sphatik Shila. Sita used to took her bath at Janki Kund near Chitrakoot. Kamadgiri 2 km away is a place of prime religious significance. The Bharat Milap temple is loacted here marking the spot where Bharat is said to have met Ram, to persuade him to return to Ayodhya. Swami Tulsidas was born at Rajpur, 18 km form Chitrakoot.

HOW TO REACH

AIR : Nearest airport – Khajuraho 185 km
RAIL : Nearest railway station – Karvi 8 km
ROAD : Chitrakoot is well connected by road. There are regular bus services from Banda, Allahabad, Jhansi, Varanasi, Chhatapur, Satna, Kanpur Faizabad and Lucknow.

HOTEL ACCOMMODATION (STD CODE 05198)

— Pramod Van – Dharamshala
— Mata Sri Anand Ram Jaipuria Smriti Bhawan. PH 2221
— Kamad Giri Bhawan, Annapuran (Vinod Lodge)
— M.P. State Tourist Bungalow, Roopali Lodge, near railway station. PH 326
— Tourist Bungalow UPSTDC, PH2219, Yatri Niwas "Chitrakoot"

KALPI

Kalpi is believed to have been originally founded by Kalib Dev, a ruler of the area in ancient times. One of the eight forts of the Chandelas, the earliest authentic mention of Kalpi is found in the annals of its capture by Qutb-ud-din Aibak in 1196 AD. After this Kalpi saw long days of struggle for its possession- not only by the Sarqi Kings of Jaunpur, but also by successive rulers - Daulat Khan Lodhi, Hoshang Shah of Malwa, Beholol Lodhi and Babar. Under Akbar Kalpi became the "GATEWAY OF THE WEST" and the starting point for expeditions to central India. In the 17th century the famous Bundela chief Chhatrasal made Kalpi his stronghold. Rani Laxmibai of Jhansi also held possession of the fort for some time. Finally it fell into the hands of the British in 1857 AD. The principal remains at Kalpi are the tombs of Madar Sahib, Ghafue Zanjani, Chol Bibi and Bahadur Shahid and the great enclosure commonly known as the Chaurasi Gumbaz, attributed to Lodhis.

KALINJAR

Located in the ancient land of Jejakbhukti, an integral part of Bundelkhand this fort and town were of strategic importance during medieval times. The fort was a Chandela stronghold from 9th to the 15th centuries and remained invincible up to times of the Mughals. Akbar finally conquered it in 1569 AD and gifted it to Birbal. From Birbal it went to the legendary Bundela warrior, Chhatrasal and thence to Hardev Shah of Panna before being captured by British in 1812 AD. Kalinjar Fort, situated at a height of 700 feet, is accessible through seven gateways - Alamgir Darwaza, Ganesh Dwar, Chandi or Chauburji Darwaza, Budha Bhadra Darwaza, Hanuman Dwar, Lal Darwaza and Bara Darwaza. Within the fort are the remains of two palaces, the Raja Mahal and Rani Mahal. There are several other places of interest within the fort.

HOW TO REACH

AIR : Nearest airport – Khajuraho 130 km

RAIL : Nearest railway station – Atarra – 36km on the Banda – Satna route

ROAD : Kalinjar is connected by road with major regions by regular bus services.

HOTEL ACCOMMODATION

— Forest Rest House, Rain Bashera

KHAJURAHO

Refer Madhya Pradesh

RISHIKESH

BASE CAMP TO VISIT FOUR PILGRIM SPOTS—

BADRINATH, KEDARNATH, YAMUNOTRI AND GANGOTRI

RISHIKESH

Situated 24 km upstream from Haridwar, at the confluence of the Chandrabhaga and Ganga, Rishikesh has long been a spiritual centre. It is said that the sage Raibhya Rishi did severe penance here and as a reward, God appeared to him in the form of Hrishikesh, hence the name. Rishikesh has numerous Ashrams, some of which are internationally recognised as center of philosophical studies, yoga and meditation.

PLACES OF INTEREST

TRIVENI GHAT : A bathing ghat where every evening an "AARATI" to river Ganga is performed.

LAKSHMAN JHOOLA : A suspension bridge across the Ganga along the old route to the holy shrines of Badrinath and Kedarnath.

SHIVANANAD OR RAM JHOOLA : Recently completed suspension bridge which spans the river near Swarg Ashram.

There are many other temples, ashrams and yoga institutues.

HOW TO REACH

AIR : Nearest airport-Jolly Grant (Dehradun) 18 km.

RAIL : Rishikesh is connected by rail via Haridwar which is on the main route. Haridwar is connected directly with Mumbai, Lucknow, Howrah, Kalka, Sri Ganganagar, Allahabad and Delhi.

ROAD : Regular bus services available from Delhi (238 km), Haridwar (24 km), Dehradun (42 km), Mussoorie (77 km), Yamunotri (288 km), Gangotri (258 km), Uttarkashi (154 km), Kedarnath (228 km), Badrinath (301 km) and Chandigarh (252 km).

TOURIST INFORMATION OFFICES

— Tourist Bureau, Railway Road, PH 302 09
— Yatra Office, Garhwal Mandal Vikas Nigam, Muni-ki-Reti, PH 317 93, 303 72

HOTEL ACCOMMODATION (STD CODE 01364)

— Hotel Ganga Kinare, 16, Virbhadra Road
  PH 305 66, 316 58
— Hotel Natraj, Dehradun Road
  PH 310 99, 312 61; Fax 315 01
— Hotel Mandakini International, 63 Haridwar Road
  PH 307 81, 310 81
— Hotel Indralok, Railway Road. PH 305 55/56; Fax 311 86
— Hotel Akash Ganga, 87/2 Haridwar Road
  PH 308 70, 304 51

BADRINATH

Badrinath is considered the holiest of the main four shrines of Uttarkhand and is one of the four Dhams. A devout Hindu has to visit it in his lifetime to attain salvation. The temple is dedicated to Lord Vishnu and was built about two centuries ago by kings of Garwal. The temple is divided into three parts—the Garbha, the Darshan Mandap and Sabha Mandap. The principal idol is of black stone and represents Vishnu seated in a meditative pose and flanked by Nara-Narayana TAPT KUND and SURYA KUND are famous springs of sulphurous water with 55 C. A dip, considered holy and refreshing the body as well as soul, is a must before offerings prayers to Shri Badrinathji.

KEDARNATH

Kedarnath, at the head of the Mandakini river, is amongst the holiest pilgrimage for the devout Hindu. Kedarnath temple built in the 8th century AD is dedicated to Lord Shiva. The conical rock in its sanctum is the idol and outside the temple door a large statue of Nandi stands

as a guard. According to legend Lord Shiva wished to elude the Pandavas and had taken refuge in Kedarnath in the form of a bull. When the Pandavas followed him here, too, he dived into the ground leaving behind him a hump on the
surface. His conical protrusion is worshipped as the idol in the shrine. The remaining parts of the body are worshipped at four other places —the arms (bahu) at Tungnath, mourh (mukh) at Rudranath, Navel (nabhi) at Mahamaheshwar and hair (jata) at Kalpeshwar. Together with Kedarnath these places are known as the Panch Kedar. The lingam is one of the 12 Jyotirlingas. The Shrine is closed on the first day of Kartik and reopened in Vaishakh. During its nine month of closure the shrine remains submerged in snow and worship is performed at Ukmimath. The Samadhi of Adi Shankaracharya is located behind the Kedarnath temple where the saint gave up his life. To the south of the main temple stands the temple of Lord Bhairav, the deity who guards the Kedarnath temple in winter, when it is closed for worship.

GANGOTRI

Gangotri is one of the Char Dham of Uttarakhand. It is situated in Garhwal Himalayas at an elevation of 3048 meters. The Gangotri shrine is seen as spiritual source of Hinduism's most sacred river "THE GANGA ". According to Hindu mythology, Ganga, the stream of life, was granted as a reward to King Bhagirath for severe penance, and the river is worshipped as deity. The physical source of the river is at Gaumukh, 18 km southwest of Gangotri, along the Gangotri Glacier. GANGOTRI TEMPLE - A Gorkha Commander Amar Singh Thapa in the early 18th century built the temple. The ruler of Jaipur renovated it in the early 20th century. The 20 feet high temple is made of white granite. The shrine of Gangotri is situated at an elevation of 3048 meters. above sea level. It is said that Raja Bhagirath used to worship Lord Shiva at the sacred stone nearby. The SUBMERGED SHIVLING is a natural rock Shivling, which according to legends, is where Lord Shiva sat to receive the Ganga in his matted locks. It normally shows up during the winter months when the waters are clearer.

YAMUNOTRI

One of the four sacred dhams of Uttarkhand and revered in Hindu mythology Yamunotri is the source of Yamuna river. The Yamunotri shrine stands on the western flank of the Bandarpunch peak (20,731 ft). The origin of the Yamuna river is the Champsar Glacier near Yamunotri. Though it is very difficult to reach the exact source of the holy river, pilgrims flock to the shrine which is open from May to November. Legend has it that the sage, Asti Muni, used to reside at this secluded spot. The hot springs here are also an attraction. The YAMUNOTRI TEMPLE—the present temple was—built by Maharani Gularia of Jaipur in 19th century. Here a holy dip in the tank filled by hot springs and cooking rice in its water are part of the rituals.

SURYA KUND - there are a number of thermal springs in the vicinity of Yamunotri. The most important of these Surya Kund has a temperature of 190° F. Pilgrims tie rice and potatoes in a muslin cloth, and immerse in the water to be cooked. DIVYA SHILA - a rock pillar, worshipped before entering the Yamunotri temple.

PACKAGE TOURS OPERATED BY U.P. TOURISM

TOUR No. 1 : Rishikesh-Kedarnath-Badrinath; 6 Days.

TOUR No. 2 : Delhi-Kedarnath-Badrinath; 8 Days.

TOUR No. 3 : Delhi-Yamunotri-Gangotri-Kedarnath-Badrinath; 12 Days

TOUR No. 4 : Rishikesh-Yamunotri-Gangotri-Kedarnath-Badrinath; 11 Days

TOUR No. 5 : Delhi-Yamunotri-Gangotri-Gaumukh-Kedarnath-Badrinath; 12 Days

TOUR No. 6 : Rishikesh-Badrinath; 4 Days (Departure Rishikesh)

TOUR No. 7 : Rishikesh-Yamunotri-Gangotri-Gaumukh; 7 Days (Departure Rishikesh)

TOUR No. 8 : Rishikesh-Kedarnath-Badrinath; 6 Days (Departure Rishikesh)

TOUR No. 9 : Delhi-Kedarnath Badrinath; 7 Days

TOUR No. 10 : Rishikesh-Yamunotri-Gangotri-Kedarnath-Badrinath; 10 Days

TOUR No. 11 : Delhi-Yamunotri-Gangotri-Kedarnath-Badrinath; 12 Days

TOUR No. 12 : Rishikesh-Valley of Flowers-Hemkund-Badrinath
              : 7 Days
TOUR No. 13 : Rishikesh-Yamunotri-Gangotri-Gaumukh-
              Kedarnath-Badrinath;12Days

DEHRADUN

Nestled in a wide and thickly forested valley of the Shivalik ranges, Dehradun is known for its Salubrious climate. Once a stronghold of Garhwal kings and later appropriated by the British as a residential resort, the town has several institutions and public schools. Dehradun is famous for its fruit orchards.

PLACES OF INTEREST

FOREST RESEARCH INSTITUTE : Established by the British, it is one of the finest of its kind in the world.

WADIA INSTITUTE OF HIMALAYAN GEOLOGY : The institution has a museum containing rock samples, semi-precious stones.

ROBBER'S CAVE : Popularly known as Guchu Pani is a picnic spot situated 8 km away from the city. The last kilometre has to be covered on foot.

HOW TO REACH

AIR : Nearest airport-Jolly Grant 24 km.

RAIL : Dehradun is directly connected by rail with Delhi, Howrah, Varanasi and Allahabad.

— 2017 Shatabdi Express D Delhi 0710 Hrs; A Dehradun 1240 Hrs.

— Return 2018 Shatabdi Express D Dehradun 1705; A Delhi 2230 Hrs.

ROAD : Dehradun is well-connected by road with all major centres of the State. There are regular buses operated by private and UP Government from Delhi (225 km), Haridwar (54 km), Rishikesh (43 km), Agra (382 km), Shimla (221 km), Yamunotri (174 km), Kedarnath (274 km), Nainital (297 km).

CONDUCTED TOURS

The Garhwal Mandal Vikas Nigam organises tours to Gangotri, Yamunotri during the season. Tours to kempty falls, Sarkhanda Devi temple are also available.

For further details contact :
— Regional Tourist Office, Hotel Drona, 45 Gandhi Road, PH 65863
— Director, Tourism, (Hills),3/3,Industrial Area, Patel Nagar, PH 624147, 623585
— Garhwal Mandal Vikas Nigam Ltd.74/1 Rajpur Road, PH 656817,654921

HOTEL ACCOMMODATION (STD CODE 0135)

— Hotel Madhuban (3 Star), 97 Rajpur Road
PH 749 990/4; fax746 496
— Hotel President (2 star) 6 Astley Hall, Rajpur Road
PH 657 386, 657 082; FAX 658 883
— Hotel Relax (2 Star), 7, Court Road
PH 657 776, 656 608; FAX 651 116
— Hotel Great Value 74-C, Rajpur Road,
PH 744 086; FAX 746 058
— Hotel Hilton, 54 Haridwar Road
PH 629 592-92, 622 268
— Indralok Hotels Pvt. Ltd., Anekant Palace, 29 Rajpur Road.
PH 658 113/ 652744; FAX 652 111
— Hotel Drona(GVNM), 45, Gandhi Road
PH 654 371, 652 794

MUSSOORIE

MUSSOORIE lies 38 km from Dehradun. Mussoorie offers views of both the Himalayan ranges to the north and the Shivalik hills and plains to the south. This erstwhile aristocratic resort is now a popular hill station and promises a variety of entertainment round the year. BHADRAJ TEMPLE is dedicated to Lord Balbhadra, brother of Shri Krishna. GUN HILL is known for ropeway ride and offers a beautiful view of the Himalayan ranges. MUNICIPAL GARDEN is a picnic spot and has artificial lake for boating. The MUSSOORIE LAKE is a delightful spot where paddle boats are available. It commands an enchanting view of the Doon Valley; GEORGE EVEREST HOUSE - The park estate of Sir George, the first Surveyor-General of India, who had his office and residence here, 8 km from Mussoorie. Mt.Everest, the highest peak of the Himalayas is named after him; KEMPTY FALLS -15 km from Mussorie is a picturesque waterfall at an altitude of 4500 ft; SURKHANDA DEVI - 35 km is an important pilgrimage centre.

The temple is located atop the hill. ASAN BARRAGE – 42km is a water sport resort with water skating sailing boating facilities. All types of accommodation is available in the city.

AULI

Auli, 16 km from Joshimath nestles in the lap of the snow-capped peaks of the Garhwal Himalayas and is an ideal ski resort with its slopes comparable to the best in the world. At an altitude of 2,500 to 3,050 metres above sea-level, Auli's well-dressed slopes are flanked by coniferous and oak forests and offer panoramic view of Mt. Nanda Devi, Mana parbat, Dungagiri, Beethartoli, Nilkanth Hathi Parbat and Ghori Parbat.

GMVN provides following facilities at Auli for the tourists -

A state-of-the art Ski lift which has been imported from France. The Ski lift is 500 metres long which makes it the longest in the country.

The slopes of Auli also have the luxury of an 800 meters long chair lift linking lower slopes with upper slopes.

There are two snow-beaters imported from Germany.

Dressed and improved ski slopes which make Auli ideal for hosting skiing festivals and competitions.

A 3.9 km long ropeway links Joshimath with the upper slopes of Auli. It covers a track distance of 4.5 km and is the longest ropeway in Asia in zig back system. It has ten towers of self supporting steel structures with saddles and shoes. Remote controlled hydraulic and pneumatic braking system makes it the safest ropeway. Besides, most sophisticated elctronic circuitry with telemetry and storm warning devices are used to minimise human error.

HOW TO REACH

AIR : Nearest airport-Jolly Grant (17 km from Rishikesh, 26 km from Dehradun)

RAIL : Nearest railway station-Haridwar and Dehradun.

ROAD : Auli is 13 kms from Joshimath. State transport and private buses ply regularly between Joshimath and Rishikesh (253 km), Haridwar (276 km), Dehradun (295 km), Delhi (500 km)

BY CABLE CAR : The most popular way to drop in at Auli is by the famed cable car service which runs for 3 km.

HOTEL ACCOMMODATION

GMVN has a unit at Auli with a 110 bed-capacity. The tariff ranges from the budget (dormitory) to luxury rooms. Alpine cottages and long huts are available with catering services,heating arrangements and round-the-clock hot water supply.

NAINITAL

The Kuman hills have long been known for their idyllic beauty. Nainital, a most beautiful resort of North India is a beautiful settlement around a blue green lake—Naini from which the town takes its name.

According to local belief the origin of Nainital dates back to mythological times when Sati, Lord Shiva's consort, committed suicide at the Yajna of Daksha Prajapati her father, in protest against no respect and recognition being shown to her husband.  When Lord Shiva roamed the universe in a frenzy carrying her body, Sati's eyes fell near the lake where The Naina Devi temple now stands. The waters of the lake are therefore considered sacred and the Naina Devi temple is the venue of an annual fair. In ancient times, the lake was known as the Tri-rishi Sarovar, the lake of the three rishis— Atri, Pulstya and Pilaha.

Nainital offers varieties of adventure sports as well as popular entertainment. This hill resort can be enjoyed at any time of the year.

HOW TO REACH

AIR : Nearest airport – Nainital (Pantnagar)

RAIL : Nearest railway station – Kathagodam which is connected by metre gauge to Agra, Bareilly and Lucknow.

ROAD : Nainital is connected by road to major centres of northern India.

TOURIST INFORMATION OFFICES

— U.P. Government Tourist Office, The Mall. PH 35337
— Parvat Tours and Information Centre, (KMVN) Dandi House, The Mall. PH 35656
— Kumaon Mandal Vikas Nigam, Oak Park House Telefax 36209

HOTEL ACCOMMODATION (STD CODE 05942)

— Vikram Vintage Inn(4 Star) Mallital near A.T.I. TELEFAX 36177/79
— Hotel Arif Castle (3 Star) Jahamgirabad House, Mallital. PH 35801-03, FAX36231

- Shervani Hilltop Inn : (3 Star), Mallital. PH 36128, 37418
- Grand Hotel : (2 Star) The Mall. PH 35406/08
- Swiss Hotel : (2 Star) Mallital. PH 36013, 35927, 35988
- Hotel Channi Raja, The Mall. PH 35643, 35624

EXCURSIONS

RANIKHET : (50 km) Situated at 1829 meters offers interesting mix of hill and military culture. It is an ideal holiday resort. Golf course, the orchards of Chaubatia and Jhoola Devi Temple are the palces of interest.

Ranikhet has forests of Oak wood, pine and is a fine place to enjoy a panoramic view of the Himalayas. Golf course is the main attraction of the city.

ALMORA : (90 km) Situated at an elevation of 5400 ft in the Kumaon Hills Almora is known for its healthy climate. The town was founded about 1560 AD by Balo Kalyan Chand, Raja of Champavat, who later made it the capital of Chand kingdom. Almora is the cultural centre of Kumaon district and a picturesque mountain resort.

KAUSANI : (180 km) A scenic hill station—compared with Switzerland, in the Himalays is located at 53 km north of Almora. It is also the bitrhplace of Hindi Poet Sumitra Nandan Pant. Mahatma Gandhi stayed at Anasaki Ashram, which offers a good resting place for travellers.

HARIDWAR

Haridwar is associated with both Lord Shiva as well as Lord Vishnu. It is among the seven sacred cities of India. Haridwar is situated on the right bank of the holy Ganga and is the point where the river spreads over the northern plain. It is also one of the four venues for the Kumbha Mela held in its magnitude every twelfth year . Essentially a religious centre which holds the promise of salvation for devotees, it is also a centre of herbal medicines and traditional studies at Gurukual kangri.

Main places of interest are CHANDI DEVI temple, BHARAT MATA temple; SHANIKUNJ; MAYA DEVI temple, BHIMGODA, MANSA DEVI temple; PAWAN DHAM; VAISHNO DEVI temple.

HARI-KI-PAIRI—Most important ghat on the Ganga river, where a holy dip is a must for every devotee. The Ganga Arati performed every evening is a spectacular sight when thousands of lighted lamps are set afloat the river.

GURUKUL KANGRI UNIVERSITY : A centre of learning where education is imparted in the traditional Indian way. Ved Mandir at the university houses many archaeological exhibits.

HOW TO REACH

AIR : Nearest airport-Jolly Grant, Dehradun 35 km.

RAIL : Haridwar is connected directly by train with Mumbai, Delhi, Varanasi Allahabad, Lucknow, Kalka.

ROAD : Haridwar is connected by roads with major citites in the State. There are regular bus services from Delhi, Agra, Nainital, Saharanpur, Gangotri and Yamunotri.

TOURIST INFORMATION OFFICE

— Regional Tourist Office, Government of UP, Rahi Motel PH 427 370

HOTEL ACCOMMODATION (STD CODE 0133)

— Hotel Himgiri International, Devpura
  PH 424 506 : Fax 426 433
— Hotel Arati, Railway Road. PH 427 456, 426 365
— Hotel Deluxe, Vishnu Ghat, Haridwar. PH 424 500
— Hotel Shiva, Haridwar-Delhi by-pass road. PH 427 505
— Hotel Mansarover International, Upper Road
  PH 426 501

KANPUR

Kanpur, situated on the banks of the holy Ganga river, is the largest industrial city and is known for its historic and religious past. During the Mutiny of 1857 it was the headquarters of a large Indian garrison and was called "CAWNPORE". It still bears landmarks of the British Raj. It is also famous for its leather industry.

HOW TO REACH

AIR : Nearest airport - Kanpur and Lucknow 65 km.

RAIL : Kanpur is a major railway junction and connected directly with mian cities of the country.

ROAD : Kanpur is connected by road with all major cities of the country.

TOURIST INFORMATION OFFICE

— UP Government Tourist Office, 26/51 Birhana Road, Opp Post Office. PH 358186

HOTEL ACCOMMODATION; (STD CODE 0512)

— The Landmark Hotel (5 Star) 10th The Mall
  PH 317 601-05; FAX 315 291, 312 247
— Hotel Swagat (1Star) 80 Feet Road, Brahm Nagar
  PH 541 923, 541 900
— Hotel Meghdoot, 17/3B, The Mall   ＊
  PH 311 999; FAX 310 209
— Meera Inn, Opp. Reserve Bank of India, The Mall
  PH 319 972-76.
— Geet Hotel, 18/174-75 (Opp Phool Bagh) The Mall
  PH 311 042-46
— Hotel Deep Mayur 11/274 Sooterganj
  PH 547 114
— Hotel Gaurav : 18/54 The Mall
  PH 318 531-35 : FAX 368 616, 369 599

EXCURSIONS

BITHOOR : (22 km) Bithoor is associated with ancient mythology. It is believed that after the destruction of the universe and its subsequent restoration by Lord Vishnu, Bithoor was chosen by Lord Brahma as his abode. It is also believed to be the place where Dhruv, the legendary child who grew up to be revered as the constant northern star, meditated and had a divine visitation. Sant Valmiki meditated and later wrote the immortal epic Ramayana here. It is also the auspicious birth place of Lord Rama's twin sons, Luv and Kush. It is also the place where Lakshman left Sita when she was exiled by Rama. More recently, Bithoor was associated with Rani Laxmi Bai of Jhansi and Nana Saheb Peshwa—two historical figures—who played key role in the 1857 War of Independence. Boating is possible here in the Ganga river.

BHITARGAON : (59 km) Houses a unique architectural specimen —a brick temple belonging to Gupta era. The very first shrine with a shinkara, dates back to 600 AD.

KANNAUJ : (80 km) It was the 7th century capital of Emperor Harsha Vardhan's empire which encompassed the entire region between the Sutlej and the Narmada rivers and eastern Bengal. Kannauj is famous for its manufacture of *Itr* i.e. perfumes.

VARANASI

Varanasi is one of the oldest living cities in the world and the ultimate pilgrimage for Hindus, who believe that to die in the city is to attain instant salvation. Varanasi is the tract of holy land lying between the Ganga and the Assi rivers. The Assi river also flows into Ganga. Varanasi is also known as Kashi, the city of light since one of the twelve 'Jyortinglinga's is installed here. Varanasi has been a great cultural centre, especially in the fields of music,learning and the craft of silk weaving.

PLACES OF INTEREST

GHATS : At dawn, pilgrims, standing waist-deep in water, pray to the rising sun.

KASHI VISHWANATH TEMPLE : Also known as the Golden temple, dedicated to Lord Shiva. Varanasi is said to be the sight of the first Shivlinga. The original temple was destroyed by Mughal Emperor Aurangzeb and the present temple was built by Rani Ahalyabai of Indore in the 18th century. The Temple is open only for Hindus.

GYANVAPI MOSQUE : It was built by Aurangzeb near the present Vishwanath Temple.

DURGA TEMPLE : Commonly called the 'Monkey temple' it was built in the 18th century.

TULSI MANAS TEMPLE : Dedicated to Lord Rama it is situated at the place where Tulsidas lived and wrote his Ramacharitmanas.

BANARAS HINDU UNIVERSITY : Founded by Pandit Madan Mohan Malaviya as a centre for the study of Indian art, culture, music and also Sanskrit it is developed into a modern academic centre of various disciplines. It is believed to be the largest residential university in Asia.

RAM NAGAR FORT AND MUSEUM : A 17th century fort Ram Nagar is the home of the Maharaja of Banaras, who is revered as the representative of Lord Shiva in the city. The Museum has unique collection of furniture, palanquins, costumes, coins and weapons.

HOW TO REACH

AIR : Varanasi is connected by air with Delhi, Agra, Khajuraho, Calcutta, Mumbai, Lucknow, Bhubaneshwar and Kathamandu.

RAIL : Varanasi is an important railway junction having train connections with all major cities of India

ROAD : Varanasi is well-connected by road to rest of the country.

CONDUCTED TOURS

(1) Half Day river trip – visiting bathing ghats on the river side, temples and Benaras Hindu University.

(2) Half Day Sarnath and Ramnagar Fort.

For further details contact :

— U.P. Government Tourist Office, Parade Kothi
   PH 411 162

— U.P. Government Tourist Information counter, Main Hall, Railway Station, PH 46370

— Government of India Tourist Office, 15B The Mall, PH 437 44 and at Airport

— Bihar State Tourist Office, Englishya Market, Sher Shah Suri Market, PH 438 21

HOTEL ACCOMMODATION (STD CODE 0542)

— Hotel Taj Ganges (5 Star), Nadesar palace Grounds
   PH 345100-18; FAX 348 067

— Hotel Clarks Varanasi (5 Star) The Mall
   PH 348 501-10; FAX 348 186

— Hotel Hindustan International (4 Star), C-21/3, Maldahiya
   PH 351 484-90; FAX 350 931

— Hotel Ashok (4 Star), The Mall
   PH 346 020 B 30; FAX 348 089

— Hotel De Paris (3 Star) 15, The Mall
   PH 346 601-08; FAX 348 520

— Hotel Ideal Best Western (3 Star) The Mall
   PH 348 091/2; FAX 348 685

— Diamond Hotel (2 Star) B 20/44 AC3, Bhelpur
   PH 310 696; FAX 310 703

— Hotel India, 59 Patel Nagar
   PH 342 912, 343 309; FAX 348 327

EXCURSIONS

SARNATH : The place where Budddha delivered his first sermon, set in a motion of Wheel of Law. On the day before his death Lord Buddha included Amarnath along with Lumbini, Bodh Gaya and Kushinagar as the four places he thought to be sacred to his followers.

Emperor Ashoka visited Sarnath around 234 BC and erected a stupa. Several Buddhist structures were raised at Sarnath between 3rd century BC and the 11th century AD and today it presents the most expansive ruins amongst the places containing Buddhist relics. The ruins, the museum and the temple are all within walking distance.

CHUNAR : (70 km) It has a immense fort overlooking the Ganga river. This place has been the scene of battles since 1540 when Sher Shah Suri took it from Humayun. Akbar recaptured it in 1575. In the mid-18th century it was appropriated by Awadh and finally by the British.

ITINERARY FOR PILGRIM CIRCUIT

Varanasi-Allahabad-Chitrakoot-Vindhyachal-Varanasi—5 Days

Varanasi-Ayodhya-Allahabad-Varanasi—4 Days

Delhi-Ayodhya-Varanasi-Vindhyachal-Allahabad-Chitrakoot-Delhi—5 Days

Delhi-Mathura-Baldeo-Vrindavan-Nandgaon-Barsana-Govardhan-Gokul-Mathura-Delhi—2 Days

Delhi-Almora-Baijnath-bageshwar-Jageshwar-Devidhura-Punyagiri-Delhi—7 Days

KUSHINAGAR

Kushinagar, one of the principal centres of Buddhist pilgrimage, is the place of Mahaparinirvana.

The monuments of Kushinagar are situated in three distincts comprising the main site of the Nirvana Temple, the central stupa and surrounding monasteries. Nirvana Temple houses over 6 meter long statue of the reclining Buddha The image was unearthed during the excavations in 1876. An inscription below dates the statue to the 5th century BC Mathakuar shrine is a black stone image of Lord Buddha in the Bhumi Sparsha Mudra (a posture showing him touching earth) was recovered here. It is believed that the last sermon by Buddha was given here. Ramabhar Stupa rises to a height of 49 ft and marks the site where the Lord Buddha was cremated. In ancient Buddhist texts, this stupa has been referred to as Mukut Bandhar Vihar. Kushinagar Museum houses finds from excavations at the site.

HOW TO REACH

AIR : Nearest airport-Gorakhpur 44 km

RAIL : Nearest railway station Gorakhpur 51 km, which is the headquarters of North Eastern Railways. Gorakhpur is connected directly with Mumbai, Delhi, Barauni and Cochin.

ROAD : Kushinagar is well connected by bus with Gorakhpur 51 km, Lumbini 175 km, Kapilvastu 148 km, Sravasti 274 km and Sarnath 261 km.

TOURIST INFORMATION OFFICE

— Government of UP Tourist Bureau, Buddha Marg, Kushinagar

HOTEL ACCOMMODATION (STD CODE 01364)

— Hotel Nekko Lotus. PH 2129
— Pathik Niwas. PH 7138 (UPSTDC)
— International Guest House
— Hindu, Birla, Buddha Dharamshala
— Nepali Dharamshala
— Chandramani Bhikushu Dharamshala

SRAVASTI

Sravasti, capital of the ancient Kosala kingdom is sacred to Buddhists because it is here that Lord Buddha performed the greatest of his miracles to confound the Tirthika heretics. These miracles include that of the Lord Buddha creating multiple images of himself and have been among the favourite themes of Buddhist art. Buddha himself spent many summers here to deliver important sermons. Here Anathapindaka was built in the garden of Prince Jeta for the reception of the Buddha. Today, the remains unearthed testify to the flourishing condition of this sacred spot in the Gupta period.

PLACES OF INTEREST

MAHETH : Covering an area of 400 acres, excavations here testify to the prosperity of ancient Sravasti.

SOBHNATH TEMPLE : Believed to be the birthplace of Jain Tirthankar Sambhavnath, it is revered by Jain pilgrims.

SAHETH : Covering an area of 32 acres, this was the site of the Jetavana monastery. This area was sanctified by Buddha's association. It became an important place of pilgrimage, adorned with numerous shrines, stupas and monasteries. The stupas belong mostly to kushan period while the temples are in Gupta style. The remains date from the Maurya era (3rd century BC) to the 12th century AD, when Buddha was waning in India.

HOW TO REACH

AIR : Nearest airport-Lucknow - 176 km, from where Sravasti can be reached by rail upto Balrampur via Gonda.

RAIL : Nearest railhead Balrampur 17 km.

ROAD : Bus services are avaliable from all major neighbouring centres.

TOURIST INFORMATION OFFICE

— Government of U.P. Tourist Bureau, Balrampur

HOTEL ACCOMMODATION

— Inspection Bungalow, PWD
— Burmese Temple Rest House
— Chienese Temple Rest House
— Jain Dharamshala

KAPILVASTU

Kapilvastu, modern Piprahwa lies at a distance of 20km from Siddarthnagar. Kapilvastu was the ancient capital of the Sakya clan whose ruler was the father of the Buddha. Prince Gautam, as the Buddha was then known, left his palace in Kapilvastu at the age of 29, and revisited it 12 years later after he had attained enlightenment.

A large stupa stands at the ancient site which is said to have housed the bone relics of the Buddha. The presence of these relics are testified by an ancient Brahmi inscription discovered at Piprahwa. The ruins of the palace are spread over a large area.

Lumbini, 95 km from Kapilvastu, is situated across the border in Nepal which is the birthplace of Lord Buddha. Buses ply upto the border from where the remaining 8 km has to be covered by private vehicles or cycle rickshaws.

HOW TO REACH

AIR : Nearest airport-Gorakhpur 104 km, Khajuraho 130 km
RAIL : Nearest railway station-Siddharth Nagar 20 km
ROAD : Kapilvastu is approchable by road from Gorakhpur 97 km, Kushinagar 148 km, Varanasi 312 km, Lumbini 95 km, Sravasti 147 km, Lucknow 308 km.

TOURIST INFORMATION OFFICE

Tourist Office, Siddharth Nagar, 20 km from Kapilvastu.

Hotel accommodation is available at Sri Lankan Temple Dharamshala and Motel run by the UPSTDC.

BUDDHAM SHARANAM—SAMPLE ITINERARY.
GORAKHPUR-PIPARIYA-KUSHINAGAR-SARNATH-KAUSHAMBI-SRAVASTI-GORAKHPUR

DAY 1

Gorakhpur to Piparahwa and back (216 km) enroute visit,
Pharenda (43 km); Nowgarh (32 km);
Biradpur (12 km); Piparahwa (3 km);
and return to Gorakhpur for overnight.

DAY 2

Gorakhpur to Kushinagar and back (106 km) enroute visit,
Kushinagar (53 km) visit many shrines and stupas
and return to Gorakhpur (53 km).

Day 3

Gorakhpur to Sarnath (208 km) enroute visit,
Kauriam (31 km)—N.H.29 from Gorakhpur,
Dohrighat (32 km); Mau (38 km); Sultanpur (25 km),
Sarnath (31 km) visit Dhamek Stupa, ruined monasteries, temples
and stay overnight at Sarnath.

DAY 4

Sarnath to Allahabad (270 km) enroute visit,
Varanasi (9 km); Allhabad (125 km); Serai Akil;
Kaushambi (25 km) - visit ancient remains of architectural and
sculptural importance and the ruined fort and proceed to Allahabad for
overnight stay.

DAY 5

Allahabad to Balarampur via Sravasti (285 km)
enroute visit Sultanpur (101 km); Faizabad (58 km); Gonda (51
km); Balrampur (41 km); Sravasti (17 km)—many temples, Ashoka's
pillars and proceed to Balrampur (17 km) for overnight stay.

DAY 6

Balrampur to Gorakhpur (163km) enroute visit
Utraula (28km); Basti (69km); Gorakhpur (66km) visit temple of
Gorakhnathji and Gita Press, End of tour.

SUGGESTED ITINERARIES
FOR BUDDHIST CIRCUIT

—   Varanasi-Sarnath-Kushinagar-Sunauki-Lumbini-Kapilvastu-
    Balarampur-Sravasti-Lucknow (6 Days).

- Lucknow-Sarnath-Kushinagar-Kapilvastu-Sravasti-Lucknow (7 Days).
- Gorakhpur-Kushinagar-Sarnath-Kaushambi-Sravasti-Kapilvastu-Gorakhpur (5 Days).
- Lucknow-Sravasti-Kapilvastu-Lumbini-Kushinagar-Bodhgaya-Sarnath-Lucknow (7 Days).
- Lucknow-Kapilvastu-Lumbini-Kushinagar-Sarnath-Bodhgaya-Rajgir-Nalanda-Patna (8 Days).

For further details and bookings contact U.P. TOURISM offices at Delhi, Chandigarh, Chennai, Ahmedabad, Calcutta, Lucknow, Mumbai, Agra and Varanasi.

SUGGESTED ITINERARY FOR WILDLIFE

- Lucknow-Dudhwa-Lucknow (2 Days)
- Delhi-Corbett National Park - Nainital-Delhi (3 Days)
- Kumaon Paradise Trekking Territory

The region of Kumaon is celebrated for offering enchanting vistas of the Himalaya, forested glades, fertile valleys and foaming rivers. The most stupendous and well-known of the glaciers of Kumaon is Pindari, followed by Kafni, Sunderdhunga and Namik (in Almora district)

PINDARI GLACIER : 3820 m ROUTE Bageshwar-Song(by bus) – Loharkhet (3 km) – Dhakuri (11 km) – Khati (8 km) – Dwali (11 km) – Phurkia (5 km) – Zero Point (8 km) Total Days 12.

KAFNI GLACIER : 3800 m ROUTE Bageshwar-Song (by bus) – Loharkhet (3 km) – Dhakuri (11 km) – Khati (8 km) – Dwali (11 km) – Byali (11 km) – Kafni glacier (2 km) Total Days 14.

SUNDERDHUNGA GLACIER : 3806 m ROUTE TO SUKHRAM GLACIER Song (by Bus) – Loharkhet (3 km) – Dhakuri (11 km) – Umla (4 km) – Jatoli (6 km) – Dungiadong (7 km) – Kathalia (6 km) – Sukhram (7 km) Total Days 14.

ROUTE TO MAIKTOLI GLACIER : Bageshwar-Song (by Bus)-Loharkhet-Dhakurfi-Umla (4 km) – Khati (4 km) – Jatoli (6 km) – Dungaidong (7 km)–Kathalia (6 km)–Maiktoli (7 km) – Total Days 14.

MILAM GLACIER : 4267 m ROUTE Munsiari – Lilam (16 km) – Bugadiar (16 km) – Rilkote (12 km) – Milam village (15 km) – Milan glacier (2 km) Total Days 12.

FAIRS AND FESTIVALS

FEBRUARY—INTERNATIONAL YOGA WEEK : A week long event to promote yoga is held in Rishikesh, a picturesque town in the foothills of the Himalayas. Detailed lectures and demonstrations of various 'Asanas' by prominent exponents of yoga are the major highlights of the Yoga Week.

MARCH—JHANSI FESTIVAL : This week-long annual event is a display of the arts, crafts and culture of the splendid city Jhansi. The cultural programmes include folk songs, dances and mushairas.

HOLI : During spring, the festival of colours is celebtrated all over India. Holi is a time to make merry. People smear each other with coloured powder. Singing and dancing add to the gaiety of the occasion. The holi celebrations in Mathura – the land of Sri Krishna are spectacular. The Rang Gulal Festival is celebrated for a week with exuberant processions, songs and music. Especially famous is the 'Lathmar Holi' of Barsana and Nandgaon.

AUGUST—JANMASHTAMI : The birth of Lord Krishna is celebrated with great fervour all over the country. In Mathura and Vrindavan – where Lord Krishna spent his childhood and youth, the Janmashtami celebrations are quite elaborate. The Krishna Leela stories of his eventful youth are enacted.

In Maharashtra, earthen pots of curd and butter are hung up over the streets. Young men enacting an episode from Krishna's childhood form human pyramids by climbing on each other's shoulders and try to break these up.

NOVEMBER—LUCKNOW FESTIVAL : This festival celebrates Lucknow's living culture. Capital alight during this ten day long event. Colourful processions, traditional dramas Kathak dances in the style of the famous Lucknow gharana, sarangi and sitar recitals alongwith ghazals, qawalis and thumri create a festive atmosphere. Exciting events like ekka races, kite flying, cock fighting and other traditional village games recreate an atmosphere of Avadh's nawabi days.

KUMBH MELA : The biggest congregation, perhaps of the entire world, Kumbh Mela is held at Allahabad every twelfth year. Ardh Kumbha Mela is also held at these places every sixth years.

MAGH MELA : This mela is celebrated every winter in January. People come and settle there for a month to have a dip in the holy Sangam every morning.

JHOOLA FAIR : The fortnight long Jhoola fair of Mathura and Vrindavan and Ayodhya, when dolls are placed in the gold or silver jhoolas or cradles is worth witnessing.

BATESHWAR CATTLE FAIR : A famous cattle fair is held at Bateshwar in Agra district.

WEST BENGAL

WEST BENGAL
AT A GLANCE

AREA : 88,752 Sq. km.

CAPITAL : Calcutta

BOUNDRIES : East : Bangladesh and Assam; West : Orissa, Bihar and Nepal; North : Sikim and Bhutan; South : Bay of Bengal.

LANGUAGES : Bengali, Hindi and English

ROADS : The length of roads as on March 31, 1995 was 68,375 km including 1,710 km national highways. The length of roads under PWD as in March 1997 were State highways 3,378 km, district roads 9,618 km and rural/village roads 5,527 km respectively.

AIRPORT   : Dumdum, Calcutta.

Other Airfields in the State are Balurghat, Cooch Behar, Malda, Bagdogra, Panagarh, Behola, Barrackpore and Kalai Kunde.

IMPORTANT MUSEUMS

Calcutta : Indian Museum; Rabindra Bharati Museum; Birla Academy of Art and Culture; Birla Industrial and Technological Museum; Asutosh Museum of Indian Art; Nehru Children's Museum; Victoria Memorial Hall Museum.

Darjeeling : Himalayan Mountaineering Institute Museum and Natural History Museum.

HILL RESORTS

Darjeeling (2127m) Railhead – Darjeeling

Kalimpong (1450m) Railhead – Siliguri 68km; New Jaipaiguri 77 km

Kurseong (1450m) Railhead – Darjeeling 32 km.

Mirik (170m) Railhead – Darjeeling 49km – Siliguri 52 km.

PILGRIM CENTRES (A : Air; R : Rail)

Bakreswar : Bakarnath Shiva Temple and Mahisasurmardini temple; A - Calcutta 209 : R - Bolapur.

Bansberia : Temples of Haneswari and Vasudev; A and R - Calcutta 47 km.

Belur Math : Headquarters of Ramakrishna Mission founded by Swami Vivekananda; A and R - Calcutta 17 km.

Calcutta : Temple of Kali; A and R - Calcutta.

Dakshineshwar : Kali temple associated with Ramakrishna Parmahansa; A and R - Calcutta133 km.

Ganga Sagar : Famed for Ganga Sagar Mela in january and for Kapil Muni Temple; A - Calcutta 133 km, R - Diamond Harbour 71 km.

Kamarpukur : Birthplace of Saint Ramakrishna; A - Calcutta 132 km, R - Tarkeswar 60 km.

Mayapur : Temple of Gouranga. Headquarters of ISCON; A - Calcutta 120 km, R - Krishnagar 20 km.

Nabadwip : Birthplace of Sri Chaitanya; A - Calcutta, R - Krishnagar 14 km.

Tarapith : Temple of Tara Devi.A centre of Tantrik cult; A - Calcutta 214, R - Rampurhat 14.

West Begal—a sojourn through its historic plains, snow-clad

mountains, rolling hills, beautiful coastline or through its deep forests in Sundarbans or Sub-Himalayan doors – imprints memory on the minds of the visitors.

HISTORY

Bengal finds a coveted place even in pre-historic times. At the time of Alexander's invasion a powerful king called Gangaridai ruled over Bengal Ascendancy of the Guptas and the Mauryas had little effect on Bengal. Later Sasanka became King of Bengal and is said to have played an important role in north-eastern India in the early half of the seventh century. He was succeeded by Gopala, who founded the Pala dynasty which ruled for centuries and had created a huge empire. The Palas were followed by the Sena dynasty which was ended by Muslim rulers from Delhi. Various Muslim rulers and governors till the Mughal period in 16th century ruled Bengal.

After the Mughals, history of modern Bengal begins with the advent of European and English trading companies. The Battle of Plassey in 1757 changed the course of history when the English first gained a strong foothold in Bengal and India. In 1905 it was partitioned to achieve some political returns but people's growing movement under the auspices of the Congress Party led to the reunion in 1911. This triggered of the hectic movement for freedom which culminated with Independence in 1947 and partition.

After 1947, the merger of native settlement began which ended with its final reorganisation in 1956 when some Bengali speaking areas of a neighbouring State were transferred to West Bengal.

CALCUTTA

Calcutta is over 300 years old and had a fairy tale beginning. Amongst the British merchants sailing down the river Hooogly was one Job Charnock who rowed ashore to Sutanati, one of a cluster of three villages, the other two being Govindpur and Kalikata. Calcutta owes its origin to this English gentlemen as he did pronounce the name of the last village.

During the British Raj Calcutta was known as the Jewel of the East and was the Capital of the country till 1911. It still bears the Victorian imprint on its streets and structures. Today, it is still the most important city in the east, the nerve centre of trade and industry of the State.

PLACES OF INTEREST

VICTORIA MEMORIAL : A splendid architectural structure in white marble, modelled on the Taj Mahal, was built in the early 20th century. in memory of Queen Victoria and was formally inaugurated by the Prince of Wales in 1921 who later became King Edward VIII of England. The stately bronze statue of the queen near the entrance, the brass canons, wrought iron street lamps, manicured lawns, gardens and pathways, the magical lighting effect in the evening and a fairy tale 'Fountain of Joy' facing the memorial building create an atmosphere of unforgettable charm.

BOTANICAL GARDENS : There Gardens have great variety of flora and fauna, all carefully classified. There is also a 250 years old great Banyan tree measuring around 400 meters in circumference.

HORTICULTURE GARDENS : Gardens especially renowned for its display and exhibition of seasonal flowers.

ZOO : One of the largest zoological gardens in India, with a good collection of fabled white tigers of Rewa. It is also well-known for its large gathering of winter birds.

LAKE : In south Calcutta an artificial lake over a large area provides opportunities for competitive boating and swimming. There is also a sport complex with a stadium, meant for taking walks, also has a yoga centre with idyllic surroundings.

NATIONAL LIBRARY : The sprawling structure of the National Library, with a most imposing facade and staircases in Belverde near Alipore houses collection of precious books in India.

There are many museums in the city which, pay testimony to the cultural richness of India's heritage. The Indian Museum, one of the largest of its kind in India, housing relics of ancient civilisations, and an art gallery is located in Chowringhee. The Academy of Fine Arts, Nehru Childrens Museum, Netaji Museum, Birla Academy of arts and Culture, Birla Indurtrial and Techonological Museum, Rabindra Bharati Museum and the Ashutosh Museum of Indian Art are some of the museums that contain invaluable and rare objects of art.

HOW TO REACH

AIR : Calcutta is connected by air with Jorhat, Lucknow, Mumbai, Nagpur, Patna, Port Blair, Ranchi, Silchar, Tezpur, Visakhapatnam, Amritsar, Delhi and Leh.

RAIL : Calcutta is connected by rail with all major cities of the country.

ROAD : Calcutta is well connected by road with all major parts of the country.

DISTANCES FROM CALCUTTA

Belur Math 16 km; Darjeeling 665 km; Durgapur 182 km; Digha 163 km; Shantiniketan 216 km; Kalimpong 654 km; Kursiyong 633 km; Murshidabad 222 km; Siliguri 585 km and Vishnupur 152 km.

CONDUCTED TOURS

(1) Calcutta city tour – Half day and full day
(2) Nepal by air – 4 Nights and 5 Days or 7 Nights and 8 days
     Kathmandu - Pokhara - Nagarkot
(3) Andman by air – 4 Nights and 5 days. Calcutta – Port Blair-
     Calcutta
(4) Bhutan and Sikkim – 7 Nights and 8 Days
     A - Calcutta – Siliguri – Jaldapara – Phuntsholing – Paro –
     Thimpu – Phuntsholing – Jaldapara – Siliguri and back to
     Calcutta
     8 Nights and 9 Days
     Calcutta – Siliguri – Mirik – Drajeeling –Pemayamgtse –
     Gangtok – Kalimpong – Siliguri and back to Calcutta.
(5) Jungle Safari : 7 Nights and 8 Days
     Calcutta – Siliguri - Chapramari – Garumara – Jayanti -
     Bhutanghat – Jakadspar-Siliguri - Calcutta

(6) Digha : 2 Nights and 3 Days.Calcutta – Digha, Shankarpur – Chandaneswar – Calcutta

(7) Murshidabad : 1 Night and 2 Days, Calcutta – Behrampur – Murshidabad – Lalbagh – Hazardurai – Calcutta

(8) Vishnupur : 2 Nights and 3 Days. Calcutta – Vishnupur – Mukutmanipur – Joyrmbati – Kamarpur – Calcutta

(9) Malda : 1 Night and 2 Days.Calcutta – Malda – Gour – Pandua –Calcutta

(10) Mayapur : 1 Night and 2 Days. Calcutta – Nabadwip – Maypur – Calcutta

(11) Bandel Church and Gadiara
Calcutta – Bandel – Calcutta (One day) By Bus / By Launch
Calcutta – Gadiara – Calcutta (One Day) By Bus / By Launch

For Detailed information contact –

— West Bengal Tourism Centre, 3/2 B.B.D. Bag (East), Calcutta 700001. PH 248 5168/5917, FAX 248 5168

HOTEL ACCOMMODATION (STD CODE 033)

— The Oberoi Grand : (5 Star Deluxe) 15, Jawaharlal Nehru Marg. PH 249 2323; FAX 249 1217
Taj Bengal : (5 Star Deluxe) 34-B, Belvedre Road, Alipore

— PH 223 3939; FAX 223 1766

— Hotel Airport Ashok : (5 Star) Dum Dum Airport
PH 5119111; FAX 5119137

— The Park Hotel : (5 Star)17, Park Street
PH 249 7336, 2493121; FAX 249 7343

— Hotel Hindustan International : (5 Star) 235/1 A.J.C. Bose Road. PH 280 2323, 247 2394; FAX 280 011

— The Kenilworth : (4 Star)1 and 2, Little Russel Street
PH 282 8394/5; FAX 2825136

— Peerless Inn : (4 Star) 12 J.L. Nehru Road
PH 2280301; FAX 2287833, 2286650

— Hotel Rutt Deen : (3 Star) 218, Loudon Street
PH 247 5240/6911 FAX 2475210

— Hotel Shalimar : (2 Star) 3 G.N.Banerjee Road, Near Calcutta Corporation Building. PH 228 5030, 228 5016; FAX 228 0616

— Astoria Hotel : 6/2 Sudder St.
PH 244 9679, 226 1227; FAX 244 8589

EXCURSIONS

BELUR MATH : (16 km) Headquarters of the Ramkrishna Mission, a Hindu service organisation set up by Swami Vivekananda, disciple of great Saint Ramkrishna Paramhansa.

BOTANICAL GARDENS : (19 km) An impressive oasis of green trees and plants especially noted for its gigantic over 200 years old Banyan tree at the Dakshineshwar. Kali Temple is famous for its associations with Sri. Ramkrishna.

GANDHI GHAT : (25 km) A memorial to Mahatma Gandhi on the banks of the Hoogly river.

DIAMOND HARBOUR : (51 km) The Hoogly river turns here towards the sea. Bakkhali (132 km) is famous for gold beach.

KRISHNAGAR : (100 km) Krishnagar can be reached by road or rail from Calcutta (100 km). The town on the banks of the Jalani river, is famous for its toy and clay models. The Krishnanagr Palace and the Roman Catholic Church are worth seeing.

NABADWIP : (114 km) : The birth place of Saint Chaitanya is the scene of many colourful festivals.

DIGHA : (185 km) A beautiful beach and a popular holiday resort with a 6 km long beach, is said to be one of the widest in the world. It is a five hours drive from Calcutta which is well-connected with Calcutta by good motorable road. Shankarpur is another virgin beach, 10 km from Digha. Frazergani is entirely a different beach. It is pure and holds the charm of a unspoilt beach. It can be accessed from Calcutta. It is also famous for the migratory birds that can be sighted over here.

GANGA SAGAR : A culturally and religiously important destination it also has an exceptionally good beach for tourists. Situated on the island in the Sunderbans, it holds the charm of a completely unspoilt beach on the estuary of the mighty Ganga. It can be approached from Calcutta by bus.

SUNDERBANS TIGER RESERVE : (166 km) Sunderbans is a large unbroken swamp criss-crossed by a network of rivers, channels and creeks at the mouth of rivers, the Ganga and the Brahmputra rivers. Sunderbans covers a vast area of 1,629 sq.km and was declared a reserve between 1928 and 1943. The tiger leads an almost amphibious life in Sunderbans. Sunderbans' estuaries support a variety of marine life which include the salt water crocodile and the Olive Ridley turtle. Leopards and fishing cats are also found in fair numbers in Sunderbans. Accommodation is available at Forest Lodge at Sajankhali.

SHANTINIKETAN

Shantiniketn is 211 km from Calcutta and there are regular bus services.

Maharshi Debendranath, father of Rabindranath Tagore, had founded an Ashram here in 1863 AD. Almost 40 years later, Rabindranath started an open-air school at Shantiniketan that gradually developed into an international univeristy named Visva Bharati where the cultures of the East and the West meet in common fellowship and thereby strengthen the fundamental conditions of world peace. KANKALITALA : 9 km from Shantiniketan, has one of the sacred Satipithas and temple. DERR PARK : Located at Ballavpur forest is 4 km from Shantiniketan.

DARJEELING

Darjeeling, centre of India's most celebrated tea growing district, has possibly the most picturesque views among all Indian hill resorts. The view across the snowy peak of Kanchenjunga and other mountains down to the swollen rivers in the valley are simply  magnificent.Darjeeling is a fascinating place, where one can see Buddhist monasteries visit a tea plantation and is a convenient base for trekking.

PLACES OF INTEREST

OBSERVATORY HILLS : One can have a magnificent view of Kanchenjunga from here.

HIMALAYAN MOUNTAINEERING INSTITUTE : Training institute for the mountaineers. It has a museum of mountaineering equipment, specimen of Himalayan flora and fauna.

THE ZOOLOGICAL PARK : The park has high altitude animals such as Siberian tiger, Himalayan black bear, panda etc.

LEBONG RACE COURSE : One of the smallest and highest race course of the world.

LLOYD BOTANICAL GARDENS : It has spectacular ferns, rhododendors and multitudes of trees and plants.

DHIRDHAM TEMPLE : It is built in Nepali style.

DARJEELING RANGEET VALLEY ROPEWAY : It links Darjeeling with singe Bazar.

HOW TO REACH

AIR : Nearest airport-Bagdogra 90 km.

RAIL : Nearest railhead-New Jalpaiguri/Siliguri. One has to travel by toy train to Darjeeling

ROAD : Darjeeling is connected by road with Siliguri, Bagdogra, Gangtok and Kathmandu.

CONDUCTED TOURS

Half day city tour visiting the Ava Art Temple, Dhirdham Temple, Himalayan Mountaineering Institute, Lebong Race Course etc.
— Full day tour to Mirik
— Full day tour to Kalimpong
— 2 Days tour to Kalimpong, Gangtok, Orchid Sanctuary
— Tiger Hill tour (early morning)
For detailed information contact –
— West Bengal Government Tourist Office, Nehru Road
    PH 54050

HOTEL ACCOMMODATION (STD CODE 0354)

— Windamere Hotel : (Heritage) Observatory Hills
    PH 354 540412 :FAX 54043
— Hotel Sinclairs Darjeeling : (3 Star) 18/1 Gandhi Road
    PH 54355; FAX 54355
— Hotel Mohit : (3 Star) Mount Pleasant Road
    PH 54723/54351; FAX 54351
— Hotel Chancellor : (3 Star) 5 DR. S.M. Das Road
    PH 52935; FAX 54582
— New Elgin Hotel : (3 Star) 18, H.D.Lama Road
    PH 54114, 54082 FAX 54267
— Hotel Garuda : (2 Star) 64, Ladenla Road
    PH 546263; FAX 56110
— Hotel Seven Seventeen : (2 Star) H.D. Lama Road
    PH 55099; FAX 54717
— Central Hotel : (Heritage) Robertson Road
    PH 56047; FAX 56048 / 50
— Hotel Apsara : 6, Ladenla Road
    PH 52983, 56285; FAX 54484

EXCURSIONS

GHOOM MONASTERY : (8 km) Built in the Tibetan style it enshrines a statue of Maitreya Buddha.

TIGER HILL : (11 km) One can see sunrise over Mount Everest and other Himalayan ranges from here.

TAKDAH : (26 km) Here are several nurseries growing Himalayan Orchids.

KURSEONG (32 km) and **KALIMPONG** (51 km) There are other hill resorts on the way to Darjeeling.

MIRIK : (49 km) Hill station 6000 feet high with a beautiful lake in the centre

SANDAKPHU : (58 km) Located at a height of 3,657 metres, a favourite place for trekkers – there are trekkers huts along the trekking routes

GANGTOK : (139 km) Capital of Sikkim

JALARPARA WILDLIFE SANCTUARY : The sanctuary, 121 km from Siliguri is remarkable for its treasure of one-horned Rihnos. Trained elephants are available to take the tourist around. There is a tourist bungalow inside the forest.

Himalayan Mountaineering Institute holds demonstrations in season on mountain climbing, rock climbing etc.

There are number of Himalayan treks that can be undertaken from Darjeeling as a base. A popular one is Sandakphu which can be approached by different trekking routes.

MURSHIDABAD

Murshidabad, named after Nawab Murshid Quli Khan, the Dewan of Bengal, Bihar and Orissa under Emperor Aurangzeb, is related to events that ultimately changed the history of India, At Plassey near Murshidabad the historic battle between Nawab Siraj-ud-Daula and Lord Clive had taken place. The relics strewn today speak of those times. But the history of this region date back perhaps further. The famous Chinese traveller Hiuen Tsiang, who made the long journey to India in 629-645 AD, in his world famous travelogue describes Karanasubarna near Murshidabad as the first capital of the ancient Bengal.

The region is rich in textile and handicrafts. Baluchari sari, now a product of Vishnupur was originally woven at Jiaganj.

HOW TO REACH

AIR : Nearest airport-Calcutta 223 km.

RAIL and ROAD : Easily accessible by rail (197 km) and road. Several buses ply between Calcutta and Behrampore. Behrampore, the district headqaurters, is about 12 km from Murshidabad.

FESTIVALS

JANUARY—CALCUTTA FESTIVAL : Held every year in the centrally located maidan area of the city of Calcutta. Ethnic food stalls displaying Bengali cuisine and cultural events make this a lively occasion.

FEBRUARY—VASANT PANCHAMI : The ceremonial welcome to spring when people, colourfully attired, especially in bright shade of yellow, dance, sing and make merry. 'Saraswati' the Goddess of Learning, is worshipped. The festival is celebrated with great fervour in the university town of Santiniketan.

Calcutta believes that Goddess Durga comes to the city during the Durga Puja and this is the cathartic festival of Bengal that is observed with utmost gusto.

The Vishnupur Festival takes place in December, the Book and Food Festival in winter and the Kali Puja at Diwali.

Shantiniketan is the host to the most mesmerising festival of all known as the Paus Mela falling in the fourth week of December. The winter festival attracts international tourists. Holi and birth anniversary of Rabindranath Tagore are other celebrations at the Shantiniketan.

BIBLIOGRAPHY

Discover Andhra Pradesh, Andhra Pradesh Travel & Tourism Development Corporation.

Chotanagpur, D.O.T. Govt. of Bihar

Bihar, D.O.T. Govt. of Bihar

Discover Delhi, Delhi Tourism & Transportation Development Corp. Ltd.

Hello! Goa, Sesa Seat Information Systems Ltd.

Wildlife in Gujarat, Directorate of Information, Govt. of Gujarat.

Enchantment of an Old World Splendour, Tourism Corp. of Gujarat Ltd.

Memories of Mahatma, Tourism Corp. of Gujarat Ltd.

Ahmedabad, Tourism Corp. of Gujarat Ltd.

Gujarat-Family Friendly Holiday, Tourism Corp. of Gujarat

Kashmir A-Z, J & K Tourism.

Ladakh, Department of Tourism Govt. of India

Jammu— You won't believe your eyes, J & K Tourism

Unforgettable KASHMIR, J & K Tourism

The World's Most Romantic Adventure—KASHMIR, J & K Tourism

Come, Holiday with us, Haryana Tourism

A Winter Paradise—Himachal Pradesh, Dept. of Tourism Govt. of HP.

Himachal Tourism A-Z, HP Tourism Development Corp.

The Himalaya Country, HPTDC

The State for Adventure, HPTDC

MANALI, HPTDC

Karnataka—A tourists Guide, Vasan Book Depot 1st Cross, Gandhinagar, Bangalore— 560009.

Karnataka—The Global Destination, Karnataka State Tourism Development Corp.

Kerala, Kerala Tourism Development Corp.

The Great Kerala Gateways, Kerala Tourism Development Corp.

Kerala—The emerald land, The Director of Tourism Govt. of Kerala.

Backwaters—The complete Magazine of Kerala Tourism, Indian Express Group.

Madhya Pradesh, D.O.T. Govt. of India

Gwalior—A Living Heritage of Heroism, MP State Tourism Development Corp. Ltd.

Orchha—Medieval Legacy in Stone, MP State Tourism Development Corp. Ltd.

Omkareshwar—Maheshwar—Sanctified by Faith, MP State Tourism Development Corp. Ltd.

Mandu—Legends of Love in City of Joy, MP State Tourism Development Corp. Ltd.

Ujjain, MP State Tourism Development Corp. Ltd.

Pachmarhi—Verdant Jewal of the Hills, MP State Tourism Development Corp. Ltd.

Bhopal—A many Splendoured City, MP State Tourism Development Corp. Ltd.

Forts of Maharashtra, Maharashtra Tourism Development Corporation.

AJANTA—A world Heritage Site, Maharashtra Tourism Development Corporation.

Aurangabad, Maharashtra Tourism Development Corporation.

ELLORA—A World Heritage Site, Maharashtra Tourism Development Corporation.

Kolhapur, Maharashtra Tourism Development Corporation.

Ajanta & Ellora—Lyrics in Stone, Maharashtra Tourism Development Corporation.

Discover India—Destination Maharashtra, Media Transasia Ltd. Room No. 202-203, Hollywood Centre, 233, Hollywood Road, Central Hong Kong.

Locations & Facilities, MTDC

Enchanting Hills, Assam Tourism

Temples & Monument of Assam, Directorate of Tourism Govt. of Assam.

MAJULI—The treasure isle of culture, Directorate of Tourism Govt. of Assam

Water Palace—Neer Mahal, Information, Cultural Affairs & Tourism Dept. Govt. of Tripura.

Orissa—The soul of India, Orissa Tourism.

ORISSA—Tourist Guide, Hotel & Restaurent, Association of Orrisa.

Discover India—Destination Orissa, Media Transasia Ltd. (for address ref Maharashtra).

Konark—The black Pagoda, Orissa Tourism Development Corp. Ltd.

Punjab—A Delightful destination, Punjab Tourism Development Corp.

This is Punjab, Punjab Tourism Development Corp.

Discover Rajasthan, Department of Tourism Govt. of Rajasthan.

Sawai Madhopur, Department of Tourism Govt. of Rajasthan.

Discover Rajasthan, Dept. of Tourism, Art & Culture, Govt. of Rajasthan.

Tamil Nadu—A land of enduring heritage, Dept. of Tourism, Govt of Tamil Nadu.

Adventure Trails, Dept. of Tourism, Govt. of Tamil Nadu.

KANNIYAKUMARI—Where the seas meet, Dept. of Tourism, Govt. of Tamil Nadu.

MAMALLAPURAM—Blend of Beach & Monuments, Dept. of Tourism, Govt. of Tamil Nadu.

AULI, U.P. Tourism.

NAINITAL, U.P. Tourism.

Uttar Pradesh A to Z, U.P. Tourism.

Uttar Pradesh Itinerary Guide, U.P. Tourism.

Bundelkhand, U.P. Tourism.

Tourist Facilities Guide, West Bengal Tourism.

South India—Travel information Guide, Kerala Tourism.

Tourist Information Booklet, Dept. of Tourism Govt. of India.

Tourist Information Booklet, Dept. of Tourism Govt. of India.

Museums & Art Galleries, Dept. of Tourism Govt. of India.

India—Destinations of 90's, Dept. of Tourism Govt. of India.

Fairs & Festivals, Dept. of Tourism Govt. of India.

White Water Rafting in India, Dept. of Tourism Govt. of India.

Trekking in Himalayas, Dept. of Tourism Govt. of India.

A Golfing Guide, Dept.of Tourism Govt. of India.

India by Rail, D.O.T. Govt. of India.

Mountaineering in the Himalayas, Ministry of Tourism Govt. of India.

Wild life, Ministry of Tourism Govt. of India.

Insight guides India, APA Products (CHK) Ltd. Orchard Point P.O. Box 219, Singapur—123.

India 1999, The Director Publication Division Ministry of Information And Broadcasting Govt. of India, Patiala House New Delhi-110001.

India, Plan Your Own Holiday, Vakis Fetter and Simons Hgue Building 9 Sprott Road Ballard Estate, Bombay-40001.
By : Shokunthala Jagannathan.

Manorama Year Book 1997, 98, 99, 2000, Malyalam Manorama Co. Ltd. Kottayam.

Wheeler's New General Knowledge Manual 1998, AH Wheeler & Co., 23 L.B. Shashtri Marg, Allahabad-211001.
By : Edger Thorpe, Showick Thorpe.

Wheeler's Concise General Knowledge Digest, AH Wheeler & Co. 23 L.B., Shastri Marg, Allahabad-211001.

India Travel Planner 1992, Cross Section Publications Ltd. F-74, Shahid Bhagat Singh, Market, New Delhi-110001.

IATO 1996, 404 Padma Tower II, 22, Rajendra Place, New Delhi-110008.

India A Cultural Voyage, Udit Narain Tiwari, Gaziabad.

Encyclopedia of India 1972.

Indus Valley Civilisation—"An outline History of the World." By : H.A. DAVIES, IIIrd 'edition, 1957, Oxford University Press. London.

Emperor Ashoka—Cambridge History of India Vol-I, S. Chand.

History of Ancient India (1942 edition), Motilal Banarsidas. *By :* R. S. Tripathi.

Hinduism, Crest Publishing House. *By :* Dr. Chitralekha Singh & Premnath

INDEX

589

Delhi

Delhi, with its ancient temples, mosques and forts and the cultural diversity of its peoples of all races, religions and languages, is a true microcosm of India. Mingling the old with the new, the congested bazaars with the wide tree-lined avenues, Delhi tells the story of the India of the past and the India of the future. Khushwant Singh, passionately in love with the city, writes vividly about its history and its present-day attractions.

Khushwant Singh, author and freelance journalist, was born in 1915. He studied law in London and practised in Lahore before joining the Ministry of External Affairs as a public relations officer. Singh was the editor of the *Illustrated Weekly of India,* and editor-in-chief of *National Herald.* He was also editor of *Hindustan Times.* In addition, he has written for most national dailies and several foreign journals like *The New York Times, Observer* (London), *New Statesman* (London), *Harpers* (U.S.A.)

He has a number of publication to his credit, including *Train to Pakistan,* which won him the Grove press Award for best work of fiction. He was also awarded the Padma Bhushan in 1974.

Crest Publishing House

(A JAICO ENTERPRISE)
G-2, 16 Ansari Road, Darya Ganj, New Delhi-110 002

Jaipur

Jaipur, the jewel in the desert, also has its share of treasures — the forts of a warrior class renowned for their valour, and the palaces of legendary rulers that conjure up images of romance and gallantry of a bygone era. But Jaipur is more than history. It is a city pulsating with life, as can be seen in the vigour of its people, the brilliance of their clothes and the richness of their music and dance. Rajmata Gayatri Devi, who embodies its glorious past and is an impassioned crusader for its future, gives a detailed account of Jaipur and its history.

Maharani Gayatri Devi, wife of the late Maharaja Sawai Man Singh II of Jaipur, was born in London in 1999. She was educated in Shantiniketan and later in London and Switzerland. Chairman of the governing council of Maharani Gayatri Devi Girls' Public School and the Maharaja Sawai Man Singh Vidyalaya in Jaipur, the Maharani is also trustee of several trusts to promote the handicrafts of Rajasthan. She takes a keen interest in sports and has been president of the Badminton association of India, Vice president of the All India Lawn Tennis Association and founder of Rambagh Golf Club. An active supporter of wildlife, she held the position of international trustee of the World Wildlife Fund. Maharani Gayatri Devi entered politics in 1960 and has also been a member of the Lok Sabha from 1962 to 1977

Crest Publishing House
(A JAICO ENTERPRISE)
G-2, 16 Ansari Road, Darya Ganj, New Delhi-110 002

Rajasthan

You cannot truly understand colour till you have seen Rajasthan. You see it here in all its brilliance, in myriad forms, in a rainbow of shades. In the people and their dresses. In the history echoing from forts and palaces. In legends that have left their footprints in the sand.

In Rajasthan colour goes beyond the white turbans and the swirling skirts. It has seeped into the very lifestyle and ambience of this golden state, even as yesterday gives way to today. Where a thousand swords flashed fire once, you may see a quiet village. Battlegrounds have become fairgrounds. In timeless Rajasthan, camles stand majestic against the endless sandy desert while music celebrates tales of chivalry and romance.

A personal adventure, a private romance have blossomed into an album of unforgettable images, brought alive in the words of Dom Moraes, who has seen in Rajasthan a splendour in the wilderness.

Born in Mumbai in 1938, Dom Moraes spent much of his childhood outside India with his father, Frank Moraes. His education was divided between Mumbai and Oxford. His first book, *A Beginning*, published while he was at Oxford, won him the 1958 Hawthornden Prize for Literature; He was its youngest and the first non-English recipient. He also published several books of prose, including an autobiography, *My Son's Father* (1968). He was Features Editor, *Nova* magazine; roving correspondent, *The New York Times Sunday Magazine*; Associate Editor, *The Asia Magazine* (Hong Kong). He has also scripted several television documentaries for BBC and TV.

He now lives in India, writing books and columns and articles for several newspapers and magazines.

Crest Publishing House
(A JAICO ENTERPRISE)
G-2, 16 Ansari Road, Darya Ganj, New Delhi-110 002

Taj Mahal

Dotted with the domes and minarets that are a legacy of the Mughals, Agra is more than just a city of ruins of old monuments — it is the home of the Taj Mahal. A visit to the city is a pilgrimage for lovers around the world who are drawn by the beauty and the romance of this marble piece. This book presents various facets and moods of this world-famous symbol of love, and Anees Jung bring alive with her words the lives and times of a glorious period of Indian history.

Anees Jung, born in 1944 studied at the Osmania University and subsequently in America. She worked briefly as researcher/editor of *India Embassy News* in Washington and as researcher/Scriptwriter for the National Film Board of Canada. She has written several books, including a book of essays titled *When a Place Becomes a Person*, and a book on India's population problem, *Unveiling India-A Womens's Journey.* She has travelled extensively and written about her travels in both the *Youth Times* and *The Times of India.* She has also contributed articles to such foreign newspapers and magazines as *The New York Times, Christian Science Monitor* (U.S.A.), and *Vogue.*

Crest Publishing House
(A JAICO ENTERPRISE)
G-2, 16 Ansari Road, Darya Ganj, New Delhi-110 002

Anywhere.
Anytime.

- 91% on-time performance
- Convenient connections
- Extensive network with
  our airline partners

 **AIR·INDIA**

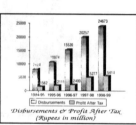

Flowers of envirocare bloom, at all our plants

At NTPC, we believe in leading the way when it comes to environmental care. over one crore trees bloom around our power plants and stand lush green testimony to our environmental activities including regular monitoring programmes, enviro-audits, reviews, renovation, retrofitting, ecological impact studies and afforestation.

India's largest power utility with installed capacity of 19291 MW 14 Coal and 7 gas based power plants spread all over the country produces almost one fourth of total power generated in India

Silver Jubilee Year

National Thermal Power Corporation Ltd.
(A Government of India Enterprise)

naa/NTPC/197/99

THE GREEN POWER NAVARATNA

With

Best Compliments

from :

S. J.
FINANCIAL &
MANAGEMENT
CONSULTANTS
LTD.

TIME

PEOPLE

PLACES

THE CANVAS IS INDIA

WE KNOW INDIA BEST

Your home in the sky इंडियन एयरलाइन्स
Indian Airlines

॥वसुधैव कुटुम्बकम्॥
(Estd. 1971)

SYMBIOSIS, PUNE
(Estd : 1971)

Senapati Bapat Road, Pune-411 004
Phone : 5652444 Fax : 91-020-5659209

INSTITUTIONS OF THE SYMBIOSIS SOCIETY

1. Symbiosis International Cultural Centre
2. English Language Teaching Institute Symbiosis (ELTIS)
3. Symbiosis Society's Law College
4. Symbiosis Institute of Business Management (SIBM)
5. Dr. Ambedkar Institute of Research in Law & Development of Law
6. Symbiosis Society's College of Arts and Commerce
7. Symbiosis Nursery School
8. Symbiosis Primary School
9. Symbiosis Institute of Computer Studies and Research (SICSR)
10. Indira Gandhi National Open University's Symbiosis Study Centre
11. Symbiosis Institute of Mass Communication (SIMC)
12. Symbiosis Society's Dr. Babasaheb Ambedkar Museum & Memorial
13. Symbiosis Secondary School
14. Symbiosis Law Times
15. Symbiosis Institute of Foreign Trade (SIFT)
16. Symbiosis Institute for Management Studies (SIMS) (For Defence Personnel and their Dependents)
17. Symbiosis Centre for Management and Human Resource Development
18. Symbiosis SPA
19. Symbiosis Institute of Telecom Management
20. Symbiosis Centre of Health Care (SCHC)
21. Symbiosis Society's Vidyavardhini High School, Harali, Dist. Kolhapur.
22. Symbiosis Centre for Information Technology (SCIT)
23. Symbiosis Society's High School, Nasik

Managing Committee :

Sh. Lalit Sangtani	**Dr. S.B. Mujumdar**	**Sh. P.L. Gadgil**
President	*Founder Director*	*Vice-President*

1. Sh. J.N. Desai; 2. Sh. S.D. Ghali; 3. Sh. V.G. Hande;
4. Sh. Y.K. Jejurikar; 5. Mrs. S.S. Mujumdar;
6. Dr. A.V. Sangamnerkar; 7. Dr. Vidya R. Yerawadekar

With Best Compliments From

Kodak Professional

&

KODAK
PROCESS MONITORING SERVICE

E-6

KODAK INDIA LIMITED
Vinay Bhavya Complex,
159-A, CST Road, Mumbai-400 098
Tel: 91-22-6528331; Fax : 91-22-6526004

With Best Compliments From

Supriya
bar & restaurant

Shrin Mansion, N.B. Marg, Opp. Grant Rd.
Rly St. (W), Mumbai-7
Tel: 382 42 02, 380 99 01, 387 18 01

PHILOSOPHY AND RELIGION TITLES FROM JAICO

In present times of stress and ceaseless striving for material gains, we often find ourselves in no man's land—lost in oblivion. We, then, tend to turn to seek the truth in great men's experiences with life and spiritual Guru's Sermons. These books-satiate the hunger for quest of truth of our existence on the Earth.

JAICO PUBLISHING HOUSE
Mumbai ● Delhi ● Bangalore
Calcutta ● Hyderabad ● Chennai